ECONOMIC SCENES

Microeconomics for Business Decisions

Microeconomics for Business Decisions

Eric J. Solberg

California State University, Fullerton

D. C. Heath and Company
Lexington, Massachusetts   Toronto

Address editorial correspondence to

D. C. Heath and Company
125 Spring Street
Lexington, MA 02173

Cover: Charles Demuth, *My Egypt* (1927). Oil on composition board. 35¾ x 30 inches. Collection of Whitney Museum of American Art, New York. Purchase, with funds from Gertrude Vanderbilt Whitney 31.172. Photography by Steven Sloman © 1987.

Copyright © 1992 by D. C. Heath and Company.

All rights reserved. No part of this publication may be reproduced or transmitted in any form or by any means, electronic or mechanical, including photocopy, recording, or any information storage or retrieval system, without permission in writing from the publisher.

Published simultaneously in Canada.

Printed in the United States of America.

International Standard Book Number: 0-669-16705-3

Library of Congress Catalog Number: 91-75399

10 9 8 7 6 5 4 3 2 1

for
Robyn Ray
Dana Dahl
and
Micah Dean

Preface

The focus of this text is on the relevance and application of microeconomics to managerial and public policy decision making. For students of economics, business administration, and public policy, microeconomics is one of the most relevant subjects they can study.

My motivation for writing this book arose from the usual dissatisfaction with alternatives. Existing books were either traditional managerial economics texts or traditional price theory texts. Neither type is well suited for serving the needs of students of business and administration. Managerial economics texts tended to be too mechanical. They either required extensive prerequisites such as calculus, finance, and statistics, or they were filled with "tools" chapters covering those same topics. Instructors found themselves teaching optimization techniques and statistics rather than microeconomics. At the same time, most managerial economics books do not adequately cover consumer choice, technological efficiency, and social welfare. In contrast, the price theory books tend to be far too theoretical and abstract, and far too sparse in the application of microeconomics to business decision making. Existing intermediate-level microeconomics texts were rich in content but failed to convey the relevance of price theory to managerial decision making.

Microeconomics for Business Decisions is a hybrid. I have covered the most relevant topics from both price theory and managerial economics. No prerequisites beyond an ability to understand graphs and do simple algebra are required. There is an appendix, "Functions, Graphs, and Optimizing with Calculus," that is intended primarily for students who need to review functions and graphs. However, it can be assigned to establish the use of calculus if the instructor wishes to supplement the text with calculus applications. But the text itself is not calculus based. Other material, such as the application of statistics to decision making, is developed in context when needed.

Unique Aspects

Microeconomics for Business Decisions is unique in its organization, presentation, and application of microeconomics:

- **Information, Risk, and Uncertainty** An early introduction to problems associated with imperfect information enables the student to integrate such considerations into later analysis, thereby making topics more realistic. Topics include asymmetric information, the principal-agent problem, and the value of information. Also covered are the important topics of risk aversion and the use of hedging to reduce uncertainty.
- **Global Perspective** The increasing importance of the international business environment is a recurring theme. A series of applications highlight aspects of the international business and economic environment.
- **Strategic Interaction** Game theory and strategic interaction between oligopolists are a major focus of the chapter on oligopoly. Topics include mixed strategies, the prisoners' dilemma, tit-for-tat, and first-mover advantage.
- **Duality** The important dual relationship between profit-maximizing output supply and input demand decisions is first explored in the chapter on pure competition. This duality is continued in later chapters so that separate chapters on input markets are unnecessary.
- **Technological Efficiency** Stress is placed on the efficient use of resources in production and the importance of technology in determining the productivity of inputs in an increasingly competitive international environment. Topics include input demand, economic growth, scale effects, economies of scope, and linear technologies.
- **Rent Seeking** Economic rent, quasi rent, and rent-seeking behavior are introduced in the chapter on monopoly power. Topics include the social loss associated with directly unproductive activities that lead to reductions in social welfare through the transfer of rent.
- **Pricing Decisions** Rather than being scattered through several chapters that deal with the various market structures, pricing decisions have been collected into a single chapter. Topics include cost-plus pricing, quality, advertising, peak-load pricing, price discrimination, bundling and tied sales, the two-part tariff, transfer pricing, fair trade, and pricing joint products.
- **Regulation and Antitrust** The increasingly important topic of environmental regulation by transferable permits is included in the chapter on regulation and control. Other topics include protective regulation, advances in public utility regulation, the most recent DOJ merger guidelines, and pricing practices and the law.
- **Forecasting** The decomposition of time series into trend, seasonal, cyclical, and random components is used as the basis for a descriptive introduction to simple forecasting models. Included are an introduction to consensus forecasting and to autoregressive-moving-average forecasting models.
- **Financial Markets** The 1990 Nobel Prize in Economics called attention to the analysis of financial markets as an important area of inquiry in economics. Topics include the capital-asset pricing model and portfolio choice.
- **Intertemporal Choice** An early introduction to saving and investment decisions and to cost-benefit analysis makes those topics available for continued use in later chapters.

- **Revealed Preference** The use of observed choice serves as the basis for understanding consumer demand. The presentation reverses the historical development of the theory of consumer choice by starting with revealed preference and then moving through indifference curve analysis to utility maximization.
- **Welfare Economics** There is no separate chapter on welfare economics, but rather this topic is woven throughout the text. Economic welfare maximization, the market solution, externalities, and the Coase Theorem are introduced in Chapter 1. The roles of firms and governments are introduced in Chapter 2. Gains from exchange, consumer and producer surpluses, and deadweight loss are introduced in Chapter 3. These topics and the objective of efficient resource use then become recurring themes in subsequent chapters.
- **Statistical Literacy** The chapters on estimation and forecasting illustrate how data can be used to reduce uncertainty and manage risk by estimating quantitative models. The analysis is simple and primarily descriptive, but all of the major pitfalls of regression analysis are covered. This coverage serves to enhance the use of actual empirical analysis in other chapters, but subsequent chapters are written so that the chapters on estimation and forecasting can be skipped at the discretion of the instructor.

Pedagogy

This book is organized into sixteen chapters that are grouped into five major parts. Each part starts with a survey of what topics will be covered and why. Each chapter starts with an outline and ends with a summary of major findings. Within each chapter, sections marked with an asterisk can be skipped, at the discretion of the instructor, without loss of continuity. There are several end-of-chapter appendixes that present the calculus version of some models.

The style and organization of this book follows a pedagogical principle from educational psychology: when presenting complex new knowledge, first sketch a schematic structure that is too simple to reflect the complex reality of the subject; only then modify and qualify that structure. The risks of this approach are that the simple structure may seem superficial and that the student will learn it only as a caricature. The alternative, however, is to embody the presentation with conceptual clutter that only serves to confuse the learner. So I have attempted to keep the presentation as simple as possible at first by starting with basic principles. As the presentation progresses, the analysis becomes ever more realistic.

Microeconomics for Business Decisions uses three kinds of applications. The first, called simply **An Application,** is either a traditional real-world application based on empirical evidence or an analytical extension of the theory. The second kind of application, called **Global Perspective,** consists of examples that emphasize the international economic environment in order to increase students' global awareness. The third kind of application, called **Economic Scene,** comprises short stories that illustrate contemporary microeconomic events in a newspaper style. In addition, I have chosen several cartoons to illustrate microeconomic problems or events. These cartoons, hopefully, will help stimulate student interest.

A great deal of care has been given to the production of illustrations. All graphs have been kept simple. I have tried to provide two or more figures whenever needed to avoid the clutter and complexity of trying to show too much on one diagram. As a consequence, there may be more graphs than in comparable texts, but this is consistent with the way most economists teach. All figures are captioned and described separately from the prose so they can be used easily by students in reviewing the material.

Sources and references are given in footnotes. Suggested readings appear at the end of each chapter. The suggested readings are of two types; some are "classical" in nature, and others are listed because they represent alternative viewpoints.

Practice problems appear at the end of each chapter. Some problems are fairly simple and require only a short algebraic, graphical, or verbal response. Other problems are more extensive and require analysis. Some problems are designed to help the student identify areas of misunderstanding; others are intended to be provocative and controversial. Check solutions to all odd-numbered problems appear at the end of the book. Full solutions to all problems are provided in the instructor's manual.

Concept boxes are used to emphasize important definitions and results. All new terms are indicated in **boldface** print when they first appear. A full **Glossary of Terms** with definitions is included at the end of the book. For easy reference, there is a **Glossary of Symbols** on the inside of the back cover.

Organization

The outline of the text is as follows:

Part I Markets: Demand and Supply
Chapter 1 Preliminaries
Chapter 2 The Economic Problem
Chapter 3 The Basics of Demand and Supply
Chapter 4 Elasticities of Demand and Supply

Part II Microeconomic Choice
Chapter 5 Individual Choice and Demand
Chapter 6 Time and Intertemporal Choices
Chapter 7 Information, Risk, and Uncertainty

Part III Estimation and Forecasting
Chapter 8 Model Estimation
Chapter 9 Business and Economic Forecasting

Part IV Technology, Production, and Cost
Chapter 10 Technology and Production
Chapter 11 Measuring the Costs of Production

Part V Market Structure and the Price System
Chapter 12 Purely Competitive Market Behavior
Chapter 13 Monopoly and Monopolistic Competition
Chapter 14 Oligopoly and Game Theory

Chapter 15 Pricing Strategy and Practices
Chapter 16 Government Regulation and Antitrust

This organization is somewhat nontraditional, but all important topics are covered. Experienced instructors will notice that there is no separate chapter on factor markets; instead, this material is woven into the fabric of the text. The supply of labor time is covered in the chapter on individual choice, the supply of capital services is covered in the chapter on intertemporal choices, and the demand for inputs is covered in the chapters on competition and monopoly behavior. Similarly, topics such as the efficient use of resources, social welfare, technical progress, and international business are woven into the fabric of many chapters.

There is no separate chapter on welfare economics. Instead, consideration of social welfare appears in every chapter from the first. Economists rely heavily on welfare economics to assess the consequences of human behavior, and leaving that for a separate ending chapter risks its exclusion from the course of study.

The overall organization is designed to be flexible so that the book can be used in either a semester or quarter course format. The first four chapters that make up Part I are intended to give students some perspective on how markets work. Chapter 1 covers preliminaries such as scope and method, the role of property rights, and externalities. Chapter 2 defines the economic problem, production possibilities, comparative advantage, and opportunity costs, and it introduces the circular flow model of the market economy. Chapter 3 covers the basics of market pricing, buyer and seller surpluses, and interdependent markets. Chapter 4 deals with the elasticities of demand and supply. If your course has a prerequisite of principles of economics, it may be possible to review these chapters quickly.

Part II deals with microeconomic choices. Chapter 5 starts with the budget constraint and revealed preference to study consumer choice rather than starting with indifference curves or utility functions. The decomposition of price effects into income and substitution effects is accomplished using revealed preference. Besides avoiding the necessity of being able to construct indifference curves and utility functions, the revealed preference approach has an empirical connotation that appeals to business students. And all students, in my experience, have an easier time understanding indifference curve analysis if they are first exposed to the concept of revealed preference. Extensions of the model of consumer choice to selling a good that is owned, the supply of labor time, and the use of price indexes—topics that are very important to students of business and administration—are included. Other topics that may receive treatment in a price theory book, topics such as equivalent and compensating variations, and the Giffen good paradox, have been avoided to keep things simple. The next two chapters cover material important to the understanding of real-world events. Chapter 6 applies the model of consumer choice to the intertemporal decisions of saving and investing, and Chapter 7 deals with information, risk, and uncertainty. Topics include asymmetric information, the principal-agent problem, expected utility, risk aversion, portfolio choice, capital asset pricing, decisions under uncertainty, hedging, and the value of information. Thus *Microeconomics for Business Decisions* covers the consumer choice model more extensively than most managerial economics texts but less extensively and with a different focus than most intermediate price theory texts.

Part III deals with how information, historical data, and events can be used to reduce uncertainty. Chapter 8 concentrates on the use of regression to estimate economic models.

The focus is primarily on model specification and interpretation, but the treatment is more extensive than that found in microeconomics books, because a superficial treatment leads to naive application. However, this chapter, as well as Chapter 9, which deals with forecasting, can be skipped without loss of continuity if the instructor wishes to emphasize other topics.

Part IV lays the foundation for the study of the behavior of firms under different forms of market structure. Chapter 10 starts with the production technology and introduces the production function. Special attention is given to the roles of technology and productivity. Although the main focus is on the smooth model, the linear (activity analysis) version of production is also included. This chapter ends with an optional section on the linear programming model of production. Chapter 11 then introduces input prices so that the production technology can be used to construct cost functions. Topics include scale effects, economies of scope, and statistical cost estimation.

Part V integrates the previous material into a comprehensive model of the market economy. This is where the student will really begin to understand how markets work. We begin with pure competition in Chapter 12. This chapter starts with short-run profit maximization by the price-taking firm, short-run output supply, and short-run input demand decisions, and progresses through long-run competitive equilibrium and efficiency. Chapter 13 deals with the consequences of monopoly power. Topics include pure monopoly, monopolistic competition, the dominant firm model, contestable markets, monopsony, and bilateral monopoly. Chapter 14 covers oligopoly, strategic behavior, and game theory. Topics include Nash equilibria, cartels, gaming, the prisoner's dilemma, and tit-for-tat strategies. Chapter 15 focuses on pricing strategies and practices under all forms of market structure. Cost-plus pricing is seen to be consistent with profit maximization under particular conditions. Other topics include new product pricing, quality, advertising, peak-load pricing, price discrimination, bundling, the two-part tariff, transfer pricing, resale price maintenance, and pricing joint products. All of the elements of our microeconomic model come to bear in this essential chapter. Chapter 16, the final chapter, starts with protective regulation, environmental regulation, and public utility regulation. It continues with a look at past and recent antitrust policy. Landmark cases are examined, and the most recent merger policy guidelines are examined. The chapter concludes with a look at pricing practices and the law.

I am able to cover all sixteen chapters in a one-semester (sixteen-week) course in business microeconomics taught at the upper-division level, where prerequisites include calculus and principles of economics and where statistics is a corequisite. Similarly, I am able to cover all sixteen chapters in a course on the price system and resource allocation taught to graduate business students where the only prerequisite is calculus. But graduate students are capable of an accelerated pace, and I don't use calculus in either course. For a quarter length course (twelve weeks), you can probably cover Part I quickly (assuming a principles prerequisite) and omit Part III altogether. The core chapters are contained in Parts II, IV, and V. In a two-quarter sequence, I would cover Chapters 1–9 in the first quarter, and after a short review I would cover Chapters 10–16 in the second quarter.

Supplementary Materials

The *Instructor's Manual* provides full answers to all of the end-of-chapter practice problems. Also included are a summary of the key points contained in each chapter and some teaching suggestions. The graphs, concept boxes, key expressions, and important tables in each chapter are replicated in the manual so they can be used to make transparencies. It should be possible to structure lectures around transparencies. Also, as a pedagogical device, the graphs and other transparency masters in the *Instructor's Manual* could be used to package "handouts." Then, as in many professional workshops, students can use a handout to structure their note taking while avoiding the necessity of replicating graphs. In this way students could concentrate more on understanding the lecture than on mere note taking.

We have chosen not to package any software with this book because there are many suitable generic programs available. For example, the student versions of *Micro TSP* or *Minitab* could be used if the instructor wants students to actively do regression. If should be noted, however, that the text was designed to be used without the necessity of having students do any cumbersome or lengthy calculations that might require the use of a computer.

Acknowledgments

I have used various versions of this text for several semesters during its development. My students were patient and helpful experimental subjects, and I am sorry that I cannot thank each of them personally.

Many of my colleagues read drafts and made useful suggestions: Vic Brazer, Andrew Gill, Maryanna Lanier, and Joyce Pickersgill from the CSUF economics department; John Erickson and Nindy Sandu from our finance department; and Nicholas Farnum, Herbert Rutemiller, and LaVerne Stanton from our management science department. Johannes van Lierop from the Southern California Gas Company also made several helpful suggestions. I thank them all. Special thanks are extended to Andrew Gill, who read practically every word of every draft of every chapter.

I would also like to thank the publisher's reviewers:

Jack Adams
University of Arkansas, Little Rock

Parviz Asheghian
St. Lawrence University

Erol Balkan
Hamilton College

Shaun Bamford
Rutgers University

Larry G. Beall
Virginia Commonwealth University

Orn B. Bodvarsson
St. Cloud State University

Ashok Bhargava
University of Wisconsin, Whitewater

Semoon Chang
University of South Alabama

Mark B. Cronshaw
University of Colorado, Boulder

Paul G. Farnham
Georgia State University

Simon Hakim
Temple University

Jack W. Hou
California State University, Long Beach

B. Patrick Joyce
Michigan Technological University

Gordon V. Karels
University of Nebraska

Leonard Lardaro
University of Rhode Island

Jon R. Miller
University of Idaho

Robert McAuliffe
Babson College

W. Douglas Morgan
University of California, Santa Barbara

Craig M. Newmark
North Carolina State University

Seth W. Norton
Washington University

Allen M. Parkman
University of New Mexico

James H. Peoples
Rutgers University

Arthur J. Raymond
Tufts University

Bruce Seaman
Georgia State University

Ved P. Sharma
Mankato State University

Stephen Shmanske
California State University, Hayward

Jennifer P. Wissink
Cornell University

Special recognition is due to Professors Cronshaw and Lardaro for their especially thorough reviews. I expect all reviewers to be pleasantly surprised at how many of their suggestions have been incorporated into the published version. Of course, I assume responsibility for any remaining errors or omissions. Suggestions for improvement would be welcome and can be sent to me or the publisher.

E. J. S.

Contents

PART IV   Technology, Production, and Cost   385

PART V   Market Structure and the Price System   511

12.   Purely Competitive Market Behavior   513

Contents

Contents

Microeconomics for Business Decisions

Markets: Demand and Supply

Microeconomics is the study of how society and individuals make decisions that affect what is produced, how production occurs, and who consumes the goods produced. Our goal is to see how a private-ownership market-oriented economy answers these questions. Our focus is also on how businesspersons and government officials can use microeconomics to understand the economic environment and make more intelligent decisions.

We start in Chapter 1 with a few preliminaries such as the meaning of competition and the primary forms of market structure. Well-defined property rights are essential to the efficient operation of a private-ownership market economy. The chapter ends with a consideration of externalities in consumption and production. In Chapter 2 we see that the basic economic problem facing all societies is scarcity. All forms of economic organization must answer three fundamental questions: What to produce? How to produce? For whom to produce? After defining an economy's production possibilities and opportunities, we define the important concept of opportunity cost. Because gains can be made from specialization and trade, individuals, firms, and nations should specialize in various types of production. We also look at the role played by the firm in seeking profits and the roles played by government: providing public goods, mitigating market imperfections, and providing an economic environment so that markets can operate efficiently.

Chapter 3 introduces the basics of market demand and market supply, the determination of market clearing prices, the gains from market exchange, and interdependent markets. Chapter 4 continues with an examination of the relationship between market demand and a firm's demand. We will measure the responsiveness of quantity demanded to changes in prices and income and other determinants of demand, and we will measure the responsiveness of quantity supplied to changes in price.

In Part II we build a theory of microeconomic choice. Chapter 5 covers the decisions of individuals and how their choices give rise to demands for products and to supplies of the factors of production. Our choice model is extended to making intertemporal decisions and to making decisions under conditions of uncertainty and risk in Chapters 6 and 7.

In Part III, we look at how to reduce uncertainty using real-world information. Chapter 8 covers how economic models can be estimated from real-world data, and in Chapter 9 we examine some relatively simple forecasting techniques.

In Part IV, we begin to build a theory of the firm. Chapters 10 and 11 begin by looking at production technology and the costs of production.

Part V fits the pieces of our microeconomic puzzle into a recognizable and useful picture. In Chapter 12 we examine how the behavior of competitive firms gives rise to demands for inputs and supplies of outputs. In Chapters 13 and 14 we investigate other forms of market structure including monopoly, monopolistic competition, and oligopoly. In Chapter 15 we examine various forms of pricing strategy and practices. Finally, in Chapter 16, we look at the social response to market imperfections and monopoly power. Topics include protective regulation and antitrust. If you make it to the end, you will have all the tools and knowledge necessary to understand the microeconomic environment as it relates to business decision making.

Chapter
1

Preliminaries

The study of economics is divided, somewhat imperfectly, into microeconomics and macroeconomics. Microeconomics deals with pieces of the economy and how the parts fit together and interact. It also deals with the behavior of individual economic actors such as consumers and producers, workers and managers, and investors and entrepreneurs. Microeconomics is the study of how society and individuals deal with the economic problem of scarcity and how their choices affect what is produced, how production occurs, and who consumes the goods produced. Thus **microeconomics** is the study of the principles governing production and consumption decisions, the allocation of resources, and the distribution of income. In contrast, **macroeconomics** is the study of such economic aggregates as the level and growth of national output, national employment and unemployment, and changes in the general price level and interest rates. Macroeconomics deals with the economy as a whole and such issues as the national debt and the balance of payments.

The application of microeconomics and, to some extent, macroeconomics to business decision making is called **managerial economics.** As a discipline, managerial economics has evolved from application of tools supplied by such decision sciences as inferential statistics and operations research, to integration of those tools with microeconomic models. Early textbooks on managerial economics were heavy with the mechanics of optimization using calculus and linear programming. Today, however, those topics are taught by departments of management science, and economics faculties teach economic analysis as it relates to private and public decision making. The book you are reading now covers important topics in microeconomics that are relevant to making managerial and business decisions.

1.1 Scope of Analysis

We limit the scope of analysis in this book to the study of the private-ownership market-exchange economy in which money is used as a medium of exchange. The analysis is focused on how markets direct the use of resources in the production of products and services, how markets influence what will be produced, and how markets affect the distribution of that output among members of society.

In a modern free-enterprise economy, most productive activities are carried out by profit-maximizing firms. But other production activities are conducted by nonprofit organizations and by governments. In all cases, managing resources used in production is crucial in maximizing social welfare. Therefore, managers of businesses and government agencies need to understand how their actions affect society as a whole. Why do businesses, whose primary objective is usually to maximize profit, need to understand how their actions affect society? Because they are subject to government regulation and constraint. Managers should understand and appreciate why society, through government, regulates business behavior. At the same time, managers need to understand how public policies affect markets. Therefore, my major goal in this book is to help you better understand how markets work.

1.2 Positive and Normative Analysis

Microeconomics deals with both positive and normative questions. Positive economic analysis describes, explains, or predicts. **Positive questions** ask what happened, why it happened, and what will happen if something changes. For example, suppose the U.S. government decides to impose stronger emission standards on the use of internal combustion engines. What will be the effect on the costs of consuming automobiles and trucks? How will prices change? Will fewer vehicles be produced? Will there be layoffs in the industry? How will the rest of the economy be affected?

In contrast, **normative questions** ask what ought to be. Should the government impose stronger emission standards? If unemployment is created as a consequence, what should the government do? Answers to questions like these involve value judgments.

Consider the event in which a Texas child fell into a sump hole near her house a few years ago. The community spared no expense in saving her. For several days national radio and television media reported the efforts of the rescue team. The team consisted of hundreds of police officers, paramedics, doctors, nurses, and construction workers as well as massive amounts of equipment. Suppose an economist had informed the city mayor that the cost of the rescue would be $300,000. Surely you would agree that the little girl's life was worth it. But what if you also knew the expenditure would be taken from the planned budget of a new trauma center that would now have to be postponed for at least one year. Suppose further that the trauma center could save about eighteen lives per year. Wouldn't it be reasonable to decide that eighteen lives are worth more than the life of the little girl? Why then did the community, without hesitation, spend the resources on rescuing her?

When value judgments are involved, microeconomics cannot tell us which the best policy is. Positive analysis can be used, however, to predict the consequences of actions. Moreover, positive microeconomic analysis can be used to examine alternatives, thereby facilitating the decision-making process.

1.3   Using Models for Analysis

Although economics is a social science, economic analysis uses the scientific method. The scientific method consists of five steps:

- defining the problem
- assembling facts
- formulating hypotheses
- deducing or predicting
- testing the validity and accuracy of the predictions

After the problem has been specified, relevant facts are gathered and observations are made. The next step is to construct a tentative explanation called a *hypothesis* or *proposition*. In formulating a hypothesis, assumptions must be made. Assumptions describe the components of the theory and their relationships. Together, the assumptions and the resulting predictions are called a **model** or **theory**. Models are not usually intended to replicate the real world. Why not? Because the real world is too complicated. We therefore build models that are abstractions and simplifications of the real world.

Economic models are a dime a dozen. Or as the *Pepper . . . and Salt* cartoon suggests, the price of economic theories may have increased to 25¢ each. Anyway, models abound—but which of them are any good? How should we judge the validity of any model?

From the *Wall Street Journal*. Permission, Cartoon Features Syndicate.

The last step in the scientific method is to test the validity of a model. One criterion is that a good model should lead to testable predictions. If the model fails to predict accurately under conditions for which the prediction was made, the model is invalid. An alternative criterion for judging a model's validity is its explanatory power. According to proponents of this view, predictive power without explanation is of no consequence from a scientific standpoint. In choosing between models with explanatory significance, the one with the greatest predictive ability is best. Predictive ability, however, is not a necessary consequence of a logical causal relationship.

Both criteria have merit. A model should not be judged invalid because it fails in any one application. Even the laws of physics have to be judged in the context set by the "uncertainty principle"—the more accurately one can measure the position of a particle the less accurate the measurement of its velocity, and vice versa. Nature has a randomness that makes it impossible to predict anything with complete certainty. Moreover, some useful explanatory models may never be empirically testable. The model may never again match the conditions and events it was designed to explain. Astronomical events like the big bang and black holes can never be observed directly. Although mathematical models of these events can be constructed that explain the universe, they cannot be directly tested. The theoretical existence of things like black holes can be tested only indirectly by their effects on other things. Most of the microeconomic models in this book have both explanatory power and predictive ability.

The primary method of analysis used in this book is called comparative statics. **Comparative statics** makes conditional predictions based on changing only one thing at a time. This technique is like taking before-and-after pictures. We take a picture before an event, use a model to make a prediction based on the event, and then take a picture after the event to see if the prediction was true. Comparative statics will enable us to make qualitative predictions. The method will also help us to interpret data in order to make quantitative predictions. Thus the comparative statics models in this book can be valuable in structuring empirical investigations and can be useful in interpreting empirical results.

1.4   Competition and Market Structure

Probably no concept in economics is more fundamental than competition. Yet the term *competition* is often misunderstood because economists frequently give it special meanings. Adam Smith's concept of competition was a behavioral one, where each individual seller set out to undersell, and each individual buyer tried to outbid, rivals in the marketplace.[1] Frank Knight argued that competition was a situation in which competing units are numerous and act independently.[2] Knight also argued that "what competition actually means is simply the freedom of the individual to 'deal' with any and all other individuals and to select the best terms as judged by himself, among those offered."[3]

---

1. Adam Smith, *The Wealth of Nations* (University of Chicago Press [1904] 1976).
2. Frank H. Knight, "Immutable Law in Economics: Its Reality and Limitations," *American Economic Review* 36 (May 1946).
3. Frank H. Knight, "The Meaning of Freedom," *Ethics* 52 (October 1941), p. 103.

Joseph Schumpeter argued that, at least from the standpoint of economic growth, "It is not . . . [price] competition which counts but the competition from the new commodity, the new technology, the new source of supply, the new type of organization . . . competition which commands a decisive cost or quality advantage and which strikes not at the margin of the profits and the outputs of the existing firms but at their foundations and their very lives."[4]

When applied to market structure, competition describes a set of conditions that lead firms to behave as price-takers. In this context, we can regard competition as the opposite of monopoly market structure. But economic competition might also be associated with the verb *to compete,* and competitive behavior may be associated with market rivalry. Oligopoly (rivalry among few firms) and monopolistic competition (rivalry among many firms through product differentiation) are forms of competition that are characterized by market rivalry, yet these forms of market structure are not *purely* competitive. Clearly, misunderstanding is possible when the term *competition* is used.

Pure competition exists when many small buyers and sellers acting independently trade a homogeneous product. No product differentiation occurs across firms. Because of the many small buyers and sellers, no buyer or seller acting alone can influence market price. Pure competition has been described as "atomistic" competition, stressing the insignificant role played by separate but numerous buyers and sellers in the market. Pure competition exists in selected parts of the U.S. economy, most notably in some agricultural and financial markets. The market for wheat is one example; the market for consumer savings is another. In each market large numbers of buyers and sellers trade a homogeneous product.

The consequence of pure competition is that all buyers and sellers act as "price-takers" because individually they cannot perceptibly influence market price. Market price is determined by the forces of supply and demand in the market, and buyers and sellers react to that price. Collectively and without collusion they influence market price, but separately, individual buyers and sellers are too small to perceptibly influence market price.

Perfect competition is pure competition with two additional characteristics. The first is *perfect mobility* of resources into, out of, and within every market. With no barriers to entry and exit, adjustment occurs instantaneously: the economic environment of perfect competition is "frictionless." Second, buyers and sellers possess *perfect knowledge* about the market. Risk and uncertainty may be there, but all information is equally available to everyone. Because perfectly competitive markets have no secrets, they also have no room for behavior like "insider trading." Obviously, the real world has no perfect competition, but some markets come close. The stock and securities markets have large numbers of buyers and sellers, information about prices and performance are readily available, and investments move rapidly from one alternative to another in response to market changes. The price of grain futures will change almost instantaneously with news about changes in the weather. The model of perfect competition to be developed therefore does have some immediate applications.

---

4. Joseph A. Schumpeter, *Capitalism, Socialism and Democracy* (Harper and Row, 1962), p. 84.

Because some of its characteristics are desirable, the idealized environment of perfect competition is also used as a standard to which other forms of market organization can be compared. Moreover, given enough time, resources and knowledge do move rather freely. With unhindered entry and exit, resources will flow into and out of markets in response to price changes in the long run. Moreover, knowledge itself is an economic good. The purely competitive firm must use knowledge as efficiently as any other resource if the firm is to survive. In the long run, then, pure competition may closely approximate perfect competition.

Effective competition, or "workable" competition, may exist when buyers and sellers act independently even though the market is not pure or perfect. To be effective, the competitive system needs to be open and free, and the competitors must be comparable. A contest between unequals is not genuine competition. And yet, as a few firms succeed where most others fail, the contest becomes less competitive. If only one contestant wins, the resulting monopoly prevents future effective competition. And, as we will see, unregulated monopoly is less desirable from society's viewpoint than the effects of pure competition. We will return to this theme after we examine the effects of different forms of market structure.

When monopoly power is exercised, the price system will no longer allocate resources efficiently. The monopoly price is generally too high, so that too few units are produced and too few resources are directed toward producing the monopoly good. Therefore, one important objective of government intervention is to ensure an environment in which effective competition takes place.

Monopoly power can develop in three ways. First, when large size substantially decreases unit production cost—that is, when economies of scale are significant—the size of the market may support only one firm or a few large firms. These relatively few large firms have the power to influence price. As a consequence, economic efficiency is sacrificed, and firms with monopoly power gain at the expense of the rest of society so heavily that national output is reduced. Second, mergers can lead to a single or dominant firm. Third, government regulations and restrictions can give rise to monopoly. Examples of this third path to monopoly include cable-television franchises and taxicab licenses. Even the government-created patent creates a property right that may lead to monopoly power. Inventions that have led to true monopolies are Polaroid's early patents on self-developing films, Xerox's early patents on photocopying, and pharmaceutical companies' patents on unique drugs. The patent system grants property rights, of course, to encourage entrepreneurs to take risks and to develop new technologies. While technological change expands production possibilities, monopoly power causes inefficient use of available resources.

Regulation and government ownership have been the most frequent ways of dealing with monopoly in the United States. When production technology dictates a need for large firms, we usually regulate that industry as a public utility. The idea is to take advantage of the low production costs provided by large size while regulating price in a way that encourages economic efficiency. Public ownership is an alternative. The most familiar examples are the U.S. Postal Service and the Tennessee Valley Authority.

Antitrust law has also been used to deal with monopoly power. Since the Sherman Act of 1890, antitrust law prohibits monopoly, attempts to monopolize, and conspiracies in

GLOBAL PERSPECTIVE: *All the World's a Cab**

The taxi trade should be a textbook example of pure competition. The market has lots of sellers (drivers), lots of buyers (passengers), and low barriers to entry (the price of a car). It isn't. Instead, taxis are a worldly lesson in the way business really works. Throughout the world, the taxi-service business is distorted by government rules, political lobbies, mafiosi, racial exclusiveness and every other sin against free trade.

As most businesses become more international, national peculiarities dissipate. You would think that with international travel so extensive, suppliers would respond to the demands of their internationally experienced customers. A taxi ride should be the same in Washington, Mexico City, and Rome. But it isn't.

Every country tries to regulate its taxis. The rules are meant to protect customers from drivers, and drivers from competition. Taxi drivers have long been a powerful lobby, using their influence to restrict entry. New York City has 11,787 licensed cabs—the same number as in 1937. To operate a cab in New York, you must hold a medallion. Medallions currently sell for $125,000. In Rome, the price of a license to operate one of the city's 5,300 yellow cabs is 180 million lire ($160,000). In Paris, the going rate for a license for one of the city's 40,300 cabs is 230,000 French francs ($46,000).

In response to the entry restrictions, taxi shortages breed pirates. In the South Bronx, where regular cabs fear to tread, Gypsy cabs flourish. But if a Gypsy strays into other areas, baseball bats come out. In London, catching a pirate cab on the street is like buying drugs—you wait to spot an unmarked car cruising slowly by the curb.

All cities that limit cab numbers also control fare rates. Taxi service, however, can be price-controlled out of existence. In Moscow, fares are absurdly low—20 kopecks (36¢) for hailing a cab plus 20 kopecks per kilometer. But the fare is barely relevant because so few cabs are there to hire. East Berlin drivers discovered that overpricing could be as damaging as underpricing. Taxi prices were unified along with the German economies, and the new hard-currency rates in the east wiped out the taxi market. Ladas and Volgas lost out to the Mercedes—riders felt that if they were paying proper fares they should ride in proper cars.

* Based on an article in *The Economist* (December 22, 1990).

restraint of trade. Other antitrust laws prohibit such monopoly behavior as price discrimination when it substantially lessens competition. The policy objective has been to encourage effective competition in order to promote economic efficiency.

1.5 Property Rights

Ownership is essential to a private-ownership market economy. But what does ownership mean? Ownership of property gives you the right to use or dispose of the property as you choose *as long as you do not violate the rights of others.* The law defines and supports your property rights because the alternative—a society without law—would force you to defend claims by brute force and violence.

> **Property rights:** *Property rights are defined by the legal rules that describe the conditions of ownership—the right to own, use, and sell.*

A legal system is needed to define and enforce property rights if society is to avoid brute force as a method for determining property rights. Without enforceable property rights, contracts would be worth little and trade would be inhibited. One of the most important roles of government is to provide a legal system by which property rights can be defined and enforced. The legal system must also provide mechanisms whereby property rights can be redefined through changes in statutes and legal opinions.

Property rights include the right to trade, give, or dispose of assets in any way you choose as long as you do not infringe on the rights of others. If you own a house you can sell it, rent it, give it away, or destroy it. But you cannot give it to someone who doesn't want it. And you can't burn it down if local laws prohibit that. You can, however, raze the house with a bulldozer if you have a legal permit to do so. Many restrictions control ownership of property. It is illegal in most countries to own a fully automatic AK-47 assault rifle. Many restrictions also apply to the use of property. In most communities it is illegal to shoot someone for trying to steal property, and it is illegal to shoot animals or people for trespassing.

A functioning system of law provided by government for the purpose of defining property rights is crucial for the efficient operation of a capitalistic economy. Without property rights, trade would be more difficult because contracts would be difficult to enforce.

1.6 Externalities and Coase's Theorem

In the following story, dumping tomato waste into local sewers is called an externality in production because the firm did not bear all the disposal costs itself. An **externality** is the effect of one economic agent's actions on the decisions of others directly rather than through market prices. It is called an externality because the action of one person has external effects on the welfare of another person.

> **Externality:** *An externality exists when the actions of one economic agent affect the welfare of others directly.*

The costs borne by society resulting from economic activities are called *social* costs. The costs borne by economic agents directly engaged in an activity are called *private* costs. The difference between private and social costs provides a measure for any externality resulting from a production or consumption activity.

Externalities can cause external economies or diseconomies in consumption or production. Production by a firm located on a river upstream from a town results in an external diseconomy if taxpayers in that town must pay for water purification required because of the firm's behavior. Another external diseconomy is failing to include in the cost of buying and operating an automobile the costs of air pollution created by using the car. Positive, beneficial externalities also arise. Both citrus growers and honey producers derive external benefits from beehives located near orchards.

ECONOMIC SCENE: *Tomato Waste Strains Sewers*

A major West Coast cannery has been quietly peeling and washing tomatoes, cooking them to a pulp, and then turning them into catsup, paste, and pulp. Whatever was left over was flushed into city sewers.

Over the past several years the local sanitation district quietly accepted the tomato waste, treated it along with other sewage, and then discharged it out to sea. Until now.

Faced with expansive urban growth that has severely taxed the sewage-treatment system, the sanitation agency has now ordered the producer, Hunt-Wesson, to drastically reduce its discharge of tomato scraps. The sheer volume of tomato waste is clogging the sewage-treatment system. In a season, the producer generates about 2.3 million pounds of tomato waste. In one day the cannery accounts for as much discharge as generated by surrounding cities—an area encompassing a population of about 350,000. A sanitation official also pointed out that unless the tomato waste is reduced, oceanic plant and animal life ultimately could suffer.

The sanitation agency's leverage is an annual waste-discharge permit. At first the Hunt-Wesson plant responded by cutting daily output of tomato waste from as much as 50,000 pounds to about 25,000. But the plant balked when the agency ordered an additional 15 percent cut and a total of 62 percent over a five-year period. The agency ultimately wants a discharge of no more than 10,000 pounds of tomato waste a day.

Company officials responded by filing a lawsuit on October 27, 1989, against the sanitation agency. Hunt-Wesson employs about 3,500 people, 1,200 of whom work in the cannery, making it one of the area's largest employers. The corporation has revenue of $2 billion a year. In its lawsuit, the company states that its volume of tomatoes has remained essentially unchanged since 1970 while development around the area has grown dramatically. The firm claims that the agency is making unreasonable demands in trying to force the firm into building an on-site waste-treatment plant. "We're in the tomato-processing business, not the sanitation business," said a company representative.

Does the producer's established practice over twenty years give it property rights to use the local sewage-disposal system without added sanctions? Or does the community at large retain those property rights? And what about the environmental impact? If the firm complies with the reduction, how will that affect the costs of production? How will that affect the returns paid to its owners and investors? Will the firm respond by reducing production, or perhaps by moving its operation outside the community? What will be the employment effects? How will tax revenue be changed? How will other local markets be affected? If the firm is not required to comply, what will be the effect on local development? Will taxes be raised to expand the district's waste-treatment capacity?

When externalities are present, private markets produce too much or too little of any good. Such inefficiency is caused by diverging social and private costs and benefits. A firm will produce too much of a good when it causes a negative externality in production if the firm's private costs are less than the social costs from production. A private consumer will consume too much of a good if the cost of buying the good is less than its social cost. Specific examples include air pollution from automobiles and noise pollution from "boom boxes."

The key to removing an externality is to *internalize* it. The producer of the externality internalizes it by treating all social costs and benefits as private costs and benefits. In this way producers of externalities bear the true social costs of their actions. Producers of negative externalities are not likely to bear these costs voluntarily, however.

Society can force the internalization of externalities in several ways. Fines can be imposed on producers of external diseconomies, or subsidies can be paid for activities that eliminate externalities. Governments can issue licenses granting holders the right to engage in the activity causing the externality. If such licenses are then sold in markets, as taxi medallions are in New York City, then the license fee will become a cost of production. Similarly, taxes can be levied on consumption of goods that cause negative externalities. The major difficulty in internalizing externalities through licensing or tax and subsidy programs is the practical difficulty of measuring the difference between private and social cost.

Under specific circumstances, an alternative to government intervention can bring about the internalization of externalities. Ronald Coase points out that direct bargaining between affected parties can cause an externality to be internalized if the property rights to the externality are well defined and if transactions costs are zero.[5]

> **Coase's theorem:** *If property rights are well defined, if costless negotiation is possible, and if the effects of income transfers between parties are equal, then the allocation of resources will be efficient and identical for any assignment of property rights.*

Notice that the Coase theorem does not say that assigning property rights has no effect on the allocation of resources. Rather, it says that although resources may be diverted from one allocation to another, the allocation will be efficient. Efficiency means that the economy is making the most of its limited resources and national output is at a maximum.

For the Coase theorem to work, however, the redistribution of income that results from the change in property rights must have negligible effects on individual demands for goods and services. But only changes in the wealth of individuals is relevant because only individuals are the ultimate source of demand. Changes in the assets of firms do not affect the theorem's validity.

To see how the Coase theorem works, consider an auto body shop that produces a loud noise adversely affecting the quiet atmosphere in a nursing home next door. If a

5. Ronald H. Coase, "The Problem of Social Cost," *Journal of Law and Economics* (October 1960).

property right to the externality is granted, say by a court, a market for the noise is created, and a socially optimal outcome will be established regardless of who owns the property right.

The producer of the externality will continue to produce more noise as long as the extra revenue generated from the noise is greater than the extra cost associated with its production. Profit increases as long as the extra revenue is greater than the extra cost. In the absence of a market, the extra cost of producing more of the externality is zero, and so the body shop continues to produce more and more noise until the extra revenue generated from the last unit of noise produced falls to zero. But if the shop is granted a property right, it can sell a reduction in the noise. The nursing home will buy reductions in the noise level as long as its price is less than the extra cost (lost revenue) of the last unit bought. (We can suppose that the lower noise level will enable the nursing home to charge a higher price.) The noise level will continue to fall until it reaches a level where the marginal value to the producer is equal to the marginal cost of the receptor.

Now let's see what happens if the receptor of the externality, the nursing home, is granted the property right. In the absence of a compensating payment from the producer, the nursing home would prefer complete quiet. That is, it would consume zero units of the externality. The receptor can gain, however, by accepting a payment from the producer— a payment that compensates for the cost of the externality. The auto body shop will be willing to pay a price for the right to make noise as long as that price is less than the extra value of the externality. In both cases, bargaining stops where the marginal value to the producer is equal to the marginal cost to the receptor. Significantly, the final result does not depend on who owns the property right.

The existence of significant transactions costs, however, is a deterrent to internalization even when property rights are well defined. Transactions costs include the time that it takes to reach a solution as well as direct costs in negotiating a contract. Lawyers' fees are a transactions cost. The time lost waiting for a legal judgment is another transactions cost. Typically, transactions costs increase rapidly as the number of negotiating parties increases, and so transactions costs are likely to become greater than potential gains when the number of affected parties is large. As a consequence, the market process may not be a practical way to achieve internalization. Then, government intervention is required to force the internalization required to reach an efficient solution.

The Coase theorem has been used as an argument against the need for centralized decision making—the view that centralized government is not necessary because people can enter into negotiations that result in socially optimal results when property rights are well defined. As we have just seen, however, significant transactions costs are one deterrent to the effective operation of the Coase theorem. For another reason, the Coase theorem may not work to achieve efficiency even when costless negotiation is possible.[6] The theorem ensures a socially optimal result only when everyone has perfect information about everyone else's preferences, which they do not. This failure is to be expected

---

6. See Joseph Farrell, "Information and the Coase Theorem," *Economic Perspectives* 1(2) (Fall 1987), pp. 113–129.

AN APPLICATION: *Bees and Orchards*

One frequently cited example of positive externalities in production is beekeepers, who provide pollination services for neighboring citrus growers, whose orchards in turn provide nectar for the bees. Citrus growers provide a positive externality to the beekeepers when the latter do not pay for the nectar. Beekeepers provide a positive externality to the citrus growers when the latter do not pay for the pollen. Economists have used this exchange as an example of social benefits that are not reflected in the price system. Positive externalities in production flow both ways in this example.

An economist, after a careful empirical study of this case, discovered that bee-keepers paid for access rights to orchards that produced superior nectar.* On the other hand, citrus growers whose orchards produced little suitable nectar had to pay beekeepers to provide pollination services. These contracts in the production of citrus and honey are consistent with the theoretical predictions of the Coase theorem.

* S. N. S. Cheung, "The Fable of the Bees: An Economic Investigation," *Journal of Law and Economics* (April 1973).

---

because bargaining is typically inefficient when, as is likely, each bargainer knows something relevant that the other does not. Thus the Coase theorem's claim that property rights and negotiation lead to socially efficient outcomes is false when bargainers possess asymmetric information.

Summary

Microeconomics is the study of society's way of dealing with the economic problem of scarcity. Positive economic analysis describes, explains, or predicts. Normative economic analysis asks what ought to be. Microeconomics cannot answer normative questions because value judgments are involved, but positive analysis can be used to examine alternatives.

Pure competition is the form of market structure with many small independent buyers and sellers of a homogeneous product. Perfect competition is pure competition with perfect knowledge and perfect mobility of resources. Effective competition occurs when competitors are nearly equal and buyers and sellers act independently without collusion. In contrast, monopoly power arises when there is no competition or when one or a few firms dominate a market.

For the market system to operate efficiently, the exercise of monopoly power must be absent. Government must foster a competitive environment in which the profit motive induces efficient use of resources. Such an environment is ensured under pure competition, where many small buyers and sellers trade a homogeneous product. But the costs of production may be lower when there are a few large firms or one large firm. Then government must regulate monopoly behavior to achieve a socially efficient outcome.

An externality is the direct effect of one person's actions on the welfare of others. When externalities are present, private markets provide too much or too little of any good because social and private costs diverge. This source of inefficiency can be removed by *internalizing* the externality so that producers of externalities bear the true social costs of their actions. According to the Coase theorem, the assignment of property rights will lead to the internalization of externalities if costless negotiation is possible and if income effects between parties are equal. Other methods of internalization are government-imposed fees and subsidies. Direct government regulation is also an alternative. Government must provide for a system of law under which property rights can be assigned and disputes litigated in a nonviolent way. A legal structure is required to protect private property rights and permit private transactions whether or not externalities are present.

Further Readings

A substantial principles of economics textbook is always a fertile source of information—a helpful place to start and a good place to review. These three books are excellent:

- J. Vernon Henderson and William Poole, *Principles of Economics* (D. C. Heath, 1991).
- Paul A. Samuelson and William D. Nordhaus, *Economics,* 13th ed. (McGraw-Hill, 1989).
- Richard G. Lipsey and Peter O. Steiner, *Economics,* 9th ed. (Harper Collins, 1990).

On the scope and method of economics, the student might wish to read these highly regarded and now classic articles:

- Milton Friedman, "The Methodology of Positive Economics," in *Essays in Positive Economics* (University of Chicago Press, 1958).
- Lionel Robbins, *The Nature and Significance of Economic Science,* 2d ed. (Macmillan, 1935).

An interesting and readable article on the Coase theorem is provided by

- Joseph Farrell, "Information and the Coase Theorem," *Economic Perspectives* 1(2) (Fall 1987), pp. 113–129.

Practice Problems

1. Which of these statements involves positive economic analysis and which normative? How do the two kinds of analysis differ?
   (a) An increase in the excise tax on gasoline to encourage conservation is a poor economic policy because it interferes with the competitive price mechanism.
   (b) An excise tax on gasoline, when revenues are used for road construction and maintenance, is good economic policy because it works like a user's fee.
   (c) An excise tax on gasoline will reduce gasoline consumption and will therefore serve a policy for conserving fuel.
   (d) An increase in the gasoline excise tax will make more people worse off than are made better off.

2. I have a theory that two aspirin tablets will cure my headache. If I have a headache and take two aspirin and the headache is not cured, is my theory invalid? What relevance does your answer have to the validity of economic models?

3. What is a property right? Why are property rights essential to the operation of a private-ownership market economy?

4. What is the economic definition of competition?

5. What is an externality in production? In consumption? Give examples of each.

6. The Built-Right corporation, a producer of wooden bedroom furniture, has just learned that it will be required to completely eliminate the effluents arising from the varnish used in finishing its products:

   (a) As the chief executive officer of this firm, what do you see as some of the options facing the firm? What types of information would you require in making decisions about the company's future?

   (b) As a local-government leader, do you see any alternatives to complete prohibition of the effluents resulting from the use of varnish? Why would you consider such alternatives?

7. In 1990 the Southern California Edison Company announced its intention to merge with San Diego Gas and Electric. Edison would become the major supplier of electricity over an area ranging from the Mexican border north past Los Angeles. Both the Justice Department and the Federal Energy Commission can take positions for or against the merger. What issues should government policy makers consider?

The Economic Problem

The cosmos, for all practical purposes, is composed of a limitless quantity of star stuff, but the raw materials available to human beings are limited.[1] Changes in technology enhance our ability to transform available raw materials into goods and services, and changes in human capital occur through changes in health, knowledge, and population. Nevertheless, with present technology and human capital, the quantities of goods and services that can be produced from available resources are finite.

The **basic economic problem** is how to produce goods and services to satisfy virtually insatiable wants from limited resources. The problem would not arise if resources were not scarce.

The economic problem arises because wants are insatiable in the sense that people always desire more of something. This statement does not mean that you never have

---

1. Recent evidence suggests that the universe is finite, though unbounded.

enough of any one thing. Rather, it means that no matter how rich you are, there is always something that you want more of—better health, more time, or a piece of rare art. The marriage between at least one insatiable want and scarcity means that choices must be made.

Any economic system must address the basic problem of scarcity. At least three questions face all economies: What is to be produced and in what quantities? What combination of resources and which method are to be used in production? Who gets the resulting output and in what quantities? Every form of economic organization must answer these questions. A fourth question arises when we consider the timing of the other decisions. Every economy must make choices about when to consume scarce resources.

2.1   What? How? For Whom? When?

Three fundamental questions face every economic system:

> **The fundamental questions:**
> - *What to produce?*
> - *How to produce?*
> - *For whom to produce?*

The first question deals with choosing which goods to produce and in what quantities. Should society produce more roads and automobiles or a rapid-transit system? Should we produce more hospitals or more schools? More police protection or more parks? More national defense or more food? We can't have more of everything; choices must be made.

The second question deals with how to organize and transform scarce resources into the goods being produced, with using resources efficiently. Efficiency involves using resources without waste. It isn't efficient to produce a good using two workers when one worker will do. Technological optimization of available resources is hard to achieve, however. Lack of information, inadequate training and education, managerial bureaucracies, and government regulations may all contribute to inefficiency. Efficiency also consists of finding the lowest-cost combination of resources to produce any good. If labor is scarce relative to land and capital, a labor-intensive method wouldn't be very efficient in producing wheat.

The third fundamental question deals with the distribution of output among members of society. Should output be distributed on the basis of talent, effort, and contribution to production? Or should it be distributed according to need? Or should everyone have an equal share?

Some economists add a fourth fundamental question: When to produce and consume? The timing of production and consumption is the issue here, because timing influences the society's way of answering the preceding fundamental questions. Some resources are not renewable—crude oil, for instance. Only a finite amount of crude oil is available for extraction. Should we save some of that crude for later use, or should we use it up as fast as we can? Other resources are renewable—trees, for instance. But it takes time to grow a tree. What is the optimal rate of forest consumption? These are important intertemporal issues: How much should we consume today and how much should we save for the future?

Investment in new capital equipment and in developing new technologies will increase future consumption possibilities at the expense of reducing current consumption.

2.2 Production Possibilities

The economic problem of making choices when resources are scarce is illustrated by a model of production possibilities. Let's imagine an economy that produces two goods, X and Y. Good X might be clothing, and good Y might be food. Or X and Y might be guns and butter. Any two goods will do to illustrate the tradeoffs. Assume that available resources can be used to produce either good. Finally, assume that technology is constant.

Table 2.1 lists some combinations of X and Y that fully employ this economy's resources. If all resources were used to produce good X, the quantity of X produced would be $X = 700$ and the quantity of Y would be $Y = 0$. If all resources are used to produce good Y, the quantity of X produced would be $X = 0$ and the quantity of Y would be $Y = 1,100$. In Table 2.1 the other combinations of X and Y are some of the other production possibilities when resources are used to produce some of both goods efficiently. These points are plotted in Figure 2.1.

Table 2.1 Efficient Production Possibilities for Goods X and Y

Good X	Good Y	$-\Delta Y/\Delta X$
700	0	
600	500	5.0
500	680	1.8
400	825	1.45
300	950	1.25
200	1,025	0.75
100	1,075	0.50
0	1,100	0.25

The shaded area in Figure 2.1 is the set of possible combinations of goods X and Y permitted by the limited resources under present technology.

> **Production possibilities set:** *The collection of all possible combinations of goods that can be produced using limited resources under a given technology.*

The *boundary* of the production possibilities set is called the **production possibilities curve.**

> **Production possibilities curve:** *A curve showing the technologically feasible combinations of goods that can be produced under full and efficient employment of limited resources.*

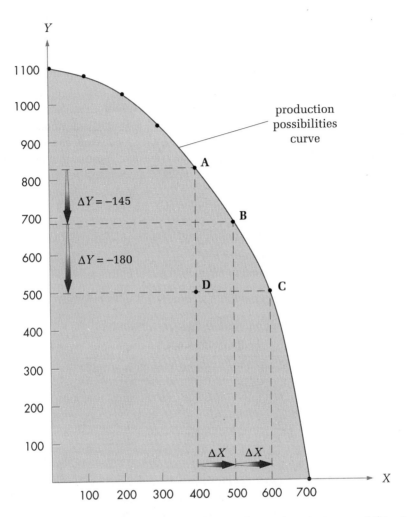

Figure 2.1 **Production possibilities curve:** Given fixed inputs, the set of production possibilities is identified by the shaded area. The boundary identifies the production possibilities curve—the possible combinations of the goods when the available inputs are used efficiently under the present technology.

Full employment of resources and the technologically efficient use of the available resources requires that the economy be on its production possibilities curve. If the economy produces a combination of goods below its production possibilities curve, such as point **D** in Figure 2.1, that economy is using its limited resources in an inefficient way, and unemployment or underemployment of resources is the cause. To maximize national output, any economy must be on its production possibilities curve.

The production possibilities curve is also called the **transformation curve** because it can be used to measure the rate at which one good can be transformed into another when the economy is operating efficiently. For example, returning to Table 2.1, suppose that this economy is producing $X = 400$ and $Y = 825$. If the economy wants to produce $X = 500$ units of X instead, the economy must reduce its production of Y to $Y = 680$. The *cost* of producing the *extra* 100 units of X, $\Delta X = 100$, is a *reduction* in the production of Y by 145 units, $\Delta Y = -145$. The cost of each extra unit of X is $-\Delta Y/\Delta X = 1.45$ units of Y as the economy moves from point **A** to point **B** along the production possibilities curve.

The real cost of producing more X is the reduction in Y. This is called an opportunity cost.

> **Opportunity cost:** *The cost of forgone alternatives.*

The opportunity cost of producing an additional 100 units of X between points **A** and **B** is the 145 units of Y forgone.

Notice that the opportunity cost of X *increases* as we move down the production possibilities curve. Between points **A** and **B** the opportunity cost of 100 units of X was 145 units of Y. But between points **B** and **C**, the opportunity cost of 100 units of X is 180 units of Y. An increasing opportunity cost of any good gives the production possibilities curve a characteristic bulge. Increasing reductions in Y are necessary to produce an extra unit of X as the economy moves along its production possibilities curve. The reason for the bulge is that resources become less productive as more and more of them are devoted to the production of any good. In making any good, the most productive resource will be used first. As more resources are used to increase output, less-productive resources are used. The extra units of these resources contribute less to increasing output than previously used units. For instance, consider the use of land in producing wine and corn. Suppose that all land is originally used to produce corn. To produce wine, some land is reallocated away from corn production and toward wine production. Naturally, the land most suitable for wine production is used first. As wine production increases, more land is reallocated to use as vineyards. But this land is less suitable than the first land allocated, because some land is more suitable for growing corn and other land for growing grapes. This situation leads to specialization in resource use. As resources are reallocated and the economy moves along its production possibilities curve, increases in the production of any good require greater use of resources that are becoming less and less productive. We shall investigate these diminishing returns in production in more detail later on.

For any quantity of X, the opportunity cost of X in terms of Y can be measured using the slope of a tangent line.[2] Because the production possibilities curve always has negative slope, we will use a sign convention and multiply the slope by minus one to get a positive value in measuring the rate of product transformation.

> **Marginal rate of transformation (MRT):** *The MRT is the negative of the slope of the production possibilities curve. The MRT measures the opportunity cost of an extra unit of one good in terms of a decrease in another good.*

---

2. See Appendix A for a review of functions and graphs.

The marginal rate of transformation of X from Y is

$$MRT_{XY} = -\frac{\Delta Y}{\Delta X}$$

In Figure 2.2, for instance, the MRT_{XY} at point **A** can be measured by the negative of the slope of the line tangent at point **A**. Notice that the MRT_{XY} is greater at point **B** because the production possibilities curve is steeper at **B**. The bulge in the production possibilities curve reflects the *increasing* opportunity cost of producing more X and results in a *decreasing* rate of product transformation.

The answer to the fundamental question of *how* goods should be produced is found in using resources efficiently along the production possibilities curve. An inefficient use of

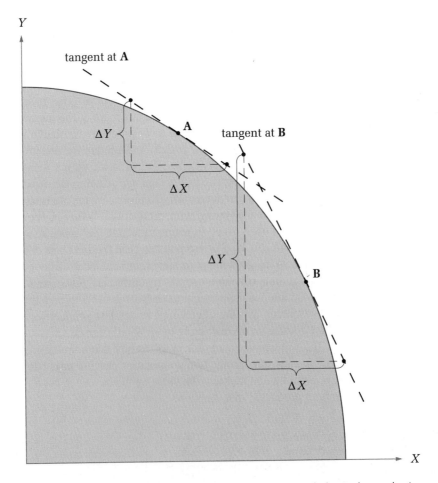

Figure 2.2 **Diminishing rate of product transformation:** The characteristic bulge in the production possibilities curve reflects a diminishing rate of product transformation as measured by the slopes of tangent lines. The opportunity cost of X increases as more X is produced.

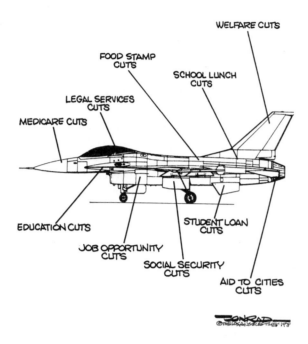

WELFARE CUTS

FOOD STAMP CUTS

SCHOOL LUNCH CUTS

LEGAL SERVICES CUTS

MEDICARE CUTS

EDUCATION CUTS

JOB OPPORTUNITY CUTS

SOCIAL SECURITY CUTS

STUDENT LOAN CUTS

AID TO CITIES CUTS

CONRAD

Copyright, 1981, Los Angeles Times. Reprinted by permission.

resources will result in a total level of output below the curve. Deciding *what* to produce involves choosing an output combination along the curve. This decision is likely to be normative. As illustrated by the Conrad cartoon, differences in opinion will arise in deciding on whether to produce more guns or butter, more hospitals or schools, because one person may value a good more than another does. The economy must also decide *for whom* the goods are to be produced—how the goods should be distributed among members of society. This decision will involve more value judgments. One thing is definite: no matter what is produced and who gets what, society always wants to be on the production possibilities curve. Why? Because if the economy is operating below its production possibilities curve, it can produce more of some good by using resources more efficiently. The increase in output can then be distributed to someone without making anyone else worse off. Who would ever oppose such an improvement through more efficient use of resources?

2.3 Comparative Advantage and Free Trade

Individuals, firms, and nations can frequently gain by trading with one another. Trade provides mutual benefits because economic actors have different strengths and weaknesses.

One of the first trading principles was enunciated in Adam Smith's *Wealth of Nations* in 1776. Smith argued that trade permits specialization and division of labor into the most productive areas, which increases the general level of production and total output. Smith maintained that the productivity of factor inputs is the major determinant of factor cost. He reasoned that individuals, firms, or nations should specialize in producing goods that can be produced using fewer inputs. Smith's trading principle is called the **principle of absolute advantage.**

Specialization and trade are beneficial whenever each party has an *absolute* cost advantage (uses fewer resources) in producing some product. But the principle does not explain why trade occurs when every party does not have an absolute advantage in producing at least one good.

Dissatisfied with Smith's theory, David Ricardo (1772–1823) developed a trade principle to show that mutually beneficial trade can occur when one party has an absolute advantage in producing all goods. Ricardo stressed relative or *comparative* costs.

> **Principle of comparative advantage:** *Persons, firms and nations should specialize in producing goods where their opportunity costs are lowest.*

Every party can be made better off if each specializes in producing goods at which they are comparatively more efficient—their comparative advantage is greatest. Less efficient parties should specialize where their comparative disadvantage is least. Then total world output will be greatest, and voluntary trade will make all trading partners better off. No one will be worse off as long as trade is voluntary.

The principle of comparative advantage can be illustrated using the production possibilities curve. Let's start with a simple case of two persons, one hunting and one fishing. Both are capable of both hunting and fishing, but one person is better at fishing than hunting and the other person is better at hunting than fishing. The one fishing, however, is better at both fishing and hunting than the hunter. If the possibility of trade exists, we will see that the person having a comparative advantage in fishing should specialize in fishing and will be called a fisher. The other person should specialize in hunting and will be called a hunter.

To keep the example simple, each person's production possibilities curve is assumed to have a constant marginal rate of transformation between producing fish and game. In Table 2.2, part A shows the hours of labor required to produce one unit of fish and one unit of game. Part B of Table 2.2 shows the hourly production possibilities for both persons. Figure 2.3 illustrates the production possibility sets for the person hunting and the one fishing. These production possibilities curves are both linear, reflecting the assumption of constant rates of transformation. The *MRT* of fish from game for the one fishing is $MRT_{FG} = 1/2$, this person must give up one-half a unit of game for every fish caught. The *MRT* of fish from game for the hunter is $MRT_{FG} = 1$, this person must give up one unit of game for every fish caught. The opportunity costs of fish and game are constant but different for both persons. The opportunity costs of an extra unit of each good for each person are reported in part C of Table 2.2.

The fisher has an *absolute advantage* in both hunting and fishing because the fisher is better in both activities. But the fisher has a comparative advantage in fishing whereas the hunter has a comparative advantage in hunting, as we can see by their opportunity costs. Therefore, gains can be made by specializing and trading. Part D of Table 2.2 reports the

Table 2.2 Gains from Specialization with Differing Opportunity Costs

	Part A: Hours of labor required to produce one unit	
	Fish	Game
Fisher	$1/8$	$1/4$
Hunter	$1/3$	$1/3$

	Part B: Hourly production possibilities	
	Fish	Game
Fisher	8	4
Hunter	3	3

	Part C: Opportunity costs	
	Fish	Game
Fisher	$1/2$	2
Hunter	1	1

	Part D: Gains from specialization[a]	
	Fish	Game
Fisher	$+1$	$-1/2$
Hunter	-1	$+1$
Total	0	$+1/2$

[a]Each person produces one more unit of the good having the lower opportunity cost.

gains in total production when the fisher produces one more unit of fish and the hunter produces one more unit of game. The individual decreases in production are determined by each person's *MRT*. Although no net gain in the production of fish appears in this example, a net gain appears in the production of game. This net gain from specialization provides the basis for gains from trade.

Gains from trade arise from differing opportunity costs. These costs depend on the *relative* costs of producing the two goods, not the absolute costs. When opportunity costs are the same for all parties, there is no comparative advantage and no possibility of further gains from specialization and trade. But when opportunity costs differ and both

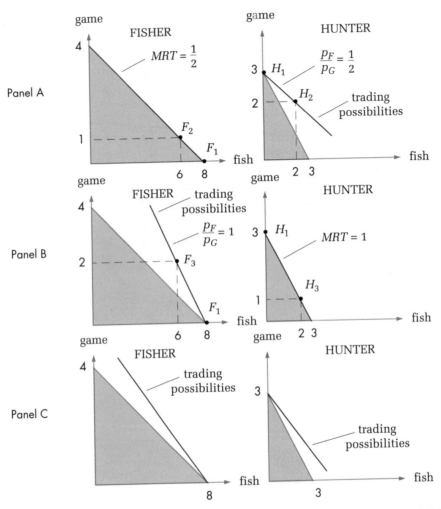

Figure 2.3   **Production possibilities and gains from trade: Panel A** The terms of trade are $p_F/p_G = 1/2$. **Panel B** The terms of trade are $p_F/p_G = 1$. **Panel C** The intermediate terms of trade are $1/2 < p_F/p_G < 1$.

parties are producing both goods, it is always possible to increase total production and expand the consumption possibilities of one or both trading partners.

How will the gains from specialization and trade be shared? A full answer to this question requires us to consider the relative prices of the goods as determined by demand and supply. But a partial answer can be given by considering the terms of trade—the price ratio. The **terms of trade** depends on the quantity of one good that can be obtained per unit of the other good as measured by the price ratio:

> **Terms of trade:** *The terms of trade is given by the quantity of one good that can be obtained per unit of another good as measured by the price ratio.*

If the price of fish is p_F and the price of game is p_G, the price ratio is p_F/p_G. The price ratio p_F/p_G measures the units of fish that have to be sold to buy one unit of game.

Autarky implies self-sufficiency and a total absence of trade. In autarky, you can consume only what you produce. Thus, in autarky, a party's production possibilities curve (whether that party is an individual, firm, or nation) also represents that party's consumption possibilities. But with trade, gains in consumption will be possible as long as the terms of trade, the price ratio, lies between the *MRT*s of the potential traders. With constant opportunity costs, complete specialization will yield the maximum potential gain from trade. Let's assume then that the person fishing produces at point F_1 and the hunter produces at point H_1 in Figure 2.3.

Suppose that the terms of trade as given by the price ratio is $p_F/p_G = 1/2$, as shown in panel A. The hunter's consumption possibilities can now be increased beyond the hunter's production possibilities by trading game for fish. If the hunter trades one unit of game for two units of fish, as dictated by the terms of trade, the hunter will be able to consume at point H_2 if the fisher is willing to consume at point F_2. Thus the hunter's consumption possibilities have been increased beyond his production possibilities.

Instead, suppose that the terms of trade is given by $p_F/p_G = 1$ in panel B. Now the fisher's consumption possibilities increase beyond the fisher's production possibilities. If the fisher trades two units of fish for two units of game in accordance with the terms of trade, the fisher will be able to consume at point F_3 if the hunter is willing to consume at point H_3.

We haven't yet determined how prices are set, but the final price ratio will lie between the two *MRT*s of the hunter and fisher, $1/2 < p_F/p_G < 1$, as shown in panel C. When this arrangement happens, both the hunter's and the fisher's consumption possibilities are increased by specializing in production and engaging in trade. The slope of the consumption, or trading, possibilities curve for each person is equal to the negative of the price ratio. Where trade will occur along the trading possibilities curve will depend on the tradeoffs between consuming fish and game the hunter and the fisher are willing to make. But whenever both wish to consume some of each good, collective consumption possibilities will be greater with specialization and trade than under autarky. Their choices will be influenced by their preferences and by prices determined by market supply and by market demand for fish and for game. Demand and supply and price determination are the topics in Chapter 3.

2.4 Trades and Increasing Opportunity Costs

A production possibilities curve bulges outward when there is a diminishing marginal rate of transformation. Complete specialization is unlikely because of the increasing opportunity costs in production. And yet trade still leads to an expansion of the set of goods that can be consumed in two ways: by allowing the bundle of goods consumed to differ from the bundle produced and by permitting a profitable change in the production mix. With trade, the consumption and production bundles can be altered independently.

Figure 2.4 shows a production possibilities curve for an economy producing two goods, X and Y, say xylophones and yams. Under autarky, if the economy produces bundle **A** it must consume bundle **A**. Given the terms of trade, trading possibilities extend the trading possibilities to bundles like **B**. They do so because ΔY units of yams, given the price of yams p_Y, generates just enough income to buy ΔX units of xylophones, given the price of xylophones p_X. That is, the price ratio p_X/p_Y determines the rate of exchange, $\Delta Y/\Delta X$, which is possible along the trading possibilities curve. If this economy prefers **B** to **A**, it can export ΔY units of yams and import ΔX units of xylophones.

Even greater gains can be made by changing the production bundle until the marginal rate of transformation of X from Y is equal to the rate of exchange of X for Y, $MRT_{XY} =$

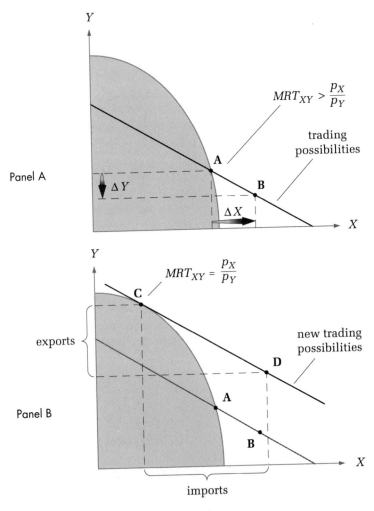

Figure 2.4   **Gains from trade: Panel A** With trade, the economy producing at **A** can consume at **B**. **Panel B** With a change in production to point **C**, the economy can now afford to consume a bundle like **D**.

GLOBAL PERSPECTIVE: *The Rusting Steel Industry*

The steel industry in the United States performed poorly during the 1970s and 1980s. Industry profits were subnormal after the late 1950s, but employment decreased dramatically during the 1970s. This slump was caused primarily by a rapid increase in steel imports and a subsequent decline in the domestic production of steel.* The U.S. steel industry faced tough new competition from foreign producers as changes in technology and costs altered the comparative advantages in steel making.

Earlier, abundant supplies of coal and iron ore, along with high labor productivity, gave the United States a cost advantage. Discovery of rich iron-ore deposits in several other parts of the world, however, plus decreased costs in ocean shipping, began to reduce the U.S. advantage. The growth in steel consumption in such countries as Japan allowed them to build new, technologically efficient plants. The resulting productivity growth, combined with lower wage rates, reduced the unit cost of labor further below the U.S. level. The average hourly compensation for iron and steel workers in the United States grew faster than in foreign importing countries. This imbalance would not have been a problem if increases in labor productivity had kept pace with wage increases, but productivity gains were sluggish in the United States.

All this change meant that the United States experienced an increase in the opportunity costs of producing steel and lost its comparative advantage. By insisting on high wages, steelworkers themselves were partly responsible for the decline, but labor was not solely to blame. Management failure to invest in more efficient technologies and to organize production more efficiently also had a lot to do with the decline.

* There was also a sharp decrease in steel demand because of steel substitutes like aluminum, plastics, and composites.

---

p_X/p_Y. In Figure 2.4, an expansion of consumption possibilities occurs by increasing the production of the good being exported and decreasing the production of the good being imported. Why? Because this economy has a comparative advantage in producing good X at the current terms of trade. This advantage can be seen by noticing that $MRT_{XY} > p_X/p_Y$ at point **A.** Production should shift toward producing more yams and fewer xylophones until the trading possibilities curve is just tangent to the production possibilities curve at a point like **C** where $MRT_{XY} = p_X/p_Y$. Then, under the current terms of trade, bundles like **D** become affordable.

This classical model of the gains from trade leads to the conclusion that people, firms, and nations should tend to specialize in producing goods in which they have a comparative advantage. Increasing opportunity costs and the resulting bulge in the production possibilities curve means that complete specialization is not likely. Nevertheless, economic actors tend to specialize in a narrow range of activities. The engineer may be a better auto mechanic than Mr. Goodwrench, but still hires the mechanic because the engineer has a comparative advantage in engineering.

On a world scale, the pattern of international comparative advantage is greatly influenced by a country's natural endowments. Some nations are rich in fertile land, others are rich in petroleum. Canada produces wheat and Saudi Arabia produces oil. Some comparative advantages are static and determined by natural endowments, but others are dynamic. Changes in technology, physical capital, education, and experience cause changes in comparative advantages. A nation can lose its comparative advantage if it does not preserve its natural resources and the health of its people. Another nation can gain a comparative advantage if it invests in physical and human capital.

2.5   Technology and Growth

Technology is the state of the art in production. Any production possibilities curve is drawn assuming constant technology. As technology changes, the production possibilities set expands. Suppose that technological change makes it possible to produce more of good X with the resources available. The maximum of X that can be produced increases as shown in Figure 2.5. The technology used in producing good Y does not

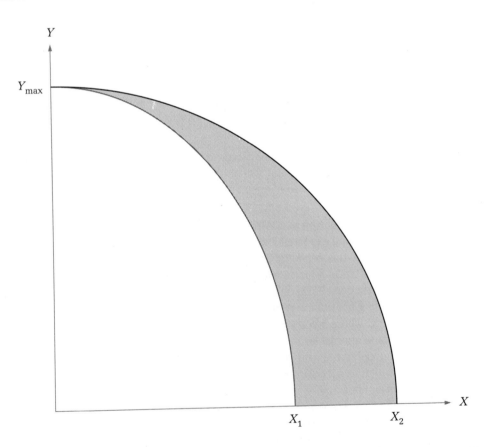

Figure 2.5 **Technological change in producing X:** A change in the technology used in producing good X increases the maximum amount of X that can be produced from X_1 to X_2. The technology used in producing good Y is unchanged, and so the maximum amount of Y that can be produced is unchanged.

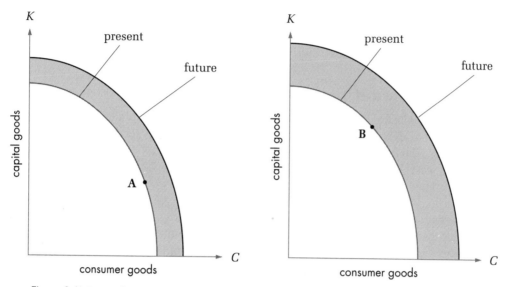

Figure 2.6 **Present choice and growth:** If the economy chooses bundle **A** in the present, it experiences some growth in its production possibilities curve because capital can be used to enhance future production. But if the economy chooses bundle **B** in the present, the economy grows faster because more capital is available to enhance future production.

change, but the technological improvement in producing X shifts the production possibilities curve outward as shown.

Other things too can cause the production possibilities curve to shift outward. For instance, a general increase in the productivity of labor due to, say, a general improvement in health will cause the maximum quantities of all goods to increase. The discovery of a new source of raw material or other inputs will expand the production possibility set.

The choice of goods produced today may affect future production possibilities. Diverting consumption in the present into saving to be used for investment and capital creation will also affect the position of the curve in the future. Suppose we classify all goods as either consumer goods or capital goods. Such capital goods as industrial machinery can be used to increase future production and consumption. Figure 2.6 shows two examples. If the economy chooses bundle **A** along its present production possibilities curve, the capital produced can be used to increase future production and consumption of

ECONOMIC SCENE: *Japan's Growth*

Japan has experienced rapid economic growth since the middle of the twentieth century. One of the reasons was its high savings rate. In the 1960s and early 1970s when output in Japan was growing at about 10 percent per year, the Japanese were saving about 25 percent of their income. This saving was channeled into investment in new capital and research. The Japanese were adopting and developing newer technologies in production. This expansion has contributed to an outward shift in Japan's production possibilities curve at a rate more rapid than that experienced in the West.

both goods. But if the economy chooses the more capital-intensive bundle **B** in the present, the economy grows faster because more capital is available to enhance future production. The economy faces a choice between current consumption and future growth.

2.6   The Market Solution

The production possibilities model is a very simple picture of the choices available to society. All modern economies produce thousands of goods and services, not just two. Nevertheless, the model does illustrate some important concepts—scarcity, choice, and opportunity cost. The model emphasizes the basic economic problem of making choices when confronted with scarce resources, but it does not answer the questions of what, how, for whom, and when.

Different societies use different ways to answer the fundamental questions. The market mechanism is the major device used in the United States. Private buyers and sellers exchange money for resources or products in markets. Money prices are used to ration scarce resources and products among competing uses with very little centralized control. Queuing, random selection, tradition, brute force, and command are alternative ways of rationing scarce resources and products. Although the market system is the main mechanism in the United States, it also uses elements of a command economy by providing public goods and government income transfers. The United States thus has a *mixed* economic system, but the emphasis is on decentralized decision making in markets.

Economic systems can also be described by their pattern of ownership—private or public. Under **capitalism** the means of production are owned primarily by individuals and decisions are decentralized. Under **fascism** the means of production are also privately owned but decisions are centralized. Public ownership is a characteristic of **socialism** and **communism,** but decision making is decentralized under socialism and centralized under communism. The system in the United States is perhaps best described as **mixed capitalism** because it has some public ownership and some centralized decision making.

The private-ownership market system can be illustrated by the **circular flow model** in Figure 2.7. The two sets of markets are product markets and factor markets. A **market** is any situation in which buyers and sellers interact. Buyers make offers to exchange money for things, and sellers make offers to exchange things for money. Barter is possible, but we are assuming that money is used as a medium of exchange. The economy is divided into two sectors: households and firms. We assume that the household (which may consist of one individual) is organized for the purpose of consumption. The firm (which may also consist of one individual) is organized for the purpose of production.

Members of society perform dual roles as consumers and producers. Individuals own the factors of production: land, labor, and capital. People sell and organize the factors to produce goods and services to consume, making a real flow of resources from members of households to firms. Firms transform the factors of production into products that are then sold back to households, creating a real flow of goods and services from firms to households.

As households buy the goods and services, money flows through the product market to firms. This consumer expenditure becomes revenue to the firms. The firms use this

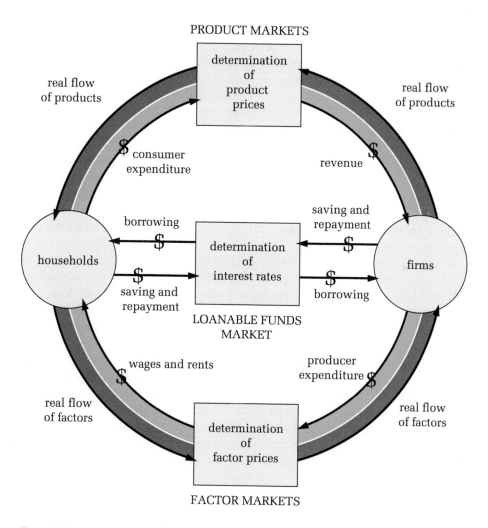

PRODUCT MARKETS

determination
of
product
prices

real flow
of products

real flow
of products

$ consumer
expenditure

revenue $

borrowing
$

saving and
repayment
$

households

determination
of
interest rates

firms

$
saving and
repayment

$
borrowing

LOANABLE FUNDS
MARKET

wages and rents
$

producer
expenditure $

real flow
of factors

real flow
of factors

determination
of
factor prices

FACTOR MARKETS

Figure 2.7 **The circular-flow model:** In a counterclockwise direction is a real flow of factors of production being transformed into goods and services. In the other direction is a balancing flow of money in the form of consumer expenditure becoming revenue to firms that is paid to the factors of production becoming household income.

revenue to buy the factors of production from owners, making a money flow through the factor market to households, completing the cycle. The producer expenditure, the firms' costs of production, becomes the money income of members of households. Money circulates through the economy in one direction, and the real factors being transformed into products flow in the opposite direction.

Not all individuals wish to spend their current income on consumption. Some people save current income for future use. Other people spend more than their current income will allow and must borrow from their future income. Similarly, firms frequently borrow from future revenue. Other firms may spend less than their current revenue and generate positive cash flow. A **loanable funds market** facilitates the flow of funds between savers and borrowers. Financial intermediaries like banks, savings and loans, and stock and bond brokers act as agents in the money market. Financial intermediaries are a special type of firm providing a service to both savers and borrowers.

The forces of demand and supply interact in all markets to determine market clearing prices. Prices communicate information that coordinates the separate actions of different firms and households. These prices ration the limited goods and services produced and also signal which goods and services should be produced and in what quantities. In the factor markets, the prices are wage rates for labor services and rental rates for the use of land and capital. These factor prices influence the level and distribution of incomes to households. In the loanable-funds market the price for lending and borrowing money is called the interest rate.

The operation of the price system answers the fundamental questions. Product prices determine what is produced as firms react to consumer demands. Factor prices determine how inputs should be combined in producing products to meet the consumer demands. In turn, both factor prices and product prices determine how total income is allocated among members of this society. All this activity happens without centralized decision making as each individual makes choices and exercises free will.

This simplified picture of the price system disregards intra-firm and intra-household transactions. The model also ignores flows of imports and exports between this economy and other countries. It is, therefore, a model of a closed economy, but where withdrawals and injections between it and the foreign sectors occur, it could be expanded to become a model of an open economy. Moreover, this simplified model disregards the public sector and the role of government. We shall expand the model to include the public sector and the role of government following a closer look at the role of the firm and profit seeking.

2.7 The Firm and the Role of Profit

A firm combines and organizes resources for the purpose of producing goods and services for sale. Firms produce about 88 percent of the goods and services consumed in the United States. The remainder are produced by governments.

In principle, firms are not necessary. All production and distribution could be organized by contractual agreements between economic agents. Firms arise, however, for two reasons. First, the *transactions costs* of engaging in individual contracts are usually high. Information and the act of negotiating contracts are costly. Such transactions costs may be lower when inputs are bought by a firm and organized to produce and distribute a good. Second, *group production* is usually more efficient. Group production may permit specialization that is not possible when one person works alone. Moreover, inputs may be complementary in that the productivity of inputs may be enhanced when used jointly. For example, it is more efficient for a tender to toss a brick to a mason atop a wall than for the mason to climb up and down to set each brick. Group production permits specialization. As the group becomes larger, though, the cost per unit of production will eventually increase, and additional costs will be incurred for organizing and supervising the group.

Nevertheless, the gains made possible by organizing production and exchange in firms are usually greater than the initial costs.

Most proprietorships and partnerships seek to maximize the wealth of their owners, which can be accomplished by maximizing profits. In a corporation, however, ownership and control are frequently separated in that the managers are distinct from the owners. Owners define the goals of the corporation and then must monitor the managers to see that they work toward the stated goals. We will assume, for simplicity, that the goal of the firm is to maximize profit. But profit in this model is *not* accounting profit. Profit is equal to revenue minus costs. Revenue is easy to measure—it is the price per unit multiplied by the number of units sold. Cost, however, is not so easy to measure.

Economic analysis uses the concept of opportunity cost in measuring the costs of production. From an economic perspective the "real" cost of producing a product is what could have been produced if the resources had been used in other employment. Thus the natural way to measure the cost of producing a good is to add the values of the inputs used in producing the good. But how should the values be measured? The concept of opportunity cost indicates that the value of any resource is the payment required to keep that resource in its current employment. We will refer to such cost as **economic cost:**

> **Economic cost:** *The payment that a resource would receive in its best alternative employment opportunity.*

Economic cost is likely to differ from bookkeeping or accounting measures of cost. Accounting costs are bookkeeping entries for explicit or imputed expenditures on productive activities. Expenditures on labor services are explicit costs. Depreciation of physical capital is an imputed cost. Economists frequently assume that the wage rate measures the opportunity cost of alternative employment of labor, so that accounting and economic costs would be the same for labor. In contrast, accounting and economic costs differ greatly in measuring the cost of capital services.

Accounting practice usually takes the historical cost of acquiring a piece of capital equipment and then applies some more-or-less arbitrary depreciation rule to determine how much of the historical cost to impute to the current period. Economists regard the historical cost as a "sunk" cost. Sunk costs are irrelevant to making production decisions in the current period. In determining the economic cost of capital, it makes no difference whether the firm owns the capital or not, and it makes no difference what the capital originally cost. If the firm does not own the capital, the opportunity cost of capital is the rental rate that must be paid to obtain the capital service. If the firm does own the capital, the opportunity cost is still the rental rate that would have to be paid if the capital service were obtained from the market.

One form of labor deserves special attention: the labor services provided by entrepreneurs.

> **Entrepreneurs:** *These are the risk takers, innovators, and organizers of the factors of production.*

Entrepreneurs provide three services. They organize the factors of production as managers. They innovate by introducing new products and developing new technologies. They also assume the risks associated with producing goods and services to be sold in a world of uncertainty. Without the innovative, risk-taking propensity of entrepreneurs, the market economy would not operate as efficiently as it can. In a quest for economic profit, entrepreneurs are motivated to use the most efficient production methods in transforming inputs into products under the present technology, and they are motivated to innovate by developing new products and new technologies. In this way, entrepreneurs contribute to the efficient operation of the economy and to economic growth.

Just like any other input, the economic cost of the entrepreneurial service is its opportunity cost. Accounting profit and economic profit are therefore measured differently. **Accounting profit** is the difference between revenue and accounting costs, so that accounting profit may or may not include all the opportunity cost of the entrepreneurial service. The cost can go either way because the compensation paid to the entrepreneur may not be equal to the entrepreneur's opportunity cost. In contrast, **economic profit** is the difference between revenue and economic costs, and economic costs always include the opportunity cost of the entrepreneurial service.

> **Economic profit:** *Economic profit is revenue less all the opportunity costs of inputs associated with the activity.*

All inputs have an opportunity cost. The opportunity cost of capital services is its market rental rate. The opportunity cost of labor is the wage rate that could be earned elsewhere. The opportunity cost of the entrepreneurial service is its earning capacity in the next best alternative. Thus if we take revenue less the opportunity costs of labor, capital, and materials, we still have to subtract the opportunity cost of the entrepreneur to get economic profit. Thus economic profit is *net* revenue in excess of the earning capacity of the entrepreneur's abilities in the next best alternative. An engineer may be able to earn $60,000 per year. If this engineer starts his own consulting business and earns an accounting profit of $70,000 per year, the business yields an economic profit of $10,000 per year.

In this book, as you might expect, we use the economic definitions of cost and profit. We do so because these definitions are broadly applicable to all firms regardless of their accounting practices. Moreover, the economic definitions are most suitable for decision making and best suited for the theoretical analysis of optimal resource allocation. For instance, we may be interested in predicting how a tax on profits may affect the firm's supply decision in order to judge whether or not the firm is using resources efficiently. To achieve this prediction the opportunity costs of resources need to be considered, and the use of economic definitions of cost are consistent with that need.

In a world of perfect certainty, owners' wealth can be maximized by maximizing the present value of the firm, and that is achieved by maximizing the present value of a stream of future profits obtained with certainty. This result applies even to a corporation because *shares* are bought and sold in the stock market. The price of each share is the present value of the stream of dividends that the owners expect to receive. The total value of all stocks is the present value of the stream of profits and capital gains that the firm is expected to generate. In a world of perfect certainty, the goal of maximizing profit is equivalent to maximizing stock-market value, and the owners' wealth will be as large as possible.

In a world of uncertainty, corporation owners expect to be compensated for risk. As usual, managers expect to be compensated for their organizational ability. When the entrepreneurial function is divided between risk takers and managers, maximization of the expected profit may not lead to maximization of owners' utilities—especially if managerial decisions do not reflect the owners' attitudes toward risk. Nevertheless, maximizing stock-market value still gives a well-defined goal for the firm.[3] Moreover, profit maximization usually results in the maximizing stock-market value if managers accurately judge and respond to the owners' attitudes toward risk. In any case, we will begin by assuming that firms act "as if" they strive to maximize profits because, in a competitive environment, the market makes firms behave as profit maximizers if they are to remain competitive.

The assumption of profit maximization has been criticized as narrow and unrealistic. Alternative assumptions have been proposed. Among these is a model of sales maximization proposed by William Baumol.[4] According to the **sales maximization model,** managers of corporations seek to maximize sales subject to a constraint that an adequate return to stockholders is generated. But the empirical evidence is mixed, and the model becomes one of profit maximization if the "adequate" return to stockholders accurately measures their opportunity costs. Another alternative is a model of **management utility maximization** proposed by Oliver Williamson.[5] According to this model, corporate managers maximize their own utility in terms of salaries and fringe benefits. Such managers may be replaced, however, once owners become aware of their managerial behavior—or owners may link managerial rewards to the profit of the company. A third alternative is proposed by Richard Cyert and James March, building on the work of Herbert Simon.[6] They propose that managers strive for "satisfactory" performance in a world of uncertainty. Simon called this **satisficing behavior.** Satisficing is not, however, inconsistent with the maximization of expected profit in a world of uncertainty.

Profit seeking serves a crucial role in the private-ownership, market economy. Profits compensate entrepreneurs for their willingness to take risk. Without the expectation of profit, there would be no reward for risk taking. Profits also compensate for innovation. Without the expectation of profit there would be no reward for introducing new technology. Profits are the reward for greater efficiency. Profits also arise from changing market

---

3. Maximizing stock-market value will usually maximize *expected* utility, the sum of the separate utilities of uncertain outcomes weighted by their probabilities of occurrence, if the owners' attitudes toward risk are reflected in the stock price.
4. W. J. Baumol, *Business Behavior and Growth* (Macmillan, 1959).
5. O. E. Williamson, "A Model of Rational Managerial Behavior," in R. M. Cyert and J. G. March, eds., *A Behavioral Theory of the Firm* (Prentice-Hall, 1963).
6. R. M. Cyert and J. G. March, eds., *A Behavioral Theory of the Firm* (Prentice-Hall, 1963), and H. A. Simon, "Theories of Decision-Making in Economics," *American Economic Review,* 49 (June 1949).

conditions. High profits cause industry expansion and reallocation of resources into that industry. Low profits or losses cause industry contraction and release of resources to be used elsewhere. Therefore, profits provide crucial signals for reallocating the economy's resources in order to satisfy buyer demands.

2.8   The Role of Government

The circular-flow model of the market economy can be modified to include the public sector. One of the primary roles of government is providing public goods.

> **Public good:** *a good that is either nonexclusive or nonexhaustive in consumption.*

A public good has one or both of these characteristics: nonexclusivity or nonexhaustibility in consumption. What do these terms mean?

A good is **nonexclusive** in consumption if its consumption by one person makes it available to everyone else at no additional cost. Examples include national defense, public health, public parks, and police protection. Once these goods are made available to society at large, they are available to everyone whether they want them or not. In some cases, exclusion is possible but impractical. For instance, charging a toll for using a public sidewalk would be too costly to administer.

A good is **nonexhaustive** in consumption when its consumption by one person does not preclude its consumption by another. Until a sidewalk becomes crowded, its use by one person does not diminish its availability to another. Clean air provided by an environmental program is available to everyone equally. The characteristic of nonexhaustion is rarely an absolute. The use of a turnpike is available to everyone, but it may become so crowded that the service provided is reduced. But until some degree of overcrowding is reached, an additional user causes no extra cost to society or any reduction in service to previous users.

Public goods are rarely provided by the private sector because it is so difficult to recover the costs of providing such goods. No one person is willing to pay the whole cost of providing a public good, and sharing expense is difficult because of the "free-rider" problem. A **free rider** is a person who enjoys a benefit without paying any share of the cost. Once a public good is provided, any one person might wish to become a free rider and still enjoy the good. Individually people are better off as free riders even though collectively they are worse off if everyone tries to be a free rider. The price system does not function well in the provision of public goods. Therefore, government usually provides public goods. Taxes are imposed to pay for the public good as a way to mitigate the free-rider problem, and the good is available to society as a whole. And so everyone pays and everyone benefits to one extent or another.

Providing public goods is one of the major functions of government. In the United States, about 20 percent of total output in the economy is purchased using public revenues. About 60 percent of that 20 percent is produced in the public sector and 40 percent is produced through contracts with private profit-oriented and not-for-profit firms. Figure 2.8 illustrates a modified version of the circular-flow model. The public sector

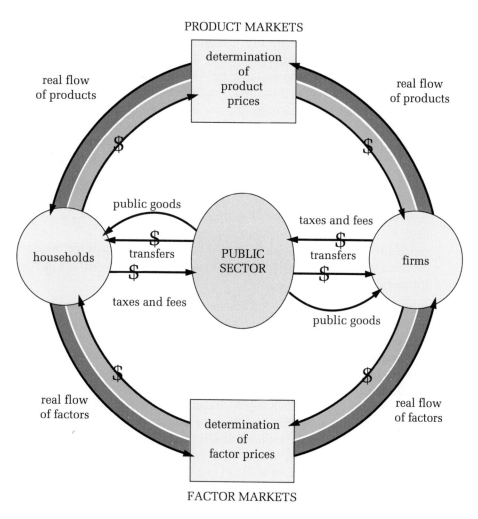

PRODUCT MARKETS

determination
of
product
prices

real flow
of products

real flow
of products

$

$

public goods

$

taxes and fees

$

households

transfers

$

PUBLIC
SECTOR

transfers

$

firms

taxes and fees

public goods

$

$

real flow
of factors

real flow
of factors

determination
of
factor prices

FACTOR MARKETS

Figure 2.8 **Circular flow with public sector:** A real flow moves to the public sector and an opposite money flow to the factors of production. A real flow goes from firms to the public sector, which is transformed, along with the real flow of other inputs, into a real flow of public goods and services to households. Money flows in the form of fees and taxes from firms and households, and money flows in the form of income transfers or payments to households and firms.

functions as a special type of market and as a special type of decision maker. In a democracy, collective decisions are made about which public goods to produce and how to produce them. To raise money to pay for public goods, taxes and fees are imposed on members of households and on firms. This public revenue is used to purchase inputs from the factor markets and to purchase goods and services from the product market. These real flows of inputs and products are transformed into public goods that then flow back to households and firms. The government also transfers some of its revenue back to households and firms in the form of subsidies or welfare payments.

The modified model of Figure 2.8 does not show all the money and real flows. For instance, there can be real flows directly from households to the public sector—like military service under a draft or the transfer of property when the right of eminent domain is exercised. This modified model also no longer includes the financial sector. These exclusions are made only to keep the illustration simple. Nevertheless, the model is useful to emphasize one important role of government, providing public goods.

Government has several other roles in a market economy. Government involvement is required because a private-sector economy alone cannot perform all the necessary microeconomic functions. Besides providing public goods, the government must:

- regulate the activities of individuals when their behavior deviates from the public interest;
- regulate the activities of firms when their behavior deviates from the public interest;
- provide a functionally operable (equitable) distribution of income and wealth;
- provide a legal structure that establishes property rights and permits private transactions.

We will examine these functions more closely as we progress through this text. All these functions are required to provide an environment in which the price system can operate most efficiently and fairly.

Efficient resource use requires that we know what to produce. For any combination of goods and services being produced, resource use influences the distribution of income. That income distribution will in turn affect output decisions as people make choices. Starting from some initial distribution of wealth, the efficient use of resources may lead to a socially unacceptable distribution of income. We may choose, then, as a society, to redistribute income. When we do so, we must make value judgments, which are unavoidable in making such decisions.

Primitive societies, for example, were forced to sacrifice the lives of physically handicapped newborn children and mentally impaired adults to attain a level of efficiency necessary for their societies to subsist. Most modern societies, however, are not forced to sacrifice their least productive members if they cannot produce as much as they consume. We therefore redistribute income from the more fortunate to the least fortunate and equity takes precedence over efficiency.

Summary

Every economic system must answer three fundamental questions: What is to be produced? How is it to be produced? For whom is it to be produced? These questions arise because of the fundamental problem of scarcity. Scarcity occurs because resources are limited and wants unlimited. Therefore, society is faced with making choices about what to produce, how to organize and use the limited resources in production, and how to distribute the real income and wealth created by transforming inputs into outputs. Society is also faced with the question of when to produce and consume. The timing of production and consumption affects savings and the level of investment and hence influences the position of the production possibilities curve in the future.

The production possibilities curve identifies the production tradeoffs with full and efficient employment of all resources. The negative of the slope of the production possibilities curve is called the marginal rate of transformation (*MRT*). The *MRT* measures the opportunity cost of producing an extra unit of one good in terms of the required decrease in the other good. Opportunity cost is the cost of forgone alternatives. The characteristic bulge in the production possibilities curve results in a *diminishing MRT* and reflects an *increasing* opportunity cost in the production of any good.

An individual, firm, or economy has an *absolute* advantage in trade when fewer resources are needed to produce a good than are needed by another. An individual, firm, or economy has a *comparative* advantage when the opportunity costs are lower than another's. Economic actors should specialize in production when they have a comparative advantage and then engage in trade to increase consumption beyond their production possibilities. When opportunity costs are increasing, economies will not completely specialize. Rather, they should produce along their production possibilities curve where the *MRT* is equal to the terms of trade as measured by relative prices.

Discovery of new resources and changes in technology can increase production possibilities. Moreover, production possibilities can be increased through increases in factor productivity. Thus, investments in physical and human capital can increase production possibilities and influence choice.

In a market system, decentralized decisions are made by individuals. When money is used as a medium of exchange, money prices are used to ration scarce resources among competing uses. Markets arise where trades take place. Under capitalism, the means of production are owned primarily by individuals and decision making is decentralized. All economic systems, however, have some centralized decision making and some public ownership and regulation because of the existence of public goods and externalities.

A market is the event of buyers and sellers interacting. The forces of demand and supply interact in markets to determine market clearing prices. The prices communicate information and coordinate the separate actions of economic actors.

Firms arise to organize inputs efficiently and to reduce the transactions costs of organizing inputs. Owners and entrepreneurs are motivated by the search for profit. Entrepreneurs are the risk takers and organizers of the factors of production. Without the innovative, risk-taking propensity of entrepreneurs in their search for profit, the market system would not operate as efficiently as it can. Without the expectation of profit, entrepreneurs would not be willing to take the risks associated with innovation. Without profits, markets would not operate efficiently in reallocating resources to satisfy buyers' demands.

Markets do not always operate perfectly. Public goods, for instance, are not traded efficiently in markets because such goods are either nonexclusive or nonexhaustive in consumption. These characteristics make it difficult for private firms to recover the costs of providing such goods. Therefore public goods are usually provided by government. Taxes and fees are imposed to pay for the public goods.

In this chapter we have surveyed the workings of the price system and its failures in answering the fundamental questions. But we only hinted at how the system works. For instance we observed that prices are determined by demand and supply. What is demand?

What is supply? And how are prices determined? Those are the topics in the next two chapters.

Further Readings

The Chapter 1 references remain relevant. Add these two authors, who present highly persuasive but contradictory views of the role of government—if you read one you should read both:

- John Kenneth Galbraith, *The Affluent Society* (Houghton Mifflin, 1958).
- Milton Friedman and Rose Friedman, *Free to Choose* (Harcourt Brace Jovanovich, 1980).

For a hard-headed liberal economist's recent and passionate defense of economics as a tool for advancing the common good, see

- Alan S. Blinder, *Hard Heads, Soft Hearts* (Addison-Wesley, 1987).

I also recommend

- Robert H. Frank, *Choosing the Right Pond: Human Behavior and the Quest for Status* (Oxford University Press, 1985).

Frank argues that some government programs and policies arise because of collective needs to circumvent individual tendencies to spend too much private income on "positional" goods in a quest for status.

If, at this juncture, your instructor is supplementing the text with calculus-based extensions and applications, you might wish to review the use of functions and graphs in Appendix A. For an excellent calculus textbook, see

- Roland E. Larson, Robert P. Hostetler, and Bruce H. Edwards, *Calculus,* 4th ed. (D. C. Heath, 1990).

Practice Problems

1. What is the basic economic problem and what causes it?
2. How do a nation's natural endowments influence the position and shape of its production possibilities curve? How does this effect determine the kinds of outputs for which a nation has comparative advantages?
3. The Banana Computer Company uses silicon memory chips in making its products. Because of its technical skills and production experience, Banana can produce chips more cheaply than any other manufacturer, domestic or foreign. Thus Banana has an absolute advantage in manufacturing memory chips. Should Banana ever buy chips from any other company? Why or why not? Should Banana specialize in producing
4. Given the quantities of wheat and cloth that can be produced in America and Korea as shown in the table, calculate the opportunity cost of wheat and cloth in America and Korea. Which country has an absolute advantage in producing each good? Which country has a comparative advantage in producing wheat? In producing cloth?

	Wheat (bushels)	Cloth (yards)
America	100	60
Korea	5	10

Calculate the gains from specialization when each country produces one more unit of the good for which it has the lowest opportunity cost.

5. Ms. Smith has a reputation for being a dedicated and efficient manager. She is also a phenomenal typist. Ms. Smith, however, does not do her own typing. Rather, she assigns that task to Mr. Jones, her secretary, who types only half as fast. Why does the slower typist do all the typing? Who is the more efficient typist?

6. A recent study estimated that quotas on imported Japanese automobiles in the early 1980s cost American consumers about $160,000 per year for each auto worker's job that was saved (Robert W. Crandall, "Import Quotas and the Automobile Industry," *Brookings Review* [Summer 1984]):

   (a) If you were an American automobile manufacturer, would you favor or oppose import quotas? Why?

   (b) If you were an auto worker in the United States, would you favor or oppose import quotas? Why?

   (c) If you were an auto worker in the United States, would you take a single cash payment of $160,000 in return for leaving the industry to look for work elsewhere? Why or why not?

   (d) As an American consumer, do you favor or oppose import quotas on Japanese automobiles? Why?

7. Draw a diagram of the circular-flow model of the private-ownership, market economy with both a public sector and the financial sectors included. Show both money flows and real flows. Now add a foreign sector with imports and exports.

8. Classify these things as public or private goods. For each, briefly explain your choice:

   (a) service of a traffic cop   (b) service of a security guard
   (c) information   (d) knowledge
   (e) mosquito control   (f) a giant redwood tree
   (g) a pair of jeans   (h) city sidewalks
   (i) strawberries   (j) the Statue of Liberty

The Basics of Demand and Supply

Every market is composed of demand and supply, and market price is determined by the interaction of demand and supply. But what is market demand? And what is market supply? Moreover, how do they interact to determine market price?

Demand is a complex subject, but managers and policymakers need to understand it thoroughly to help them make decisions that will achieve their goals. Market demand can be found by aggregating all consumers' demands. To see how that works, suppose there are only two consumers, and suppose we know how much of a good each wants to buy at any price. Then all we need to do to find market demand at any price is to add the quantities being demanded by both consumers. Because each consumer's choice is influenced by other prices, income, preference, and expectations, market demand is a function of other prices and consumers' incomes, preferences, and expectations. In general, market demand for any good is a function of the good's price, other prices, and consumers' incomes, preferences, and expectations as well as the number of consumers.

Once we have market demand, then each firm's demand can be found by disaggregating market demand into each firm's share. This is an important step because the firm's share determines how its revenue varies with price and quantity and hence influences whether or not it will be able to make a profit.

Consumers' choices, then, determine the market demand for a good and influence the demand for each firm's products. This influence applies even to intermediate goods used by other firms in producing goods for final consumption. Consumers' choice influences the demand for intermediate goods because that demand is derived from the demand for the final good. In a later chapter, however, we will fully consider the demand for intermediate goods and other inputs in the production process; first we need to examine technology's influence on production. For now, be aware that the demand for inputs in any production process is a *derived* demand—demand for raw materials, labor, and capital is derived from the demand for the good being produced.

Supply too is a complex subject. For any product, market supply is found by aggregating all individual firms' supplies. Each firm's decision about how much of the product to supply is a function of product price, input prices, production technology, and expectations. Once we know the supply decision of each firm, we can construct market supply by aggregating their individual supply decisions. We will examine the firm's supply decision in later chapters in the context of different market structures. For now, we concentrate on the consequence of those individual decisions as summarized by market supply. Similarly, supplies of land, labor, and capital—the so-called factors of production—are found by aggregating all individual owners' supplies. We will examine individual factor supply decisions in later chapters in the context of individual choice.

In this chapter we study the basics of market demand and market supply, learning how market price is determined. In Chapter 4, methods are assembled for analyzing the strength of demand and the responsiveness of demand to changing conditions. Our investigation will also help us to specify models that can be used to estimate demand functions, a topic in another chapter. Later, we will consider in detail how individual consumer choice determines market demand. Also later, after examining how technology affects production possibilities and costs, we examine how firms decide how much to supply. For now, we concentrate on the basics of *market* demand and supply.

3.1   Market Demand

Many things influence market demand for a good—consumers' preferences, their incomes, the prices of other goods, and the good's own price. If Q_X is the quantity of some good X, p_X is that good's price, p_Y and p_Z are the prices of other goods, M is the money income of all consumers, T denotes the current set of tastes held by consumers, E denotes consumers' expectations, and n is the number of consumers, the demand for good X as a function of these variables can be denoted by

$$Q_X = D_X (p_X, p_Y, p_Z, M, T, E, n)$$

Thus the quantity of good X demanded is a function of all those variables as well as some others that are not listed.

We start, however, by holding everything constant except the good's own price. Let $Q = D(p)$ denote the relationship between the quantity demanded and the good's price in a market. The function $D(p)$ represents market demand as a function of price, with everything else held constant.

> **Market demand:** *Market demand* D(p) *is the aggregation of all consumers'* *demands at every price.*

When graphed, as illustrated by Figure 3.1, quantity demanded as a function of price alone is called a **demand curve.**

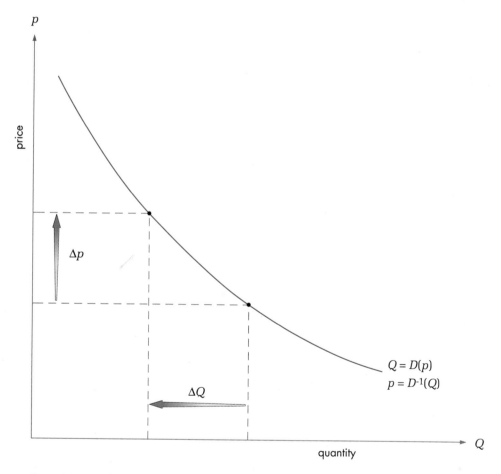

Figure 3.1 **A market demand curve:** The market demand curve $Q = D(p)$ has negative slope, $\Delta Q / \Delta p < 0$, for two reasons. First, as price increases, consumers look for substitutes. Second, as price increases, consumers' real incomes fall. The inverse market demand curve $p = D^{-1}(Q)$ treats price as a function of quantity.

> **Demand curve:** *The market demand curve is the graph of quantity demanded as a function of price,* $Q = D(p)$.

We expect quantity demanded to be inversely related to price, and so the graph of this function will have negative slope,

$$\text{slope } = \frac{\Delta Q}{\Delta p} < 0$$

The slope measures the change in quantity demanded when price changes. Care must be taken, however, in measuring and in interpreting the slope of the demand curve because economists usually graph the demand curve with quantity, the dependent variable, on the horizontal axis, as illustrated by Figure 3.1. This practice is contrary to the mathematical convention of graphing the dependent variable on the vertical axis. Economists break with that convention for good reasons, but this departure can be a source of confusion.[1]

For two reasons we expect the demand curve to have negative slope. First, as the good's price increases, consumers find substitutes that become relatively less expensive. For example, if the price of Coca-Cola increases, consumers look for substitutes like Dr Pepper or 7-Up whose prices have not changed. This is called the **substitution effect:**

> **Substitution effect:** *Quantity demanded decreases when price increases alone because consumers look for substitutes.*

Second, as the good's price increases, each dollar spent will buy fewer units than before. Consumers' real incomes, or purchasing power, fall with a price increase, and they normally buy less of any good.[2] This reaction is called the **income effect:**

> **Income effect:** *Quantity demanded normally decreases when price increases because consumers' purchasing power falls.*

Normally, both substitution and income effects of price changes will contribute to the inverse relationship between price and quantity demanded.

When the demand curve $Q = D(p)$ is inverted to get $p = D^{-1}(Q)$, it is called the **inverse demand curve:**

> **Inverse demand curve:** *An inverse demand curve is price as a function of quantity demanded—the demand curve* $Q = D(p)$ *is inverted to get* $p = D^{-1}(Q)$.

The inverse demand curve has slope $\Delta p/\Delta Q$, the inverse of the demand-curve slope.

---

1. One reason is that we will be interpreting demand curves as average revenue curves, and average revenue equals price. The role of price is thus emphasized by placing price on the vertical axis. Another reason is that later we will superimpose average revenue curves on top of average cost curves, and so if price were not already on the vertical axis we would have to switch axes at that time.
2. Exceptions are called inferior goods compared to the normal-good case. We look at inferior goods later in this chapter.

3.2   Shifts in Demand

When determinants of demand other than price change, the whole demand curve shifts. Shifts in the demand curve are called **changes in demand:**

> **Change in demand:** *A shift in the demand curve caused by changes in the determinants of demand other than the good's own price.*

A change in demand is illustrated by Figure 3.2. The whole demand curve shifts. At any given price, say $p = p_1$, the quantity demanded increases from Q_1 to Q_2. Changes in demand are caused by changes in the prices of other goods and consumers' incomes, preferences, and expectations. Market demand also changes when the number of consumers in the market changes. When demand increases, the demand curve shifts to the *right*. When demand decreases, the demand curve shifts to the *left*.

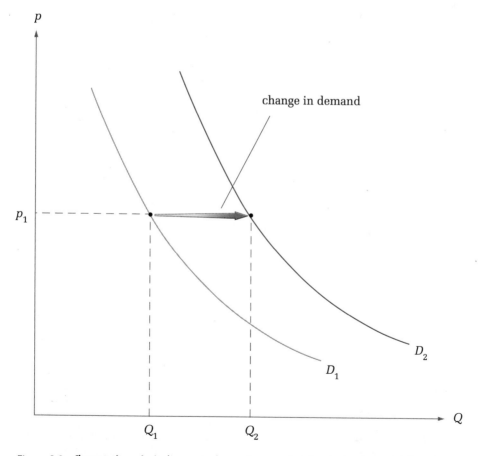

Figure 3.2   **Change in demand:** A change in demand means that the demand curve shifts—the quantity demanded increases, say, from Q_1 to Q_2 when price remains constant at $p = p_1$.

ECONOMIC SCENE: *Champagne Tastes**

Nearly a decade ago, the historic and staid champagne houses of France decided to change the image of their products. Slick and flashy promotional campaigns featured long-legged blondes and bubbly froth to lift champagne sales. Successfully. Sales increased by 75 percent between 1982 and 1990, and exports doubled. Prices, of course, increased sharply. Premium champagne may cost more than $40 a bottle.

Such increases will, in all likelihood, provide greater profits to the champagne makers. But they describe their situation as regrettably being forced to ration shipments to clamoring retailers. Many people wonder why champagne houses do not increase production in response to the increase in demand. The reason is that the French government has limited the area where grapes for champagne can be grown. In an international agreement signed by many countries, but not the United States, only sparkling wines made in a specified region in France may be called champagne.

Even with fixed supply, the rising prices caused by the outward shift in demand will soon force quantity demanded to equal quantity supplied. The rising prices will motivate many customers to turn to respectable, less-expensive sparkling wines from California, Spain, Australia, and Brazil.

In contrast to worldwide growth, champagne sales in the United States have declined in recent years. This drop reflects both growing antialcohol sentiment and the weaker dollar. With a decline in the value of the dollar relative to the franc, champagne prices are even higher in the United States. Not only has a growing distaste for alcoholic beverages decreased demand in the United States, increasing relative prices have also cut the quantity demanded.

---

*This vignette is based on Steven Greenhouse, "Champagne Taking an Elite Turn," *The New York Times,* Thursday, October 18, 1990.

In summary, the market demand *curve* relates quantity demanded to price alone because other things are held constant. The market demand *function,* however, relates quantity demanded to price *and* all the other things that influence consumers' choice. Thus, in addition to a good's own price, market demand is a function of other prices, the level and distribution of consumers' incomes, preferences, expectations, and attitudes, and of the number of consumers. Demand *changes,* the demand curve *shifts,* when determinants of demand other than price change. Most of those other things are beyond the firm's control. Although the firm may be able to set its own price, it has no control over other prices. Likewise, the firm may be able to influence preferences with advertising, but it has little or no control over individual consumer preference or any of the other things that influence demand. How these things influence demand matters, however, because the firm needs to be able to forecast demand.

As an example of how demand changes, consider what happened to the demand for gasoline during the early days of the Persian Gulf crisis late in 1990. After Iraq invaded Kuwait, the United Nations imposed an embargo on crude oil exported by Iraq. Moreover, a U.N. military response was led by the United States, and several nations sent troops into the region to prevent Iraq from also invading Saudi Arabia and other oil-producing countries. The threat of war caused consumers to react by increasing their demand for gasoline. Many consumers, both individuals and firms, began to stockpile or hoard gasoline, expecting shortages and price increases. The demand curve shifted to the right as the demand for gasoline increased. We will later see how this reaction contributed to the short-run increase in gasoline prices.

3.3 Normal Goods and Inferior Goods

Normally, we expect demand to increase when consumer income increases. Therefore, when the demand curve for a good shifts to the right, that good is called a **normal good:**

> **Normal good:** *A good the demand for which increases when consumer income alone rises.*

Occasionally the demand for a good decreases when consumer income rises, and the demand curve shifts to the left. Such a good is called an **inferior good:**

> **Inferior good:** *A good for which demand decreases when consumer income alone rises.*

In the United States the market demand for potatoes decreases slightly when consumer income rises, and so potatoes are classified as an inferior good. Not that Americans don't like potatoes; rather, collectively they decrease their demand for potatoes when their incomes rise.

A change in consumers' incomes affects their ability to purchase goods and hence influences their choices. Thus, a change in consumers' income, or a change in the distribution of income, may influence market demand. The market demand for a good depends on its own price, the price of related goods, and consumers' money incomes. For two goods X and Y, the demand function for good X may be written

$$Q_X = D(p_X, p_Y, M)$$

where p_X is the price of good X, p_Y is the price of good Y, and M is consumers' money income. The other determinants of demand are being held constant, and so their role is suppressed in our notation. When market demand is written as a function of price alone, the market demand *curve* may be written

$$Q_X = D(p_X; p_Y, M)$$

to emphasize that p_Y and M are being held constant while p_X is allowed to vary. Similarly, when market demand is written as a function of income alone, it may be denoted

$$Q_X = D(M; p_X, p_Y)$$

to emphasize that p_X and p_Y are being held constant while M is allowed to vary. When quantity demanded is expressed as a function of income alone, it is called an **Engel curve:**

> **Engel curve:** *An Engel curve is a graph of quantity demanded as a function of money income.*

An Engel curve and two demand curves for good X are illustrated in Figure 3.3. The Engel curve is drawn for price p_1, which denotes that price is fixed at $p_X = p_1$. When the Engel curve has positive slope, demand increases when income increases, and the good is a normal good. The positive slope of the Engel curve in panel A of Figure 3.3 means that consumers collectively behave as if good X were normal. As M increases to $M + \Delta M$,

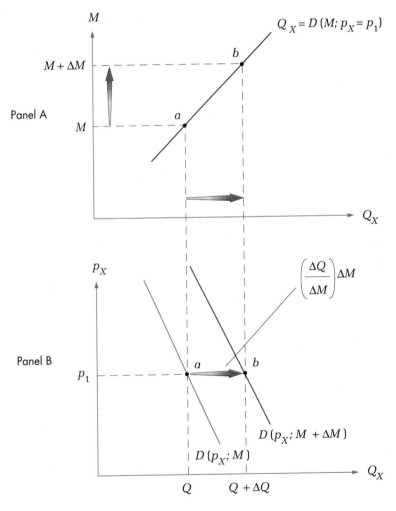

Figure 3.3   **Income change and a normal good: Panel A** For a normal good, an increase in income causes a slide along the Engel curve from **a** to **b** and $\Delta Q > 0$. **Panel B** A corresponding increase occurs in demand—a rightward shift in the demand curve.

quantity increases from Q to $Q + \Delta Q$, given $p_X = p_1$. Thus in panel B, market demand shifts to the right in response to the increase in income. The direction of the shift is indicated by the sign of the slope of the Engel curve, and the size of the slope measures the magnitude of the shift in demand.

As an algebraic example, suppose the demand function is

$$Q_X = D(p_X, M) = 50 - 10p_X + 5M$$

To graph the Engel curve, we must know price. Suppose price is equal to $p_X = 5$, then the Engel curve becomes

$$Q_X = D(M; p_X = 5) = 5M$$

If $M = 10$, then $Q_X = 50$. If $M = 20$, $Q_X = 100$. Notice that the slope of the Engel curve is $\Delta Q_X / \Delta M = 5$. Now let's fix M and find the ordinary demand curve. If $M = 10$, then

$$Q_X = D(p_X; M = 10) = 100 - 10p_X$$

When $p_X = 5$, $Q_X = 50$, as before. If $M = 20$, then

$$Q_X = D(p_X; M = 20) = 150 - 10p_X$$

When $p_X = 5$, $Q_X = 100$, as before. If graphed, it is easy to see that the demand curve would shift to the right as income increases.

When the Engel curve has negative slope, demand decreases when income increases, and the good is an inferior good. Figure 3.4 illustrates the inferior-good case. As consumers' income changes from M to $M + \Delta M$, a slide occurs along the negatively sloped Engel curve in panel A. Quantity decreases from Q_X to $Q_X + \Delta Q_X$ where $\Delta Q_X < 0$. At price $p_X = p_1$ is a corresponding shift in the market-demand curve in panel B. The demand curve shifts to the left in response to an increase in income when consumers collectively view the good as inferior. The sign of the slope of the Engel curve indicates the direction of the shift, and the size of the slope of the Engel curve measures the magnitude of the shift.

3.4 Market Substitutes and Market Complements

Shifts in demand may also occur in response to changes in the price of another good. Again, for two goods X and Y, the market demand for good X may be written

$$Q_X = D_X(p_X, p_Y, M)$$

When the other price and income are held constant, the demand curve may be written

$$Q_X = D_X(p_X; p_Y, M)$$

to emphasize that the position of the demand curve depends on p_Y, the other good's price, as well as money income. When the price of the other good changes, the demand for X shifts. The good X is called a **market substitute** for Y when a direct relationship

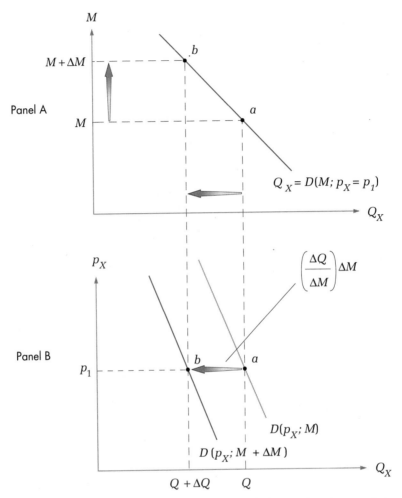

Figure 3.4   **Income change and an inferior good: Panel A** For an inferior good, an increase in income causes a slide along the Engel curve from **a** to **b** and $\Delta Q < 0$. **Panel B** A corresponding decrease occurs in demand—a leftward shift in the demand curve.

connects the demand for X to the price of Y. The good X is called a **market complement** for Y when an inverse relationship applies between the demand for X and the price of Y.[3]

Figure 3.5 illustrates X as a market substitute for Y. Suppose good X represents IBM personal computers and good Y represents Apple Macintosh PCs. Given an increase in the price of the Macintosh (Y), the quantity of Macs demanded decreases. If consumers

3. The labels *market substitute* and *market complement* emphasize that a good is classified according to a response in the market by all consumers. We can distinguish between *gross* and *net* substitutes or complements; these labels describe the behavior of one consumer. *Gross substitute* and *gross complement* describe one consumer's choices as price changes. *Net substitutes* and *net complements* describe a consumer's willingness to trade between two goods as determined by the consumer's preferences and the consumption technology—topics for a later chapter.

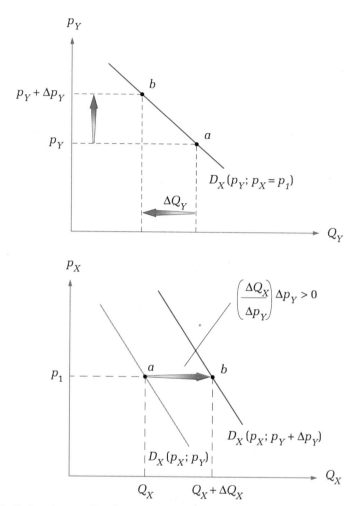

Figure 3.5 **Market substitute:** Good X is a market substitute for good Y because the demand for X increases to $Q_X + \Delta Q_X$ with $\Delta Q_X > 0$ in response to the decrease in Y to $Q_Y + \Delta Q_Y$ with $\Delta Q_Y < 0$ caused by the increase in p_Y. That is, X is substituted for Y when the price of Y increases.

respond by increasing their demand for IBMs (X), then X has been substituted for Y.

Figure 3.6 illustrates X as a market complement of Y. Now suppose that good X represents software by Microsoft for the Mac. Good Y is the Macintosh. When the price of the Macintosh (Y) increases, again the quantity of Macs demanded decreases. If consumers respond by decreasing their demand for Microsoft software (X), a complementary change follows in the demand for X with respect to Y.

Our observations lead to these definitions:

> **Market substitute:** *A good is a* **market substitute** *for a second good when the demand for the first good* increases *in response to an increase in the price of the second good.*

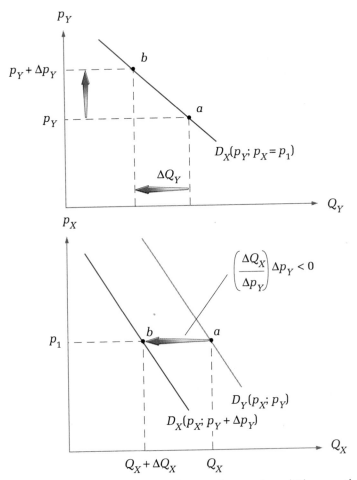

Figure 3.6 **Market complement:** Good X is a market complement of good Y because the demand for X decreases to $Q_X + \Delta Q_X$ with $\Delta Q_X < 0$ in response to the decrease in Y to $Q_Y + \Delta Q_Y$ with $\Delta Q_Y < 0$ caused by the increase in p_Y. That is, a complementary decrease occurs in X as Y decreases when the price of Y increases.

> **Market complement:** *A good is a **market complement** of a second good when the demand for the first good decreases in response to an increase in the price of the second good.*

Suppose the price of gasoline increases dramatically, as it did in response to the OPEC oil embargo early in the 1970s and again late in the 1970s. The American consumer responded by switching to smaller, more fuel-efficient cars. The demand for large cars decreased, which proved to be market complements with respect to gasoline. The demand for smaller cars increased and they proved to be market substitutes for gasoline. Consider also the short-run 1990 increase in the price of gasoline in response to the Persian Gulf crisis caused by Iraq's invasion of Kuwait. This rise followed a resurgence of the demand for "muscle cars" during the 1980s. If the price of gasoline increased permanently, what do you predict would happen to the demand for large and small cars even though a substantial portion of the American public preferred large cars?

3.5 Market Supply

The supply of any *product* depends on its price, the prices of inputs, the current production technology, the competition between firms, the goals of producers, and the producers' expectations and attitudes about taking risks. The same things will influence a firm's demand for factors of production. The supply of any *factor* depends on its price and all the things that affect consumer demand. Factor supply and consumer choice are connected because consumers in a private-ownership economy own the factors of production.

Market supply is the aggregation of the supplies by all potential sellers. Again, however, we start by holding everything constant except the good's price. Let $Q = S(p)$ denote the relationship between the quantity supplied with the good's price in a market. The function $S(p)$ represents market supply as a function of price, with everything else held constant.

> **Market supply:** *Market supply* S(p) *is the aggregation of all firms' supplies at every price.*

We expect quantity supplied to be directly related to price, and so the graph of this function will have positive slope, $\Delta Q/\Delta p > 0$. When graphed, quantity supplied as a function of price alone is called a **supply curve.**

> **Supply curve:** *The supply curve is the graph of quantity supplied as a function of price,* Q = S(p).

Figure 3.7 illustrates a positively sloped supply curve. The main reason supply curves have positive slope also explains why production possibilities curves are "bulged" outward. Opportunity costs are increasing because of diminishing returns from variable inputs used in producing any good.

When the supply curve $Q = S(p)$ is inverted to get $p = S^{-1}(Q)$, it is called the **inverse supply curve:**

> **Inverse supply curve:** *The inverse supply curve is the graph of price as a function of quantity supplied—the supply curve* Q = S(p) *is inverted to get* p = S⁻¹(Q).

The inverse supply curve has slope $\Delta p/\Delta Q$, the inverse of the slope of the supply curve.

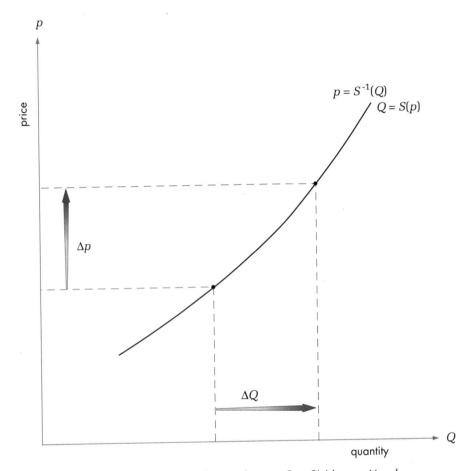

Figure 3.7 **A market supply curve:** The market supply curve $Q = S(p)$ has positive slope, $\Delta Q/\Delta p > 0$, because of diminishing returns to variable inputs. The inverse supply curve $p = S^{-1}(Q)$ treats price as a function of quantity.

3.6   Shifts in Supply

Shifts in the supply curve are called **changes in supply:**

> **Change in supply:** *A shift in the supply curve caused by a change in the determinants of supply other than the good's own price.*

A change in supply is illustrated by Figure 3.8. The whole supply curve shifts. At any given price, say $p = p_1$, the quantity supplied increases from Q_1 to Q_2. This change in supply may have been caused by a technological improvement in producing the product, a reduction in the price of any factor of production, or an increase in the number of firms producing the product. When supply increases, the supply curve shifts to the *right*. When supply decreases, the supply curve shifts to the *left*.

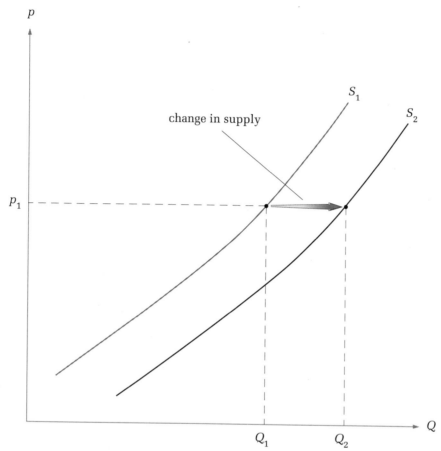

Figure 3.8 **Changes in supply:** A change in supply means that the supply curve shifts—the quantity supplied increases, say, from Q_1 to Q_2 when price remains constant at $p = p_1$.

In summary, the market supply curve relates quantity supplied to price while other things are held constant. The market supply *function*, however, relates quantity supplied to price and all other things that influence suppliers' decisions. For a good being produced, market supply is a function of the good's price, the price of inputs used in production, the underlying production technology, the goals of producers, their expectations and attitudes, and the number of producers. If any of these other things change, the whole supply curve will shift.

Consider again the Persian Gulf crisis of 1990. The cutoff of crude oil from Iraq and Kuwait decreased the number of producers supplying oil. At the same time the opportunity costs of oil reserves to be used in making gasoline increased. Uncertainty was rampant about potential future supplies. The risks associated with being in the oil business increased, and, in compensation, firms required a higher rate of return. Although other countries reacted by increasing their planned production, the adjustment took time, and so the market-supply curve of gasoline shifted to the left as the supply of oil decreased. We will see later how these things also contributed to the rising price of gasoline in the short run and the eventual decline in the price of gasoline in the long run.

3.7 Market Equilibrium and Changes in Equilibrium

A market is in equilibrium at some price when quantity demanded is equal to quantity supplied. The market clearing price, or equilibrium price, is the price at which quantity demanded is equal to quantity supplied.

A market equilibrium is illustrated by Figure 3.9. The market clears at price p_e, where quantity demanded is equal to quantity supplied, $D(p_e) = S(p_e)$. At any price like p_1 that is lower than p_e, the quantity demanded is greater than the quantity supplied, creating a shortage, and price will be bid up. At any price like p_2 that is higher than p_e, the quantity demanded is less than the quantity supplied, so that a surplus exists and price will be bid down. The market is at rest—reaches an equilibrium—at p_e, where no further change in price will occur as long as no change occurs in demand or supply.

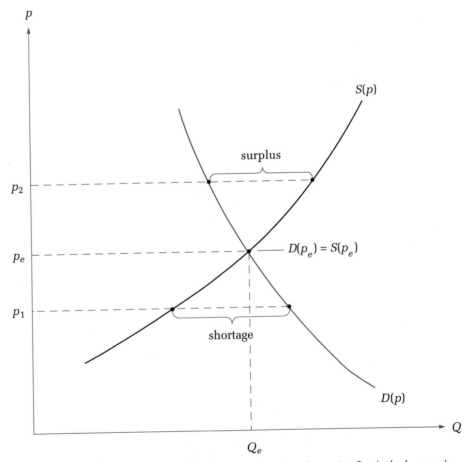

Figure 3.9 **Market equilibrium:** The market clears at price p_e and quantity Q_e. At the lower price p_1 a shortage occurs because quantity demanded is greater than quantity supplied, and so price rises. At the higher price p_2 a surplus appears, and so price falls.

Do not fall into the habit of saying that equilibrium occurs when demand equals supply, because demand *never* equals supply. If it did, that would imply that the demand curve coincides with the supply curve.

This algebraic example illustrates how equilibrium price is determined. Suppose demand and supply are given by

$$\text{demand:} \quad Q = D(p) = 80 - 4p$$
$$\text{supply:} \quad Q = S(p) = -10 + 6p$$

The equilibrium price occurs where quantity demanded equals quantity supplied:

$$D(p_e) = S(p_e)$$

Substitution yields

$$80 - 4p_e = -10 + 6p_e$$

Solving for price yields

$$p_e = 9$$

Equilibrium quantity can be found by evaluating either demand or supply at p_e:

$$Q_e = D(p_e) = S(p_e) = 44$$

You might wish to reinforce your understanding of market equilibrium by computing the quantity demanded and quantity supplied at prices other than $p = 9$.

Changes in equilibrium occur when demand or supply change, as illustrated by Figure 3.10. In panel A, an increase in supply leads to a decrease in equilibrium price. Of course a decrease in supply would lead to an increase in price. In panel B, an increase in demand leads to an increase in equilibrium price. Similarly, a decrease in demand would lead to a decrease in price.

Markets do not remain static. Changes occur in both demand and supply, especially as time passes. In Figure 3.11, equilibrium price has been drifting down as supply has increased faster than demand. This is the change that happened, for instance, in the market for personal computers. When the personal computer was introduced by Apple, demand gradually increased as people learned how to use the machine. At an accelerated pace, the personal computer became common in the home and the office. If demand had increased alone with no change in supply, equilibrium price would have risen. Instead, other firms, such as IBM and Compac, entered the market while Apple was introducing its Macintosh line. This entry and expansion in the industry caused supply to increase faster than demand, resulting in a downward drift in the price of personal computers.

The forces of demand and supply work in input markets, too. Consider a case wherein two employees, one male and the other female, face a wage adjustment. If the two workers have equivalent skills in performing the tasks required by the employer, if the risks associated with hiring either person do not differ, and if discrimination is not present, both workers should be paid at the same wage rate. Later we will see that these conditions must apply in competitive markets, because the firm will not be able to maximize profit and practice discrimination at the same time.

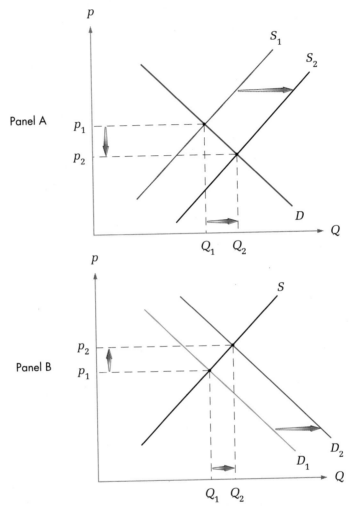

Figure 3.10 **Changes in equilibrium: Panel A** An increase in supply causes a decrease in equilibrium price. **Panel B** An increase in demand causes an increase in equilibrium price.

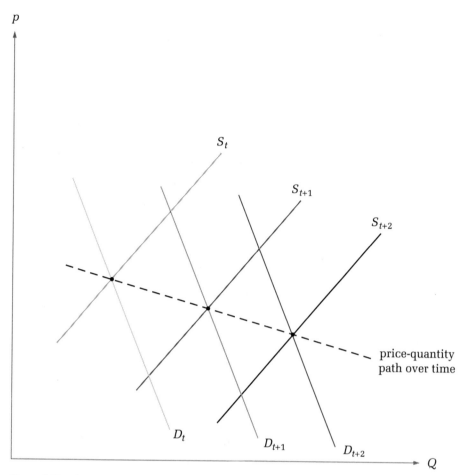

Figure 3.11 **Changes in demand and supply:** In this market, demand has increased more slowly than supply over time, and so the equilibrium price has been drifting downward.

ECONOMIC SCENE: *Gasoline Price Changes in 1990*

Late in 1990, the Persian Gulf crisis resulted in a dramatic short-run increase in the pump prices of gasoline across the United States and around the world. As illustrated by the *B.C.* cartoon "Warp Speed" by Jonny Hart, consumers were amazed at how fast suppliers responded to the threat of decreased supplies of crude oil. The rapid response and the large price increases of 30 percent or more at the pump led consumers to accuse the big oil companies of price "gouging." In fact, however, we can see more plausible explanations for the gasoline price increases.

By permission of Johnny Hart and NAS, Inc.

Figure 3.12 illustrates what happened in the market for gasoline. Demand increased from D_1 to D_2 as consumers stocked up on gasoline as a hedge against possible shortages. Market equilibrium price increased from p_1 to p_2. At the same time, crude oil supplies from the Gulf decreased. The decrease in the supply of crude along with the increased risks of doing business in the Gulf, and the increased opportunity costs of reserves of crude and gasoline caused a decrease in the supply of gasoline. The decrease in supply caused the price to rise from p_2 to p_3, and equilibrium quantity decreased from Q_2 to Q_3.

One company, ARCO, was so sensitive to the charge of price gouging that it froze the pump price at its service stations. This freeze lasted only a few days, for ARCO experienced shortages.

The decrease in domestic supply was magnified further when the United States began to export oil to Europe. Higher prices in Europe made it profitable to export oil from the United States in spite of the cost of transportation. In summary, U.S. firms were responding to changing market conditions and making rational profit-maximizing decisions. Evidence of the collusion that would be necessary for price gouging is distinctly lacking.

To top it all off, a 5¢-a-gallon hike in the federal gasoline tax took effect in December 1990, but pump prices nationally rose only 2.1¢ a gallon in response. "I had no choice," said a Shell dealer in California who raised his pump prices only 2 to 3¢ a gallon.* "It was either eat the difference or lose my [sales] volume."

---

*As reported by Patric Lee, *Los Angeles Times,* Wednesday, December 5, 1990.

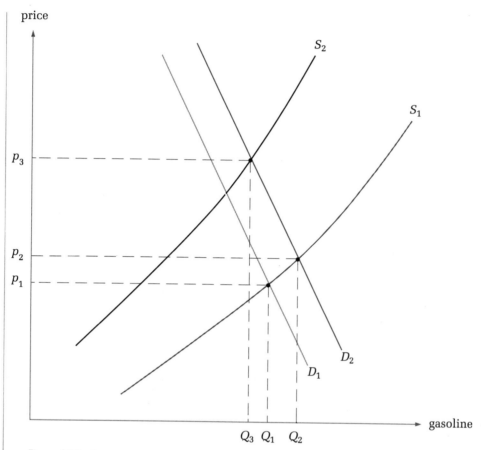

Figure 3.12 **Short-run gasoline price increase:** Late in 1990, the Persian Gulf crisis caused consumers to increase their demand for gasoline as a hedge against potential shortages and price increases. At the same time, crude oil supplies from the Gulf decreased. This dual change, along with the increased risks of doing business in the Gulf and the increased opportunity cost of reserves of crude and gasoline, caused a decrease in supply. The increased demand and the decreased supply caused the equilibrium price of gasoline to increase.

The automobile association reported that the national average retail price for self-service regular unleaded gasoline increased 2.1¢ in response to the 5¢ increase in the tax. Why were retailers unable to pass along the entire tax? The answer is found in the market, where the supply curve has positive slope and the demand curve has negative slope. As the inverse supply curve shifted up by an amount equal to the tax hike, the equilibrium price changed by an amount less than the tax hike. If consumers had not been responsive to price changes, retailers would have been able to pass along the entire tax. Said one Chevron dealer: "Regardless of what happens, if you don't stay competitive on the street, you don't stay in business."

AN APPLICATION: *An Excise Tax on Gasoline*

In 1990, the state of California imposed a 5¢ excise tax on each gallon of gasoline sold. How will that tax affect the pump price of gasoline? Who pays the tax, the consumer or the supplier? An excise tax is levied on a product such as gasoline. The tax is imposed by government but collected by firms that act as government's agents. Each firm's supply decision is based on the part of the price charged to consumers that the firm retains, and so the supply decision is based on the market price less the excise tax. That is, if p is the market price and t is a per unit excise tax, then the part of the market price retained by the supplier is $p - t$. Because the effective supply price to each firm is reduced by the tax, each firm will decrease its quantity supplied at every market price, and supply decreases.

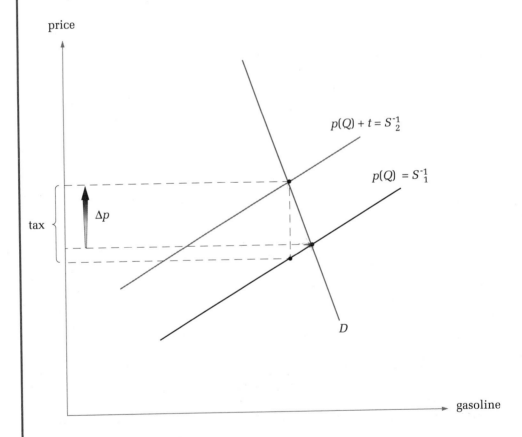

Figure 3.13 **An excise tax on gasoline:** The vertical distance between the old and new supply curves is equal to the excise tax. Supply has decreased because quantity supplied is lower at any market price. The change in equilibrium price is less than the excise tax as long as the supply curve has positive slope—as long as the demand curve is not vertical.

Figure 3.13 illustrates what will happen. Each service station will attempt to pass on the financial burden of the tax by increasing its price. That is, if a firm is to continue to produce the same quantity as before, the firm must receive the same supply price as before. The firm will therefore raise the price at every quantity supplied. If $p(Q) = S^{-1}$ is the supply price before the tax, given the supply curve S_1, after the tax the supply price will be $p(Q) + t$, and supply shifts to curve S_2. The vertical distance between the old supply curve and the new is equal to the per unit tax, and the effect on the supply curve is to shift the curve to the left. At every market price the quantity supplied is less than it was before the tax.

In the typical case, where the demand curve has negative slope and the supply curve has positive slope, the increase in the equilibrium price will be less than the tax. The proportion of the per unit tax paid by the consumer can be measured by dividing the price change by the tax:

$$\text{consumers' share} = \Delta p/\text{tax}$$

The producers' share is that proportion of the tax not successfully passed on to consumers:

$$\text{producers' share} = 1 - (\Delta p/\text{tax})$$

Thus, in the typical case, part of the tax will be borne by consumers and part by suppliers.

GLOBAL PERSPECTIVE: *Flexible Exchange Rates*

The exchange rate is the ratio at which one country's currency can be converted into another's. How are exchange rates determined? Well, one way is by government dictate. The government sets the exchange rate as, say, one dollar is equal to so many marks, so many yen, so many pounds, and so on. This exchange can be accomplished by setting a fixed price on some common means of payment—historically, it was gold. If the exchange rate is fixed and the country is importing (buying abroad) more than it is exporting (selling abroad), the resulting deficit in its balance of payments will cause an outward flow of the accepted means of payment (gold).

At the opposite extreme are completely flexible exchange rates. The forces of demand and supply determine the rates of exchange between currencies. If Germans desire to import goods from the United States, ignoring international investment flows, this exchange generates a supply curve of German marks seeking to buy U.S. dollars, as shown in Figure 3.14. The supply of German marks is upward sloping because, as the price of the mark in dollars goes up, U.S. goods become cheaper in marks and Germans will want to buy more U.S. goods. The demand curve for marks is downward sloping because, as the price of the mark in terms of the dollar goes down, German goods become cheaper in dollars and Americans will want to buy more German goods. The exchange rate is determined where supply intersects demand. The equilibrium "price" becomes $/m, the dollar price of one mark.

dollars per mark

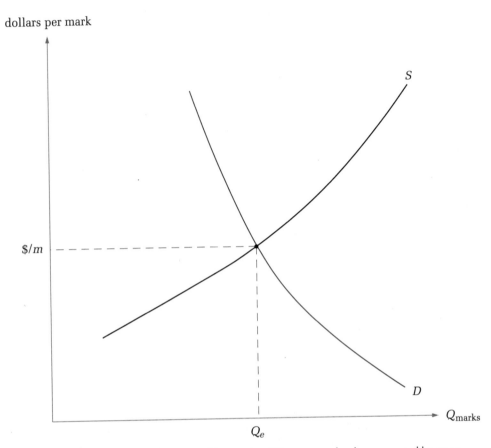

Figure 3.14 **Determining an exchange rate:** The supply of German marks slopes upward because, as the price of the mark in dollars goes up, U.S. goods become cheaper in marks and Germans will want to buy more U.S. goods. The demand curve for marks slopes downward because, as the price of the mark in terms of the dollar goes down, German goods become cheaper in dollars and Americans will want to buy more German goods. The exchange rate is determined where supply intersects demand. The equilibrium "price" becomes $/mark, the dollar price of one mark.

3.8 Gains from Equilibrium Pricing: Buyer Surplus and Seller Surplus

In any market, social gains can come from trading at the equilibrium price, and you will learn eventually that those gains are maximized under the form of market structure called perfect competition. That is why economists use the results of perfect competition as a benchmark to measure the effects of other forms of market structure and the effects of departures from equilibrium pricing.

To the buyer, the *marginal* value of the *last* unit consumed is the market price. In contrast, the *use* value of *each* unit consumed is the price that the consumer would have paid to get each unit. All buyers, however, pay only the market price or marginal value of

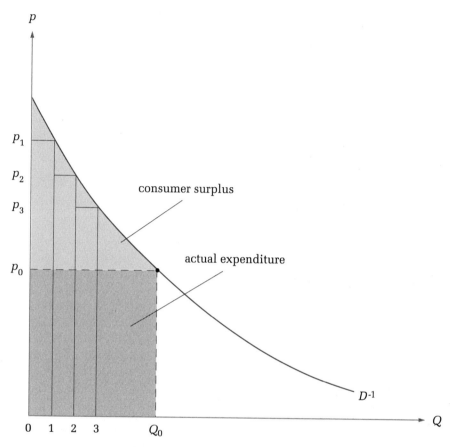

Figure 3.15 **Consumer surplus:** The total use value of Q_0 units at price p_0 is equal to the area under the inverse demand curve D^{-1} between $Q = 0$ and $Q = Q_0$. Consumer surplus equals the difference between total use value and actual expenditure.

the last unit for all units. As illustrated by Figure 3.15, as the quantity demanded increases from $Q = 0$ to $Q = Q_0$, buyers would have been willing to pay $p(Q)$ for each unit Q. For instance, consumers would pay p_1 to get the first unit, p_2 to get the second, p_3 to get the third, and so on. Thus, the *total* value of Q_0 is the sum of the prices that buyers would have been willing to pay for all units up to Q_0. The total value of Q_0 units can be approximated by adding up the use values of all units consumed; that is, by adding the areas of the rectangles at p_1, p_2, p_3, and so on, up to p_0. The total value can be measured exactly by the total area under the inverse demand curve $p(Q)$ from $Q = 0$ to $Q = Q_0$. The buyers, however, pay only the marginal value p_0 for the Q_0 units consumed, and so a *surplus* value is received by buyers at the current price, p_0. That surplus, the difference between the total value and the actual expenditure, is called **consumer surplus:**

> **Consumer (buyer) surplus:** *Consumer surplus is the total benefit, or value, that buyers receive beyond what they pay for a good.*

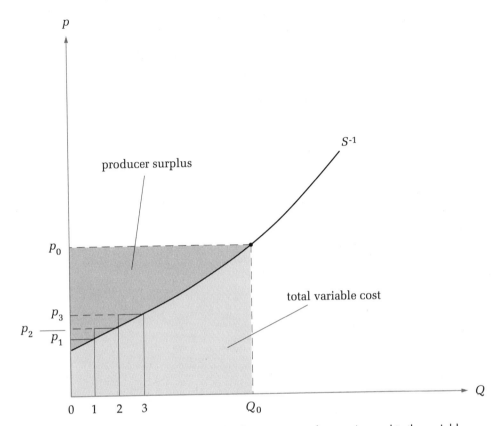

Figure 3.16 **Producer surplus:** The area under the inverse supply curve is equal to the variable cost of producing Q_0 units. Producer surplus equals total revenue received, $p_0 Q_0$, less total variable cost.

Given the market price for a good, the value of the good to some buyers exceeds the market price paid by those buyers, and those consumers would pay more for the good if they had to. Consumers who value the good less than market price will not purchase the good. At the current market price, consumer surplus equals the total amount that demanders would have been willing to pay for all units consumed, less the actual expenditures.

Similarly, sellers of a good receive a surplus also. The price of each unit sold must at least equal its average variable cost of production. In other words, the producer must receive a price not less than the unit variable cost. If the price is less than the unit variable cost, the producer will shut down and supply zero units. Otherwise the seller will not be able to cover the variable costs of production. As illustrated by Figure 3.16, as the quantity supplied increases from $Q = 0$ to $Q = Q_0$, suppliers would have been willing to sell at price $p(Q)$ for each unit. Thus, the area under the inverse supply curve between $Q = 0$ and $Q = Q_0$ must be equal to the total variable cost of producing Q_0 units. This area can be approximated by adding up the areas of the rectangles at p_1, p_2, p_3, and so on up to p_0, and total variable cost can be measured exactly by the area under the supply

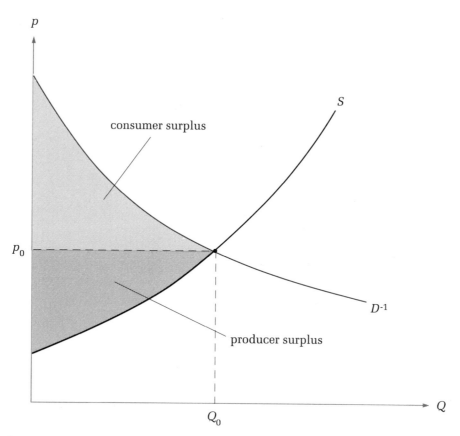

Figure 3.17 **Welfare gain from market trading:** The total welfare gain from trading at the equilibrium price is the sum of consumer surplus and producer surplus—the entire shaded area between the supply and demand curves at the equilibrium point.

curve. But the seller receives price p_0 for all units sold up to Q_0, and so total revenue is $p_0 Q_0$, which is greater than the total variable cost of producing Q_0 units. Thus, the seller receives a surplus over the variable costs of production. **Producer surplus** is equal to the area to the left of the supply curve at the current price and is equal to revenue less total variable cost.[4]

> **Producer (seller) surplus:** *Producer surplus is the total value that sellers receive beyond the amount required to supply the good.*

We are now ready to measure the social gain, or welfare gain, resulting from the existence of the market. Trade creates welfare gains that did not exist before trading took place. As shown in Figure 3.17, the welfare gain from trade at the equilibrium market

---

4. Later you will learn that, when the supply curve coincides with the marginal-cost curve, the surplus to each producer is equal to profits plus the payments to fixed inputs (fixed cost) because the area under the marginal-cost curve is equal to total variable cost.

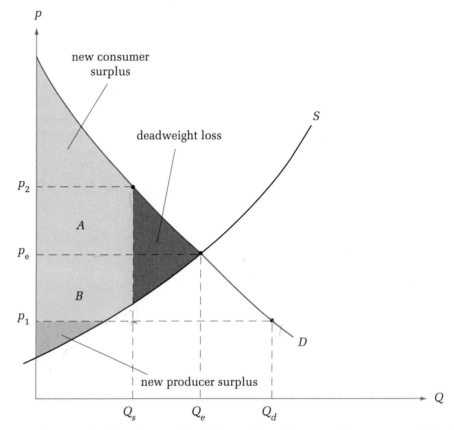

Figure 3.18   **Deadweight loss of a price ceiling:** Given a price ceiling p_1, producers want to sell Q_s units and consumers want to buy Q_d units. Because only Q_s will be traded, consumers are willing to pay the price p_2. Part of the old producer surplus (area of rectangle B) is transferred out of old producer surplus to consumers. The "actual" price paid increases to p_2 as transactions costs increase or as buyers resell the good. Nevertheless, consumers retain part (area of rectangle A) of the old consumer surplus. But part of old consumer surplus and part of old producer surplus is lost to society—a deadweight loss.

price is the sum of consumer surplus and producer surplus. Notice that *both* consumers (demanders) *and* producers (suppliers) have gained and *no one* has lost.

What happens when market interference occurs?[5] Suppose a price ceiling is imposed, as illustrated by Figure 3.18. At the price ceiling p_1 below the equilibrium price p_e, producers want to sell Q_s units. Because Q_s is less than the equilibrium quantity Q_e, producer surplus shrinks. At the same time consumers want to buy Q_d units at the ceiling

---

5. When the market demand curve is used to measure the change in consumer welfare caused by a change in the market, we cannot measure which consumers gain and which lose without looking at their individual demand curves.

price, and so a market shortage follows. Only Q_s will be traded, but consumers are willing to pay price p_2 for Q_s units. That price is greater than the original equilibrium price. What price will consumers actually pay? Because some consumers will be willing to resell at a higher price, and because consumers incur extra transactions costs in acquiring the good—like waiting in a queue, the "actual" price paid will ultimately increase to p_2. Consumer surplus changes because part of the old consumer surplus is retained and part of the old producer surplus is transferred to "consumers" acting as intermediaries. The intermediaries are better off, pure consumers are worse off, and producers are worse off. Moreover, now we find a loss to society.

The price ceiling has caused a net reduction in the welfare gains from trade. This reduction is called a **deadweight loss** because no one recovers the loss—it is gone forever.

> **Deadweight loss:** *A deadweight loss is the social loss (welfare loss, or efficiency loss) caused by a departure from competitive pricing.*

The measurement of deadweight loss and changes in producer and consumer surpluses is a useful way to evaluate the effect of many forms of market interference and market imperfections.

GLOBAL PERSPECTIVE: *Tariffs and Trucks*

Small trucks are produced both domestically and abroad. Suppose that both America and Japan produce identical small trucks—light utility vehicles or LUVs. The domestic demand and supply curves for LUVs is shown in Figure 3.19. Japan is assumed to be willing to supply any amount demanded at price p_I, and so the supply price for imports is constant and the supply curve of imports is horizontal at that price. To keep the analysis simple, let's assume that domestic production is consumed first, and any shortfall in domestic production below domestic demand is covered by imports.

Panel A illustrates the situation before a tariff is imposed. The quantity demanded is Q_2 at the import price. Domestic producers are willing to sell Q_1 units at that price. The difference between Q_2 and Q_1 is the quantity imported to America from Japan. The consumer surplus and the producer surplus for domestic producers are calculated in the usual way.

In panel B we see the effect of a tariff on imported trucks. If the tariff is t dollars per truck, the price increases to $p_I + t$. The quantity of trucks demanded shrinks to Q_4 at the higher price, and consumer surplus is reduced. Part of the reduction in consumer surplus goes to domestic producers in the form of an increase in producers' surplus because domestic production increases to Q_3 at the higher price. The number of imported trucks shrinks from $Q_2 - Q_1$ units to $Q_4 - Q_3$ units. Tax revenues are generated in the amount $t(Q_4 - Q_3)$, and this tariff revenue is a gain to the country. The tariff still causes a deadweight loss, however, because consumers lose more than all other groups gain. Economists describe the tariff as socially *inefficient* because of the net welfare loss to society.

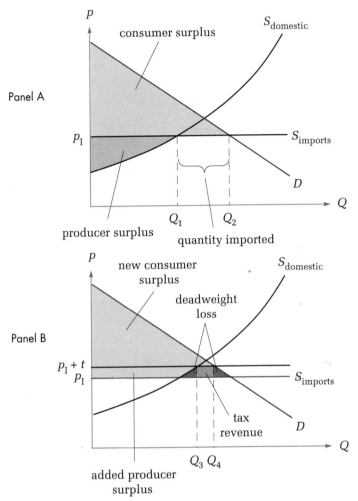

Figure 3.19 **Deadweight loss of a tariff: Panel A** The consumer surplus and domestic producer surplus at the import price p_I. **Panel B** The deadweight loss due to a tariff that raises the import price to $p_I + t$.

3.9   Interdependent Markets

Markets are interdependent because the demand for a good depends on the prices of other goods. If price changes in one market, that may shift the demand curve in other markets, causing price changes in those markets. Those price changes may induce further price changes in all markets. Thus, one price change may cause other price changes, which ripple through other markets, causing further price changes. The initial price change may have been caused by a change in market supply that affected the market price, or the initial price change may have been caused by a change in consumers' incomes or preferences that affected market demand. Where will it all end? Presumably at some set of prices that clear all markets simultaneously.

A concept that is particularly useful in analyzing interdependent markets is excess demand:

> **Excess demand:** *Excess demand is quantity demanded less quantity supplied.*

Consider a two-market system for goods X and Y. Quantity demanded for good X is a function of the price of X given the price of the other good and consumer money income:

$$Q_X = D_X(p_X; p_Y, M)$$

The semicolon denotes the conditional relationship with respect to p_Y and M. Let $Q_X = S_X(p_X)$ denote the quantity of X supplied as a function of the price of X alone. Let's assume that quantity supplied increases with price. The excess demand for X may now be written

$$E_X = D_X(p_X; p_Y, M) - S_X(p_X)$$

We will fully consider supply decisions in a later chapter, but for now we assume that quantity supplied increases with price.

Equilibrium in the X market requires that quantity demanded be equal to quantity supplied. Another way of stating this equilibrium condition is that excess demand must be equal to zero. Figure 3.20 illustrates excess demand in the X market. The market is in equilibrium when $E_X = 0$, where the demand curve intersects the supply curve. At any price below the equilibrium price, excess demand will be positive, signaling that an increase in price will occur. Similarly, at any price above the equilibrium price, excess demand will be negative, signaling that a decrease in price will occur. Thus, positive excess demand will be followed by a price increase, and negative excess demand will be followed by a price decrease.

Similarly, in the Y market, the excess demand for Y may be written

$$E_Y = D_Y(p_Y; p_X, M) - S_Y(p_Y)$$

Equilibrium in the Y market requires that $E_Y = 0$.

Both markets are in equilibrium at the same time when $E_X = 0$ and $E_Y = 0$ simultaneously. In general, multimarket equilibrium requires that all excess demands be equal to zero simultaneously in all markets being analyzed:

> **Multimarket equilibrium:** *Multimarket equilibrium occurs when all markets being analyzed have zero-excess demands simultaneously.*

With multimarket equilibrium no price in these markets is likely to change, and the prevailing set of prices are multimarket equilibrium prices. Now it's easy to see why working with excess demands is so useful. Because we find one excess demand and one price for each good, the number of equations equals the number of the unknown prices. The multimarket equilibrium prices can be found by setting all excess demands equal to zero at the same time.

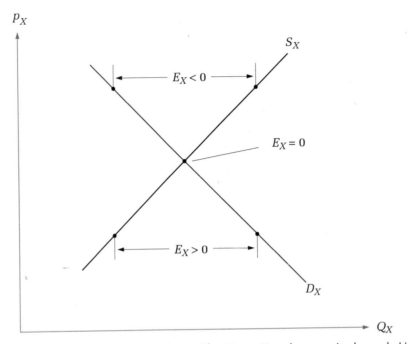

Figure 3.20 **Excess demand:** The excess demand for X is positive when quantity demanded is greater than quantity supplied. The excess demand for X is negative when quantity supplied is greater than quantity demanded. Zero excess demand is another way of saying that this market is in equilibrium.

Let's take the simple two-good case. The set of prices, p_X and p_Y, which generates simultaneous equilibrium, can be found by setting the excess demands in each market equal to zero simultaneously. Figure 3.21 illustrates a simultaneous equilibrium at p_Y^a in the Y market and p_X^b in the X market. To simplify this example, we make additional assumptions. First, assume that the demand for X is independent of money income, and assume that Y is a normal good—the demand for Y will increase when income increases. Second, assume that X is a market substitute for Y, and that the demand for Y is independent of the price of X.

Suppose we find an exogenous change in M to $M + \Delta M$, where $\Delta M > 0$. The increase in M causes the demand for Y to increase, and D_Y shifts to the right in Figure 3.21. At the initial price p_Y^a, the excess demand for Y is now positive, $E_Y > 0$. The Y market thus is now out of equilibrium, and so price in the Y market will begin to increase to point **c**, where $E_Y = 0$ once more. But the increase in p_Y to $p_Y + \Delta p_Y$ will cause a shift in the demand for X. Because X is a market substitute for Y, the D_X curve shifts to the right from point **b** to point **c** at the current price of X. Now the X market is out of equilibrium, for the excess demand for X is now positive, $E_X > 0$. Hence the price of X will increase as the X market moves to a new equilibrium.

In the example of Figure 3.21, the new multimarket equilibrium under the new set of prices and income will occur at $p_X^b + \Delta p_X$ and $p_Y^a + \Delta p_Y$, where quantity demanded equals

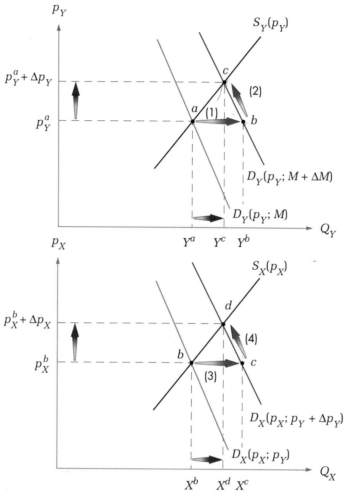

Figure 3.21 **Interdependent markets:** Here Y is normal, but X is independent of income. Also, X is a market substitute of Y, but Y is independent of p_x. If (1) consumers increase their demand for Y in response to an increase in income, then (2) the price of Y increases as that market adjusts, and (3) the demand for X increases in response to the increase in p_y. Finally, (4) the price of X increases as that market adjusts to a new equilibrium.

quantity supplied simultaneously in both markets. No further change will occur because of the assumptions made. But what if the demand for X had shifted when income changed? And what if the demand for Y depended on the price of X? Well, myriad shifts and slides would become hard to trace graphically, but the new equilibrium set of prices could be determined by setting the excess demands equal to zero simultaneously:

$$E_X(p_X, p_Y; M) = 0$$
$$E_Y(p_X, p_Y; M) = 0$$

Thus, for any given level of *M,* the set of prices that yield simultaneous equilibrium could be found.[6]

An analysis of multimarket equilibrium that does not include all the markets is called **partial equilibrium** analysis. Examining all markets at the same time is known as **general equilibrium** analysis. General equilibrium will be considered in a later chapter after we examine production decisions. Recognize that the preceding illustration is an example of *partial* equilibrium analysis because a general equilibrium analysis would require including all markets including input markets.

---

6. A relationship known as **Walras's Law** states that as long as the expenditure by each consumer equals that consumer's money income, the aggregate value of all excess demands for goods is zero. Walras's Law is an accounting identity and holds whether or not markets are in equilibrium. This relationship means that if some markets have positive excess demands, at least one market must have negative excess demand, and *vice versa.* Thus, when we examine only two markets at a time, in order for both markets to have positive (negative) excess demands at the same time, a third market must have negative (positive) excess demand.

AN APPLICATION: *A Dual Labor Market and the Minimum Wage*

One of the most important unresolved public debates is the influence of minimum wages on the economy. Late in 1987, for instance, the state of California increased its minimum wage to $4.25 an hour from $3.35 an hour, the federal minimum established in 1981. The state legislature also approved a controversial "sub-minimum" of $3.50 an hour for workers who earn at least $60 a month in tips.* The changes were scheduled to be implemented July 1, 1988, and the state estimated that 600,000 workers would be affected. Representatives of the state's major business organizations—including the California Manufacturers Association and the California Restaurant Association—predicted layoffs, slowdowns in hiring, and increased prices as a result. On the other hand, a full-time worker under the old minimum earned $6,968 a year, an amount that is 60 percent of the poverty level for a family of four in 1988.

The likely effect of a minimum wage in low-paying labor markets is predictable. When the minimum wage is above the equilibrium wage that would have prevailed, quantity supplied will be greater than the quantity demanded and unemployment will increase. Total wages—the "revenue" to the workers selling their services—will increase if quantity demanded is relatively unresponsive to the change in the wage rate, but total wages will decrease if quantity demanded is very responsive. The magnitude of the change in employment will depend also on the responsiveness in quantity supplied. Further adjustments, however, will occur because labor markets are interdependent.

---

*California's Supreme Court subsequently ruled the "sub-minimum" wage unconstitutional.

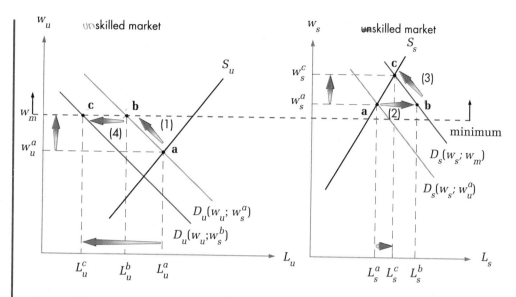

Figure 3.22 **Minimum wage and dual labor market:** Without the minimum wage, w_m, a multimarket equilibrium appears at **a** in both markets. Then: (1) the minimum wage causes a slide along D_u from **a** to **b** and the unskilled wage becomes $w_u = w_m$; (2) skilled workers are substituted for unskilled as D_s shifts from **a** to **b** in the skilled market; (3) as the skilled market adjusts to a new equilibrium, a slide occurs along D_s from **b** to **c** and w_s increases to w_s^c; and (4) the D_u curve shifts from **b** to **c** in response to the increase in w_s—a complementary decrease follows in D_u. The new multimarket equilibrium at points **c** in both markets results in higher wage rates in both markets, but the level of employment is higher than before in the skilled sector and unemployment has been created in the unskilled sector.

Labor markets not directly affected by the minimum wage will be affected indirectly if previously higher-paid labor is substituted for less-skilled, lower-paid labor. A partial equilibrium model of two labor markets can be used to analyze possible reactions. Consider the labor market as divided into two sectors: a market for "skilled" labor and a market for "unskilled" labor. Assume that unskilled labor is a market complement of skilled labor and skilled labor is a market substitute for unskilled. Physicians and nurses might fit this pattern, or engineers and technical writers. The designation as skilled and unskilled is relative. The idea is that skilled labor may be substituted for the unskilled, but unskilled may not be substituted for skilled labor, at least not in the short run. The implication is that the demand for unskilled labor is inversely related to the skilled wage rate, but the demand for skilled labor is directly related to the unskilled wage rate.

Suppose we wish to examine how such a dual labor market reacts to a minimum-wage rate above the prevailing wage in the unskilled sector. The labor categories might be machinists and apprentices, or waiters and busboys. Such a dual labor market is illustrated in Figure 3.22, where the subscripts denote skilled and unskilled. The quantity of skilled labor is denoted by L_s, and the quantity of unskilled labor by L_u. Market supply is determined by aggregating individual labor-supply decisions for individuals who have the requisite skills. Market demand is determined by aggregating separate firms' labor-demand decisions for each skill category. Without the minimum wage, each market is at equilibrium at point **a.**

Suppose now that a minimum wage w_m is imposed that is above the current unskilled market wage w_u so that $w_m > w_u$. At the same time, suppose the current skilled wage w_s is above the minimum wage, so that $w_m < w_s$. Thus, the skilled sector is not affected directly by the minimum wage. The legal requirement, however, is that the wage in every market must be no less than the minimum, so that the wage in the unskilled sector must increase immediately to w_m. Quantity demanded for L_u will decrease to L_u^b, as illustrated by the slide from **a** to **b** along the unskilled demand curve. This change is followed by a shift in the D_s curve from **a** to **b** as skilled labor is substituted for unskilled. The skilled sector is now out of equilibrium and w_s will begin to rise. As the skilled market moves toward a new equilibrium at **c**, L_s decreases as w_s increases, as shown by the slide along the new D_s curve from **b** to **c**. Finally, the D_u curve shifts from **b** to **c** in the unskilled sector because of a complementary decrease in the D_u curve. The unskilled sector is at a new equilibrium at **c** even though excess demand is negative because of the constraint imposed by the minimum wage.

Employed unskilled workers are paid the minimum wage that is higher than their previous wage, but employment for unskilled workers has fallen. The difference between quantity supplied and quantity demanded at w_m provides us with a measure of unemployment. Part of the measured unemployment is caused by the increase in quantity supplied, induced by the increase in the wage rate, but part also results from the decrease in demand for unskilled workers. Skilled labor, however, enjoys both a higher wage and more employment.

These conclusions remain essentially unaltered when we assume that both types of labor are substitutes in a stable system. That problem is left as an exercise. Thus, many economists believe minimum wages contribute to unemployment. Strong arguments, however, can also be made in favor of the minimum wage. One such argument is that the minimum wage counters market power exercised by large firms in hiring labor. Another argument would point out that the analysis above used a partial-equilibrium model, and that income effects may increase the demand for unskilled workers so that employment levels increase above the levels that prevail in the absence of the minimum wage. Moreover, some proponents of the minimum wage cite fairness considerations apart from positive economic analysis.

Summary

Market demand is the aggregation of consumers' demands. Thus, market demand depends on the price of the good; the prices of other goods; the level and distribution of consumers' money incomes, preferences, and expectations; and the number of consumers. The market demand curve is a graph of the quantity demanded when price alone changes.

For two reasons we expect the demand curve to have negative slope. First, a substitution effect causes quantity demanded to decrease when price increases alone because consumers look for substitutes. Second, an income effect causes quantity demanded to decrease when price increases, at least for normal goods, because consumers' purchasing power falls. Inferior goods also tend to have negatively sloped demand curves because substitution effects usually dominate income effects of price changes.

The demand for a normal good increases, the demand curve shifting to the right, when money income alone increases. The demand for an inferior good decreases, the demand curve shifting to the left, when money income alone increases. The demand for a market substitute increases when the price of another good increases, and the demand curve for the market substitute shifts to the right. The demand for a market complement decreases when the price of another good increases, and the demand curve for the market complement shifts to the left.

Market supply for a good is the aggregation of firms' supplies for goods being produced. Market supply depends on the price of the good, the prices of all factor inputs, the current production technology, and the number of firms producing the good. The market supply curve is a graph of the quantity supplied when price alone changes. Short-run supply curves tend to have positive slope because of diminishing returns to variable inputs used in production. A market is in equilibrium at some price when the quantity demanded is equal to the quantity supplied.

Consumer surplus is the total benefit, or value, that buyers receive beyond what they pay for a good. At the current market price, consumer surplus equals the area under the demand curve less total buyer expenditure for the good. Producer surplus is the total value that suppliers receive beyond the amount necessary to induce them to supply the good. Producer surplus equals total buyer expenditure for the good less the area under the supply curve at the current price. The total welfare gain from trading at the equilibrium price is the sum of buyer and seller surpluses. The gains from trade are maximized when price is such that quantity demanded equals quantity supplied. Trading at any other price results in a deadweight loss.

Markets are interdependent because demand for any good depends on the prices of other goods. The concept of excess demand, quantity demanded minus quantity supplied, is particularly useful in analyzing interdependent markets. Positive excess demand in any market signals that the price in that market will increase, and negative excess demand signals a decrease in that price. Multimarket equilibrium requires zero excess demands in all markets simultaneously, and this requirement can be used to find the set of all prices consistent with multimarket equilibrium. Economists usually assume that observed prices in markets are equilibrium prices determined by stable systems.

Further Readings

The principles textbooks listed at the end of Chapter 1 remain relevant. For an introduction to the application of microeconomics to international trade issues, see

- Robert J. Carbaugh, *International Economics,* 3d. ed. (Wadsworth Publishing Company, 1989).
- Miltiades Chacholeades, *International Economics* (McGraw-Hill, 1990).
- Steven Husted and Michael Melvin, *International Economics* (Harper & Row, 1990).
- Peter H. Lindert, *International Economics,* 9th ed. (Richard D. Irwin, 1991).

Practice Problems

1. Given the demand curve $Q = D(p) = 100 - 5p$:
   (a) What is the slope of this demand curve?
   (b) Find the equation for the inverse demand curve.
   (c) What is the slope of the inverse demand curve?
2. Given the market demand and market supply schedules for a good:

Price	Quantity demanded	Quantity supplied
$8	45	75
6	55	55
4	65	35
2	75	15

   (a) Find the linear equation for both the demand curve and the supply curve.
   (b) Solve algebraically for the equilibrium price and quantity.
3. Consider the demand for television sets over time. If you were retained by a television manufacturer, what economic variables would you recommend be followed to help forecast demand?
4. On a graph, show that the total value of water is greater than the total value of diamonds even though the marginal value (price) of diamonds is greater than the marginal value (price) of water.
5. A per unit tax on any good affects the quantity supplied at each price. If t is the per unit tax, then the supply price to the sellers of the good is $(p - t)$, the market price less the per unit tax. If Q denotes the quantity of the good, and if the market demand and supply curves are:

$$Q_d = D(p) = 1000 - 100p$$
$$Q_s = S(p) = 500 + 100p$$

   (a) Graph the demand and supply curves and determine the equilibrium price and quantity before the tax.
   (b) On the same graph, plot the new supply curve after a $2 tax is imposed. What are the new equilibrium price and quantity?
   (c) Calculate the proportion of the tax borne by the producer and that borne by the consumer.
   (d) Indicate the area on the graph that measures the deadweight loss, then calculate the deadweight loss.
6. On a graph, show the deadweight loss due to a minimum wage in one labor market without considering feedback effects from other markets.
7. Suppose that all cameras are imported into the United States, and that Americans face a flat supply curve. Show that in this case a tariff always reduces the welfare of Americans.

8. Suppose all cameras are imported into the United States, but the supply curve facing Americans has positive slope. A tariff is then imposed and all tax revenues are distributed to Americans. Identify the gains and losses to all parties and any deadweight loss. Do Americans gain or lose in this case?

9. Given the demand and supply functions:

$$D_X = 50 - p_X + p_Y \qquad S_X = -50 + 4p_X$$

(a) Determine the excess demand function $E_X(p_X, p_Y)$.
(b) If $p_Y = 50$, set $E_X = 0$ and find p_X.
(c) If $p_Y = 100$, set $E_X = 0$ and find p_X.
(d) Does the equilibrium price for X increase or decrease as p_Y increases? Why?

10. In a two-market system, suppose the excess demands for good X and good Y are:

$$E_X = 50 - 6p_X + 2p_Y$$
$$E_Y = 35 - 3p_X - 4p_Y$$

(a) Determine whether each good is a market substitute or a complement of the other. Explain your answer.
(b) Solve for the multimarket equilibrium prices.
(c) If $p_X = 5$ and $p_Y = 10$, will the price of X increase or decrease? Why? Will the price of Y increase or decrease? Why?

11. Suppose the two types of labor are the skilled and the unskilled. The skilled labor might be drywall construction workers who have taken a formal training program offered by their union. The unskilled might be relatively inexperienced workers who have not undergone comparable training. Here *each* type of labor is a market *substitute* for the other type. If a wage floor is imposed that is greater than the current equilibrium wage in the unskilled sector but less than the current wage in the skilled sector, graphically trace the effects on wages and employment in both markets. Assume that own-wage effects on demand are larger than cross-wage effects.

Chapter 4

Elasticities of Demand and Supply

Total revenue equals quantity sold multiplied by price, and average revenue is total revenue divided by quantity. Average revenue therefore equals price. Price typically is inversely related to quantity demanded, and so total revenue may rise, fall, or not change as price increases. Thus, understanding how quantity demanded varies with price is crucial to understanding how revenue varies with price and quantity.

Most firms are profit maximizers, but even nonprofit firms strive to operate without losses. Profit is the difference between revenue and cost, and revenue is determined by demand. Thus, no matter how cost effective production operations may be, a firm cannot operate profitably with insufficient demand.

A firm may be able to influence demand in two ways. One way is to influence quantity demanded by changing price. Another way is to try to increase demand by influencing consumers' preferences or by introducing a new product. Given existing demand, the pricing and production decisions are profoundly influenced by the demand function for the firm's product. This influence is exerted because the firm must set prices so that the expected quantity demanded will match the planned quantity produced in order to maximize expected profit.

4.1   The Firm's Demand and Average Revenue

Market demand must be shared among the firms in the industry. Dividing demand is easy if all firms have equal market share. It is easy because, with equal market shares, market demand at every price is just divided by the number of firms to get each firm's demand. When the firms have different market shares because, say, they are each producing a slightly differentiated product, identifying each firm's demand curve may not be quite so easy. The firm's demand curve, its average revenue curve, is influenced by everything that influences market demand. The demand curve, the firm's share of the market at every price, is also influenced by the structure of the market. Market structure is determined by the number and size of firms, whether all produce the same or slightly different products, and the degree of interdependence between firms in the industry. In all cases, however, a firm's demand curve for its product coincides with its average revenue curve.

The two polar extremes of market structure are pure monopoly and pure competition. A firm has a **pure monopoly** when it is producing a unique product that has no close substitutes. In the pure-monopoly case, the market demand curve is the firm's demand curve because the industry has only one firm. At the other extreme, a firm is **purely competitive** when it is one of many small, independent firms, all producing the same good. A purely competitive firm reacts to the market-determined price, and the firm is described as a price-taking firm. Other forms of market structure include oligopoly and monopolistic competition. In **oligopoly,** a few large firms produce substitutable products. Usually we find a great deal of business rivalry and interdependence among oligopoly firms. In **monopolistic competition** many relatively small firms produce differentiated but substitutable products. Product differentiation is the essential characteristic that distinguishes monopolistic competition from pure competition. These and other forms of market structure are investigated in detail in a later chapter. But whatever the form of market structure, the firm's demand curve coincides with its average revenue curve.

> **Firm's demand curve:** *The firm's demand curve coincides with its average revenue curve.*

The monopoly case is illustrated by Figure 4.1. **Average revenue** is equal to price because it is found by dividing total revenue by quantity. The *monopolist's* average revenue curve is equal to the *inverse* market demand curve because price is equal to average revenue,

$$AR = p(Q) = D^{-1}$$

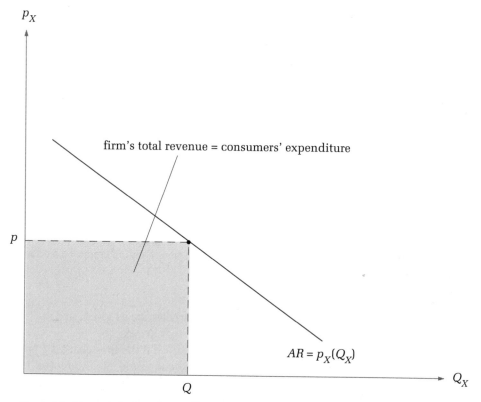

Figure 4.1 **The monopoly demand curve:** The monopolist's average revenue curve, its demand curve, is the inverse market demand curve, $AR = p(Q)$, because price is equal to average revenue. Total revenue is given by multiplying price times quantity demanded, $R = pQ$, at any point. For the monopolist, the firm's total revenue also equals consumers' expenditure.

That is, average revenue to the monopolist is found by inverting the market demand curve $Q = D(p)$ to get price as a function of quantity. The firm's demand curve coincides with its average revenue curve because this curve indicates the relationship between price and quantity demanded that faces the firm. **Total revenue** is equal to price multiplied by quantity at any point along the average revenue curve,

$$R = pQ$$

For the monopolist, the firm's total revenue also equals consumers' expenditure on the good.

The case of the purely competitive firm is illustrated by Figure 4.2. In a purely competitive market, each firm produces the same good, and each firm is too small by itself to have a discernible influence on the market. The market price p_e is determined where market demand intersects market supply. At the market price, the area of the rectangle under the market demand curve is equal to consumers' expenditure. But consumers' expenditure is not equal to the individual firm's total revenue because that total expenditure must be shared among all the firms. Average revenue is determined, however,

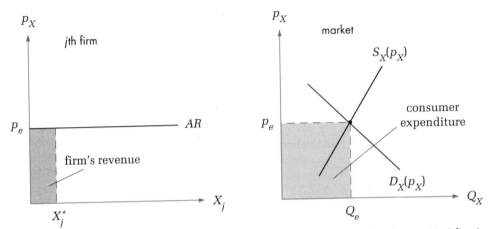

Figure 4.2 **Competitive demand:** The average revenue curve for the price-taking (competitive) firm is determined by the market clearing price in a market where many firms are producing the same good.

by the market price. The competitive firm takes the market price as given, and its average revenue remains *constant* at that market price.

Why is the competitive firm a price-taking firm? Because if the firm charges a price above the market price, all consumers will purchase the good elsewhere. Moreover, the firm can sell as much as it wants to at the current market price. The exact quantity sold by each firm, X_j^* for the jth firm in Figure 4.2, will be determined by the firm's motivation to maximize profits. Profit maximization is the subject in later chapters. For now, realize that if all firms are identical, the quantity sold by each firm will be equal to the equilibrium quantity Q_e divided by the number of firms in the industry. In any case, as shown by Figure 4.2, the firm's total revenue is equal to the market price multiplied by the quantity sold by the firm, and average revenue is equal to market price.

These principles can be generalized to firms operating under any form of market structure, from pure monopoly to pure competition. Once the firm's average revenue or total revenue curve is found, the average revenue curve may be interpreted as that firm's demand curve. Except for the price-taking firm, average revenue will decrease as quantity increases because price must be lower to sell more—a consequence of the inverse relationship between quantity demanded and price. Total revenue to the firm is determined along the average revenue curve by multiplying price by quantity.

In summary, the firm's demand curve coincides with its average revenue curve. The position of the average revenue curve is influenced by all the things that determine the position of the market demand curve. The position of the firm's demand is also influenced by the form of market structure: the degree of product differentiation and the forms of strategic behavior chosen by all the firms in the market. But before we look more closely at shifts in demand and average revenue, it will be constructive to examine very closely how responsive revenue is to changes in price and quantity.

4.2   Total Revenue and Price Elasticity

Any seller will quickly recognize that, when quantity demanded varies inversely with price, the seller's average revenue curve will be negatively sloped. This relationship means that when price is increased, quantity demanded will decrease and vice versa. Therefore, as illustrated by Figure 4.3, the net change in total revenue is ambiguous. As price increases from p to $p + \Delta p$, quantity decreases from Q to $Q + \Delta Q$, where $\Delta Q < 0$. There is a gain in revenue due to the price increase, but a loss in revenue caused by the quantity decrease. The net change in revenue may be positive or negative depending on whether the gain is larger or smaller than the loss.

Whether revenue increases or decreases with a change in price depends on how responsive quantity demanded is to the change in price. If quantity decreases a lot relative to a price increase, then revenue will fall. But if the decrease in quantity is small, then revenue will rise. Therefore, it would be useful to have a measure of the responsiveness of quantity demanded to price changes that would indicate the direction of the change in revenue. The responsiveness of quantity demanded to price change can be measured by

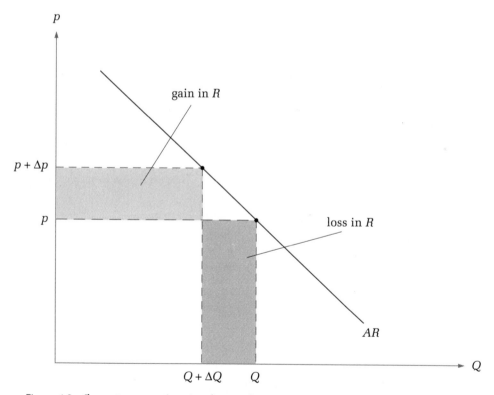

Figure 4.3 **Changes in revenue:** As price changes from p to $p + \Delta p$ (where $\Delta p > 0$), quantity changes from Q to ΔQ (where $\Delta Q < 0$). The net change in total revenue may be positive or negative, depending on whether the gain is larger or smaller than the loss.

the slope of the demand curve, $\Delta Q/\Delta p$.[1] But slope is not a good measure of responsiveness when we are trying to determine whether revenue will increase or decrease with changes in price. To see why it is inadequate, consider a linear demand curve,

$$Q = a - bp; \; a > 0, \; b > 0$$

The slope of this linear demand curve is

$$\frac{\Delta Q}{\Delta p} = -b$$

and revenue is given by

$$R = pQ = p(a - bp) = ap - bp^2$$

When graphed, this function is mound-shaped. Revenue is zero when price is $p = 0$. Revenue increases at a decreasing rate as price increases from zero until a maximum is reached. Then revenue decreases at an increasing rate until revenue again equals zero at price $p = a/b$, where $Q = 0$. Thus, even though the slope of the linear demand curve remains constant, revenue first increases and then decreases as price increases.

Another problem with using slope to characterize the responsiveness of quantity to changes in price is that slope is not invariant to changes in the scale of measurement. If price is converted from dollars to cents, or if quantity is converted from tons to ounces, the slope will change also. We need a measure of responsiveness that is invariant to changes in scale and, at the same time, one that can be used to predict how revenue will vary with price.

The scaling problem can be avoided by calculating *percentage* changes. The ratio of the percentage change in quantity to the percentage change in price is known as **price elasticity:**

> **Price elasticity:** *Price elasticity of demand is the percentage change in quantity demanded divided by the percentage change in price.*

The price elasticity of demand is denoted by the Greek letter "eta,"

$$\eta = \frac{\% \text{ change in } Q}{\% \text{ change in } p}$$

When the percentage change in quantity is *greater* than the percentage change in price so that $\eta > 1$, revenue will *decrease* when price increases, and demand is said to be **elastic.** When the percentage change in quantity is *less* than the percentage in price so that $\eta < 1$,

---

1. It is easy to get confused beyond this juncture because of the economic tradition of graphing demand curves with quantity demanded, the dependent variable, on the horizontal axis. Thus if you calculate the slope as the "rise over the run" from a graph, you will get $\Delta p/\Delta Q$ rather than $\Delta Q/\Delta p$. The slope of the *inverse* demand curve is $\Delta p/\Delta Q$, but the slope of the demand curve is $\Delta Q/\Delta p$. In this book we always calculate the slope as the change in the dependent variable divided by the change in the independent variable.

revenue will *increase* when price increases, and demand is said to be **inelastic.** In summary, when demand is elastic, revenue will decrease with a price increase, but when demand is inelastic, revenue will increase with a price increase.

ECONOMIC SCENE: *Beyond the Pink Bus Line*

In the late 1950s and early 1960s, a bus line operating in Orange County, California, was called the pink bus line because of the paint jobs on its buses. It provided cheap transportation to the beach during the summer months. This story, however, is not about the pink bus line but its successor, the South Coast Transit Company, also now defunct. As a student of economics, I found that this story caught my attention because I used to ride the Pink Bus Line to the beach.

> The South Coast Transit Co. plans to abandon its daily bus service to [the beach areas]...[because] it sustained a $3,000 loss during August [even though an official] said his company received a rate increase from the PUC last March, adding that while per passenger revenues are up 20 percent over the previous period, passenger loads are down 29 percent.*

Because the changes described in the article took place over a relatively short period, it is probably safe to assume that other things remained unchanged as the price changed.

Per passenger revenue is average revenue, and average revenue is price. Passenger load, the number of passengers per trip, is a measure of quantity demanded. Thus, quantity demanded fell 29 percent in response to the 20 percent increase in price. Simple arithmetic yields a price elasticity of $\eta = 1.45$. At this time the demand curve for bus transportation was price *elastic* over the routes cited because $\eta > 1$. Thus the increase in price could be expected to cause a decrease in revenue.

It takes more than a decrease in revenue to explain the loss, however, because a loss is a negative profit—and profit is total revenue less cost. It seemed reasonable to me, and it still does, that the cost of operating a bus between two points would remain relatively constant. Whether the bus is empty or full, the cost of the bus itself and the wage of the driver remain constant. The bus would be more fuel efficient when operating empty, and it would require less maintenance. Fuel was cheap in those days, however, and buses were cleaned by teenagers at minimum wage. Thus, assuming some empty seats on the buses, the maximization of revenue would maximize profit (or minimize losses) if cost was constant. It is clear, then, that the price change was in the wrong direction. With elastic demand, a price increase causes a decrease in revenue. Moreover, the request for another increase in price would make the situation worse if granted. Ironically, the company was using the loss to threaten a shutdown of that route unless the Public Utility Commission agreed to another rate increase while, the article went on to indicate, the transit company was looking for a new general manager.

Los Angeles Times, October 19, 1971.

4.3   Point-Price Elasticity of Demand

Price elasticity of demand is the percentage change in quantity demanded divided by the percentage change in price. A percentage change is computed by dividing the change by the total and multiplying by 100. The percentage change in quantity of a good thus is $(\Delta Q/Q) \times 100$, where Q is the quantity. Likewise, the percentage change in price is $(\Delta p/p) \times 100$, where p is the price. Thus, price elasticity of demand for any good may be computed by

$$\eta = -\frac{\Delta Q/Q}{\Delta p/p}$$

The negative sign is used because ΔQ and Δp have opposite sign.[2] Notice that the 100s have canceled out of the equation, and so price elasticity also measures the proportionate change in quantity demanded divided by the proportionate change in price.

A rearrangement of terms in this expression reveals that

$$\eta = -\frac{\Delta Q}{\Delta p} \cdot \frac{p}{Q}$$

Recall that $\Delta Q/\Delta p$ is the slope of the demand curve, and so price elasticity may be written as

$$\eta = -\text{slope} \cdot \frac{p}{Q}$$

the negative of the slope weighted by price divided by quantity. When the change in the price is small, the slope of the demand curve is measured by the slope of a line tangent at the point defined by p and Q. This condition leads to a measure of the elasticity known as **point-price elasticity** of demand.

> **Point-price elasticity of demand:** *Point-price elasticity is the negative of the slope of the demand curve at a point multiplied by the ratio of price divided by quantity at that point.*

Consider the demand curve shown on Figure 4.4. The slope of the demand curve at point a can be found by identifying the slope of the tangent line at point a. If at a we see that $\Delta Q/\Delta p = -2$, and if $p = 5$ and $Q = 20$ at point a, then the elasticity of demand at a is

$$\eta = -\frac{\Delta Q}{\Delta p} \cdot \frac{p}{Q} = -(-2)\frac{5}{20} = 0.50$$

Thus, this demand curve is price inelastic at that point.

Although elasticity depends on the slope, slope and elasticity are not the same. In two special cases, however, slope determines the elasticity exactly, as illustrated in Figure 4.5. In panel A, the demand curve is perfectly vertical over some range of prices, so that

---

2. This sign convention is not used in all books. Some authors take the absolute value in order to obtain a positive measure; others just work with negative own-price elasticities.

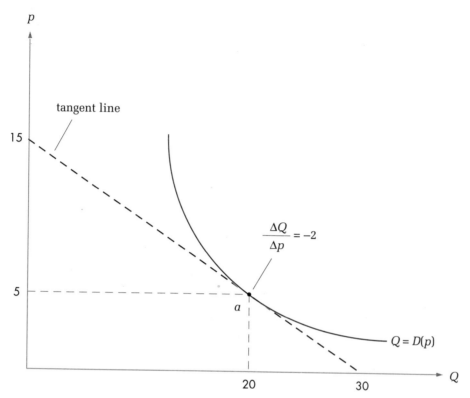

Figure 4.4 **Point-price elasticity of demand:** The slope of the demand curve $D(p)$ is determined at any point along the curve. Elasticity is measured at that point by taking the negative value of the slope and multiplying by the ratio of price divided by quantity at the point. At point **a**, $Q = 20$, $p = 5$ and $\Delta Q/\Delta p = -2$, and so elasticity is $\eta = -(-2)(5/20) = 1/2$, and demand is inelastic at point **a**.

$\Delta Q/\Delta p = 0$ and $\eta = 0$ everywhere. This demand curve is said to be **perfectly inelastic** because quantity is completely unresponsive to price. The demand for insulin by a diabetic may be perfectly inelastic over a wide range of prices.[3] In panel B, the demand curve is nearly horizontal and $\Delta Q/\Delta p$ approaches negative infinity, and so the price elasticity of demand is $\eta \cong \infty$. Demand is said to be **perfectly elastic** when $\eta \cong \infty$. The firm's demand for a product where perfect substitutes are available will be perfectly elastic because consumers switch completely away from the good when its price exceeds the substitute's price. In all other cases, care must be taken not to confuse elasticity and slope. Two examples illustrate why.

---

3. It is impossible for the diabetic's demand for insulin to be perfectly inelastic everywhere because, once total expenditure equals the diabetic's money income, quantity demanded must eventually fall with an increase in price. In addition, even if the diabetic's demand is perfectly inelastic at some price, the market demand does not have to be perfectly inelastic. Nor does the firm's demand curve have to be perfectly inelastic. Can you think of some reasons why?

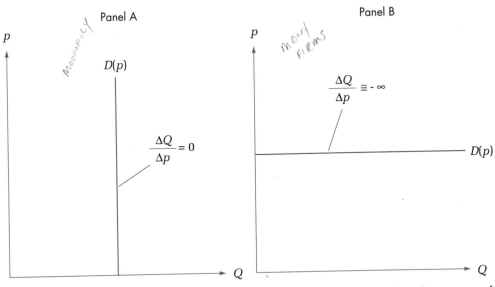

Figure 4.5   **Limiting cases and elasticity: Panel A** Demand is perfectly vertical over the relevant range of prices so that $\Delta Q/\Delta p = 0$ and $\eta = 0$ everywhere. Demand is perfectly inelastic. **Panel B** Demand is nearly horizontal so that $\Delta Q/\Delta p \cong -\infty$ and $\eta \cong \infty$. Demand is perfectly elastic.

As a first example of how slope and elasticity differ, consider again the linear demand

$$Q = a - bp;\; a > 0,\; b > 0$$

The slope remains constant at $\Delta Q/\Delta p = -b$. And yet, elasticity for this linear demand curve is

$$\eta = -\,\text{slope} \cdot \frac{p}{Q} = \frac{bp}{a - bp}$$

The elasticity of the linear demand curve is not constant because elasticity varies as price varies.

As a second example of how slope and elasticity differ, consider this demand curve

$$Q = \frac{k}{p};\; k > 0$$

Quantity demanded is inversely related to price, and the term k is a constant. A graph of such a demand curve is shown in Figure 4.6. The slope of this demand curve is given by[4]

$$\text{slope} = \frac{-k}{p^2}$$

When these equations are substituted into the point-elasticity formula, it is easy to see

---

4. This is a special case of a class of demand curves called constant-elasticity demand curves, having functional form $Q = kp^{-\eta}$, where η is the constant elasticity. The slope of this demand curve is given by the derivative $\partial Q/\partial p = -\eta k/p^{\eta+1}$.

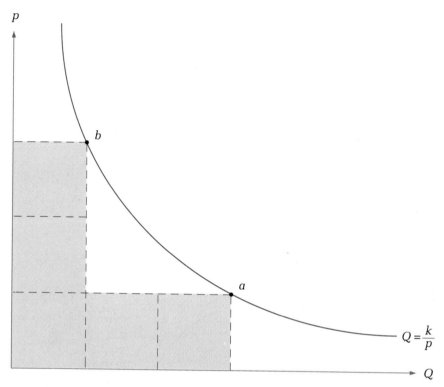

Figure 4.6 **Constant elasticity of demand:** This demand curve graphs as a rectangular hyperbola because the area of the rectangle under the curve remains constant. This demand curve has unitary elasticity of demand everywhere. But the slope varies as price changes while elasticity remains constant at $\eta = 1$. Notice that revenue remains constant at $R = k$ everywhere along this demand curve.

that $\eta = 1$ everywhere along this demand curve. And yet the slope of this demand curve, though negative everywhere, does not remain constant. This condition can be seen easily by graphing this demand curve as shown in Figure 4.6. The slope varies as price changes and elasticity remains constant.

4.4   Marginal Revenue and Price Elasticity

Revenue increases as price increases when demand is price inelastic. Revenue decreases as price increases when demand is price elastic. This relation implies that revenue will be maximized at some price–quantity combination. Managers and economic analysts would, of course, find it useful to identify that point of revenue maximization. Moreover, further insights can be gained by relating revenue maximization to price elasticity through **marginal revenue:**

> **Marginal revenue:** *Marginal revenue is the change in total revenue for an incremental change in quantity.*

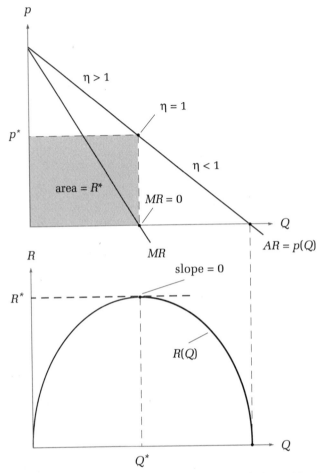

Figure 4.7 **Revenue maximization and elasticity:** Revenue is maximized where MR = 0 at Q*. Price must be set at p* to sell Q* units. At that point on the average revenue curve (the firm's demand curve), price elasticity is $\eta = 1$, and demand is said to have unitary elasticity.

By "incremental change" is meant a one-unit change. Marginal revenue is a highly useful concept that can be used to find the revenue-maximizing quantity and price. Later, we will also use marginal revenue to find the profit-maximizing quantity and price.

Marginal revenue can be measured by the slope of the firm's *total* revenue curve, $MR = \Delta R/\Delta Q$. As illustrated by Figure 4.7, when the firm moves along its average revenue curve, price must decrease as quantity increases. Total revenue equals price multiplied by quantity, $R = pQ$, and so when quantity is zero, revenue is zero. As price falls and quantity becomes positive, revenue increases initially. Eventually revenue will peak and begin to fall. Surely, if price falls to zero, revenue will equal zero also. Thus, as quantity increases, marginal revenue is positive when revenue is increasing, equal to zero when revenue is maximized, and negative when revenue is decreasing.

Notice that marginal revenue is below average revenue when the average is falling. That is a consequence of falling average revenue, the inverse relationship between price and quantity demanded. When average revenue is falling, the marginal must be below the average, drawing the average down. How then is *elasticity* related to marginal revenue?

An *elastic* demand means that revenue will *decrease* with an increase in price. If price *decreases,* revenue will *increase* with the increase in quantity when demand is elastic. Marginal revenue is positive when demand is elastic ($MR > 0$ when $\eta > 1$) because revenue is increasing with the increase in quantity.

When demand is *inelastic,* revenue will *increase* with an increase in price. If price *decreases,* revenue will *decrease* with the increase in quantity when demand is inelastic. Marginal revenue is negative when demand is inelastic ($MR < 0$ when $\eta < 1$) because revenue is decreasing with the increase in quantity.

When marginal revenue is equal to zero, revenue is maximized and price elasticity must be unitary ($MR = 0$ when $\eta = 1$). Demand is said to have **unitary elasticity** when $\eta = 1$. Unitary price elasticity implies revenue maximization and *vice versa.*

These results are fairly easy to remember. When demand is inelastic, quantity demanded is relatively unresponsive to price, meaning a direct relationship between revenue and price. When elasticity is unitary, revenue is maximized. When demand is elastic, quantity demanded is relatively responsive to price, indicating an inverse relationship between revenue and price. These results are summarized in this table:

Price Elasticity	Type	Marginal Revenue	Revenue Change
$0 \leq \eta < 1$	inelastic	$MR < 0$	$\dfrac{\Delta R}{\Delta p} > 0$
$\eta = 1$	unitary	$MR = 0$	maximum R
$1 < \eta \leq \infty$	elastic	$MR > 0$	$\dfrac{\Delta R}{\Delta p} < 0$

We can develop a useful equation that expresses MR as a function of elasticity. Let price change from p to $p + \Delta p$ so that quantity changes from Q to $Q + \Delta Q$. The new revenue is

$$R + \Delta R = (p + \Delta p)(Q + \Delta Q)$$

The change in R can be found by subtracting the old revenue from the new revenue to obtain

$$\Delta R = (p + \Delta p)(Q + \Delta Q) - pQ$$
$$= p\Delta Q + Q\Delta p + \Delta p\Delta Q$$

For small changes in price, the term $\Delta p\Delta Q$ will be small, and so the change in revenue will be approximately

$$\Delta R = p\Delta Q + Q\Delta p$$

Now divide this expression by ΔQ to obtain

$$MR = \frac{\Delta R}{\Delta Q} = p + Q\frac{\Delta p}{\Delta Q}$$

Now let's factor out p to obtain

$$MR = p\left[1 + \frac{Q}{p}\cdot\frac{\Delta p}{\Delta Q}\right]$$

Inspecting this expression reveals that the second term inside the bracket is the negative of the inverse of price elasticity, and so

$$MR = p\left[1 - \frac{1}{\eta}\right]$$

Recall that marginal revenue is equal to zero when revenue is maximized. Now it's easy to see that marginal revenue is equal to zero when price elasticity is unitary—just substitute $\eta = 1$ into the last MR equation.

As an algebraic example, take the linear demand curve

$$Q = a - bp$$

The inverse of the firm's demand curve yields price as a function of quantity, the firm's average revenue curve. For the linear demand curve, average revenue is

$$AR = p(Q) = \frac{a}{b} - \frac{Q}{b}$$

Total revenue as a function of quantity is

$$R(Q) = p(Q)Q = \left[\frac{a}{b} - \frac{Q}{b}\right]Q$$

Marginal revenue is given by[5]

$$MR = \frac{\Delta R}{\Delta Q} = \frac{a}{b} - \frac{2}{b}Q$$

Notice that this linear marginal revenue curve is twice as steep as the linear average revenue curve. To find Q^*, the revenue-maximizing quantity, set marginal revenue equal to zero,

$$MR = \frac{a}{b} - \frac{2}{b}Q^* = 0$$

which yields

$$Q^* = \frac{a}{2}$$

Because a is the intercept of the demand equation, Q^* occurs at the halfway point along the average revenue curve where $MR = 0$ and $\eta = 1$. The revenue-maximizing price is

$$p^* = \frac{a}{2b}$$

---

5. This is the derivative $\partial R/\partial Q$.

This result shows that price p^* occurs at the midpoint of the linear demand curve. At that point, elasticity is unitary and $MR = 0$.

4.5 Arc-Price Elasticity of Demand

Sometimes the slope of the demand curve is not known but price-quantity pairs are observed. Or sometimes economists wish to characterize the elasticity of demand over a range of prices even though the slopes at given points along the curve are known. Either way, a decision is to be made about how to measure total price and total quantity, and usually another is to be made about how to measure slope.

Suppose that we know two price-quantity pairs along the unknown demand curve. Let's denote the two price-quantity pairs as (p_1, Q_1) and (p_2, Q_2), as illustrated by Figure 4.8. The slope of the unknown demand curve between these two points can be approximated by dividing the finite change in quantity by the finite change in price,

$$\frac{\Delta Q}{\Delta p} = \frac{Q_1 - Q_2}{p_1 - p_2}$$

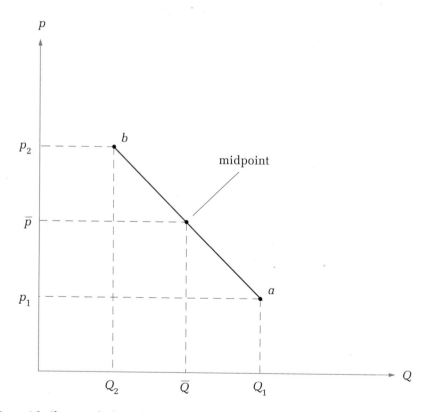

Figure 4.8 **Elasticity and unknown demand:** The arc-elasticity formula is used to calculate elasticity using $\Delta Q = Q_1 - Q_2$ and $\Delta p = p_1 - p_2$ and average price $\overline{p}$ and average quantity $\overline{Q}$ as measures of total price and total quantity. Thus, elasticity is calculated at the midpoint of a straight line drawn between the observed price-quantity pairs.

ECONOMIC SCENE: *Vanity Plates and Flowers*

In 1985, North Carolina started a roadside-beautification program and has been planting black-eyed Susans, wildflowers, and dogwoods.* Fees for vanity plates supported the program. But when the state legislature increased the price of vanity plates from $30 to $40, orders fell from 60,354 between October 1988 and June 1989 to 31,122 in the comparable period in the following year. As a result, only 280 new areas of roadside will be planted in 1990, compared to 350 areas added in 1989.

Revenue from the sale of vanity plates declined because quantity sold fell by a greater proportion than the increase in price. Demand for vanity plates was price elastic. An estimate of the price elasticity can be generated by the arc elasticity formula,

$$\text{arc } \eta = -\frac{\Delta Q}{\Delta p} \cdot \frac{\bar{p}}{\bar{Q}} = 2.236$$

where $\Delta p = 10$, $\Delta Q = -29,227$, $\bar{Q} = 45,740.5$ and $\bar{p} = 35$. If the goal is to maximize revenue from the sale of vanity plates in order to maximize the money available to plant roadsides each year, price should be reduced until price elasticity is unitary.

*As reported in *Time* (July 16, 1990), p. 28.

Now we need measures of total price and total quantity, but we have two choices for each. When the alternative measures for total price and total quantity are substituted into the elasticity formula, the answer will vary depending on whether we start at point *a* or point *b*.[6] The usual solution to this problem is to compute *average* quantity and *average* price:

$$\bar{Q} = \frac{Q_1 + Q_2}{2}$$

$$\bar{p} = \frac{p_1 + p_2}{2}$$

Substitution into the definition of elasticity yields

$$\text{arc } \eta = -\frac{\Delta Q}{\Delta p} \cdot \frac{\bar{p}}{\bar{Q}} = -\frac{Q_1 - Q_2}{p_1 - p_2} \cdot \frac{p_1 + p_2}{Q_1 + Q_2}$$

Notice that you don't have to bother to do the averaging because the 2s cancel.

This formula is called the **arc-price elasticity** formula because the calculation takes place at the midpoint of a secant line drawn between two points along an arc of the demand curve:

---

6. If you are making $4 per hour and get a raise of $1 per hour, you'll say you got a 25 percent increase. But if you're making $5 per hour and get cut $1 per hour, you'll say you got a 20 percent decrease. In each case the wage varied between $4 and $5 for a $1 change, but the percentage of change depends on where you start.

> *Arc-price elasticity of demand:* *The arc-price elasticity is the negative of the slope of a straight line between two points along a demand curve weighted by average price divided by average quantity.*

The arc elasticity formula uses the slope of the straight line between two observed points to measure the slope of the demand curve. The formula then uses the price and quantity that correspond to the midpoint of that line. Notice that, unless the demand curve is linear, this midpoint of the straight line will not lie on the demand curve.

4.6   Estimated Demand and Mean-Price Elasticity

The arc elasticity formula was a special case of using only two price-quantity pairs to measure price elasticity. Other cases might have several data points that could be used. Figure 4.9 shows several price-quantity pairs plotted in a "scattergram" or scatterplot. The observed points do not fall along a straight line or simple curve. If they did it would be easy to fit a linear equation to the points.[7] But in the case shown, some variation in the quantity demanded occurs independently of changes in price. That variation may be caused by other determinants of demand or by simple measurement error. The usual solution here is to use the information in the scattergram to estimate the unknown demand curve.

Estimation methods are covered in a later chapter, but estimation always proceeds to "fit" an equation to the observations. As illustrated in Figure 4.9, the estimated demand $\hat{D}(p)$ has been fitted by some criterion to the observations.[8] That is, $\hat{D}(p)$ is the estimate of the true but unknown demand curve $Q = D(p)$. Once we have the estimate $\hat{D}(p)$, we can use its slope to calculate price elasticity at any point along $\hat{D}(p)$ using the point elasticity formula. Frequently, econometricians also report an estimated elasticity at the point of the means:

> *Mean-price elasticity:* *Mean-price elasticity is the negative of the slope at the point of the means for an estimated demand curve weighted by average price divided by average quantity.*

The most frequently used method for estimating demand is called least-squares regression. You will learn how to use least squares in a later chapter. For now, understand that the least-squares method always generates an estimated equation that passes through the point of the means. Thus, for Figure 4.9, the estimated demand curve $\hat{D}(p)$ will pass through the point $(\bar{p}, \bar{Q})$. Mean elasticity is then computed at this point by taking the slope of the estimated demand curve at the point of the means and weighting it by the ratio of the mean price divided by the mean quantity. Care needs to be exercised in using mean

---

7. See Appendix A for fitting deterministic equations to points.
8. The notation $\hat{D}$ is read "dee-hat."

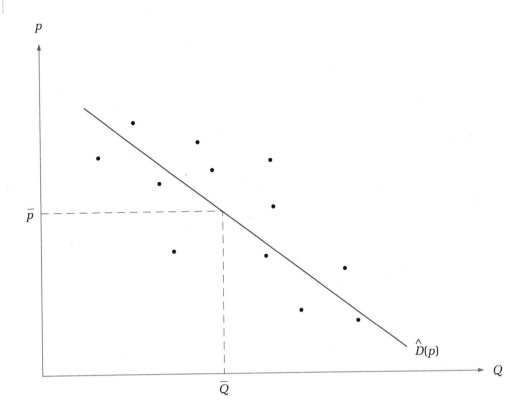

Figure 4.9   **Elasticity and estimated demand:** The unknown demand curve $Q = D(p)$ is estimated as $\hat{D}(p)$ from several price-quantity pairs. Demand may be characterized by calculating its elasticity at the average price and average quantity even though the point of the means was not one of the observed price-quantity pairs.

elasticities, however. Because elasticity usually varies from one point to another along a demand curve, concluding that demand is elastic or inelastic based on the means could be quite misleading.

4.7   Income and Cross-Elasticities

Shifts in demand and average revenue curves may occur whenever any of the underlying determinants of demand change. The most important of these are consumers' incomes and the prices of other goods. Other important determinants of market demand are consumers' preferences, consumers' expectations, and the number of potential consumers. Other important determinants that affect the firm's demand, its average revenue curve, include the number of other firms in the industry and the market structure. For instance, some product differentiation will affect market share through consumers' tastes for differences in product characteristics. The firm needs to be able to predict changes in demand in order to be prepared to react to those changes.

We can extend the concept of elasticity to measure the responsiveness of demand to changes in any of the underlying determinants. For instance, if consumer preference is related to the degree and type of advertising, an elasticity in advertising expenditure would indicate how responsive demand is to changes in advertising. Firms frequently use advertising expenditures as an explanatory variable when estimating demand. Estimates of the advertising elasticity of demand may allow the firm to judge the effectiveness of advertising in influencing demand and the firm's market share. Public utilities calculate weather elasticities of demand for their products. The gas company may use the deviation of temperature from 65 degrees F (18° C) as a variable in explaining the variation in the demand for natural gas. Or it may use an index of the technological efficiency of consumer gas appliances and forced-air heating units to forecast demand. Therefore, the concept of elasticity is quite general and useful in a variety of ways.

Again, the reason for using an elasticity rather than a slope is to purge the measure of responsiveness of any scale sensitivity. We start by considering a change in income, and we then consider a change in the price of some other good. Realize, though, that elasticities may be computed for any of the determinants of demand.

Income elasticity of demand is defined as the percentage change in quantity divided by the percentage change in income.

> **Income elasticity:** *Income elasticity is the percentage change in quantity divided by the percentage change in income.*

Income elasticity can also be measured by the proportionate change in quantity divided by the proportionate change in income, elasticity for normal good would be +pos

$$\eta_M = \frac{\Delta Q/Q}{\Delta M/M}$$

where η_M denotes elasticity with respect to income. Income elasticity may be positive or negative, and we wish to know which it is because that indicates the direction of the shift in demand. Rearranging the terms yields

$$\eta_M = \frac{\Delta Q}{\Delta M} \cdot \frac{M}{Q}$$

Income elasticity of demand is equal to the slope of the Engel curve multiplied by the ratio of income divided by quantity.

The sign of income elasticity is determined by the slope of the Engel curve. Therefore, $\eta_M > 0$ when the good is normal, and $\eta_M < 0$ when the good is inferior. If $\eta_M = 0$, then the demand for the good is said to be *independent* of money income. The sign of income elasticity indicates the direction of the shift in demand as income increases. Because elasticity is independent of scale, we can compare the income elasticity of apples sold by the bushel in Washington to that of oranges sold by the crate in Mexico.

Knowledge of a good's income elasticity can be very useful to managers and analysts. If, for instance, you know that a good's income elasticity is 0.50, then you can predict a 1/2 percent increase in demand when consumer income increases 1 percent. Thus if consumer income is expected to increase 5 percent, other things remaining constant, you may predict an approximate increase in demand of 2.5 percent. Then, if you can also predict how market shares will be determined, you will be able to predict changes in a firm's average revenue curve.

The income elasticity of market demand for most products is positive. Table 4.1 presents some estimated income elasticities in ascending order. Estimates are presented for both the short run and the long run. Long-run elasticities are usually greater than short-run elasticities because consumers have more time to react over longer periods. The only inferior good in the list is potatoes; all others are normal goods. As you might

Table 4.1 **Estimated Income Elasticities of Demand**

Item	Short Run	Long Run
Potatoes	−0.20	−0.81[a]
Pork[b]	0.27	0.18
Beef[b]	0.51	0.45
Furniture	2.60	0.53
Water	0.90	0.60
Electricity, residential[c]	0.30	0.70
Dental services	0.38	1.00
Chicken[b]	0.49	1.06
Automobiles	5.50	1.07
Physicians' services	0.28	1.15
Clothing	0.95	1.17
Gasoline and oil	0.55[d]	1.36
Household appliances	2.72	1.40
Shoes	0.90	1.50
Jewelry and watches	1.00	1.60
Housing, owner-occupied	0.07	2.45
Foreign travel	0.24	3.09

Note: Estimation methods and data types vary from source to source, and so estimates should be taken as approximations.
Sources: Unless otherwise indicated, estimates are from Hendrick S. Houthakker and Lester D. Taylor, *Consumer Demand in the United States* (Harvard University Press, 1970):
[a] Dale M. Heien, "The Structure of Food Demand: Interrelatedness and Duality," *American Journal of Agricultural Economics* (May 1982).
[b] Michael K. Wohlgenant and William F. Hahn, "Dynamic Adjustment in Monthly Consumer Demand for Meats," *American Journal of Agricultural Economics* (August 1982).
[c] G. R. Lakshmanan and William Anderson, "Residential Energy Demand in the United States," *Regional Science and Urban Economics* (August 1980).
[d] Robert Archebald and Robert Gillingham, "An Analysis of Short-Run Consumer Demand for Gasoline Using Household Survey Data," *Review of Economics and Statistics* (November 1980).

expect, such necessities of life as food, water, shelter, clothing, medical services, and transportation are relatively income inelastic in the short run. In the long run, such goods as owner-occupied housing and foreign travel are much more responsive to changes in income than in the short run. This variation makes sense because these are big-ticket items that require some planning to change. In contrast, furniture is very sensitive to short-run changes in income because it is easy to postpone purchase of this type of durable good, but furniture is income inelastic in the long run.

The magnitude of income elasticity is also influenced by each consumer's expenditure on the good relative to that consumer's budget. Consumers are usually much more responsive to changes in income when the required expenditure on a good is relatively large. For instance, notice that the short-run income elasticities for pork and beef are small, but the short-run elasticity for furniture is much larger. Furniture, after all, is a big-ticket item in most consumers' budgets.

The extent of income elasticity is important to both managers and policy analysts. The long-run elasticity for owner-occupied housing was estimated to be about 2.5. The demand for housing will increase by about 2.5 percent for each 1 percent increase in consumer income. But the short-run income elasticity for housing is only 0.07; consumers' response to rising income will be slow.

When the income elasticity is unity, $\eta_M = 1$, demand for the good increases by 1 percent for each 1 percent increase in consumer income. This relation has important implications in an expanding or contracting economy. If $\eta_M < 1$ for a good, producers of that good will not share proportionately in increases in national income. Similarly, if $\eta_M > 1$ for a good, producers of the good will gain more than a proportionate share of increases in income. Thus, firms having demand functions with high income elasticities will have good growth opportunities in an expanding economy. On the other hand, firms with low income elasticities may be better protected against a contraction in the national economy. Thus, knowledge of a firm's income elasticity of demand can be most useful in forecasting its demand.

Income elasticity can also strongly affect the marketing decisions of firms. For instance, as America grays with the baby-boom bubble moving through the 1990s, a firm may find it useful to know the income elasticity for that age group as it plans marketing strategies for the future. Knowing income elasticities for different demographic groups and geographic regions could lead to better decisions about where to locate distribution centers and where to target advertising. With the young urban professional occupations growing in the 1980s, many firms directed their promotional efforts at the so-called Yuppies because of the anticipated increase in their income. Automobile companies have aimed their advertising more and more toward women in response to upward trends in female participation in the labor force and their moving into higher-paying occupations.

An elasticity can be used to measure the responsiveness of demand to changes in other prices independently of scale. When the price of some other good changes, the reaction is called **cross-price elasticity.**

Cross-price elasticity: Cross-price elasticity is the percentage change in the quantity demanded for one good divided by the percentage change in a second good's price.

Cross-price elasticity may be measured by the proportionate change in quantity divided by the proportionate change in the other price:

$$\eta_{p_Y} = \frac{\Delta Q_X / Q_X}{\Delta p_Y / p_Y}$$

Where η_{p_Y} denotes the cross-price elasticity of demand for X with respect to the price of Y. Rearranging terms results in

$$\eta_{p_Y} = \frac{\Delta Q_X}{\Delta p_Y} \cdot \frac{p_Y}{Q_X}$$

The term $\Delta Q_X / \Delta p_Y$ is *positive* when X is a market *substitute* for Y because when the quantity of Y demanded decreases in response to an increase in p_Y, the demand for X increases. The term $\Delta Q_X / \Delta p_Y$ is *negative* when X is a market *complement* for Y because when the quantity of Y demanded decreases in response to an increase in p_Y, the demand for X decreases. Thus, the sign of the cross-price elasticity coefficient corresponds to the direction of the shift in demand for X when the price of Y increases.

As an algebraic example, suppose the demand function for good X is

$$Q_X = D(p_X, p_Y) = 100 - 10p_X + 4p_Y$$

The slope of the demand curve is $\Delta Q_X / \Delta p_X = -10$. The change in quantity due to a one-unit change in the price of Y is $\Delta Q_X / \Delta p_Y = 4$. The position of the demand curve is determined by p_Y. If $p_Y = 5$, then the demand curve is $Q_X = 120 - 10p_X$. If $p_Y = 10$, then the demand curve is $Q_X = 140 - 10p_X$. Because the demand for X increases as the price of Y increases, X is a market substitute for Y. Substituting $\Delta Q_X / \Delta p_Y = 4$ into the cross-price elasticity formula yields

$$\eta_{p_Y} = \frac{\Delta Q_X}{\Delta p_Y} \cdot \frac{p_Y}{Q_X} = \frac{4p_Y}{Q_X}$$

To evaluate this function further, we must choose values for p_Y and Q_X. For the values determined by $p_X = 8$ and $p_Y = 5$, the quantity is $Q_X = 40$; therefore,

$$\eta_{p_Y} = \frac{1}{2}$$

A positive cross-price elasticity equal to 1/2 means that the demand for X will increase by 1/2 percent for a 1 percent increase in p_Y as X is substituted for Y in the neighborhood of the point on the demand curve determined by the values $p_X = 8$ and $p_Y = 5$.

Table 4.2 lists some long-run cross-price elasticities of demand. Notice that the demand for subcompact cars was not responsive to changes in the price of full-sized cars. Apparently, consumers did not consider subcompacts a close substitute for full-sized automobiles. At the other extreme, the cross-price elasticity of demand was high for an Impala when the price of a Chevelle changed. The Impala was a close substitute for the Chevelle during this period. Not only were these models close in size, they were also made by the same manufacturer. Margarine was a good substitute for butter. Pork was a substitute for beef, but it was not a close substitute because the cross-price elasticity was fairly small. In manufacturing use, electricity and natural gas were substitutes but not

Table 4.2 **Estimated Long-Run Cross-Price Elasticities**

Item	Other Price	Cross-elasticity
Subcompact cars	Full-sized models	0.0[a]
Pork	Beef	0.4[c]
Natural gas, manufacturing	Electricity	0.4[b]
Electricity, residential	Natural gas	0.5[d]
Natural gas, residential	Electricity	0.8[d]
Margarine	Butter	1.5[c]
Impala (1968–1973)	Chevelle	11.0[a]

Note: Estimation methods and data types vary from source to source, and so estimates should be taken as approximations.

Sources:

[a] F. Owen Irvine, Jr., "Demand Equatons for Individual New Car Models Estimated Using Transactions Price with Implications for Regulatory Issues," *Southern Economic Journal* (January 1983).

[b] Robert Halvorsen, "Energy Substitution in U.S. Manufacturing," *Review of Economics and Statistics* (November 1977).

[c] Dale M. Heien, "The Structure of Food Demand: Interrelatedness and Duality," *American Journal of Agricultural Economics* (May 1982).

[d] G. R. Lakshmanan and William Anderson, "Residential Energy Demand in the United States," *Regional Science and Urban Economics* (August 1980).

close substitutes. In residential use, electricity and natural gas were much better substitutes; however, consumers were more responsive in substituting natural gas for electricity than they were in substituting electricity for natural gas.

Cross-price elasticity may be very useful to the firm in formulating its pricing strategy relative to other prices. If a firm's product is a market complement with respect to some other good and the price of that other good increases by 2 percent, you can predict the percentage decrease in demand if you know the cross-price elasticity. Or, if a firm's rival is likely to match a price cut, an increase in the quantity demanded due to the price decrease may be muted by a decrease in demand as the rival firm also cuts its price. Alternatively, if the rival firm ignores an increase in your price, you are likely to experience a relatively large decrease in quantity demanded because the responsiveness to the increase in your price will not be muted by a matching increase in your rival's price.

Cross-price elasticity is also useful in forecasting. Forecasters frequently use a general price index and the prices of close substitutes and complements as predictors. Computer software is likely to be a complement with respect to computer hardware. Given the downward trend in the price of computer hardware, an increasing trend in the demand for computer software can be expected. Knowledge of the cross-price elasticity of demand for software to changes in the price of computers would enable you to predict the percentage increase in the demand for software.

Cross-price elasticity is frequently used in antitrust cases to measure the degree of competition. The producers of aluminum for containers may appear to have considerable monopoly power. But if the cross-price elasticities of demand are positive and large compared to the prices of plastic, glass, and waxed cardboard containers, the degree of competition from these related industries is high. The producer of aluminum containers may not be able to raise its price without losing considerable business to these related industries. We will return to this theme in a later chapter dealing with market structure.

GLOBAL PERSPECTIVE: *Cars in Canada*

When gasoline prices increased dramatically in the early 1970s, the demand for small, fuel-efficient cars increased in Canada and the United States. The Canadian experience was studied and demand elasticities were estimated for new cars, large and small.* Pooled data were used for each of five years, from 1971 to 1975, for each of eight Canadian provinces, yielding forty observations. The estimated demand elasticities are reported in Table 4.3.

Table 4.3 Estimated Demand Elasticities for New Cars in Canada

	Own-price Elasticity	Income Elasticity	Cross-price Elasticity with Other Car Type	Cross-price Elasticity with Gasoline
Large Cars	1.26	0.34	0.86	−0.63
Small Cars	2.30	0.37	1.73	0.18

Source: A. G. Blomquist and W. Haessel, "Small Cars, Large Cars, and the Price of Gasoline," *Canadian Journal of Economics* (August 1978), pp. 470–489.

The own-price elasticity of demand for large cars was smaller than for small cars. Although both types of cars had elastic demand curves, consumers were more responsive to changes in small-car prices. Because both types of cars had positive income elasticities, both types of cars can be classified as normal goods. The cross-price elasticities of demand for a change in the price of the other type of cars are both positive, so that each type of car was a market substitute for the other. Notice, however, that the cross-price elasticity for large cars compared with the small-car price is much smaller than the cross-price elasticity for small cars compared to the large-car price. Consumers were switching to small cars more rapidly when the price of large cars increased alone than they switched to large cars when the price of small cars increased alone.

When the price of gasoline increased, the demand for large cars *decreased,* as indicated by the negative cross-price elasticity compared with a change in the price of gasoline. Large cars were market *complements* for gasoline. In contrast, when the price of gasoline increased, the demand for small cars also *increased.* The *positive* cross-price elasticity of demand for small cars in the price of gasoline indicates that small cars were market *substitutes* for gasoline. These results are not too surprising. When the price of gasoline increased alone, consumers stopped buying as many large cars and began buying more small cars that were more fuel efficient.

---

* A. G. Blomquist and W. Haessel, "Small Cars, Large Cars, and the Price of Gasoline," *Canadian Journal of Economics* (August 1978), pp. 470–489.

AN APPLICATION: *Estimated Elasticities for Consumer Durables*

Microeconomic theory may be used to interpret the results of estimated demand functions. One such application involves estimating monthly wholesale-industry demand for consumer durable goods.* Monthly data were observed from January 1963 to April 1970. The estimated demand function is†

$$\hat{Q} = 10{,}468.4 - 175.6P + 5{,}585.6M - 76.2R$$

where

Q = retail inventory of department stores in durable goods
P = consumer price index for durable goods
M = average hourly gross earnings of workers
R = open-market rate on prime 4–6 month commercial notes

The dependent variable Q is a measure of the quantity demanded from manufacturers of durable goods, and $\hat{Q}$ denotes its predicted value, given values for the explanatory variables. This market-demand function is linear in its specification. The first coefficient is the estimated intercept term. The other coefficients are the estimated slope terms. The explanatory variables were chosen to conform to the model of consumer demand. Variable P is a measure of own price, M is a measure of consumers' income, and R is a measure of the price of a "good," a financial asset, which is expected to be a market substitute. The variable R may also be serving as a proxy for the price of obtaining short-term financing. This estimated equation explained 93 percent of the variation observed in the dependent variable.

Elasticities are not constant along linear demand functions, so that mean elasticities are commonly calculated by computer programs used to estimate the demand equation from the data. Such mean-elasticity coefficients are calculated as follows:

$$\eta_P = -(-175.6)\frac{\overline{P}}{\overline{Q}} = 2.269$$

$$\eta_M = 5{,}585.6\frac{\overline{M}}{\overline{Q}} = 2.031$$

$$\eta_R = -76.2\frac{\overline{R}}{\overline{Q}} = -0.049$$

where $\overline{P} = 105.10$, $\overline{M} = 2.96$, $\overline{R} = 5.28$ are the variable means, and $\overline{Q} = \hat{Q}$ at the point of the means.

By examining the estimated elasticities, the quantity demanded of durable goods is seen to be quite sensitive to changes in price. The price elasticity of 2.269 implies that demand is elastic at the point of the means, and a 1 percent increase in price might be expected to lead to a decrease in quantity demanded of more than 2 percent. The

---

* Adapted from Robert S. Pindyck and Daniel L. Rubenfeld, *Econometric Models and Economic Forecasts,* 3d ed. (McGraw-Hill, 1991).
† Chapter 5 is devoted to such estimation.

income elasticity is 2.031, and the positive sign indicates that durable goods are a normal good. Demand might be expected to increase slightly more than 2 percent in response to a 1 percent increase in hourly earnings. The cross-elasticity is -0.049. The negative sign is consistent with an interpretation that durable goods is a market complement for the alternative good; however, the cross-elasticity is close to zero. Moreover, that coefficient was not estimated with much precision, and so a better conclusion is that the demand for durable goods is independent of the price of the alternative.

4.8   Determinants of Elasticity

One of the most important determinants of demand elasticity is the ability to substitute among available goods. The inverse relationship between quantity demanded and price will be more pronounced if close substitutes are available. Thus, demand will be more elastic for goods having close substitutes and less elastic for goods having few, if any, substitutes.

Another determinant of demand elasticity is the income effect associated with price changes. Price-induced income effects are larger for some goods than others. The size of the price-induced income effect is determined by two things: the quantity currently being purchased and the size of the pure income effect. If the good is being consumed in large quantities, consumers are likely to be more responsive to a price change than if they are consuming the good in small quantities.

One clue to the importance of this determinant of price elasticity, the size of the income effect, is the proportion of total income used to purchase the good in question. The larger the total expenditure on the good in relation to income, the more responsive the consumer is likely to be. For example, income effects caused by a change in the price of housing may be large even though housing as a whole has few if any substitutes. Thus, housing may be relatively price elastic. In contrast, the demand for pencils may be price inelastic even though close substitutes are available. Expenditure on pencils is a small share of consumers' incomes, and price-induced income effects are small.

A second clue is gained by looking at the income elasticity of demand. The pure income effect is larger as demand for the good becomes more elastic, and so goods that are more income elastic in demand usually are also more price elastic, other things being equal.

The time frame or period of analysis also influences demand elasticities. For most goods, demand is more elastic over longer periods because consumers have more time to search for substitutes. Close substitutes may also be developed and made available to consumers in the long run. Consumers have more time to react and have more alternatives available to them over longer periods. In the mid-1970s the price of gasoline soared in response to the Organization of Petroleum Exporting Countries (OPEC) oil embargo. The response by the consumer in the short run appeared to be very inelastic. Queues at service stations became so long that tempers flared and fights for positions in the queue occurred. In the long run, however, consumers shifted to smaller, more efficient automobiles and switched to such alternative modes of transportation as van pools.

Table 4.4 lists some estimated price elasticities for several goods. Except for water, quantity demanded is more responsive to price changes in the long run than in the short run. Most of the goods listed have price-elastic demand in the long run, but many of the goods have price-inelastic demand in the short run. Notice the inelastic short-run and long-run demands for residential use of electricity, and compare them to the elastic demand for residential use of natural gas. In residences natural gas is used primarily for heating and substitutes are available, but in residences electricity is used primarily for lighting and appliances, and little substitution is possible. Tobacco products are price inelastic in the short run, but they are price elastic in the long run. New automobiles are quite price elastic in both the short run and long run, but this effect is to be expected because purchase of a new car usually takes a big chunk out of the budget. Foreign travel is insensitive to short-run changes in price and quite sensitive to long-run changes.

Table 4.4 Estimated Price Elasticities of Demand

Item	Short Run	Long Run
Water	0.2	0.1
Electricity, residential[a]	0.3	0.7
Jewelry and watches	0.4	0.7
Shoes	0.7	1.2
Gasoline	0.4[b]	1.5[c]
Foreign travel	0.1	1.8
Housing, owner-occupied	0.3	1.9
Tobacco products	0.5	1.9
Natural gas, residential[a]	1.4	2.1
New automobiles	1.2	2.4
Rail travel	1.4	3.2
Movies	0.9	3.7

Note: Estimation methods and data types vary from source to source, and so estimates should be taken as approximations.
Sources: Unless otherwise indicated, estimates are from Hendrick S. Houthakker and Lester D. Taylor, Consumer Demand in the United States (Harvard University Press, 1970):
[a] G. R. Lakshmanan and William Anderson, "Residential Energy Demand in the United States," Regional Science and Urban Economics (August 1980).
[b] Robert Archebald and Robert Gillingham, "An Analysis of Short-Run Consumer Demand for Gasoline Using Household Survey Data," Review of Economics and Statistics (November 1980).
[c] J. M. Griffin, Energy Conservation in OECD, 1980–2000 (Cambridge University Press, 1979).

ECONOMIC SCENE: *A Wrigley Price Hike*

On March 30, 1987, the Wrigley Jr., Company raised the price of its chewing gum to 5¢ per stick. At the same time Wrigley introduced a new small pack with five sticks for 25¢ and raised the price of its seven-stick pack to 35¢. Wrigley's smaller packs and higher prices were quickly criticized by competitor American Chicle Group, the makers of Chiclets, Trident, and Dentyne brands. The president of American Chicle was quoted as saying, "The trend in the confectionery industry has been to offer consumers more for less; Wrigley is giving them less for more."*

Wrigley makes Spearmint, Doublemint, Juicy Fruit, and Extra brands and has a 50 percent market share. American Chicle has a 28 percent market share. The next largest supplier of gum is Nabisco, which makes Bubble Yum and has a 20 percent market share. Other manufacturers make up the remaining 2 percent of the market. Industry sales were $2.8 billion in 1986.

Why is Wrigley increasing its price? One reason might be that the firm thinks its revenue will increase with the increase in price. That will come about if its demand curve, its average revenue curve, is inelastic. Is this expectation reasonable? First, some consumers do *not* feel that Bubble Yum, a sugarless bubble gum, is a close substitute for the Wrigley brands. Similarly, Dentyne and Trident seem to cater to a special segment of the market. Second, expenditure on chewing gum by the individual is not a large share of the typical consumer's budget. Thus, it seems likely that the demand for chewing gum will be price inelastic. Both of Wrigley's competitors also raised the price of their brands in the past two years. Industry-wide, the average price of gum had risen 50 percent during the past six years as sales volume (quantity) declined 39 percent. The price elasticity of about 0.8 indicates that market demand was price inelastic over that period. Thanks to the average price increase, the dollar volume of industry sales (revenue) had increased by an average of 14 percent per year.

Wrigley was also betting on a threshold effect. By packaging the gum in five-stick packs, it made the price per pack 25¢ rather than 35¢. Wrigley thinks that the consumer will be more likely to "plunk down a quarter" for a pack of gum than to pay 35¢ per pack.

*As reported by Jesus Sanchez, *Los Angeles Times,* Part IV, April 15, 1987.

4.9   Constant Elasticity Demands

When demand functions are estimated, the first step is to specify its functional form. One frequent choice is to specify the demand equation as linear in all the explanatory variables. In such cases elasticities are computed and reported at the point of the means. A frequently used alternative to the linear specification is illustrated by this example:

$$Q_X = \beta_0 p_X^{\beta_1} p_Y^{\beta_2} M^{\beta_3}$$

where the β_0 is an arbitrary constant and β_1, β_2, and β_3 are unknown parameters. Quantity demanded is a function of the prices of X and Y and money income. If other things that influence demand are changing, those should be included as explanatory variables also, and so let's assume that all else remains constant or has a negligible effect on the demand for X.

A convenient way of expressing this function is to take logarithms and write

$$\log Q_X = \log \beta_0 + \beta_1 \log p_X + \beta_2 \log p_Y + \beta_3 \log M$$

Expressed in this way, the demand function becomes linear in terms of the coefficients β_1, β_2, and β_3. The change in the logarithm of a number can be approximated by dividing the change in the number by the number, and we can write:

$$\beta_1 = \frac{\Delta \log Q_X}{\Delta \log p_X} \cong \frac{\Delta Q_X / Q_X}{\Delta p_X / p_X} = -\eta_{p_X}$$

$$\beta_2 = \frac{\Delta \log Q_X}{\Delta \log p_Y} \cong \frac{\Delta Q_X / Q_X}{\Delta p_Y / p_Y} = \eta_{p_Y}$$

$$\beta_3 = \frac{\Delta \log Q_X}{\Delta \log M} \cong \frac{\Delta Q_X / Q_X}{\Delta M / M} = \eta_M$$

Thus the coefficients β_1, β_2, and β_3 yield direct measures of the elasticities. Notice that these elasticities remain constant. When the logarithm of the quantity demanded is linearly related to the logarithms of the explanatory variables, the demand function is called a **constant elasticity** demand. As you will see in the chapter on estimating, the constant-elasticity demand specification is easy to estimate and easy to interpret.

As an example, let's look at an application.[9] The demand for textiles over time is expected to be a function of textile price, other prices, consumer income, and the number of consumers. Suppose that we have data on the textile consumption per capita (Q) over several years. Further, suppose that we have measured the relative price of textile goods (P) by dividing the retail price index for clothing by a general cost-of-living index, and suppose we have measured real per capita income (M) by dividing the money income of all consumers by a cost-of-living index and the population size. Measuring the quantity demanded, the good's price, and consumers' income in real per capita terms helps to control for variations in the cost of living and the size of the population over time.

We can then specify a constant elasticity demand equation as

$$\log Q = \beta_0^* + \beta_1 \log P + \beta_2 \log M + \varepsilon$$

where β_1 and β_2 represent elasticity coefficients and ε is a random error term.[10]

---

9. Adapted from Henri Theil, *Principles of Econometrics* (John Wiley, 1971), pp. 102, 106–108, 115–117.
10. The term β_0^* represents the term $\log \beta_0$

When annual data were observed for several periods and applied using a computer program, the resulting estimated demand equation might be

$$\widehat{\log Q} = 1.467 - 0.821 \log P + 1.089 \log M$$

Because this demand function is of the constant-elasticity variety, the estimated coefficients can be interpreted as direct estimates of the elasticities.

The estimated coefficient attached to $\log P$ yields an estimate of 0.821 for price elasticity. Likewise, the estimated coefficient attached to $\log M$ yields an estimate of 1.089 for income elasticity. Thus, when real income per capita increases by 1 percent and the relative price of textile goods decreases by 2 percent, the change in textile consumption can be predicted to increase by $(1.089 - 2(-0.821)) = 2.7$ percent approximately. Of course, this prediction is subject to the condition that any other neglected variables will remain constant.

4.10 Elasticity of Supply

The slope of the supply curve measures the change in quantity supplied in response to a change in price. But the slope does not remain invariant to changes in the scales of measurement. This scaling problem can be avoided by calculating *percentage* changes. The ratio of the percentage change in quantity supplied to the percentage change in price is a **price elasticity of supply:**

> **Price elasticity of supply:** *The price elasticity of supply is the percentage change in quantity supplied divided by the percentage change in price.*

The supply-price elasticity will be denoted by η_s,

$$\eta_s = \frac{\% \text{ change in } Q}{\% \text{ change in } p}$$

where Q is quantity supplied and p is price. Price elasticity of supply is positive when quantity supplied is directly related to price.

The supply-price elasticity may be computed by

$$\eta_s = \text{slope} \cdot \frac{p}{Q}$$

This formula is almost the same as that used to calculate the price elasticity of demand. The differences are that now we use quantity supplied and the slope of the supply curve, and we don't have to apply a sign change. You can use either an arc-elasticity or a point-elasticity formula depending on the type of data on hand or your objective in describing the supply curve. You can calculate elasticities for short-run supply curves and for long-run supply curves.

It is easy to determine whether a linear supply curve is elastic or inelastic. To see how, take the linear supply curve $Q = a + bp$. The elasticity of supply is

$$\eta_s = \text{slope} \cdot \frac{p}{Q} = \frac{bp}{a + bp}$$

Now, if $a = 0$ so that the linear supply curve passes through the origin, $\eta_s = 1$, and supply has *unitary* elasticity. Alternatively, if $a > 0$ so that the line cuts the quantity axis before it cuts the price axis, then $\eta_s < 1$ and supply is price *inelastic*, because the denominator is greater than the numerator in the formula. Similarly, if $a < 0$ so that the line cuts the price axis first, then $\eta_s > 1$ and supply is price *elastic*.

This technique can also be applied to nonlinear supply curves. As shown in Figure 4.10, when a tangent line cuts the price axis first, the supply curve $S(p)$ is elastic ($\eta_s > 1$) at the point of tangency. When the tangent line passes through the origin, the supply curve $S(p)$ has unitary elasticity at the point of tangency. When a tangent line cuts the quantity axis first, supply curve $S(p)$ is inelastic ($\eta_s < 1$) at the point of tangency. This relation provides a quick and easy way to determine whether a supply curve is elastic or inelastic at a point.

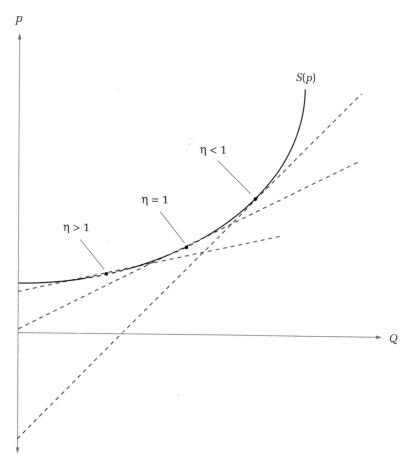

Figure 4.10 **Supply-price elasticity:** When the tangent line cuts the price axis first, supply is elastic ($\eta > 1$) at the point of tangency. When the tangent line cuts the origin, supply has unitary elasticity ($\eta = 1$) at the point of tangency. When the tangent line cuts the quantity axis first, supply is inelastic ($\eta < 1$) at the point of tangency.

A long-run supply curve is usually more elastic than the short-run supply curve because there are fewer constraints in the long run. For the firm, all inputs are variable in the long run, and so the firm can be more responsive to price changes. In the market, industry supply curves are more responsive in the long run because entry and exit of firms occurs. Changes in input prices may partially mitigate the effect that entry has on long-run prices, but as long as entry and exit are easy, the long-run industry supply will be more elastic than short-run industry supply. Moreover, technical progress affects both the firm and the industry in the long run.

Supply elasticity depends greatly on how costs behave as output is varied. Supply will tend to be less elastic if costs rise rapidly as output increases. The stimulus to increase production will be muted by the increase in costs. On the other hand, if costs rise slowly as production increases, a rise in price that raises profit will induce a larger increase in output than would occur otherwise.

Summary

The firm's demand curve is found by allocating market demand to the firms in the industry. The firm's demand curve is coincident with its average revenue curve. Thus, average revenue is influenced by the firm's market share. Market share depends on the form of market structure in the industry: the number and size of firms in the industry; the degree of product differentiation; and the extent and type of rivalry and strategic behavior.

Two polar cases tend to bracket the possibilities of demand at the firm level. A pure monopolist's average revenue curve is coincident with the market demand curve because the firm is the only one in the industry. At the other extreme, a purely competitive firm is a price-taker, and its average revenue is constant. That is, the price-taking firm has a perfectly elastic demand curve, determined by the going market price. Under other forms of market structure, the elasticity of each firm's demand curve depends on the determinants of that market structure as well as all else that influences market demand. For the most part, firms have little control over the position of their average revenue curves except through product differentiation.

Price elasticity of demand measures the responsiveness of quantity demanded to changes in price in a way that is independent of the scale of measurement. Price elasticity is defined as the percentage change in quantity divided by the percentage change in price. There are two basic formulas for calculating elasticity. Point-price elasticity weights the negative of the slope of the demand curve at a point by the ratio of price divided by quantity at that point. Arc-price elasticity weights the negative of the slope between two points by the ratio of average price divided by average quantity between two points. A mean-price elasticity can also be calculated by weighting the negative of the slope of an estimated demand curve at the point of the means by the ratio of average observed prices divided by average observed quantities. Demand elasticity is influenced by the consumers' abilities to substitute among available goods. Thus, demand elasticities are usually larger in the long run because consumers have more time to search for substitutes.

Price elasticity of demand is related to the expenditure of buyers, and hence to the revenue of sellers. When the firm's demand is price inelastic, revenue is directly related to price. When the firm's demand is price elastic, revenue is inversely related to price. Revenue is at a maximum when demand has unitary elasticity.

Income elasticity of demand is defined as the percentage change in quantity divided by the percentage change in income. Income elasticity also equals the proportionate change in quantity divided by the proportionate change in income. Income elasticity may be measured by weighting the slope of the Engel curve by the ratio of income divided by quantity, using either a point formula or an arc formula. The sign of the income-elasticity coefficient corresponds to the direction of the shift in the demand curve when income increases. The magnitude of the income-elasticity coefficient measures the change in demand as a percentage. Normal goods have positive income elasticity, and inferior goods have negative income elasticity.

Cross-price elasticity of demand is defined as the percentage change in quantity divided by the percentage change in the other good's price. Cross-price elasticity also equals the proportionate change in quantity divided by the proportionate change in the other price. Cross-price elasticity may be computed by using either a point formula or an arc formula. The sign of the cross-price elasticity coefficient corresponds to the direction of the shift in the demand curve when the other price changes. A positive cross-price elasticity indicates that the good is a market substitute for the good whose price has changed. Similarly, a negative cross-price elasticity indicates that the good is a market complement of the good whose price has changed. The magnitude of the cross-price elasticity coefficient measures the change in demand as a percentage.

Supply-price elasticity is the percentage change in quantity supplied, divided by the percentage change in price. Supply-price elasticity may be computed at a point or between two points. When you have a graph of the supply curve, it is easy to see whether it is elastic or inelastic at any point or between two points. Extend the tangent line at a point, or a secant line between two points, back to the origin. Supply is inelastic if the line cuts the quantity axis before it cuts the price axis. Supply is elastic if the line cuts the price axis first. Long-run market-supply curves are usually more elastic than short-run supply curves because fewer constraints apply in the long run.

Further Readings

The student interested in a mathematical description of elasticity might wish to read

- John M. Kulman and Russel G. Thompson, "Substitution and Values of Elasticities," *American Economic Review* (June 1965).

The topics of substitutability and complementarity are covered nicely in

- Paul A. Samuelson, "Complementarity: An Essay on the 40th Anniversary of the Hicks-Allen Revolution in Demand Theory," reprinted in *The Collected Papers of Paul A. Samuelson,* vol. IV, ed. by H. Nagatani and K. Crowley (MIT Press, 1977).

That article includes an informative example of the relationships among tea, coffee, lemon, and cream.

Practice Problems

1. Given the demand curve $Q = D(p) = 100 - 5p$:
   (a) What price will maximize revenue?
   (b) What is the price elasticity of demand at that price?
2. Given the market-demand and market-supply schedules for a good (the same as in problem 2 of Chapter 3):

Price	Quantity Demanded	Quantity Supplied
$8	45	75
6	55	55
4	65	35
2	75	15

   (a) Find the equilibrium price and quantity, then compute the elasticity of demand at the equilibrium. Is demand elastic or inelastic at this equilibrium?
   (b) Will consumer expenditure increase or decrease if supply decreases? Why?
3. If the market demand curve is

$$Q = 1,000 - 10p$$

   and the industry has identical firms, what is the equation for each firm's average revenue (inverse-demand) curve?
4. Suppose the demand equation for a good is $Q = 20 - 3p$. What is the price elasticity at $p = \$1$? At $p = \$4$?
5. A marketing analyst observes that when the price of a good was $50 the quantity demanded was 1,000 units and when the price of the good was $40 the quantity demanded was 1,400 units. What is the elasticity of demand? What elasticity formula must be applied, and why?
6. Demonstrate that the elasticity of demand is unitary for any demand curve of the form $Q = k/p$ having slope $= -k/p^2$ for k any positive constant.
7. Given that the demand equation for a good is

$$Q = 500 + 0.10M$$

   where M is average family income:
   (a) Determine the income elasticity at $M = \$15,000$, $M = \$20,000$, and $M = \$25,000$.
   (b) Explain why income elasticity is changing in the direction indicated.
   (c) Would you characterize this industry as susceptible to recession?
   (d) Would a sustained inflation in the economy tend to alter this demand equation? What is likely to happen to the income elasticity of demand?

8. Given the demand equation $Q_X = 80p_Y - 0.5p_Y^2$ where other things have been held constant:
   (a) Given that $\Delta Q_X/\Delta p_Y = 80 - p_Y$, determine the cross-price elasticity when the price of the other good is $p_Y = \$10$.
   (b) Is good X a market substitute or complement with respect to good Y?
   (c) How strong is the relationship?

9. Would you expect the demand for IBM personal computers to be more or less price elastic than the demand for personal computers in the industry as a whole?

10. Explain why the market demand for cigarettes might be price inelastic in the short run but price elastic in the long run.

11. Budget studies conducted in the United States indicate that the income elasticity of demand for servants is about +2. Over the last half century, however, the income of the average American family has risen but the number of servants has fallen. How can these results be reconciled?

12. According to an analyst at the U.S. Department of Agriculture, the price elasticity of demand for cigarettes is about 0.35, and the income elasticity is about 0.50. What effect would a 10 percent excise tax have on consumption? Suppose that incomes are expected to increase 50 percent over the next decade. Would such a prediction cause you to invest in tobacco stocks? Why or why not?

13. Explain why the price elasticity of demand for water is inelastic in both the short run and the long run but the price elasticity of demand for movies is inelastic in the short run but elastic in the long run.

14. Suppose that the cross-price elasticity for large cars with respect to the price of gasoline is -0.2 and the cross-price elasticity of demand for compact cars with respect to the price of gasoline is $+0.3$:
    (a) If the price of gasoline goes up by 10 percent, what is the percentage change in the demand for large cars? For compact cars?
    (b) Are large cars market substitutes or complements with respect to gasoline? Are compact cars market substitutes or complements with respect to gasoline? How can they be? Doesn't this relation defy common sense and technological requirements?

15. Explain how information about cross-price elasticity of demand might be useful to a firm facing an antitrust suit.

16. Given the demand function $Q_X = 50p_X^{-1.2}p_Y^{0.6}M^{0.02}$
    (a) What is the own-price elasticity of demand?
    (b) What is the cross-price elasticity of demand?
    (c) What is the income elasticity of demand?

17. Suppose the demand equation has been estimated to be

$$\hat{Q} = 18.35 - 1.2p + 4.3M$$

where p is price and M is money income. Given that average price is $\bar{p} = 8.1$ and average income is $\bar{M} = 5.9$, what is the mean price elasticity? What is the mean income elasticity?

18. Suppose that the demand curve for a good is given by

$$Q = 1.5p^{-0.8}M^{0.9}A^{0.2}$$

where p is price, M is income, and A is advertising expenditure.
    (a) What is the price elasticity of demand?
    (b) Will consumer expenditure increase or decrease with an increase in price? Why?
    (c) What is the income elasticity of demand?
    (d) Is the good a normal or inferior good? Why?
    (e) What is the advertising elasticity of demand?
    (f) Will demand shift to the right or the left with an increase in advertising? How do you know?
    (g) Is it reasonable to expect the advertising elasticity to remain constant as advertising increases?
19. Suppose the market supply curve for a good is given by $Q_s = 80 + 5p$. Is this supply curve elastic or inelastic? How do you know?
20. Usually, a long-run industry supply curve is more elastic than its short-run industry supply curve. Why?

Microeconomic Choice

T he foundation of microeconomic analysis rests on an understanding of how individuals make choices. Individual choices influence the market demands for goods and market supplies of inputs used in producing those goods. Therefore, managers and policymakers can benefit from a clearer understanding of individual choice in our economic environment. Chapter 5 covers individual choice and the determination of individual demand for goods and the individual supply of labor. You will see how market demand curves are found by aggregating individual demand curves. In Chapter 6 we extend the individual choice model to making decisions over time. Topics include saving and borrowing, investment, the determination of interest rates, and cost-benefit analysis. Additional realism is added in Chapter 7 with a consideration of decision making under conditions of risk and uncertainty. Topics include expected utility maximization, risk-return trade-offs, hedging, the value of information, and how asymmetric information introduces a market imperfection.

Chapter

Individual Choice and Demand

Why is the study of individual economic choice important? Because the individuals' choices influence market outcomes, determining the market demand for every good. This relation influences the revenue received by firms producing the goods. Revenue considerations in turn influence producers' decisions about how much to produce and how to organize and use resources in production. More-over, in a private-ownership economy, individuals own the factors of production: land, labor, capital, and entrepreneurial ability. Individual choices thus influence the supply of these factors and the determination of factor prices.

As members of households, individuals make decisions about how much of each good to buy. As the owners of factors of production, they make decisions about how much of those factors to supply. These decisions interact with the production decisions that firms make to determine prices for inputs and the goods being produced. Thus, individual choices influence the allocation of resources and the distribution of income in the economy.

In our economic environment managers can benefit from clearer understanding of individual choice. The effectiveness of managers of profit and nonprofit organizations, and of administrators of private or public enterprises will be enhanced by understanding how and why individuals choose among alternative goods and activities. Let us say a firm contemplates introducing a new product. The chief executive officer wants to predict the effect on corporate profit, the financial manager wants to estimate the effect on cash flow, the production manager wants to forecast input requirements, and the marketing manager wants to forecast sales as a function of advertising outlay. All depend on the market demand for the product, and so understanding how individuals choose will assist in making qualitative and quantitative estimates of consumers' behavior, reducing the uncertainty of decision making.

The body of economic thought known as **consumer choice** analyzes how individuals make decisions when confronted with constrained opportunities. Opportunities are constrained by the money income available to spend and by the prices of the commodities and services being sold. The model of consumer choice can be applied and extended in many ways. It can be applied where individuals are endowed with goods that can be consumed or traded for other goods. It can be applied to the allocation of time between leisure and work. It can be extended to analyze saving out of current income to increase future consumption. The consumer-choice model provides the foundation upon which most microeconomic and macroeconomic analyses rest.

5.1   The Budget Constraint

The economic theory of individual choice is straightforward. Economists assume that individuals choose the best alternative available. Consumer choice is viewed as selection among available alternatives to obtain the preferred combinations of goods. But as the Greg Howard cartoon illustrates, the choices you make are constrained by your income.

Choice is constrained by the existence of goods, by their prices, and by the individual's money income. As a student, you are a consumer of paper and pencils. How do you decide how much paper and how many pencils to buy? To simplify the analysis, let's assume that these are the only two goods you purchase. Suppose pencils cost 10¢ each and paper costs 2¢ per sheet, and suppose you have $5 to spend on both pencils and paper. Thus the maximum number of pencils you can buy is 50, the $5 you have to spend divided by the price of pencils. Likewise, the maximum number of sheets of paper that you can buy is 250, $5 divided by the price per sheet.

SALLY FORTH By Greg Howard

Reprinted with special permission of North American Syndicate, Inc.

Of course you are not likely to spend the whole $5 on just paper or just pencils. If you want some of both, you must decide how much of each to buy. You could afford to buy 10 pencils and 200 sheets of paper with the $5. A specific collection of goods is referred to as a **bundle.** The bundle of 10 pencils and 200 sheets of paper is shown at point **A** in Figure 5.1. Point **A** lies on the straight line drawn between the maximum number of pencils that

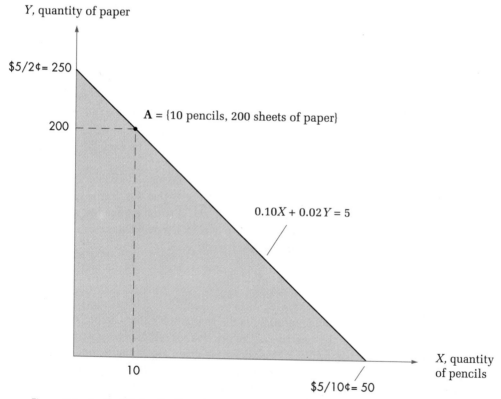

Figure 5.1 **An affordable bundle:** If you have $5 to spend on pencils (X) and paper (Y) when pencils cost 10¢ each and paper costs 2¢ per sheet, you can buy at most 50 pencils or 250 sheets of paper. You are more likely to buy some bundle like **A** that costs $5. Any other bundle that satisfies the equation 0.10X + 0.02Y = 5 also costs $5. Any bundle in the shaded area costs less than $5.

are affordable and the maximum quantity of paper that is affordable. Any other bundle of pencils and paper that lies on that straight line also costs $5. Bundles of pencils and paper below the straight line, the shaded area in Figure 5.1, are also affordable because they cost less than $5. Bundles above the straight line cost more than the income you have to spend.

Let's begin to generalize. Let X denote the quantity of pencils having price p_X. Likewise, let Y denote the quantity of paper having price p_Y. The expenditure on X units of pencils is determined by its price multiplied by quantity, $p_X X$. Likewise, the expenditure on Y units of paper is $p_Y Y$. Total expenditure on both goods is the sum of the expenditure on pencils and on paper:

$$p_X X + p_Y Y$$

Total expenditure may not exceed money income, and so the **budget constraint** is

$$p_X X + p_Y Y \leq M$$

where M denotes money income from all sources. The equality part of the budget constraint, the straight line $p_X X + p_Y Y = M$, is called the **budget line.**

The budget constraint identifies the **attainable set,**

The attainable set: *The attainable set is all affordable bundles of goods.*

That is, any bundle of X and Y is attainable if it is affordable. The attainable set is illustrated in Figure 5.2, where quantities of X and Y are measured along the axes. On the X axis, the maximum quantity of X that may be purchased is M/p_X. Likewise, on the Y axis the maximum quantity of Y that may be purchased is M/p_Y. The straight line drawn between these two points is the budget line.

The budget line represents quantities of X and Y that are just affordable. As illustrated by Figure 5.2, the purchase of some bundle like **A** that lies on the budget line requires that expenditure equal income. But a bundle like **B** is too expensive, and purchasing a bundle like **C** requires an expenditure less than money income.

The budget line, $p_X X + p_Y Y = M$, can be written

$$Y = \frac{M}{p_Y} - \frac{p_X}{p_Y} X$$

When written in this way, the intercept M/p_Y is the amount of Y that can be purchased when $X = 0$ and the slope is the negative of the price ratio, $\Delta Y/\Delta X = -p_X/p_Y$. This slope measures the amount by which Y must decrease given a one-unit increase in X when expenditure equals income. Thus, the price ratio measures the *opportunity cost* of consuming X. For the simple paper-and-pencils example, the cost of one pencil is five sheets of paper. The price ratio is the rate at which you are able to "trade" Y for X—a **rate of exchange.**

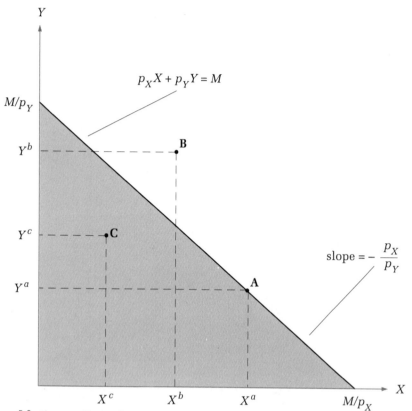

Figure 5.2 **The attainable set:** Given prices and money income, the boundary of the attainable set is given by the budget line. The maximum quantity of X that may be purchased is M/p_X, and the maximum quantity of Y that may be purchased is M/p_Y. Bundle **A** is just affordable, bundle **B** is too expensive, and bundle **C** leaves part of money income unspent.

Changes in prices or changes in money income affect the budget constraint. Figure 5.3 illustrates the effects of an increase in the price of X and an increase in money income. When the price of X increases alone, the maximum quantity of X that can be purchased, M/p_X, decreases. As the budget line rotates toward the origin, real income decreases because the purchasing power of the fixed money income decreases. The steeper slope reflects the increase in the opportunity cost of X as it becomes more expensive. In our earlier example, if the price of pencils increases to 20¢ each, the cost of one pencil rises to ten sheets of paper. An analogous change occurs if the price of Y alone increases.

Changes in money income cause *parallel* shifts in the budget line. As M increases, as shown in Figure 5.3, the attainable set expands while the slope of the budget line remains constant. Similarly, decreases in M alone will result in parallel inward shifts in the budget line.

At this juncture, you can understand intuitively that real income increases when the attainable set expands. Moreover, real income decreases when the attainable set

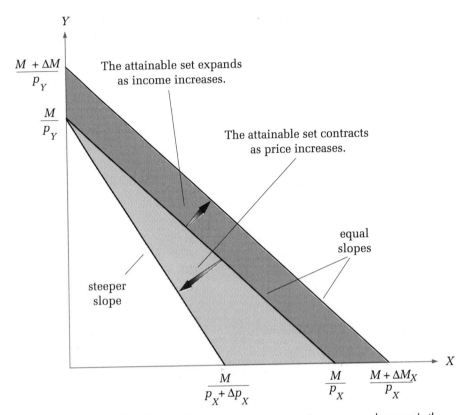

Figure 5.3 **Changes in the budget line:** An increase in p_X to $p_X + \Delta p_X$ causes a decrease in the maximum amount of X that can be purchased. The steeper slope reflects the increase in the opportunity cost of X, and real income decreases. An increase in M to $M + \Delta M$ causes an increase in the maximum amounts of both X and Y that can be purchased and an increase in real income. When the slope remains unchanged, opportunity cost also remains constant.

contracts. Real income *changes* whether the expansion or contraction is caused by price changes or money-income changes or both. Real income remains constant, however, for proportionate changes in all prices and money income.

What happens if prices and money income all change at the same time but not proportionately? If M increases while prices decrease, real income increases as the attainable set expands. Similarly, if M decreases while prices increase, real income decreases as the attainable set contracts. But if some price changes in the same direction as the change in money income, real income will increase or decrease depending on the magnitude of the changes. One thing is certain: whenever the price of good X increases relative to the price of any other good, the opportunity cost of X increases as it becomes more expensive regardless of changes in money income. For example, when the price of pencils doubles from 10¢ to 20¢ while the price of paper remains at 2¢ per sheet, the opportunity cost of one pencil doubles from 5 to 10 sheets of paper.

Notice that the two-good case is more general than you might think. If we are interested primarily in the demand for good X, it is useful to group all other goods into a **composite good.** This composite good may then be treated as the amount of money available to spend on these other goods. Under this interpretation, the price of Y will be $p_Y = 1$ when Y is the composite good, for the cost of one dollar's worth of other goods is one dollar. This relation permits us to use the two-good diagram to analyze the choice of X. The budget constraint becomes

$$p_X X \leq M - Y$$

The budget line can be written

$$Y = M - p_X X$$

In other words, the maximum level of X is M/p_X and the maximum level of the composite good Y is given by M, the level of money income. When any one of the prices is set equal to unity, say $p_Y = 1$, while adjusting the other price and income accordingly, that price is called the **numeraire** price, and then all prices and income are expressed in terms of the numeraire price.[1]

5.2 Revealed Preference

Let's conduct a conceptual experiment that has an empirical connotation—choice is observed given prices and money income. If the consumer buys a bundle because it is preferred to any other bundle in the attainable set, the consumer thereby reveals a preference for that bundle over all others that were also affordable. **Revealed preference** states that when bundle **A** is chosen, **A** is revealed to be preferred over all other bundles that were also affordable:

> **Revealed preference:** *When **A** is chosen over **B** when both are affordable, then **A** is revealed preferred to **B**.*

Revealed preference is illustrated in Figure 5.4. Let p_X^a and p_Y^a denote the prices when **A** is chosen, and let X^a and Y^a be the quantities of goods X and Y in bundle **A**, then the expenditure required to purchase **A** is

$$p_X^a X^a + p_Y^a Y^a$$

Likewise, if X^b and Y^b are the quantities of good X and Y in bundle **B**, then the expenditure required to purchase **B** when **A** is chosen is

$$p_X^a X^b + p_Y^a Y^b$$

---

1. When Y is treated as a composite good, p_y becomes the numeraire price and p_y is pegged at $p_y = 1$. But any good can become the numeraire good—even in the many-good case.

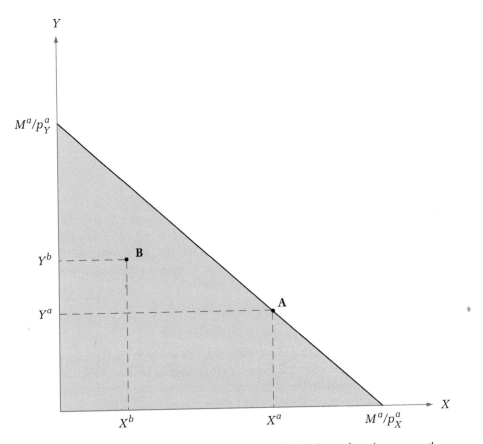

Figure 5.4   **Revealed preference:** When **A** is chosen, **A** is revealed to be preferred over any other bundle **B** that is also affordable.

In other words, if **A** is chosen when **B** is affordable,

$$p_X^a X^a + p_Y^a Y^a \geq p_X^a X^b + p_Y^a Y^b$$

then **A** is revealed preferred to **B**. The choice of a bundle from the attainable set reveals a preference for that bundle over any other bundle that costs as much.

Besides the assumption that choice reveals preference, two more assumptions are needed. One assumption is called **completeness and uniqueness:**[2]

> **Completeness and uniqueness:** *There must be at least one set of prices and income at which each bundle is chosen and, except for proportional changes, there is only one set of prices and income at which each bundle is chosen.*

The effect of this assumption is a unique budget line that corresponds to the choice of any

---

2. Strictly speaking, uniqueness is not necessary, but the exposition is much simpler with it.

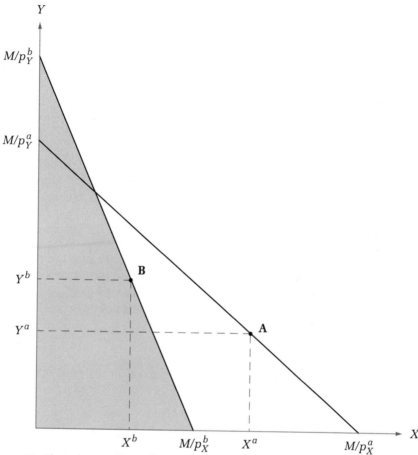

Figure 5.5 **The weak axiom:** If **B** is affordable when **A** is chosen, then **A** must be too expensive when **B** is chosen.

bundle. That is, the completeness-and-uniqueness assumption means that, for any bundle chosen, we can find a unique budget line.

Another needed assumption is called **consistency:**

> ***Consistency:*** *If A is revealed preferred to B, then B must never be revealed preferred to A.*

Consistent consumer behavior requires that once the consumer reveals a preference for one bundle over another, and as long as the consumer's tastes remain unchanged, the consumer will never act inconsistently by choosing that other bundle over the preferred bundle when both are affordable.

The consequence of these assumptions is illustrated by Figure 5.5. The attainable set corresponding to the choice of **A** is identified by the budget line through **A**. The choice of bundle **A** reveals **A** to be preferred to any bundle like **B** within this attainable set. But according to the completeness assumption, there must be some set of prices and income that would induce the consumer to choose **B**. The attainable set corresponding to the choice of **B** is shaded in Figure 5.5. Consistency then requires that the attainable set corresponding to **B** not include **A**.

These observations lead to a restatement of the consistency assumption called the **weak axiom of revealed preference:**

> *The weak axiom: If B is affordable when A is chosen, then A must be too expensive when B is chosen, if consumers' behavior is consistent.*

The weak axiom of revealed preference is sometimes called the WARP condition. That condition requires consistent, rational behavior—not "warped" behavior. Most of the important theorems of consumer behavior are directly derivable from the weak axiom.[3]

5.3 From Individual to Market Demand

Revealed preference indicates that, given the consumer's tastes and preferences, the consumer's choice is a function of the prices of all goods and the consumer's money income. This relation implies that the individual's demand for every good is a function of all prices and money income. For the two-good case, the demand functions can be denoted

$$X = X(p_X, p_Y, M)$$
$$Y = Y(p_X, p_Y, M)$$

As the price of good X changes alone, the quantity demanded for that good may be depicted

$$X = X(p_X; p_Y, M)$$

where the semicolon denotes the conditional relationship to the other price and income, p_Y and M, which are being held constant. The relationship between quantity and the good's price is the individual's **demand curve.**

As the price of X changes, the budget line rotates. As shown in Figure 5.6, for instance, the budget lines rotate outward as the price of X falls. As the affordable set expands with this price decrease, the consumer can afford to buy more of either good or more of both goods. The path of bundles chosen as price changes is called a **price expansion path (PEP)** or **offer curve.** The PEP represents offers to buy various amounts of X and Y as a function of the price of X, holding other things constant.

Figure 5.6 illustrates the PEP_X and the resulting demand curve for X. This consumer chooses bundle **A** when the price of X is p_X^a. As the price decreases to p_X^b, this consumer will choose some bundle like **B**. In this case, the quantity demanded increases from X^a to X^b as price decreases from p_X^a to p_X^b. Similarly, if price were to increase from p_X^b to p_X^a,

---

3. Actually, a slightly stronger assumption is needed in the many-good case, the **strong axiom of revealed preference:** a series of bundles ranked with respect to each other cannot be ranked in reverse order in any combination, and revealed preference is transitive.

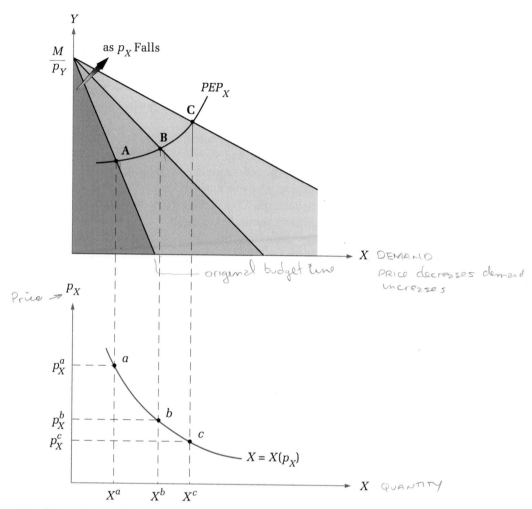

Figure 5.6 **Choice and demand:** The demand curve $X = X(p_X)$ is determined as the consumer moves along the PEP_X from one chosen bundle to the next.

quantity demanded would fall from X^b to X^a. There is an inverse relationship between price and quantity demanded.

An inverse relationship between quantity demanded and own price means that the slope of the demand curve is negative, $\Delta X/\Delta p_X < 0$. Quantity demanded usually falls with an increase in price for two reasons. First, real income falls as price increases. Second, the opportunity cost of a good increases when its price increases, and the consumer will search for substitutes. These price-induced income and substitution effects are examined more formally in following sections.

An individual's demand curve for a good must be negatively sloped once price rises so high that all money income is spent on that good. To see this effect, suppose that a diabetic "needs" 100 units of insulin per week. Let's say the price is $10 per unit. This diabetic must have an income of at least $1,000 a week to buy the 100 units. What happens when price rises to $20 per unit? If income stays constant at $1,000 per week, the quantity demanded must fall to 50 units. The diabetic's demand curve is thus negatively sloped once expenditure on the drug exhausts money income. The only way in which this diabetic can satisfy the "need" for 100 units as price rises above $10 is for money income to rise proportionately. In summary, with other things remaining constant, quantity demanded will eventually fall as price rises.

Consumers' demand (all consumers), or **market demand,** depends on the choices of all consumers. To see how consumers' demand curves are aggregated to determine market demand, let's start with the consumer choosing good X in the amount $X = 0$. As the price of X falls, the consumer may eventually be motivated to buy some X. The price at which the consumer switches from $X = 0$ to $X > 0$ is called the consumer's **reservation price.** The quantity demanded is zero for any price above the reservation price. The change in quantity demanded from $X = 0$ to $X > 0$ as price falls below the reservation price is called a change on the **extensive margin.** Once quantity demanded is positive, subsequent reductions in price cause changes on the **intensive margin.**

The horizontal summation of the individual consumer's demand curves yields the market demand curve. Other things that affect demand remain constant. Let $X_i = X_i(p_X)$ denote the demand curve of the ith consumer. Let n be the total number of consumers in the market. If the preferences of one consumer are not affected by the choices of another, the market demand as a function of price is,

$$Q_X = D(p_X) = \sum_{i=1}^{n} X_i(p_X)$$

where Q_X denotes the quantity demanded.

As an example of deriving market demand, Figure 5.7 illustrates a case with only two consumers. For simplicity, each consumer is shown having a linear demand curve, but each has a different reservation price. The reservation price for the first consumer is p_1^*, and the second consumer's reservation price is p_2^*. The market demand at p_0 is $X = 9$ because $X_1(p_0) = 4$ for the first consumer and $X_2(p_0) = 5$ for the second consumer. The market demand *curve* is the horizontal summation of the demand curves for the two consumers, $D(p_X) = X_1(p_X) + X_2(p_X)$.

Notice that Figure 5.7 shows two kinks in the market demand curve. The first kink occurs where price equals the first consumer's reservation price. Above that price the quantity demanded is zero, and so $Q_X = 0$. As price falls below p_1^*, the first consumer demands more and more as price continues to fall. The second kink occurs where the market price equals the second consumer's reservation price. As price falls below p_2^*, the second consumer demands more and more as price continues to fall.

When several consumers are involved, the market demand is the horizontal summation of the demand curves for all potential consumers:

Market demand: *Market demand is the aggregation of all consumers' demands at every price. Changes in quantity in response to changes in price reflect changes at both the extensive and the intensive margins.*

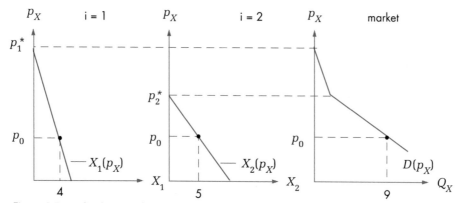

Figure 5.7 **Market demand:** The market-demand curve $Q_X = D(p_X)$ is the horizontal summation of consumers' demands, $X_1(p_X)$ and $X_2(p_X)$, for two consumers, $i = 1, 2$.

As price decreases, some consumers will choose to consume the good in positive amounts for the first time. Or, as price increases, some consumers will stop consuming the good altogether. Thus, changes at the *extensive* margin tend to reinforce the typical inverse relationship between quantity and price at the *intensive* margin. Jumps in demand may occur as consumers make choices at the extensive margin. With many consumers in the market, however, any jumps and "kinks" in the *market* demand curve will be nearly indiscernible and the curve will be nearly smooth. Therefore, we will proceed as if market-demand curves are continuous and smooth, always having negative slope.[4]

5.4 Pure Income Effects

As income changes alone, relative prices remaining constant, a parallel shift appears in the budget line. The path of bundles chosen for parallel shifts in the budget line is called an **income-expansion path** (*IEP*). An *IEP* is illustrated in Figure 5.8. Given the prices of both goods, bundle A is chosen when income is M^a, and bundle B is chosen when income increases to M^b.

The individual's Engel curve for good X may be written

$$X = X(M; p_X, p_Y)$$

when p_X and p_Y are held constant. An individual's Engel curve for X is illustrated in Figure 5.8. As the consumer moves along the *IEP* in response to the change in income, the quantity demanded can be related to income. When quantity demanded increases with increases in the consumer's income, the consumer views the good as a normal good. The

---

4. The possibility that a *market* demand curve might have positive slope is remote because all consumers do not have identical preferences, nor do they have identical incomes. Even if a few consumers' demand curves have positive slope over some price range, the market demand curve will still have negative slope so long as enough consumers have demand curves with negative slope. Moreover, the changes on the extensive margin will always cause an increase in quantity demanded as price falls below consumers' reservation prices. Changes at the extensive margin make the possibility of a positively sloped market demand curve even more unlikely.

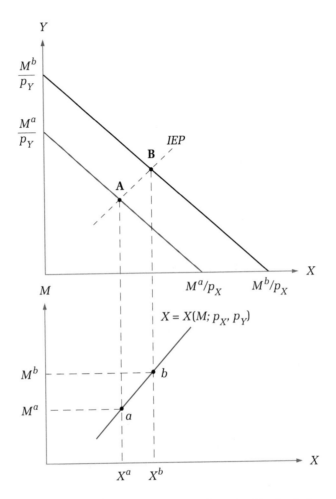

Figure 5.8 **The Engel curve:** The demand for Good X is determined by the choices made along the income-expansion path, *IEP*, as income alone varies.

Engel curve for a normal good has positive slope, reflecting the direct relationship between quantity and price. The slope of the Engel curve, $\Delta X/\Delta M$, measures a **pure income effect** because $\Delta X/\Delta M$ is being measured when prices are constant.

Of course, not all goods are normal. Consider how your demand for potatoes might change if your income increased. The demand for potatoes may decrease as the consumer's income increases, and the individual's Engel curve will have negative slope. When quantity demanded decreases with increases in the individual's income, the consumer views the good as an inferior good.

In the two-good case, all possible income-expansion paths are illustrated in Figure 5.9, where the arrows indicate the direction of the path as income increases. Notice that it

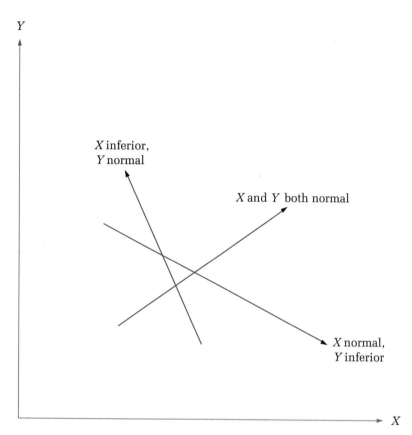

Figure 5.9 **Alternative income-expansion paths:** When income increases, at least one good must be a normal good.

is not possible for both goods to be inferior at the same time. Why? Because even if income were to increase without limit, expansion would just stop at some bundle at which the consumer was satiated in the consumption of both goods. Even if satiation consumption of both goods were to occur, there would be no decrease in the consumption of either good as income continued to rise. This conclusion extends to the many-good case as well.

Whether a good is revealed to be normal or inferior depends on the consumer's choices as income varies. Not all consumers will make the same choice, and any one consumer may react differently depending on the level of income. A consumer may view a good as normal at low levels of income, but as inferior for high levels of income. For example, a person with low income might behave as if ground beef were normal, but that same person with a high income might behave as if it were inferior. Ask yourself how you might behave if your income increased from $10,000 to $25,000—your demand for ground beef might increase. But you might consume less ground beef and more steak and lobster if your income increased from $25,000 to $40,000.

5.5 Substitution and Price-Induced Income Effects

Now we are ready to examine the inverse relationship between quantity demanded and price, the *negatively* sloped demand curve, in more detail. You must admit that a direct relationship between quantity demanded and price would be strange, because then more could be sold at a higher price and the revenue to the seller would always increase as price increased. Why do economists usually assume that demand curves have a negative slope? Does this relation mean that no consumer can ever want more of a good just because it is expensive? Is it possible to have a positively sloped demand curve? If the demand curve for some good has a positive slope, can that slope remain positive regardless of the level of price?

When the price of a good changes, the consumer is motivated to change the quantity of that good demanded for two reasons. First, because relative prices change, the tendency now is to substitute less expensive goods for the relatively more expensive good as its opportunity cost increases. Second, as price changes with money income constant, real income changes, causing a price-induced income effect.

For example, when the price of pencils rises from 10¢ to 20¢ with the price of paper remaining at 2¢ per sheet, the relative price of pencils rises from 5 sheets per pencil to 10 sheets per pencil. The opportunity cost of pencils has increased, and you have to give up more paper than before to consume each extra pencil. Your consumption of pencils is thus likely to fall—a substitution effect. In addition, your real income has fallen with the increase in the price of pencils. With $5 to spend, the maximum number of pencils you can now afford falls from 50 to 25. You are likely to reduce your consumption of pencils because of this change in real income. This price-induced income effect reinforces the substitution effect, and your consumption of pencils decreases.

In the two-good case, given an increase in the price of X alone, the consumer will substitute some Y for X. The change in quantity demanded resulting from the change in relative price alone is called the **substitution effect**. At the same time, real income changes. The change in quantity demanded as a result of the change in real income alone is called the **price-induced income effect**. The **total effect** of the price change is the sum of the substitution and price-induced income effects.

The total effect of a price change is illustrated in Figure 5.10, where **A** is chosen from the original attainable set. As the price of X increases, the attainable set contracts, real income falls, and a new bundle like **B** is chosen. The total effect is the decrease in the quantity of X demanded, associated with the movement along the PEP_X from **A** to **B**.

Hypothetically, we can compensate this consumer for the loss in real income by granting a lump-sum increase in M. How much of a compensating change is required? The answer depends on how we define real income. If real income is defined as the ability to purchase a particular bundle, then the compensating change in M required to permit the consumer to continue to purchase **A** is easy to calculate.

For Figure 5.10, the consumer moves from **A** to **B** in response to the price increase. The old bundle **A** is no longer affordable under the new set of prices, and **B** is chosen.

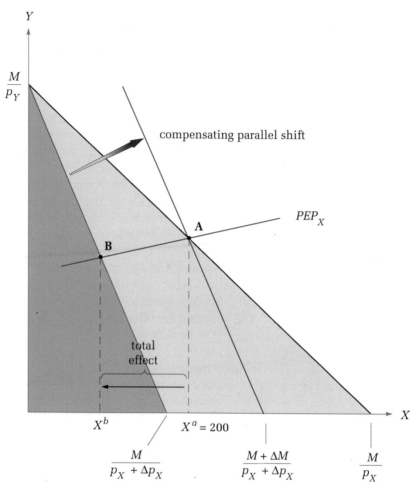

Figure 5.10 **Compensated price change:** The consumer moves from **A,** where $X^a = 200$, to **B,** in response to the price change $\Delta p_X = 2$. A compensating change in income of $\Delta M = X^a \Delta p_X = 400$ dollars will cause a shift in the new budget line so that **A** is affordable once more.

The compensating change in income must be positive, $\Delta M > 0$, because the change in price was positive, $\Delta p_X > 0$. The new budget line for **B** must be shifted outward until **A** is just affordable once more. The ΔM required to enable the consumer to purchase **A** under the new set of prices is given by $\Delta M = X^a \Delta p_X$. For example, suppose that the price change was $\Delta p_X = \$2$ and the original quantity demanded was $X^a = 200$. The required compensating change in income is then $\Delta M = X^a \Delta p_X = \$400$. That is, because the consumer pays an extra Δp_X per unit of X to be able to afford X^a units of X under the new set of prices, the required compensating change in income is calculated by multiplying the original quantity X^a by the price change. The budget line after the compensating change in income has the same slope as the budget line for **B**, but now **A** is affordable once more.

The consumer cannot be worse off than before the price change, because now **A** is affordable again, and real income must be at least as great as it was before the price change.[5]

Will the consumer choose **A** after the compensating shift in the budget line? No, because, according to the assumption of uniqueness, only one budget line is associated with the choice of each bundle. The consumer will thus not choose **A** even though it is again affordable. Will the consumer choose a bundle on or below the initial budget line? No, because the choice of any bundle previously affordable when **A** was chosen would violate the weak axiom. The consumer has revealed a preference for **A** over all other bundles in the initial attainable set. Thus, after the price change and a compensating change in income, the consumer will choose a newly affordable bundle.

We are now ready to decompose the total effect of the price change into the substitution and price-induced income effects. Consider Figure 5.11. After the compensating change in income, the set of newly affordable bundles is shown as the lightly colored area. That part of the original attainable set no longer affordable is grey. According to the weak axiom, a bundle like **C** will be chosen. Notice that **C** was not affordable when **A** was chosen, but **C** is revealed as preferred to **A** because **A** is affordable when **C** is chosen. The movement from **A** to **C** is caused by the change in price while real income, in the sense of being able to purchase the original bundle, is held constant—a movement associated with a substitution effect. The **substitution effect** is measured by the change in quantity, $X^c - X^a$, caused by the change in price alone while real income is held constant. The movement from **C** to **B** is caused by the change in real income alone—a movement along an *IEP*. The **price-induced income effect** is measured by the change in quantity, $X^b - X^c$, caused by the change in real income induced by the price change. Notice that the total effect, $X^b - X^a$, is equal to the sum of the substitution and the price-induced income effects:

$$(X^b - X^a) \quad = \quad (X^c - X^a) \quad + \quad (X^b - X^c)$$

$$\begin{pmatrix} \text{total} \\ \text{effect} \end{pmatrix} = \begin{pmatrix} \text{substitution} \\ \text{effect} \end{pmatrix} + \begin{pmatrix} \text{price-induced} \\ \text{income} \\ \text{effect} \end{pmatrix}$$

The substitution effect must always be inverse or the weak axiom will be violated. By "inverse" we mean that the dependent variable (quantity) is inversely related to the independent variable (own price).

Application of price-induced income and substitution effects lead to the **fundamental theorem** of consumer choice:

> *The fundamental theorem: Any good [simple or composite] that is known always to increase in demand when money income alone rises must definitely shrink in demand when its price alone rises.*[6]

---

5. Shortly you will learn that this method of compensation actually overcompensates the consumer.
6. Paul A. Samuelson, "Consumption Theorems in Terms of Overcompensation Rather Than Indifference Comparisons," *Economica* (February 1953).

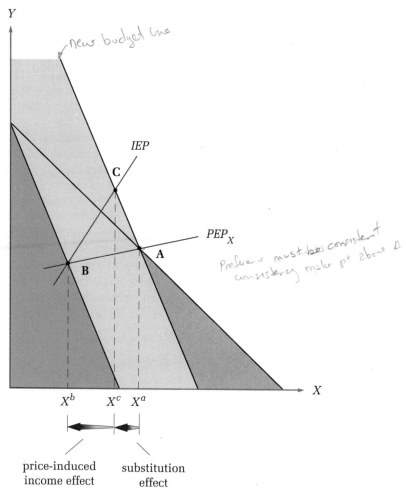

Figure 5.11 **The fundamental theorem:** The price-induced income effect reinforces the always-inverse own-price substitution effect when the good is normal. The weak axiom guarantees that **C** is left of **A**, and **B** must be left of **C** if X is normal; hence, **B** must be left of **A.** Thus, the demand curve must have negative slope, $\Delta X/\Delta p_X < 0$, whenever X is normal.

The fundamental theorem deals with normal goods, as in Figure 5.11. The total effect of the price change causes the consumer to move to **B** from **A** along the PEP_X. This total effect, $\Delta X = (X^b - X^a)$, can be decomposed into a substitution effect and a price-induced income effect. The substitution effect, $(X^c - X^a)$, must be inverse according to the weak axiom—the relationship between the change in quantity and the change in price associated with the substitution effect is *always* inverse. If the good is normal, the price-induced income effect, $(X^b - X^c)$, will also be inverse—the relationship between the change in quantity and the change in price associated with the price-induced income effect is also inverse *if the good is normal.* Thus, the price-induced income effect of a normal good will reinforce the always-inverse own-price substitution effect.

AN APPLICATION: *Gasoline Taxes and Rebates*

Suppose that an excise tax has been imposed on gasoline in order to promote conservation of fuel. This tax has caused an increase in the price of gasoline at the pump by 50¢ per gallon. Furthermore, suppose Congress has proposed a rebate to compensate consumers for the loss in real income associated with the tax. How much should the rebate be, and will the scheme promote a reduction in average consumption of gasoline?*

Suppose that before the tax the current average consumption of gasoline is 400 gallons per year per person. Let X denote the quantity of gasoline measured in gallons, and let Y denote the consumption of all other goods. Because Y is a composite good, let's treat Y as the numeraire with $p_y = 1$. The before-tax choice by the average consumer is labeled bundle **A** in Figure 5.12, where $X = 400$ gallons. Given the 50¢ increase in the price of gas, the pump price of gasoline will increase to $(p_X + 50¢)$, and the budget line becomes steeper. The average consumer will move along a PEP_X to a bundle like **B**. If gasoline is a normal good, or if it is inferior but the substitution effect dominates, consumption of gasoline will decrease to a quantity like X^b.

Let ΔM denote the compensating change in income under the rebate. If the budget line is shifted so that **A** becomes affordable once more after the tax, the expenditure for bundle **A** would be

$$(p_X + 50¢) \, 400 + Y^a = M + \Delta M$$

Before the tax and rebate, the level of expenditure was

$$p_X \, 400 + Y^a = M$$

The required rebate ΔM is found by subtracting the original level of expenditure from that required to purchase **A** after the tax. Therefore, the required rebate is

$$\Delta M = 400 \times 50¢ = \$200$$

After the compensating rebate, the consumer will be able to purchase **A** after the tax and will be at least as well off as before the tax.

According to the weak axiom the bundle chosen after the rebate will never be to the right of **A**. Therefore a bundle like **C** will be chosen, and the average level of gasoline consumption decreases. This conditional argument—that the average consumer would never be worse off under this tax-rebate plan—should not be interpreted as an argument in favor of the plan. One issue is that the taxes collected will not be sufficient to cover the rebates, and so added revenues are required. Several other extensions might be considered in the analysis. For instance, individuals consume more or less than the average level of gasoline consumed, so that some individuals consuming more than the average might be made worse off. If you are consuming more than the average but are compensated according to the average, the compensation may be too small. Compensation could be based on calculating each individual's rebate on his or

---

*This hypothetical proposal actually is fairly close to one proposed in a presidential campaign by George McGovern. The rebate was to be made in the form of a reduction in the payroll tax.

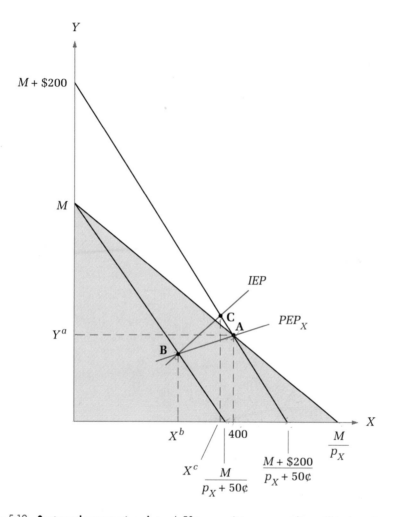

Figure 5.12 **Gas tax and compensating rebate:** A 50¢ per unit tax on gasoline will induce the average consumer to decrease the level of consumption from 400 gallons to X^b. A cash rebate of $200 (the 50¢ increase in price multiplied by 400 gallons) will enable the consumer to purchase **A** once more. Bundle **C** will be chosen because the consumer will be better off, and the average level of consumption of gasoline will fall according to the weak axiom.

her actual consumption, but this technique would increase the costs of administration. Moreover, it is likely that the excise tax would be greater than the price increase, because suppliers usually are not able to pass the whole tax on to consumers, and so part of the burden of the tax would be borne by suppliers who have not been compensated under the tax-rebate plan. In addition, other prices are likely to change eventually, and a careful analysis of changes in each consumer's budget line would be necessary to predict whether each consumer would be worse off or better off. Nevertheless, if gasoline is a normal good, the average consumption of gasoline will fall.

So far so good, but what about inferior goods? An inferior good is illustrated by Figure 5.13. As before, the substitution effect, $(X^c - X^a)$, is always inverse. But the price-induced income effect, $(X^b - X^c)$, is *direct* when X is *inferior.* It is direct because an increase in price causes a decrease in real income, and a decrease in real income causes an increase in demand for inferior goods. In the case shown, the total effect is inverse because the inverse substitution effect dominates the now-direct price-induced income effect, and so the demand curve still has negative slope.

An interesting question arises for an inferior good. Is it possible for the now-direct price-induced income effect of an inferior good to be so strong that it overwhelms the

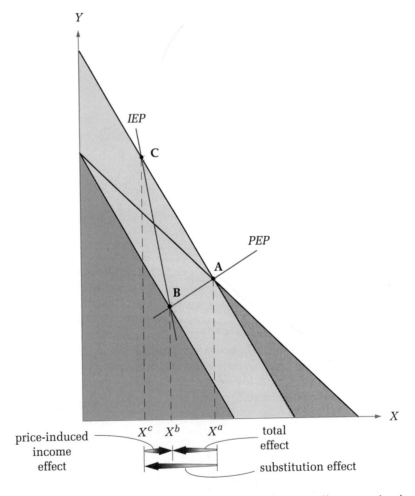

Figure 5.13 **An inferior-good case:** The now-direct price-induced income effect mutes the always-inverse substitution effect. The total effect is inverse if the substitution effect dominates the price-induced income effect, and the demand curve will have negative slope, $\Delta X/\Delta p_X < 0$.

always-inverse substitution effect? The answer is yes, at least theoretically. Such a **Giffen good** is a *special* inferior good whose price-induced income effect is larger in magnitude than its substitution effect. A Giffen good occurs when a direct price-induced income effect is larger in magnitude than the inverse substitution effect. The magnitude of the price-induced income effect is larger when the quantity of the good being consumed is larger. This relation implies that a Giffen good must be a highly inferior good that is being consumed in large quantity, a somewhat paradoxical situation that most consumers would not accept easily. We have little empirical evidence that Giffen goods exist, and that is fortunate—for economists at least—because a large part of economic analysis is based on having negatively sloped demand curves.

5.6 Preference and Indifference

We have seen how to represent bundles that a consumer is *able* to purchase—the affordable set. The consumer will be constrained to make a choice from the affordable set, and we say that such a choice reveals a preference for the bundle chosen. But because preference *precedes* choice, we need to find a way to represent the rankings of all bundles—the preference set. This model of consumer preference requires four new assumptions.

The first assumption is that preferences are **complete:**

Completeness: *The consumer can compare and rank all bundles.*

Completeness of the preference set means that for any two bundles **A** and **B,** the consumer will prefer **A** to **B,** will prefer **B** to **A,** or will be indifferent between the two bundles. Indifference means that the two bundles are equally ranked, and neither is preferred to the other. This ability to rank all bundles is independent of the ability to purchase bundles. Preference is not the same as choice, and preference is not influenced by price.[7]

The second assumption is called **transitivity:**

Transitivity: *If the consumer prefers A to B and prefers B to C, then A is preferred to C also. If the consumer is indifferent between A and B and is indifferent between B and C, then the consumer is indifferent between A and C also.*

---

7. This hypothesis eliminates cases of "prestige" goods or "conspicuous" consumption, where the price of goods influences the consumer's rankings of bundles of the goods.

Transitivity ensures that the consumer's preferences are "rational" in the sense that contradictions do not arise when ranking bundles. Transitivity also means that two bundles can be compared indirectly by comparing them to other bundles.

A third assumption is called **nonsatiation** in consumption:

Nonsatiation: *More is preferred to less.*

That is, the consumer must always prefer more to less with respect to every good. At first glance it may seem unreasonable to assume that more is always preferred to less for every good. But once we consider the possibility of exchange for other goods, even if you don't want to consume more of some good yourself, more will still have value. The nonsatiation assumption has other forms, but this version is simplest and most suitable for our purposes. [8]

The fourth assumption is called **convexity**:

Convexity of preference: *Means are preferred to the lower-ranked of two extremes.*

One implication of convexity is that half a loaf of bread is better than no loaf. Convexity implies that any weighted average of two bundles is preferred to the lower-ranked bundle.

These assumptions can be used to describe consumer preferences. When a series of bundles are equivalent in the individual's ranking, the consumer is indifferent among those bundles. In the two-good case, a consumer's preferences can now be illustrated graphically with **indifference curves:**

An indifference curve: *A set of bundles among which the consumer remains indifferent.*

A typical map of consumer preference is shown in Figure 5.14. Each curve is a set of bundles that are equally ranked. That is, any indifference curve represents a set of bundles that provide the same level of satisfaction. Taken together, the curves represent a topological map of consumer preference.

The indifference curves shown in Figure 5.14 have distinctive properties. One of these is that indifference curves may not "touch" one another. If two indifference curves were to touch, that contact would violate the transitivity assumption. Therefore, no two indifference curves may share any point as long as transitivity holds.

Another property of indifference curves is that a new curve can be drawn between any two other curves. This condition is a consequence of the completeness assumption. Because the consumer can rank all bundles, an indifference curve must be associated with each and every bundle.

---

8. A more general and less restrictive assumption is offered by Gerard Debreu. His nonsatiation assumption says that the consumer will never be satiated with respect to all goods simultaneously. Debreu's version of nonsatiation allows the consumer's indifference curves to bend inward but not close on themselves. The resulting model generates the same results as our model that uses the more restrictive assumption.

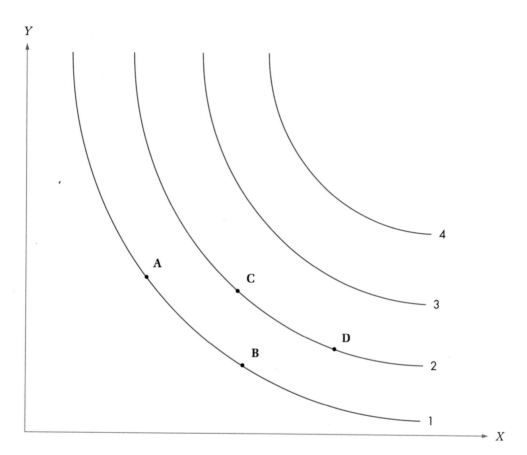

Figure 5.14 **An indifference map:** Indifference curves represent a mapping of consumer preference. Each curve identifies a set of bundles that have the same ranking. Different curves identify bundles having different rankings. Bundles **A** and **B** are equally ranked, and bundles **C** and **D** are equally ranked. But **C** and **D** are preferred to and have greater ranking than **A** and **B.**

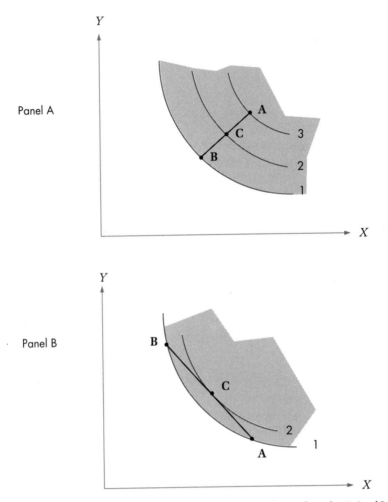

Figure 5.15 **Panel A** If **A** is preferred to **B**, then bundle **C** must also be preferred to **B**. **Panel B** If **A** is equivalent to **B**, then bundle **C** must be preferred to **A** and to **B**.

A third property of indifference curves is that they all have negative slope. This property follows from our nonsatiation assumption. When an indifference curve has negative slope, it is possible to compensate the consumer for decreases in the consumption of one good by giving the consumer an appropriate-sized increase in the other good.

A fourth property of indifference curves is that they are "bowed" toward the origin. This shape follows from the assumption of convexity. As long as the consumer requires successively larger amounts of one good in compensation for successive incremental decreases in the other good, each indifference curve will be convex. The geometry of convexity is illustrated by Figure 5.15, where bundle **C** is a weighted average of bundles **A** and **B**. When **A** is preferred to **B**, the weighted average **C** must also be preferred to **B**. When the consumer is indifferent in choosing between **A** and **B**, the weighted average **C** must be preferred to **B** and to **A**.

ECONOMIC SCENE: *Beer and Martinis*

I had a teacher of economics who was very particular about martinis. Not only did the gin and vermouth have to be mixed in just the right proportions, the glass had to be chilled to just the right temperature. Now, I know it's hard to believe, but he was so particular that he had an engineering student build a martini-making machine. Coils chilled the gin and vermouth as these ingredients were dispensed in an exact proportion. When the weight of the glass and ingredients reached a specified limit, an olive would fall from a chute, halting the procedure. The result was his "perfect" martini.

What do this professor's indifference curves look like for gin and vermouth? Before proceeding, let's assume that extra quantities of either ingredient may be set aside to be used later. Then, suppose the professor's perfect martini consists of four units of gin, to be mixed with one unit of vermouth. Panel A of Figure 5.16 illustrates the indifference curves resulting in $M = 1$ martinis and $M = 2$ martinis. Each indifference curve is L-shaped, with the corners occurring along a ray determined by the required fixed proportions. These two goods, gin and vermouth, are called *perfect net complements* according to this consumer's tastes and preferences.* They are perfect complements because they must be consumed in fixed proportion. The horizontal and vertical segments are a result of the ability to set aside extra amounts of the two goods.

In contrast, the professor's taste for beer was not so refined.† In fact, when expressing a choice between Dos Equis and Budweiser, the professor was indifferent, saying, "Beer is beer." This attitude implies that when offered a six-pack of XX or a six-pack of Bud, each was equally preferred. Moreover, any combination of XX and Bud that resulted in six bottles of beer generated the same satisfaction. The resulting indifference curve is shown in Panel B of Figure 5.16. These two goods are called *perfect net substitutes* because the negative slope of the curve is constant.

Indifference curves for perfect net substitutes or perfect net complements are not strictly convex everywhere, but in both cases the "goods" can be combined to form one good. Gin and vermouth can be combined into one good called martinis. Because the brands of beer are indistinguishable according to this consumer's tastes, they can be combined to make one good called beer. Perhaps the preference set that should be considered is the one related to beer and martinis.

---

*The modifier *net* is used so as not to confuse preference with choice when classifying goods as *market* substitutes or complements.

†Allison and Uhl conducted blind taste tests on various brands of beer and found that beer drinkers could not distinguish one brand from another and could not identify their favorite brands. In a separate study, Ackoff and Ernshoff conducted blind taste tests using one brand of beer by placing different labels on the same brand. They found that all subjects believed the "brands" were different and could tell the difference by tasting; moreover, most of the subjects felt that at least one of the four "brands" was not fit for human consumption. See R. Ackoff and J. Ernshoff, "Advertising Research at Anhaueser-Busch, Inc. (1968–74)," *Sloan Management Review* 16 (Spring 1975), pages 1–15, and R. Allison and K. Uhl, "Influence of Beer Identification on Taste Perception," *Journal of Marketing Research* 1 (August 1964), pages 36–49.

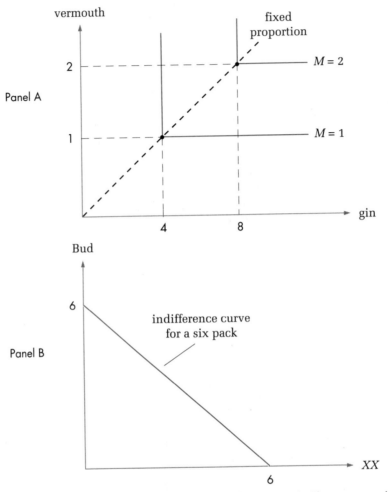

Figure 5.16 **Panel A** These two goods are perfect net complements. **Panel B** These two goods are perfect net substitutes.

Indifference curves for beer and martinis might look like those shown in Figure 5.17. This consumer views bundles **A, B, C,** and **D** as yielding the same level of satisfaction. This consumer achieves maximum satisfaction when four units of beer are consumed along with four martinis. This is called a **bliss point** because extra consumption of either good beyond the bliss point results in a decrease in satisfaction. Beyond the bliss point both goods become "bads." The existence of a bliss point violates our assumption of nonsatiation because more is not always better. Nevertheless, this example shows that positively sloped indifference curves are consistent with rational behavior as long as there is no bliss point.‡

‡Bliss points are inconsistent with the attainment of general equilibrium in the economy as a whole.

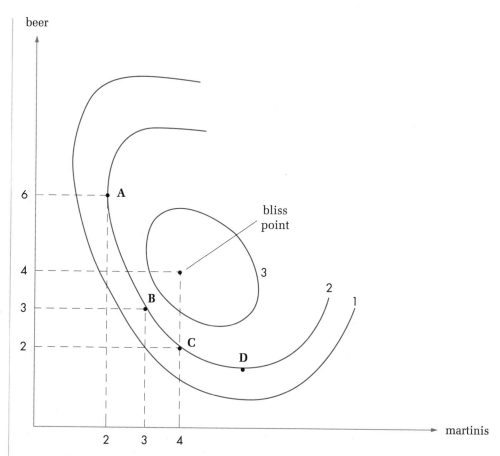

Figure 5.17 **Preference for beer and martinis:** This consumer reaches a bliss point when consuming four units of each good. The existence of a bliss point violates the assumption of nonsatiation because more is not always better. If we wish to permit indifference curves that bend inward, we need to modify the assumption of nonsatiation. Better yet, if we assume that this person can trade for other goods, the indifference curves will have negative slope everywhere.

5.7 Maximizing Utility

Economists have found it convenient to refer to the level of satisfaction associated with any choice as the "utility" of that choice. The idea is that every individual—consumer, producer, or manager—assesses the utilities of alternatives and chooses the alternative that yields the greatest utility. But what is utility? Utility is an abstract, but highly useful, concept that can be inferred from individual behavior. We have seen that each indifference curve represents a different level of preference. Alternatives along the same indifference curve are equally ranked and must therefore yield the same level of utility. Alternatives on different indifference curves yield different utilities. It is possible, therefore, to assign a numerical value called **utility** that is consistent with the ranking of each indifference curve.

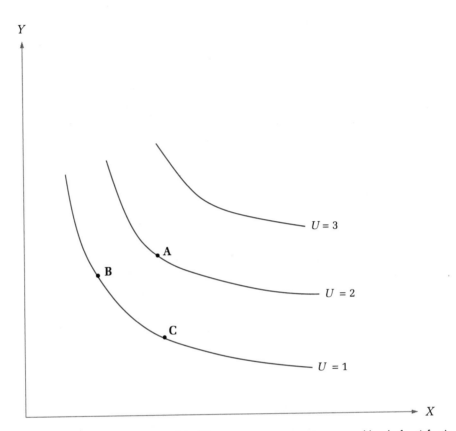

Figure 5.18 **Utility and preference:** Each indifference curve represents an equal level of satisfaction and utility. Thus a legitimate utility assignment would be $U = 2$ for bundle **A** and $U = 1$ for bundles **B** and **C** because **A** is preferred to **B** and **C** and **B** and **C** lie on the same indifference curve. Higher-ranked bundles must have greater utility, and equal-ranked bundles must have the same utility.

In our model of consumer choice, a utility assignment may be made to every bundle. Bundles of equal ranking are assigned equal utility values, and bundles of higher ranking are assigned greater utility values. This utility assignment can be represented by a function called the **utility function:**

> ***The utility function:*** $U(A) > U(B)$ *when **A** is preferred to **B**;* $U(A) = U(B)$ *when **A** is indifferent to **B**.*

That is, the utility of **A** is greater than the utility of **B** when **A** is preferred to **B**, or the utility of **A** is equal to the utility of **B** when the individual is indifferent between **A** and **B**. The utility function generates numbers in accordance with the ranking determined by the consumer's preferences.

Consider the preference set represented by the indifference curves in Figure 5.18. Given this consumer's preferences, the indifference map reflects the consumer's ranking of

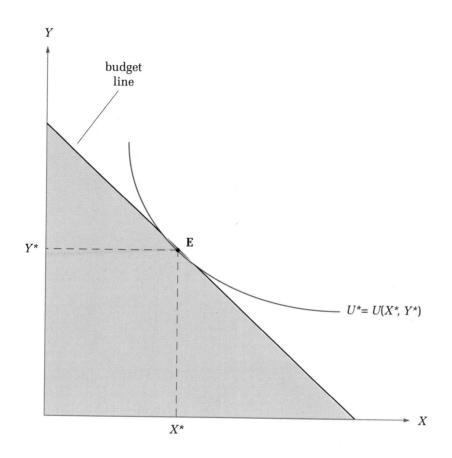

Figure 5.19 **Utility maximization:** The consumer chooses the best-affordable indifference curve $U^* = U(X^*, Y^*)$. In this case there is an interior solution, for both X^* and Y^* are positive.

all bundles and the consumer's willingness to substitute amounts of one good for another. Because bundles along any indifference curve are equally ranked, bundles on that indifference curve must be assigned the same numerical ranking. Thus bundles **B** and **C** must have the same utility assignment, $U(\mathbf{B}) = U(\mathbf{C})$. Bundles on higher-ranked indifference curves must have a greater utility assignment. For instance, bundle **A** is ranked greater than **B** and **C**, and so $U(\mathbf{A})$ must be greater than $U(\mathbf{B})$. The utility assignment $U(\mathbf{B}) = 1$, $U(\mathbf{C}) = 1$ and $U(\mathbf{A}) = 2$ is consistent with that ranking.

Recognize that utility is an **ordinal** ranking of bundles. The numerical assignment can be quite arbitrary as long as it is consistent with the ranking. Moreover, any other numerical assignment that corresponds to the preference ordering would serve as well. Thus, any order preserving transformation of any original utility function would serve as well.

The utility-maximizing choice of the consumer can now be represented graphically. As shown in Figure 5.19, the consumer chooses bundle **E,** the most preferred bundle that is affordable. More of either good beyond bundle **E** would increase utility, but such choices are not affordable. Affordable bundles other than **E** yield less satisfaction because they must lie on lower-ranked indifference curves.

When both goods are being consumed in positive amounts, as in Figure 5.19, we call that an *interior* solution. When one of the goods is chosen in zero amount, as in Figure 5.20, we call that a *corner* solution.

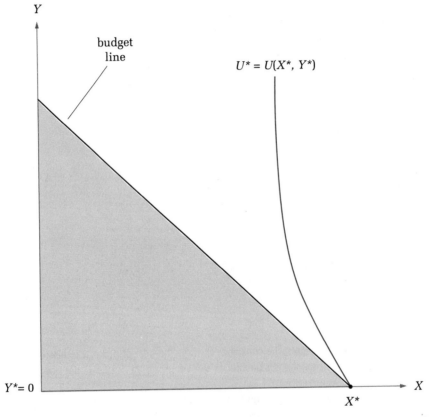

Figure 5.20   **A corner solution:** When this consumer maximizes utility, the best-affordable bundle occurs at a corner point. The utility-maximizing quantities of X and Y are $X^* = M/p_X$ and $Y^* = 0$.

AN APPLICATION: *Employee Fringe Benefits*

Employers frequently compensate employees with fringe benefits in addition to wage payments. These benefits often amount to more than 25 percent of a worker's compensation. Fringe benefits are a form of income-in-kind. Typical benefits include medical and life insurance, recreational and educational benefits for employees and their children, and use of a company car or van pool. Increasingly, benefits include day care for children and frail elderly. Instead of providing fringe benefits the employer could pay workers increased cash wages. What are the consequences of offering fringe benefits instead of cash?

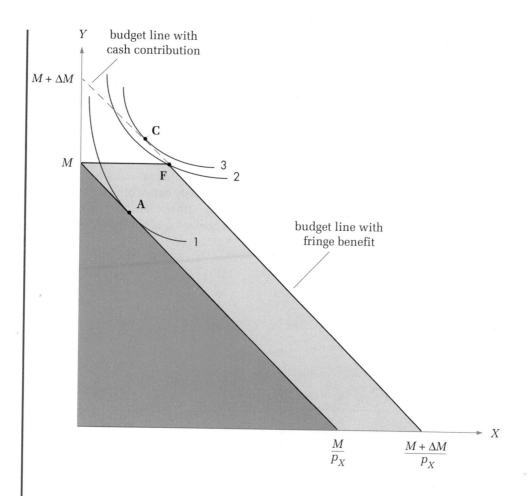

Figure 5.21 **Cash compensation or fringe benefit:** An increase in cash compensation of ΔM dollars permits the employee to choose bundle **C.** A fringe benefit of equal dollar value on X restricts the choice to a maximum of M dollars that can be spent on other goods. With the in-kind fringe benefit, this employee will choose bundle **F.** This individual is better off with the cash compensation.

To answer this question, let's look at a case in which the benefit offered is health insurance. Let X denote the quantity of health insurance consumed and Y denote expenditure on all other consumption, a numeraire good. Figure 5.21 illustrates a case in which the employer considers offering to its employees increasing cash compensation by ΔM dollars or providing an equal-value fringe benefit of ΔM dollars of health insurance. As shown in Figure 5.21, the employee's budget line will shift outward as real income increases under either alternative. Choice is restricted more by the fringe benefit, however, because the maximum amount of other goods affordable does not change under the fringe benefit. An employee like the one depicted will be better off with the extra cash because the cash compensation bundle **C** is preferred to the fringe-benefit bundle **F.** Other employees will be indifferent between the extra cash contribution and the fringe benefit if their preferences result in choices to the right of **F.**

No employee will prefer this fringe benefit to an increase of equal value in money income. This preference results because all affordable alternatives under the fringe benefit remain affordable with the equal-value increase in income. Some employees will be worse off with the fringe benefit, however, because they end up with a less-preferred bundle. Why then do employers offer fringe benefits? Several explanations are possible.

Fringe benefits frequently are exempt from income taxation. Suppose the extra income of ΔM dollars is subject to a tax rate of t. The after-tax change in income is thus $(1 - t)\Delta M$. As illustrated by Figure 5.22, the maximum amount of X that can be consumed is greater under the fringe benefit than under an equal-value cash grant. Some individuals, like the one shown, who were previously better off with the extra cash, may now be better off with the fringe benefit. Other individuals who were previously indifferent to the alternative forms of compensation will definitely be better off with the fringe benefit.

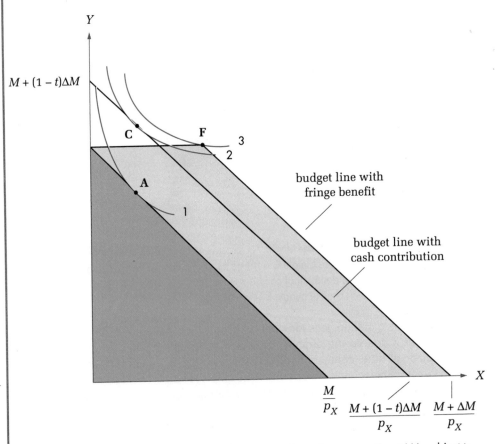

Figure 5.22 **Fringe benefit exempt from taxes:** If the increase in cash compensation ΔM is subject to an income tax where t is the tax rate but a fringe benefit of equal value is exempt from the tax, this individual will now prefer the fringe benefit to the cash compensation because **F** is preferred to **C.**

Fringe benefits like health insurance are usually cheaper for the employer because group rates or other quantity discounts are usually available to the employer but not to the employee. Figure 5.23 illustrates the case in which the price of X is lower by f dollars per unit to the employer. Once again, an individual who was previously better off with the extra cash may now be better off with the fringe benefit. Moreover, employees previously indifferent between the extra cash and the benefit will now be better off with the fringe benefit.

When fringe benefits are not tax exempt or when employers cannot purchase the benefit at a lower price than the worker, the employer will discourage some workers from seeking employment with the firm. Workers without other dependents, for example, may prefer employment with a firm offering cash compensation rather than family medical insurance. As we have just seen, this effect is mitigated somewhat when the fringe benefit is tax exempt and when the benefit can be purchased at a group discount. In either case, the firm can influence the type of worker attracted for employment.

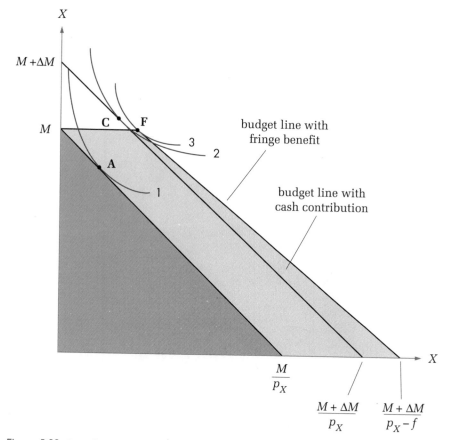

Figure 5.23 **Fringe benefit and group rate:** If the good subject to the fringe benefit may be purchased at a group rate, its price to the employee will be lower by f dollars per unit. This individual will now prefer the fringe benefit to the cash compensation because **F** is preferred to **C**.

5.8   Substitution and Marginal Utility

Usually the consumer is willing to substitute amounts of one good for another. Movement along any indifference curve measures the amounts of one good that the consumer is just willing to substitute for another. This rate of substitution is so important in economics that it is given a special name:

> **Marginal rate of substitution (MRS):** *The MRS measures the amount of one good that the consumer is willing to exchange for small amounts of another good in order to remain on the same indifference curve.*

What is the *MRS* implied by the *Far Side* cartoon?

The marginal rate of substitution may be measured by the negative of the slope of an indifference curve:

$$MRS_{XY} = -\frac{\Delta Y}{\Delta X}$$

where $\Delta Y / \Delta X$ is the slope of the indifference curve at a point. The measurement of the marginal rate of substitution by the slopes of tangent lines is illustrated in Figure 5.24. At **A,** the slope of the tangent line measures the amount of Y that must be sacrificed to get

THE FAR SIDE   By GARY LARSON

"And always — *always* — remember this: A swimmer in the water is worth two on the beach."

THE FAR SIDE COPYRIGHT 1987 and 1991 UNIVERSAL PRESS SYNDICATE. Reprinted with permission.

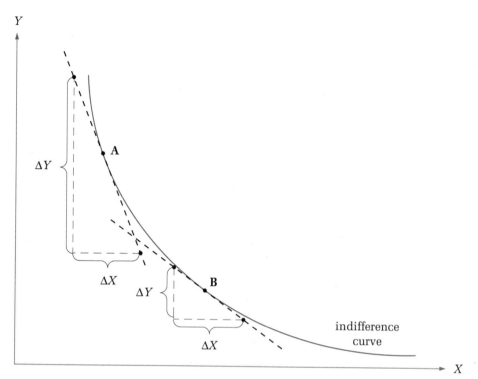

Figure 5.24 **The marginal rate of substitution:** The MRS_{XY} can be measured by the slope, $\Delta Y/\Delta X$, of a tangent line to a point along an indifference curve. Convexity of the curve implies a diminishing MRS_{XY} as the consumer acquires more X relative to Y.

an extra unit of X near **A** to stay on the same indifference curve. At **B,** the slope of this tangent line measures the amount of Y that must be sacrificed to get an extra unit of X near **B** to stay on the same indifference curve. Notice that the marginal rate of substitution is smaller near **B** than near **A.** In other words, the consumer subjectively values X in terms of Y less and less as consumption of X is greater. A diminishing marginal rate of substitution is the economic meaning behind convex indifference curves.

To convince yourself that a diminishing MRS is a reasonable condition, consider how much water you would be willing to give up to get one high-quality diamond. Would you stop bathing for a month to get one more diamond? Now suppose that you have traded most of your water this month for several diamonds so that all you have left is drinking water. How much water would you be willing to give up now? Could you, would you, give up drinking water for a month to get one more diamond? If not, your indifference curves for water and diamonds are convex.

When only one good changes, utility changes too. The change in utility when one good changes alone can be measured by **marginal utility:**

> **Marginal utility:** *Marginal utility is the change in utility divided by an incremental change in consumption of one good alone.*

Thus the ratio

$$MU_X = \frac{\Delta U}{\Delta X}$$

is the marginal utility of a one-unit change in X when Y is held constant. Likewise, the marginal utility of Y is

$$MU_Y = \frac{\Delta U}{\Delta Y}$$

when X is held constant.[9]

Suppose a consumer states: "If you halve X and double Y, I am equally well off." This set of preferences can be represented by $U = XY$ because utility remains constant if X is divided by any constant and Y is multiplied by that constant, or vice versa. Indifference curves for $U = 50$, $U = 100$, and $U = 200$ are illustrated in Figure 5.25. Other equally good utility functions for this consumer would be $V = \sqrt{XY}$ and $W = X^2Y^2$, because each of these yields a constant when X is halved while Y is doubled, or vice versa. Indeed, the indifference curves for U, V, and W all coincide.

For the original utility function $U = XY$, the marginal utility of X between bundles **A** and **B** is

$$MU_X = \frac{\Delta U}{\Delta X} = \frac{50}{5} = 10$$

and the marginal utility of X between **B** and **C** is

$$MU_X = \frac{\Delta U}{\Delta X} = \frac{100}{10} = 10$$

When $Y = 10$ in this example, utility is $U(X; Y = 10) = 10X$. The marginal utility of X thus remains constant at $MU_X = 10$ for the utility function $U = XY$ when $Y = 10$. For the consumer of Figure 5.25, the transformations $V = \sqrt{U}$ and $W = U^2$ generate indifference curves that coincide with those of $U = XY$, and so U, V, or W all represent the same set of preferences. It is easy to show that MU_X diminishes as X increases when utility is being measured by V. Also, it is easy to see that MU_X increases as X increases when utility is being measured by W. You might want to graph indifference curves for U, V, and W to verify this interpretation. Thus, whether the marginal utility of a good diminishes, increases, or remains constant has no behavioral interpretation.[10]

One way of calculating the marginal rate of substitution is to make use of a relationship with marginal utilities. Along any indifference curve the change in total utility must be zero, and so the MU_X multiplied by the change in X added to the MU_Y multiplied by the change in Y together must be zero,

$$MU_X\Delta X + MU_Y\Delta Y = 0$$

---

9. In terms of the calculus, marginal utilities are partial derivatives: $MU_X = \partial U/\partial X$; $MU_Y = \partial U/\partial Y$.
10. This result is not true of the marginal utility of income, however. A diminishing marginal utility of income does have a behavioral interpretation, as we shall see in a later chapter.

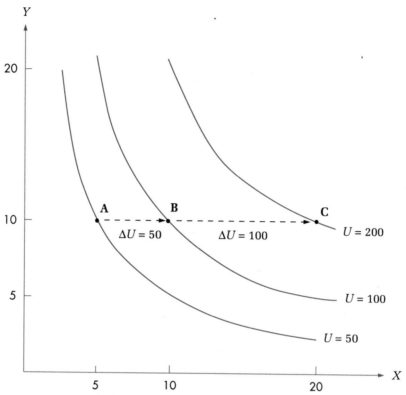

Figure 5.25 **Utility U = XY:** This set of indifference curves represents the statement: "If you halve X and double Y, I am equally well off." The utility function $U = XY$ is one utility assignment consistent with this set of preferences.

Rearranging the terms leads to

$$\frac{MU_X}{MU_Y} = -\frac{\Delta Y}{\Delta X}$$

The right-hand side of this equation is the marginal rate of substitution. Thus, the marginal rate of substitution is $MRS_{XY} = MU_X/MU_Y$.

An example is provided by the earlier utility function $U = XY$. Because the $MU_X = Y$ when X changes alone, and $MU_Y = X$ when Y changes alone, the marginal rate of substitution is $MRS_{XY} = MU_X/MU_Y = Y/X$ for this utility function. Notice that the marginal rate of substitution diminishes as X increases relative to Y—as it must if the indifference curves are convex.[11]

---

11. Earlier we saw that $V = \sqrt{U}$ or $W = U^2$ would serve as well as $U = XY$ for this consumer's preferences. The MRS thus should be the same for U, V, or W at any bundle. That the MRS_{XY} equals Y/X for the utility functions V and W is left as an exercise.

5.9 Utility Maximization and Demand

Given preferences, the consumer chooses the bundle that maximizes utility subject to the budget constraint:

Utility maximization:

$$\text{maximize} \quad U = U(X,\ Y)$$
$$\text{subject to} \quad p_X X + p_Y Y \leq M$$

An interior solution is illustrated in Figure 5.26. Bundles like **A** cannot be chosen. Bundles like **B**, **C**, and **D** are affordable but will not be chosen because a better bundle like **E** is affordable. Notice that the utility-maximizing bundle **E** coincides with a point of tangency of the highest attainable indifference curve and the budget line.[12] At the point of tangency, the utility-maximizing quantities of X and Y are denoted by $X = X^*$ and $Y = Y^*$. The level of utility can be measured by evaluating U at X^* and Y^*, and so maximum utility is $U^* = U(X^*,\ Y^*)$.

Tangency can be represented by two conditions. First, the utility-maximizing consumer must be on the budget line and *not* at bundles like **A** and **B**. This result comes about because **A** is not affordable and **B** leaves unspent some income that can be used to increase utility when spent. Thus, expenditure must equal money income, $p_X X + p_Y Y = M$. Second, the slope of the indifference curve must be equal to the slope of the budget line because at **C** the consumer can sell X and buy Y at the price ratio given by the budget line, thereby increasing utility, and at **D** the consumer can sell Y to buy X in order to increase utility. Thus, the utility-maximizing consumer will *not* choose bundles like **C** or **D**. Recall that the price ratio determines the *ability* of the consumer to exchange one good for the other along the budget line. Recall also that the *MRS* measures the *willingness* of the consumer to exchange amounts of one good for the other along an indifference curve. At a bundle like **C**, the consumer's willingness to exchange Y for X is lower than the ability to exchange Y for X along the budget line, $MRS_{XY} < p_X/p_Y$, and so the consumption of X is too high relative to Y.

Once again, suppose that good X is pencils and good Y is paper. The price of pencils is 10¢ each, and the price of paper is 2¢ per sheet. Along the budget line, the consumer is able to "buy" five sheets of paper with one pencil—the price ratio is five to one. Suppose this consumer has plenty of pencils but little paper and is at a point like **C**. This condition implies that this consumer would be willing to trade a pencil for just a few more sheets of paper because the *MRS* of pencils for paper is lower than the price ratio. At **C** this consumer subjectively values pencils less than paper relative to the ability to exchange pencils for paper, and so an exchange will be made by reducing the consumption of pencils and increasing the consumption of paper. Similarly, at a point like **D**, the consumer's willingness to exchange Y for X is higher than the ability to exchange Y for X along the budget line, $MRS_{XY} > p_X/p_Y$, and so the consumption of X is too low relative to Y. At **D** this consumer subjectively values pencils more than paper relative to the ability to

---

12. Corner solutions in which either $X = 0$ or $Y = 0$ are also possible—as can be seen geometrically—but such choices cannot be interpreted as points of tangency. Thus, strictly speaking, the tangency condition holds only for *interior* solutions in which both $X > 0$ and $Y > 0$.

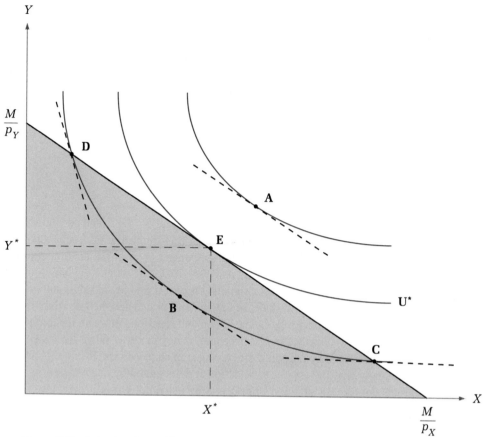

Figure 5.26 **An interior solution:** The consumer will choose the bundle **E**, which yields maximum utility $U^* = U(X^*, Y^*)$. This bundle is identified by the tangency of an indifference curve to the budget line. Tangency requires that $p_X X + p_Y Y = M$ and $MRS_{XY} = p_X/p_Y$.

exchange pencils for paper, and so an exchange will be made by increasing the consumption of pencils and decreasing that of paper. Thus, the consumer can equalize the *MRS* with the price ratio by moving to **E**. The consumer is said to be optimizing at **E** along the budget constraint where the willingness to exchange is just equal to the ability to exchange, and utility is maximized.

The **tangency requirement** for utility maximization can now be stated concisely:

> **Tangency conditions for utility maximization:**
>
> (1) *expenditure must equal income,*
>
> $$p_X X + p_Y Y = M$$
>
> (2) *the MRS must equal the price ratio,*
>
> $$MRS_{XY} = \frac{p_X}{p_Y}$$

A numerical example will help to illustrate how tangency can be applied. Suppose utility is given by $U = X^2Y$. This relation means that $MU_X = 2XY$ and $MU_Y = X^2$ are the marginal utilities.[13] Given prices $p_X = 4$ and $p_Y = 2$, and given income of $M = 60$, the consumer will choose $X = X^*$ and $Y = Y^*$, so that utility is maximized. We know that utility maximization occurs at the point of tangency of an indifference curve and the budget line. We also know that the MRS can be measured by the ratio of marginal utilities, $MRS_{XY} = MU_X/MU_Y$. Substituting the ratio of marginal utilities and the known prices and income yields two equations in terms of two unknowns, X and Y:

$$4X + 2Y = 60$$

$$\frac{2Y}{X} = \frac{4}{2}$$

These equations can be solved simultaneously for $X = X^*$ and $Y = Y^*$. The second equation reveals that $Y = X$ at the current prices. Substituting into the first equation results in $6X = 60$ or $X = 10$. We find that $Y = 10$ because $Y = X$ at the current set of prices. Thus, the optimizing values are $X = 10$ and $Y = 10$.

The utility-maximizing values of X and Y depend on prices, money income, and preferences. The demands for X and Y thus are functions of prices and income when the consumer's preferences remain unchanged. These demand functions must be invariant with respect to proportionate changes in all prices and money income. Why? Because the budget line remains unchanged by proportionate changes in all prices and income. Now you can see more clearly that the level of satisfaction is determined by quantities consumed. Utility is not directly affected by prices—prices do not enter directly into the utility function.

5.10 Substitution and Income Effects Reconsidered

Previously, when we decomposed the total effect of a price change into substitution and price-induced income effects, we found the compensating change in income by multiplying the original level of consumption by the price change. As illustrated by Figure 5.27, the ΔM required to purchase bundle **A** under the new set of prices is given by $\Delta M = X^a \Delta p_X$. Under the original set of prices, bundle **A** was chosen. When the price of X increases, bundle **A** is no longer affordable. After compensating the consumer for the loss in purchasing power by giving the consumer $\Delta M = X^a \Delta p_X$ dollars, bundle **A** is affordable once more, but the consumer will choose a bundle like **C** according to the weak axiom.

The original level of utility was $U(\mathbf{A})$. After compensating for the price change the level of utility is $U(\mathbf{C})$. The consumer has a greater utility than before because $U(\mathbf{C}) > U(\mathbf{A})$—the consumer has been *overcompensated* in terms of utility. It would be possible, then, to give the consumer a smaller compensating change in income that would enable the purchase of a bundle **D** on the original indifference curve. The consumer is indifferent between bundles **D** and **A**.

---

13. $MU_x = \partial U/\partial X = 2XY$ and $MU_y = \partial U/\partial Y = X^2$. See the Appendix on optimization and the use of functions.

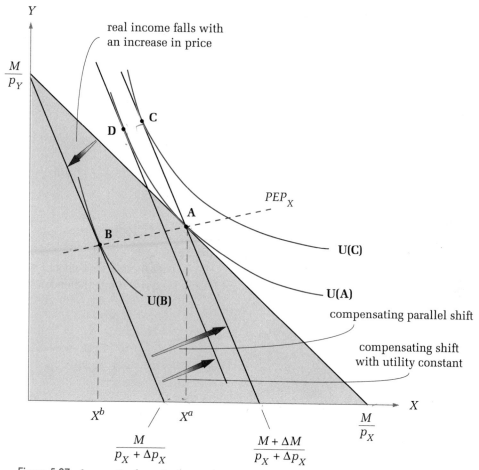

Figure 5.27 **Compensating for a price change:** A compensating change in income of $\Delta M = X^a \Delta p_X$ dollars will shift the budget line so that **A** is affordable once more after the increase in price of $\Delta p_X > 0$. The weak axiom implies that some bundle like **C** will be chosen after the compensating change in income. But $U(C) > U(A)$, and so the consumer has been overcompensated in utility terms because utility is greater than before the price change. Another way to compensate for the loss in real income caused by a price increase is to give the consumer a compensating change in income sufficient to restore the original level of utility. Bundle **A** is no longer affordable, but the consumer is just as well off as before because $U(D) = U(A)$.

Wouldn't it be better, then, to determine the required compensating change in income so that utility is restored to its original level? After all, isn't real income best measured in terms of utility because constant utility implies the same level of satisfaction? Yes, but that can be done only if the utility function is known as illustrated by Figure 5.27. To work directly with the utility function, economists sometimes observe reactions to price changes in order to estimate the *typical* consumer's utility function. Moreover, in theory, it is usually sufficient to assume that consumers behave as utility maximizers to make qualitative, conditional predictions about consumers' behavior. In practice, however, it is much easier to measure substitution and income effects using revealed preference.

5.11 Buying and Selling

How does one obtain income? Well, one way is to sell something, either your time or something you own. Selling your time amounts to providing labor services. Selling something you own—your time, accumulated assets, or something produced—is a decision to supply that good for a price. Our choice model can be extended to analyze such decisions. Production decisions are examined in a later chapter, and so for now we will start with a model in which the individual is endowed with two goods.

For two goods X and Y, let X^e and Y^e denote the *endowments* of X and Y owned by the individual. The budget constraint can now be written

$$p_X X + p_Y Y = p_X X^e + p_Y Y^e$$

Money income is determined by

$$M = p_X X^e + p_Y Y^e$$

Money income is equal to the value of the endowment.

The budget line is illustrated by Figure 5.28. The individual can always choose to consume $X = X^e$ and $Y = Y^e$, and so the budget line must pass through the endowment

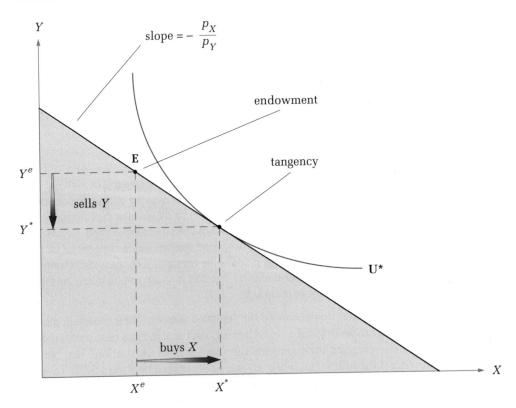

Figure 5.28 **The endowment budget line:** When endowed with X^e and Y^e units of X and Y, money income is determined by $M = p_X X^e + p_Y Y^e$. The budget line must have slope equal to $-p_X/p_Y$, and the budget line must pass through the endowment bundle.

bundle. As before, the slope of the budget line is $-p_X/p_Y$. To see why, suppose we start at the endowment bundle. To buy an extra unit of X, $\Delta X = 1$, the individual must sell p_X/p_Y units of Y; therefore, the change in Y must be $\Delta Y = -p_X/p_Y$. At any point along this budget line, the individual must exchange Y for X at the rate p_X/p_Y.

The individual will choose the bundle for which the marginal rate of substitution equals the price ratio along the budget line. In the case shown in Figure 5.28, the individual *sells* $\Delta Y = Y^e - Y^*$ units of Y and *buys* $\Delta X = X^* - X^e$ units of X in order to consume the utility-maximizing amounts X^* and Y^*.

What happens to the budget line when the individual's endowment changes? The slope of the budget line remains the same, and the budget line shifts in a parallel fashion. An increase in the endowment works just like an increase in money income, and the budget line shifts outward. Likewise, a decrease in the endowment shifts the budget line inward.

What happens to the budget line when prices change? Because the endowment bundle is always affordable, the endowment point remains the same. The slope of the budget line changes, however, as the price ratio changes. As illustrated by Figure 5.29, the budget line rotates clockwise as X becomes relatively more expensive. Likewise, the budget line rotates counterclockwise as Y becomes relatively more expensive.

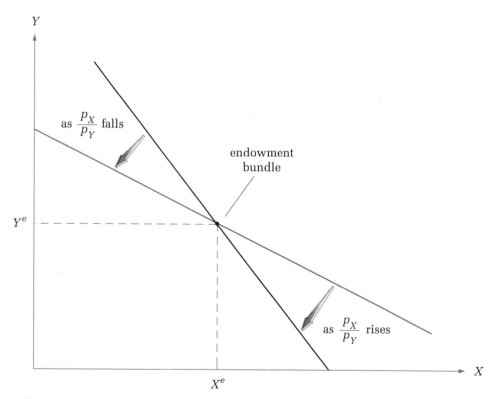

Figure 5.29 **A change in relative prices:** The endowment bundle is affordable for any set of prices. The budget line rotates clockwise as X becomes relatively more expensive. The budget line rotates counterclockwise as Y becomes relatively more expensive.

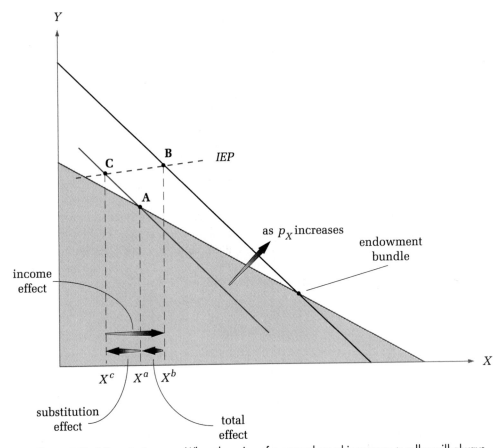

Figure 5.30 **Selling price increases:** When the price of a normal good increases, a seller will always remain a seller, but the substitution and income effects of the price change work in opposite direction because the income of the consumer increases when the price of the good being sold increases.

The most interesting cases occur for changes in the price of a good being sold. First, let's examine the case in which price increases. As illustrated by Figure 5.30, when the selling price of X increases, the budget line rotates in a clockwise direction. The individual moves from a bundle like **A** to one like **B**. As before, the total effect of the price change can be decomposed into a substitution effect and an income effect.[14] The substitution effect is always inverse according to the weak axiom. The income effect, however, is now direct if X is normal because the increase in the price of X causes an increase in money income to the seller of X. The total effect will be direct if the income effect dominates the substitution effect of the normal good being sold. Then the quantity

---

14. The price-induced income effect, however, is not quite an ordinary price-induced income effect because the value of the endowment changes with a change in price.

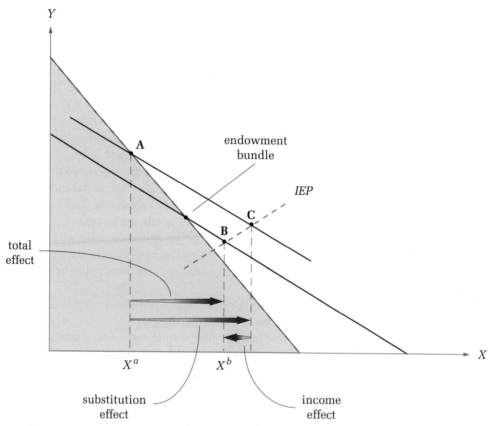

Figure 5.31 **Selling-price decreases:** When the price of a normal good decreases, a seller may become a buyer if the substitution effect is large enough.

of the good sold decreases because consumption increases. If, however, the substitution effect dominates the income effect, the price increase will cause an increase in the quantity sold because consumption decreases. Thus, the total effect of a price change for a normal good being *sold* is indeterminate because the substitution and income effects of a price change work in opposite directions. One thing is clear: A seller will always remain a seller when the price of the good being sold increases.

What happens when the selling price decreases? As illustrated by Figure 5.31, the budget line rotates counterclockwise. A seller of good X choosing a bundle like **A** may move to a bundle like **B**, where he becomes a buyer of X. Once again the substitution and the income effects move in opposite directions when X is normal. The substitution effect causes the seller to sell less or buy more of a normal good. But the income effect will cause the seller to sell more and buy less of a normal good. The total change is indeterminate because it depends on the magnitude of the two effects. One thing is clear: A seller who remains a seller will be worse off when price falls, because the new bundle is inside the old budget line.

5.12 Work–Leisure Choices: Supply of Labor Time

Everyone is endowed with time. Your time can either be consumed as leisure or sold in the market as labor. The consumption of your own time has a price—the wage rate that could have been earned by selling your time as labor. Our choice model can be applied to analyze how an individual chooses to allocate time between work and leisure. The work–leisure decision is important for managers to understand because they will benefit from a clearer understanding of how labor time supplied varies with wage rates and other income. After all, labor time is frequently the most costly input in any production process. The model can also be used to analyze the effect of income transfers and taxes.

Let's divide total time T per period into work time $\mathscr{L}$ and leisure time ℓ, so that $\mathscr{L} + \ell = T$. Work time is defined as the time associated with earning a wage in the current period. Earnings from work can be added to nonwork income to obtain the total income available to purchase goods. To simplify the analysis, those goods can be treated as a composite good called consumption, C. Leisure is also a type of consumption, and its price is the wage rate because the wage rate is the opportunity cost of devoting time to leisure rather than to work. Both leisure time and the composite good are assumed to be normal goods.

Figure 5.32 illustrates the consumer's utility-maximization problem, where utility is a function of leisure time and the consumption of the composite good, $U = U(\ell, C)$. Choice is constrained by a physical constraint that leisure time may not exceed total time available, T. Likewise, labor time may not exceed total time, where labor is found by $\mathscr{L} = T - \ell$. Thus, the attainable set must lie to the right of the C-axis, where $\ell = 0$ and to the left of the time constraint, where $\mathscr{L} = 0$.

The budget line is determined as before. Expenditure may not exceed money income. It may be measured by C when the composite good is the numeraire, and income is the sum of work income and nonwork income. Thus the budget constraint is

$$C \le w\mathscr{L} + N$$

where $w\mathscr{L}$ is work income, the wage rate multiplied by the time spent working, and N denotes nonwork income. The budget line is plotted on Figure 5.32. One point can be determined by finding the endowment bundle. The individual is endowed with $\ell = T$ units of leisure time. At the endowment point $\mathscr{L} = 0$, only nonwork income is available, and the consumer may purchase N units of C. Another point along the budget line can be determined by finding the level of consumption possible when $\ell = 0$. Because $\mathscr{L} = T$ when $\ell = 0$, total income is $wT + N$, and the consumer may purchase $wT + N$ units of C. The maximum level of income possible is sometimes referred to as full income. The budget line is drawn between the full-income point and the endowment point. Notice that the slope of the budget line is equal to the negative of the wage rate—each extra hour of leisure time costs w dollars in forgone consumption.

The consumer's choice is ℓ^* and C^*, where utility is maximized. As before, nonsatiation requires that expenditure equal income,

$$C = w(T - \ell) + N$$

where $(T - \ell)$ is substituted for $\mathscr{L}$. For interior solutions, tangency requires that the MRS be equal to the price ratio as measured by the real wage rate, $MRS_{\ell C} = w$.

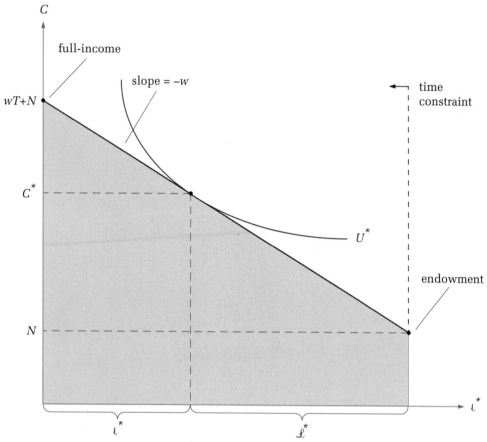

Figure 5.32 **The consumption-leisure model:** The consumer's choice determines the demand for consumption, C^*, the demand for leisure time, ℓ^*, and the supply of labor time, $\mathcal{L}^*$. Choice is limited by a physical time constraint as well as the budget constraint.

As the wage rate increases, the attainable set expands, as shown in Figure 5.33. The price-expansion path can be used to construct the demand for leisure curve $\ell = \ell(w)$. The supply-of-labor curve can be found by subtracting leisure demanded from total time, $\mathcal{L}(w) = T - \ell(w)$. In the example shown in Figure 5.33, the demand-for-leisure curve is forward bending and has positive slope at high wage rates. How is it possible, if leisure is a normal good, to observe a direct relationship between leisure and the price of leisure? Well, leisure is a good that is sold, not bought—at least in the absence of slavery. Thus, an increase in the price of leisure (the wage rate) increases real income. If leisure is a normal good, the wage-induced income effect will be direct. Because own-price sub-stitution effects are always inverse, the wage-induced income effect must be larger than the substitution effect when the demand for leisure has positive slope. Leisure *must* be normal if its demand curve has positive slope.

A **backward-bending labor-supply** curve occurs when the substitution effect dominates the wage-induced income effect for initial increases in the wage rate, but as the

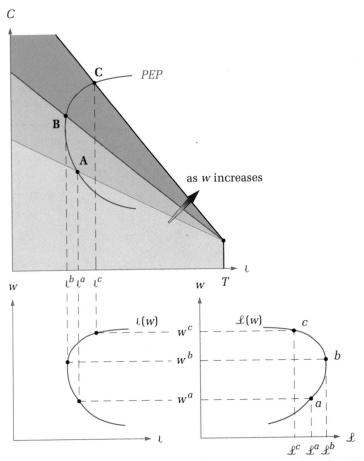

Figure 5.33 **Demand for leisure and supply of labor time:** The consumer moves along the *PEP* as the wage rate increases. Leisure demanded $\ell(w)$ is subtracted from total time T to determine the labor supply $\mathcal{L}(w)$ at each wage rate.

level of consumption of the composite good becomes relatively high—and the consumption of leisure becomes relatively low—the wage-induced income effect begins to dominate the substitution effect. Whether or not the consumer's labor-supply curve has positive or negative slope becomes an empirical question, because normalcy of a good is not sufficient to sign the total effect of a change in price when the good is sold rather than bought.

AN APPLICATION: *Why Pay Overtime?*

Suppose a manager wishes to induce employees to work longer hours. You might expect that an offer of a higher wage rate might cause the desired positive incentive on work time. But when the higher wage rate, say time and a half, is paid for all hours worked, the budget line rotates about the endowment point, as illustrated in Figure 5.34. An individual worker may choose a bundle like **B** to the right of **A** if the substitution effect is dominated by the income effect of the price change. At **B** the

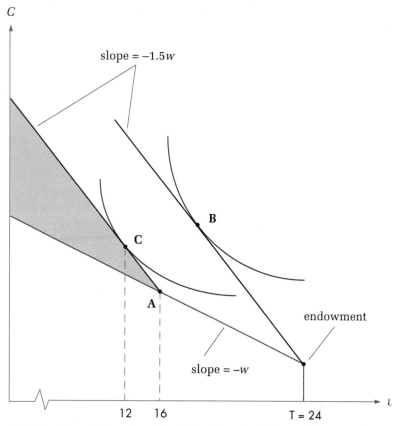

Figure 5.34 **Overtime and labor supply:** An individual choosing 16 hours of leisure and 8 hours of work may choose a bundle like **B** and offer to work less at the higher wage rate. But if the higher wage applies only to time worked more than the standard time of 8 hours, the attainable set expands only by the shaded area. The weak axiom guarantees that more work will be offered at the overtime rate.

individual wants to work fewer hours rather than more. The consequence may be an increase in absenteeism. Production schedules become more difficult to meet as the manager's plans are thwarted.

Alternatively, suppose the increased wage rate is paid only for work beyond standard time, say $1.5w$ for $\mathcal{L} > 8$ hours per day. The overtime premium causes a kink in the budget line where $\mathcal{L} = 8$. The attainable set is expanded only when the individual works more than the standard time. The weak axiom guarantees that no individual will work less than before. Moreover, if an individual's choice is affected by the overtime premium, that individual will definitely wish to work more. In conclusion, the overtime premium will never cause a disincentive effect on labor supply for any employee, and overtime is expected to cause an increase in labor supply for some employees. Absenteeism will never increase under the overtime premium, and the manager's plan will be easier to achieve.

5.13 Gains from Voluntary Exchange

When two individuals, firms, countries, or other economic agents are endowed with goods, there is a potential for gains from exchange between agents. One of the most important principles in economics is the **fundamental theorem of exchange:**

> **Fundamental theorem of exchange:** *Voluntary trade is mutually beneficial.*

This principle is obviously true because, if economic agents behave rationally, each will engage in voluntary trade only if it is advantageous to the individual to do so. Therefore, such barriers to trade as protective tariffs and import quotas frequently leave the potential traders worse off. This realization does not mean that people will not make errors in judgment that they later regret. Nor does free trade protect you from being swindled. But free trade does make both parties better off *at the time of the trade,* or the trade would not occur.

Voluntary exchange carries two potential sources of gain. Voluntary exchange is mutually beneficial because traders can: (1) change consumption patterns so that each achieves a preferred bundle; (2) specialize in production to increase the quantities of goods to be consumed. Production is considered in a later chapter. Our simple two-good model of consumer choice, however, can be extended to analyze the gains from *pure* exchange when no production takes place.

A simple model of **bilateral pure exchange** consists of two agents, each endowed with a bundle of two goods. We refer to the two agents as person A and person B—Alvin and Betty, if you like. The model is illustrated graphically by an "Edgeworth box" in Figure 5.35. Alvin's consumption of X and Y is measured in the usual way. For Betty, the axes are inverted. The two sets of axes are superimposed so that the endowment bundles coincide on the graph at **E.** Alvin's initial endowments are X_a^e and Y_a^e units. Betty's initial endowments are X_b^e and Y_b^e units. The total stocks of goods that may be consumed by the two agents are $(X_a^e + X_b^e)$ units of X and $(Y_a^e + Y_b^e)$ units of Y. The area of the total stocks is shaded in Figure 5.35, and both shaded areas define the Edgeworth box. Given the endowments and preferences, the pure theory of exchange describes how the total stocks will be allocated and consumed.

The potential for trade can be illustrated by starting at the endowment bundle. At **E,** Alvin's utility is U_a^e and Betty's utility is U_b^e. Both agents would be better off at a trading point like **T,** where Alvin trades Y for more X and Betty trades X for more Y. Any bundle in the shaded region between U_a^e and U_b^e represents a trade that would leave both agents better off than at **E.** This region is called the **trading set**—a region of mutual advantage.

Any trade must take place within the trading set. Some trades are more "efficient" than others. A trade is **efficient** when there are no potential gains from trade for one agent without making the other agent worse off. The set of efficient trades can be identified with help from the concept called **Pareto efficiency.**

> **Pareto efficiency in exchange:** *An allocation of goods is Pareto efficient if any further exchange of goods will leave someone worse off.*

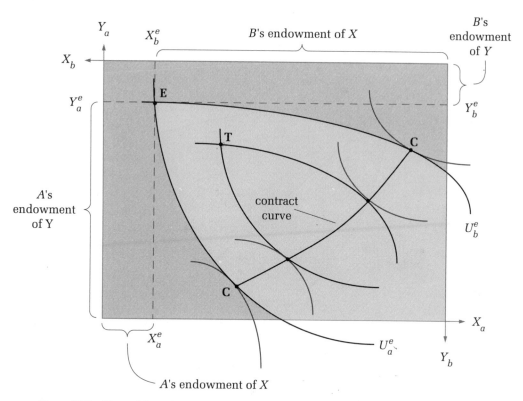

Figure 5.35 **Edgeworth box and trading set:** The Edgeworth box corresponds to the shaded areas and is determined by the sum of the endowments. The trading set is the darker region between U_b^e and U_a^e. All trades like bundle **T** will make both agents better off. All Pareto-efficient trades occur along the contract curve CC where, once attained, any movement along the curve leaves one agent worse off.

The set of Pareto-efficient allocations is called the **contract curve.** The contract curve is identified by points of tangency between A's indifference curves and B's indifference curves.

The traders will select some bundle along the contract curve. How is that bundle determined? And how is the exchange rate—the price ratio—between X and Y determined? Recall that each budget line must pass through the endowment point. Thus, given prices p_X and p_Y, the budget line separates the Edgeworth box into two regions: A's attainable set and B's attainable set.

Figure 5.36 illustrates how to determine the equilibrium price ratio when both agents are *competitive* traders or "price-takers." Suppose initially that prices are such that the dashed line is the budget line. Alvin prefers bundle **A,** and Betty prefers bundle **B.** These positions desired by each agent cannot be attained simultaneously, however, because the markets are not cleared. Alvin wants more X at **A** than at the original bundle **E.** Thus Alvin wants to buy X, but Betty does not want to sell as much as Alvin wants to buy. Alvin

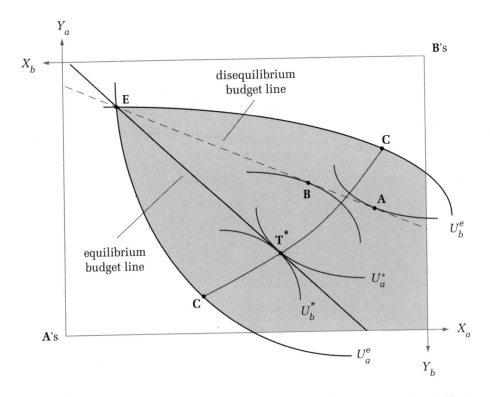

Figure 5.36   **Competitive equilibrium in pure exchange:** Both markets will be cleared at a bundle like T*
within the trading set where both agents' indifference curves are tangent with one another and with
a common budget line that establishes the market clearing exchange rate.

also wants to sell Y. Betty wants to buy Y, but not as much as Alvin wants to sell. The
total demand for X is less than the stock available. These conditions mean that the price of
X must be higher relative to the price of Y for the markets to clear, and the budget line
must rotate about the endowment point.

The market will be cleared at a bundle like **T*** along the contract curve where the
prices are just sufficient to clear both markets. At any other bundle along the contract
curve the markets will not be cleared simultaneously. The equilibrium rate of exchange,
the price ratio that clears both markets, is established by the budget line that passes
through bundle **T***.

> **Competitive equilibrium in pure exchange:** *A trading bundle that lies along
> the contract curve and establishes market clearing prices.*

In summary, the conditions for competitive equilibrium in pure exchange are: (1) the
trading bundle must lie in the trading set, and (2) the bundle must represent a tangency of
both agents' indifference curves with one another and with a common budget line.

![world map icon] **GLOBAL PERSPECTIVE:** *Trading Food for Crude*

Suppose North America has a surplus of grain it would like to trade for crude oil produced by Persia. Persia has a shortage of grain but a surplus of crude. The conditions of exchange can be analyzed in the Edgeworth-box diagram of Figure 5.37. Persia's origin is placed at the lower left-hand corner. North America's origin is placed at the upper right-hand corner of the box. Bundle **E** shows the initial endowments for Persia and North America. Persia has a relatively large endowment of crude oil, and North America has a relatively large endowment of grain.

The contract curve *CC* identifies the set of Pareto-efficient trades. The price-expansion paths for Persia and North America are derived by varying the price ratio, the price of grain (p_G) divided by the price of crude (p_C). The budget line must pass through the endowment bundle. The budget line, which also passes through the point of intersection of the price-expansion paths, determines the market clearing exchange rate.

Now suppose Persian preferences change in favor of retaining more oil for future export. Their new preferences result in a whole new set of indifference curves for Persia. Hence, we find a new price-expansion path for Persia. The old and new expansion paths are shown in Figure 5.38. The expansion paths identify offers to trade at alternative exchange rates. A new equilibrium is established where the price of grain in relation to that of crude is lower than

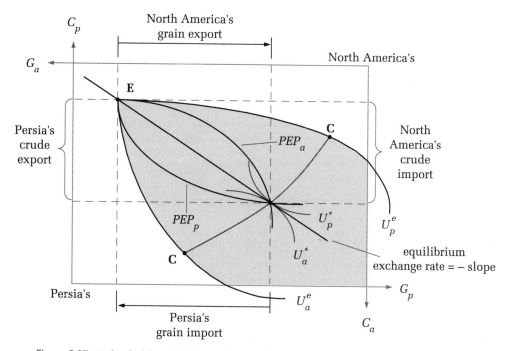

Figure 5.37 **Trading food for crude:** Two trading partners trade food (grain), denoted by G, and crude oil, denoted by C. The equilibrium amounts of export and import are determined on the contract curve CC, where the market clearing price ratio (the exchange rate) equals the marginal rates of substitution for each partner. That is, equilibrium occurs where the price-expansion paths (offer curves) for Persia and North America cross.

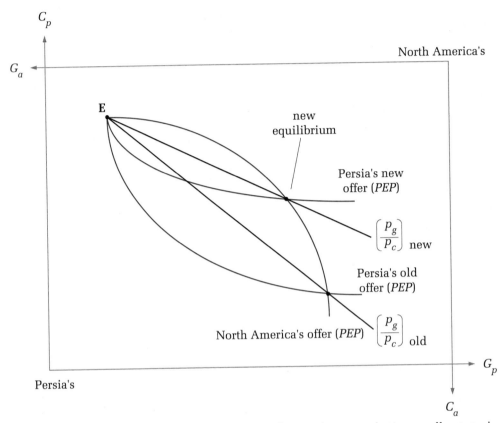

Figure 5.38 **Change in equilibrium exchange:** Persia's preference changes so that its new offers to trade, its new price-expansion path, reflects willingness to exchange less crude oil for grain than before. The price of crude oil will increase relative to the price of grain in order to clear both markets at the new exchange rate.

before. That is, the quantity of crude North America demands will fall in response to the relative increase in the price of crude.

What happens if North American public opinion also changes, shifting its price-expansion path? If, for instance, preference changed because Americans desired to be less dependent on foreign oil imports, North America's price-expansion path would shift to the left in Figure 5.38. The equilibrium point would move even closer to the endowment bundle. Conceivably, preferences in both regions could change so that all trade would cease.

One thing is clear: With voluntary exchange, both Persia and North America are better off at the equilibrium bundle, whatever the equilibrium exchange rate turns out to be in response to their preferences. Free trade does have some potential disadvantages, however. Some goods may be of strategic importance. North America may not wish to become too dependent on oil imports. Government may therefore have to restrict imports in response to public opinion if that does not happen naturally. Other goods may be subject to export restriction. For example, the United States has restricted sales of military-related products to some countries. Or government may wish to protect an infant industry from foreign competition while the industry becomes established. Or too much specialization may cause a country to become vulnerable to events outside its control. When the price of oil increased in 1979, Mexico borrowed heavily to finance its development. Later, when the price of oil fell, Mexico had great problems paying the interest and principal on those loans. The same happened to Iraq late in the 1980s. Nevertheless, most arguments in favor of trade barriers are based on fallacious economic reasoning because the disputants fail to recognize the obvious truth that voluntary trade is mutually beneficial.

5.14 Using Index Numbers*

Because the buying power of a dollar changes when prices change, it is necessary to adjust the value of that dollar, which we accomplish with a price-index number. To compare the relative expenditure for a college education today and in 1980, we would first have to determine the buying power of the dollar today compared with that in 1980. Price-index numbers are computed for such purposes and are used every day by managers and economists to make comparisons when prices have changed.

A price-index number merely expresses the reference-period price as a percentage of the base-period price. If the price of some good increases from $1.25 to $1.50, the price-index number is

$$\frac{\$1.50}{\$1.25}(100) = 120$$

The new price is 20 percent higher than the old price.

When calculating a price-index number for a bundle of goods, it is not sufficient to add all prices together for a reference period and then divide that sum by a sum of base-period prices because prices depend on how quantity is measured. Price per pound will differ from price per ton, and the index will vary when price is measured differently even though the bundle consumed remains the same. We need an index that weights each price by the amount of each good consumed:

> **Weighted aggregate index:** The ratio of the sum of weighted reference-period prices $p^k_i q^k_i$ to the sum of weighted base-period prices $p^0_i q^0_i$, expressed as a percentage,
>
> $$WI_k = \frac{\sum_{i=1}^{n} p^k_i q^k_i}{\sum_{i=1}^{n} p^0_i q^0_i}(100)$$
>
> where the q^k_i and q^0_i are the quantity weights associated with the n goods.[15]

---

* This section may be skipped without loss of continuity.

15. The superscripts in these formulas are indexes, not exponents.

To simplify the notation, the weighted aggregate index can be written

$$WI_k = \frac{\Sigma p^k q^k}{\Sigma p^0 q^0} (100)$$

where the summation takes place over the n price-quantity multiples.

Practical applications of index numbers are usually associated with comparing income or expenditure required to buy a bundle of goods when prices have changed. Price changes may cause real income to change—consumers may be better off or worse off when relative prices and incomes change. Frequently it is necessary to adjust income or expenditure for inflation or deflation in prices. The U.S. Department of Labor uses a special form of a weighted aggregate index for several of its published indexes. This measure is called the **Laspeyres Price Index:**

> **Laspeyres Price Index:** *A weighted index of prices using* base-*period quantities as the weights,*
>
> $$LPI = \frac{\Sigma p^k q^0}{\Sigma p^0 q^0} (100)$$

The reason for using the base-period quantities as weights is that they do not change from year to year—the bundle being compared between the two periods is the same.

An alternative called the **Paasche Price Index** uses the reference-period quantities rather than the base-period quantities as weights:

> **Paasche Price Index:** *A weighted index of prices using* reference-*period quantities as the weights,*
>
> $$PPI = \frac{\Sigma p^k q^k}{\Sigma p^0 q^k} (100)$$

The Paasche index is used less frequently than the Laspeyres index because base-period prices of some of the reference-period goods usually are not known. If the reference period is the current period, some of the current-period goods may not have existed in the past base period, and so their prices did not exist. Yet both the Laspeyres index and the Paasche index are useful, as we shall see next.

Index numbers may be used to make comparisons between bundles purchased at different prices. In particular, sometimes we can use the concept of revealed preference in conjunction with index numbers to tell whether an individual is better off or worse off when prices have changed. Looking at panel A of Figure 5.39, if **B** is revealed as preferred to **A** we know that

$$\Sigma p^b q^a \leq \Sigma p^b q^b$$

That is, **A** was affordable when **B** was chosen. To clarify, we suppose that p^b is the set of prices in 1970 when **B** was chosen. But **A** was chosen under the set of 1955 prices p^a. If **A** remains affordable under the 1970 prices p^b when **B** was chosen, the consumer must be better off with **B.** In other words, an unambiguous increase in the standard of living has occurred.

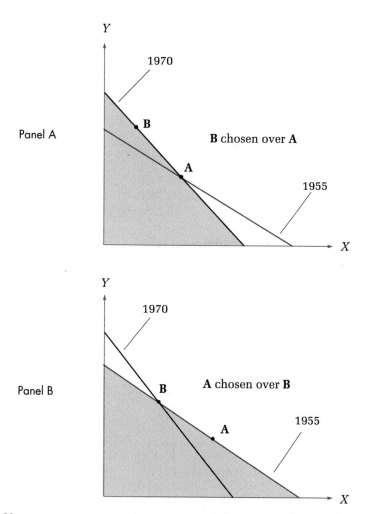

Figure 5.39 **Using index numbers: Panel A** The consumer is better off in 1970 when the *LPI* ≤ income index. **Panel B** The consumer is worse off in 1970 when the *PPI* ≥ income index.

Now let's divide both sides of this equation by $\Sigma p^a q^a$, the expenditure on **A** when **A** was chosen. The result is

$$\frac{\Sigma p^b q^a}{\Sigma p^a q^a} \leq \frac{\Sigma p^b q^b}{\Sigma p^a q^a}$$

When multiplied by 100, the left-hand side is just a Laspeyres Price Index. The right-hand side is just the ratio of reference-period income to base-period income. When multiplied by 100, the right-hand side becomes an income index. Thus, the relation becomes

$$LPI \leq \frac{M^b}{M^a} (100)$$

Therefore, if the Laspeyres index is *not greater than* the income index, the consumer is *better off* in the reference period (year 1970).

Next, consider panel B of Figure 5.39, where **A** is revealed as preferred to **B**. Revealed preference requires that

$$\Sigma p^a q^b \leq \Sigma p^a q^a$$

That is, the consumer could have chosen **B** in 1955 but chose **A** instead. Bundle **A** was chosen when **B** was affordable, and the consumer is now worse off with **B**. Now let's divide both sides into $\Sigma p^b q^b$, the expenditure on **B** when **B** was chosen. The result is

$$\frac{\Sigma p^b q^b}{\Sigma p^a q^b} \geq \frac{\Sigma p^b q^b}{\Sigma p^a q^a}$$

When multiplied by 100, the left-hand side is just a Paasche index. The right-hand side is again the ratio of reference-period to base-period income. When it is multiplied by 100, the right-hand side becomes an income index. The relation becomes

$$PPI \geq \frac{M^b}{M^a} (100)$$

Therefore, if the Paasche Price Index is *not less than* the income index, the consumer is *worse off* in the reference period (year 1970).

Two criteria for welfare change have been established, measuring welfare by whether the consumer is better off or worse off. Consumer welfare has increased if the Laspeyres Price Index is *not greater than* the income index. Consumer welfare has decreased if the Paasche Price Index is *not less than* the income index. If neither of these cases holds, then definitive changes in consumer welfare are not discernible by applying index numbers.[16] In practice, however, the difference between the computed values of the Laspeyres and Paasche index numbers is small.

---

16. Another way to look at this problem of discerning changes in welfare is to use *quantity* index numbers. As before, in a Laspeyres quantity index the base prices are used as weights and in a Paasche index the reference prices are used as weights. This extension is not developed in this text.

AN APPLICATION: *The Consumer Price Index*

The Consumer Price Index (CPI) tells us what changes are taking place in the purchasing power of the dollars we spend. It shows how the cost of the same market basket of goods changes as time passes by recording the prices of goods an average family buys—from fruit to footwear. The CPI compares what the bundle costs this month against what it cost a month ago, a year ago, or ten years ago. Employees of the U.S. Bureau of Labor Statistics (BLS) survey stores and other business establishments across the country to gather the prices of specific goods such as hamburger and other cuts of meat. For each survey they price the same goods. The CPI is a Laspeyres index because the base-year quantities are always used as weights.

Almost everyone is affected in some way by the CPI because of the many ways in which it is used. The CPI is used as an *escalator* in collective-bargaining agreements, in pension plans, and in income-transfer plans to help keep payments in line with changing prices. The CPI is also used to shape government policy, because it is a major yardstick by which the success or failure of policies is judged. Business and union leaders and other private citizens use the index as a guide in making decisions.

Although the CPI is often used as a cost-of-living index, it is in fact a price index, reporting changes in prices for a fixed group of goods. The CPI does *not* reflect the changes in *buying patterns* that consumers make in response to price changes because it is a Laspeyres index. But we know that substitution does take place when relative prices change. Thus, because the CPI takes the same bundle of goods, in the same proportions (or weights), month after month, it is not a cost-of-living index. Moreover, though the CPI includes taxes that are directly associated with prices— such as sales taxes—it does not include income and payroll taxes. A complete cost-of-living index would include all taxes. Investment items, such as stocks and bonds, are also excluded from the CPI.

Because price data are used for different purposes by different groups, the BLS publishes seasonally adjusted as well as unadjusted changes each month. Seasonally adjusted changes are usually preferred for analyzing general price trends because they eliminate the effect of regular, periodic price movements resulting from climatic conditions, production cycles, model changeovers, holidays, and sales. The unadjusted data are of primary interest when the question is about prices that consumers actually pay. Most collective-bargaining agreements and pension plans, for example, link compensation changes to the unadjusted CPI. Special care should be exercised when using the seasonally adjusted index because each year the seasonal status of every series is reevaluated. Analysts therefore need to make sure that consistent series are chosen when using adjusted indexes.*

The CPI is divided into seven major expenditure groups—food and beverages, housing, apparel and upkeep, transportation, medical care, entertainment, and other goods and services. Prices are collected in eighty-five urban areas. In 1978, the BLS began publishing two CPIs: (1) An index for all urban consumers (CPI-U), which covers approximately 80 percent of the civilian noninstitutionalized population; and (2) an index for urban wage earners and clerical workers (CPI-W). The CPI-U includes, in addition to wage earners and clerical workers, such groups as professional, managerial, and technical workers, the self-employed, short-term workers, the unemployed, retirees, and others not in the labor force.

In a fixed-weight index such as the CPI, the quantity of each good used in calculating the index remains fixed. Therefore, to reflect current expenditure patterns, the BLS revises the base periodically. One recent revision began in January 1987 with weights based on the *1982–1984 Consumer Expenditure Survey.* Previously, the CPI was revised in January 1978, with weights based on the *1972–1973 CES.* Revised weights also reflect the geographic distribution of consumers derived from the census of population.

All prior revisions of the price index have used 1967 as the base.† Thus the price index in 1967 is entered as 100, and changes are indicated in relation to that number. A

---

*For a report that gives some guidance on developing escalator clauses, see *Using the Consumer Price Index for Escalation,* Report 761, U.S. Department of Labor, Bureau of Labor Statistics (Washington, D.C.: U.S. Government Printing Office), January 1989.

†With publication of the January 1988 data, the BLS changed the standard reference base period for the Consumer Price Index (CPI) series and many of the Producer Price Index (PPI) series. The CPI was rebased to 1982–84 = 100. Most PPI series were rebased to 1982 = 100. Previously, the base for both series was 1967 = 100.

reference index of 110 means that prices increased 10 percent since the base period. Similarly, a reference index of 90 means a 10 percent decrease. Movements of the index from one date to another can be expressed as changes in *index points,* but it is more useful to express the movements as *percentage* changes because index points are affected by the base period, but percentage changes are not. For example, the CPI-U changed from 330.0 in reference-period September 1986 to 344.4 in reference-period September 1987, with 1967 = 100. The change in index points was 14.4, but the percentage increase for the period was 4.36 percent.

The influence of the 1987 revision of the CPI-U for the seven major expenditure categories was reported by the BLS.‡ Comparisons between the revised (1987) and old (1978) series by major category for the first six months of 1987 relative to December 1986 are summarized in Table 5.1. For all goods the new index rose 2.7 percent based on 1982–84 expenditure patterns and the old index rose by 3.1 percent, based on the 1972–1973 expenditure patterns. This difference comes primarily from differences in the relative weights of goods in the index based on the changes in expenditure patterns.

Notice that the CPI and the market basket on which it is based represent the experience of the average household, not that of your specific family. It is unlikely that your own experience will correspond in detail with either of the two national indexes or to those for specific cities or regions. If you spend a larger share of your income than most people do on goods whose prices remain constant or rise less than other prices, your own rate of inflation will probably be lower than average. If your income is keeping pace with general inflation, you will be better off as a consequence. But if your income is spent mostly on goods whose prices are rising rapidly relative to your income, you will be worse off.

Table 5.1 Comparison of the Revised (1987) and Old (1978) CPI-U for the First Six Months of 1987

Category	Relative Importance (December 1986)		Percentage Change	
	Revised CPI	Old CPI	Revised CPI	Old Cpi
All items	100.0	100.0	2.7	3.1
Food and beverage	17.82	20.12	2.6	2.7
Housing	42.95	38.13	2.5	2.7
Apparel and upkeep	6.34	5.01	1.7	1.7
Transportation	17.22	19.89	3.9	5.2
Medical care	5.42	6.87	3.2	3.4
Entertainment	4.40	4.29	3.2	3.4
Other goods and services	5.86	5.69	2.2	2.3

Note: Because of independent rounding, components may not add to totals.
Source: Monthly Labor Review, U.S. Department of Labor, Bureau of Labor Statistics (Washington, D.C.: U.S. Government Printing Office), November 1987.

‡Mary Lynn Schmidt, "Comparison of the Revised and the Old CPI," *Monthly Labor Review* (November 1987), pages 3–6.

Summary

The basic postulate of the theory of consumer choice is that consumers choose among alternatives in a manner consistent with their individual evaluations of self-interest. Choice is constrained by the availability of goods, their prices, and the consumer's income. The budget line is determined by the combinations of goods that, when purchased, just exhaust the consumer's income. The slope of the budget line is determined by the price ratio, and the price ratio measures the available rate of exchange between the goods.

The choice of any bundle that is affordable reveals a preference for that bundle over other bundles that were also affordable. A consumer who acts consistently, according to the weak axiom, never reveals a preference for a bundle over another bundle previously chosen when both were affordable. The weak axiom leads to the fundamental theorem of consumer choice stating that normal goods must always have negatively sloped demand curves.

Because choice is determined by all prices and money income given consumer preference, demand is a function of all prices and income is given preference. The demand curve relates quantity to a good's price, all else remaining constant. The Engel curve relates quantity to the consumer's income, all else remaining constant.

The total effect of a price change may be decomposed into a substitution effect and a price-induced income effect. The change in quantity demanded due to the change in price while real income remains constant—the substitution effect—must be inverse. The change in quantity demanded due to the change in real income caused by the price change—the price-induced income effect—will be inverse if the good is normal and direct if the good is inferior.

Consumers' preferences can be represented by indifference curves, which cannot touch one another. Indifference curves are usually assumed to be strongly convex, and so they have no flat segments. Indifference curves are negatively sloped if more is always preferred to less.

The utility function assigns ordinal numerical values to bundles in accordance with the consumer's preferences. Indifference curves represent bundles having equal ranking and utility. When all goods are consumed in positive amounts, utility-maximizing choice can be represented by the tangency of an indifference curve to the budget line. At the tangency point, expenditure equals income and the marginal rate of substitution equals the price ratio. Thus, a consumer chooses to allocate income so that the required rate of exchange equals the willingness to exchange goods. In other words, utility maximization requires that the ratio of marginal utilities equal the price ratio for all pairs of goods chosen.

When the utility function is known, demand equations can be derived by applying the tangency conditions for utility maximization: expenditure must equal income; and the MRS must equal the price ratio. The solution procedure is always the same: express the tangency condition as a function of the quantities, prices, and income; then express quantity demanded for each good as a function of all prices and income, given current preferences.

One way to obtain income is to sell something that you own. In each period, every person is endowed with time and goods. Exchange occurs between economic agents as a means to increase utility. Because the endowment bundle is always affordable, the budget line rotates about the endowment point if relative prices change. We know that the price-induced income effect will reinforce the substitution effect for any normal good being bought. But the total effect of a price change for a normal good being sold has indeterminate sign because the price-induced income and substitution effects work in opposite directions.

Everyone is endowed with time. The model of consumer choice can be applied to analyze how individuals allocate their time. Choice is limited by a physical time constraint as well as the budget constraint. As the wage rate changes, the demand for leisure is determined. The supply of labor time is determined simultaneously. If leisure is a normal good, the wage-induced income effect and the substitution effect move in opposite directions. Whether or not the individual's labor supply curve has positive or negative slope becomes an empirical question.

When economic agents are endowed with wealth, there are potential gains in utility from exchange between agents. Voluntary trade is always mutually beneficial. A trade is efficient when no further gains from trade can be gotten by any agent without making another agent worse off. Pareto efficiency in exchange occurs when further exchange will make someone worse off. Pareto-efficient allocations occur along the contract curve—the points of tangency between the agents' indifference curves. A competitive equilibrium in pure exchange occurs along the contract curve when the price ratio equals the *MRS* for both agents.

Index numbers can be used to make welfare comparisons when prices have changed. Consumer welfare has increased if the Laspeyres Price Index is *not greater than* the income index. Consumer welfare has decreased if the Paasche Price Index is *not less than* the income index. The CPI reported by the Bureau of Labor Statistics is a Laspeyres Price-Index number.

Further Readings

Several authors concentrate on consumer choice, but my favorites are

- H. A. John Green, *Consumer Theory,* rev. ed. (Academic Press, 1978).
- George J. Stigler, *The Theory of Price,* 4th ed. (Macmillan, 1987).

The now-classic and most frequently cited advanced book is

- Paul A. Samuelson, *Foundations of Economic Analysis* (Harvard University Press, 1966).

Samuelson's writings on revealed preference are reprinted in *The Collected Papers of Paul Samuelson,* vol. 1, Joseph E. Stiglitz, ed. (MIT Press, 1976). Samuelson and Stigler have been awarded Nobel prizes in economics for their lifelong contributions to the discipline.

For applications of the consumer-choice model to decisions on labor supply see

- Michael C. Keeley, *Labor Supply and Public Policy* (Academic Press, 1981).
- Mark R. Killingsworth, *Labor Supply* (Cambridge University Press, 1983).
- Orley Ashenfelter and Richard Layard, editors, *Handbook of Labor Economics,* vol. 1 (Elsevier Science Publishers, 1986).

- Ronald G. Ehrenberg and Robert S. Smith, *Modern Labor Economics,* 3rd ed. (Scott, Foresman, 1988), chapters 6, 7.

An interesting extension of the standard model of consumer choice, called attribute analysis, formulates consumer utility as a function of the attributes or characteristics of goods. Utility is a function of attributes, and the consumption of goods is the way in which attributes are gained. See

- Kelvin Lancaster, "Change and Innovation in the Technology of Consumption," *American Economic Review* (May 1966).
- K. Lancaster, "A New Approach to Consumer Theory," *Journal of Political Economy* (April 1967).

For more on the use of kinked budget constraints, see this very readable article:

- Robert Moffitt, "The Econometrics of Kinked Budget Constraints," *Journal of Economic Perspectives* 42(2) (Spring 1990).

Practice Problems

1. For two goods X and Y, the budget line is $p_X X + p_Y Y = M$:
   (a) Graph the budget lines when $p_X = \$2$, $p_Y = \$1$, and $M = \$20$. What is the slope of this budget line? What is the opportunity cost of X?
   (b) On the same graph, plot a new budget line when the price of X becomes $p_X = \$1$. What is the slope of this new budget line? What is the opportunity cost of X?
   (c) Plot the bundles: $\mathbf{A} = \{X = 5,\ Y = 10\}$; $\mathbf{B} = \{X = 10,\ Y = 10\}$. Calculate expenditure required for both bundles for both sets of prices. Verify that $\mathbf{B}$ is too expensive when $\mathbf{A}$ is just affordable, and verify that $\mathbf{A}$ is affordable when $\mathbf{B}$ exhausts money income.

2. Given this information:

   $$\mathbf{A} = \{X = 20,\ Y = 20\} \text{ is chosen when } p_X = \$2,\ p_Y = \$2$$
   $$\mathbf{B} = \{X = 30,\ Y = 10\} \text{ is chosen when } p_X = \$2,\ p_Y = \$4$$

   (a) Is $\mathbf{A}$ revealed preferred to $\mathbf{B}$ consistent with the revealed-preference approach to consumer choice?
   (b) Is $\mathbf{B}$ revealed preferred to $\mathbf{A}$ consistent with the revealed-preference approach to consumer choice?

3. Suppose a consumer is consuming 20 units of a good and the price of the good increases by \$3. What change in income is required to restore this consumer's purchasing power? Instead, suppose the price of decreases by \$2. Now what is the compensating change in income?

4. Given the utility function $U = XY$, we know that $MU_X = Y$ and $MU_Y = X$. Given the alternative utility functions $V = \sqrt{U}$ and $W = U^2$, show that the $MRS = Y/X$ for all three of these functions. What does this result imply about the indifference curves for all three utility functions?
   [Hint: $MU_X = \sqrt{Y}/(2\sqrt{X})$ and $MU_Y = \sqrt{X}/(2\sqrt{Y})$ for $V = \sqrt{XY}$. Calculus can also be used to find MU_X and MU_Y for $W = (XY)^2$.]

5. A friend of mine likes beer but is not particular about the brand. He has said, "Beer is beer!" What do his indifference curves look like between the brands Bud and XX? Are these indifference curves consistent with the model of consumer choice as presented in the text?

6. A special kind of ranking called a **lexicographic ordering** is ruled out by our consumer-choice model. A lexicographic ordering is like arranging words alphabetically, where the order is determined by ranking the first item in a set, then the second item, and so on.

    Suppose a judge in a beauty pageant says, "I always prefer contestants with poise over beauty, but among contestants with poise I rank contestants regarding their beauty." Try representing this judge's preferences graphically. Can you draw indifference curves to represent this type of preference set? Show why or why not.

7. Advertising is used to try to influence consumers' choice. Use indifference curves to illustrate how this effect might happen. Although all product advertising is intended to influence choice, not all advertising is intended to influence preferences. Can you think of an example?

8. Suppose $U = XY$ is the utility function and prices are $p_X = \$2$, $p_Y = \$2$.
    (a) Graph the indifference curves $U = 100$, $U = 400$, and $U = 900$.
    (b) Graph the IEP by changing money income.
    (c) Using the information gained, plot the Engel curve for X.
    (d) Is X normal or inferior? Why?

9. Given the special utility function $U = XY$, use the tangency conditions to find an equation for $X = X(p_X, p_Y, M)$, the demand function.

10. Given a good for which the demand curve for a typical consumer is $X = 20/p_X$, if 100 consumers have identical tastes, what is the market demand curve $Q_X = D_X(p_X)$?

11. What is the difference between the pure income effect and the price-induced income effect?

12. Suppose the utility function is $U = XY$, where $MU_X = Y$ and $MU_Y = X$, and given $p_X = \$1$, $p_Y = \$1$, and $M = \$40$, find X^* and Y^*. Then suppose that p_X changes to $p_X = \$2$ and determine the new maximizing quantities. Graph the budget lines and show the bundles chosen, and then find and identify the substitution and income effects of the price change on the graph.

13. For a good that is purchased, what are the conditions for a negatively sloped consumers' demand curve? In other words, what conditions are required for $\Delta X / \Delta p_X < 0$ to be true? Your answer should include careful consideration of substitution and income effects.

14. Suppose $U = \ell C$, where ℓ is leisure time and C is consumption, a composite good with price $p_C = \$5$. Given that $T = 24$ and $N = 0$:
    (a) When the wage rate is $w = \$2$, determine the choice of ℓ and C for this consumer.
    (b) Find labor supply as a function of w, and graph the supply curve. [Hint: repeat part (a) for, say, $w = \$1, \$2, \$3, \$4$, and $\$5$. Or better yet, you might just find ℓ as a function of w and then find $\mathcal{L}(w) = T - \ell(w)$.]
    (c) What can you conclude about the substitution and income effects of the change in the wage rate in this case?

15. Normalcy is a sufficient condition for a negatively sloped demand curve for a good that is purchased. Explain the paradox that, when the demand-for-leisure curve has positive slope, leisure must be a normal good.

16. Using an Edgeworth box, identify the trading region and the contract curve. Explain why trade will always lead to a point that is both in the region and on the curve.

17. Using an Edgeworth box, explain how you know the competitive equilibrium is on the contract curve.

18. A consumer first chooses **A** but then chooses **B** under these conditions:

$$\mathbf{A} = \{X = 20, \ Y = 20\} \text{ is chosen when } p_X = \$2, \ p_Y = \$2$$
$$\mathbf{B} = \{X = 30, \ Y = 10\} \text{ is chosen when } p_X = \$2, \ p_Y = \$4$$

Suppose **A** is the base bundle and **B** is the reference bundle. Compute the Laspeyres and Paasche price-index numbers. Is it possible to state that the consumer is better off or worse off as a result of the inflation and change in income?

19. During a given base and reference period, price p and quantity of traded shares q for two stocks were

	Base Period		Reference Period	
	p	q	p	q
Stock A	$15	12,500	$18	15,000
Stock B	$41	9,000	$37	11,000

Calculate a weighted aggregate index, a Laspeyres Price Index, and a Paasche Price Index, using these data. Comment on the differences in values obtained.

20. Given this information on consumer price indexes (1967 = 100) for all items, 1987 revision:

	CPI-U	CPI-W
1985	322.2	318.5
1986	328.4	323.4

(a) Each index applies to a different average consumer unit. Can you think what some of those differences might be?

(b) What is the percentage increase in the CPI-U between 1967 and 1986?

(c) What is the percentage increase in the CPI-U between 1985 and 1986?

(d) Was the average wage earner and clerical worker experiencing greater or less inflation between 1985 and 1986 compared to the average professional?

(e) If you live in a rural area, would it be more appropriate to use the CPI-U or the CPI-W in calculating the change in your cost of living between 1985 and 1986?

21. For each of these situations, explain how an index number might be used in making a decision.
    (a) A public utility wishes to increase its rates to compensate for inflation. The current rates were established in 1978.
    (b) A homeowner wishes to establish a price for her home, which cost $50,000 in 1980.
    (c) A union wishes to know the real buying power of a dollar two years ago when the union last made a wage contract.
    (d) Public officials in California want to know how much of an increase in the $3.35 per hour minimum wage established in 1981 would be required to lift the minimum wage to the standard of living in 1967.
22. Criticize these uses of index numbers:
    (a) A consultant observes that the CPI rose from 105.2 in 1965 to 131.6 in 1975. He concludes that costs of living increased by 26.4 percent during that time.
    (b) Rather than negotiate a 3.1 percent increase for the first six months of a fiscal year followed by another 3.1 percent for the second six months, a union accepts a 6.2 percent increase for the last six months only. The union then tells its membership that they are better off with the 6.2 percent increase.

Chapter 5 Appendix: *Laws of Demand*

In the indifference-curve model of consumer choice, calculus can be used to study the properties of demand functions. Assuming only two goods, X_1 and X_2, the consumer's problem is:

$$\text{maximize } U(X_1, X_2) = U$$
$$\text{subject to } p_1X_1 + p_2X_2 \le M$$

where M is money income. Assuming an interior solution, and that both goods are chosen in positive quantities, the Lagrangian function can be defined.*

$$L = U(X_1, X_2) + \lambda(M - p_1X_1 - p_2X_2)$$

where λ is the Lagrange multiplier. (If corner solutions were allowed or if explicit recognition of the inequality constraint were included, then Kuhn-Tucker conditions would provide necessary conditions for optimization.)

The first-order conditions for an interior solution are:

$$U_1(X_1, X_2) = \lambda p_1$$
$$U_2(X_1, X_2) = \lambda p_2$$
$$p_1X_1 + p_2X_2) = M$$

where

$$U_i(X_1, X_2) = \partial U/\partial X_i = MU_i$$

denotes the marginal utility of X_i. The second-order conditions for utility maximization require convexity of the indifference curve tangent to the budget line.

The solution to the first-order conditions yields the utility-maximizing quantities X_1^* and X_2^* as well as λ^*. The first-order conditions require that:

$$\frac{MU_1}{MU_2} = \frac{p_1}{p_2}$$
$$p_1 X_1 + p_2 X_2 = M$$

The first equation states that the ratio of marginal utilities (the marginal rate of commodity substitution) must equal the ratio of prices. The second equation states that expenditure equals money income. Together the two equations require tangency of the indifference curve to the budget line.

Because the first-order conditions depend only on prices, income, and the utility function, the demand functions

$$X_1 = X_1(p_1, p_2, M)$$
$$X_2 = X_2(p_1, p_2, M)$$

exist for a given utility function. (The multiplier λ is also a function of prices and income.) The properties of these demand functions can be examined by evaluating the first-order conditions with respect to price and money income as the consumer moves along an expansion path. The first-order conditions are differentiated with respect to a price or money income—this effect amounts to movement along an expansion path because the first-order conditions remain satisfied. (See the following section on the derivation of the Hicks-Slutsky equation.)

The total effect of a price change is consequently

$$\frac{\partial X_i}{\partial p_j} = \left(\frac{\partial X_i}{\partial p_j}\right)_{U=\text{const}} - X_j\left(\frac{\partial X_i}{\partial M}\right)$$

This expression is known as the Hicks-Slutsky equation. The first term on the right-hand side is an expression that measures the substitution effect, the change in quantity in response to a change in price while utility remains constant:

$$\left(\frac{\partial X_i}{\partial p_j}\right)_{U=\text{const}} = \text{pure substitution effect}$$

The second term on the right-hand side is an expression that measures the price-induced income effect:

$$-X_j\left(\frac{\partial X_i}{\partial M}\right) = \text{price-induced substitution effect}$$

The price-induced income effect is composed of two parts. One part measures the pure income effect:

$$\left(\frac{\partial X_i}{\partial M}\right) = \text{pure income effect}$$

The other part measures the quantity of X_j required to compensate for a small change in p_j.

The slope of a demand curve is given by the Hicks-Slutsky equation for a change in own-price, $i = j$. For the first good,

$$\frac{\partial X_1}{\partial p_1} = \left(\frac{\partial X_1}{\partial p_1}\right)_{U=\text{const}} - X_1\left(\frac{\partial X_1}{\partial M}\right)$$

If X_1 is a normal good, the pure income effect is positive, $(\partial X_1/\partial M) > 0$. If X_1 is an inferior good, the pure income effect is negative, $(\partial X_1/\partial M) < 0$. Thus, the sign and magnitude of the pure income effect is changed by $-X_1$ in the equation. The price-induced income effect has sign opposite that of the pure income effect.

The pure substitution effect is always negative for changes in own-price because the change in quantity occurs along a negatively sloped segment of a convex indifference curve. The slope of the demand curve will therefore be negative if the good is a normal good because an inverse price-induced income effect will reinforce the always-inverse substitution effect. If the good is inferior, the demand curve will also have negative slope if the now-direct price-induced income effect is smaller in magnitude than the inverse-substitution effect.

Cross-price effects can be examined for $i \neq j$. Setting $i = 1$ and $j = 2$ results in

$$\frac{\partial X_1}{\partial p_2} = \left(\frac{\partial X_1}{\partial p_2}\right)_{U=\text{const}} - X_2\left(\frac{\partial X_1}{\partial M}\right)$$

The first term on the right-hand side measures a compensated cross-price effect. The second term measures the price-induced income effect of a change in the other good's price. In the two-good case, the compensated cross-price effect must be positive, and the two goods are said to be net substitutes. But in the many-good case the compensated cross-price effect may be negative, and then the two goods are said to be net complements.

Derivation of the Hicks-Slutsky Equations

The following derivations require some knowledge of matrix algebra. The change in marginal utility with respect to a change in quantity is denoted by $U_{ij} = \partial U_i/\partial X_j$, where $U_i = \partial U/\partial X_i$. The U_{ij} are second-partial derivatives. In the two-good case, the bordered Hessian is

$$\begin{bmatrix} U_{11} & U_{12} & -p_1 \\ U_{21} & U_{22} & -p_2 \\ -p_1 & -p_2 & 0 \end{bmatrix}$$

This matrix is symmetric because $U_{ij} = U_{ji}$. If this matrix has the mathematical property of being negative definite, then the second-order condition for utility maximization is satisfied—the indifference curve has the proper convexity at the point of tangency. In the two-good case, then, the determinant of the bordered Hessian is positive:

$$D = -p_2^2 U_{11} + 2p_1 p_2 U_{12} - p_1^2 U_{22} > 0$$

As money income changes alone, the consumer moves along an income-expansion path. The pure income effect may be derived by differentiating the first-order conditions with respect to money income alone. The resulting equations are:

$$U_{11}\frac{\partial X_1}{\partial M} + U_{12}\frac{\partial X_2}{\partial M} - p_1\frac{\partial \lambda}{\partial M} = 0$$

$$U_{21}\frac{\partial X_1}{\partial M} + U_{22}\frac{\partial X_2}{\partial M} - p_2\frac{\partial \lambda}{\partial M} = 0$$

$$-p_1\frac{\partial X_1}{\partial M} - p_2\frac{\partial X_2}{\partial M} = -1$$

The simultaneous solution to these equations for pure income effects results in

$$\frac{\partial X_1}{\partial M} = \frac{p_2 U_{12} - p_1 U_{22}}{D}$$

and

$$\frac{\partial X_2}{\partial M} = \frac{p_1 U_{21} - p_2 U_{11}}{D}$$

These expressions are indeterminate in sign even though $D > 0$; however, both may not be negative at the same time because at least one good must be a normal good.

As price changes alone, the consumer moves along a price-expansion path. Differentiating the first-order conditions with respect to the first price alone results in:

$$U_{11}\frac{\partial X_1}{\partial p_1} + U_{12}\frac{\partial X_2}{\partial p_1} - p_1\frac{\partial \lambda}{\partial p_1} = \lambda$$

$$U_{21}\frac{\partial X_1}{\partial p_1} + U_{22}\frac{\partial X_2}{\partial p_1} - p_2\frac{\partial \lambda}{\partial p_1} = 0$$

$$-p_1\frac{\partial X_1}{\partial p_1} - p_1\frac{\partial X_2}{\partial p_1} = X_1$$

The simultaneous solution for the total effects of a change in the first price alone results in

$$\frac{\partial X_1}{\partial p_1} = \frac{-\lambda p_2^2}{D} - X_1\left(\frac{p_2 U_{12} - p_1 U_{22}}{D}\right)$$

and

$$\frac{\partial X_2}{\partial p_1} = \frac{\lambda p_1 p_2}{D} - X_1\left(\frac{p_1 U_{21} - p_2 U_{11}}{D}\right)$$

The terms in parentheses are seen to be the pure income effects. The first terms on the right-hand side of each equation are substitution effects. Thus, the equations may be written

$$\frac{\partial X_1}{\partial p_1} = \left(\frac{\partial X_1}{\partial p_1}\right)_{U=\text{const}} - X_1\left(\frac{\partial X_1}{\partial M}\right)$$

and

$$\frac{\partial X_2}{\partial p_1} = \left(\frac{\partial X_2}{\partial p_1}\right)_{U=\text{const}} - X_1\left(\frac{\partial X_2}{\partial M}\right)$$

These are the Hicks-Slutsky equations.

Because the first-order conditions require that $\lambda = U_i/p_i > 0$ and the second-order condition requires that $D > 0$, the compensated own-price effect must be negative,

$$\left(\frac{\partial X_1}{\partial p_1}\right)_{U=\text{const}} = \frac{-\lambda p_2^2}{D} < 0$$

Thus, we can conclude that all normal goods have negatively sloped demand curves, for an inverse price-induced income effect will reinforce this inverse-compensated own-price effect. Likewise, the compensated cross-price effect must be positive,

$$\left(\frac{\partial X_2}{\partial p_1}\right)_{U=\text{const}} = \frac{\lambda p_1 p_2}{D} > 0$$

We can therefore conclude that the two goods must be net substitutes because this compensated cross-price effect is symmetrical.

Chapter 6

Time and Intertemporal Decisions

Everyone has heard the expression "Time is money," but the notion has many nuances. We already know, for instance, that the opportunity cost of leisure time is the wage rate. Why, then, are you spending your time reading a textbook on microeconomic decision making? Well, apart from the pursuit of knowledge for its own sake—the consumption component of becoming educated—you are making an investment in your own human capital. All investments require time to realize a return.

When you invest a dollar today you expect to realize a return of more than a dollar later on. It is also true that a dollar today is worth more than that same dollar tomorrow. Today's dollar is worth more for three reasons, even without inflation. First, to get a dollar tomorrow you could invest less than a dollar today at a positive interest rate—today's value of tomorrow's dollar is less than a dollar today. Turning that idea around, the future value of today's dollar is greater than a dollar today. Therefore, when you make intertemporal decisions, you need to adjust the value of money as time passes. Second, almost all decisions made today about future consumption plans are subject to risk. Not all outcomes have the same likelihood of occurring. Some events are more probable than others, and the possible outcomes of some decisions are more variable than those of others. Therefore a dollar received with certainty is worth more than a chance at that same dollar if you are averse to risk. Third, the real world is full of uncertainty. Natural disasters and catastrophes are unpredictable facts of life. Nature is not discerning or discriminating. For these reasons a sure dollar is worth more than a chance at receiving that same dollar subject to the whims of nature. Thus, the three things in addition to inflation that affect the value of a dollar are time, risk, and uncertainty.

Anyone engaging in economic analysis or managerial decisions should be aware of how time, risk, and uncertainty affect economic behavior and the operations of markets. In this chapter we focus on the element of time; in Chapter 7 we consider risk and uncertainty. Decisions that affect the future as well as the present are referred to as

Berry's World

© 1987 by NEA, Inc. 9-C

"Pity ain't it? I have plenty of time and no money, an' YOU have plenty of money an' no time."

Reprinted by permission of NEA, Inc.

intertemporal decisions. Saving, borrowing, and investment decisions are intertemporal decisions that interact to determine interest rates. Such decisions depend on a person's patience, present and future income and wealth, assessment of risk and uncertainty, attitude toward taking risk, and the present and anticipated prices of goods and interest rates. Intertemporal choice in consuming and in acquiring real and financial assets is one of the most important topics that managers can study.

6.1 The Time Value of Money

If a friend asked to borrow $3 for lunch with a promise to pay you back tomorrow, you would probably loan the $3 without further thought. Why? Because $3 isn't very much to lose even if your friend doesn't pay you back. Moreover, any interest lost by not investing the $3 is insignificant. But if your friend asked to borrow $3,000 for a year, you would probably expect that the loan would be repaid with interest even if collateral were provided in case of default. The interest, therefore, is not compensation for any risk associated with making the loan; rather, it is compensation for the forgone interest income that you could have earned, say, by placing the money in a savings account. Of course you might ask for greater interest if you have a safe alternative that pays interest greater than the savings account, or if the loan is not risk free. But if you see no other alternatives and considerations, money has a time value because by not spending it today you have to postpone consumption of goods today.

Initially, to focus on the implications of the time value of money for decision making, let's assume that the outcomes of all alternatives are known with perfect certainty. A dollar given up today is not equivalent to a dollar received in the future as long as we have the alternative of earning a positive return on the dollar in the interim. Let's denote the **rate of return,** the interest rate, as $i \times 100\%$. An interest rate of 5 percent means that $i = 0.05$.

Suppose an amount of money M is invested at an interest rate $i \times 100\%$ per year. The return, or future value, at the end of one year is

$$FV_1 = M + iM = (1 + i)M$$

where FV_1 denotes the future value of M dollars at the end of one year. If $1,000 is invested at 8 percent, the return at the end of one year is

$$FV_1 = (1.08)1,000 = \$1,080$$

At the end of two years, the total return is

$$
\begin{aligned}
FV_2 &= FV_1 + iFV_1 \\
&= (1 + i)M + i(1 + i)M \\
&= (1 + i)(1 + i)M \\
&= (1 + i)^2 M
\end{aligned}
$$

where FV_2 denotes the future value of M dollars invested for two years. If compounded for two years, the return on $1,000 invested at 8 percent is

$$FV_2 = (1.08)^2\, 1,000 = \$1,166$$

If compounded for five years, the return is

$$FV_5 = (1.08)^5 \, 1{,}000 = \$1{,}469$$

Thus, at the end of t years,

$$FV_t = (1 + i)^t M$$

where FV_t is the **future value** of compounding M dollars at an interest rate i for t years. This expression is called the **future-value formula.**[1]

Just as an amount of money invested today has a future value, an amount of money to be received in the future has a present value. The term **present value** refers to the present or current value of an amount of money that will be received at some time in the future. To calculate present value, the compounding of an investment to determine future value is reversed. That is, a future return is *discounted* to determine its present value. The **present-value formula** for an amount of money M_t received in period t is

$$PV = \frac{M_t}{(1 + i)^t}$$

where i is the discounting interest rate. For instance, the present value of $\$1{,}469$ to be received in $t = 5$ years and discounted at a rate of 8 percent is

$$PV = \frac{\$1{,}469}{(1.08)^5} = \$1{,}000$$

Notice how this result compares to the numerical example in the preceding paragraph. The present value PV of any future amount of money M_t is merely the amount that if invested in the present would equal the future amount FV_t. An amount to be received in the future is worth less in the present.[2]

---

1. The future-value formula can be modified to reflect periods of less than a year and continuous compounding, but we will leave that subject for a finance text because it is the basic idea that matters here.
2. If there is within-period compounding and f is the frequency of compounding per period, the present-value formula becomes

$$PV = \frac{M_t}{\left[1 + \dfrac{i}{f}\right]^{ft}}$$

For example, if $\$1{,}000$ is received in $t = 5$ years at 6 percent per year compounded $f = 2$ times per year, the present value is

$$PV = \frac{1{,}000}{\left[1 + \dfrac{0.06}{2}\right]^{10}} = 744.09$$

Beyond this note, we will ignore the complexities of within-period compounding in order to concentrate on the principles important in making economic decisions.

6.2   Saving and Borrowing

The time value of money has important implications about choosing to save or borrow. Changes in the interest rate will affect the levels of present and future demands for goods as well as the amount of loanable funds in the economy. Therefore, every business decision maker and economic analyst needs to know how interest rates affect economic decisions.

One of the "goods" available to the consumer is the decision either to save part of current income and increase future consumption or to borrow from future income and increase current consumption. **Saving** is the decision to postpone consumption in the present period in order to increase future consumption. **Borrowing** is the decision to reduce future consumption in order to increase present consumption.

Our analysis is restricted to two periods, but it could be extended to many. Consumption in each period is represented by a composite good. The consumption in the initial period is C_1, and consumption in the subsequent period is C_2. The composite good C is treated as numeraire, and so we must assume that the prices of all goods between periods remain in fixed proportions. Thus, except for a general inflation that causes a proportionate increase in all prices, and except for a discounting of price between periods because of the changing time value of money, price ratios do not change within a period or between periods. In addition, goods must be consumed in the period acquired, so that the analysis is not appropriate for durable goods.[3]

The budget constraint for the two-period planning horizon is shown in Figure 6.1. In the absence of saving or borrowing, the amount of money the consumer has to spend in each period is denoted by M_1 and M_2. These amounts of money determine the levels of consumption possible in each period as $C_1 = M_1$ and $C_2 = M_2$ when there is no saving or borrowing. The consumption possibilities $C_1 = M_1$ and $C_2 = M_2$ are the consumer's initial endowment. The endowment is always available to the consumer, and so the budget line must pass through that bundle. What about the rest of the budget line?

Let S denote *saving* out of present income when S is *positive*, and let S denote *borrowing* from future income when S is *negative*. Suppose the consumer can borrow or lend at interest rate i per period. The level of expenditure on *present* consumption is

$$C_1 = M_1 - S$$

Present expenditure on present consumption equals the endowment income M_1 less saving (or plus borrowing). For example, if present income is $M_1 = 100$ and saving is $S = 10$, the present level of consumption is $C_1 = 90$. The level of expenditure on *future* consumption is

$$C_2 = M_2 + S(1 + i)$$

The level of expenditure on future consumption equals the endowment income M_2 plus savings and interest earnings. If future income is $M_2 = 100$ when savings was $S = 10$ in

---

3. Durable goods may be considered a special form of asset. The valuation of assets and investment decisions are discussed later in this chapter.

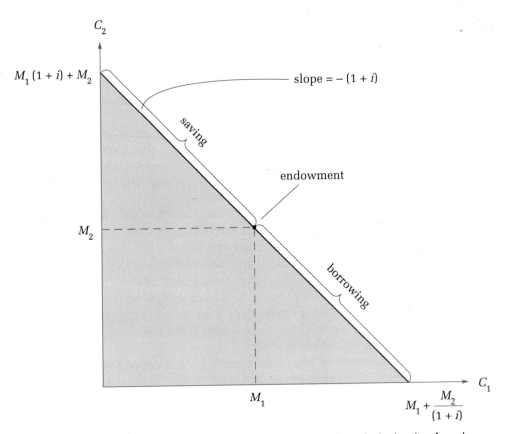

$$C_2$$

$$M_1(1+i) + M_2$$

slope $= -(1+i)$

saving

endowment

$$M_2$$

borrowing

$$M_1$$

$$M_1 + \dfrac{M_2}{(1+i)}$$

$$C_1$$

Figure 6.1 **The two-period budget constraint:** A leftward movement along the budget line from the initial endowment is made possible by saving (and lending) in the first period. If all the first-period endowment is lent, then the maximum level of consumption in the second period is $M_1(1+i) +$ M_2. A rightward movement along the budget line from the initial endowment is possible by borrowing from future consumption. If borrowing equals M_2, then the maximum level of consumption in the first period is $M_1 + M_2/(1+i)$.

period 1, the future consumption will be $C_2 = 100 + 10(1.10) = 111$, the future income plus past savings plus the return on the past savings.

Total consumption over both periods may not exceed the total value of the endowments. In terms of the two-period budget line,

$$C_1 + C_2 = [M_1 - S] + [M_2 + S(1+i)]$$
$$= M_1 + M_2 + iS$$

Substituting $S = M_1 - C_1$, moving all consumption terms to the left-hand side, and dividing both sides by $(1+i)$ yields

$$C_1 + \frac{C_2}{(1+i)} = M_1 + \frac{M_2}{(1+i)}$$

The term $C_2/(1 + i)$ represents the value of C_2 in the present period, and the term $M_2/(1 + i)$ represents the value of M_2 in the present period. This budget line states that the present value of present and future consumption equals the present value of present and future endowment income.

The budget line is illustrated in Figure 6.1. The C_1 intercept will be

$$C_1 = M_1 + \frac{M_2}{(1 + i)}$$

when $C_2 = 0$. In other words, when future consumption is zero, present consumption can be increased beyond present income by the present value of future income. The C_1 intercept is just the present value of present plus future income. For example, if $M_1 = 100$ and $M_2 = 110$ and the consumer borrows 110 from the future at 10 percent, the maximum present consumption is $M_1 = 100$ plus $M_2/(1 + i) = 110/(1.10) = 100$. Thus the C_1 intercept is 200 when $C_2 = 0$. If the consumer borrows $M_2/(1 + i)$ dollars in the first period at interest rate i, the future income of M_2 dollars will be just sufficient to pay back the loan.

The C_2 intercept will be

$$C_2 = M_1(1 + i) + M_2$$

when $C_1 = 0$. That is, when present consumption is zero, future consumption can be increased by $(1 + i)M_1$ dollars by lending $S = M_1$ dollars in the first period and adding the return to future income. For example, if $M_1 = 100$ and $M_2 = 110$ and the consumer saves $S = M_1$ dollars, the return will be $100(1.10)$ at 10 percent. Thus, when $C_1 = 0$, the C_2 intercept is $C_2 = M_1(1.10) + M_2 = 220$. The C_2 intercept is just the future value of present income plus future income.

The slope of this budget line is

$$\frac{\Delta C_2}{\Delta C_1} = -(1 + i)$$

This slope measures the *required rate of exchange* in consumption between periods. At a 10 percent interest rate, the slope is -1.10. If the interest rate were zero, then the slope would be -1, and a one-for-one exchange in consumption would occur between periods. The term $(1 + i)$ can be interpreted as the *opportunity cost* of a one-unit increase in present consumption.

As the interest rate rises, the cost of present consumption rises because the consumer must forgo a larger amount of future consumption for each unit of present consumption. If the interest rate increases from 10 percent to 20 percent, the slope of the budget line changes from -1.1 to -1.2. The effect of an increase in the interest rate in the budget line is illustrated by Figure 6.2. The budget line rotates about the point of the initial endowment as the interest rate changes. The budget line becomes steeper as i increases, reflecting the increased opportunity cost of present consumption.

The consumer's *preferences* between present and future consumption can be represented by a utility function:

$$U = U(C_1, C_2)$$

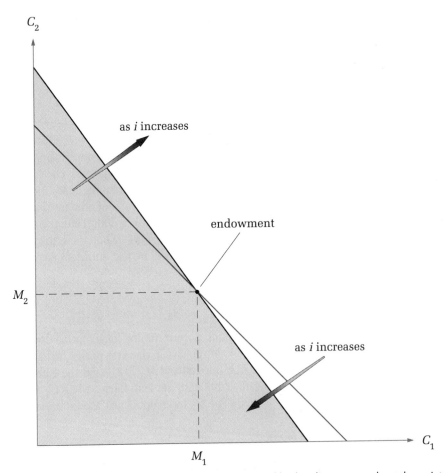

Figure 6.2 **An increase in the interest rate:** The intertemporal budget line rotates about the point of the initial endowment as i changes. The slope of the two-period budget line increases as i increases.

Indifference curves can be identified with each level of utility. If the consumer doesn't distinguish between present and future consumption, all indifference curves will be straight lines having slope of -1 everywhere. More realistically, the consumer will be willing to exchange future for present consumption at different rates depending on the levels of present and future consumption, and so the indifference curves will be convex.

The slope of each indifference curve reflects the willingness to substitute future for present consumption. Thus, the marginal rate of substitution (MRS) measures the consumer's willingness to sacrifice future consumption to increase present consumption. The utility-maximizing choices of two consumers are illustrated in Figure 6.3. The convexity of the indifference curves implies that the MRS diminishes as C_1 increases relative to C_2. That is, along any indifference curve, future consumption is subjectively valued more as the level of present consumption increases.

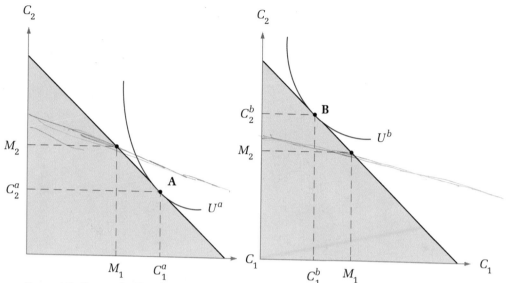

Figure 6.3 Borrowing and lending: Given identical initial endowments and facing identical interest rates, person A is a borrower because $C_1^a > M_1$, and person B is a lender (a saver) because $C_1^b < M_1$. Person A has a greater time preference for present over future consumption.

As before, the utility-maximizing choice occurs at a point of tangency. At such points, the MRS equals the price ratio,

$$MRS = (1 + i)$$

In Figure 6.3, the budget lines facing each of the consumers are identical because both consumers have identical endowments and face identical interest rates. Thus, the difference in choices reflects only their differences in time preference. Obviously, choices would be influenced by differences in endowments as well as in the interest rates to be paid by each person, but the focus here is on the differences in preferences. Person A has a greater preference for present over future consumption than person B. Person A is a borrower because present consumption is greater than present endowment. Person B is a saver (and a lender) because present consumption is less than present endowment.

Saving is a function of the interest rate because $S = M_1 - C_1$ and C_1 is influenced by the interest rate. For the consumer who is borrowing, the level of borrowing must decrease as the interest rate rises if consumption is a normal good. As shown in Figure 6.4, the borrower may become a saver as the interest rate rises further. For a saver, the price-induced income effect causes consumption to increase because the attainable set expands in the saving region when i increases. Eventually the now-direct income effect may dominate the substitution effect, causing the supply curve $S(i)$ to bend backward. It is not possible, however, for a lender to become a borrower as the interest rate rises because that would violate the weak axiom. Likewise, it is not possible for a borrower to become a lender as the interest rate falls.

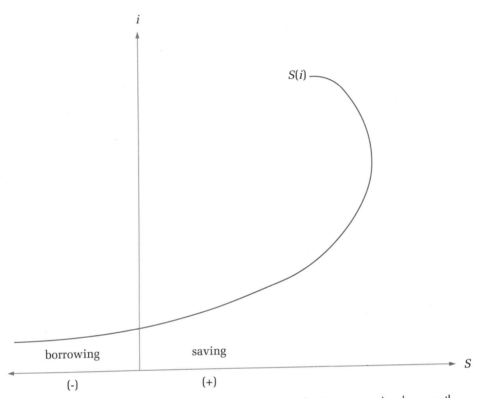

Figure 6.4 **Supply-of-savings curve:** Borrowing will decrease as the interest rate rises because the price-induced income effect will reinforce the substitution effect. The consumer may decide to save at a higher interest rate, but the supply-of-savings curve may eventually bend backward as i increases if the now-direct income effect dominates the substitution effect.

AN APPLICATION: *Anticipated Inflation*

Suppose inflation increases all prices in the second period. Let α denote the anticipated inflation. An inflation rate of 3 percent means that $\alpha = 0.03$. If the consumer anticipates this inflation with certainty, so that the actual rate of inflation equals the anticipated rate, the price of future consumption is $(1 + \alpha) = 1.03$. The effect on the attainable set is illustrated by Figure 6.5. The endowment in the first period is unaffected by inflation, but in the second period it is reduced. Similarly, the maximum possible level of C_1 is not affected by inflation, but that of C_2 is reduced. The slope of the budget line becomes

$$-(1 + i)/(1 + \alpha) = -(1 + i)/1.03$$

Inflation has the effect of increasing the relative price of future consumption.

The influence of inflation can be analyzed by examining the income and substitution effects of the price change. Figure 6.5 illustrates the case of a saver having a positively sloped supply curve. The price-induced income and substitution effects are

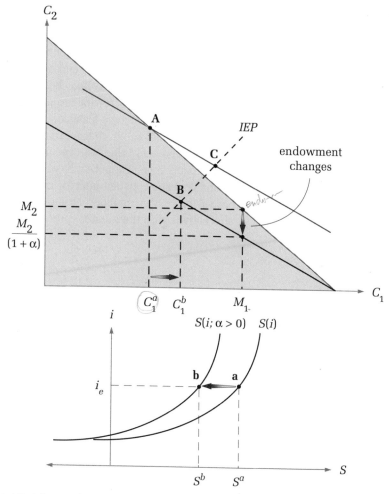

Figure 6.5 Inflation and saving: For a saver having a positively sloped savings curve, anticipated inflation causes a reduction in saving at any interest rate because the substitution effect dominates the price-induced income effect. If inflation is great enough, the saver may become a borrower.

opposite in sign, but the substitution effect dominates. Thus, at any given interest rate the supply of saving will be less than before the inflation, and the supply curve shifts to the left. If inflation is high enough, the saver may become a borrower.

If present and future consumption are normal goods, future consumption will always fall in response to inflation, and a borrower will always borrow more in response to inflation. But the response of a saver depends on the magnitude of the substitution and income effects of the price change. For the example in Figure 6.5, saving decreased because the consumer had a positively sloped supply curve. For the consumer on a backward-bending portion of a saving supply curve, however, saving will increase with inflation because the income effect of the price change dominates the substitution effect.

6.3   Evaluating Alternatives

The intertemporal-choice model can be used to demonstrate an important principle: present value is the *only* correct way of converting a stream of payments into current dollars. Figure 6.6 illustrates why. Consider two alternative endowment bundles, **A** and **B**. If saving and borrowing are prohibited, this individual would choose **A** over **B** because **A** generates greater utility. But when saving and borrowing are permitted, all consumption possibilities along each of the budget lines become feasible. The individual now chooses **B** over **A** because **B** permits the choice of **C**, which has greater utility than **A**. The budget line associated with **B** has greater present value than the budget line for **A**. Therefore, an individual will *always* prefer the pattern of income that has the highest present value if the individual can borrow and lend at a constant interest rate.

One very useful application of present value is in valuing different income streams from alternative investments. Because alternatives with the greatest present value always

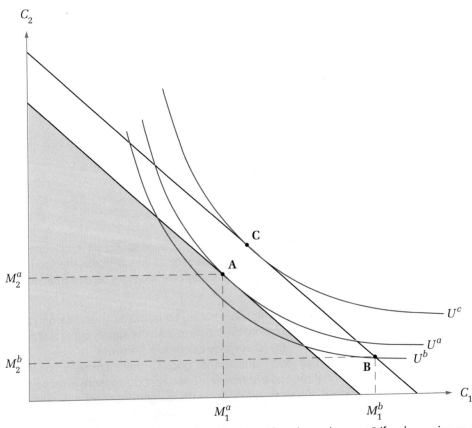

Figure 6.6 **Comparing present values:** Endowment **A** is preferred to endowment **B** if no borrowing or saving is permitted. If borrowing or saving is permitted at a positive interest rate, however, bundle **C** becomes available because its present value is the same as that of **B**. Therefore, **B** is chosen over **A** because the present value of **B** is greater than the present value of **A**.

add more to wealth than alternatives with smaller present values, you should always choose the alternative with the highest present value. Of course, which one yields the greatest present value depends on the interest rate.

Consider two investments, A and B. Alternative A yields $220 at the end of the first year, $242 at the end of the second, and nothing thereafter. Alternative B yields $440 at the end of the first year and nothing thereafter. Which alternative should you choose? The answer depends on the interest rate. If the interest rate is zero, the answer is easy—just add up the returns to see that

$$PV_a = 220 + 242 > PV_b = 440$$

when $i = 0$, and so A should be chosen over B. But if the interest rate is high enough, the later return on alternative A will be discounted more heavily. This result suggests that at some interest rate the two alternatives have the same present value. To find that rate, we set $PV_a = PV_b$:

$$PV_a = \frac{220}{(1 + i)} + \frac{242}{(1 + i)^2} = PV_b = \frac{440}{(1 + i)}$$

For this example, the present values are both equal to $400 when $i = 0.10$. Thus, A should be chosen when the interest rate is less than 10 percent, but B when the rate is greater than 10 percent.

6.4 What Interest Rate?

We have just seen that the discounting interest rate is crucial in calculating the present value of any continuing stream of payments. Therefore, the interest rate is crucial in evaluating alternatives over time. Then what interest rate should you use? Given a perfectly competitive lending market, the appropriate discounting interest rate is the *market* rate of interest, because any consumer or firm can lend or borrow at the market rate. But in real life we find many market rates.

Passbook savings accounts have rates, and checkbook balances do too. Government securities and privately issued bonds carry rates. Rates are allowed that banks charge their best and most reliable corporate borrowers, and rates are allowed by financial intermediaries charged for more risky loans. All "market" rates refer to an average cost of borrowing and average return to lending in a specific type of market. Moreover, we find short-term rates and long-term rates, as well as nominal rates and real rates. Which rate then should you use in calculating present values?

The choice of the appropriate discounting interest rate should be guided by the following principle. The interest rate measures the *opportunity cost* of funds, and so any stream of payments should be compared to your next best alternative investment that carries similar risk and uncertainty. If the stream of payments is risky, you should use an interest rate of an investment with a similar risk. If the stream of payments will continue for several years, then you should use a long-term interest rate.

Once you choose the appropriate market rate, recognize the difference between a *nominal* rate and a *real* interest rate. The **nominal rate** of interest is expressed in current dollars. The **real rate** adjusts the nominal rate to measure purchasing power after expected price changes have been considered. Economists always prefer real rates because they convey information about how individuals are faring in purchasing power.

We have seen that inflation reduces the real value of future income. Moreover, the return from saving out of current income must be discounted using the rate of inflation to determine the real return to future consumption. The interest rate i in dollars is called the **nominal** rate of interest. With an inflation rate of $\alpha 100$ percent, the rate of exchange between present and future consumption is

$$-\frac{(1 + i)}{(1 + \alpha)}$$

This is the slope of the budget line when inflation is considered. Thus, the **real interest rate** ρ is defined by

$$1 + \rho = \frac{(1 + i)}{(1 + \alpha)}$$

The value $(1 + \rho)$ measures how much extra future consumption you can get if you give up one unit of present consumption. That is why ρ is called the **real** rate of interest. When inflation is present, and as long as the anticipated income stream is not adjusted upward by the rate of inflation, the appropriate discounting interest rate is the real rate of interest. If, on the other hand, the next period's cash flow is projected to increase at the rate of inflation, then the nominal interest rate is the appropriate discount rate.

The preceding equation can be solved to get an expression for the real interest rate:

$$\rho = \frac{(i - \alpha)}{(1 + \alpha)}$$

Thus when the rate of inflation is 4 percent and the market rate of interest is 12 percent, the real rate of interest is

$$\rho = \frac{(0.12 - 0.04)}{(1.04)} \cong 0.077$$

If the rate of inflation is fairly small, then $1 + \alpha$ will be just slightly greater than unity. Thus, when α is small, the real rate of interest may be approximated by

$$\rho \cong i - \alpha$$

This approximation is easy to use. If, for instance, the rate of inflation is 4 percent and the market rate of interest is 12 percent, the real rate of interest is approximately 8 percent. This approximation slightly *overstates* the real rate of interest.

6.5 Assets and Present Value

Assets are goods that provide a flow of services over time. The two types are financial assets and real assets. **Financial assets** provide a *monetary* flow of services in the form of interest payments. **Real assets** provide a *real* flow of services in the form of consumption.

Financial assets are of many types. One type, the **annuity,** is a financial agreement consisting of a series of payments made at the end of each period over a fixed number of periods. Examples of annuities are mortgage payments, retirement-plan payments, and sinking-fund payments. The present value of an annuity payment of R dollars per period over T periods is

$$PV = \frac{R}{(1 + i)} + \frac{R}{(1 + i)^2} + \cdots + \frac{R}{(1 + i)^T}$$

That is, the present value of an annuity is the sum of the discounted payments.

This formula for calculating the present value of an annuity can be simplified. Multiplying both sides of the equation by $(1 + i)$ and subtracting the result from the original equation results in

$$PV - PV(1 + i) = -R + \frac{R}{(1 + i)^T}$$

Solving for present value yields

$$PV = \frac{R}{i}\left[1 - \frac{1}{(1 + i)^T}\right]$$

For example, the PV of a $1,000 per year payment over $T = 10$ years with a discounting interest rate of 6 percent is

$$PV = \frac{\$1,000}{0.06}\left[1 - \frac{1}{(1.06)^{10}}\right] = \$7,360$$

Thus, the present value of $1,000 per year for 10 years is $7,360 when the discounting interest rate is $i = 0.06$.

A **perpetuity** is an annuity that lasts forever. In the past, the British government issued bonds that never matured called *consols*. A consol yields an annual payment determined by multiplying its face value by a fixed rate of interest. For instance, if the face value of the consol was $100 and the rate of interest was 6 percent, the annual payment would be $6. A passbook savings account can be used as a perpetuity. Given an initial deposit, the interest earnings could be withdrawn forever. The present value of a perpetuity is determined by the same formula as an annuity except that T approaches infinity. As T approaches infinity, the term $1/(1 + i)^T$ goes to zero. Thus, the present value of a perpetuity is

$$PV = \frac{R}{i}$$

where R is the periodic return. This formula tells you how much money you would need to invest at an interest rate i to get R dollars per period forever. This formula is particularly easy to use. For example, an asset paying $8 per year forever has a PV of $100 when the interest rate is 8 percent, but the same asset has a PV of $200 when the interest rate is 4 percent.

The present value of a long-term financial asset can be approximated by using the formula for the perpetuity. This approximation works because, for the interest rates we usually encounter, the term T might as well be infinity when T is big. If you hold a 30-year asset with periodic return of $1,000 at 10 percent, the present value formula R/i for a perpetuity gives you a quick and easy way to approximate the value of this long-term asset as $10,000 approximately.

Another type of financial asset closely related to annuities and perpetuities is the **bond.** Bonds can be issued by governments or corporations as a means for borrowing money. The borrower promises to pay a periodic payment of C dollars called the **coupon** until a maturity date T. At the maturity date the borrower must pay an amount F, called the **face value.** The present value of a bond is

$$PV = \frac{C}{(1 + i)} + \frac{C}{(1 + i)^2} + \cdots + \frac{C}{(1 + i)^{T-1}} + \frac{F}{(1 + i)^T}$$

Notice that this is the same as the formula for annuities except for the final fixed-face-value payment.

Of course, these are not the only types of financial assets. But for all types of financial assets, the thing to notice is that their present values are *inversely* related to the interest rate. When the interest rate goes up, the present value of a financial asset will fall because the value of a future dollar goes down as the interest rate goes up.

The other type of asset, **real assets,** yields a "return" in the form of consumption over time. If you own a house that you live in, then you don't have to pay rent. Part of the return from owning the house is the rent that you implicitly pay to yourself. By choosing to rent the house to yourself, you have forgone the opportunity of earning rental payments from someone else. Therefore, the periodic payment that you receive is the *imputed rental rate* on your house, the opportunity cost of not renting the house to someone else. The capital equipment owned by a firm is a real asset. The value of such capital is determined by its present value. The original cost of such capital has no bearing on its present value because that outlay is a sunk cost. Rather, the present value of capital is determined by discounting the *imputed rental rate* of the capital. The imputed rental rate of capital is the price that would have to be paid to rent the capital services in each period. The imputed rental rate is the opportunity price of the services provided by the capital. If the periodic rents are $R_1, R_2, \ldots, R_T$ over the useful life of the capital, and if at period T the capital good has scrap value S, the present value of the capital good is

$$PV = \frac{R_1}{(1 + i)} + \frac{R_2}{(1 + i)^2} + \cdots + \frac{R_T}{(1 + i)^T} + \frac{S}{(1 + i)^T}$$

Thus, the valuation of real assets like houses or capital goods works in the same way as for financial assets.

6.6   Valuing Assets Under Certainty

Asset markets are well developed. All sorts of financial intermediaries facilitate trade of financial assets, including banks, savings and loan institutions, and stock exchanges. Real asset markets are well developed also, such as markets for both residential and commercial real estate, and businesses that rent capital equipment. Remark-

ECONOMIC SCENE: *A Market Meltdown*

In October 1987, the Dow Jones industrial average lost 13 percent of its value in a week and closed nearly 800 points below the previous high of August on the New York Stock Exchange. Similar changes took place in exchanges in Great Britain, West Germany, Japan, and other markets worldwide. Quickly, many people started to draw parallels with the great crash of 1929. Most economists, however, said that this would not be a rerun of the Great Depression that followed the crash of 1929. But the day now called Black Monday—October 19, 1987—had stripped $500 billion from the market value of U.S. securities.

In looking for explanations, analysts began to point the finger at automatic trading by computer programs in index-futures markets. The trade deals not in actual stocks but in bets on what stock indexes may be on future dates. With *index arbitrage,* investors seek profit from tiny price differences between stock index futures and stock prices by selling whichever is more expensive and buying the cheaper. As they buy and sell millions of shares of stocks and futures contracts, the price changes are magnified and tend to feed on themselves.

Criticism was directed less toward the practice of arbitrage itself than toward the use of computers programmed to trigger trading. That is, as arbitrage began to force the average price of stocks down to their present values, the computer programs triggered unchecked trading. In response, the New York Stock Exchange tightened restrictions on the use of its SuperDot index-arbitrage program. Members of the exchange were temporarily prohibited from using the program on any day when the Dow Jones industrial average moved more than 50 points in a day's session. The objective was to limit potential market volatility caused by computer program trading. In an earlier action, Shearson Lehman Hutton Inc. announced that it would cease all index computer-programmed trading for its own account. In a separate but related action, futures margin requirements were raised to 15 percent on the Chicago Mercantile and the Chicago Board of Trade, where 80 percent of stock futures trading occurs. These actions may slow down some risk takers, but they won't stop the practice of arbitrage.

ably, when asset markets operate under conditions of complete certainty about the future flow of services provided by the assets, all assets will have identical rates of return.

The process guaranteeing that all assets will have the same rate of return under certainty is called **arbitrage.**

> **Arbitrage:** *Arbitrage is the process by which market participants eliminate the difference in returns between assets by selling one asset to buy another.*

Here is how arbitrage works: Consider two assets, A and B. Asset A has a price of p_1 in the current period and p_2 in the subsequent period. Asset B pays an interest rate i

between the two periods. Now consider investing $1 in either asset A or B. One dollar will buy

$$Q = \frac{1}{p_1}$$

units of A. The future value of q units of A is

$$FV_a = p_2 Q$$

Therefore, the future value of A is

$$FV_a = \frac{p_2}{p_1}$$

Alternatively, one dollar invested in asset B will yield

$$FV_b = (1 + i)$$

Now, if $FV_b > FV_a$, then any owner of asset A can sell one unit for p_1 dollars and buy asset B. This transaction will return $p_1(1 + i)$ dollars, which is sufficient to repurchase asset A in the second period because $FV_b > FV_a$ implies that $p_1(1 + i) > p_2$. An original owner of A will own A once more and will have extra money besides, thereby earning a sure return.

But who would buy asset A if $FV_b > FV_a$? No one would be willing to buy A at price p_1 because they would earn a greater return by spending p_1 dollars on B. Plenty of people are willing to sell A, though, and so supply exceeds demand and the price of A will fall. How far will it fall? Until the future values of A and B are equal,

$$\frac{p_2}{p_1} = (1 + i)$$

This arbitrage condition can be rewritten

$$p_1 = \frac{p_2}{(1 + i)}$$

The conclusion is that the current price of an asset must be equal to its present value.

We have just seen that the price of any asset, whether a capital good or other asset, can be measured by its present value. The present value of any asset depends on the discounting interest rate and the amounts and timing of the returns generated by the asset. On choosing which asset to hold, Irving Fisher (1930) developed the **separation theorem:**

> **Fisher's separation theorem:** *Given a perfect lending market, individuals choose among assets by comparing present values using a market rate of interest, and the choices are not influenced by preferences about the timing of consumption.*

A lending market is perfect when perfect information is available to large numbers of buyers and sellers in the market. The following extension of an earlier example will demonstrate the Fisher proposition.

Suppose you learn about two assets, A and B, and the market rate of interest is 10 percent. Asset A provides $220 at the end of the first year, $242 at the end of the second year, and nothing thereafter. Asset B provides $440 at the end of the first year and nothing thereafter. Both of these assets have equal present values.

Now consider an individual who strongly prefers present consumption over future consumption. Suppose that this intertemporal impatience is so strong that this person decides to spend $440 this year and nothing in the second. Clearly, asset B permits this spending pattern. But asset A also permits the same spending pattern because $220 is returned in one year and an additional $220 can be borrowed at 10 percent interest. The loan requires a $242 payback, but the loan can be repaid exactly from the return from asset A in the second year. Thus, equal spending patterns can be achieved from either asset, and the individual will be indifferent between them. Time preference has no influence on choice of asset.

We can demonstrate the previous conclusion—that the price of any asset will equal its present value—with this same example. Any person having $400 can lend $200 for repayment in one year and $200 for repayment in two years. At the 10 percent interest rate, the first-year return is $220, and the second-year return is $242. Thus, no one would be willing to pay more than $400 for asset A because its payment stream can be duplicated by lending $400. Likewise, no one would be willing to pay more than $400 for asset B because its payment stream can be duplicated by lending $400 at 10 percent for one year. If either asset sells for less than $400, it becomes profitable to borrow funds to purchase the assets. The subsequent arbitrage forces the asset prices up to their present values.

6.7 Investment Decisions

The **net present value** (*NPV*) of an investment project is

$$NPV = \sum_{t=1}^{T} \frac{\pi_t}{(1 + i)^t} - I$$

where $\pi_t = R_t - C_t$ is the net return per period (revenue less cost in each period), i is the discounting interest rate, and I is the initial cost of the investment. When the firm has unlimited funds to invest it should undertake every project that has a positive *NPV*. Determining the *NPV* is far from simple in the real world. The firm must predict what revenues will be generated by the project, and what costs. Moreover, it must determine what discount rate to use, and i may not remain constant over the life of the project.

Once the net periodic returns and the discount rate are set, however, calculating the *NPV* is relatively simple. Suppose a firm considers investing $98,500 on equipment that will be used over a five-year period. The equipment is expected to have a scrap value of $55,000 at the end of the five years. The project is expected to generate $40,000 per year in revenue, and operating costs are expected to be $19,200 per year. Finally, the discounting interest rate is taken to be 12 percent. The *NPV* of the project is

$$\sum_{t=1}^{5} \frac{R_t - C_t}{(1.12)^t} + \frac{\text{scrap value}}{(1.12)^5} - 98,500$$

$$= \sum_{t=1}^{5} \frac{40,000 - 19,200}{(1.12)^t} + \frac{55,000}{(1.12)^5} - 98,500$$

$$= \frac{20,800}{1.12} + \frac{20,800}{(1.12)^2} + \frac{20,800}{(1.12)^3} + \frac{20,800}{(1.12)^4} + \frac{20,800}{(1.12)^5} + \frac{55,000}{(1.12)^5} - 98,500$$

$$\cong 18,571 + 16,582 + 14,805 + 13,219 + 11,802 + 31,208 - 98,500$$

$$= \$7,687$$

As long as there are no better alternatives, the project should be undertaken, because it has a positive *NPV*.

6.8 The Internal Rate of Return and Investment Alternatives

The source of investment funds may be retained earnings, bond sales, stock sales, or a bank loan. Investment funds are therefore limited. The firm should still undertake an investment that has a positive *NPV* as long as the funds are available, but how does the firm choose between alternative investments?

An alternative measure for the profitability of a possible investment project is its internal rate of return. If an investment generates a return, called the **internal rate of return,** greater than any market alternative, and if the price of the investment is determined by the market interest rate, the investment will be profitable.

> **Internal rate of return (m):** *The internal rate of return is the discounting interest rate that makes an investment's net present value equal to zero.*

The internal rate of return is also referred to as the **marginal efficiency of investment.** If properly used, the internal rate of return can be used to make investment decisions. If an investment's internal rate of return is greater than an appropriate alternative interest rate, the investment will increase the investor's wealth.

The internal rate of return (*m*) is determined by setting the stream of net returns equal to the initial cost of the investment,

$$\sum_{t=1}^{T} \frac{\pi_t}{(1 + m)^t} = I$$

The value of m can be found from this equation. A solution to this polynomial function of degree T is usually found with the help of a computer program or a preprogrammed financial calculator.

Calculating m is easier when the periodic returns are equal. When the return is R dollars per year over T years, the internal rate of return is found from the formula

$$\frac{R}{m}\left[1 - \frac{1}{(1 + m)^T}\right] = I$$

For example, the rate of return for an investment of $7,360 returning $1,000 for each of 10 periods is found by evaluating

$$\frac{1,000}{m}\left[1 - \frac{1}{(1 + m)^{10}}\right] = 7,360$$

or

$$1 - \frac{1}{(1 + m)^{10}} = 7.36m$$

Trial and error reveals that the rate of return is very close to $m = 0.06$ or 6 percent.

Ordinarily the PV of an investment is inversely related to the discounting interest rate. This relation will always be true if the periodic returns are either constant or increasing. Consider the PV of a perpetuity costing $250 and yielding a return of $10 per period:

i	$PV = R/i$	$NPV = PV - 250$
0.01	1,000	750
0.02	500	250
0.04	250	0
0.08	125	-125

The present value of this perpetuity is plotted as a function of the interest rate in Figure 6.7. The net present value of this perpetuity is $NPV = (10/i) - 250$ because $PV = R/i$ for a perpetuity and $R = 10$. For the initial investment of $250, the internal rate of return is $m = 0.04$ where the $NPV = 0$ for this investment. Notice that if the internal rate of return is *greater* than the interest rate, $m > i$, the investment will yield a *positive NPV* and will *increase* the investor's wealth.

It is tempting, therefore, to formulate a decision rule in terms of m and i: undertake the investment if $m > i$. When $m > i$ the NPV of the investment is greater than its cost. For instance, the net present value is $NPV = \$500$ for the $250 perpetuity yielding a periodic return of $10 when the interest rate is $i = 0.02$. The internal rate of return of

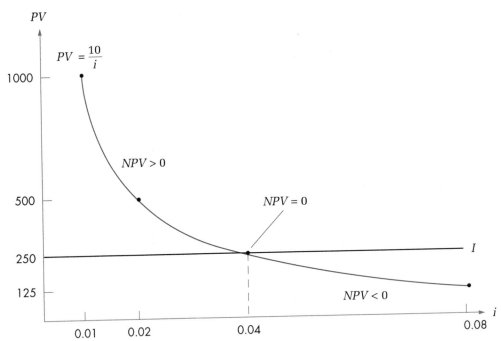

Figure 6.7 **The present value of a perpetuity:** The present value of a perpetuity is given by $PV = R/i$, where R is the periodic return and i is the discounting interest rate. When the periodic return is $R = \$10$, the PV is $PV = 10/i$. If the cost of the investment is $I = \$250$, then the internal rate of return is $m = 0.04$, where NPV = 0.

$m = 0.04$, greater than the interest rate of $i = 0.02$, signals that the NPV will exceed the cost of the investment. It is tempting, therefore, to decide in favor of any investment having a rate of return greater than the discounting interest rate. But we find two problems in such a rule.

The first problem is that the internal rate of return that yields $NPV = 0$ may have more than one value. If the cash flows for an investment are negative for early periods, becoming positive in later periods, as is typical for most investment projects, then the internal rate of return will be unique. But if later periods also bring very low negative cash flows, the NPV may fall to zero once more.

The second problem occurs with two mutually exclusive investments. As illustrated by Figure 6.8, suppose we have two alternatives, A and B. Investment A yields small early returns but large returns later, and investment B yields a more uniform flow. At lower-discounting interest rates, A will have a greater NPV than B because late returns dominate the NPV calculation at low discount rates. At higher discount rates, B will have a greater NPV because early returns dominate the calculations. Comparison of internal rates of return would lead us to choose B because $m_b > m_a$. But if the discounting

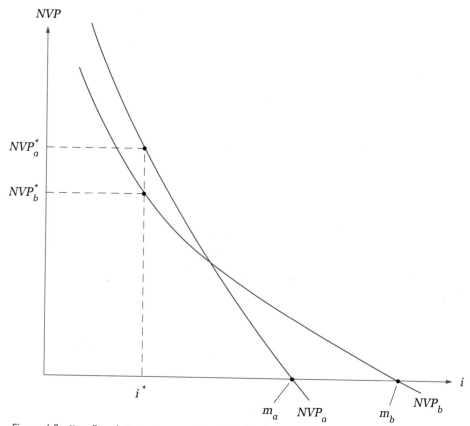

Figure 6.8 **Mutually exclusive investments:** When i^* is the discounting interest rate, investment A should be chosen over B because A has a greater NPV at i^* even though B has a greater internal rate of return.

interest rate is $i = i^*$, then $NPV_a^* > NPV_b^*$, and A should be chosen first. You can see a danger in choosing the wrong alternative.

The investment with the greater NPV adds more to wealth, and so the best rule for deciding on investments is:

> **NPV investment decision rule:** *Choose all feasible investments having positive* NPV *at the appropriate discount rate. Between mutually exclusive investments, choose the one with the greatest* NPV.

This investment rule, properly implemented, always ranks projects correctly.[4]

---

4. In practice, the internal rate-of-return rule is usually consistent with the net present-value rule. The *NPV* rule, however, *always* leads to the correct decision.

AN APPLICATION: *Investments in Education and Training*

Investments that directly affect people's productivity, improving skills, knowledge, or health, are called investments in **human capital.*** The concept of human capital is that a worker's skills are like a *stock* of productive capital that generates services that can be "rented out" to employers. Education and training affect the productivity of that stock of human capital, and so education and training can be viewed as investments in human capital. Although investments in human capital create benefits in the form of psychic returns from greater job satisfaction and deeper appreciation for the "finer things in life," in this application we concentrate on their effect on expected earnings. In particular, we look at schooling and on-the-job training.

Let's first consider formal schooling and especially the demand for a college education. A person who considers attending college has a choice between two income streams such as those illustrated in Figure 6.9. Income stream *A* is a stylized version of the expected age–earnings profile of someone entering the labor force at age 18 who has a high-school education. Income stream *A* corresponds roughly to the actual profile observed in 1984 data. This income stream for high-school graduates peaked at about 47 years of age. Income stream *B* is drawn to reflect the 1984 profile for college graduates, which peaked at about 55 years of age. The age–earnings profiles for workers with more education are generally steeper than those of workers with less education. The initially negative returns from college education reflect the direct costs of such things as tuition and books. To those we add the opportunity cost of earnings forgone while attending college. The income stream for college graduates must eventually rise above the alternative income stream to induce someone to invest in a college education—unless psychic returns are large.

Investing in a college education is worthwhile if the present value of benefits (monetary and psychic) is at least as great as the cost of going to college. If the cost is *C* and the benefit in period *t* from stream *B* is B_t, the net present value of going to college is

$$NPV_b = \sum_{t=1}^{T} \frac{B_t}{(1 + i)^t} - C$$

Similarly, if the benefit at period *t* from stream *A* is A_t, we can measure the net present value of finishing only high-school education:

$$NPV_a = \sum_{t=1}^{T} \frac{A_t}{(1 + i)^t}$$

Thus, for the person to choose college over stopping after high school, it must be true that $NPV_b \geq NPV_a$.

The internal rate-of-return approach can be applied as an alternative method for evaluating this investment decision. For each alternative, we can set the *NPV* equal to

---

*See Gary S. Becker, *Human Capital,* 2nd ed. (National Bureau of Economic Research, 1975).

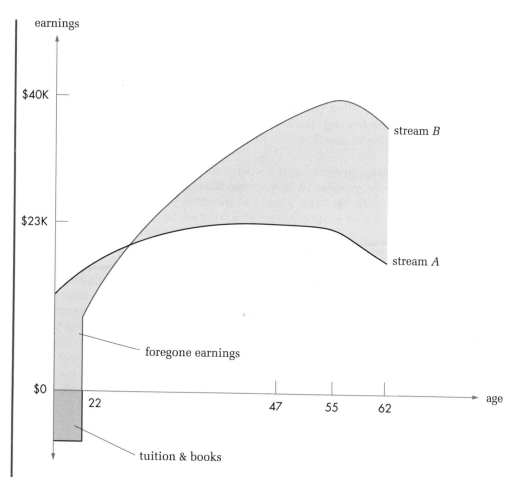

Figure 6.9 **Investment in college:** Persons with a high-school education typically have earnings stream A. Persons investing in college expect earnings stream B. Although college may provide greater earnings later in life, two investment costs are incurred—the direct cost of things like books and tuition plus the opportunity cost of forgone earnings while attending school.

zero and calculate the discounting interest rate, $i = m$. The best alternative is the one with the highest internal rate of return. Empirical studies using only money returns have estimated rates of return ranging between 5 and 15 percent after adjusting for inflation. Notice, however, that the exclusive use of monetary returns tends to *understate* the true rate of return because psychic returns are excluded in the calculations. At the same time, these studies tend to *overstate* the true rate of return because they cannot separate the contribution that ability makes to earnings from the contribution made by schooling alone. Another source of bias is that people select themselves into occupations in which they have a comparative advantage. I might choose to go to college because I have limited mechanical aptitude and know I'd have little chance of making a good living as a carpenter or electrician. Therefore the benefits of going to college for those who choose to go may be greater than indicated by the measured rates of return in empirical studies. One should always be aware too that returns to schooling vary quite a bit from one occupation to the next. Nevertheless, it is interesting that empirical estimates of rates of return from schooling are quite close to the returns generated by investment in physical capital and financial assets.

Another form of investment in human capital is **on-the-job-training,** OJT for short. The two forms of OJT are, first, *general training,* which is useful to many firms besides the one providing the training. General training increases the productivity of the worker on any job. Second, *specific training* increases the worker's productivity only on a specific job.

Why do firms provide general training when that training is transferable to other jobs? If general training increases a worker's productivity, isn't the worker more likely to quit for a higher-paying job? If so, a firm that invests in general training will lose its investment. And how about specific training? If a firm pays for specific training and the worker subsequently quits, that expenditure too is wasted. Under what conditions will firms be willing to pay for general and specific training? Investment analysis can help evaluate these questions.

To simplify our analysis, let's assume that all input and output markets are purely competitive. Under pure competition, labor is paid a wage equal to the *value of its marginal product* in each period, $w_t = VMP_t$, where the value of the marginal product of labor measures the extra revenue generated from the added output produced by the last unit of labor used in production.[†] Thus, VMP_t is the marginal revenue generated by using an extra unit of labor in period t. Anything that increases the productivity of labor will increase its VMP_t. Over the term of employment in competitive markets, because the wage is equal to labor's marginal value, the present value of the returns from labor to the employer will be equal to the present value of the expenditure on labor. But what happens when the productivity of labor is changed because of OJT?

Let's assume that wage payments are made at the end of each period t, and that training occurs only in some initial period. We denote the value of labor's marginal product and the wage rate in the initial period as VMP_0 and w_0. The two costs to the employer associated with OJT are, first, direct training costs D. Second is the opportunity cost of lost output during the training period, increasing the total investment outlay to I. Under pure competition, the present values of expenditures and receipts over a term T of employment must be equal:

$$VMP_0 + \sum_{t=1}^{T} \frac{VMP_t}{(1 + i)^t} = w_0 + \sum_{t=1}^{T} \frac{w_t}{(1 + i)^t} + D$$

The net present value from training can be found by discounting the difference between VMP_t and w_t over time,

$$NPV = \sum_{t=1}^{T} \frac{VMP_t - w_t}{(1 + i)^t}$$

†This consequence of pure competition will be proved in Chapter 12.

The initial wage rate therefore is

$$w_0 = VMP_0 + NPV - D$$

That is, the training-period wage will be equal to the value of the marginal product of labor *plus* the net present value of the returns from training *less* the direct training costs.

We still need to consider the opportunity cost of lost output during the training period. If VMP_0^* is the extra revenue that could have been generated during the initial period, the opportunity cost of the lost output is

$$VMP_0^* - VMP_0 > 0$$

If I measures the total cost of training as the sum of direct cost and opportunity cost, then

$$w_0 = VMP_0^* + NPV - I$$

This equation shows that, in the initial period, the wage rate will equal the marginal revenue from labor only when $NPV = I$.

Now let's look at general training. Firms providing general training in competitive markets will capture none of the returns, because $VMP_t = w_t$ for all periods, so that $NPV = 0$. The wage equation becomes

$$w_0 = VMP_0^* - I$$

In actual marginal revenue, the wage is

$$w_0 = VMP_0 - D$$

The wages paid will be equal to the marginal revenue from labor *less* the direct cost of the general training. That is, workers will be paid a wage equal to their marginal contribution to revenue *less* the direct cost of the general training. Wages paid during the training period are *lower* because the firm must recover both direct and indirect costs of training. The cost of general training is paid by the worker in the form of a lower wage during the training period.

Next let's look at specific training. Completely specific training has no effect on productivity that is useful to other firms. Thus the wage a worker can get elsewhere is independent of specific training received, and the firm will pay the market wage. The firm therefore does not have to reduce the wage to compensate for the training costs, but it will be willing to pay that cost only if it can collect a return in the form of higher productivity. The NPV after training must then be equal to the total cost of training, $NPV = I$. The initial wage, then, will be equal to the value of labor's marginal product in the absence of training,

$$w_0 = VMP_0^*$$

Is it plausible that firms pay for and collect the returns from specific training? If the worker subsequently quits, the expenditure is wasted. Likewise, a worker fired after paying for the specific training would suffer a loss. Thus the willingness of firms and workers to pay for specific training depends on the likelihood of labor turnover.

Most training has general and specific components. Because firms pay none of the general costs and only part of the specific costs, the proportion of the training cost paid by firms will be directly related to the specific component. Another implication of the OJT model is that firms will pay generally trained workers the same wage they could get elsewhere, but specifically trained workers will be paid more than they could get elsewhere in order to reduce turnover. Workers with specific training have less incentive to quit, and firms have less incentive to fire them, than workers having general training or no training. Quitting and layoff rates, then, are inversely related to the amount of job-specific training.

6.9   Investment Demand and the Supply of Capital

In the aggregate economy, investment is the portion of national output that adds to the nation's stock of physical assets or replaces worn-out physical assets. Such investment in real assets includes new plants, new equipment, and changes in inventory. Inventories of raw materials, parts, and finished goods are real assets that businesses use to produce revenues. Changes in the stock of such goods are called *inventory* investment. Investments in structures and equipment are called *fixed* investments.[5] The sum of all fixed and inventory investments is called *aggregate* investment.

The **investment-demand schedule** is a relation between the aggregate investment and the interest rate. To see how aggregate demand for investment is determined, let's consider two alternative investments. Investment A has an internal rate of return of $m_a = 0.10$. Investment B has an internal rate of return of $m_b = 0.05$. Neither investment will be chosen at interest rates of 10 percent or greater. When the interest rate falls below 10 percent, the level of investment will be I_a because $m_a > i$. When the interest rate falls below 5 percent, the level of investment will be $I_a + I_b$, because $m_a > m_b > i$. Aggregate investment *increases* as the interest rate *falls* because more investments qualify by having positive *NPV* at the lower interest rates.

The true investment-demand schedule will graph as a step function if the investment alternatives are lumpy. But if the number of firms is large or if small investments are possible, a smooth curve $I = I(i)$ will provide a close fit to the true investment demand. Such an investment-demand curve is illustrated in Figure 6.10. The slope of $I(i)$ is negative because more investments have a positive *NPV* at lower interest rates. The investment-demand curve is referred to as the **marginal efficiency of investment** (*MEI*) curve.

Investment leads to creation of capital by increasing inventories, buying machinery, expanding the physical plant, and so on. To keep things simple, however, let's assume only

---

5. An owner of a home can be viewed as a business that rents its home to itself. This view is consistent with the treatment of home ownership in the National Income and Product Accounts, which include in the measure of national output the "imputed rent on owner occupied dwellings."

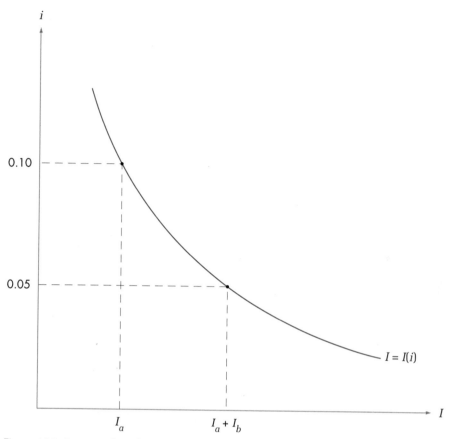

Figure 6.10 **Investment-demand curve:** Aggregate investment demand can be represented by a smooth curve $I = I(i)$ when the number of firms is large or when small investment alternatives are available. The slope of $I(i)$ is negative because more investments have positive net present values at lower interest rates.

one capital good. With only one capital good, the MEI curve can be interpreted as either the demand for investment funds or the supply of capital value. The supply of capital value is given by multiplying the quantity Q of newly produced capital by its price. The price, as we have seen, is equal to its present value. Present value is inversely related to the interest rate. Thus the value of new capital is given by $V(i) = Q(i)PV(i)$, and $V(i)$ increases when i decreases because both Q and PV increase when i decreases.[6] An inverse relationship applies between the value of new capital and the interest rate. Moreover, when new capital is the only asset available, the MEI curve $I(i)$ coincides with the supply of capital value as a function of the interest rate.

---

6. The expression $Q(i)$ is the supply of physical capital. Later you will learn that $Q(i)$ has positive slope because of increasing marginal cost caused by the diminishing productivity of inputs used to produce capital.

6.10 Determining the Market Interest Rate

The interest rate is important in directing economic activity between consumption and formation of capital. Saving is a function of the interest rate, and so the supply of loanable funds for investment depends on the interest rate. If all individual saving decisions are added at each level of the interest rate, the result is an aggregate savings curve, which represents the supply of loanable funds as a function of the interest rate. Denoted by $S(i)$, the aggregate savings curve can be interpreted as the demand for new capital in value terms if new capital is the only form of investment. On the other side of the market, the demand for investment funds is represented by the MEI curve $I(i)$. This curve can be interpreted as the supply of new capital in value terms if capital is the only form of investment.

The equilibrium interest rate is determined where the supply of savings (loanable funds) intersects the demand for investment, where $S(i) = I(i)$, as Figure 6.11 illustrates. The equilibrium interest rate is $i = i_e$, and the equilibrium level of savings is determined by $S_e = S(i_e)$. Similarly, the equilibrium level of investment is determined by $I_e = I(i_e)$.

Because the price of new capital is its present value, its price is determined by the interest rate. If we continue to assume that new capital is the only form of investment, then the MEI curve $I(i)$ and the capital-supply curve $V(i)$ coincide. The supply of capital value is $V(i) = Q(i)PV(i)$, where Q is the quantity of new capital and PV is its price, and

---

ECONOMIC SCENE: *Japanese Save More**

The average Japanese family had stashed away $86,250 in savings as of 1989, confirming Japan's place as one of the most frugal countries. The average Japanese family added 15.3% to its already large nest egg in 1989, the biggest contribution since 1979. By comparison, Americans saved an average of only 6.3% of their income in 1989. The British saved 4.9%, and the French and West Germans saved about 12%. These household savings rates do not include the value of the family home or other real estate.

Americans have argued that the Japanese tendency to save large portions of their income keeps their spending down. The result is they buy fewer goods, including imported goods from the United States. The U.S. has complained in trade negotiations that Japan's high saving rate is a contributing factor to the massive U.S. trade deficit with Japan, which stood at $49 billion in 1989.

The Japanese have turned the argument around, saying the United States could improve its economic situation if it saved more. They argue a high savings rate makes more money available for investments and pushes interest rates lower, leading to higher capital creation. Both countries have listed savings rates as a structural barrier to balanced trade during trade negotiations dubbed the Structural Impediments Initiative.

---

*From United Press International.

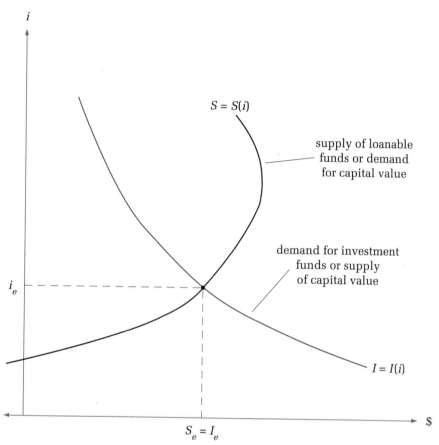

Figure 6.11 **Determining the market interest rate:** The market interest rate is determined by the equilibrium condition that the supply of investment funds $S(i)$ intersects the demand for investment funds $I(i)$. At interest rate i_e, where $S_e = S(i_e) = I_e = I(i_e)$, the demand for capital value will be equal to the supply of capital value if new capital is the only form of investment.

so $I(i) = Q(i)PV(i)$. Thus the quantity of new capital can be determined as $Q_e = Q(i_e)$ because $I(i_e)$ and $PV(i_e)$ are determined in equilibrium. Once the interest rate is settled, it determines the market value of all assets, the output of new capital and other investment goods, the amount of consumption and saving, and the volume of lending and borrowing in the economic system.

Anything that affects the position of the $S(i)$ curve or the $I(i)$ curve will cause a change in the market interest rate. An increase in the cost of producing new capital will decrease the supply of new capital and the $I(i)$ curve will shift to the left. Thus, a *decrease* in the market interest rate can be predicted when the cost of producing new capital *rises.* Similarly, if consumers become more impatient in their preferences for consumption, the $S(i)$ curve will shift to the left. Thus an *increase* in the market interest rate can be predicted when consumers save *less.*

AN APPLICATION: *Interest Rates and Inflation*

Earlier in this chapter we examined what happens to the $S(i)$ curve when consumers anticipate inflation with certainty. As shown in Figure 6.5, the $S(i)$ curve shifts to the left when the $S(i)$ curve has positive slope. Such a shift in the $S(i)$ curve is superimposed on the $I(i)$ curve in Figure 6.12. As you see, the decrease in savings because of the anticipated inflation causes an increase in the nominal market interest rate. The link between the price of the consumption good and the interest rate is direct.

The results of the greater inflation anticipated are a rise in present consumption, a corresponding fall in saving, an increase in the market interest rate, and a decrease in investment in equilibrium. This result is ensured if the substitution effect of the change in the rate of inflation dominates the income effect of a change in that rate. Otherwise the $S(i)$ curve would shift to the right.

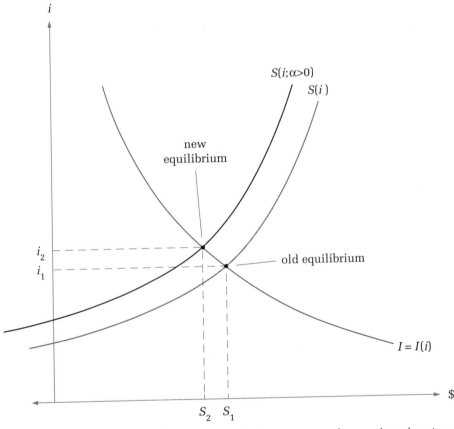

Figure 6.12 **Inflation and the interest rate:** Anticipated inflation causes a decrease in saving at every interest rate if the savings curve has positive slope. The leftward shift in the $S(i)$ curve causes a rise in the market rate of interest. The investment in new capital will fall, reducing future productive capacity. This decline may lead to higher actual inflation.

An interesting cycle of self-fulfilling expectation can occur as the equilibrium level of investment falls in response to the higher interest rate. Investment in new capital will fall and overall productive capacity in the economy will be less than it would have been. At the same time the demand for current consumption has increased. If the growth in demand for consumption goods exceeds the growth in productive capacity and hence the growth in the supply of goods, general prices will rise. The higher anticipated inflation leads to higher actual inflation. This progression can lead to a further increase in anticipated inflation, and an inflationary spiral has begun.

6.11 Public Investment Decisions and Cost-Benefit Analysis

Recall that public goods are either nonexclusive or nonexhaustive in consumption. The characteristic of **nonexclusion** means that consumption of the good cannot be confined to those who pay for the good. The characteristic of **nonexhaustion** means that use of the good by one person does not reduce its availability to others. Because of these characteristics, public goods are rarely provided by profit-seeking firms.

The total demand for a public good is determined differently than the market demand for a private good. For any good, the demand price measures the marginal benefit (marginal value) of the last unit consumed. Thus each consumer's inverse demand curve can be interpreted as a **marginal benefit** (*MB*) curve. Figure 6.13 shows the individual demand curves for two consumers. If this is a public good (because each unit is consumed by each individual at the same time), the total marginal benefit is determined by adding together the individual marginal benefits. The aggregate demand for a public good is thus the *vertical* summation of the individual demand curve.

> **Demand for a public good:** *The aggregate demand for a public good is equal to the vertical summation of all individuals' demand curves. This aggregate demand measures the total marginal benefit to society for each unit consumed.*

But what is the optimal amount of the public good to be provided?

Let's suppose that society decides to provide the good in such amounts that its price equals the marginal social cost of each unit supplied. **Marginal social cost** (*MSC*) is the extra cost per unit to society for each extra unit produced, and social cost is measured as an opportunity cost of the next-best forgone alternative. This interpretation implies that the supply curve will coincide with the marginal social-cost curve. Marginal social cost will, of course, increase with increases in the quantity supplied. It increases because of diminishing returns and increasing opportunity cost. The optimal quantity of the good is determined where aggregate demand intersects the supply curve. Why? Because at that level of output the total marginal benefit is equal to the total marginal social cost. When total marginal benefit exceeds the marginal social cost, net benefit to society will increase by producing more. And as soon as marginal social cost exceeds the total marginal benefit, the net benefit to society will decrease with an extra quantity of the good. In summary,

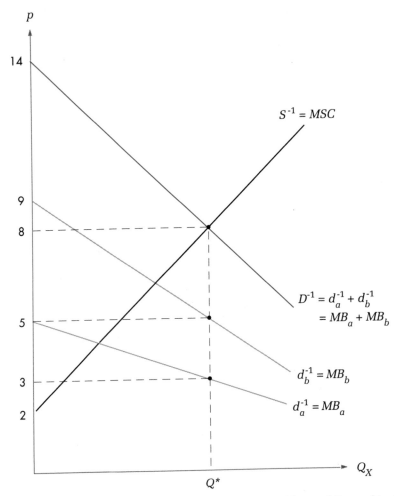

Figure 6.13 **Optimal amount of a public good:** The aggregate demand for a public good is obtained by vertical summation of the individual demand curves because each unit is consumed by each consumer at the same time. The optimal amount of the good occurs where the sum of the marginal benefits to all consumers is equal to the marginal social cost.

more of the public good should be provided until the aggregation of individual marginal benefits equals marginal social cost.

For two reasons, the optimal amount of a public good will not be provided by the private sector. First is the free-rider problem. Each person perceives that the good will be provided even if he or she does not contribute to its payment. Second, each person is motivated to disguise his or her preferences for the good. If an individual's preferences are not revealed, no one will be able to measure the price the individual would be willing to pay, and the individual's demand curve will not be measurable. Therefore, the price to charge each person cannot be found, and the price system fails to provide signals to demanders and suppliers so that the social optimum can be reached.

GLOBAL PERSPECTIVE: *The SST Concorde*

In 1977, the United States declined to jointly develop a supersonic transport (SST) with the British and French governments. This decision was based on cost-benefit analysis. The British and French went ahead on the project, spending about $4 billion in developing the Concorde. Only twenty planes were built, and only eleven are used to fly between Europe and the United States. The Concorde never proved to be commercially viable because of inefficient use of fuel and limited range.

Not until 1984 did the operation of the Concorde generate a profit. Even by the end of the decade, current revenues were just slightly above operating costs. The one-way price to fly between the United States and Europe on the Concorde is about $5,000, about five times as much as is charged to fly on the Boeing 747. The SST saves three hours compared to a 747; to make it worthwhile, a passenger's opportunity cost would have to exceed $1,333 per hour. It appears that the British and French greatly overstated the benefits and understated the costs of the project because the $4-billion investment will never, it seems, be recovered. Of course, the technological advances derived from the project may pay social dividends in the future.

In May 1990, Aerospatiale and British Aerospace said they would study plans for a new SST to succeed the Concorde. The "son of Concorde" would carry twice as many passengers and have double the range. Through advances in engine technology, the super-Concorde would be more fuel efficient than the current SST, and therefore commercially viable. Marketing studies indicate that there would be a market for 300 to 500 of the super-Concorde between 2005 and 2025.

The main technical hurdles to the new SST are environmental problems—noise and air pollution.* The Concorde is ten times noisier than conventional airliners. The sonic boom from such a large plane shakes the earth like a small earthquake. And the pollution from its engines may release more hydrofluorocarbons than all the aerosols used around the world, further damaging the ozone layer.

Concorde's replacement could cost more than $20 billion in development alone, which is why aerospace companies believe it can work only as an international collaboration. The new SST would carry more passengers, about 250 compared to 100 on the Concorde. Its range would be greater, and it would be able to fly from Los Angeles to Tokyo in about 4½ hours, compared to 10 hours on a conventional airliner.

*As reported in *The Economist,* February 9, 1991.

If the price system fails in providing public goods, and if the market demand curve cannot be measured, how can society determine how much of a good to supply? How should society decide whether or not to undertake a public project such as flood control or police protection? The technique used is called **cost-benefit analysis.**

> **Cost-benefit analysis:** *Cost-benefit analysis is the public-sector counterpart to private-sector investment decisions.*

As with capital budgeting in the private sector, the benefits and costs of a public project must be evaluated on a marginal basis. As long as the marginal benefit exceeds the marginal cost of a public good, more of the good should be provided.

Cost-benefit analysis consists of five steps:

- Identify the project or projects.
- Determine all effects, favorable and unfavorable, direct or indirect, present and future.
- Assign monetary values to the stream of direct and indirect benefits and costs.
- Decide on an appropriate discount rate to use in calculating the net present value of the project.
- Choose projects that have positive net present values, and, between competing alternatives, choose the project that produces the greatest net benefit.

These steps are straightforward in principle, but their implementation can be difficult in practice. For one reason, the list of effects may be extensive, especially when confronted with an uncertain future. For another, it can be difficult to assign monetary values to benefits and costs. The goods and services flowing from a public project are not priced in private markets, and so it is difficult to assign a value to them. Moreover, many of the benefits and costs may be indirect. How, for instance, would you assign a dollar value to the runoff of water through a canyon to the ocean caused by the construction of a public park? How do you assign a dollar value to the increased risk to children at a nearby school caused by the increased traffic during and after construction of the park? Still another problem arises in choosing the appropriate discount rate.

The **social discount rate,** or public cost of capital, is the discount rate used to calculate the net present value of a public project. Many economists advocate applying a discount rate that reflects the opportunity cost of using the funds in the private sector.[7] A good estimate would be the rate of return on government securities. Or the pretax rate of return on private investments could be used as the opportunity cost of funds. The pretax rate is used because business taxes represent income redistributed from the private to the public sector. In practice, the social-discount rate used in evaluating public projects varies from application to application, but most often it is below the true opportunity cost of capital in the private sector. Using a discount rate that is too low leads to acceptance of projects that might not otherwise be justified. Too low a discount rate also leads to a bias in favor of long-lived projects.

If any public project makes someone better off without making anyone else worse off, then the project is Pareto optimal. Most projects, however, are opposed by someone. Very few public projects, therefore, would pass a Pareto-optimality criterion. An alternative test, the **Kaldor-Hicks criterion,** says that as long as gainers could compensate losers, a public project should be undertaken. Compensation need not actually be made. But as long as gainers could compensate losers, benefits will exceed costs and the project will generate a net social benefit.

---

7. See William J. Baumol, "On the Social Rate of Discount," *American Economic Review* (February 1977), pp. 788–802.

AN APPLICATION: *Polio Research*

Cost-benefit analysis was used to estimate the internal rate of return from polio research.* The internal rate of return can be compared to an appropriate social-discount rate to see if the project was worthwhile. The net present value of this project was calculated as

$$NPV = \sum_{t=1}^{T} \frac{B_t\,(N_t - W_t) - V_t - C_t}{(1 + i)^t}$$

where

B_t = benefit per case of disease prevention
N_t = number of cases occurring in the absence of research
W_t = number of cases occurring in the presence of research
V_t = cost of applying the results of the research program
C_t = direct research costs

In the formula, T is the time horizon beyond which benefits and costs are nearly zero because of discounting. After assigning monetary values to the costs and benefits, and estimating the number of cases with and without research, the internal rate of return can be calculated by setting the *NPV* equal to zero.

Weisbrod concluded that the internal rate of return was positive and about 12 percent. This rate of return, however, probably underestimated the true rate of return, because the calculation did not include an estimate for the cost of pain and suffering, or the value to individuals of reduced illness or longevity.

*Burton A. Weisbrod, "Cost and Benefits of Medical Research: A Case Study of Poliomyelitis," *Journal of Political Economy* (May–June 1971), pp. 527–544.

Summary

The present value of any future amount of money is the amount that must be invested to generate the future amount. The savings decision can be analyzed with a two-period model of consumer choice. Each consumer has preferences over alternative combinations of present and future consumption. A consumer can increase present consumption by borrowing, or increase future consumption by saving.

In the two-period model, the budget line must pass through the consumer's endowment point. The slope of the budget line is $-(1 + i)$, where i is the interest rate, and the slope measures the possible rate of exchange in consumption between periods. The marginal rate of substitution measures the consumer's willingness to sacrifice future consumption to increase present consumption. Utility maximization requires that $MRS = (1 + i)$.

The supply of savings is a function of the interest rate. Examining substitution and income effects of a change in the interest rate reveals that borrowing falls as the interest rate rises. As the interest rate rises, a borrower may become a saver. Saving continues to rise with increases in the interest rate as long as the substitution effect dominates the income effect. Saving may decrease as the interest rate rises, however, if the income effect dominates the substitution effect. Thus, the intertemporal choice model permits a backward-bending supply-of-savings curve.

Assuming that borrowing or lending can occur, present value is the only correct way to convert a flow of dollars into current dollars. Under certainty, an alternative that has the greatest present value always adds more to wealth than alternatives with smaller present values, so that you should always choose the alternative with the greatest present value. Present value depends crucially on the discounting interest rate. The appropriate discounting interest rate is the inflation-adjusted interest rate for investments of similar risk.

An asset is a good that provides a flow of services over time. An annuity is a financial asset consisting of a series of payments over time. A perpetuity is an annuity that lasts forever. The present value of an annuity is the sum of its discounted time payments. For a perpetuity having constant periodic returns, the present value is equal to the periodic return divided by the discount rate. This calculation also provides an easy way to approximate the present value of a long-term annuity having a reasonable interest rate.

All assets yield the same rate of return under conditions of certainty because of arbitrage. Moreover, given a perfect lending market, choices are not influenced by preferences about the timing of consumption, and individuals choose among assets by comparing present values using the market rate of interest.

The internal rate of return, or marginal efficiency of investment, is the discount rate that equates the present value of the net returns to the cost of the investment. Net present value is present value less the initial cost of the investment. Thus the internal rate of return can be found where *NPV* equals zero. As an investment rule, all feasible investments that have positive *NPV* should be undertaken. Investment alternatives should be ranked according to their net present values, and this principle is always a correct capital-budgeting strategy.

The investment-demand curve summarizes the relationship between physical assets in the economy and the interest rate. Here, investment includes creation of new structures and equipment and changes in inventories. Usually, more investment alternatives are undertaken at lower interest rates because the *NPV*s of more alternatives become positive.

When new capital is the only physical asset, the interest rate is determined in the market for new capital. The supply-of-savings curve can be interpreted as the supply of loanable funds or the demand for new capital. The demand-for-investment curve can be interpreted as the supply of capital value. The quantity of new capital can be found once the interest rate is known because quantity supplied, multiplied by the price of capital, is equal to capital value. The investment-demand curve has negative slope because both quantity and present value are inversely related to the interest rate.

Cost-benefit analysis of public projects is the public counterpart to private capital budgeting. A public project should be undertaken whenever the present value of future benefits exceeds the present value of social costs. The provision of public goods is complicated by the fact that demand for a public good is the vertical summation of individual demands, the free-rider problem, and individuals' motive for not revealing their preferences. The failure of the market to provide public goods motivates society's use of cost-benefit analysis in choosing public projects.

Further Readings

The classical reference work on interest rates is

- Irving Fisher, *The Theory of Interest* (Macmillan, 1930).

Fisher was the first to recognize that the same good at different dates could be treated as two different goods. For a recent article on arbitrage in economics, see

- Hal R. Varian, "The Arbitrage Principle in Economics," *Journal of Economic Perspectives* (Fall 1987).

For a survey of the complications that arise in attempting to measure the cost of capital and determining the proper discount rate in investment decisions, see

- William J. Baumol, *Economic Theory and Operations Analysis,* 3d ed. (Prentice-Hall, 1972).
- Jack Hirshleifer, "On the Theory of Optimal Investment Decisions," *Journal of Political Economy* (August 1958).

For surveys of capital budgeting practices, see:

- J. C. T. Mao, "Survey of Capital Budgeting: Theory and Practice," *Journal of Finance* (May 1970).
- J. M. Fremgen, "Capital Budgeting Practices: A Survey," *Management Accounting* (May 1973).
- L. J. Gitman and J. R. Forrester, "A Survey of Capital Budgeting Techniques Used by Major U.S. Firms," *Financial Management* (Fall 1977).
- Suk H. Kim and Edward J. Farragher, "Current Capital Budgeting Practices," *Management Accounting* (June 1981).

For a general survey of investment behavior, see

- D. W. Jorgenson, "Econometric Studies of Investment Behavior: A Survey," *Journal of Economic Literature* 9 (December 1971).

For more extensive coverage of cost-benefit analysis, see:

- Ezra J. Mishan, *Cost-Benefit Analysis: An Introduction* (Praeger, 1977).
- A. R. Prest and R. Turvey, "Cost-Benefit Analysis: A Survey," *Economic Journal* (December 1965), pp. 683–735.

Practice Problems

1. Suppose an airlines company has been sued for negligence in a crash killing all passengers aboard a plane. In addition to damages for negligence and court costs, the plaintiffs are asking for a settlement equal to the total earnings over the expected lifetimes of all passengers. As the defendant, how might the airlines company respond?

2. What is the present value of $100 received one year from now if the interest rate is 10 percent? What is the present value if the interest rate is 5 percent?

3. A consumer expects that future income will increase by $2,100. The market rate of interest is 5 percent. If this consumer increases present consumption by $1,100, how much will future consumption increase?

4. In a study of intertemporal food purchases, would it make sense to assume that the goods are perfect substitutes?

5. As the interest rate rises, does the intertemporal budget constraint become steeper or flatter? Why?

6. In the two-period choice model, what happens to the budget line if the rate of interest for borrowing is greater than the interest rate on saving? Illustrate this attainable set on a graph.

7. If a consumer who is initially a lender remains a lender after a decline in the interest rate, is the consumer better off or worse off after the change in the interest rate? Why?

8. If a consumer who is initially a lender becomes a borrower after a decline in the interest rate, is the consumer better off or worse off after the change in the interest rate? Why?

9. In the two-period model of intertemporal choice, suppose a consumer's preferences become more impatient:
   (a) How does this change affect the slope of the indifference curves?
   (b) If other things remain the same, how does the change in preference affect the $S(i)$ curve?

10. Suppose asset A can be sold for $11 next period. If similar assets are paying a rate of return of 10 percent, what is the price of asset A? Why?

11. A durable consumer good such as a house or automobile can be treated like an asset that yields a stream of services as time passes:
   (a) What are the appropriate values to assign to the periodic services of a durable good?
   (b) What investment rule should be applied by consumers in deciding to purchase a durable good?

12. Determine the yearly payment for an $80,000 loan amortized over 30 years at 10 percent interest. Now treat the payment as a return to a perpetuity when the discounting interest rate is 10 percent to approximate the present value of the payment as a periodic return. How close is the approximation?

13. Given two mutually exclusive investments:

	Investment Cost	Perpetual Return
Investment A:	$3,800	$1,000
Investment B:	$7,000	$1,400

   (a) Which alternative will be chosen if the discounting interest rate is 10 percent?
   (b) Which alternative will be chosen if the discounting interest rate is 15 percent?

14. What will happen to the savings supply curve if all prices—the prices for goods and for inputs—change by the same proportion? What then do you think will happen to the market rate of interest?

15. Suppose the quantity supplied of a good X is given by $Q_s = p$. Suppose further that only two individuals have these demands, respectively, for good X:

$$X_1 = 8 - 2p$$
$$X_2 = 12 - p$$

   (a) If Q_d denotes the aggregate quantity demanded, and if the good is a public good, what is the aggregate demand curve?
   (b) What is the optimal level of production of this public good?
   (c) What prices will each consumer be willing to pay for the optimal quantity?
   (d) Answer each of the preceding questions if the good were a private good.

16. Several studies have reported very low private and social rates of return from graduate education in many disciplines, including economics. Nevertheless, more and more universities are offering advanced degrees. How do you think the rates of return from education are calculated? How can you explain the seemingly inefficient allocation of resources?

Chapter

Information, Risk, and Uncertainty

Risk occurs when an alternative carries more than one possible outcome and the probabilities of the outcomes are known. Uncertainty occurs when the outcomes cannot be described or when probabilities cannot be assigned. How should you judge alternatives amid inevitable risk and uncertainty? Some uncertainty arises because we lack knowledge and information about processes governing events, perhaps the primary reason managers should study the economic environment. But even perfect knowledge does not imply perfect foresight, and so risk is there because some events are randomly determined.

Institutions and markets have evolved in response to risk and uncertainty and the need for information. Public universities conduct research and communicate information that might not otherwise be produced because knowledge, once produced, becomes public property. Futures markets help reduce risk for some people by transferring it to others for a price. Insurance is sometimes available to pool the risk associated with events which are *uncertain* for the individual that are merely *risky* for a group of individuals. Investors learn to diversify their portfolios in order to hedge against possible poor performance by any one investment.

Our primary objective in this chapter is to gain an understanding of how people make decisions when the outcomes of choices are risky or uncertain. Some of the models we use are abstract. Moreover, though implementing some of these models is theoretically possible, it may be impractical. Thus, a secondary objective in this chapter is to examine some *practical* decision rules that capture the essence of the theoretical models. You will learn some valuable tools of analysis as you learn more about how markets work.

7.1   Asymmetric Information

For most of the decision models discussed so far, we have assumed that buyers and sellers have equivalent information about relevant decision variables. Often, however, some parties know more than others—we have **asymmetric information:**

> **Asymmetric information:** *Information is asymmetric when some parties know more than others about economic decision variables that are relevant.*

Information is asymmetric when the seller knows more than buyers do about the quality of a product, when one firm knows more than rivals do about its market conditions, and when managers know more than owners do about their firms.

Pure competition is predicated on the assumption that information is perfect. All buyers and sellers have equal access to information and equal knowledge about all decision variables. Asymmetric information, therefore, is a source of market imperfection and can lead to economic inefficiency.

One possible consequence of asymmetric information is that people's decisions will be different than under complete information. Traders' choices will be altered, the market

AN APPLICATION: *The Market for "Lemons"*

The influence of asymmetric information on product quality was first analyzed by George Akerlof in a classic paper.* Akerlof looked at the market for used cars, but he recognized that sellers know much more about the quality of used cars than buyers do. As a consequence, information about quality is asymmetric, and this imbalance influences the market outcome.

Figure 7.1 illustrates the problem of having two types of used cars: those of high quality and low quality. Initially, let's suppose that both sellers and buyers have complete information—they both know the quality of a specific used car. The price of a high-quality used car is $8,000, where demand D_H intersects supply S_H. The price of a low-quality used car is $4,000, where demand D_L intersects supply S_L.

What happens if the seller knows the quality, but the buyer discovers that quality only after the car is bought? The effective demand for high-quality cars will decrease because, on average, a buyer may buy a car that is a "lemon." At the same time, the effective demand for low-quality cars will increase because, on average, a buyer may get a "cherry." The total demand for used cars has shifted to demand for a car of average quality. As a result, fewer high-quality cars and more low-quality cars are sold. This preponderance increases the proportion of low-quality cars on the market. Because buyers can't tell the quality before purchase, they lower their expectations about quality, and total demand will decrease. This time both of the demand curves will shift to the left, increasing the proportion of low-quality cars even more. The shifts may even continue until only low-quality used cars are sold. The fraction of high-quality cars sold is less, certainly, than it would be if consumers had complete information before purchasing a car. The asymmetric information has caused a market distortion.

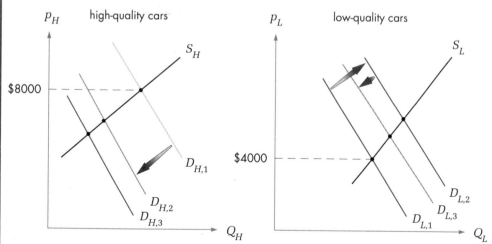

Figure 7.1 **Markets for used cars:** With complete information, the price of a high-quality used car is $8,000 and the price of a low-quality used car is $4,000. With aysmmetric information, the demand for used cars falls, and the proportion of "lemons" for sale increases.

*George A. Akerlof, "The Market for 'Lemons': Quality, Uncertainty, and the Market Mechanism," *Quarterly Journal of Economics* (August 1970) pp. 488–500.

outcome will be different, and the trading process and outcome are less efficient than otherwise. Asymmetric information may cause **adverse selection:**

> **Adverse selection:** *The procedure by which "less-desirable" traders (buyers or sellers) are more likely to participate in voluntary exchange.*

Credit-card companies must charge all borrowers the same interest rate, which attracts low-quality borrowers, and their presence forces interest rates up. Credit-card companies try, at least partially, to discriminate between low-quality and high-quality borrowers by denying credit to applicants with undesirable credit histories, but that strategy doesn't entirely eliminate adverse selection.

7.2   The Principal-Agent Problem

An *agency relationship* is established whenever you hire someone to perform a task that affects your welfare. The person who does the hiring is called the *principal,* and the other person is called the *agent.* Consider the cartoon by Brad Anderson in which Marmaduke is charged with being the agent. Lawyers act as agents for clients. Doctors act as agents for patients. Business managers act as agents for business owners.

In most corporations, owners can't monitor the performance of their managers because information is neither complete nor costless. This limitation gives rise to an asymmetric information problem—managers know more than the owners about the firm's

"Guard the cookies for a minute, will you, Marmaduke?"

© 1990 United Feature Syndicate, Inc.

Reprinted by permission of UFS, Inc.

performance and business conditions. The asymmetric-information problem is especially acute in the modern corporation for small stockholders investing in large firms.

Separating ownership from control, coupled with asymmetric information, makes it difficult for owners to monitor the managers' behavior. Managers can then pursue their own goals, which may not be consistent with the wealth-maximizing goal of owners. Although a manager's ability to deviate from the goals of owners has some limitations, separating ownership from control can lead to inefficient use of resources. One solution to the principal-agent problem is to design an incentive system that rewards agents for achieving the goals that principals set. Such incentives as profit sharing or stock options are likely to induce behavior by the agent that is consistent with the principal's goals. Another solution is suggested by the *Marmaduke* cartoon—place an effective constraint on the principal's behavior.

The principal-agent problem also arises in public enterprise and government. A politician may be more interested in keeping his or her constituency happy than in maximizing overall social welfare. In some ways, controlling public officials' behavior is harder because market forces that keep private managers in line are lacking.

7.3 Uncertainty and Risk

Certainty occurs when a decision maker knows in advance the outcome of any alternative. Everyone knows, however, that uncertainty arises for many reasons. Some economic events are governed by the randomness of nature, such as the weather. Other economic events are governed by nations' political decisions, which can be very unpredictable. Civil disorder or war in one part of the world may affect the prices of energy, precious metals, and rare art elsewhere and may affect the balance of payments among nations. An accident in a nuclear power-generating plant may affect the production of dairy products and timber products in adjacent geographic regions. Business rivals and trading nations sometimes make punitive, unpredictable, and seemingly irrational decisions.

Some uncertainty persists because information about the processes governing events is limited. Even with perfect information, some events would be randomly determined, and so decisions whose outcomes depend on those events remain risky. Knowing the probabilities of outcomes of events may help assess the risks associated with making choices. Such information is often costly, and uncertainty may persist when no one is willing to pay the price to obtain the information. Information is one way, though, to reduce uncertainty or to convert uncertain events into risky alternatives. Thus, institutions and practices have evolved in response to uncertainty.

In this book I distinguish between decisions made under *risk* or under *uncertainty*. Frank Knight (1921) proposed this classification, illustrated by Figure 7.2. **Certainty** is a situation without speculation and guesses. Certainty implies no room for probability. **Noncertainty** is an absence of certainty, so noncertainty exists when the outcome of or occurrence of an event is in doubt. Decisions under noncertainty can be divided into cases of uncertainty and cases involving risk. In cases of **decisions under uncertainty,** no probabilities can be assigned to the events. The Knightian view of uncertainty has two branches: (1) the possible events of an action are unknown; (2) the probabilities of events

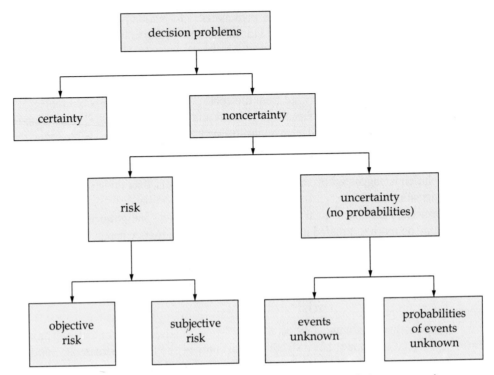

Figure 7.2 **Classifying decision problems:** Certainty is the condition in which the outcome of any decision is known. Noncertainty occurs when the outcome is in doubt. Uncertainty describes cases in which the probabilities of outcomes cannot be assigned. Risk describes cases in which either objective or subjective probabilities of the outcomes are known or can be assigned.

are unknown. In cases of **decisions under risk,** the probabilities of the events are known. Decision making under risk also has two branches: (1) the probabilities of events can be assigned objectively; (2) the probabilities of events must be assigned subjectively.

Knight's classification scheme is not universally accepted. Some statisticians known as Bayesians argue that probabilities can always be assigned subjectively. If probabilities can always be assigned, the distinction between noncertainty and uncertainty is muted. Another departure from Knight's classification scheme relates to the term *risk*. Risk is sometimes used to describe an attitude toward the willingness to accept or avoid gambles. When we use the word in that context, we will refer to *risk aversion*.

7.4 How to Assign Probabilities to Risky Alternatives

The label *risk* is used to describe an alternative in which the payoff is not known with perfect certainty, but for which an array of possible payoffs and their probabilities are known. That is, the payoffs follow a probability distribution. When historical experience about the frequencies of the payoffs of an alternative are known, those frequencies can be used to assign probabilities to the outcomes. Likewise, when technological or logical information about the likelihood of the payoffs can be had, objective probabilities can also be assigned. On some occasions, however, we have little experience or other information to draw upon. Decisions must then be based on subjective probabilities assigned according to personal or expert opinion about the likelihood of the payoffs.

Despite general agreement on the properties of probabilities, no general agreement has been reached on a definition for probability. Some see probability as a property of empirical phenomena—probabilities are assigned by the frequencies of events. A coin tossed many times comes up heads half the time. Others see probability as an extension of logic—equally likely events are assigned equal probabilities. The coin has only two sides, and we have no reason to expect bias. Still others see probability as a measure of the confidence a person has that an event will occur—the odds that will be acceptable in a bet that the event will occur. Even odds will be assigned to the coin toss.

The **objectivist view** interprets probability as the relative frequency of an event in an infinite sequence of replications of an experiment. For the coin toss, the frequency interpretation of the probability of heads as 1/2 follows from an experiment in which a coin is tossed many times and we observe that the event heads occurs one-half the time. It matters not that you might never actually perform the experiment because you know what would happen if you ever did.

The **subjectivist (Bayesian) view** says that hunches about likely states of nature can be transformed into numerical values that follow the laws of probability. Subjective probabilities can be assigned to a real-world gamble by confronting the decision maker with a choice between the real-world gamble and a hypothetical gamble, having equal payoffs. Suppose the best payoff of a gamble is b dollars and the worst payoff is w dollars. The individual can then be confronted with a hypothetical gamble having the same payoffs. The probabilities of the payoffs can be varied until the individual is indifferent between the gambles, and these probabilities can then be assigned to the payoffs of the real-world gamble.

Suppose the real-world gamble has payoffs b = $60 and w = $30. We wish to determine the probability of the best payoff, Prob(b) = P, and the probability of the worst payoff, Prob(w) = $(1 - P)$. Now consider this hypothetical gamble or "game." An urn contains n black balls and $(100 - n)$ white balls—black for best and white for worst. One ball is picked at random. A black pays off $60 when picked, and a white pays off $30 when picked. Next, suppose we set n = 80 and the individual chooses the game over the real-world alternative. Thus the individual must believe that P is *less than* 0.80. Now, suppose we reduce the odds of winning to, say, n = 50. If the individual now chooses the real-world alternative over the game, the decision maker must believe that P is *greater than* 0.50. The probability P must lie between 0.50 and 0.80. Let's try n = 75. Then, for n = 75, if the person is indifferent between the game and the real-world alternative, the subjective probabilities for this person are P = 0.75 and $1 - P$ = 0.25.

This method of assigning subjective probabilities illustrates that, if events and outcomes can be described, subjective probabilities can always be found. The technique is presented, however, as a hypothetical example of how subjective probabilities could be found. The technique is not intended as an everyday, practical device. Rather, it is a theoretical argument that subjective probabilities exist and could be assigned to any set of events—even when the decision maker says, "Gee, I really don't know the odds." Assignments of probabilities provide a basis for describing potential choices among actions that yield risky payoffs. The example shows that probabilities can be assigned without experimental information. This finding is fortunate, because business decisions do not always include repetition of events, and so we may have too little information to set probabilities according to objective standards.

7.5 Expected Utility and Risk Aversion

In the real world, consumption possibilities are contingent upon specific events' occurring. It is convenient to think of random events as **states of nature.** If your house happened to burn down, your consumption possibilities would be different than if your house didn't burn down. If you win a lottery, your consumption possibilities change. Your consumption possibilities also depend on your employment, and the probability that you may become too ill or disabled to work is positive. The expected return on an investment may depend on whether or not a downturn hits the business and economic environment. These different states of nature have positive probabilities of occurring.

A **contingent consumption plan** specifies what would be consumed under each state of nature. An investment manager may specify such a plan. People have preferences between different contingent plans, just as they have preferences between actual consumption and investment alternatives. If we have preferences about contingencies, we can apply a utility function to describe those preferences. Because the outcome depends on the probabilities that events will occur, utility is a function of those probabilities, and decisions will depend on the utility that is *expected* to occur.

Expected utility means a utility index constructed within the context of random events:

> **Expected utility:** *The expected utility of a chance at random payoffs is the sum of the utilities of the payoffs weighted by their probabilities.*

The expected utility of an action A that has n payoffs a_j that occur with probabilities P_j is

$$E[U(A)] = \sum_{j=1}^{n} U(a_j) P_j$$

where $\Sigma P_j = 1$. The payoffs must be mutually exclusive and exhaustive: either your house burns down or it doesn't. The construction of the expected utility index is illustrated by a type of gamble called a lottery.

A **lottery** is a gamble undertaken by buying a ticket. Consider a lottery ticket, denoted by T, which has two payoffs.[1] The best payoff is b and has probability P, and the worst payoff is w and has probability $(1 - P)$. The *expected value* of this lottery ticket is

$$E(T) = bP + w(1 - P)$$

The *expected utility* of this lottery is

$$E[U(T)] = U(b)P + U(w)(1 - P)$$

where the utilities of the two payoffs are $U(b)$ and $U(w)$. The expected utility of the chance at having one or the other of the two payoffs is the sum of their separate utilities weighted by their probabilities. If calculating the expected utility depends on the utilities of the payoffs, how can $U(b)$ and $U(w)$ be measured?

Because utility assignments are ordinal, you can choose any values for $U(b)$ and $U(w)$ as long as $U(b) > U(w)$ because the best payoff b is preferred to the worst payoff w. Conventional utility assignments are $U(b) = 1$ and $U(w) = 0$. Once this initial assignment is made, the expected utility of the chance at the best or worst outcome is determined by the expected-utility formula.

Once the initial utility assignments have been made, they can be used to measure the utility of any intermediate outcome obtained with certainty. Suppose an individual is confronted with an alternative C that has a certain payoff c, which lies between b and w. The payoff c is received with certainty. The utility of the certain alternative C can be found by finding the probability at which the individual is indifferent between C and the lottery T. For high probabilities, the lottery T will be preferred to C because if $P = 1$ the lottery yields a payoff of b that is greater than the payoff c. For low probabilities, the alternative C will be preferred to the lottery because if $P = 0$ the lottery yields a payoff of w that is less than the payoff c. Thus, at some probability P_c the individual is indifferent between the lottery and the certain alternative.

When the individual is indifferent between the lottery T and the alternative C at $P = P_c$, the *expected utility* of the lottery must be equal to the *utility* of the payoff c from the alternative,

$$U(b)P_c + U(w)(1 - P_c) = U(c)$$

---

1. That the lottery has only two payoffs is not restrictive because multiple payoffs can be combined into a compound lottery. That is, payoffs of x, y, and z, each having probability of 1/3, can be represented by a compound lottery having expected value

$$\left[x\left(\frac{1}{2}\right) + y\left(\frac{1}{2}\right) \right]\left(\frac{2}{3}\right) + z\left(\frac{1}{3}\right)$$

This expected value is equivalent to that of the original lottery.

When the conventional assignments $U(b) = 1$ and $U(w) = 0$ are made, substitution into the equality above indicates that the utility of C is $U(c) = P_c$. Thus, a numerical utility index can be assigned to C by asking the individual to identify the probability that results in indifference between the lottery and the alternative certain payoff.

A numerical example will help reinforce these ideas. Suppose an individual is faced with a chance at $30 or $60. One or the other outcome will occur, but not both. As an alternative, $45 can be obtained with certainty. How can the utility of $45 be measured? The certain payoff is $c = 45$, and the best and worst payoffs of the lottery are $b = 60$ and $w = 30$. We know that at some probability P_c the expected utility of the lottery is equal to the utility of the certain alternative,

$$U(60) \, P_c \, + \, U(30)(1 - P_c) \, = \, U(45)$$

Using the conventional assignments $U(60) = 1$ and $U(30) = 0$, substitution into the equality above indicates that $U(45) = P_c$. Now all you have to do is find P_c.

How do you find P_c? That is easy: just use the method for assigning subjective probabilities outlined in the preceding section. Vary the probability of obtaining the best payoff until the individual is indifferent between the lottery and $45. Suppose that, after several trials, the value $P_c = 3/4$ is identified. Thus the utility of $45 is $U(45) = 3/4$ when $U(60) = 1$ and $U(30) = 0$.

The method for measuring the utility of alternative C having certain payoff c is illustrated by Figure 7.3. The money payoffs are measured along the horizontal axis, and the utility assignments are measured along the vertical axis. The best and worst payoffs for the lottery T are represented by points B and W and are assigned conventional utilities $U(b) = 1$ and $U(w) = 0$. As the probability of winning the best payoff increases, point T moves upward along the straight line between points W and B. Point T is fixed at the point where indifference occurs between T and C. That indifference occurred when $P = 3/4$, so that probability was assigned as the *expected* utility of the lottery, $E[U(T)] = 3/4$. Because P was chosen so that indifference occurred between T and A, the utility of $c = 45$ is fixed at $U(45) = 3/4$ also. Therefore the *money value* of the gamble is equal to $45 and is *less than* the *expected value* $E(T)$ of the gamble. In other words, the expected value of the gamble $E(T)$ must be *greater* than the certainty equivalent c in order to compensate for the risk associated with the gamble. The expected value of T is $E(T) = 52.5$. The amount of money $c = 45$ is called the **certainty equivalent** to the gamble because they have the same expected utility, $U(c) = E[U(T)]$.

In Figure 7.3, the curved line represents the utility of money $U(M)$. We determined one point on this curve when $M = c$ by finding $U(c)$. Other points along $U(M)$ can be determined by changing the payoff of C and then finding the probability where indifference occurs. Therefore, curve $U(M)$ represents the **measured utility of money.** Notice that the money value of the lottery, its certainty equivalent, is less than the expected value of the lottery. The resulting curvature of the utility of money curve $U(M)$ indicates diminishing marginal utility of money or *aversion to risk.*

In the context of decision making under uncertainty, the diminishing marginal utility of money (or wealth) means nothing more or less than risk aversion:

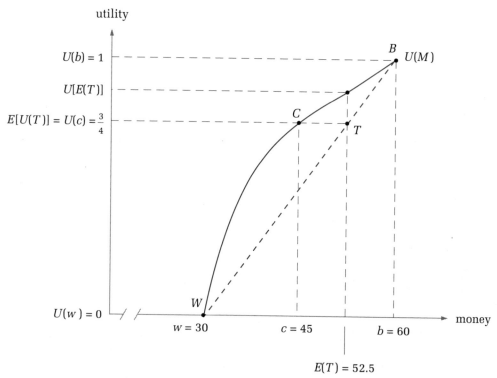

Figure 7.3 **Measurable utility under uncertainty:** When confronted with a chance at a lottery T with payoff $w = 30$ and $b = 60$ under uncertainty, and an alternative C with certain payoff $c = 45$, we find some probability of obtaining the best payoff b, where the individual is indifferent between T and A. If that probability is $P_c = 3/4$, where $E[U(T)] = U(c)$, then $U(c) = 3/4$ if $U(w) = 0$ and $U(b) = 1$. The certain payoff c is called the certainty equivalent to the gamble T because they have the same expected utility.

> **Risk aversion:** *When the certainty equivalent of a gamble is less than the gamble's expected value, diminishing marginal utility of money is implied, and the person is risk averse.*

As you can see in Figure 7.3, diminishing marginal utility of money implies that $U[E(T)] > E[U(T)]$. Risk aversion does *not* mean that all gambles will be avoided. The probability of winning the best payoff may be high enough or the amount of the best payoff great enough that the expected utility of the gamble is greater than its price.

Of course, not everyone is risk averse. A person is called a **risk lover** when the certainty equivalent of a gamble is greater than the gamble's expected value. The gamble is preferred to the expected value of the gamble. A risk lover's preferences result in *increasing* marginal utility of money. A third possibility occurs when the utility-of-money

ECONOMIC SCENE: *Why Play Lotto?*

State lotteries have become an important source of public revenue, yielding $108 per capita in 1989. Sixty percent of adults in lottery states play at least once a year.*

Setting aside its value as recreation, as an amusing pastime, why do people play when the expected value of prizes typically is only half the ticket price? The negative net expected value makes a lottery ticket a bad sort of risky financial asset. The net expected value of a ticket may actually become positive when jackpots accumulate over a series of drawings when no one wins, and that helps to explain why large jackpots draw many players who would not otherwise buy tickets. But lotteries have rather broad appeal even when jackpots are not exceptionally large.

The challenge is to understand why the risky prospects of lottery games appeal to people who exhibit risk-averse behavior in other circumstances. It has been shown that most people, when given a choice between a 50 percent chance of receiving $1,000 and a sure thing of $400, prefer the latter.†

Milton Friedman and L. J. Savage suggest that people may perceive a disproportionate benefit in a prize that is large enough to elevate their social standing, and so they are willing to pay a premium for that chance.‡ This appeal helps explain why lottery games with relatively modest prizes appeal primarily to low-income players, but games with larger jackpots begin to attract higher-income players.

Another explanation for rational, risk-averse people's accepting the unfair bets at long odds in the typical lottery says that players do not have good intuitions about their chances. In this view, the typical lottery consumer is a rational but poorly informed decision maker. Someone who spends $20 a week on a 6/49 lotto over his or her lifetime would have less than a 1 in 200 chance of winning any jackpot. Perhaps this handicap explains the eventual decline in the number of players as they gain experience in losing.

---

*See Charles T. Clotfelter and Philip J. Cook, "On the Economics of State Lotteries," *Journal of Economic Perspectives,* 4(4) (Fall 1990), pp. 105–119.

†Daniel Kahneman and Amos Tversky, "Prospect Theory: An Analysis of Decision Under Risk," *Econometrica,* 47 (March 1979), pp. 263–291.

‡M. Friedman and L. J. Savage, "The Utility Analysis of Choice Involving Risk," *Journal of Political Economy,* 56 (August 1948), pp. 279–304.

curve is linear: the person is **risk neutral.** A risk-neutral person doesn't care about the riskiness of the gamble—but does care about its expected value.

Introducing utility into the analysis of decision making under uncertainty leads to the conclusion that it is *not* the actual payoffs that matter. Rather, it is the *subjective* values of the payoffs that we should consider. Therefore, in choosing among actions under uncertainty and in making contingent plans, the decision maker should choose the action having the greatest expected utility rather than the action having the greatest expected value.

Directly applying utility maximization as a decision rule is impractical in most real-world situations in which you may be asked to justify your choice to others. Can you see your boss or the board of directors react to your explanation that you chose an action because it gave *you* the greatest subjective utility? Therefore, we will next examine operational decision rules that, although they reflect the insights gained from utility analysis, are not set out explicitly in terms of utilities.

7.6 Using Expected Values

Sometimes it is sufficient to choose the alternative that has the greatest expected value. If you are risk neutral and don't care about risk, then you will maximize utility by choosing the action (strategy, or alternative) that has the greatest expected value. If you are risk averse, you will maximize utility by choosing the action that has the greatest expected value from among actions with equal risk, and you will maximize utility by choosing the action that has the smallest risk from among actions with equal expected utility.

These rules can be simplified when making decisions that are replicated. Replication means that the decision will be made many times under identical circumstances. In replication, the law of large numbers can be applied. The **law of large numbers** states that if an event occurs k times in n identical trials (replications), then k/n approaches the probability of the event as n gets large. That would be the result when playing poker or roulette for a long time, and also when providing insurance against an event that has a historically established and slowly changing frequency of occurrence.

> **Expected value rule:** *When a decision will be replicated many times, choose the action with the greatest expected value if you want to maximize the expected payoff from the action.*

Expected value is a fairly intuitive concept. Nevertheless, it is so important that it needs to be formalized. Expected value is particularly serviceable because it is used to measure the values of risky alternatives in decision making.

The outcome or payoff of an event can be treated as a **random variable,** a variable with a value that is determined by a chance or random occurrence. The daily closing price of an industrial stock is a numerical event that may be treated as a random variable. Whether or not a salesperson closes a deal can be treated as a random variable by assigning a zero or one to the outcome and assigning a probability to each event. The **probability distribution** of a random variable assigns a probability to each possible value of a random variable. A sales manager might state, "We have a 70 percent chance of closing this deal." The random variable may be assigned value $X = 1$ with probability 7/10 and value $X = 0$ with probability 3/10 as its probability distribution.

Random variables can be discrete or continuous. A **discrete** random variable has a countable number of values. Closing a sales deal is a discrete random variable. A **continuous** random variable can assume an infinitely large number of values corresponding to points on a line interval. The time it takes you to get to work or school is a continuous random variable.

The **expected value** or **mean** of a random variable is the weighted average of the possible values, with the probabilities serving as weights. The expected value of a random variable X is denoted by $E(X)$. For a discrete random variable having n outcomes X_1, $X_2, \ldots, X_n$, the expected value is[2]

$$E(X) = \sum_{i=1}^{n} X_i f(X_i)$$

where $f(X_i)$ is the probability that X_i occurs. Each outcome X_i is multiplied by its corresponding probability $f(X_i)$ and the products are added. The expected value, or mean, of a distribution is a measure of central tendency. The mean is a balance point—if you place a distribution on a fulcrum at its mean, the distribution will just balance because it has equal weight on either side of its mean.

When working with a statistical *population*—all possible observations of a random variable—the expected value is denoted by the Greek letter μ.[3] The mean of a random variable X is denoted by μ_x, where the subscript indicates the variable.[4]

As an example of calculating expected value, suppose a firm is considering two actions in the form of two investment alternatives, each calling for an equal outlay. Payoffs on the two investments depend on general economic activity. Three levels of economic activity are identified as recession, normal, and boom. For each investment, payoffs can be matched with each state of the economy, along with the probability that each state will occur. This information is summarized in this **payoff table:**

	State of the Economy		
Action	Recession	Normal	Boom
Project A	$400	$500	$ 600
Project B	$100	$500	$1200
Probabilities	0.2	0.6	0.2

2. For simplicity, we concentrate on discrete random variables. For a continuous random variable, substitute an integral for each summation and indicate the variable of integration in all the formulas for expected value.

3. The Greek letter "mu" is pronounced "mew."

4. When working with a *sample* from the population of a random variable X, the *sample* mean is

$$\bar{X} = \frac{1}{n} \sum_{i=1}^{n} X_i$$

where the sample size is n. The probability of each observation is $1/n$ when each observation X_i is equally likely.

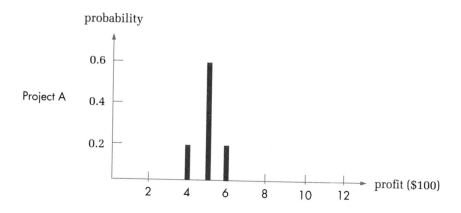

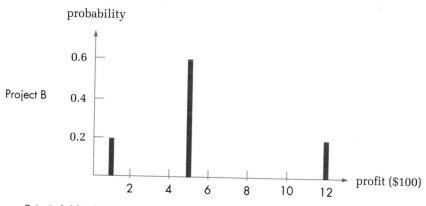

Figure 7.4 **Probability distributions for two alternatives:** Project B has greater expected value, but B also has greater risk than A because the probability distribution for B has greater dispersion than the distribution for A.

The corresponding probability distributions are illustrated by Figure 7.4. A **payoff table** is a list of alternative actions and an array of their payoffs that depend on which state of nature occurs along with their probabilities. Thus, the alternatives are described as if the decision maker were playing a game against nature. This example includes three states of nature—the three possible levels of economic activity.

Now let's calculate the expected values for the alternative actions of choosing project A or project B. The expected return from choosing A is

$$\mu_a = \$400(0.2) + \$500(0.6) + \$600(0.2) = \$500$$

The expected return from choosing B is

$$\mu_b = \$100(0.2) + \$500(0.6) + \$1200(0.2) = \$560$$

Project B has the greatest expected value, and B will be chosen under the expected-value rule.

One of the most obvious flaws in applying the expected-value rule is that the dispersions in the payoffs of the alternatives are not considered. Consider the payoff table in the example above as illustrated by Figure 7.4. Although project B has the greatest expected value, the project also has the greater risk because its lowest payoff is smaller than the lowest payoff for A. A decision maker may wish to choose A in order to guarantee a return of at least $400. Whether or not the highest payoff of $1,200 for B compensates for the added risk depends on the individual's attitude about taking risk and the consequence of the worst outcome.

7.7 Why Buy Insurance?

An insurance company sells policies to individuals or firms that are trying to avoid risk. Consider an example of insurance against illness. Suppose the loss to the individual is $6,000 if the individual becomes ill. If 1 in 1,000 persons becomes ill, the probability of becoming ill is 1/1,000, according to the law of large numbers. How much would an individual be willing to pay for insurance to avoid the gamble of losing $6,000? And how much would the insurance company have to charge?

The expected loss is $6,000 \times (1/1,000) = $6. Thus the insurance company would have to charge at least $6 per policy to cover the average loss, and would have to sell many policies for the law of large numbers to apply. If only one policy were sold for $6 and the individual became ill, the insurance company would lose $5,994. If, however, several thousand policies were sold at $6 and 1 in 1,000 people became ill, the company could just cover the average loss.

Of course the insurance company will set price in excess of the expected loss. Even apart from the need to cover operating costs and the desire to earn a profit, the policy price must also compensate for the transfer of the risk. But would an individual pay more than the expected loss?

In other words, would an individual be willing to lose with certainty an amount greater than the expected loss in order to avoid the gamble of losing an even greater amount? For example, an individual will pay more than the $6 if the loss in utility of the uncertain loss of $6,000 is greater than 1,000 times the loss in utility of the certain loss of $6. How much more than $6 depends on the individual's attitude toward risk. A risk-averse person will pay a premium to replace the gamble having a given expected value with a certain alternative having equal value.

Risk aversion explains the demand side of insurance. The supply side is explained by the law of large numbers. The law of large numbers works only when the probability distributions are statistically independent and identical for all individuals being insured.[5] In such cases it is possible to convert uncertainty for the individual into certainty for the population as a whole.

---

5. Statistical independence of two probability distributions requires that the realized outcome from one distribution not affect the probabilities of outcomes in the other distribution. When two random variables X and Y are statistically independent, their joint probability can be calculated as $f(X, Y) = f(X)f(Y)$.

AN APPLICATION: *Reservation Price for Buying Insurance*

Insurance for sale is always an unfair gamble if the price exceeds the expected loss. And it will always be unfair in the private marketplace because the seller will offer the insurance only if price exceeds the expected payoff. Therefore, only risk-averse people buy insurance.

How much will a risk-averse person be willing to pay to insure against a loss? Suppose this person has the utility function $U(M) = \sqrt{M}$, as shown in Figure 7.5. This person has invested $900, with utility $U(900) = 30$. Now suppose this person faces the prospect of losing $800, which would decrease utility to $U(100) = 10$. What will this person be willing to pay to insure against this loss if the probability of the loss is $P = 1/2$? The expected value of the gamble is

$$E(\text{gamble}) = 900 \left(\frac{1}{2}\right) + 100 \left(\frac{1}{2}\right) = 500$$

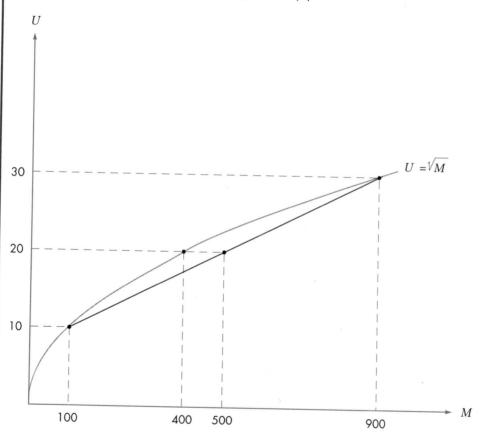

Figure 7.5 **The reservation price for insurance:** Given $U = \sqrt{M}$ and initial wealth of $M = \$900$, utility is $U = 30$. Confronted with a possible loss of $800, utility may fall to $U = 10$. If $P = 1/2$ is the probability of the loss, the expected value of the gamble is $500, and the expected utility of the gamble is $U = 20$. The certainty equivalent of this gamble is $400, and so this person will not pay more than $900 − $400 = $500 to avoid this gamble.

The expected utility of this gamble is

$$E[U(\text{gamble})] = U(900)\left(\frac{1}{2}\right) + U(100)\left(\frac{1}{2}\right) = 20$$

Therefore, the money value of this gamble—its certainty equivalent—is $400, because $\sqrt{M} = 20$ implies that $M = 400$. This person would not be willing to pay more than $400 to take this gamble, and so would not be willing to pay more than $900 - $400 = $500 for insurance to avoid risking the $800 loss.

The expected payoff by the insurance company is $400 because the $800 loss occurs with probability $P = 1/2$. But the price the person is willing to pay is greater than $400 and less than $500. Thus, the insurance company may be able to cover its opportunity costs at a price in that range between the expected payoff and the consumer's reservation price. If so, this insurance will be offered.

In general, suppose a risk-averse individual with utility $U(M)$ has an initial wealth M_0. If this person faces a loss L with probability P, the expected utility is

$$U(M_0 - L) P + U(M_0)(1 - P)$$

This person's reservation price R for insurance will be given by

$$U(M_0 - R) = U(M_0 - L) P + U(M_0)(1 - P)$$

That is, the reservation price is the value R that yields the same utility as the expected utility when insurance is not purchased because this person is indifferent between buying insurance and remaining self-insured at that price.

The requirement that the probability distributions be independent and identical leads insurance companies to identify classes of risk. Automobile insurance is higher for young drivers because as a class they are riskier to insure. Similarly, insurance rates vary over different geographic locations when the probability distribution depends on location. The likelihood of an accident or theft may vary greatly from one neighborhood to the next. To ensure the independence of probability distributions, insurance companies diversify over different geographic locations when the distributions depend on location. A company offering earthquake insurance will cover a wide geographic area rather than concentrate solely, say, in San Francisco.

A problem related to the need for independent probability distributions is **moral hazard,** which occurs when the distribution is affected by the insurance. Individuals having fire insurance may be less careful about preventing fires. Moral hazard is the reason life-insurance policies do not cover suicides. One method used to mitigate the effects of moral hazard is deductible provisions in policies. People will drive more carefully when their collision insurance does not pay a first fixed amount of damage per accident. Similarly, deductible health-insurance provisions decrease frivolous trips to the doctor.

7.8 Using Variance and Standard Deviation to Measure Risk

Looking back at the payoffs associated with the two alternative investment projects and their probability distributions, as shown on Figure 7.4, it is easy to see that B has greater dispersion than A. The spread or dispersion of a distribution is frequently used as a proxy for risk.

The most frequently used measure of the spread or dispersion is the variance. The **variance** of a random variable X is

$$\text{Var}(X) = E\{[X - E(X)]^2\}$$

The variance is the expected value of the squared deviations of a random variable about its mean. Because the variance is an expected value, it can be computed by

$$\text{Var}(X) = \sum_{i=1}^{n} [X_i - E(X_i)]^2 f(X_i)$$

Because the variance includes only squared terms, it must be nonnegative. When the variance of a random variable from a population is being measured, the *population* variance is denoted by σ^2, where σ is the Greek letter sigma.[6]

The variance is measured in *squared* units of the random variable. It is useful to have a measure of the dispersion that is expressed in terms of the original units. This interpretation is provided by the **standard deviation** of a random variable, which is the positive square root of the variance. The standard deviation of a *population* is denoted by σ. The standard deviation is measured using the same scale as the original random variable. The mean and standard deviation are convenient ways of characterizing a probability distribution. Indeed, the mean and standard deviation completely describe some probability distributions such as the familiar bell-shaped normal distribution. The mean provides a measure of central tendency, and the standard deviation is a measure of the dispersion expressed in the same units of measurement.

Let's calculate the variance and standard deviation for each of the two projects previously considered. We already know that their expected values are $\mu_a = \$500$ and

---

6. When working with data from a random sample where $f(X_i) = 1/n$ and n is the sample size, the **sample variance** is

$$S^2 = \frac{1}{n} \Sigma (X_i - \mu_x)^2$$

Because the population mean μ_x is usually unknown when estimating σ^2, the sample mean is used in place of μ_x, and the estimator of σ^2 becomes

$$S^2 = \frac{1}{n-1} \Sigma (X_i - \bar{X})^2$$

The division by $(n - 1)$ rather than by n corrects for a known bias in estimating σ^2.

μ_b = \$560. To determine a variance of a random variable, we first calculate the deviation of each possible outcome from the mean, then square it, and then multiply this term by the probability of its occurrence. These products are then summed to get the variance. For project A we have

$$\sigma_a^2 = (400 - 500)^2(0.2) + (500 - 500)^2(0.6) + (600 - 500)^2(0.2)$$
$$= (100)^2(0.2) + (0)^2(0.6) + (100)^2(0.2) = 4,000$$

The standard deviation of the payoffs to project A is σ_a = 63.25 approximately. For project B, the variance is

$$\sigma_b^2 = (100 - 560)^2(0.2) + (500 - 560)^2(0.6) + (1,200 - 560)^2(0.2)$$
$$= (460)^2(0.2) + (60)^2(0.6) + (640)^2(0.2) = 126,400$$

The standard deviation for the payoffs to project B is σ_b = 355.53 approximately. Comparing the standard deviations of the two projects verifies that B is indeed the riskier project, but that doesn't mean project A is necessarily better.

It is clear that a project with greater expected value is better than another project with equal or greater standard deviation. It is also clear that a project with equal or greater expected value is better than another project with equal standard deviation. This distinction leads to a decision rule called the **mean-variance rule:**

> **Mean-variance rule:** *Between two investment alternatives having equal variance, choose the one having the greater mean return. Between two investment alternatives having equal means, choose the one having the smaller variance.*

All too frequently, however, the riskier alternative has the greater expected return. We need then a measure of the *relative* riskiness of alternatives.

One measure of relative risk is the **coefficient of variation,**

$$v = \frac{\sigma}{\mu}$$

The coefficient of variation is the standard deviation divided by the mean. This relation leads to this decision rule:

> **Coefficient of variation rule:** *Choose the alternative that has the smallest coefficient of variation, σ/μ.*

This rule is better than the expected-value rule because the coefficient of variation depends on both the size of the expected value and the standard deviation. A proportionately larger expected value is necessary to induce a risk-averse decision maker to undertake the additional risk as measured by the standard deviation.

Although the coefficient-of-variation rule is superior to the expected-value rule, and the coefficient-of-variation rule can be applied to cases that cannot be resolved by the mean-variance rule, the coefficient-of-variation rule does not reflect the *degree* of risk aversion. That is, just because a riskier alternative has a proportionately greater mean does not imply that choosing that alternative will necessarily maximize utility.

7.9   Mean-Variance Utility and Portfolio Choice

One approach to choosing among risky alternatives is to assume that utility depends only on the mean and variance of any alternative.[7] The mean indicates the expected payoff, and the variance indicates the riskiness of the payoff. The idea is that a larger mean tends to compensate for the larger risk, but the required compensation depends on the decision maker's aversion to risk. That is, a trade-off appears between the mean and the variance of any distribution of payoffs among alternatives. When measuring the risk, we can use either the variance or the standard deviation. It is natural, then, to think of a utility function that depends on the mean and standard deviation, $U = U(\mu, \sigma)$.

When preferences depend only on the mean and standard deviation, indifference curves can be used to illustrate an individual's preferences for return and risk. If people are risk averse, a greater mean return makes them better off and a greater standard deviation makes them worse off. That is, the mean is a "good," but the standard deviation is a "bad," and any indifference curve will have positive slope, as shown in Figure 7.6. The slope of any indifference curve at any point measures the marginal rate of substitution between risk and return,

$$MRS = \frac{\Delta U/\Delta \sigma}{\Delta U/\Delta \mu} > 0$$

The indifference curves will be concave to the mean axis if, for successively equal increases in the standard deviation, the individual must be compensated with successively larger increases in the mean. Risk and return are not perfect substitutes.

To fix ideas, let's use this model to analyze a simple portfolio problem. As shown in Figure 7.6, suppose you find only two assets, and you can divide your wealth between the two. That is, you don't have to choose one or the other; you can buy some of each. One asset is a riskless asset with certain rate of return denoted by c. The certain rate of return c will be positive because money has a time value. Suppose c is 6 percent. The riskless asset might be a Treasury bill that pays a fixed rate of interest. The other is a risky asset that pays a rate of return r_j if the jth state of nature occurs. The risky asset, denoted by point **R** in Figure 7.6, might be an investment in a mutual fund. The line tangent to U^* at utility-maximizing point **P** is a "budget line," which shows all the return-risk pairs that can be achieved with the two assets. This budget line is sometimes called the "security market line." The investor chooses a portfolio along the budget line by equating the *MRS* with the price of risk. The slope of this budget line provides us with a measure of the **price of risk** because that slope measures how risk and return can be traded off in making choices.

Let μ_r be the mean return to the risky asset that yields returns r_j with probabilities $f(r_j)$. The standard deviation of the risky asset is denoted σ_r. Suppose μ_r is 18 percent

---

7. This model was originally developed in the late 1950s by Harry M. Markowitz of the City University of New York and refined in the mid 1960s by William F. Sharpe of Stanford University. Jointly, they were awarded the 1990 Nobel Prize in Economics, mainly for developing this model and applying it to portfolio choice. They are credited with laying the foundation for the creation of mutual funds and advancing the understanding of financial markets. The prize was shared with Merton H. Miller, who is credited with developing the capital-asset pricing model that we will examine later in this chapter.

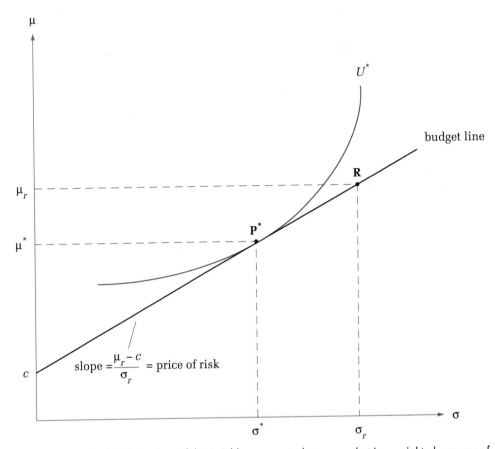

Figure 7.6 **Portfolio choice:** A portfolio **P** yields an expected return μ_p that is a weighted average of the certain return c and the expected return μ_r from the risky asset. If k is the fraction of each dollar invested in the risky asset **R**, the expected return to a portfolio **P** is $\mu_p = k\mu_r + (1-k)c$. The fraction k will be chosen to achieve μ^* and thereby to maximize utility, and so portfolio **P*** will be chosen.

and $\sigma_r = 3$. Now, suppose you can divide each investment dollar between the two alternatives. If k is the fraction of your wealth held in the risky asset so that $(1 - k)$ is the fraction held in the riskless asset, then the **expected return to a portfolio P** is

$$\mu_p = k\mu_r + (1 + k)c$$

That is, the expected return to a portfolio P is the weighted average of the expected return μ_r to the risky asset and the return c to the riskless asset. As illustrated by Figure 7.6, if you set $k = 1$ and devote all your money to the risky asset **R**, your mean return will be μ_r or 18 percent, with standard deviation of $\sigma_r = 3$. If you set $k = 0$ and devote all your money to the riskless asset, your return will be c or 6 percent, with standard deviation of zero. The slope of the straight line between these points is the *price of risk* because it measures the rate of exchange between the riskless asset and the risky asset. The slope can be measured by $(\mu_r - c)/\sigma_r$, as shown in Figure 7.6.

Because $kr_j + (1 - k)c$ is the return to the portfolio, the variance of the portfolio return is affected only by the variation in r_j because c is a constant. Thus, $\sigma_p^2 = k^2\sigma_r^2$ and $\sigma_p = k\sigma_r$—the standard deviation of the portfolio is equal to the fraction k of your wealth held in the risky asset multiplied by the standard deviation of the risky asset.[8] For the numerical example, $\sigma p = k\sigma_r$ is $1.5 = (0.5)(3)$. Investing in portfolio **P** has reduced your risk at the cost of reducing the expected rate of return. As you devote more of your wealth to the risky asset, you also incur greater risk.

Given the preferences that yield the indifference curves shown, the utility-maximizing choice is portfolio **P*** with mean return μ^* and standard deviation σ^*. Wealth will be divided between the risky asset and the riskless asset so that the marginal rate of substitution is just equal to the price of risk,

$$MRS = \frac{\mu_r - c}{\sigma_r}$$

Thus, in the market for assets, each individual will choose a portfolio in which his or her marginal rate of substitution is equal to the price of risk. When people have the opportunity to trade risks, the equilibrium price will be equal across all individuals. Therefore, in equilibrium, utility-maximizing individuals will make choices that result in equal marginal rates of substitution. Thus, the demand for assets is a function of the price of risk.

To see how the demand for assets is influenced by the price of risk, consider the example in Figure 7.7, where an individual can invest in asset **X** or asset **Y**. Here, **Y** is riskier than **X**, but **Y** yields a higher return, $\sigma_y > \sigma_x$, but $\mu_y > \mu_x$. If this person could choose only **X** or **Y** or the riskless alternative, asset **X** would be chosen because both **Y** or c yield lower utility. Both **Y** and c have indifference curves that are ranked lower than **X** for this person's preferences. But the person can invest in a portfolio, and so investing in asset **Y** and the riskless alternative is better than investing in **X** and the riskless asset. Portfolio **P$_2$**, which includes some of asset **Y**, will be chosen over portfolio **P$_1$**, which includes no **Y**.

---

8. This result follows because for any random variable X, the $\mathrm{Var}(kX) = k^2\mathrm{Var}(X)$. More formally for this specific example, the variance of the risky asset is given by

$$\sigma_r^2 = \Sigma\ (r_j - \mu_r)^2 f(r_j)$$

And the variance of the portfolio is found by summing the squared deviations of the portfolio return from its mean return weighted by their probabilities:

$$\sigma_p^2 = \Sigma\ (kr_j + (1 - k)c - \mu_p)^2 f(r_j)$$

Substitution for μ_p yields

$$\sigma_p^2 = \Sigma\ (kr_j - k\mu_r)^2 f(r_j)$$
$$= k^2\Sigma\ (r_j - \mu_r)^2 f(r_j)$$
$$= k^2\sigma_r^2$$

Thus, $\sigma_p = k\sigma_r$, the standard deviation of the portfolio is equal to the fraction k of your wealth held in the risky asset multiplied by the standard deviation of the risky asset.

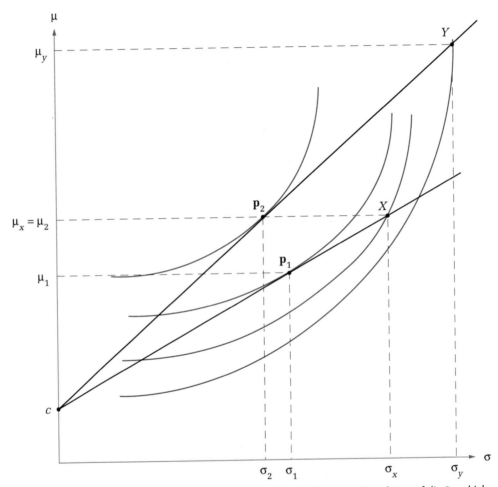

Figure 7.7 **Demand for assets:** When choosing between two risky assets **X** and **Y,** portfolio **P₂,** which includes **Y,** will be chosen over portfolio **P₁,** which includes **X,** because **P₂** yields a preferred risk-return combination.

7.10 Using Covariance to Measure Risk

When the returns to alternative assets are correlated, an individual's utility depends on the mean and variance of the *portfolio* held—not the mean and variance of any asset in the portfolio. In the mean-variance model, the utilities from alternatives depend on their means and standard deviations, an assumption that is valid only when the alternatives are independent. Two random variables are *independent* if the outcome of one does not depend on that of the other, as when we compared a risky asset with a riskless asset, because the riskless asset had a fixed return.

Often, however, the returns to alternative assets are not independent. One good may be a normal good and another an inferior good. The demand for one good will rise while the demand for the other falls as consumers' income changes. Therefore, if you wanted to hedge against the business cycle or other swings in the economy, you might buy stocks in both industries. Moreover, variability in returns usually correlates positively with the level of the return because market forces usually compensate greater risk by greater return. Therefore, when you choose two assets that are not independent and the risks of which are positively correlated, you increase your risk when you buy both.

A simple example illustrates how important this notion of dependence is. Suppose two assets are available, each having two outcomes. Asset A is worth either $100 or $-$50, with probabilities 1/2 each. Asset B is worth either $-$50 or $100, with probabilities 1/2 each. The expected value of each asset is $25. If you don't care about risk, you will be willing to pay $25 for either asset. But if you are averse to risk, you will be willing to pay *less* than $25 for either asset.

Now, suppose you can hold both assets, and you then observe that the assets are *negatively* correlated because when one is worth $100 the other is worth $-$50. When both are held, the expected value of holding both is $50. The variance of holding both is zero because a return of $50 is certain when you hold both because of the perfect negative correlation between their payoffs. Thus, this perfect negative correlation between the dependent payoffs of these assets allows you to avoid all risk by buying both. In general, risk can be reduced by holding a diversified portfolio that includes some assets whose payoffs are negatively correlated.

Some way is needed to measure the *extent* of any dependence between assets. Two related measures are used most often, **covariance** and **correlation.** Both measure the *linear* association between two random variables. Both will be useful in judging the risk associated with dependent alternatives.

First, the **covariance** of two random variables X and Y is defined as

$$\text{Cov}(X, Y) = E\{[X - E(X)][Y - E(Y)]\}$$

Covariance is the expected value of the product of the deviations of the two random variables about their means. Covariance being an expected value, it can be computed by

$$\text{Cov}(X, Y) = \sum_{i=1}^{n} [X_i - E(X_i)][Y_i - E(Y_i)] f(X_i, Y_i)$$

where $f(X_i, Y_i)$ is the joint probability that pairs of values (X_i, Y_i) will occur. When working with a population of random variables, the **population covariance** will be denoted by σ_{xy}.

A *positive* covariance indicates that the random variables tend to be above or below their means at the same time—a *direct* relationship between the two variables. A *negative* covariance indicates that one random variable tends to be above its mean when the other tends to be below its mean—there is an *inverse* relationship between the two variables.

When two random variables are *independently distributed,* their covariance will be zero. Second, the **correlation** between two random variables X and Y is defined as[9]

$$\text{Cor}(X, \ Y) = \frac{\text{Cov}(X, \ Y)}{\sqrt{\text{Var}(X)\text{Var}(Y)}}$$

The **population correlation** between two random variables is denoted by ρ_{xy}, and so

$$\rho_{xy} = \frac{\sigma_{xy}}{\sigma_x \sigma_y}$$

The population correlation is equal to the population covariance divided by the product of the population standard deviations. Correlation transforms the covariance so that correlation lies between -1 and $+1$. Thus, correlation is independent of the scales of measurement of X and Y and covariance is not. A *zero* correlation indicates that no *linear* relationship connects the variables. A correlation of $+1$ indicates a perfect linear relationship, in which all pairs fall on a straight line having *positive* slope. Likewise, a correlation of $+1$ indicates a perfect linear relationship, in which all pairs fall on a straight line having *negative* slope. The closer correlation is to $+1$ or -1, the closer the relationship is to being perfectly linear.

A numerical example will help clarify use of the formulas for covariance and correlation. Suppose two random variables X and Y have this joint distribution:

X	Y	f(X, Y)
0	0	1/10
10	0	4/10
20	10	4/10
30	10	1/10

These random variables might be the possible payoffs of two assets. The expected values of X and Y are:

$$\mu_x = 0\left(\frac{1}{10}\right) + 10\left(\frac{4}{10}\right) + 20\left(\frac{4}{10}\right) + 30\left(\frac{1}{10}\right) = 15$$

$$\mu_y = 0\left(\frac{1}{10}\right) + 0\left(\frac{4}{10}\right) + 10\left(\frac{4}{10}\right) + 10\left(\frac{1}{10}\right) = 5$$

---

9. Correlation is mentioned in this context primarily to help you understand covariance, but correlation is frequently used to describe the linear association between two random variables.

This table of computations will prove useful:

$X - \mu_x$	$(X - \mu_x)^2$	$Y - \mu_y$	$(Y - \mu_y)^2$	$(X - \mu_x)(Y - \mu_y)$
-15	225	-5	25	75
-5	25	-5	25	25
5	25	5	25	25
15	225	5	25	75

The variances of X and Y are:

$$\sigma_x^2 = 225\left(\frac{1}{10}\right) + 25\left(\frac{4}{10}\right) + 25\left(\frac{4}{10}\right) + 225\left(\frac{1}{10}\right) = 65$$

$$\sigma_y^2 = 25\left(\frac{1}{10}\right) + 25\left(\frac{4}{10}\right) + 25\left(\frac{4}{10}\right) + 25\left(\frac{1}{10}\right) = 25$$

The covariance between X and Y is:

$$\sigma_{xy} = 75\left(\frac{1}{10}\right) + 25\left(\frac{4}{10}\right) + 25\left(\frac{4}{10}\right) + 75\left(\frac{1}{10}\right) = 35$$

The correlation between X and Y is:

$$\rho_{xy} = \frac{35}{\sqrt{65 \times 25}} = 0.8682$$

There is a fairly strong linear and direct relationship between these two random variables; therefore, the variables are positively correlated and the correlation is high.

Now we are ready to measure the risk of any asset relative to the asset market as a whole. This measure, the **beta of an asset,** is denoted by the Greek letter β. If σ_{mj} is the covariance of the return to the market as a whole with the return to the jth asset, and if σ_m^2 is the market variance, then the beta of the jth asset is

$$\beta_j = \frac{\sigma_{mj}}{\sigma_m^2}$$

Thus, if $\beta_j < 1$, the asset is *less* risky than the market as a whole, and if $\beta_j > 1$, the asset is *more* risky than the market as a whole. A broad-based security-market index, such as the Standard and Poor's 500 Index or the New York Stock Exchange Index, normally is used as a measure of total market returns.

For some types of assets, including stocks and bonds and other securities, advisory services provide estimates of the betas for various assets. At other times beta is more difficult to determine, but we can estimate it from data by least-squares regression—a topic covered in Chapter 8.

7.11 Valuing Risky Assets Using Beta

How are capital assets priced when they are risky? Previously we saw that the current price of an asset with certain returns must be equal to its present value. We then saw that the potential for arbitrage guarantees that all riskless assets earn the same rate of return in the market. But when assets are risky their prices must be adjusted for risk, which we can achieve by subtracting a risk-adjustment factor from the mean return of the risky asset. That is, if μ_j is the expected return to the jth risky asset, the risk-adjusted return for that asset will be equal to μ_j *less* a risk-adjustment factor.

The risk-adjustment factor is found in this way. Let μ_m be the mean return to the market as a whole. The price of risk, $(\mu_m - c)/\sigma_m$, is multiplied by the amount of the market risk, as measured by standard deviation σ_m, to get the **cost of risk**, $\mu_m - c$. As before, c is the certain return to a riskless asset. Then the cost of risk is multiplied by the asset's risk relative to the market, β_j, to get the **risk-adjustment factor:**

$$\beta_j(\mu_m - c)$$

Thus, the **adjusted return** for any *risky* asset must be

$$\mu_j - \beta_j(\mu_m - c)$$

The adjusted return of the risky asset is its mean return minus its risk-adjustment factor.

In market equilibrium all assets must earn the same rate of return *after adjusting for risk*. Therefore, between a risky asset and a riskless alternative, market equilibrium requires that

$$\mu_j - \beta_j(\mu_m - c) = c$$

Rearranging, this equation reveals that

$$\mu_j = c + \beta_j(\mu_m - c)$$

The expected return on any asset must equal the risk-free return c *plus* a "risk premium." The risk premium is the extra amount required to compensate for the risk. This equation has many uses in studying financial markets.

The preceding equation is the main result of the **capital-asset pricing model,** commonly referred to as CAPM. The CAPM recognizes that a firm's stock will be held in someone's portfolio. In the context of the CAPM, the expected rate of return for the stock of firm j is μ_j. The term c refers to the rate of return that the firm would have to offer if its earnings were risk free. Of course, no firm can offer a risk-free return, and so rate c is usually taken to be the yield of a U.S. government security such as a Treasury bill. The term μ_m is the mean market return on all alternative investments.

To implement the CAPM, we must estimate the beta of the asset. One way to estimate beta is to fit the equation of a straight line to historical data. The model to be estimated is

$$(r_t - c_t) = \alpha + \beta(r_{mt} - c_t) + \varepsilon_t$$

where $(r_t - c_t)$ is the periodic rate of return for the asset above the risk-free rate c_t in period t, $(r_{mt} - c_t)$ is the market return above the risk-free rate, and ε_t is a random error term. The terms α and β are to be estimated from actual data, and the estimated β will

ECONOMIC SCENE: *Stock-Market Efficiency*

Most economists believe that the stock market is remarkably efficient in adjusting to all relevant information about individual stocks and the economy as a whole. According to the **efficient-market hypothesis (EMH),** the market adjusts so quickly to news that no technique for selecting a portfolio of stocks can outperform a strategy of holding a diversified portfolio such as those making up the Standard & Poor's 500 stock index. According to the EMH, a portfolio formed from randomly selected stocks would perform as well as a portfolio chosen by an expert. The EMH model predicts that stock price changes behave like random departures from previous prices, and so follow a "random walk." Leave a drunk in the middle of a field and it is impossible to predict where the drunk will be at any moment; likewise, changes in price will be independent from previous changes.*

Critics of the EMH model argue that variability in stock prices cannot be explained by a simple random walk. They say behavioral considerations and crowd psychology must be used to understand fluctuations in the stock market. As evidence, these critics point to the market meltdown of October 1987. In the week following October 19, starting on Black Monday, the Dow Jones average of 30 major industrial corporations lost 13 percent of its value. Within a month after Black Monday, the Dow Jones average dropped to one-third of its previous high. Did the stock market really reflect all relevant information about individual stocks and the economy when the index was at its peak? Did new information justify the precipitous drop?

Recently, Burton Malkiel asked these questions and concluded that reports on the death of the EMH appear premature.† In defense of the random-walk model, Malkiel mentions that any expected price change in a stock will cause an immediate adjustment. Otherwise, a profitable arbitrage opportunity would suggest itself and could be exploited to earn abnormal profits. If the flow of information is unimpeded and no prohibitive transactions costs appear, then tomorrow's price change in speculative markets will reflect only tomorrow's "news." Because news by definition is unpredictable, the resulting price changes must also be unpredictable and random. Most empirical studies tend to support the random-walk model. Very few predictable patterns have been found in stock price series.

Malkiel says one exception is the "January effect," wherein stock prices rise during the first few days in January. A "weekend effect" has also been documented, when average returns fall between the close of trading on Friday to the close of trading on Monday. Some seasonal patterns have also been discovered. But these departures from randomness are usually small, and transactions costs preclude a profitable investment strategy.

Malkiel argues that systematic opportunities for arbitrage will not persist in a market dominated by profit-maximizing traders. Malkiel supposes a "Christmas rally," with stock prices rising between Christmas and New Year's. Traders would attempt to take advantage of the rally by buying on the day before Christmas and selling just

---

*More formally, the random-walk model states that investment returns are serially independent and their probability distributions are constant over time.
†Burton G. Malkiel, "Is the Stock Market Efficient?" *Science,* 243 (March 10, 1989), pp. 1313–1318.

before New Year's. But as traders follow this practice, soon it will be necessary to buy two days before Christmas and then sell two days before New Year's. Further adjustments by traders will find all the buying done long before Christmas so that the Christmas rally disappears. Malkiel concludes that any regularly occurring trading opportunity that can be discovered is bound to self-destruct.

A stronger version of the EMH states that all public information has been figured into current market prices. Empirical evidence tends to support this view that public information is rapidly assimilated into current market prices. Stock splits are usually followed by dividend increases, which convey information about management's confidence in the future. The market generally adjusts immediately with higher prices for stocks just split. Substantial gains can be made by those who already own the split stocks, but no evidence appears of abnormal returns after the split. Similarly, merger announcements can raise stock prices substantially. But no evidence indicates abnormal price changes after the public release of merger information. Thus it appears that the only way to profit on stock splits, dividend increases, and merger announcements is to have advance information. But such trading is illegal.

If the stock market is efficient, how can we explain Black Monday? Or are psychological factors more important in understanding the stock market? In defense of the EMH, Malkiel numerically illustrates how sensitive stock prices can be to small changes in interest rates and perceptions of risk.

The capital-asset pricing model predicts that the price of a stock will be equal to its risk-adjusted present value. Thus, if the growth rate (g) of the current dividend (D) remains constant, the stock's price today will be

$$P = \frac{D(1 + g)}{(1 + i)} + \frac{D(1 + g)^2}{(1 + i)^2} + \cdots + \frac{D(1 + g)^T}{(1 + i)^T}$$

where i is the appropriate discount rate. If the number of periods T is allowed to go to infinity, the price equation simplifies to

$$P = \frac{D(1 + g)}{(i - g)}, g < i$$

If the stock's expected growth rate is 6 percent, and if the period's dividend $[D(1 + g)]$ is $5, the price of the stock will be

$$P = \frac{\$5}{(i - 0.06)}$$

Suppose the rate of interest on government bonds is 9 percent and the additional risk premium required by investors in the stock market is 2 percent. The appropriate discounting interest rate is 11 percent ($0.09 + 0.02 = 0.11$), and the price of the stock will be

$$P = \frac{\$5}{0.05} = \$100$$

Now assume that yields on government bonds rise from 9 to 10.5 percent, and that the required risk premium rises from 2 to 2.5 percent. The appropriate discount rate then rises from 11 to 13 percent. The price of the stock becomes

$$P = \frac{\$5}{0.07} = \$71.43$$

The stock price has fallen by nearly 30 percent.

This sequence appears to be exactly what happened just before Black Monday. Yields on long-term Treasury bonds increased from about 9 to 10.5 percent just before the crash. Congress also threatened to impose a "merger tax" that would have made merger activity prohibitively expensive. At the same time, Secretary of the Treasury James Baker threatened to encourage a further fall in a recent decline in the dollar. Both of these threats increased investors' perceptions about risk. Thus, the subsequent changes in stock prices can be explained by rational response to small changes in interest rates and perceptions of risk.

be the estimate of beta for the asset. The usual estimation technique is least-squares regression. Once the beta of an asset has been estimated, it can be compared to the betas of other assets to judge relative risk, or beta can be used to predict the expected rate of return of the asset.

Table 7.1 reports some estimated betas for securities issued by selected U.S. companies. Monthly data were used from January 1979 through December 1983. The estimated intercepts (alphas) are included to capture any unmeasured influences on the dependent variables. Those intercepts are expected to be close to zero because the dependent variables are the rates of return for each asset *above* the risk-free rate. An estimated beta greater than 1 indicates that the asset is riskier than the market as a whole. Fortunately for managers, it is not necessary to compute the beta for each security every time it is needed. Several investment-advisory services, including *Value Line Investment Survey* and Merrill Lynch, regularly compute and publish individual security beta estimates.

Table 7.1 Estimates of β for Selected Securities, 1979–1983

Company	Estimated α	Estimated β
McDonald's	0.01	0.38
Coca-Cola	0.00	0.41
IBM	0.00	0.54
Kellogg	0.00	0.57
Security Pacific	0.00	0.94
Hewlett-Packard	0.00	1.10
United Airlines	−0.02	1.35
Chrysler	0.00	1.45
Lockheed	0.01	1.52
Boeing	−0.02	1.54

Source: George Foster, *Financial Statement Analysis*, 2d ed. (Prentice Hall, 1986), p. 347. Adapted by permission of Prentice Hall, Englewood Cliffs, New Jersey.

AN APPLICATION: *Airline Safety and Demand*

Airline safety has been a subject of public debate since the deregulation that began in 1978. Airlines are insured against most direct costs of an accident, but they cannot insure against loss in demand or in shareholders' wealth. The effect of serious accidents on airline equity values and demand has been studied.* A serious accident is defined as one in which at least one on-board fatality occurred.

In the first part of this study the authors looked at the effect of an accident on the equity values of airlines. The capital-asset pricing model was used to separate changes caused by overall market effects from those caused by accidents. The normal relation between returns R_{jt} to a given security j on day t and a market return is

$$R_{jt} = \alpha_j + \beta_j R_{mt} + \varepsilon_{jt}$$

where R_{mt} is the market return on day t and ε_{jt} is a random error term. The parameter α_j measures the part of the average daily return that is *not* chargeable to market movements. The deviation of a stock's daily return from the value expected from the CAPM is measured by the prediction error,

$$\hat{\varepsilon}_{jt} = R_{jt} - \hat{\alpha}_j - \hat{\beta}_j R_{mt}$$

where α_j and β_j have been replaced by their estimates. If the prediction error $\hat{\varepsilon}_{jt}$ is large on any day t when an accident happened, we have evidence that the accident influenced the return on the stock.

This CAPM was estimated from daily stock-market data from the New York and American Stock Exchanges between 1962 and 1985. During this period 74 accidents occurred. After estimating the CAPM, the average abnormal returns from two days before news of the accident to 14 days after were calculated. A cumulative abnormal return was also calculated for the accident day and each of the following 14 trading days. On average, a firm's equity value went down 0.94 percent on the first trading day after an accident. Though small, this loss was statistically significant. Results also indicated that the information was almost totally absorbed into the stock price on the first day. Abnormal returns were small and mostly insignificant after the first day of information. The average value lost on the first day was $3.67 million, and the biggest was $169 million over a two-day period.

The second part of this study covered the average effect on market demand. Demand was estimated for each firm as a function of price, income, a time trend, and seasonal variables:

$$\ln RPM = \lambda_j + \phi t + \alpha_j \ln P_{jt} + \beta_j \ln I_t + \sum_{i=1}^{11} \gamma_{ij} F_{it} + \sum_{l=1}^{L_j} \sum_{k=0}^{3} \delta_{jlk} C_{jlk} + \varepsilon_{jt}$$

*Severin Borenstein and Martin B. Zimmerman, "Market Incentives for Safe Commercial Airline Operation," *American Economic Review,* 78(5) (December 1988), pp. 913–935.

where

RPM_{jt} = revenue passenger miles for firm j in month t
t = number of month
P_{jt} = average revenue per passenger mile for firm j in month t
I_t = U.S. personal income in month t
F_{jt} = eleven monthly dummies
C_{jlk} = dummy that takes a value of 1 in the kth month after the lth crash that firm j experienced and 0 otherwise

Notice that the α and β coefficients yield price and income elasticities because the equation is of the double-log form. This equation was estimated separately for each airline. The several equations estimated are not reproduced here, but the estimated coefficients were reasonable and fairly precise. As an overall measure of the responsiveness to price, the mean price elasticity was calculated to be $\bar{\eta} = 0.50$.

The primary focus in this part of the study was on the deviation from the expected demand following an accident. Again, by analyzing the prediction error during the months following a crash, the effects on demand can be examined for a statistically significant effect. The results indicate that, prior to deregulation, the effect of an accident on demand was quite small. The authors estimate that the total loss in demand caused by an accident averaged 10.9 percent of one month's traffic. Since deregulation, consumers' response to accidents appeared to increase, but the effects are not statistically significant. The loss in demand increases to 15.3 percent after 1978, but that estimate was based on only 13 accidents. The greater decreases in demand since deregulation are consistent, however, with a more competitive environment.

In summary, the loss in stockholder wealth after an accident has been small but statistically significant. Direct estimates of the demand for airline travel, however, does not indicate that the loss in asset values was caused by adverse consumer response.

7.12 Valuing Risky Cash Flows

When periodic returns are certain, wealth can be maximized by choosing the investment alternative that has the highest net present value. But this rule depends crucially on using the appropriate discounting interest rate. If you choose a discount rate for investments in a similar risk class, then you have already adjusted for risk. We can, however, adjust the *NPV* formula to include a risk-adjustment factor that may vary with time.

The **risk-adjusted NPV** is

$$NPV_a = \sum_{t=1}^{T} \frac{R_t}{(1 + i + a_t)^t} - I$$

where the R_t are periodic returns, I is the initial cost of the investment, i is the risk-free rate, and $i + a_t$ is the *risk-adjusted* discount rate. The adjustment factor a_t is permitted to vary from period to period as your assessment of risk changes.

As an illustration, let's modify one of the examples from Chapter 6. A firm considers investing $98,500 on equipment over a five-year period. The equipment is expected to have a scrap value of $55,000 at the end of five years. The project is expected to generate $40,000 per year, and the operating costs are expected to be $19,200 per year. The discounting interest rate was taken to be 12 percent, and the *NPV* of the project was calculated to be $7,686.

Now, however, the firm recognizes that the returns are risky. Suppose management uses these risk-adjusted discount rates:

Period t	Risk-adjusted Rate	Risk-adjustment Factor
1	12%	0%
2	14	2
3	16	4
4	18	6
5	20	8

The *adjusted NPV* is

$$
\begin{aligned}
NPV_a &= \sum_{t=1}^{5} \frac{R_t}{(1.12 + a_t)^t} + \frac{\text{scrap value}}{(1.12)^5} - 98,500 \\
&= \frac{20,800}{1.12} + \frac{20,800}{(1.14)^2} + \frac{20,800}{(1.16)^3} + \frac{20,800}{(1.18)^4} + \frac{20,800}{(1.20)^5} + \frac{55,000}{(1.12)^5} - 98,500 \\
&= 18,571 + 16,005 + 13,326 + 10,728 + 8,359 + 31,208 - 98,500 \\
&= -\$303
\end{aligned}
$$

The negative risk-adjusted *NPV* indicates that the expected return will be negative when adjusted for risk.

An alternative but equivalent technique for evaluating risky cash flows can be used. The goal of this method is to use an adjusted return to calculate an adjusted *NPV* denoted by *NPV**. Each expected return R_t is weighted by a factor w_t to obtain

$$
NPV^* = \sum_{i=1}^{T} \frac{R_t w_t}{(1 + i)^t} - I
$$

The weights w_t are used to convert the returns into **certainty equivalents.** The decision maker is asked to state an amount R_t^* to be received with certainty that is equivalent in

---

GLOBAL PERSPECTIVE: *Investment and Political Risk**

Direct business investment in other countries is subject to risk not associated with domestic business investment. Analysis of such risks is referred to as *political risk assessment.* Political risk arises because of uncertainty from exchange controls, expropriation, future tariffs, nontariff barriers, taxes, export controls, labor relations, and government instability. Managers and decision makers need detailed information about the international environment to make informed decisions. Decision making based on casual impressions is no longer sufficient. Increased awareness and skill in applying political and economic analysis are required.

For one thing, capital budgeting formulas should be adjusted to take into account politically related risks. The unadjusted *NPV* formula is

$$NPV = \sum_{t=1}^{T} \frac{R_t}{(1 + i)^t} - I$$

where R_t are the expected periodic returns from investment I. If no political risk is present, this formula can be applied without modification. An adjustment should be made, however, to take into account politically relevant risks. One way is to use a *risk-adjusted* discount rate. The risk-adjusted *NPV* is

$$NPV_a = \sum_{t=1}^{T} \frac{R_t}{(1 + i + a_t)^t} - I$$

where $i + a_t$ is the risk-adjusted discount rate. This commonly used method for adjustment has the advantage of allowing intuitive judgments of politically related risks to be simply applied to the calculations. This approach, though, often overcompensates for political risk because even small upward adjustments in the discount rate have rather large negative effects on net present value. Therefore, the certainty equivalent method may be better for this application.

The certainty-equivalent method adjusts the periodic return using weights to convert the periodic returns into certainty equivalents:

$$NPV^* = \sum_{i=1}^{T} \frac{R_t w_t}{(1 + i)^t} - I$$

The formula can be simplified by assuming that the weights are constant, $w_t = w$, where $0 < w < 1$. The formula becomes

$$NPV^* = w \sum_{i=1}^{T} \frac{R_t}{(1 + i)^t} - I$$

---

*This application is based on Thomas L. Brewer, "Political Risk Assessment for Foreign Direct Investment Decisions: Better Methods for Better Results," *Columbia Journal of World Business,* 16(1) (Spring 1981), pp. 5–11.

The coefficient w represents the ratio that would make the decision maker indifferent between a riskless cash flow and a given risky cash flow,

$$w = \frac{\text{riskless cash flow}}{\text{risky cash flow}}$$

Hence, w is a function of the decision maker's utility preferences on risk-return trade-offs.

Using the certainty-equivalent method does not eliminate subjectivity. Nor does it preclude the need for estimating the probabilities and magnitudes of politically related events such as exchange controls or expropriations. Nevertheless, carefully applying the certainty-equivalent approach will improve investment decisions in the context of international political risk.

---

utility to a chance at R_t. The amount $R_j^* = R_t w_t$ is called the **certainty equivalent** of R_t. The weights, then, are

$$w_j = \frac{R_j^*}{R_j} = \frac{\text{certain return}}{\text{risky return}}$$

These weights, the certainty equivalent factors, are then used in the numerator of the NPV equation.

The certainty-equivalence approach uses weights in the numerator of the NPV formula. In contrast, the risk-adjusted discount-rate approach uses a risk-adjustment factor in the denominator of the NPV formula. When the decision maker is consistent in setting the certainty equivalents and the risk-adjusted discount rates, the adjusted net present values will be the same for both techniques, $NPV_a = NPV^*$. The two techniques are simply alternative procedures for making the same adjustment for risk, and the choice of technique should not affect the decision.

In real-world applications, managers must set estimates for a_t or w_t for various investment alternatives. Deriving estimates can be a formidable task. Frequently, adjustment factors are determined subjectively. In other cases the historical performance of similar investments can be useful. Once the beta of an asset has been determined, the capital-asset pricing model can be used to determine the risk-adjustment factor. Recall that the CAPM concludes that the expected return on any asset must equal the risk-free return plus the risk adjustment:

$$\mu_j = c + \beta_j(\mu_m - c)$$

The risk-adjustment factor is $\beta_j(\mu_m - c)$. If the risk-free rate is 5 percent and the market rate is 12 percent, the risk-adjustment factor for an asset having $\beta_j = 1.3$ is

$$\beta_j(\mu_m - c) = 1.3(12\% - 5\%) = 9.1\%$$

The required return for this asset is

$$\mu_j = c + \beta_j(\mu_m - c) = 5\% + 9.1\% = 14.1\%$$

This risk-adjusted rate of return can then be used in calculating the risk-adjusted *NPV*.

7.13 Avoiding Uncertainty by Hedging

A **futures contract** promises delivery of a fixed quantity at a future date at a fixed future price. Markets in which futures contracts are bought and sold are called **futures markets.** A buyer and seller agree on the price of a good to be determined at some specified date in the future. The holder of the futures contract can demand delivery of the good at the future date. Futures markets deal in grains, potatoes, cotton, frozen orange-juice concentrate, cocoa, precious metals, Treasury bonds, and several other goods and assets. Futures markets handle stocks, government-issued mortgages, and other financial securities. Transactions in futures markets consist of buying and selling futures contracts. A crucial function of any futures market is eliminating uncertainty about price.

The market in which a good or asset is purchased today is called a **spot** (or **cash**) market. The price of the good in the current period is the **spot price.** In the spot market, buyers and sellers agree on a spot price for delivery of the good now.

Futures markets work quite differently from spot markets. The price of the good that is specified in the futures contract is the **futures price.** The *buyer* of a futures contract agrees to purchase a specified quantity of a good at a specified price, the futures price, in the future. Both delivery and payment are to be made in the future. The *seller* of a futures contract is obligated to supply the good at the futures price, but the seller need not own the good at the time of sale.

When the seller does not own the good or asset being sold, the seller is in a **short position.** The buyer is in a **long position** because the good or asset cannot be acquired until sometime in the future. To ensure that both the buyer and the seller conform to the contract, each must put up cash called a *margin requirement.* Traders can sometimes deposit assets with brokers to satisfy the margin requirement, which is usually some small percentage, say 5 to 15 percent, of the value of the contract.

The seller or buyer of a futures contract can *close out* the contract before the delivery date by engaging in an offsetting transaction. A seller can close out a contract by buying another with the same delivery date. Similarly, a buyer can close out a contract by selling another with the same delivery date. Most futures contracts are settled before their maturity date by paying the difference between the future price and the spot price.

A **hedge** occurs when an individual simultaneously sells in the futures market and buys in the spot market, or *vice versa.* The possibility of a loss from *any* fluctuation in the spot price can be reduced by simultaneously selling a futures contract and purchasing the good.

Consider a wheat farmer who is planting a crop to be harvested at some time in the future. The farmer may take a short position and sell a futures contract to deliver a specific amount of wheat at a future date. The price of wheat to be received by the farmer is the futures price. Thus the uncertainty about the price of wheat to be received by the farmer has been removed. Uncertainty about the physical delivery of the wheat remains, however. On the other side of the market, a miller who is planning to purchase wheat in the future can take a long position and buy the farmer's contract. In this way the miller can also eliminate the uncertainty about the price to be paid on some future date.

Suppose the current spot price of wheat is $4.00 per bushel. The miller needs 1,000 bushels in the future to make flour. If the miller buys now and the price of wheat *rises* to $4.25 per bushel, the miller will experience an *increase* in profit of ($4.25 − $4.00) × 1,000 = $250. But if the price *falls* to $3.75 per bushel, then the miller will experience a *decrease* in profit of ($3.75 − $4.00) × 1,000 = −$250. Although the chance at an extra $250 would be welcome, the possibility of a $250 decrease in profit might be enough to bankrupt the miller.

A hedge will permit the miller to eliminate the uncertainty. At the time of purchasing wheat, suppose the miller enters into a futures contract to deliver wheat at $3.90 per bushel. That is, the miller promises to deliver 1,000 bushels in the future at $3.90 per bushel. But the miller intends to convert wheat into flour, and so a simultaneous purchase of wheat in the future will be necessary. Now a price increase in the future to $4.25 will result in a loss because of the futures contract. The loss would be ($3.90 − $4.25) × 1,000 = −$350. The *net* change in profit if the price of wheat rises will be $250 − $350 = −$100, the $250 increase in profit less the $350 loss from the futures contract. If the price of wheat should fall to $3.75, the gain from the futures contract would be ($3.90 − $3.75) × 1,000 = $150. The *net* change to the miller if the price of wheat falls will now be ($150 − $250) = −$100 once again. The hedge means that the net reduction in profit will be the same whether price increases or decreases by the same amount. The hedge has converted the uncertainty associated with a possible loss of $250 into a certain loss of $100 when the price change is ±25¢.

The net reduction in profit may be an acceptable price to pay to avoid the possibility of an even larger loss. The guaranteed reduction in profit results from the futures price being less than the initial cash price. That is the usual arrangement because the buyers of futures contracts expect to make a profit from risk transferred to them from hedgers like the miller who must pay to reduce that risk. Most buyers and sellers of futures contracts are not farmers or millers; they are called **speculators** because they are betting that the spot price will be higher than the futures price. Futures markets perform the role of transferring risk caused by uncertainty from hedgers to speculators.

Hedgers and speculators are important to the economy. Hedgers are primarily interested in making a profit by selling a good, but if they are risk averse they are also interested in reducing the risks to acceptable levels. Speculators, on the other hand, specialize in information about future supply and demand, and they are willing to assume some of the risk, expecting to make a profit based on their superior knowledge about the price of the good in the future. Speculators anticipate the price of the good in the future. If the futures price is above the current spot price, the speculators must believe that the good's price will rise. Thus, if you want to predict what the price of a good will be in the future, you might use the futures price as an indicator of what the expert speculators think it will be.

AN APPLICATION: *Managing Stock-Market Risk**

Investments in stocks are risky because stock prices and dividends vary. One source of this variability is *firm specific.* If a pharmaceutical company discovers a new drug, its stock price may rise. If the company does not obtain approval from the Food and Drug Administration to market the drug, the company's stock price will fall. Such a change in a company's stock price will not, however, perceptibly influence other stock prices. A second source of variability is *market risk.* Market-wide events affect all stocks: a general increase in interest rates might lower expected earnings for nearly every firm in the economy.

To successfully manage risk, investors must manage both firm-specific risk and market risk. Firm-specific risk is traditionally managed by holding a diversified portfolio of stocks. Diversification across stocks, however, may not reduce market risk. If an increase in interest rates causes all stock prices to fall, the change in one stock's price will not offset the change in another.

Market risk can be managed in two ways. One way is to reduce the share of all stocks in a portfolio and increase the share of other assets such as bonds. A second way is to reduce the share of stocks that have large market risk and increase the share of stocks with smaller risk. Both of these methods usually involve a trade-off between the return to the portfolio and its volatility.

Since 1982, as an alternative to traditional risk management, stock index futures have grown popular as a way to manage market risk. A financial futures contract is an agreement to buy or sell a financial asset at a set time in the future for a predetermined price. Stock index futures are future contracts wherein the asset is a *group* of stocks included in calculating a major stock price index. Nothing is exchanged when the contract is written because it is an agreement to make an exchange at a future date. Moreover, physical delivery of the asset rarely occurs because, even if permitted, a buyer or seller settles the contract by taking an offsetting position in the same futures contract before delivery. Stock index futures contracts actually *require* traders to settle contracts by taking an offsetting position.

Traders in stock index futures make profits or suffer losses when they settle a contract. A *buyer* makes a profit when the price rises and suffers a loss when price falls. A *seller* suffers a loss when the price rises and makes a profit when the price falls. Buyers and sellers are betting on changes in price.

The use of stock index futures has grown because they permit management of market risk by hedging. To hedge market risk, an investor must be able to take a position in a hedging asset so that profits or losses on the asset offset changes in the value of the stock portfolio. When events cause the value of an investor's portfolio to fall, the investor needs to make a profit on the hedging asset.

Stock index futures work as a hedge because their prices are highly correlated with changes in stock portfolio values caused by market-wide events. Investors who hold stock portfolios hedge market risk by selling stock index futures. If the market falls, the loss in the value of the portfolio is offset by the profit made when the price of the index future falls also. Of course when the market rises, the increase in value of the portfolio

---

*This application is based on Charles S. Morris, "Managing Stock Market Risk with Stock Index Futures," *Economic Review* 74(6), Federal Reserve Bank of Kansas City, June 1989.

is partially offset by the losses occurring when the price of the index future rises. The cost of reducing risk is a reduction in the expected return.

Managing market risk by hedging with stock index futures is relatively inexpensive because transactions costs are low. Fees paid to brokers and traders are quite small. Moreover, because buyers are allowed to use U.S. government securities to meet margin requirements, investors can earn interest on the initial margin outlay. Investors using stock index futures as a hedge also do not have to otherwise alter their portfolio. Despite these advantages over the traditional method of diversification to manage risk, some limitations apply. One problem is that stock index futures provide no protection against firm-specific events. A second is that futures traders must cover their futures losses at the end of each day, meaning that immediate cash settlements are required daily. A third limitation is the existence of *managerial* risk associated with using stock index futures inappropriately. It is possible for managers to "overhedge" by selling too many futures contracts so that, if the market rises, the losses on the futures position will be greater than the gains on the portfolio. Thus, managers must understand the complexities of hedging with stock index futures.

7.14 Decisions Under Uncertainty

Occasionally managers and other decision makers have to decide under uncertainty when they have no information about the probabilities of outcomes. Without such information, decision theory is usually presented as a game against nature. We cannot think of nature as malevolent, and so we don't need to consider the strategies that an opponent may adopt. In a later chapter, when we examine oligopoly, we will consider games with strategic behavior.

In games against nature, the player must be able to list alternative actions, identify the states of nature, and match the payoffs of any action with the states of nature. When we organize this information into an array, the result is called a **payoff table,** which will look like this:

	States of Nature			
Action	S_1	S_2	$\cdots$	S_n
A_1	a_{11}	a_{12}	$\cdots$	a_{1n}
A_2	a_{21}	a_{22}	$\cdots$	a_{21}
$\vdots$	$\vdots$	$\vdots$		$\vdots$
A_m	a_{m1}	a_{m2}	$\cdots$	a_{mn}

The payoff of action A_i is a_{ij} if state of nature S_j occurs.

Any rule for choosing actions requires that the player's attitude toward risk be known. That is, both the player's attitude toward taking gambles and financial position are necessary ingredients in concocting any decision rule. Because attitudes toward taking gambles and financial positions vary from person to person, appropriate rules vary likewise. As you'd expect, therefore, we have no universally valid decision rule under uncertainty. As an initial step in devising decision rules under uncertainty, let's look at two relatively naive rules.

First, the **maximin rule** says, Choose the action that yields the best of the worst payoffs. Consider this payoff table:

	S_1	S_2	S_2	Minimum Payoff
A_1	99	3	0	0
A_2	96	93	-3	-3

$$\text{maximin} = 0$$

The minimum payoff for action A_1 is 0, and the minimum payoff for action A_2 is -3. Thus, action A_1 is indicated by the maximin rule because maximin $= 0$. This rule might be appropriate for the pessimist who always expects the worst.

A second rule has been proposed for the optimist. The **maximax rule** says, Choose the action that yields the best of the best outcomes. The maximax rule always results in choosing the action with the greatest possible payoff. For the preceding payoff table:

	S_1	S_2	S_2	Maximum Payoff
A_1	99	3	0	99
A_2	96	93	-3	96

$$\text{maximax} = 99$$

The maximax rule—choose the maximum of the maximum payoffs, also indicates that action A_1 should be chosen because maximax $= 99$.

Both the maximin rule and the maximax rule disregard intermediate payoffs. A third, more sophisticated, rule is known as the **minimax regret rule.** This rule seeks to minimize the opportunity cost of an incorrect action, and it does cover intermediate payoffs. **Regret** is measured by the absolute value of the difference between the payoff for an action and the greatest payoff within the same state of nature. For a given column in the payoff table, the greatest payoff is found. The absolute value of the difference between that highest payoff and other payoffs in the same column measures the opportunity cost of choosing any action if that state of nature occurs.

To illustrate the regret rule, consider again the preceding payoff table. If you choose action A_1 and the state is S_1, the regret is 0. But if you choose A_2 and the state is S_1, the regret is 3. The regrets for the other states are found in the same way and can be arranged as a payoff table:

	S_1	S_2	S_2	Maximum Regrets
A_1	0	90	0	90
A_2	3	0	3	3

$$\text{minimax} = 3$$

The minimax regret rule indicates that action A_2 should be chosen because A_2 has the minimum of the maximum regrets, minimax regret = 3.

The minimax regret rule considers large differences in intermediate payoffs. The rule still disregards intermediate *regret* values, however. Another criticism of the regret rule is that differences between payoffs for any state of nature may not be an appropriate measure of regret. We need to measure the payoffs for their utilities. Then regrets will be marginal disutilities of choosing the wrong action, and the minimax regret rule will then select the action having the smallest marginal disutility.

7.15 Bayesian Decisions

Bayesian decisions force us to use probabilities. One rule, the **Laplace rule,** says that equal probabilities should be assigned to the states of nature if we have no better information. If we find n states of nature, the equiprobable assignment is $1/n$ to each. Then the action with the greatest expected value is chosen. From the standard payoff table, the expected value of action A_i is

$$E(A_i) = \sum_{j=1}^{n} a_{ij} \left(\frac{1}{n}\right)$$

The Laplace rule considers all possible payoffs.

As an example of the Laplace rule, the standard payoff table for the preceding example was:

	S_1	S_2	S_2	Expected Value
A_1	99	3	0	34
A_2	96	93	-3	62
probabilities:	1/3	1/3	1/3	max = 62

Because of the three states of nature, the probability of each is taken to be 1/3. The expected value of A_1 is

$$E(A_1) = 99\left(\frac{1}{3}\right) + 3\left(\frac{1}{3}\right) + 0\left(\frac{1}{3}\right) = 34$$

The expected value of A_2 is

$$E(A_2) = 96\left(\frac{1}{3}\right) + 93\left(\frac{1}{3}\right) - 3\left(\frac{1}{3}\right) = 62$$

The Laplace rule indicates that we should choose action A_2 because $E(A_2) > E(A_1)$. Of course, if we know the utility function, we can calculate expected utilities and we should choose the action that yields the greatest expected utility.

The Laplace rule suffers from a serious limitation imposed by the equal-probability assignments because, even without information, the decision maker may believe some states of nature are more likely than others. A rule called the **Bayesian rule** extends the Laplace rule by assigning subjective probabilities to the states of nature. The Bayesian rule, like the Laplace rule, then says to choose the action with the greatest expected value—or, if you know the utility function, to choose the action with the greatest expected utility.

Which of the several rules is best we do not know clearly. It may seem that the minimax regret rule and the Bayesian rule are superior to the others, but the indications of the rules are not always consistent—as illustrated by a practice problem at the end of this chapter. In general, which rule to apply depends on several factors. First, the frequency of the decision is important. If the decision is to be replicated many times, then it is reasonable to expect to win or lose in the same proportions as the general population does. As experience is gained, relative frequencies can be used as probabilities and expected value maximization can be applied. But if the decision is to be made only once, then the worst and the best outcomes may occur. Then the player's attitude toward risk and the player's ability to afford the worst outcome becomes important.

7.16 The Value of Information*

Information has value. If an individual could predict with certainty which state of nature would occur, any action could be chosen for the utilities of the payoffs associated with that state of nature. Thus, information about which state would occur must have both *utility* and *money* value. An individual would be willing to pay up to the money equivalent of the utility value of the information to acquire the information.

Let's denote the money payoff of action A_i when state S_j occurs as a_{ij}, and the utility of the payoff as $U(a_{ij})$. Then with probabilities P_j that state S_j occurs, the expected utility of any action A_i is

$$E[U(A_i)] = \sum_{j=1}^{n} U(a_{ij})\, P_j$$

The expected utility of any action is the sum of the products of the utilities of the payoffs and their respective probabilities. But you already know all that.

---

* This section may be skipped without loss of continuity.

The action that maximizes expected utility will be denoted by A_m. That action will have an expected value not less than the expected value for any other action; thus, for all i

$$E[U(A_m)] \geq E[U(A_i)]$$

Consider this payoff table:

	S_1	S_2
A_1	16	16
A_2	81	1
	1/3	2/3

Suppose the utility function is given as $U(a_{ij}) = \sqrt{a_{ij}}$. In terms of utility, the payoff table becomes:

	S_1	S_2	Expected Utility
A_1	4	4	12/3
A_2	9	1	11/3
	1/3	2/3	

Because $E[U(A_1)] > E[U(A_2)]$, these expected utilities indicate that action A_1 should be chosen.

Now suppose *perfect* information is available on which state will occur. For the numerical example above, if S_1 occurs, A_2 will be chosen because $U(a_{21}) = 9$ is highest for S_1. If S_2 occurs, A_1 will be chosen because $U(a_{12}) = 4$ is highest for S_2. In general, if state $\hat{S}_j$ is predicted, action A_k will be chosen when

$$U(a_{kj}) \geq U(a_{ij})$$

The *expected utility of a perfect prediction* that state S_j will occur is

$$E[U(A_k)] = \sum_{j=1}^{n} U(a_{kj}) P_j$$

That is, the expected utility of a perfect prediction is the summation of all the maximum utilities for each state, multiplied by their probabilities. For the numerical example, the expected utility of a perfect prediction is

$$E[U(A_k)] = 9 \left(\frac{1}{3}\right) + 4 \left(\frac{2}{3}\right) = \frac{17}{3}$$

because $A_k = A_2$ when S_1 is predicted and $A_k = A_1$ when S_2 is predicted. The perfect information received about which state occurs will predict S_1 with frequency $P_1 = 1/3$ and S_2 with frequency $P_2 = 2/3$.

We now know both the *maximum* expected utility and the expected utility of a *perfect prediction*. The difference between the two is the *value* of the information in *utility*. This difference is called the **utility of perfect information:**

> **Utility of perfect information:** *The difference between the expected utility of a perfect prediction and the expected utility without the information.*

The utility of perfect information that state $\hat{S}_j$ will occur will be denoted by $\hat{U}$ and is

$$\hat{U} = E[U(A_k)] - E[U(A_m)]$$

For our numerical example, the utility of perfect information is

$$\hat{U} = \frac{17}{3} - \frac{12}{3} = \frac{5}{3}$$

because $E[U(A_k)] = 17/3$ and $E[U(A_m)] = 12/3$.

How much would you be willing to pay for the information about which state will occur? We find the *value* of perfect information in *money* by evaluating the utility function of the money payoff at $\hat{U}$. That is, if $U = U(M)$ is the utility of money, then $M = \hat{M}$ can be found from $\hat{U} = U(\hat{M})$. For the numerical example, the utility function was assumed to be $U = \sqrt{M}$. When evaluated at $\hat{U} = 5/3$, this utility function yields $5/3 = \sqrt{\hat{M}}$ or $\hat{M} = 25/9$. Thus, you should pay no more than $\hat{M} = \$2.77$ to obtain the perfect information about which state will occur.

The maximum amount of money that a decision maker would be willing to pay for information is given by the money equivalent of the utility of perfect information.

> **Value of perfect information:** *The value of perfect information is equal to the money equivalent of the utility of perfect information—the maximum amount of money that will be paid for a perfect prediction.*

Of course the actual price paid for information will be less because most information is far from perfect. Nevertheless, this analysis provides some explanation for the demand for information as a good. The demand for information will be inversely related to its price and directly related to its quality.

Summary

The existence of asymmetric information can lead to market distortions and inefficient use of resources. This condition is illustrated by the "lemons" problem, in which sellers know more than buyers about quality of product. The total demand for the high- and low-quality good will decrease and the quantity of low-quality goods bought will increase. This shift may drive high-quality goods out of the market. Another manifestation of asymmetric information occurs in the principal-agent problem, where managerial behavior is difficult to monitor.

According to Frank Knight, certainty is a situation without speculation and guesses. Uncertainty occurs when no probabilities can be assigned to events. Risk occurs when events can be described by probability distributions. The term *risk aversion* is used to describe or measure an attitude toward the attraction or aversion to gambling. Risk aversion requires a diminishing marginal utility of money.

Objective probability is the frequency of an event in a sequence of infinite replications of an experiment or the frequency of an event whose outcomes follow a known probability distribution. Subjective probability is a numerical assignment that reflects an individual's feelings about the likelihood of an event. An individual can be induced to reveal subjective probabilities about events whenever he or she is willing to participate in an experiment offering a hypothetical gamble having identical payoffs as the real-world gamble.

The payoffs of any action can be characterized as a random variable. The mean of a random variable is its expected value, the weighted average of the possible values with their probabilities as weights. The variance of a random variable is the expected value of its squared deviation from its mean. The standard deviation is the positive square root of the variance. The covariance between two random variables is the expected value of the products of their deviations about their respective means. Correlation between two random variables transforms covariance into a measure of linear association that is independent of scales.

The decision rule of choosing the action having the greatest expected value is appropriate when decisions are replicated. Expected value maximization, though, is limited severely by the law of large numbers. Many economic decisions are made only once. Another flaw in the expected-value rule is that the dispersion in payoffs is not considered. Greater dispersion is associated with greater risk. An alternative rule that does consider dispersion says, Choose the alternative that has the smallest coefficient of variation, the standard deviation divided by the mean. This rule, however, does not reflect the extent of risk aversion.

Another approach in choosing among risky alternatives is to assume that utility depends on the mean and variance of the payoffs. Mean-variance analysis has been applied to portfolio choice problems. Once the utility-maximizing choice has been identified, we can measure the *price* of risk as the difference between the mean of the portfolio and the return from a riskless alternative, all divided by the standard deviation of the portfolio. When people have opportunities to trade risk, the equilibrium price of risk will be equal across all individuals.

When the returns to alternatives are not independent, diversification can be used to reduce the overall risk to the portfolio. Moreover, risk spreading can be used to spread the risk among many individuals. Also, when returns are not independent, the covariance of payoffs to alternatives can be used in measuring the relative risk of any asset. The beta of an asset is the covariance of its return with the market return divided by the market variance. The risk-adjusted return to any risky asset is its expected return less a risk-adjustment factor, which is equal to the beta of the asset multiplied by the difference between the market return and the return to a certain alternative. In market equilibrium, the prices of all risky assets will be equal *after* adjusting for risk.

Decisions under uncertainty can be characterized as games against nature. The problem is described with a payoff table. Several decision rules have been proposed for choosing among uncertain actions. The maximin rule (for pessimists) and the maximax rule (for optimists) both disregard intermediate payoffs, and so neither is very satisfactory. The minimax regret rule seeks to minimize the opportunity cost of an incorrect action, but it still considers only the largest and smallest regrets for any action. The Laplace rule assigns equal probabilities to all states of nature. The Bayesian rule assigns subjective probabilities to all states. Both the Laplace and Bayesian rules consider intermediate payoffs as well as the best and worst payoffs for every action; however, both rules are subject to the same criticism as expected value maximization.

Measurable utility and expected utility can be extended to decisions under uncertainty. Individual attitudes toward risk are considered, and the method does not depend on the law of large numbers. Although expected utility maximization is not often a practical operational tool, it does emphasize that information has value. The utility of perfect information about which state will occur is the difference between the expected utility of a perfect prediction and the expected utility without the information. The most an individual would be willing to pay for perfect information is equal to the money equivalent of the information's utility. The model also demonstrates that the demand for information is inversely related to its price and directly related to its quality, and so information can be treated just like any other good.

Further Readings

The distinction between risk and uncertainty applied in this chapter is from

- Frank H. Knight, *Risk, Uncertainty and Profit* (Houghton Mifflin, 1921).

Another useful book is provided by

- Kenneth J. Arrow, *Essays in the Theory of Risk Bearing* (North Holland, 1970).

For further insights on the utility foundations of mean-variance analysis and extending the concept of risk to investment and portfolio decisions, see

- Harry M. Markowitz, *Portfolio Selection* (John Wiley, 1959).
- J. Hirshleifer, "Investment Decisions under Uncertainty: Choice-Theoretic Approaches," *Quarterly Journal of Economics* (November 1965).
- M. S. Feldstein, "Mean-Variance Analysis in the Theory of Liquidity Preference and Portfolio Selection," *Review of Economic Studies*, 36(1) (1969).

For an argument in favor of using the coefficient-of-variation rule, see

- J. Fred Weston and Eugene F. Brigham, *Managerial Finance*, 7th ed. (Holt, Rinehart & Winston, 1981).

The capital-asset pricing model was first presented by

- W. F. Sharpe, "Capital Asset Prices: A Theory of Market Equilibrium under Conditions of Risk," *Journal of Finance*, 19 (September 1964).

For more recent developments on the use of the CAPM, see

- Stephen A. Ross, "The Current Status of the Capital Asset Pricing Model (CAPM)," *Journal of Finance* (June 1982).
- H. Levy, "The Capital Asset Pricing Model," *Economic Journal*, 93 (1983).

Measurable utility and expected utility as well as a comprehensive treatment of game theory are provided in:

- John von Neumann and Oskar Morgenstern, *Theory of Games and Economic Behavior*, 2nd ed. (Princeton University Press, 1953).

John von Neumann was a major figure in mathematics who made several important contributions in physics, computer science, and economic theory, and Oskar Morgenstern was a Princeton economist who, along with von Neumann, helped to develop game theory. A more popular book on games is

- R. D. Luce and H. Raiffa, *Games and Decisions* (John Wiley, 1966).

For a survey of measurable utility, expected utility, and decision theory, see

- William J. Baumol, *Economic Theory and Operations Analysis*, 3d ed. (Prentice-Hall, 1972).

These articles are also relevant:

- A. A. Alchian, "The Meaning of Utility Measurement," *American Economic Review* (March 1953).
- Paul A. Samuelson, "Utility, Preference and Probability" and "Probability, Utility and the Independence Axioms" (1953), reprinted in *Collected Scientific Papers of Paul A. Samuelson*, vol. 1, J. E. Stiglitz, ed. (M. I. T. Press, 1966).

For a fairly recent survey of the economics of uncertainty and information, see

- J. Hirshleifer and John G. Riley, "The Analytics of Uncertainty and Information—A Survey," *Journal of Economic Literature* (December 1979).

Also relevant are

- F. A. Hayek, "The Use of Knowledge in Society," *American Economic Review*, 35 (1945).
- George Stigler, "The Economics of Information," *Journal of Political Economy* (June 1961).

For an excellent discussion of principal-agent relationships and an extensive list of references, see

- David E. M. Sappington, "Incentives in Principal-Agent Relationships," *Journal of Economic Perspectives,* 5(1) (Spring 1991).

Practice Problems

1. Faced with an influx of foreign cars with a reputation for high quality, American car companies began to offer extensive guarantees on new cars. Explain why this shift might be a reaction to a "lemons" problem.
2. Consider these investments:

	Investment A		Investment B	
Return	Probability	Return	Probability
500	1/8	800	1/8
1,000	3/4	1,000	3/4
1,500	1/8	1,200	1/8

(a) Calculate the expected return on each investment.
(b) Calculate the variance and standard deviation of each investment.
(c) Which investment would you choose using the mean-variance rule?
(d) Which investment would you choose using the coefficient-of-variation rule?
3. Explain how the law of large numbers is related to objective probability. What relevance does this relation have to expected-value maximization?
4. Given this information:

	Investment A		Investment B	
PV	Probability	PV	Probability
100	3/10	300	3/10
400	4/10	400	4/10
700	3/10	500	3/10

(a) Which alternative will be chosen according to the expected-value rule?

(b) What alternative will be chosen to maximize expected utility if utility is given by

Money	Utility
0	0
100	20
200	39
300	57
400	73
500	87
600	98
700	105

(c) Using the table, calculate the marginal utilities of money. What can you say about the marginal utility of money in this case?

5. An individual's utility is given by

$$U(X) = \left(\frac{X}{10}\right)^2$$

Find the probability P when this individual is indifferent between two lotteries, A and B, which offer these prizes:

Lottery A		Lottery B	
Prize	Probability	Prize	Probability
110	1/2	90	P
130	1/2	150	$1-P$

6. Using a graph, show that a risk-neutral investor (one having a linear utility function) makes investment decisions in accordance with maximizing expected value.

7. A risk-averse person is offered a payment of $325 or a chance at a gamble that pays $1,000 with probability 1/4 and $100 with probability 3/4. Will this person choose the certain payment or the gamble?

8. An investor whose utility function is given by $U(X) = \sqrt{X}$, where X denotes money profits, is given a chance to choose one of these options:

Option A		Option B	
Profit	Probability	Profit	Probability
16	1/2	81	1/2
196	1/2	121	1/2

(a) Calculate expected values and expected utilities.
(b) Which option should be chosen?
(c) Graph the utility function.
(d) Calculate and identify on your graph the maximum price that the investor would be willing to pay for options A and B.
(e) What are the expected profits from A and B?

9. A newspaper columnist reported on this game: "Flip a coin. You get $1,000 if it comes up heads, nothing if tails. But if you could sell your chance just before the flip, how much would you sell it for? Odds on the flip run 50–50, and so you'd charge $500 for your chance, no? Most people queried said they'd sell for $350." Pessimists, right?

10. Suppose an individual is indifferent to $40 with certainty and Lottery A offering $0 with probability 1/2 and $90 with probability 1/2. Furthermore, this individual is indifferent to $50 with certainty, and Lottery B offering $0 with probability 1/3 and $90 with probability 2/3. What choice will be made in these situations?
(a) Lottery C, offering $40 with probability 1/4 and $90 with probability 3/4, or Lottery D, offering $50 with probability 1/2 and $90 with probability 1/2.
(b) Lottery E, offering $0 with probability 1/4 and $50 with probability 3/4, or Lottery F, offering $40 with probability 4/5 and $90 with probability 1/5.

11. Consider a lottery T that offers a chance at $w = $0 or $b = $100 at even odds. If the conventional utility assignments of $U(0) = 0$ and $U(100) = 1$ are made, suppose that the utility of $50 with certainty is measured at $U(50) = 3/5$:
(a) What is the expected value of the lottery?
(b) Given that the price of the lottery is $50, what is the gain in utility if the player wins the lottery? What is the loss in utility if the player loses the lottery?
(c) Does this player have a preference toward risk that results in a diminishing or increasing marginal utility of money? Is this player a risk averter or a risk lover?
(d) Explain why this player will or will not buy this lottery when its price is $50.

12. Suppose a stock has a β of 1.5, the market rate of return is 10 percent, and an alternative riskless asset has a rate of return of 5 percent:
(a) What is the expected rate of return on the stock according to the CAPM?
(b) If the expected value of the stock is $100, what price should the stock sell for today?

13. Use the capital-asset pricing model to determine the adjusted discounting interest rate if the risk-free return is 6 percent and the average market rate is 10 percent

when the beta of an asset is:

(a) $\beta = 2$ (b) $\beta = 1$ (c) $\beta = 1/2$ (d) $\beta = 0$

Then explain what the beta of an asset implies about its risk relative to the market as a whole. When $\beta = 0$, does that imply the asset has no risk?

14. The current spot price of wheat is $5.10 per bushel and the future price is $5.00 per bushel. Determine the profit or loss due to a hedge on 1,000 bushels if the future spot price becomes $5.25 per bushel.

15. An individual has a measurable utility function over money payoffs of the form $U = \sqrt{M}$. Given a lottery in which $0 is received with probability 2/3 and $36 is received with probability 1/3, how much would this person be willing to pay to replace the lottery with its expected value?

16. Given the table of money payoffs:

	S_1	S_2
A_1	4	4
A_2	9	1
	1/3	2/3

(a) If the measurable utility function is $U = \sqrt{M}$, where M is the money payoff, construct the payoff table of utilities.

(b) Compute the expected utilities of each action.

(c) Compute the expected utility of a perfect prediction.

(d) Compute the utility of perfect information.

(e) How much would this person be willing to pay for the perfect information?

17. For this payoff table (cited by Baumol as from John Milnor):

	S_1	S_2	S_3	S_4
A_1	1	1	1	1
A_2	0	4	0	0
A_3	1	3	0	0
A_4	2	2	0	1

(a) Which action is indicated by the maximin rule?

(b) Which action is indicated by the minimax regret rule?

(c) Which action is indicated by the Laplace rule?

Estimation and Forecasting

nformation has value in a world filled with uncertainty. Although it is said that history repeats itself, that truism is not entirely accurate because some unpredictable events occur that cannot be predicted or will not be repeated. Still, historical information can be used to predict the likelihood of some future events. Businesspeople and government officials use historical data to quantify economic relationships that they can then use for predicting and forecasting.

The most frequently used method in quantifying an economic model is estimating equations from data using least-squares regression, the subject of Chapter 8. Economic theory guides us in specifying the functional form to be estimated, and theory helps us choose explanatory variables. After estimation, economic theory then helps to interpret the quantified model.

Some of the more commonly used and practical forecasting techniques are surveyed in Chapter 9. You will see how trends can be established in time series, and you will learn how to detrend a series in order to isolate the trend from seasonal, cyclical, and random components. Topics include autoregressive, moving-average, and mixed autoregressive–moving-average models. You will learn how to use dummy variables to predict seasonal changes in a time series, and you will see how leading indicators can be used to predict cyclical variation. We also look at how simultaneous-equation models can be applied to capture relationships between sectors of the economy. All these techniques are used every day in the real world by decision makers who require information about the future.

Chapter

Model Estimation

The basic model of market equilibrium is quite useful in making *qualitative,* conditional predictions. We can predict that the demand for a good will increase if the price of a market substitute increases alone. Subsequently, the increase in demand will lead to an increase in the good's own price. The model is also useful in interpreting *quantitative* information. If we know that the price elasticity of demand is $\eta = 2$, we then know that a 1 percent increase in price will cause approximately a 2 percent decrease in quantity demanded. Furthermore, this model tells us that total consumer expenditure will fall when price increases if demand is elastic. But where does that quantitative information come from?

Demand and supply equations can be estimated from empirical information. The estimated equations can then be used to make quantitative predictions and forecasts.

Calvin and Hobbes   by Bill Watterson

Calvin & Hobbes Copyright 1989 Universal Press Syndicate. Reprinted with permission.
All rights reserved.

Presumably, the predictions and forecasts will be reliable enough to reduce the uncertainty in merely making qualitative predictions. Also, we should know how to judge the validity of economic models. You should never rely heavily on a model that appears sensible but is not founded on a sound base of empirical evidence. Unlike Calvin's view in the cartoon by Bill Watterson, research is an indispensable part of science. One way to test the validity of an economic model is to subject it to empirical verification.

In this chapter we concentrate on estimating demand and supply, but the tools learned will be useful later in estimating other economic models. We will, consider, for instance, how to estimate production functions and cost curves in later chapters. In this chapter we focus primarily on *causal* models—in which we can see a clear cause-and-effect relationship between explanatory variables and a dependent variable. In this book causation is defined as prediction according to a theory; thus, prediction without a theory is not causation.[1]

The most usual method of estimating economic models from empirical data is regression analysis, a principal technique used in a field of study called **econometrics**—economic measurement. After a brief introduction to regression analysis, we proceed from a simple linear model with one explanatory variable to estimating nonlinear models with several explanatory variables. It is very dangerous to use regression models naively, and so we examine several frequent problems and their remedies, with the objective of assembling the "best" empirical model possible.

8.1   Regression Analysis

Regression analysis is a statistical technique with which we attempt to "explain" movements in a *dependent* variable as a function of movements in *explanatory* variables. For a demand function, the dependent variable is quantity demanded, and the explanatory variables are prices, income, and other things that might influence demand. For a supply function, the dependent variable is quantity supplied, and the explanatory

---

1. For a discussion on alternative definitions of causation, see Arnold Zellner, *Basic Issues in Econometrics* (University of Chicago Press, 1984), pp. 35–74.

variables include the good's price, input prices, measures of technology, and other things that might influence supply. In the real world the determinants of demand and supply change simultaneously, meaning that any quantitative analysis of demand and supply must control for changes in any conditions that might influence demand or supply.

Economic theory makes selecting some of the explanatory variables obvious. But selecting and measuring other variables may not be so obvious. In estimating demand, we know that preference is crucial in determining choice. Therefore, unless we have strong reason to believe that preferences remain constant, we need to control for changes in preference. Because it is not easy to measure preference directly, indirect control may be exercised by using proxies. A **proxy** variable is one that is thought to vary systematically with a variable that cannot be measured directly. If consumer preference is related to age, perhaps the consumer's age or the age distribution of the population is a suitable proxy for preference. Other proxies that are frequently used are gender, education, race, religion, region of residence, and season of the year. Another variable that may affect preference is promotional advertising. Indeed, the effectiveness of advertising might be the primary focus of your empirical investigation. In estimating supply, the state of technology is crucial. One proxy used to control for a changing technology as time passes is time itself.

The two basic types of data are time-series and cross-sectional data. **Time-series** data consist of the values of variables as they occurred over different periods. Time-series data may be recorded for relatively short periods such as days or for longer periods such as annual averages. For an example of time-series data, see Table 8.1, presenting data on the price and quantity demanded for oranges over a twelve-day period. Each day the price was recorded and matched with the quantity demanded on the same day. These observations can be represented graphically on a **scatterplot,** as illustrated by Figure 8.1, a graph of the paired observations. Notice that the quantity demanded is now plotted on

Table 8.1 Hypothetical Demand for Oranges

Day(i)	Quantity (Y_i)	Cents (X_i)	($Y_i - \bar{Y}$)	($X_i - \bar{X}$)	($X_i - \bar{X}$)($Y_i - \bar{Y}$)	($X_i - \bar{X}$)^2	($Y_i - \bar{Y}$)^2
1	55	100	−45	30	−1,350	900	2,025
2	70	90	−30	20	−600	40	900
3	90	80	−10	10	−100	100	100
4	100	70	0	0	0	0	0
5	90	70	−10	0	0	0	100
6	105	70	5	0	0	0	25
7	80	70	−20	0	0	0	400
8	110	65	10	−5	−50	25	100
9	125	60	25	−10	−250	100	625
10	115	60	15	−10	−150	100	225
11	130	55	30	−15	−450	225	900
12	130	50	30	−20	−600	400	900
Sums:	1,200	840	0	0	−3,550	2,250	6,300

Source: Jan Kmenta, *Elements of Econometrics,* 2d ed. (Macmillan, 1986). Reprinted by permission of Macmillan Publishing Co., Inc. Copyright © 1986 by Jan Kmenta.

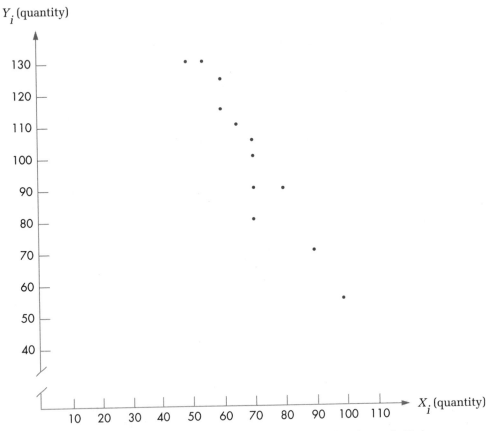

Figure 8.1   **A scatterplot of data:** Prices (X_i) and quantities demanded (Y_i) for $i = 1, 12$ days were observed and plotted as price–quantity pairs.

the vertical axis. In econometrics, it is conventional to plot the dependent variable on the vertical axis.

Cross-sectional data, the other basic type, can be recorded in the same way. **Cross-sectional** data are records of values of variables for some fixed time period. A list of regional unemployment rates is a cross-section. Census data are a cross-section of individuals and families for a survey period. Cross-sectional data may be pooled with time-series data if they are compatible. The unemployment rate by region may be recorded for several survey years and pooled into one data set.[2]

Data are then used to estimate a functional relationship between the dependent variable and the explanatory variables. Frequently, the functional form to be estimated is specified as linear. To estimate the demand curve for oranges from the data in Table 8.1,

2. Another type of data set called **longitudinal** data or **panel** data traces the values of variables relevant to a panel over time. A panel of individuals may be selected and their incomes recorded for several years. Although longitudinal data have time-series and cross-sectional characteristics, the panel being studied does not change.

the linear equation $Y = \alpha + \beta X$ might be chosen. The dependent variable representing quantity demanded is Y and X is the explanatory variable representing price. Our model of demand indicates that intercept α should be positive and slope β should be negative. One way to estimate the intercept and slope would be to place a straightedge over the scatter-plot so that it "fits" the data as closely as possible. By projecting the line through the Y-axis, we can find an estimate of α. And we can estimate β by measuring the ratio $\Delta Y / \Delta X$ along the line. Of course everyone fitting a line by eye will obtain a slightly different equation, and so it would be useful to have a technique that would generate the same equation no matter who uses the technique. Moreover, it would be useful to have some objective criteria for judging the "goodness of fit."

Linear equations may not be the best functional specification. Perhaps we have good reason to believe that demand is of the constant-elasticity variety. Thus, economic theory may also be useful in specifying the functional form to be estimated. Or perhaps you believe that advertising expenditures influence demand greatly for initial expenditures but less and less for ever-greater expenditures; you might therefore choose a cubic function to capture the expected relationship between demand and advertising. Fortunately, regression analysis is sufficiently flexible to permit many functional forms with a large number of explanatory variables. Before we examine the multivariate regression model, let's examine a linear model with just one explanatory variable.

The simplest linear regression model is

$$Y = \alpha + \beta X + \varepsilon$$

where Y is the dependent variable, X is the explanatory variable, α is the intercept, and β is the slope. Besides the variation in Y caused by changes in X, variation almost always comes from other sources as well. This additional variation is recognized by including a **stochastic (random) error** term in the model. The Greek letter epsilon, ε, is used for the random error. Initially, we assume that the random error has zero mean and constant variance. We can hope the random error is small and caused primarily by measurement error. Later, however, we will consider additional variation in Y caused by omitting important explanatory variables, misspecifying the functional form, or random and unpredictable events.

Now for an example of the simple regression model. Suppose the demand for apples is determined by the *stochastic* (random) relationship,[3]

$$Q = 11 - 0.4p + \varepsilon$$

where random error ε has this probability distribution:

ε	Prob(ε)
+1	1/4
0	1/2
−1	1/4

---

3. This example is adapted from Jan Kmenta, *Elements of Econometrics,* 2d ed. (Macmillan, 1986), pp. 204–206.

Thus, Q has some variation besides that caused by price changes. The demand schedule now may be written

Q	Prob(Q)
$12 - 0.4p$	1/4
$11 - 0.4p$	1/2
$10 - 0.4p$	1/4

This schedule implies that, for example, when $p = 0$: 25 percent of the time $Q = 12$; 50 percent of the time $Q = 11$; and 25 percent of the time $Q = 10$. Figure 8.2 indicates the stochastic demand for Q when $p = 0, 5, 10, 15, 20$, and 25. The sizes of the points correspond to the frequency of occurrence.

In Figure 8.2, notice that a positive error is just as likely as a negative error. The expected value of the error thus is zero,

$$E(\varepsilon) = (1)\frac{1}{4} + (0)\frac{1}{2} + (-1)\frac{1}{4} = 0$$

Because $E(\varepsilon) = 0$, the expected value of Q given p is

$$E(Q; p) = 11 - 0.4p$$

Thus, the *expectation* of demand as a function of price has intercept $Q = 11$ when $p = 0$ and slope $\Delta Q/\Delta p = -0.4$.

8.2   Least-Squares Regression

Returning now to the generic model, we may include reference to specific sample observations by writing

$$Y_i = \alpha + \beta X_i + \varepsilon_i$$

where subscript i denotes the ith observation with $i = 1, \ldots, n$ and n is the number of observations in a random sample drawn from the population. If the expected value of the error term is zero, $E(\varepsilon_i) = 0$, then the expected value of Y_i given X_i when X is fixed is

$$E(Y_i; X_i) = \alpha + \beta X_i$$

This equation is known as the **true regression** line. We may never know the *true* values of α and β; however, they can be *estimated*.

How can we estimate α and β? We can choose among several alternative criteria for obtaining estimates, but the method most often used is least-squares regression. **Least-squares regression** generates estimates for α and β by minimizing the sum of the

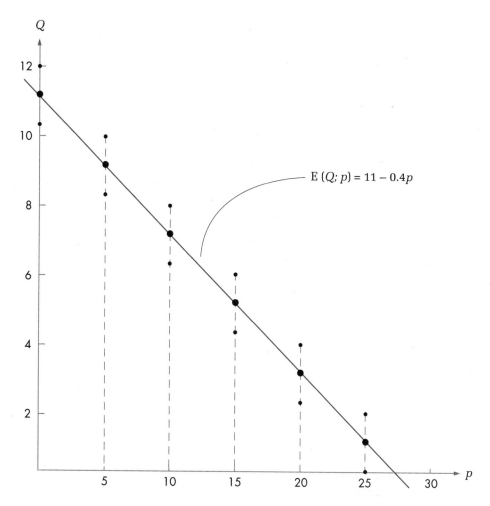

Figure 8.2 **Stochastic demand:** Quantity demanded is $Q = 11 - 0.4p + \varepsilon$, where $\varepsilon = -1$ with probability $= 1/4$, $\varepsilon = 0$ with probability $= 1/2$, and $\varepsilon = +1$ with probability $= 1/4$. Because $E(\varepsilon) = 0$, $E(Q; p) = 11 - 0.4p$.

squared errors where the error is measured by the difference between the observed value of Y and its predicted value $\hat{Y}$:

> **Least-squares regression:** *The method for finding the linear equation that minimizes the sum of squares of the residual errors for all observations.*

Data representing paired observations of the dependent and explanatory variables can be presented by a scatterplot. Figure 8.3 shows a scatterplot for which data points (X_i, Y_i) are plotted for a hypothetical sample of size $n = 6$.

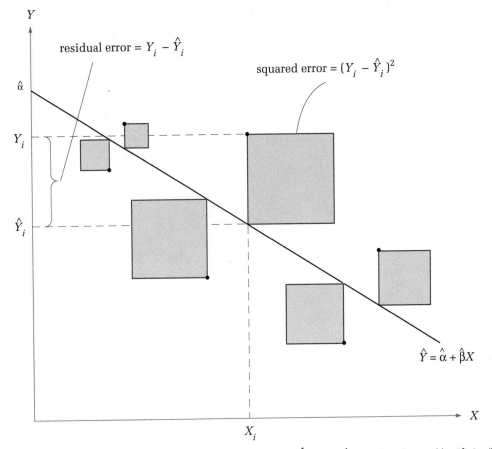

Figure 8.3   **Scatterplot and linear estimates:** A linear estimate $\hat{Y} = \hat{\alpha} + \hat{\beta}X$ may be obtained by "fitting" a straight line to the observations. The residual error for the ith observation is the difference between the actual value Y_i and the estimated value $\hat{Y}_i$.

The **estimated regression line** is denoted by

$$Y_i = \hat{\alpha} + \hat{\beta}X_i + \hat{\varepsilon}_i$$

where $\hat{\varepsilon}_i$ is defined as the **residual error,**

$$\hat{\varepsilon}_i = Y_i - \hat{Y}_i$$

and $\hat{Y}_i = \hat{\alpha} + \hat{\beta}X_i$ is the predicted value of Y_i given X_i. The *prediction* of Y given X is referred to as Y-hat, and the *estimates* for α and β are called α-hat and β-hat. Likewise, the residual error is called ε-hat.

As illustrated by Figure 8.3, each residual error $\hat{\varepsilon}_i$ is the difference between the observed value of the dependent variable and its predicted value for the ith observation. The random errors ε_i are deviations in the observations of the dependent variable from

AN APPLICATION: *Demand for Oranges*

As a numerical example, consider the preceding data on prices and quantities of oranges sold in a supermarket on twelve consecutive days, as listed in Table 8.1. To keep the example simple, we assume that the supermarket has enough oranges each day to meet its demand. In other words, change in quantity supplied is not an issue. Let X_i be the price charged and Y_i be the quantity sold on the ith day. If we assume that the stochastic demand function is

$$Y_i = \alpha + \beta X_i + \varepsilon_i$$

then the method of least squares can be used to obtain estimates $\hat{\alpha}$ and $\hat{\beta}$.

The least-squares estimators for α and β require the Cov(X, Y) and the Var(X) from the sample. The formulas are:

$$\text{Cov}(X, Y) = \frac{1}{n}\Sigma(X_i - \bar{X})(Y_i - \bar{Y})$$

and

$$\text{Var}(X) = \frac{1}{n}\Sigma(X_i - \bar{X})^2$$

Substitution results in

$$\hat{\beta} = \frac{\Sigma(X_i - \bar{X})(Y_i - \bar{Y})}{\Sigma(X_i - \bar{X})^2} = \frac{-3{,}550}{2{,}250} = -1.578$$

The required numbers for the substitutions are shown in Table 8.1. Now that we have $\hat{\beta}$, and because the sample means are $\bar{Y} = 100$ and $\bar{X} = 70$, we can find $\hat{\alpha}$ as

$$\hat{\alpha} = \bar{Y} - \hat{\beta}\bar{X} = 100 - (-1.578)70 = 210.46$$

Thus, the least-squares regression line is

$$\hat{Y}_i = 210.46 - 1.578X_i$$

This estimated demand curve is linear, and so the price elasticity of demand is different at different prices. The mean elasticity can be calculated at the point of the means, $\bar{Y} = 100$ and $\bar{X} = 70$:

$$\hat{\eta} = -(-1.578)\left(\frac{70}{100}\right) = 1.1046$$

This estimated demand curve is elastic at the point of the means.

---

the true population regression line, whereas the residual errors $\hat{\varepsilon}_i$ are deviations in the observations of the dependent variable from the estimated sample regression line.

The **squared error** is

$$\hat{\varepsilon}_i^2 = (Y_i - \hat{Y}_i)^2$$

In Figure 8.3, each squared error is shown to be equal to the area of a square, determined by squaring each residual error. To incorporate all the errors in estimating α and β for the linear equation, the sum of all the squared errors is minimized,[4]

$$\min \Sigma \, (Y_i - \hat{Y}_i)^2 = \min\Sigma \, (Y_i - \hat{\alpha} - \hat{\beta}X_i)^2$$

Minimizing this expression yields estimates $\hat{\alpha}$ and $\hat{\beta}$, and the estimated equation is $\hat{Y} = \hat{\alpha} + \hat{\beta}X$. Least squares fits a line to the scatterplot in such a way that the sum of the squared errors is minimized.

The **least-squares estimators** for α and β can be shown to be:[5]

$$\hat{\beta} = \frac{\text{Cov}(X, Y)}{\text{Var}(X)} = \frac{S_{xy}}{S_{xx}}$$

$$\hat{\alpha} = \overline{Y} - \hat{\beta}\overline{X}$$

where S_{xy} is the sample covariance of X and Y, S_{xx} is the sample variance of X, and $\overline{Y}$ and $\overline{X}$ are the sample means. The least-squares estimator $\hat{\beta}$ is equal to the sample covariance of X and Y divided by the sample variance in X. The estimated equation $\hat{Y} = \hat{\alpha} + \hat{\beta}X$ must pass through the point of the sample means because $\hat{\alpha} = \overline{Y} - \hat{\beta}\overline{X}$. Thus, if slope β is underestimated by $\hat{\beta}$, the intercept α will be overestimated by $\hat{\alpha}$, and vice versa.

8.3 Multivariate Least Squares

Quantity demanded is a function of several variables that vary simultaneously. In practice it is not usually possible to allow one variable to change while holding all other variables constant. But that configuration can be accomplished statistically by extending the regression model to include several explanatory variables. The regression model is extended by assuming that the dependent variable Y is a function of k explanatory variables and an error term:

$$Y_i = \alpha + \beta_1 X_{1i} + \beta_2 X_{2i} + \cdots + \beta_k X_{ki} + \varepsilon_i$$

$$= \alpha + \sum_{j=1}^{k} \beta_j X_{ji} + \varepsilon_i$$

The only additional assumptions required for estimating are that $n > k + 1$ and that no X_j is perfectly correlated with any of the remaining explanatory variables taken separately or in combination.

---

4. Minimizing the sum of the errors is not satisfactory because negative errors tend to cancel positive errors. Minimizing the sum of the absolute values of the errors would solve the sign problem but might ignore some observations in obtaining the estimated equation. The least-squares method not only solves the sign problem and considers all errors, it also weights large errors more heavily than small errors.
5. See the appendix to this chapter. Because we are working with a sample from an unknown population, we use the notation S_{xy} for the covariance between X and Y and S_{xx} is the variance of X that can also be written S_x^2.

Estimation requires $i = 1, \ldots, n$ matched observations for $Y, X_1, X_2, \ldots, X_k$. The sum of squared deviations of the observed value of Y from the fitted model is

$$\sum_{i=1}^{n} (Y_i - \hat{Y}_i)^2 = \sum_{i=1}^{n} \left[Y_i - \left(\hat{\alpha} + \sum_{j=1}^{k} \hat{\beta}_j X_{ji} \right) \right]^2$$

Minimizing this sum of squared errors leads to a set of $(k + 1)$ equations in terms of the $(k + 1)$ unknowns, $\hat{\alpha}, \hat{\beta}_1, \hat{\beta}_2, \ldots, \hat{\beta}_k$. The equations are called the **normal equations** and are developed in the appendix to this chapter. Solving the normal equations when several explanatory variables and many observations are included is tedious, and so computer programs have been written to do the calculations. For our purposes, realize only that the number of observations must exceed the number of unknown coefficients to be estimated, and that none of the explanatory variables may be exact linear combinations of other explanatory variables.[6]

Multivariate regression has become so common that computer programs are widely available. These programs routinely calculate estimated coefficients and important summary statistics. Table 8.2 illustrates a typical regression output, whether generated by a mainframe or personal-computer program. The example in the table is an estimated-demand equation using a program called SYSTAT. The equation to be estimated was

$$Q_d = \alpha + \beta_1 p_x + \beta_2 M + \beta_3 p_y + \varepsilon$$

Quantity demanded of good X is a linear function of own-price (p_x), consumers' money income (M) measured in hundreds of dollars, and the price (p_y) of a related good Y. Annual observations were taken over a twenty-year period, and some descriptive statistics for the variables are reproduced in Table 8.2. We will consider the information contained in that table as we proceed.

The estimated regression equation is

$$\hat{Q}_d = 121.747 - 9.462 p_x + 4.091 M - 2.210 p_y$$

The coefficient for p_x is negative, as it should be for a demand equation. The positive coefficient for M indicates that good X is a normal good. The negative coefficient for p_y indicates that good X is a market complement for good Y.

The estimated coefficients are interpreted as the partial effect of a change in their respective explanatory variable alone. That is,

$$\hat{\beta}_j = \frac{\Delta Y}{\Delta X_j}$$

and the remaining variables remain constant. For instance, the estimated coefficient for own-price from Table 8.2 indicates that the predicted Q_d decreases by 9.462 units for a

---

6. The latter condition is called **perfect multicollinearity,** and the normal equations would not be independent and do not have a unique solution.

Table 8.2 **Example of Multivariate Regression Output**

Regression Output from SYSTAT

DEP VAR: QD   N: 20   SQUARED MULTIPLE R: 0.969
STANDARD ERROR OF ESTIMATE: 7.318   ADJ SQUARED MULTIPLE R: 0.963

VARIABLE	COEFFICIENT	STD ERROR	T
CONSTANT	121.747	32.479	3.748
PX	− 9.462	1.849	− 5.118
M	4.091	1.870	2.188
PY	− 2.210	3.239	− 0.682

ANALYSIS OF VARIANCE:

SOURCE	SUM-OF-SQUARES	DF
REGRESSION	26910.039	3
RESIDUAL	856.761	16

Descriptive Statistics from SYSTAT

TOTAL OBSERVATIONS: 20

	QD	PX	M	PY
MINIMUM	72.000	4.000	20.000	14.000
MAXIMUM	198.000	10.000	39.890	25.000
MEAN	140.400	6.300	29.717	19.600
VARIANCE	1461.411	4.747	38.113	11.411
STANDARD DEV	38.228	2.179	6.174	3.378

one-unit increase in price if M and p_y are held constant. Likewise, a \$100 increase in M will increase predicted Q_d by 4.091 units if p_x and p_y are constant, and a one-unit increase in p_y will decrease predicted Q_d by 2.210 units if p_x and M are held constant.

Besides minimizing the sum of squared errors, the estimators $\hat{\alpha}$ and $\hat{\beta}_j$ have another desirable characteristic. As long as the random error has zero mean, $E(\varepsilon) = 0$, and as long as the random error ε is uncorrelated with any of the explanatory variables, the least-squares estimators will be **unbiased** in the sense that $E(\hat{\beta}_j) = \beta_j$ and $E(\hat{\alpha}) = \alpha$. That is, the estimators are unbiased if their expected values equal their true but unknown values. What does this statement mean? An estimate is generated from a random sample. If the sampling and estimation procedure is replicated over and over, a distribution of estimates will be generated. Therefore, the estimator is a random variable and has a distribution, and that distribution has an expected value, or mean. If the mean of the distribution of the estimator is equal to the true but unknown value of the random variable, the estimator is unbiased. This condition implies that, although an estimate calculated from one sample is unlikely to be exactly equal to the true value of the random variable, on average the estimator will be equal to the true value.

ECONOMIC SCENE: *The Bordeaux Equation**

Professor Orley Ashenfelter, a Princeton economist, has derived a formula for predicting the quality of red-wine vintages from France. The equation is

In Qual $= -12.145 + 0.00117$ *WintRain* $+ 0.6164$ *Temp* -0.00386 *HarvRain*

where

In Qual	= logarithmic index of quality, with 1961 = 100.
WintRain	= winter rain (October through March) in millimeters.
Temp	= average temperature during the growing season (April through September) in degrees centigrade.
HarvRain	= harvest rain (August through September) in millimeters.

Professor Ashenfelter used the most objective measure of quality he could devise: an index of auction prices for about eighty wines after they had matured in their bottles. According to this multivariate regression analysis, heavy rains in the winter followed by a hot summer improve wine quality, and rainfall before the harvest damages it. The statistical fit from 1952 through 1980 was remarkably good for the red wines of Burgundy as well as Bordeaux.

Ashenfelter's wine equation is not without its critics. The director of wines at Christie's auction house in London and a leading authority on Bordeaux, points out that the equation cannot predict differences in quality between estate-bottled wines of the same vintage. And the equation makes errors by grouping wines made from the cabernet sauvignon grape with others made from the milder merlot grape. But for most Bordeaux vintages, Ashenfelter's predictions correspond closely with the subjective rankings assigned by professional wine tasters. One wine retailer and importer writes: "I basically agree with Professor Ashenfelter and his new and interesting system of rating through weather conditions.... My selections for the 1980 decade closely parallel Professor Ashenfelter's, with 1983, 1985 and, particularly, 1989 as the greatest of vintages."

*Based on an article by Peter Parsel, *The New York Times,* March 4, 1990.

8.4   Goodness of Fit

After obtaining the least-squares equation, how does one judge how good the equation fits the data? One very useful statistic is provided by the **standard error of regression,** S, which is computed from

$$S^2 = \frac{\Sigma \hat{\varepsilon}_i^2}{n - k - 1}$$

The standard error of regression for the problem of Table 8.2 is 7.318. You can verify that S is equal to the square root of the sum of squares residual, 856.761, divided by $(n - k - 1) = 16$, which is called the *residual degrees of freedom.* The statistic S^2 is an estimate of the population variance of the random error $\sigma^2 = \text{Var}(\varepsilon)$. The division of the sum of squared errors by $(n - k - 1)$, rather than n, where k is the number of βs estimated, yields an unbiased estimator of σ^2. The standard error of regression S is minimized by minimizing the sum of squared errors.

A related measure of the goodness of fit is provided by the **coefficient of determination** R^2, called "R-squared" for short:

> ***Coefficient of determination (R²):*** *R^2 measures the proportion of the total variation in the dependent variable explained by regression.*

The variation explained by the regression is $\text{Var}(\hat{Y})$, and the total variation is $\text{Var}(Y)$.[7] Thus, the coefficient of determination is

$$R^2 = \frac{\text{Var}(\hat{Y})}{\text{Var}(Y)}$$

The least-squares method minimizes the proportion of the variation in Y that remains unexplained by the regression and thereby maximizes R^2.[8] Computer programs routinely report R^2, and so you don't need to compute R^2. But you do need to know how to interpret R^2. For the demand equation of Table 8.2, the reported "squared multiple R" is $R^2 = 0.969$. Nearly 97 percent of the variation in the quantity demanded was explained by that regression.

A perfect linear fit would result in 100 percent of the variation in the dependent variable explained by the linear regression, so that $R^2 = 1$ and $S = 0$. When a single explanatory variable is included, all points on the scatterplot will lie exactly on the estimated equation $\hat{Y} = \hat{\alpha} + \hat{\beta}X$ when $R^2 = 1$. At the other extreme, if none of the variation in Y is explained by the regression that $R^2 = 0$, no *linear* association connects Y and any of the explanatory variables.

One of the most frequent mistakes made by beginning users of least-squares regression is placing too much reliance on R^2 as a measure of the precision of the estimated equation, when several explanatory variables appear. The value of R^2 usually increases and can never decrease when an extra explanatory variable is added to the regression. This condition tempts number *crunchers* to "mine" data for a good fit without carefully considering either the theoretical consideration for including each variable or each variable's contribution to explaining the variation in the dependent variable. Good econometricians practice number *crafting* rather than number crunching.

The R^2 statistic can be artificially forced to 1 by allowing the number of explanatory variables k to approach the sample size n. Thus, R^2 is meaningful only when the ratio (k/n) is sufficiently small; that is, 0.25 or less. Thus, the number of explanatory variables should be less than $n/4$.

---

7. The variance in the estimated value of Y is $\text{Var}(\hat{Y}) = E\{[\hat{Y} - E(\hat{Y})]^2\} = E\{[\hat{Y} - \bar{Y}]^2\}$ because $E(\hat{Y}) = \bar{Y}$.
8. One problem with least-squares estimation is that there is always a "best" line $Y = \hat{\alpha} + \hat{\beta}X$ through any set of X, Y values, and so R^2 will often be high even without an underlying predictive relationship. As an extreme case, R^2 will be 1 whenever only two X, Y pairs are used—a straight line can always be drawn perfectly through two points.

To compensate for the rise in R^2 whenever an additional explanatory variable is added to the equation, an **adjusted R^2,** called "R-bar-squared," is used:

$$\overline{R}^2 = 1 - (1 - R^2)\left[\frac{(n-1)}{(n-k-1)}\right]$$

The adjusted R^2 for the demand equation reported in Table 8.2 is 0.963. When an explanatory variable is added, $\overline{R}^2$ may fall if that added variable contributes little to explaining the variation in the dependent variable. If $\overline{R}^2$ falls when you add an explanatory variable to the regression, that is a strong indication that the equation is misspecified in some way.

8.5 Precision of a Coefficient Estimate

Just because an estimated equation has a high R^2 does not imply that the equation is good, nor does a low R^2 necessarily indicate that the equation is bad. More important, the equation should have a sound theoretical justification and separate explanatory variables should make significant contributions to explaining the variation in the dependent variable. The precision of each $\hat{\beta}$ is more important than the overall fit.

Any $\hat{\beta}$ is a statistic computed from a sample—presumably a random sample. As a statistic, the value of a $\hat{\beta}$ depends on the sample. If you were to take another sample, you would compute a different value for each $\hat{\beta}$. Thus, each $\hat{\beta}$ is a random variable and each has a probability distribution.

The *mean* of the distribution of any $\hat{\beta}$ is $E(\hat{\beta})$, its expected value. The estimator $\hat{\beta}$ is unbiased when

$$E(\hat{\beta}) = \beta$$

Unbiasedness of any $\hat{\beta}$ is ensured if the random error ε is uncorrelated with any of the explanatory variables.

The *variance* of any $\hat{\beta}$ is denoted by

$$\text{Var}(\hat{\beta}) = \sigma_{\hat{\beta}}^2$$

Similarly, the standard deviation of $\hat{\beta}$ is denoted by $\sigma_{\hat{\beta}}$. As before, variance and standard deviation are measures of the dispersion of the random variable $\hat{\beta}$ about its mean. The random variable $\hat{\beta}$ is more precise if it has a smaller variance.

The variance and standard deviation of any $\hat{\beta}$ are, of course, unknown. The estimated standard deviation of a $\hat{\beta}$ is called its **standard error.** We denote the standard error $S_{\hat{\beta}}$. Computer programs calculate each estimated coefficient's standard error. For the example in Table 8.2, the standard error of the p_x coefficient is 1.849, of the M coefficient, 1.870, and of the p_y coefficient, 3.239. Small standard errors are desirable.

Standard errors are inversely related to the sample size. That is, the standard errors of the estimated coefficients will decrease as the sample size increases. Any standard error is also inversely related to the variance in the explanatory variable. Therefore the more variation in any explanatory variable the better because the standard error of its estimated coefficient will be smaller.

Econometricians look at the ratio of an estimated coefficient to its standard error as a measure of its precision. If the coefficient is large relative to its standard error, then you have statistical evidence that the estimated coefficient is more than just a random event; the estimated coefficient is then said to be statistically different from zero—statistically significant, for short. The ratio $\hat{\beta}/S_{\hat{\beta}}$ is called a ***t*-ratio**.[9] When you have a fairly large sample, large enough say, so that $n - k - 1$ is greater than 25, a rule of thumb can be used to judge the statistical significance of $\hat{\beta}$:

> **Rule of thumb:** *For relatively large samples, if the absolute value of $\hat{\beta}/S_{\hat{\beta}}$ is at least 2, then $\hat{\beta}$ is precise enough to infer that the true β is not equal to zero, and you will be correct in this judgment at least 95 percent of the time.*

When the sample size is so small that $(n - k - 1)$ is less than 25, we must assume that the random error is normally distributed and *t*-ratios must be somewhat higher than 2 in absolute value. But when the sample size is large relative to the number of coefficients, no assumption about the error distribution is required.

As an example of using *t*-ratios, consider again the statistics reported in Table 8.2. The *t*-ratios for the estimated coefficients are reported in the rightmost column. You can verify that each of the *t*-ratios is equal to the estimated coefficient divided by its standard error. For the variable p_x, the *t*-ratio of -5.118 indicates that the coefficient -9.462 is fairly precise because it is more than five times the size of its standard error. The variable M has a *t*-ratio of 2.188, and so the coefficient 4.091 is also fairly precise because it is more than twice the size of its standard error. The variable p_y has a coefficient -2.210, however, and its *t*-ratio is only -0.682. Thus, the estimated coefficient for the p_y variable is not very precise. When a coefficient is not very precise, we infer that it is not significantly different from zero, and no statistical evidence appears of a linear relationship between the dependent variable and the explanatory variable being tested.

8.6 Multicollinearity

A problem occurs in the multivariate regression model when one of the explanatory variables is highly correlated with some other explanatory variables. If an *exact* linear relationship connects explanatory variables, those variables are **perfectly collinear** and are perfectly correlated. Least-squares estimating is not possible when two explanatory variables are perfectly collinear if they are both included in the regression.[10]

As an example of collinearity, suppose you wished to estimate the demand for a good that you own. Economic theory indicates that you should include the good's price, other prices, and consumer income among the explanatory variables. If you have a competitor

---

9. One way to judge the precision of any $\hat{\beta}$ is to use probability theory and statistical inference to see if the estimated value is statistically different from zero. The *t*-ratio can be used to conduct formal statistical tests, as discussed in the appendix to this chapter.
10. The normal equations have more unknowns than there are equations.

selling a similar good, it would be natural to include your competitor's price as an explanatory variable. After all, that good is a close substitute for your good. If the price of that other good is perfectly correlated with the price of your good, the two prices will be perfectly collinear. If you were inadvertently to include both prices in your regression equation you would be unable to compute estimates of the coefficients. To proceed, you would have to exclude one of the prices from the equation.

A more likely case consists of two explanatory variables that are highly correlated but not perfectly so. In the example above, your competitor may react similarly but differently to changing market conditions. In this example, the two variables will be **nearly collinear.** When two explanatory variables are nearly collinear, estimating is possible but interpretation is difficult. Interpreting an estimated coefficient as the slope of the function while other explanatory variables remain constant is strained when one of the other explanatory variables is highly correlated with the variable that is allowed to change. It would be foolish to predict that your customers will react to a change in your price alone when you know that your competitor will closely match your price change. Another problem when near collinearity occurs is that the standard errors of the estimated coefficients will be big, so that estimated coefficients will not appear very precise.[11]

Still another problem that occurs when two variables, say X_k and X_m, have high covariance is that β_k will be overestimated when β_m is underestimated—and *vice versa.* This condition is *not* the same as bias because the β-hats remain unbiased as long as no other specification errors are made. It does mean, however, that between two nearly collinear variables, when the sample results in an overestimate of one of the slope coefficients, the other slope coefficient will be underestimated. In the demand example, if price elasticity is overestimated, cross-elasticity will be underestimated.

In practice, it is usually easy to identify two explanatory variables that are nearly collinear. All one has to do is compute the simple correlations between pairs of explanatory variables. If the correlation is nearly equal to unity, then the two variables are nearly collinear. One solution is to drop one of the offending variables from the regression. It is much more difficult, however, to detect collinearity between subsets of explanatory variables, a condition called **multicollinearity:**

> **Multicollinearity:** *A linear combination of explanatory variables is highly collinear with another explanatory variable.*

An example of perfect multicollinearity is provided by the model

$$Y = \alpha + \beta_1 X_1 + \beta_2 X_2 + \beta_3 X_3 + \beta_4 X_4 + \varepsilon$$

where

$$X_1 = 10X_2 - X_3 + X_4/2$$

---

11. Thus, using the standard statistical tests of significance, as detailed in the appendix to this chapter, is compromised. It will be *harder* to reject a hypothesis of no linear relationship with the dependent variable. Although you are *less* likely to *reject* the standard null falsely, you will be *more* likely to *accept* the null when it is false.

The variables X_2, X_3, and X_4 may not be perfectly correlated with X_1 when each is taken alone, but the linear combination defined is exactly equal to X_1. As before, estimating is not possible when multicollinearity is *perfect,* and so detection is easy. But detection is not so easy when the variables are nearly multicollinear.

We have two practical ways of detecting multicollinearity. The first way is to inspect sample pairwise correlations.[12] If the correlation between two explanatory variables is high and larger than the correlation of either or both variables with the dependent variable, multicollinearity is likely to be a problem. But paired correlations reveal near collinearity only between *pairs* of variables. A second way to detect multicollinearity is to examine the overall fit of the equation compared with the significance of individual explanatory variables. One of the consequences of multicollinearity is that the overall fit is affected far less than the significance of separate regression coefficients. Thus, the combination of a *high* R^2 with *low* t-ratios for several estimated coefficients is an indication of severe multicollinearity.

When severe multicollinearity has been diagnosed or is suspected, the next step is to decide whether anything should be done to correct the problem. Why should you even consider doing nothing about multicollinearity? Well, all remedies have drawbacks, and so doing nothing may be the correct course of action. If you are primarily interested in predicting the dependent variable and don't care about the individual effects of the explanatory variables on the dependent variable, do nothing about suspected multi-collinearity because the coefficient estimates and predicted values remain unbiased. Likewise, you should do nothing unless the remedy significantly improves the standard errors. When the explanatory variables are all statistically significant you're probably better off doing nothing rather than introducing other problems caused by the remedy.

Multicollinearity can be just a data problem, and so one attractive remedy is to take a new sample or augment the sample you have. The danger here is that the new sample may "fit better," but it may be further from the truth. Whenever you rerun a regression, you run the risk of encountering a sample that accidentally works well for the model.

8.7   Nonlinear Models and Dummy Variables

Frequently the model to be estimated is nonlinear. Sales may increase with advertising expenditures at a decreasing rate. Demand may have constant elasticity and therefore cannot be linear. Regional differences in the behavior of consumers may cause steplike shifts in average demand by region. Thus, you may see many relationships that cannot be expressed adequately by a linear equation. Fortunately, linear regression can be extended to estimate many nonlinear equations.

---

12. Recall that the correlation between two random variables X and Y is defined

$$\text{Cor}(X, Y) = \frac{\text{Cov}(X, Y)}{\sqrt{\text{Var}(X)\ \text{Var}(Y)}}$$

Consider first the possibility that an event will occur or a characteristic that is qualitative will be present. The event takes place or the characteristic is present or not. It is natural to assign the value unity when the characteristic is present and zero otherwise—such qualitative variables are called **dummy variables.**

Suppose you wish to estimate the demand for a good as a function of consumer income. Demand will increase for a normal good as income increases if other things remain the same. But your data include observations for both males and females, and you realize that females have an average income lower than that of males. Taste may also vary by gender. On average the quantity demanded at any income level may be different for females. One way to test that hypothesis would be to estimate the model with a dummy variable for gender:

$$Y = \alpha + \beta_1 X_1 + \beta_2 X_2 + \varepsilon$$

where X_1 measures income and $X_2 = 1$ for females but $X_2 = 0$ for males. The variable X_2 is a dummy variable. Panel A of Figure 8.4 illustrates a likely least-squares outcome for the problem described. It has two regression lines, one for males ($X_2 = 0$) and one for females ($X_2 = 1$). Notice that the slope of the two equations is the same and only the intercept shifts.[13]

Let's extend the dummy-variable model by including a second variable that measures a different characteristic. Suppose you can no longer measure consumers' incomes directly, but you do have the years of education to use as a proxy for income. Threshold effects are likely when using education as an explanatory variable because, say, having a college degree may cause a discrete jump in average income. To capture this threshold effect, you may write the model

$$Y = \alpha + \beta_1 X_1 + \beta_2 X_2 + \beta_3 X_3 + \varepsilon$$

where X_1 now measures years of education, X_2 is the gender dummy, and X_3 is a dummy that takes a value of unity when years of education are greater than or equal to sixteen, $X_3 = 1$ if $X_1 \geq 16$. Panel B of Figure 8.4 illustrates a likely outcome for this case. This specification results in a discontinuity in the estimated equation, but all segments have the same slope.[14]

Nonlinear equations may be estimated by least squares if the equation can be transformed into an equation that is linear in the coefficients to be estimated. Consider estimating sales as a function of advertising. You might expect that sales will increase at an increasing rate for initial advertising because repeated advertising has a reinforcing effect. Eventually, consumers may not react as strongly to repeated advertising, and sales may even begin to fall if the consumers become resentful. Sales may increase at an increasing rate initially, then continue to increase but at a decreasing rate until a maximum

---

13. If you want to permit a difference in the slopes also, you would just estimate two regressions without the gender dummy. You would estimate one from the data on males, and the other from the data on females.
14. Again, if you want to permit a difference in slopes, four separate equations can be estimated.

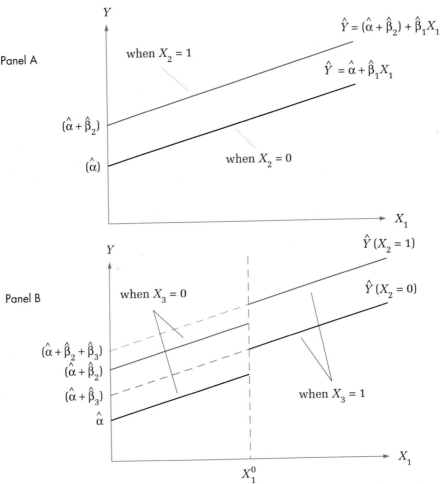

$$\hat{Y} = (\hat{\alpha} + \hat{\beta}_2) + \hat{\beta}_1 X_1$$

Panel A when $X_2 = 1$

$$\hat{Y} = \hat{\alpha} + \hat{\beta}_1 X_1$$

$(\hat{\alpha} + \hat{\beta}_2)$

$(\hat{\alpha})$ when $X_2 = 0$

X_1

$\hat{Y}(X_2 = 1)$

Panel B when $X_3 = 0$ $\hat{Y}(X_2 = 0)$

$(\hat{\alpha} + \hat{\beta}_2 + \hat{\beta}_3)$
$(\hat{\alpha} + \hat{\beta}_2)$
$(\hat{\alpha} + \hat{\beta}_3)$ when $X_3 = 1$
$\hat{\alpha}$

X_1

X_1^0

Figure 8.4 **Using dummy variables: Panel A** The model to be estimated is $Y = \alpha + \beta_1 X_1 + \beta_2 X_2 + \varepsilon$, where X_2 is a dummy variable. The intercept shifts when $X_2 = 1$, but the slope remains the same. **Panel B** The model to be estimated is $Y = \alpha + \beta_1 X_1 + \beta_2 X_2 + \beta_3 X_3 + \varepsilon$, where X_2 and X_3 are dummy variables and $X_3 = 1$ when $X_1 \geq X_1^0$. Four different intercepts are estimated for the different combinations of X_2 and X_3. A discontinuity appears in the equation estimated, but the slope of each segment is the same.

is reached, and then decrease. A *cubic* function may be a reasonable approximation to the consumers' response:

$$Y = \alpha + \beta_1 X + \beta_2 X^2 + \beta_3 X^3 + \varepsilon$$

If three new variables are defined $X_1 = X$, $X_2 = X^2$, and $X_3 = X^3$, the equation becomes

$$Y = \alpha + \beta_1 X_1 + \beta_2 X_2 + \beta_3 X_3 + \varepsilon$$

The cubic equation has been transformed into a multivariate linear-regression model that can be estimated by least squares. Any polynomial equation can be transformed into a multivariate regression model.

AN APPLICATION: *Demand for Cigarettes in the United States*

Using annual data from 1947 to 1982, an estimate was made of the demand function for cigarettes in the United States.* The estimated regression equation was

$$\widehat{\ln Q} = -2.55 - 0.29 \ln P + 0.08 \ln A - 0.09 \ln M + 0.14 \ln P_c - 0.10C - 0.06D$$
$$\quad\quad (-2.07) \quad\quad (4.48) \quad\quad (-1.00) \quad\quad (0.92) \quad\quad (-5.19) \quad (-3.60)$$

where Q is annual cigarette consumption, P is the average price of cigarettes, A is advertising expenditures, M is per capita income, and P_c is the average price of cigars. The variable C is a dummy variable that equals 1 if the year is after the 1953 American Cancer Society report linking smoking with cancer. The variable D is a dummy variable for the years 1968 to 1970. During this period the Federal Trade Commission required that one antismoking commercial be aired for every four prosmoking ads. This equation captured 91 percent of the variation in quantity demanded. The t-ratios for the estimated coefficients are in parentheses.

Applying the t-ratios to test the significance of the coefficients, using the rule of thumb, indicates that the coefficients for own-price, advertising, and both dummy variables are significantly different from zero. The coefficients for the income variable and the other price variable do not have a statistically significant effect on quantity demanded.

The estimated equation yields direct estimates of elasticities. The price elasticity of demand is 0.29. The income elasticity of demand for cigarettes is -0.09, but the coefficient is not significantly different from zero. The cross-elasticity of demand for cigarettes relative to the price of cigars is 0.14, but again this coefficient is not statistically significant. The advertising elasticity is 0.08 and is statistically significant.

That the regression coefficient of C is negative and statistically significant implies that the American Cancer Society report negatively affected cigarette smoking. Likewise, the significantly negative coefficient for D indicates that the advertising restriction also negatively influenced smoking.

*R. Porter, "The Impact of Government policy on the U.S. Cigarette Industry," in P. Ippolito and D. Scheffman, eds., *Empirical Approaches to Consumer Protection Economics,* Federal Trade Commission, 1984.

As another example of transforming a nonlinear equation into a linear regression model, consider the constant-elasticities demand function

$$Q = \beta_0 p_x^{\beta_1} p_y^{\beta_2} M^{\beta_3} \upsilon$$

where υ is a random error term. The absolute value of the β_1 coefficient is the own-price elasticity of demand, and β_2 and β_3 are cross-price and income elasticities. Taking the logarithm of both sides results in

$$\log Q = \log \beta_0 + \beta_1 \log p_x + \beta_2 \log p_y + \beta_3 \log M + \log \upsilon$$

Now, if we define $Y = \log Q$, $\alpha = \log \beta_0$, and $\varepsilon = \log \upsilon$ results in

$$Y = \alpha + \beta_1 \log p_x + \beta_2 \log p_y + \beta_3 \log M + \varepsilon$$

This equation is linear in the coefficients to be estimated, and the coefficients yield elasticities. Estimation proceeds as an exercise in multivariate linear regression.

Many kinds of nonlinear equations can be transformed into linear-regression models. The model can be estimated by least squares as long as the nonlinear equation can be transformed into an equation that is linear in the coefficients to be estimated. Of course, some models cannot be transformed into a form that is linear in the coefficients. Estimating such models requires techniques other than least squares.

8.8   Model Specification and Specification Error

The first step in estimating an economic model should be to specify the regression equation to be estimated. This step involves selecting the explanatory variables, specifying the functional form to be estimated, and choosing the correct form of the random error term. A **specification error** results when any one of these choices is made incorrectly.

In selecting the explanatory variables, be guided by the underlying economic model. Sometimes, however, an explanatory variable is omitted from the regression because it is unmeasurable or perhaps just forgotten. If a variable is omitted when it is relevant in determining the dependent variable, the estimated coefficients for the remaining explanatory variables will be affected. The estimated standard errors are also affected. More specifically, if X_m is omitted when $\beta_m \neq 0$ in the true model, and if X_m is correlated with any of the remaining variables, the estimated β coefficients will be biased for the remaining variables.[15] Only if the omitted but properly included variable has zero correlation with all the remaining variables will the β-hat coefficients be unbiased. Even if the omitted variable is uncorrelated with the included variables, all estimated coefficients will have biased estimated variances and the intercept remains biased. Thus the application of standard significance tests is compromised.

Another form of specification error occurs when you improperly choose the functional form of the equation to be estimated. For example, if the proper specification is quadratic and you omit the squared term, then the equation is misspecified. The result is the same as if you had omitted a properly included variable. Estimating the linear model when the true model is nonlinear leads to the same results as omitting a relevant explanatory variable. The same happens too when a dummy variable is excluded that should have been included. The magnitude of the bias depends on the magnitude of the curvature or discontinuity in the true relation.

Suppose instead that you err by including an irrelevant variable. Least-squares estimators then remain *unbiased,* but they are not *efficient.* Variances are also unbiased, and so the application of the rule of thumb is valid.[16]

---

15. For a proof see Henri Theil, *Principles of Econometrics* (John Wiley, 1971), pp. 548–550. By bias is meant that $E(\hat{\beta}) \neq \beta$ for the other variables when $\beta_m \neq 0$ in the true model and X_m is excluded in the estimation.
16. You lose degrees of freedom when an irrelevant variable is included in the regression, but this loss of efficiency makes it *harder* to reject a standard null hypothesis about zero slope. Thus, when we reject a null that $\beta_j = 0$, we are reasonably sure that we have not increased the probability of accepting the alternative when it is true.

ECONOMIC SCENE: *Pennies for Your Thoughts*

Once upon a time a student of econometrics decided to estimate the effect of study time on the grades received by economics students on their final exams. Along with study time, the number of pennies in pocket or purse was used as an explanatory variable. Why include pennies? That is not clear, but perhaps the investigator remembered the old saw, "A penny for your thoughts." Or perhaps the number of pennies was included as a proxy for some unmeasurable variable.

After surveying performance by many students in several classes, the estimated equation was

$$\hat{G} = 70 + 1.2H + 4.0P$$
$$\qquad\quad (0.8)\quad (1.0)$$

where G is the grade (score) between 0 and 100 percent, H is the hours of study time, and P is the number of pennies held by the student while taking the exam. The standard errors are in parentheses, and the sample correlation coefficient between H and P was 0.80. Though unreported, the coefficient of determination was said to be quite high.

By any reasonable standard, the variable that represents pennies is statistically significant because its t-ratio is high. At the same time, hours of study is not, because its standard error is relatively big. Are these results reasonable, and if not, what should be done to get more reasonable results? Is the estimated coefficient for H biased downward as a result of including P and its high correlation with H, and should H therefore be dropped from the specification before reestimating?

The multicollinearity problem is obvious because of the high correlation between H and P. Including P as an explanatory variable, however, does not bias the estimated coefficient for H. One possible solution to the multicollinearity would be to drop one of the variables. Study time is statistically insignificant, but dropping H would lead to specification bias because study time is properly included theoretically. On the other hand, P seems irrelevant and causes a loss of efficiency, and excluding an irrelevant variable does not bias remaining coefficients. Thus P should be dropped from the model even though it is statistically significant, and the model should then be reestimated. The variable H may become significant when the irrelevant variable is dropped because of the gain in efficiency and because P and H were highly correlated.

When the model is reestimated, the analyst should also consider a nonlinear specification. It seems reasonable to expect diminishing returns for study time, and so a quadratic specification

$$G = \alpha + \beta_1 H + \beta_2 H^2 + \varepsilon$$

could capture that possibility. Other explanatory variables might also be relevant, such as the grade each student received in a prerequisite course.

Consider again the estimated model reported in Table 8.2. In this demand equation, the estimated coefficient for the variable p_y was not very precise. Should you then drop that variable from the regression? No, because theoretically p_y is a properly included variable, and omitting it would be likely to bias the estimated coefficients of the remaining variables. If, on the other hand, good X is not a close substitute or complement with respect to good Y, and p_y is retained as an explanatory variable, its inclusion will not bias the remaining estimates.

In summary, the cost of improper specification is bias. In contrast, the cost of including an irrelevant variable is loss of efficiency. Therefore, if the sample is large enough when you are in doubt about a variable, you should leave that variable in the regression. On the other hand, if the sample is small, the loss of degrees of freedom when adding several variables to the model may be serious. The choice of a model becomes a bias-efficiency trade-off, and the model builder will have to exercise careful judgment.

8.9   Stochastic Explanatory Variables

In the simple regression model $Y = \alpha + \beta X + \varepsilon$, we assumed that the explanatory variable X was independent of the random error ε. When it is independent, the least-squares estimators of α and β are unbiased. To see why, take covariances for both sides of the regression equation with respect to X to obtain:

$$S_{xy} = \beta S_{xx} + S_{x\varepsilon}$$

Thus, the least-squares estimate of β is

$$\hat{\beta} = \frac{S_{xy}}{S_{xx}} = \beta + \frac{S_{x\varepsilon}}{S_{xx}}$$

Independence of X and ε guarantees that $E(S_{x\varepsilon}) = 0$ so that $E(\hat{\beta}) = \beta$.[17] The independence of X and ε is assured if X is nonstochastic (when X is fixed in repeated samples). But that is too strong an assumption when X is beyond the analyst's control.

In contrast, when X and ε are correlated, $\hat{\beta}$ is no longer unbiased or consistent because $S_{x\varepsilon} \neq 0$ even with large samples. When X and ε are correlated, the regression does not adjust for the joint effect of X and ε on Y. Because we know that

$$\hat{\beta} = \beta + \frac{S_{x\varepsilon}}{S_{xx}}$$

we will find negative bias when $S_{x\varepsilon} < 0$ because X and ε are negatively correlated, and positive bias when $S_{x\varepsilon} > 0$ because X and ε are positively correlated. Positive bias, illustrated by Figure 8.5, occurs in estimating β because positive errors are more likely when X is above its mean and negative errors are more likely when X is below its mean. Thus, some of the effect of the error is wrongly attributed to the least-squares regression coefficient when X and ε are correlated.

---

17. Independence of X and ε also guarantees that the least-squares estimators of α and β will be efficient (lowest variance) and consistent. When $S_{x\varepsilon}$ approaches zero as n gets large, then $\hat{\beta}$ is a **consistent** estimator of β.

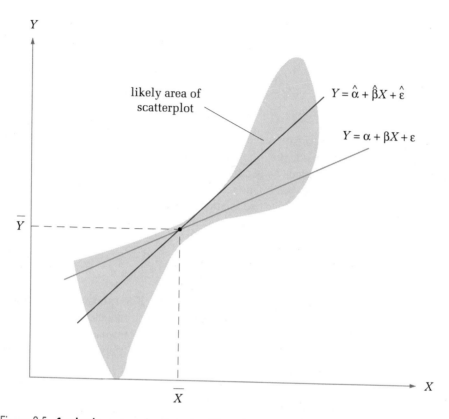

Figure 8.5 **Correlated regressor and random error:** When the regressor X is positively correlated with the random error ε so that $S_{x\varepsilon} > 0$, the fitted line will have estimated slope that is biased upward.

The solution to this source of bias is to use an **instrumental variable:**

> **Instrumental variable:** *The variable Z is an instrumental variable for X if Z and X are correlated when Z and ε are uncorrelated.*

Given an instrumental variable for X, the solution to the problem of having a correlated regressor and error is to use the instrument to obtain:

$$S_{zy} = \beta S_{zx} + S_{z\varepsilon}$$

That is, we take covariances of both sides of the regression model with respect to the instrument. The **instrumental variable estimator** for β is then defined by

$$\tilde{\beta} = \frac{S_{zy}}{S_{zx}} = \beta + \frac{S_{z\varepsilon}}{S_{zx}}$$

The estimated coefficient $\tilde{\beta}$ is read "beta tilde." The estimator $\tilde{\beta}$ is said to be a **consistent** estimator when $S_{z\varepsilon}$ approaches zero as the sample size increases. A consistent estimator may be better than an unbiased estimator when you have a large sample. The problem becomes one of finding or constructing a good instrumental variable.[18] A method for constructing appropriate instrumental variables is demonstrated in the next section.[19]

8.10 The Identification Problem

It is fairly easy to estimate a demand function when little else is varying except for price and quantity demanded. But when the other variables that affect demand are all changing at once, it can be difficult to get good estimates of demand equations and still more difficult to make good forecasts. One reason it may be difficult to obtain accurate estimates of demand relations is the close relationships among economic variables.

Consider the problem of estimating market demand when price and quantity are being determined simultaneously by supply and demand:

$$\text{supply: } Q_s = \alpha_1 + \alpha_2 P + \varepsilon_s$$
$$\text{demand: } Q_d = \beta_1 + \beta_2 P + \varepsilon_d$$

These are called the **structural equations** of the system. The random error terms ε_s and ε_d are influenced by changes in unmeasured variables that influence the position of the supply and demand curves. The supply curve may be shifting because of changes in input prices or changes in technology. The demand curve may be shifting because of changes in preferences caused by advertising or changes in expectations about inflation. As illustrated by Figure 8.6, the scatterplot of observed prices and quantities generated by shifting demand and supply curves does not allow easy estimating of demand or supply.

A solution to these structural equations can be found by setting quantity supplied equal to quantity demanded,

$$\alpha_1 + \alpha_2 P + \varepsilon_s = \beta_1 + \beta_2 P + \varepsilon_d$$

to find

$$P = \pi_1 + v_1$$
$$Q = \pi_2 + v_2$$

where

$$\pi_1 = \frac{\beta_1 - \alpha_1}{\alpha_2 - \beta_2} \quad \text{and} \quad \pi_2 = \frac{\alpha_2 \beta_1 - \alpha_1 \beta_2}{\alpha_2 - \beta_2}$$

---

18. In the multivariate regression model, the assumption of independence of the regressor to the error in the simple model is replaced by two assumptions. First, the distribution of each explanatory variable is independent of the true regression coefficients. Second, each of the explanatory variables is distributed independently of the true error of the model. The estimated regression coefficients are then estimated as *conditional* on the given values of the regressors. Under this interpretation, the least-squares estimators are unbiased in the sample.

19. Once an instrumental variable has been found for the stochastic explanatory variable, a simple test can be performed to see if the variable is correlated with the error. See J. A. Hausman, "Specification Tests in Econometrics," *Econometrica*, 46(6) (November 1978), pp. 1251–1271.

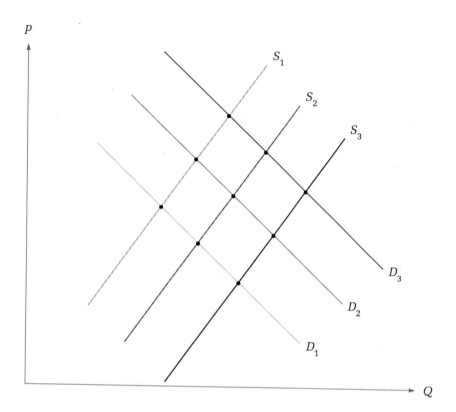

p

S_1

S_2

S_3

D_3

D_2

D_1

Q

Figure 8.6 **The identification problem:** The demand and supply curves shift in response to changing determinants of demand and supply. The observed price–quantity pairs do not provide sufficient information to identify the demand or the supply relation.

and v_1 and v_2 are random errors that are functions of errors ε_s and ε_d. This form of the system of equations is called the **reduced form.** Variables P and Q are called **endogenous variables** because they are determined by the system. The reduced form can *always* be estimated. For this simple model, the coefficients can be estimated by

$$\hat{\pi}_1 = \overline{P} \quad \text{and} \quad \hat{\pi}_2 = \overline{Q}$$

where $\overline{P}$ and $\overline{Q}$ are the variable means. The estimated coefficients for the reduced form cannot, however, be translated back into the structural coefficients without more information. The system is said to be **unidentified** when the structural coefficients cannot be estimated.

Three types of additional information will permit identification. We can identify structural equations with (1) prior information about some of the structural parameters, (2) prior information about the properties of the error terms, or (3) additional information about the structure of the model. First, if you have prior knowledge about the structural coefficients, identification may be possible. For instance, if you know α_1 and α_2 in the supply equation you can estimate β_1 and β_2 from the reduced-form equations. Second, if the error in one of the equations is small, you can identify the other equation. If the variation in ε_d is small, then the demand equation can be identified from the variation in supply. To see this result, try small shifts in the demand curve in a graph like Figure 8.6 while supply shifts more. The scatterplot will indicate that demand can be estimated. Third, and most frequently used, the exclusion of a variable in an equation may allow us to identify that equation if the variable appears in another equation in the system. Such variables must be **predetermined**—a variable that influences the outcome of the system without being affected by that outcome. Predetermined variables serve as excellent instrumental variables because they are correlated with the endogenous variables but are uncorrelated with the error.

To see how we can use inclusion of predetermined variables to identify equations that are to be estimated, consider this extension of the supply and demand model:

$$\text{supply: } Q_s = \alpha_1 + \alpha_2 P + \alpha_3 T + \varepsilon_s$$
$$\text{demand: } Q_d = \beta_1 + \beta_2 P + \beta_3 M + \varepsilon_d$$

Variable T might be a measure of technology that influences supply independently of price and quantity, and variable M might be a measure of consumer income that influences demand but not supply. Because T is excluded from the demand equation but properly included in the supply equation, and if it is a predetermined variable, then the demand equation may be identified. Similarly, because M is excluded from the supply equation but properly included in demand, and if M is exogenous to the system, then supply may be identified.

For the preceding demand and supply system, in order to estimate the demand curve, we first take covariances of both sides of the demand equation, using T as an instrument:

$$S_{qt} = \beta_2 S_{pt} + \beta_3 S_{mt}$$

Next, we take covariances of both sides of the demand equation, using M as an instrument:

$$S_{qm} = \beta_2 S_{pm} + \beta_3 S_{mm}$$

These two equations can be solved simultaneously to get estimates for β_2 and β_3, the coefficients of the demand equation. An estimate for intercept β_1 can be calculated in the usual way. Similar calculations can be performed to estimate α_1, α_2, and α_3 for the supply equation.

A variable that helps to identify an equation by its exclusion from that equation must, however, belong in the system of equations. For example, adding another variable to the supply equation to identify demand will succeed only when that variable belongs in the supply equation and is statistically significant. Simply adding irrelevant and statistically insignificant variables to achieve identification will not help. A researcher can do nothing beyond estimating the reduced form if the structural equation is not identified.

To identify any equation, this condition must be satisfied:[20]

---

20. This order condition is necessary but not sufficient for identification. The sufficient condition, the **rank** condition, is beyond the scope of this text.

> ***Order condition for identification:*** *The number of predetermined variables* excluded *from the equation, but included in the other equations, must at least equal the number of endogenous variables* included *on the right-hand side of the equation to be identified.*

In the system just considered, the demand equation satisfied the order condition exactly because T was excluded from the demand equation but P was included. Likewise, the supply equation satisfied the order condition exactly because M was excluded from the supply equation but P was included. If, however, the number of predetermined variables excluded is greater than the number of endogenous variables on the right-hand side, the equation to be estimated is **overidentified.**

An equation is **overidentified** when more than one way is available to generate estimates for the unknown coefficients. If a variable for an input price were added to the supply equation, the demand equation would be overidentified. It would be overidentified because both technology and the input price are suitable instruments, but each one generates different estimates for the coefficients of the demand equation. The solution is no longer unique.

The method used to solve the overidentification problem, which also provides instrumental variables for deriving consistent estimates, is called **two-stage least squares:**

> ***Two-Stage Least Squares:***
> **Stage I:** *Regress each of the endogenous variables in the equation to be estimated on all the predetermined variables in the system.*
> **Stage II:** *Use the predicted values of the endogenous variables from Stage I as instruments for each of the endogenous variables and estimate the equation by least squares.*

Stage I amounts to estimating the reduced form of the system. Stage II uses the Stage I predictions of each endogenous variable as its instrument that, by construction, will be correlated with the dependent variable but not the error. The overidentification problem is solved by creating new instruments that are linear combinations of the old instruments (the predetermined variables). You will have just the right number of new instruments to generate a unique solution, and using instruments means that consistent estimates will be generated.

To see how two-stage least squares works, consider this extension of the supply and demand system just used:

$$\text{supply: } Q_s = \alpha_1 + \alpha_2 P + \alpha_3 T + \alpha_4 Z + \varepsilon_s$$
$$\text{demand: } Q_d = \beta_1 + \beta_2 P + \varepsilon_d$$

where Z is a measure of an input price. The supply equation is *not* identified. The demand equation is identified, but demand is *over*identified because both T and Z are exogenous to

---

AN APPLICATION: *Market for Television Advertising*

A simultaneous-equations model of demand and supply of commercial minutes watched by television viewers was estimated using monthly data from January 1964 to December 1969.* Quantity is the number of minutes of network commercial messages watched per month by all households. Price is the price per home-minute of network commercials in real dollars paid by sponsors. The demand and supply functions were specified as:

$$\text{demand: } P = P(Q, I, U, S)$$
$$\text{supply: } Q = Q(P, T, C, W)$$

where

P = price
Q = quantity
I = real personal disposable income
U = fraction of civilian labor force unemployed
S = season of the year, monthly dummies
T = time, sequence of the month in the sample
C = an index of the real cost of studio production
W = weather (average monthly temperature)

Price is the dependent variable in the demand function—an inverse demand. Because I, U, and S appear in demand but not supply, the supply equation is identified. Similarly, because T, C, and W appear in supply but not demand, the demand equation is identified. The estimated demand equation is:

$$\hat{P} = 32.230 - 0.073Q - 120.22U + 0.032I$$
$$+ 4.830 \; Jan + 4.995 \; Feb + 4.391 \; Mar + 2.833 \; Apr$$
$$- 2.532 \; Jun - 4.284 \; Jul - 4.537 \; Aug + 2.561 \; Sep$$
$$+ 8.229 \; Oct + 7.757 \; Nov + 6.152 \; Dec$$

This equation explained more than 94 percent of the variation in price. At the point of the means, the price elasticity of demand is

$$\eta_D = \left| \frac{1}{-0.073} \cdot \frac{\bar{P}}{\bar{Q}} \right| = 0.924$$

The term $\Delta Q/\Delta P$ was found from $1/(\Delta P/\Delta Q)$, where $\Delta P/\Delta Q = -0.073$ is from the estimated equation.

The estimated supply equation is:

$$\hat{Q} = 395.92 + 0.582\tilde{P} + 0.946T - 6.479C - 2.025W$$

where $\tilde{P}$ is the instrumental variable obtained by regressing price on all the predetermined variables in the system. That is, $\tilde{P}$ is computed from the estimated stage I reduced-form equation for P. The supply equation explained almost 96 percent of the

---

*Gary W. Bowman, "Demand and Supply of Network Television Advertising," *Bell Journal of Economics* (Spring 1976).

variation in the quantity supplied. At the point of the means, the price elasticity of supply is

$$\eta_S = 0.582 \frac{\bar{P}}{\bar{Q}} = 0.040$$

The term $\Delta Q / \Delta P = 0.582$ is read directly from the estimated supply equation.

The estimated price elasticity of supply indicates that the supply curve is highly inelastic with respect to price. The estimated price elasticity of demand is close to unity. These elasticity estimates imply that small decreases in the number of hours of programming offered by the networks, small decreases in the number of commercials per hour, or small decreases in the aggregate audience size will not substantially change the revenues of the networks. Consequently, regulatory policies that decrease network output—public-service programming, the prime-time access rule, or reduced advertising during children's programs—may have little or no effect on network revenues. Furthermore, the very inelastic supply and unitary elastic demand indicate that output may be set by the networks so that demand price will be consistent with maximum revenue for them.

---

the system. To apply two-stage least squares, the first step is to regress P on T and Z:[23]

$$\text{Stage I: } \hat{P} = \hat{\pi}_1 + \hat{\pi}_2 T + \hat{\pi}_3 Z$$

Thus, the instrumental variable $\hat{P}$ is created from the estimated first-stage equation using the exogenous variables as regressors to obtain the π-hats. The second step is to regress quantity demanded on $\hat{P}$:

$$\text{Stage II: } Q_d = \beta_1 + \beta_2 \hat{P} + \varepsilon_d$$

The least-squares estimators $\hat{\beta}_1$ and $\hat{\beta}_2$ of β_1 and β_2 are *consistent* when $\hat{P}$ is used as an instrumental variable.

8.11 A Changing Variance of the Error

When the variance of the random error changes, the variance of the error may be written

$$\text{Var}(\varepsilon_i) = \sigma_i^2$$

where the subscript indicates that σ_i^2 depends on i, the observation index. Figure 8.7 illustrates an error increasing as the explanatory variable increases. Whenever the variance of the error changes, **heteroscedasticity** is present, a frequent problem when working with cross-sectional data. For a cross-section of sales of firms in an industry, it would be reasonable to expect that the sales for larger firms are subject to greater

---

21. This is just the reduced-form equation for P. The reduced-form equation for Q need not be estimated because Q does not appear on the right-hand side of the structural equation to be estimated.

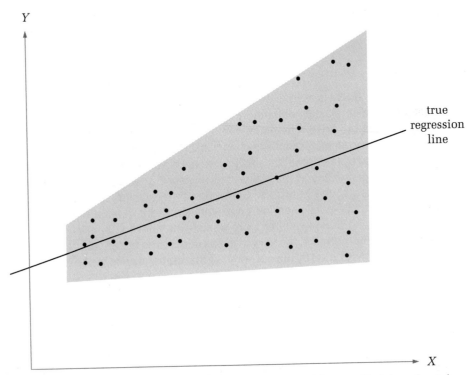

Figure 8.7 **A case of heteroscedasticity:** In this case, the variance of the error, $\text{Var}(\varepsilon_i) = \sigma^2_{i}$, gets larger as X gets larger. A loss of efficiency occurs, but the least-squares equation will remain unbiased because a positive error remains just as likely as a negative error.

variation than those of smaller ones. Sales from large firms would have greater error variance than for smaller firms. In contrast, heteroscedasticity is *not* a frequent problem when working with time-series data because changes in the dependent and explanatory variables are likely to be of the same order of magnitude as time passes. But heteroscedasticity can occur with either time-series or cross-section data when the quality of the data changes. If the sampling technique improves with time or across regions, the sampling error will be smaller for some observations than others.

As illustrated by Figure 8.7, the scatterplot of observations lies equally above and below the true regression line, even though the spread of the distribution changes. In the presence of heteroscedasticity, the least-squares coefficient estimates remain unbiased. Some efficiency is lost, however. Heteroscedasticity *increases* the variances of the β-hat distributions. Because standard tests of significance are constructed under an assumption of constant error variance, standard tests are compromised when heteroscedasticity appears.

Detecting heteroscedasticity requires specific tests for a definitive conclusion, but we leave complete consideration of the formal tests to specialized texts. An informal test is to inspect the pattern of residuals after regression. Figure 8.8 illustrates a fan-shaped pattern for the residual, and the probable cause is heteroscedasticity. This informal

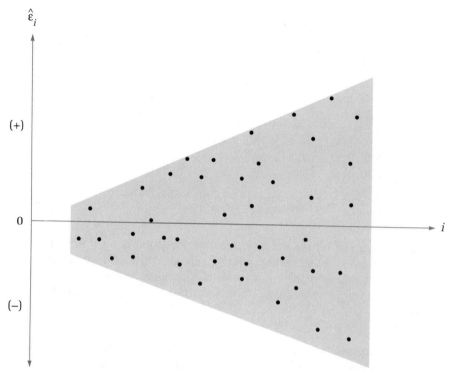

Figure 8.8 **Looking for heteroscedasticity:** If the pattern of estimated residual error, $\hat{\varepsilon}_i = Y_i - \hat{Y}_i$, is fan-shaped, the probable cause is heteroscedasticity—changing variance of the error.

procedure will not reveal heteroscedasticity unless the variance of the error is either increasing or decreasing as i increases, as when the variance of the error is related to the magnitude of an explanatory variable.[22] That variable may have been included in or excluded from the regression. If the heteroscedasticity is caused by an excluded variable, the remedy is to include it. If it is caused by an included variable, the remedy is to use a modified regression technique called weighted least squares.

Weighted least squares (WLS) works as follows. Suppose you know σ_i^2. Then, instead of estimating $Y_i = \alpha + \beta X_i + \varepsilon_i$, each observation is weighted by $1/\sigma_i$. The resulting equation is

$$\frac{Y_i}{\sigma_i} = \alpha \left(\frac{1}{\sigma_i}\right) + \beta \left(\frac{X_i}{\sigma_i}\right) + \frac{\varepsilon_i}{\sigma_i}$$

The variance of the new error term is a constant. Notice that this transformed equation must be estimated without an intercept. If several explanatory variables are included, each is weighted by $1/\sigma_i$ before estimation. Usually σ_i is unknown, and it must be estimated from the data before WLS can be performed.

---

22. For a fairly easy test assuming that the random error is related to one of the explanatory variables, see H. Glejser, "A New Test for Heteroscedasticity," *Journal of the American Statistical Association*, 64 (1969), pp. 316–323.

AN APPLICATION: *Estimating Sales Across Firms**

Sales are expected to be influenced by advertising expenditures. Consider this cross-section of data on twenty firms:

Y (Sales in $1,000)	X (Advertising $)	Number of Firms
160, 160, 180, 200, 210, 220, 230, 250	2,000	8
200, 220, 230, 300, 310, 340, 350	4,000	7
300, 300, 400, 450, 540	6,000	5

Source: Jan Kementa, *Elements of Econometrics* (Macmillan, 1986).

When the data are plotted on a scatterplot (not shown), it is easy to see that the variation in Y increases as X increases. Another indication of heteroscedasticity is that the ranges of the Y values for the three values of X increase as X increases, but fewer firms appear for the larger values of X. The relation between sales and advertising was specified to be

$$Y_i = \alpha + \beta X_i + \varepsilon_i$$

where Y is sales in thousands of dollars, X is advertising expenditures in actual dollars, and the subscript refers to the ith firm. The random error term ε_i was assumed to be normally distributed with zero mean and variance σ_i^2. Heteroscedasticity is present, because σ_i^2 varies across firms. The ordinary least-squares regression equation is

$$\hat{Y}_i = 98.8 + 0.0483 X_i$$

with $R^2 = 0.613$. The standard errors are not reported because the ordinary least-squares estimators are inefficient when heteroscedasticity is present.

Suppose the variance of the error is related to the explanatory variable in this way:

$$\sigma_i^2 = \sigma^2 X_i^2$$

This expression means that $\sigma_i/X_i = \sigma$, which is a constant. We can now obtain efficient estimates of α and β by WLS, using $1/X_i$ as a weighting factor. The WLS equation is

$$\frac{Y_i}{X_i} = \alpha \left(\frac{1}{X_i} \right) + \beta + \frac{\varepsilon_i}{X_i}$$

where the new error ε_i/X_i has constant variance. Estimation yields

$$\left(\frac{\hat{Y}_i}{X_i} \right) = \underset{(24.8)}{110.0} \left(\frac{1}{X_i} \right) + \underset{(0.0089)}{0.0450}$$

with $R^2 = 0.611$. The standard errors are in parentheses, and they clearly indicate that the estimates are statistically different from zero.

*This application comes from *Elements of Econometrics*, 2d ed., by Jan Kmenta. Reprinted by permission of Macmillan Publishing Co., Inc. Copyright © 1986 by Jan Kmenta.

Reverting to the original specification, the WLS results indicate that

$$\hat{Y}_i = 110.0 + 0.0450X_i$$
$$(24.8) \quad (0.0089)$$

The estimated elasticity of demand with respect to advertising is

$$\hat{\eta} = 0.0450 \, X_i/\hat{Y}_i$$

as a function of X_i. As X_i varies, then, we get

X_i	$\hat{\eta}$
2,000	0.45
4,000	0.62
6,000	0.71

Sales is inelastic with respect to increases in advertising expenditure, but demand becomes more responsive to increases in advertising at higher levels of advertising within the range of these data.

Rather than assuming that the variance of the random error is related to the explanatory variable in the form used above, we can estimate that variance from the data. A natural way to proceed when the data are grouped is to estimate a σ_i^2 for each group. For the three groups in this data set, the estimates are: $S_1^2 = 1,069.64$; $S_2^2 = 3,714.29$; $S_3^2 = 10,520.00$, and so the weights become $1/S_1$, $1/S_2$, and $1/S_3$ for the three groups respectively. Weighted least squares now yields

$$\hat{Y}_i = 111.10 + 0.0444X_i$$
$$(25.70) \quad (0.0092)$$

with $R^2 = 0.609$. These results are similar to those obtained under the other assumed form of the heteroscedasticity.

8.12 Serial Correlation

Serial correlation occurs when the errors between observations are correlated.[23] When the observations are made over some time, serial correlation means that the error in one period carries over into subsequent periods. When observations are made in cross-section and are ordered geographically, serial correlation is present whenever the error for one geographic location is correlated with the error in an adjacent location. Several potential sources of serial correlation are possible. A systematic pattern on the errors can be introduced inadvertently by manipulating the data, say, by interpolation or with moving averages. Momentum or inertia in time series may result in serially correlated errors,

---

23. Serial correlation is a special form of **autocorrelation**—when $\text{Cov}(\varepsilon_s, \varepsilon_t) \neq 0$ between pairs of observations s and t.

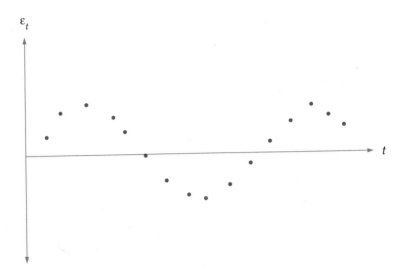

Figure 8.9 **Positive serial correlation:** Positive serial correlation results in "tracking"—subsequent errors tend to have the same sign.

especially when the time intervals are small. Not controlling for seasonal variation will introduce an element of serial correlation. Common geographic factors or meteorological events may affect observations for adjacent regions and thereby affect the error term in a systematic way. Serial correlation is most common in time-series data, however, and the shorter the time interval the greater the likelihood of serial correlation.

The consequence of serial correlation can be serious. The standard least-squares estimators are no longer efficient, and they have biased estimated variances. Thus, the standard significance tests are invalid. The estimators remain consistent, however, but they are not asymptotically efficient.

Serial correlation occurs most frequently in time series, and so we switch our observation index to $t = 1, T$, where T is the total number of observations. **First-order serial correlation** is present when the error ε_t is correlated with the preceding error ε_{t-1},

$$\varepsilon_t = \rho\varepsilon_{t-1} + \upsilon_t$$

where ρ is a correlation coefficient between successive errors and υ_t is a random error assumed to have zero mean, to have constant variance, and to be independent of ε_{t-1}. The parameter ρ is called the **coefficient of autocorrelation.** Figure 8.9 illustrates positive first-order serial correlation. With **positive serial correlation,** a positive error makes a subsequent positive error more likely, and a negative error makes a subsequent negative error more likely. The errors tend to "track" because of a positive correlation between successive errors. In contrast, with **negative serial correlation** between successive errors the signs of successive errors tend to "switch" between being positive and negative more often than if randomly determined.

One way to detect serial correlation uses a scatterplot of successive residual errors, as shown by Figure 8.10. If most of the ordered pairs $(\hat{\varepsilon}_t, \hat{\varepsilon}_{t-1})$ fall in quadrants I and III, then $\rho > 0$ is indicated. If most of the ordered pairs fall in quadrants II and IV, then $\rho < 0$

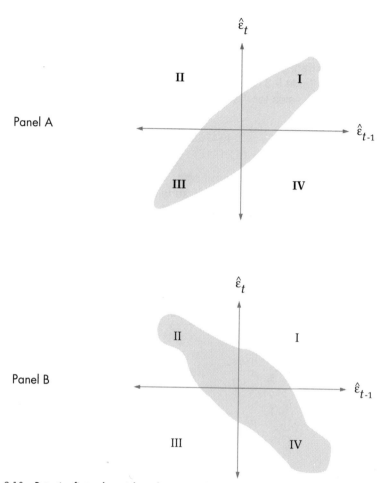

Figure 8.10 **Detecting first-order serial correlation: Panel A** Estimated residuals obtained from ordinary regression indicate that $\rho > 0$ is likely. **Panel B** Estimated residuals obtained from ordinary regression indicate that $\rho < 0$ is likely.

is indicated. The most frequent formal test for first-order serial correlation uses a statistic called the **Durbin-Watson d-statistic,** which is provided automatically by most computer programs.[24] Given the d-statistic, it can be shown that

$$d \cong 2(1 - \hat{\rho})$$

This approximation can be used to estimate ρ once d is known. A value of $d \cong 2$ indicates that $\hat{\rho} \cong 0$ and there is no evidence of serial correlation. As a rule of thumb, then, no autocorrelation is evident if d is close to 2. If d is close to zero, then positive autocorrelation is indicated. If d is close to 4, then negative autocorrelation is indicated. Otherwise a formal test needs to be conducted.

---

24. See the appendix to this chapter for the formal test.

AN APPLICATION: *Predicting Sales from Industry Sales*

Suppose a company wants to predict its sales by using industry sales as a predictor variable because accurate predictions of industry sales are available from the industry trade association. Table 8.3 displays seasonally adjusted quarterly data on company sales and industry sales for the period 1983 to 1987. Least-squares estimation yields

$$\hat{Y}_t = -1.45475 + 0.17628X_t$$
$$\quad\quad (0.21415) \quad (0.00144)$$

Estimated standard errors are in parentheses. Because the data are from a time series in which the intervals are fairly small, serially correlated errors are suspected even though seasonally adjusted data were used.

A computer program generated the d-statistic as $d = 0.735$. Because this result is fairly close to zero, the analyst decided to estimate the coefficient of autocorrelation ρ and apply a generalized differences model.* She chose to use a two-step iterative

Table 8.3 Company Sales and Industry Sales, by Quarter

Year and Quarter	t	Company Sales (Y_t)	Industry Sales (X_t)
1983: 1	1	20.96	127.3
2	2	21.40	130.0
3	3	21.96	132.7
4	4	21.52	129.4
1984: 1	5	22.39	135.0
2	6	22.76	137.1
3	7	23.48	141.2
4	8	23.66	142.8
1985: 1	9	24.10	145.5
2	10	24.01	145.3
3	11	24.54	148.3
4	12	24.30	146.4
1986: 1	13	25.00	150.2
2	14	25.64	153.1
3	15	26.36	157.3
4	16	26.98	160.7
1987: 1	17	27.52	164.2
2	18	27.78	165.6
3	19	28.24	168.7
4	20	28.78	171.7

Source: John Neter, William Wasserman and Michael J. Kutner, *Applied Linear Regression Models*, 2d ed. (Richard D. Irwin, 1989), p. 493.

*Using a 5 percent level of significance for $T = 20$ observations and $k = 1$ explanatory variables, the upper and lower values for d are $d_L = 1.20$ and $d_U = 1.41$. Because $d = 0.735$ falls below $d_L = 1.20$, the test indicates that positive autocorrelation is present. See the chapter appendix.

procedure to estimate ρ from the results of the first-step least-squares equation. She ran the regression

$$\hat{\varepsilon}_t = 0.631166 \, \hat{\varepsilon}_{t-1}$$

This procedure amounts to estimating a regression through the origin using the estimated residuals from the first-step equation as the dependent variable and the lagged value of the residual as the regressor.

The original variables are then transformed according to the generalized-differences model. The required transformations are:

$$Y_t^* = Y_t - 0.631166Y_{t-1}$$
$$X_t^* = X_t - 0.631166X_{t-1}$$

The analyst chose not to perform the special adjustment on the first observation— usually a serious mistake, as we saw in the preceding section. She got lucky in this application, because the resulting estimates turn out to be pretty good. Because she did not do the special adjustment, the number of observations used in the revised regression drops to 19. The estimated generalized-differences model is

$$\hat{Y}_t^* = -0.39396 + 0.17376X_t^*$$
$$(0.16704) \quad (0.00296)$$

where the intercept is an estimate of $\alpha(1 - \hat{\rho})$. Because $\hat{\rho} = 0.631166$, the new estimate for the intercept is -1.06811. Standard errors are in parentheses. Notice that the estimated standard error of the slope coefficient is larger than before the correction. The larger standard error is expected because ordinary least squares underestimates the standard error when positive serial correlation appears. The Durbin-Watson d-statistic for this new regression was $d = 1.65$, a value that is much closer to 2. No further iterations were performed by the analyst because she saw no further evidence of serial correlation.†

Having handled the problem of autocorrelation, the prediction model becomes

$$Y_0 = -1.06811 + 0.17376X_0$$

where X_0 is a value of X_t obtained from the industry's trade association and Y_0 is the predicted value of Y_t. The company's market share can also be approximated from the prediction model given industry sales. Market share is

$$\frac{Y_0}{X_0} = \left(\frac{-1.06811}{X_0}\right) + 0.17376$$

Now, because X_0 is likely to be large relative to $\hat{\alpha}$ (all recorded X_t values are greater than 100), the first term on the right-hand side of this last equation is small and may safely be ignored. Thus the company's market share is about 17 percent.

---

†The upper and lower values from the appendix table at the 5 percent level of significance for 19 observations are $d_L = 1.18$ and $d_U = 1.40$. Because $d = 1.65$ is greater than d_U, a null hypothesis of positive serial correlation is now rejected. A test of negative autocorrelation requires a comparison with $4 - d_L = 2.82$ and $4 - d_U = 2.60$. Because $d = 1.65$ is less than $4 - d_U$, a null hypothesis of negative serial correlation is also rejected.

![world map icon] **GLOBAL PERSPECTIVE:** *North Atlantic Air Travel*

A demand equation for air travel between the United States and Europe was estimated using data from 1965 to 1978.* Economic theory dictates that quantity demanded is a function of price and income. To generate direct estimates of the price and income elasticities, all variables were transformed into natural logarithms. The estimated equation is

$$\widehat{\ln Q} = 2.737 - 1.247 \ln P + 1.905 \ln GNP$$
$$(-5.071) \qquad (7.286)$$
$$\overline{R}^2 = 0.97 \qquad d = 1.83$$

where

Q = number of passengers per year traveling between the United States and Europe, in thousands

P = average yearly fare between New York and London, adjusted for inflation and weighted by the seasonal distribution of traffic

GNP = U.S. gross national product each year, adjusted for inflation.

Estimated t-ratios appear in parentheses. The estimated coefficients yield the elasticities, and their t-ratios indicate that both coefficients are significantly different from zero even though only $n = 14$ observations were used. The adjusted-R^2 is quite high, and so the estimated equation has a very good overall fit. The value of the Durbin-Watson statistic, $d = 1.83$, is fairly close to 2, indicating no first-order serial correlation that would compromise use of the t-ratios.

Because no close substitute is available for air transportation, excluding a price of a substitute good should not bias the estimated elasticities. Other potential explanatory variables, such as real income of Europeans, are likely to be correlated with the included variables, and so no other variables were included in the regression. Potential multicollinearity between the two variables included seems to have been avoided by deflating both the fare and income by a price index.

The estimated price elasticity of demand of $\eta_P = 1.247$ indicates an elastic demand for air travel over the North Atlantic. Revenue could therefore have been increased by reducing fares. The estimated income elasticity of $\eta_{GNP} = 1.905$ indicates that air travel is a normal good over this route. If the GNP increases 1 percent, we can predict approximately a 1.9 percent increase in the number of passengers per year.

*J. M. Cigliano, "Price and Income Elasticities for Air Travel: The North Atlantic Market," *Business Economics* (September 1980), pp. 17–21.

Correction of first-order serial correlation usually involves applying a method called generalized differences. If $\hat{\rho}$ is the estimate of ρ, the **generalized-differences model**[25]

$$Y_t - \hat{\rho}Y_{t-1} = \alpha(1 - \hat{\rho}) + \beta(X_t - \hat{\rho}X_{t-1}) + \upsilon_t$$

---

25. **Durbin's method** is an easy two-step procedure for estimating the generalized-differences model. Step one consists of estimating

$$Y_t = \alpha(1 - \rho) + \rho Y_{t-1} + \beta X_t - \rho\beta X_{t-1} + \upsilon_t$$

to get an estimate $\hat{\rho}$ from the least-squares coefficient for Y_{t-1}. Step two then uses $\hat{\rho}$ in the generalized-differences model.

can be estimated, where v_t is the random error. This transformation is motivated by the desire to obtain a new error v_t that has been purged of serial correlation.[26] Because the first observations (when $t = 1$) cannot be transformed like all the remaining observations, the appropriate transformation is to multiply Y_1 and X_1 by $\sqrt{1 - \hat{\rho}^2}$. This step is very important to perform, or the results may not be any better than ordinary regression.

Summary

Econometrics means economic measurement. The most frequent method used to estimate economic models from empirical information is called regression analysis. Regression means tendency toward the mean. Regression analysis estimates the mean of a dependent variable as a function of explanatory variables. Economic theory is useful in choosing the explanatory variables and in specifying the functional form to be estimated.

The estimating technique used most often is called least-squares regression. The method of least squares generates estimates for the coefficients of a linear equation so that the sum of the squared errors is minimized. The error is defined as the difference between the actual and predicted values of the dependent variable. A measure of the goodness of fit is provided by the coefficient of determination, R^2, which measures the proportion of the total variation in the dependent variable explained by the regression.

The method of least squares can be extended to include several explanatory variables, multiple regression, and can be used to estimate many types of nonlinear equations. All that is required is that the equation to be estimated can be transformed into an equation that is linear in the coefficients to be estimated.

Least-squares estimators have several desirable properties. When the disturbance term of the unknown but true regression equation has zero mean, the least-squares coefficient estimates are *unbiased* and *efficient* as long as the explanatory variables are independent of the random error and independent from each other. Efficiency means that the estimators have minimum variance.

We are usually most interested in judging the quality of the estimated coefficients. An estimated coefficient is more precise as its standard error shrinks. A coefficient's t-ratio is defined as the estimated coefficient divided by its standard error. A t-ratio greater than 2 indicates that the estimated coefficient is fairly precise. As a rule of thumb for large samples, if the estimated coefficient is twice the size of its standard error, you will be right more than 95 percent of the time in saying the estimated coefficient is statistically different from zero.

Naive application of regression is possible because computer programs are so readily available and so easy to use. But several potential problems appear. One frequent problem is nearly perfect multicollinearity among explanatory variables. Multicollinearity does *not* cause bias in the estimation in the coefficients. When one regressor is highly correlated with one or a combination of other regressors, though, a severe loss in efficiency can occur.

---

26. If $\rho = 1$, the model is called **first-differences** and $Y_t - Y_{t-1} = \beta(X_t - X_{t-1}) + v_t$, where the error term has constant variance and is independent of the transformed explanatory variable. The first-differences model is estimated without intercept and then α is estimated using the means of the original variables.

Another problem in regression analysis occurs by estimating an improperly specified model. If a properly included variable is inadvertently omitted, the result is biased estimators for all the remaining coefficients. A similar bias is caused by estimating the wrong functional form. Including an irrelevant variable causes a loss in efficiency, but that does not cause biased coefficient estimators.

Another source of bias occurs when a regressor is correlated with the random error. When an explanatory variable is randomly determined (stochastic), that regressor must be independent of the error so that the estimated coefficient will be *consistent.* If the regressor is not independent, one solution is to use an instrumental variable technique to obtain consistent estimators. Consistency is a large-sample property, so that here we need relatively large samples.

Any functional representation of the cause-and-effect relationship between a dependent variable and other variables is called a structural equation. To estimate a structural equation such as demand or supply from a system of equations, we must identify the structural equation. A necessary condition for identification is the order condition: the number of predetermined variables excluded from the equation must be at least equal to the number of endogenous variables included on the right-hand side of the equation.

Two-stage least squares is a two-step procedure for estimating one or more equations in a system of simultaneous equations. First, all endogenous variables are regressed on all predetermined variables in a system of equations to obtain estimated structural equations. Second, the predicted values of the endogenous variables from the reduced-form equations are then used as instrumental variables in estimating identified structural equations. Two-stage least squares yields consistent coefficient estimates and also solves the overidentification problem when it occurs.

Heteroscedasticity, or changing variance of the error, can be another problem in applying least squares. The least-squares coefficient estimators remain unbiased, but the loss in efficiency can be drastic. That loss means the standard significance tests are not valid. When detected, the most frequent solution is to perform weighted least squares to achieve constant variance in the transformed error.

Serial correlation occurs when a predictable pattern in the error values appears across adjacent observations. The consequence is that least-squares estimators are no longer efficient and have biased estimated variances. The first-order serial-correlation model assumes that successive errors are correlated. The Durbin-Watson statistic may be used to detect first-order serial correlation.

Estimating econometric models and forecasting from regression models is as much an art as it is a science. You should strive to be a number crafter rather than a number cruncher. Nothing will substitute for carefully specifying the model before estimation. Because estimating is so easy with the many computer programs available, apply caution to avoid naive use.

Further Readings

Two excellent introductory econometrics texts are

- Robert S. Pindyck and Daniel L. Rubinfeld, *Economic Models and Economic Forecasts,* 3d ed. (McGraw-Hill, 1991).

- A. H. Studenmund and Henry J. Cassidy, *Using Econometrics: A Practical Guide* (Little, Brown, 1987).

This popular paperback is also strongly recommended:

- Peter Kennedy, *A Guide to Econometrics,* 2d ed. (M.I.T. Press, 1985).

For a more advanced but relatively easy text, see

- Jan Kementa, *Elements of Econometrics,* 2d ed. (Macmillan, 1986).

For an authoritative and widely cited text, see

- Henri Theil, *Principles of Econometrics* (John Wiley, 1971).

Many computer programs perform multiple regression analysis. The most widely used mainframe programs are SPSS (Statistical Package for the Social Sciences), Biomed, and SAS (Statistical Analysis System). For a review, see

- Thomas Buchanan and Timothy King, "Comparing Statistical Packages: SPSS, Biomed, and SAS," *Social Science Journal,* 24(3) (1987).

Both SPSS and SAS come in personal-computer versions also. Those designed primarily for use on PCs are too numerous and are changing too rapidly to review in detail, but some of the better programs are Minitab, MicroTSP (time series processor) and RATS (regression and time series). Made for the Macintosh are JMP (from SAS), MicroTSP, SPSS, and SYSTAT.

Practice Problems

1. The term "regression" comes from an early study relating the height of sons (S) to the height of their fathers (F), where

$$S = \alpha + \beta F + \varepsilon$$

The study found a tendency toward the mean, or regression, in that fathers who are taller (shorter) than average tend to have sons who are also taller (shorter) than average but closer to average height. What values for α and β yield that result?
2. Assume that least-square estimates are obtained for $Y = \alpha + \beta X + \varepsilon$. You now decide to multiply X by 10. What happens to the least-squares intercept and slope?
3. Show that the simple least-squares regression line passes through the point of the means.
4. For the simple least-squares regression line, what configuration of sample points will yield $S^2 = 0$? What configuration of sample points will yield $R^2 = 1$?
5. A notable econometrician said, "What's all this concern with goodness-of-fit? Give me a polynomial of high order, and I'll fit the curl on a pig's tail!" What was he trying to tell us? Can you think of any drawbacks associated with using a polynomial of high order?
6. What makes a reasonable-sized sample? How many observations do you need to apply the rule-of-thumb test of the statistical significance of a regression coefficient?
7. A student attempted to estimate an asset-demand equation using these explanatory variables: W_t = current wealth, W_{t-1} = previous-period wealth, and $\Delta W_t = W_t - W_{t-1}$. What problem was encountered? What should be done?

8. True or false? If false, why?
   (a) Multicollinearity among explanatory variables means that the regression coefficients are biased.
   (b) Multicollinearity makes it more likely that the parameter estimates will be statistically significant.
   (c) Regression models should be purged of all traces of multicollinearity.
   (d) Multicollinearity is easy to detect by looking at all pairwise sample correlation coefficients for the explanatory variables.
   (e) Once two explanatory variables are found to be highly collinear, the best solution is to drop the variable that has the lowest correlation with the dependent variable.

9. Using annual data from 1965 to 1980, imports (M) was regressed on GNP and the CPI to obtain

$$\hat{M} = -69.97 + 0.045\, GNP + 0.931\, CPI \qquad R^2 = 0.9894$$

with both M and GNP measured in billions of dollars. Neither of the variables was statistically significant. When M was regressed on GNP and CPI separately, the results were:

$$\hat{M} = -69.97 + 0.112\, GNP \qquad R^2 = 0.9766$$
$$\hat{M} = -555.84 + 13.81\, CPI \qquad R^2 = 0.9622$$

Each of the variables was statistically significant in these regressions. Can you explain why the researcher ran, and chose to use, this specification:

$$\left(\widehat{\frac{M}{CPI}}\right) = -1.39 + 0.202\left(\frac{GNP}{CPI}\right) \qquad R^2 = 0.9142$$

10. A student interested in the effect of study time on grades estimated this equation:

$$\hat{G} = 70 + 1.2H + 4.0P$$
$$\phantom{\hat{G} = 70 +} (0.8) \quad (1.0)$$

where G is the grade (score) between 0 and 100, H is hours of study time per day, and P is the number of pennies in the pocket or purse of the person taking the exam. The standard errors are in parentheses. The sample correlation coefficient between H and P is 0.80. Explain why each of these statements is true or false:
   (a) Pennies are a significant determinant of the score.
   (b) The estimated coefficient for H is biased downward.
   (c) The variable H should be omitted from the equation because it is insignificant.
   (d) The variable P should be omitted from the equation because it is irrelevant and causes a loss of efficiency.

11. A land developer was interested in estimating the selling price of beach lots. He recorded data on these variables for each of 20 beach lots recently sold:

$$Y = \text{sale price in } \$1{,}000.$$
$$X_1 = \text{area in hundreds of square feet.}$$
$$X_2 = \text{elevation in feet above sea level.}$$
$$X_3 = \text{lot slope in degrees.}$$

The resulting regression equation, with standard errors in parentheses, is:

$$\hat{Y} = -2.491 + 0.099X_1 + 0.029X_2 + 0.086X_3$$
$$(0.058) \qquad (0.006) \qquad (0.031)$$
$$R^2 = 0.7838 \qquad S = 0.6075$$

(a) What percentage of the variation in price is explained by the regression?

(b) Determine which coefficients are statistically significant.

(c) Estimate the selling price for a 100-foot by 50-foot rectangular beach lot that is 20 feet above sea level and has a 5-degree slope toward the ocean.

12. Use the order condition to determine which of these equations may be identified in these systems with three endogenous variables (Y_1, Y_2, Y_3) and three exogenous variables (X_1, X_2, X_3):

(a) Model I:

$$Y_1 = \alpha_0 + \alpha_1 X_1 + \alpha_2 Y_2 + \alpha_3 Y_3 + \varepsilon_1$$
$$Y_2 = \beta_0 + \beta_1 X_1 + \beta_2 X_2 + \beta_3 X_3 + \beta_4 Y_1 + \varepsilon_2$$
$$Y_3 = \gamma_0 + \gamma_1 X_1 + \gamma_2 X_2 + \gamma_3 Y_1 + \gamma_4 Y_2 + \varepsilon_3$$

(b) Model II:

$$Y_1 = \alpha_0 + \alpha_1 Y_2 + \alpha_2 X_2 + \varepsilon_1$$
$$Y_2 = \beta_0 + \beta_1 X_1 + \beta_2 X_2 + \beta_3 X_3 + \varepsilon_2$$

13. Given these demand and supply equations:

$$Q_t^d = \alpha_0 + \alpha_1 R_t + \alpha_2 I_t + \alpha_3 D_t + \varepsilon_t$$
$$Q_t^s = \beta_0 + \beta_1 R_t + \beta_2 R_{t-1} + \beta_3 D_t + \beta_4 t + v_t$$

Where Q_t is the quantity of raw materials, R_t is a measure of the terms of trade for raw materials, I_t is an index price for capital, D_t is a dummy variable for the Korean war, and t is the time period for $t = 1$ to $t = T$.

(a) Which variables may safely be considered to be predetermined and which are endogenous?

(b) Are the demand and supply equations identified?

14. Given these observations on Y and X:

Y	X
4	2
7	6
4	10

(a) Calculate the ordinary least-squares equation for the model.

(b) Assume that heteroscedasticity is present where $\sigma_i = kX_i$, then calculate the new estimates of α and β.

(c) If the unknown but true equation is $Y = 3 + 0.5X$, which model gives the best estimate for β? Why?

15. The population-regression equation is

$$Y_t = \alpha + \beta X_t + \varepsilon_t$$

(a) Assume first-order serial correlation with $\rho = 1$, and write out an appropriate transformation to estimate by linear regression.

(b) What two things are different about the transformed equation?

Problems 16 and 17 require the formal t-test covered in the chapter appendix:

16. Suppose that for the single-variable regression model we obtain $\hat{\beta} = -1.578$ from a sample of size $n = 12$, and the standard error is calculated to be $S_{\hat{\beta}} = 0.176$. Conduct a one-tailed test of a null hypothesis that $\beta \geq 0$ against an alternative that $\beta < 0$ at a 5 percent level of significance.

17. Suppose that for a sample of size $n = 18$ we estimate $\hat{\beta} = 10.56$ and $S_{\hat{\beta}} = 5.16$ with $n - 2 = 16$ degrees of freedom. Is this coefficient statistically different from zero at a 10 percent level of significance? What about a 5 percent level of significance?

Problems 18 and 19 require the use of a computer program:

18. Given this data set:

i	Y	X_1	X_2
1	42	4	2
2	39	4	2
3	48	4	3
4	51	4	3
5	49	6	2
6	53	6	2
7	61	6	3
8	60	6	3

Source: Adapted from J. Neter, W. Wasserman, and M. H. Kutner, *Applied Linear Regression Models*, 2d ed. (R. D. Irwin, 1989), p. 296.

(a) What is the sample correlation between X_1 and X_2?

(b) Estimate the model $Y = \alpha_0 + \beta_1 X_1 + \beta_2 X_2 + \varepsilon_0$.

(c) Now estimate the model $Y = \alpha_1 + \beta_1 X_1 + \varepsilon_1$.

(d) Now estimate the model $Y = \alpha_2 + \beta_2 X_2 + \varepsilon_2$.

(e) Examine the estimated coefficients for all three models. Do you think you may have uncovered an important principle here? What is it?

19. Use the data on firm sales and industry sales in Table 8.3 and then:

(a) Assume that $\rho = 1$ and estimate a first-differences model.

(b) Use $d = 0.735$ to obtain an estimate for ρ and then estimate the generalized-differences model, but be sure to use the special adjustment on the first observations by multiplying Y_1 and X_1 by $\sqrt{1 - \hat{\rho}^2}$ so that you can use all 20 observations. Compare your results with those of the application in the chapter.

Chapter 8 Appendix: *Estimation and Inference in Regression*

The Normal Equations

The error of regression is measured by the difference between the observed value of Y and its predicted value. Least-squares regression generates estimates for α and β by minimizing the sum of the squared errors:

$$\min \Sigma(Y_i - \hat{Y}_i)^2 = \min \Sigma(Y_i - \hat{\alpha} - \hat{\beta}X_i)^2$$

Minimizing this expression yields estimates $\hat{\alpha}$ and $\hat{\beta}$, and the estimated equation is $\hat{Y} = \hat{\alpha} + \hat{\beta}X$. This step is accomplished by taking the partial derivatives of the sum of squared errors with respect to $\hat{\alpha}$ and $\hat{\beta}$, yielding two equations in terms of the two unknowns $\hat{\alpha}$ and $\hat{\beta}$. When these equations are set equal to zero simultaneously, the resulting equations are called the **normal equations:**

$$\Sigma Y_i = \hat{\alpha}n + \hat{\beta}\Sigma X_i$$
$$\Sigma X_i Y_i = \hat{\alpha}\Sigma X_i + \hat{\beta}\Sigma X_i^2$$

If we multiply the first equation by ΣX_i and then subtract it from the second equation multiplied by n, the result is

$$\hat{\beta} = \frac{n(\Sigma X_i Y_i) - (\Sigma X_i)(\Sigma Y_i)}{n(\Sigma X_i^2) - (\Sigma X_i)^2}$$

It is true that

$$n\Sigma(X_i - \overline{X})(Y_i - \overline{Y}) = n(\Sigma X_i Y_i) - (\Sigma X_i)(\Sigma Y_i)$$

and

$$n\Sigma(X_i - \overline{X})^2 = n(\Sigma X_i^2) - (\Sigma X_i)^2$$

Substituting into the normal equation for $\hat{\beta}$, after a little algebra, yields

$$\hat{\beta} = \frac{\text{Cov}(X, Y)}{\text{Var}(X)}$$

The least-squares estimator $\hat{\beta}$ is equal to the sample covariance of X and Y divided by the sample variance in X. The first normal equation gives

$$\hat{\alpha} = \frac{\Sigma Y_i}{n} - \beta\frac{\Sigma X_i}{n}$$

In the multivariate regression model with k explanatory variables, the model to be estimated is

$$Y = \alpha + \beta_1 X_1 + \beta_2 X_2 + \cdots + \beta_k X_k + \varepsilon$$

The following rule may be applied in obtaining the normal equations for this model. When $k = 1$, we have the simple model $Y = \alpha + \beta_1 X_1 + \varepsilon$ and the multiplier of α is 1 and the multiplier of β is X_1. The first normal equation is obtained by multiplying both sides by 1, adding all observations, and omitting the last term involving ε. The second normal equation is obtained by multiplying both sides by X_1, adding all observations, and omitting the last term involving ε. For two explanatory variables, $k = 2$, the normal equations become:

$$\begin{aligned}
\Sigma Y &= \hat{\alpha} n &&+ \hat{\beta}_1 \Sigma X_1 &&+ \hat{\beta}_2 \Sigma X_2 \\
\Sigma X_1 Y &= \hat{\alpha} \Sigma X_1 &&+ \hat{\beta}_1 \Sigma X_1^2 &&+ \hat{\beta}_2 \Sigma X_1 X_2 \\
\Sigma X_2 Y &= \hat{\alpha} \Sigma X_2 &&+ \hat{\beta}_1 \Sigma X_2 X_1 &&+ \hat{\beta}_2 \Sigma X_2^2
\end{aligned}$$

The first multiplier is 1, the second is X_1, and the third is X_2. In the general case of k explanatory variables, the normal equations are:

$$\begin{aligned}
\Sigma Y &= \hat{\alpha} n &&+ \hat{\beta}_1 \Sigma X_1 &&+ \hat{\beta}_2 \Sigma X_2 &&+ \cdots + \hat{\beta}_k \Sigma X_k \\
\Sigma X_1 Y &= \hat{\alpha} \Sigma X_1 &&+ \hat{\beta}_1 \Sigma X_1^2 &&+ \hat{\beta}_2 \Sigma X_1 X_2 &&+ \cdots + \hat{\beta}_k \Sigma X_1 X_k \\
&\quad\vdots \\
&\quad\vdots \\
\Sigma X_k Y &= \hat{\alpha} \Sigma X_k &&+ \hat{\beta}_1 \Sigma X_k X_1 &&+ \hat{\beta}_2 \Sigma X_k X_2 &&+ \cdots + \hat{\beta}_k \Sigma X_k^2
\end{aligned}$$

We have $(k + 1)$ equations in terms of $(k + 1)$ unknowns: $\hat{\alpha}, \hat{\beta}_1, \ldots, \hat{\beta}_k$. A solution to this system of equations requires that the number of observations exceed the number of unknowns and that none of the explanatory variables may be exact linear combinations of other explanatory variables.

Hypothesis Tests on Coefficient Estimates

In the simple regression model, if the random error is normally distributed, then the estimator $\hat{\beta}$ is also distributed normal and has mean β and variance $\sigma_{\hat{\beta}}^2$:

$$\hat{\beta} \sim N(\beta, \sigma_{\hat{\beta}}^2)$$

The symbol $\sim$ means "is distributed as." It follows from elementary statistics that

$$\frac{\hat{\beta} - \beta}{\sigma_{\hat{\beta}}} \sim N(0, 1)$$

where $N(0, 1)$ denotes the standard normal distribution (zero mean and unit variance). Because $\sigma_{\hat{\beta}}$ is unknown, we are forced to use an estimate $S_{\hat{\beta}}$ for $\sigma_{\hat{\beta}}$. Substituting $S_{\hat{\beta}}$ results in the ratio

$$\frac{\hat{\beta} - \beta}{S_{\hat{\beta}}} \sim t_{n-k-1}$$

where t_{n-k-1} denotes the Student's t-distribution with $(n - k - 1)$ degrees of freedom.[1] Again, k is the number of βs estimated, and so for the simple regression model, where

---

1. The Student's t-distribution and the standard normal distribution are discussed in every introductory statistics book. The t-distribution is symmetric like the normal distribution, but the t-distribution is fatter in the tails. The t-distribution is asymptotically normal, and so the normal is used when the degrees of freedom is greater than 30.

$k = 1$, the degrees of freedom is $(n - 2)$. The value $S_{\hat{\beta}}$ is the standard error of the estimator $\hat{\beta}$.

The t-distribution can be used to conduct statistical hypothesis tests about the value of β. A **statistical hypothesis test** begins by specifying a hypothetical value of the parameter. For β, this hypothetical value is denoted by β_0. The hypothesis is called the **null hypothesis,** denoted by H_0. The null hypothesis is typically a statement about a value or a range of values that could occur if the researcher's theory is *not* correct. This is a "straw-man" approach, where the null is the straw man that we hope to knock down. That is, we hope to reject the null. If the null is rejected by the test, tentative acceptance of an alternative hypothesis is indicated. The **alternative hypothesis,** denoted by H_a, is usually the value consistent with the researcher's theory. The alternative value is denoted by β_a.

When you have an opinion about the sign of β, the natural null hypothesis is to say that β is of sign opposite that expected. For example, if you expect $\beta < 0$, then the null and alternative hypotheses would be

$$H_0 \colon \beta \geq 0 \text{ and } H_a \colon \beta < 0$$

Rejection of the null lends statistical support in favor of the alternative. This is an example of a **one-tailed** (or **one-sided**) **test** because $\hat{\beta}$ must be negative to reject the null. A one-tailed test when you expect $\beta > 0$ would require that $\hat{\beta}$ be positive in order to reject the null. When performing a one-tailed test, a sign check should be performed first because the sign of the estimated parameter must conform to that indicated by the alternative or the null will not be rejected. It would be a waste of effort to do further calculations when the sign test fails.

The first step in conducting a hypothesis test is specifying the null and alternative hypotheses. The second step is to specify a decision rule for rejecting the null hypothesis. This step requires choosing the probability of wrongly rejecting a true null hypothesis. The **level of significance** is the probability of wrongly rejecting a true null hypothesis. As the analyst you choose the level of significance. The level of significance is sometimes (somewhat loosely) referred to as if it were a percentage. Levels of significance of 1, 5, or 10 percent are common, but other choices may be made. The level of significance chosen should be smaller as the wrong rejection of the null grows costlier. Conversely, the level of significance should be larger as the wrong acceptance of the null grows costlier. The only way to reduce the probability of making both wrong decisions is to increase the sample size.

The formal test is conducted using the t-distribution because

$$\frac{\hat{\beta} - \beta_0}{S_{\hat{\beta}}} \sim t_{n-k-1}$$

where β_0 is the hypothesized value of β. A one-tailed test is illustrated by Figure A8.1. The value of t under this null is denoted by t_0 and is calculated by setting β_0 equal to zero,

$$t_0 = \frac{\hat{\beta}}{S_{\hat{\beta}}}$$

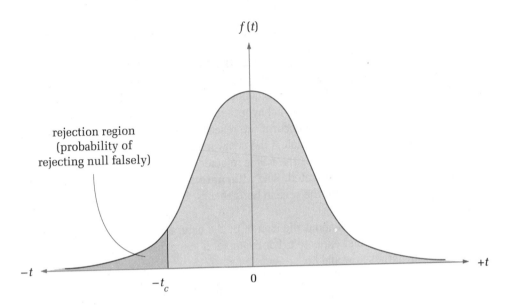

Figure A8.1 **One-tailed *t*-test:** To reject the null hypothesis that $\beta \geq 0$ against the alternative that $\beta < 0$, the test statistic $t = \hat{\beta}/S_{\hat{\beta}}$ must lie in the rejection region in the left-hand tail at the appropriate degrees of freedom and at the chosen level of significance.

This computed value is then compared to a critical value denoted by t_c. The critical value t_c, given the appropriate degrees of freedom $(n - k - 1)$ and the level of significance, can be found from the tabled values of the t-distribution in Appendix B. For H_0: $\beta \geq 0$, as illustrated by Figure A8.1, the critical value t_c will be negative because $\hat{\beta}$ must be negative for the null to be rejected. If $t_0 < t_c$, then statistical evidence is sufficient to reject the null that $\beta \geq 0$.

As an example, consider the estimated model in Table 8.2. In this case, $n = 20$ and $k = 3$, and so the degrees of freedom is $n - k - 1 = 16$. Because the own-price co-efficient is expected to be negative, a one-tailed test of a null hypothesis that $\beta_1 \geq 0$ is appropriate where β_1 is the true own-price coefficient. The estimate $\hat{\beta}_1 = -9.462$ is negative, and so we proceed by comparing the test statistic

$$t_1 = \frac{\hat{\beta}_1}{S_{\hat{\beta}_1}} = -5.118$$

to some critical value. Let's pick 1 percent as the level of significance so that the chance of wrongly rejecting the null is only 1 percent. Therefore, the test statistic t_1 will fall in the rejection region falsely 1 percent of the time. When t_1 does fall in the rejection region, then, we have fairly strong evidence that the alternative $\beta_1 < 0$ is true. The critical t-value for a 1 percent left-sided test at 16 degrees of freedom is $t_c = -2.583$.[2] Thus the null $\beta_1 \geq 0$ is rejected because $t_1 < t_c$, the test statistic lies within the rejection region. This statistical evidence lends support to the alternative hypothesis that $\beta_1 < 0$.

---

2. You should verify this statement by looking up the tabled value.

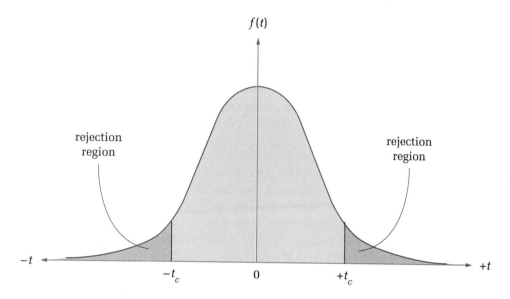

Figure A8.2 **Two-tailed *t*-test:** To reject the null hypothesis that $\beta = 0$ against the alternative that $\beta \neq 0$, the test statistic $t_0 = \hat{\beta}/S_{\hat{\beta}}$ must be compared to the rejection regions in both tails, where $\pm t_c$ is chosen so that the level of significance is divided equally between the two tails.

When you have no prior expectation about the sign of β, then a **two-tailed (or two-sided) test** is appropriate. When the sign of β can be positive or negative, the natural null hypothesis is to say that β is nonzero. The null and alternative hypotheses would be

$$H_0\text{: } \beta = 0 \text{ and } H_a\text{: } \beta \neq 0$$

Rejection of the null lends statistical support favoring the alternative that the explanatory variable does contribute to explaining the variation in the dependent variable. As illustrated by Figure A8.2, a critical value t_c is chosen so that the area in each tail is equal to one-half the level of significance.

For the application of Table 8.2, a two-tailed test is appropriate for M because its coefficient can be positive or negative. Also, a two-tailed test is appropriate for p_y because its coefficient can be positive or negative. This time, let's choose a 5 percent level of significance. At 16 degrees of freedom, the critical values are

$$t_c = \pm 2.120$$

The *t*-ratio for the variable M is $t_2 = 2.188$. Thus, we reject a null hypothesis that $\beta_2 = 0$ at a 5 percent level of significance and conclude that the estimated coefficient $\hat{\beta}_2 = 4.091$ is significantly different from zero in a statistical sense. In contrast, the *t*-ratio for the variable p_y is $t_3 = -0.682$, which does not fall outside the ± 2.120 interval. Thus, we cannot reject a null hypothesis that $\beta_3 = 0$ at the 5 percent level of significance. The estimated coefficient $\hat{\beta}_3 = -2.210$ is not statistically different from zero.

So far we have relied on an assumption that the random error is normally distributed. What happens when that assumption is not true? A remarkable result from inferential statistics known as the central-limit theorem allows us to perform the standard test whenever the sample is large even if the random error is not normally distributed *as long as* the error is not correlated with any of the explanatory variables. The central-limit theorem states that under rather general conditions, sums and means of random measurements drawn from a population tend to assume a bell-shaped distribution in repeated sampling. Applied to the regression coefficients, the central-limit theorem says that the least-squares regression coefficients are asymptotically normal. Thus, the standard statistical tests involving α and β are *asymptotically* valid *even if* the random error ε is *not* normally distributed.[3]

Experience shows that t-tests are fairly robust from departures from the normality assumption. That experience, along with the central-limit theorem, has led econometricians to apply a rule of thumb in conducting two-tailed t-tests: If the absolute value of the ratio $\hat{\beta}/S_{\hat{\beta}}$ is at least 2, then the hypothesis is that $\beta = 0$ will be rejected at a 5 percent level of significance for fairly large samples. If you have a large sample, and because the t-distribution is asymptotically normal, the critical values to reject a null hypothesis that $\beta = 0$ are ± 1.96 at a 5 percent level of significance. Thus, for a large sample, any test statistic $\hat{\beta}/S_{\hat{\beta}}$ that lies outside the interval $[\pm 1.96]$ implies rejection of $\beta = 0$, and false rejection of the null will occur only 5 percent of the time.

In summary, you can perform a hypothesis test that each coefficient is statistically different from zero by calculating

$$t_j = \frac{\hat{\beta}_j}{S_{\hat{\beta}_j}}$$

and comparing that t_j to a critical value t_c chosen from the t-table with $(n - k - 1)$ degrees of freedom. One degree of freedom is lost for each coefficient estimated, including the constant term. With a large sample, the rule of thumb for a two-tailed test at 5 percent level of significance requires that the absolute value of t_j be at least 2 in order to reject a null hypothesis that $\beta_j = 0$.

It is easy to misuse formal tests. First, rejection of a null hypothesis that $\beta_j = 0$ does not *prove* the alternative hypothesis because the statistical result depends on the sample used. A different sample may indicate a different conclusion. Thus, rejection of the null merely provides statistical evidence in support of the alternative that a *linear* relationship connects the dependent variable and the explanatory variable. Second, a statistically significant estimate for some β_j does *not* prove a *causal* relationship. The results might be spurious, or perhaps the dependent and explanatory variables are both determined by and correlated with another variable not included in the regression.

The Durbin-Watson Test for Serial Correlation

First-order serial correlation is present when error ε_t is correlated with the preceding error ε_{t-1},

$$\varepsilon_t = \rho \varepsilon_{t-1} + v_t$$

---

3. As long as the other assumptions hold and σ^2 is finite.

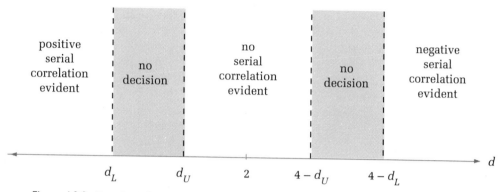

Figure A8.3 **Using the Durbin-Watson statistic:** The upper and lower values of the Durbin-Watson d-statistic define rejection regions where a null hypothesis of no serial correlation may be rejected.

where ρ is a correlation coefficient between successive errors and v_t is a random error assumed to have zero mean, to have constant variance, and to be independent of ε_{t-1}. The null hypothesis to be tested is that $\rho = 0$, that no serial correlation is present.

The Durbin-Watson d-statistic is defined as

$$d = \frac{\sum_{t=2}^{T} (\hat{\varepsilon}_t - \hat{\varepsilon}_{t-1})^2}{\sum_{t=2}^{T} \hat{\varepsilon}_t^2}$$

The test is illustrated in Figure A8.3. For critical values we find an upper limit d_U and a lower limit d_L and two zones of indeterminacy. Exact values of the upper and lower limits are found in a table of Durbin-Watson d values. Such a table is included in the Appendix of Tables. As an example of how to use the Durbin-Watson d, suppose a regression using $T = 96$ observations with $k = 4$ explanatory variables results in $R^2 = 0.69$ and $d = 0.95$. The critical values of the d statistic at a 5 percent level of significance are $d_L = 1.58$ and $d_U = 1.75$. Because $d < d_L$, the null hypothesis H_0: $\rho \leq 0$ is rejected in favor of the alternative H_a:$\rho > 0$ that positive serial correlation is present.

A few words of caution. First, don't be surprised if your d-statistic falls in the indeterminate range, because that happens frequently. Second, the test is valid only when the explanatory variables are uncorrelated with the random error. Third, the test is not valid when a lagged value of the dependent variable is used as an explanatory variable.[4]

---

4. For the case wherein a lagged value of the dependent variable is used as an explanatory variable, see J. Durbin, "Testing for Serially Correlated Errors," *Econometrica* (1970), pp. 410–421.

Business and Economic Forecasting

Studying business and economic activity often requires analyzing data that have been collected over a period of time. Any series of observations that can be arranged chronologically is called a **time series.** Time series are often analyzed by managers in making forecasts. In fact, all businesses make forecasts, even if some of those forecasts are quite crude. Forecasting is an essential part of reducing uncertainty about what the future holds.

Some of the areas in which forecasts are used are: sales projections, strategic planning, technological changes, market trends, inventory control, planning materials requirements, and projection of futures' prices. You can see the breadth of applications for which forecasting techniques may be used to gain information about what might happen in the future.

We distinguish between pure time-series models and causal models. A **pure time-series model** for predicting a dependent variable Y_t has only time t and past values (Y_{t-1}, Y_{t-2}, ...) of the dependent variable as predicting variables. A **causal model** for predicting Y_t uses predictors other than time and past values of Y_t as predicting variables. Of course, it is possible to construct mixed models in which time, past values of Y_t, and other explanatory variables, lagged and unlagged, are used as predicting variables.

9.1   Decomposition of Time Series

One approach to evaluating time series is to decompose the series into four components: a trend, seasonal variation, cyclical variation, and random or irregular variation. The four components are most easily understood by looking at a graph of a series. Figure 9.1 illustrates a series with $t = 1$, 20 quarterly measurements. First, by looking at the graph of this series, you can see a slight upward trend. Second, a seasonal component seems to be suggested by the periodic fluctuation of this series *within* each year. If you look at observations four quarters apart, you can see the seasonal variation. Third, this series seems to drift downward before it turns upward. Such cyclical variation differs from seasonal variation in two ways: cycles take place over years, not within each year, and cycles do not necessarily have a fixed length—the duration of the cycle is not always constant. Fourth, a time series almost always has a random or irregular component caused by unpredictable events or just stochastic variation in the dependent variable. Describing how the four components combine to form a series, we can adopt two basic approaches.

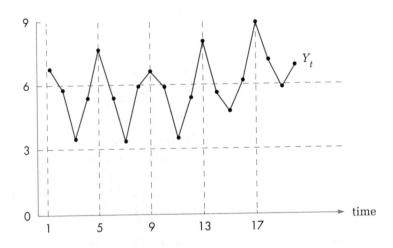

Figure 9.1   **A time series:** This time series consists of $t = 1$, 20 quarterly measurements of Y_t. The series appears to have a slight upward trend. A quarterly seasonal movement is obvious. In addition to irregular movement, there also appears to be a slight U-shaped cycle.

The **additive model** expresses the series as a sum of the four components:

> **Additive model:** *A series can be represented by an additive model as the* sum *of four components:*
>
> $$trend + seasonal + cyclical + random.$$

Table 9.1 lists the series graphed in Figure 9.1, along with some *assumed* values of the four components. For an additive decomposition, the components have the same units of measurement as the original series.

The **multiplicative model** expresses the series as the product of the four components:

> **Multiplicative model:** *A series can be represented by a multiplicative model as the* product *of four components:*
>
> $$trend \times seasonal \times cyclical \times random.$$

Table 9.1 An Additive Decomposition of a Time Series

t	Y_t	=	Trend	+	Seasonal	+	Cyclical	+	Random
1	6.750		5.000		1.5		0.000		0.25
2	5.750		5.125		0.0		0.125		0.50
3	3.500		5.250		−1.5		0.250		−0.50
4	5.375		5.375		0.0		0.250		−0.25
5	7.625		5.500		1.5		0.125		0.50
6	5.375		5.625		0.0		0.000		−0.25
7	3.375		5.750		−1.5		−0.125		−0.75
8	5.875		5.875		0.0		−0.250		0.25
9	6.625		6.000		1.5		−0.375		−0.50
10	5.875		6.125		0.0		−0.500		0.25
11	3.500		6.250		−1.5		−0.500		−0.75
12	5.375		6.375		0.0		−0.500		−0.50
13	8.000		6.500		1.5		−0.500		0.50
14	5.625		6.625		0.0		−0.500		−0.50
15	4.750		6.750		−1.5		−0.500		0.00
16	6.125		6.875		0.0		−0.500		−0.25
17	8.875		7.000		1.5		−0.375		0.75
18	7.125		7.125		0.0		−0.250		0.25
19	5.875		7.250		−1.5		−0.125		0.25
20	6.875		7.375		0.0		0.000		−0.50

Source: Nicholas R. Farnum and LaVerne W. Stanton, *Quantitative Forecasting Methods* (PWS-Kent, 1989), p. 35.

Table 9.2 A Multiplicative Decomposition of a Time Series

t	Y_t	=	Trend	×	Seasonal	×	Cyclical	×	Random
1	6.750		5.18		1.330		.951		1.030
2	5.750		5.26		1.006		0.970		1.120
3	3.500		5.34		.699		1.002		.978
4	5.375		5.42		.995		1.028		.970
5	7.625		5.50		1.330		.996		1.047
6	5.375		5.58		1.006		.997		.980
7	3.375		5.66		.699		.986		.905
8	5.875		5.74		.995		.929		1.107
9	6.625		5.82		1.330		.938		.912
10	5.875		5.90		1.006		.931		1.063
11	3.500		5.98		.699		.898		.974
12	5.375		6.06		.995		.943		.945
13	8.000		6.14		1.330		.921		1.064
14	5.625		6.22		1.006		.960		.936
15	4.750		6.30		.699		.979		1.151
16	6.125		6.38		.995		1.001		.964
17	8.875		6.46		1.330		1.048		.986
18	7.125		6.54		1.006		1.078		1.005
19	5.875		6.62		.699		1.094		1.213
20	6.875		6.70		.995		1.110		.929

Source: Nicholas R. Farnum and LaVerne W. Stanton, *Quantitative Forecasting Methods* (PWS-Kent, 1989), p. 37.

A multiplicative decomposition of the series in Figure 9.1 appears in Table 9.2. For a multiplicative decomposition, only the trend part is measured in the same units as the dependent variable. The seasonal, cyclical, and random components are "indexes" or "weights" and are unit free. The weights are frequently expressed as percentage deviations from the trend. The multiplicative model serves as the foundation for producing seasonally adjusted time-series data by the U.S. Bureau of the Census.

9.2 Linear and Nonlinear Trends

The movement of the expected value of a series, $E(Y_t)$, in *one* direction (either upward or downward, but not both) is called a **trend**. A trend is not necessarily constant, but it is assumed to be smooth. A series with a constant trend changes at a constant rate with respect to time. A series with a trend that is not constant changes smoothly and continuously with time, but the rate of change may be increasing or decreasing.

A **linear-trend model** can be used to represent a series with a constant trend:

Linear-trend model:

$$Y_t = \beta_0 + \beta_1 t + \varepsilon_t$$

where ε_t is the random component of the series Y_t.

It is usually assumed that the random component has zero mean, $E(\varepsilon_t) = 0$. The trend in this model can be expressed

$$T_t = E(Y_t) = \beta_0 + \beta_1 t$$

where the intercept β_0 is the trend value at the origin of the series, $t = 0$. In the linear-trend model, the expected change in Y_t due to a one-unit change in time is constant,

$$E\!\left(\frac{\Delta Y_t}{\Delta t}\right) = \beta_1$$

Least-squares regression can be used to obtain estimates of the intercept and slope terms for this model. Forecasts can be generated by allowing the time variable to move beyond the final period in the series.

The linear-trend model suffers from a major limitation—the trend is constant. When a time series increases or decreases at an increasing or decreasing rate, or when a time series first increases or decreases at an increasing rate and then continues to increase or decrease but at a decreasing rate, the linear model is not likely to fit the data closely. Even if it does have good fit, the linear model is not likely to generate reliable forecasts beyond the range of the original series. Therefore, nonlinear-trend models are useful.

Occasionally, a quadratic, cubic, or higher-order polynomial-trend model is appropriate in describing the path of an economic variable with passing time. The general **polynomial-trend model** is:

Polynomial-trend model:

$$Y_t = \beta_0 + \beta_1 t + \beta_2 t^2 + \cdots + \beta_s t^s + \varepsilon_t$$

where s is the degree of the polynomial.

Any polynomial-trend model can be estimated, provided that the number of observations in the series is greater than the number of parameters to be estimated. A second-degree polynomial-trend model yields a **quadratic**-trend model,

$$Y_t = \beta_0 + \beta_1 t + \beta_2 t^2 + \varepsilon_t$$

The quadratic-trend model requires at least $T = 4$ observations, where $t = 1, T$, in order to estimate by least-squares regression. The sign of β_2 determines whether the trend changes at an increasing or decreasing rate.

Sometimes your series tends to grow at a fairly constant *percentage* rate in each period. Then an **exponential trend model** can be used:

Exponential-trend model:

$$Y_t = \alpha \exp[(\beta_1 t + \beta_2 t^2 + \cdots + \beta_s t^s)]v_t$$

After taking the natural logarithm of this model, we get

$$\ln Y_t = \beta_0 + \beta_1 t + \beta_2 t^2 + \cdots + \beta_s t^s + \varepsilon_t$$

where $\beta_0 = \ln \alpha$ and $\varepsilon_t = \ln v_t$. Like the polynomial-trend model, the exponential-trend model can be used to describe movements in a time series that follows a relatively smooth but nonlinear path over time. Both models can be estimated by least-squares regression.

Let's look at a simple example to illustrate these alternative models. Consider the time series in Table 9.3 for a hypothetical corporation's net annual sales over a 26-year period. An estimated *linear*-trend model yields:

$$\hat{Y}_t = 0.297 + 5.986t \quad R^2 = 0.916$$
$$(16.205)$$

where the *t*-ratios are in parentheses. An estimated *quadratic*-trend model yields:

$$\hat{Y}_t = 34.043 - 1.263t + 0.268t^2 \quad R^2 = 0.999$$
$$(-7.139) \quad (42.098)$$

The quadratic model exhibits a much better overall fit, indicating that the trend is nonlinear. An estimated *exponential*-trend model with $s = 1$ yields:

$$\widehat{\ln Y_t} = 3.195 + 0.076t \quad R^2 = 0.993$$
$$(58.478)$$

This model also exhibits a very good overall fit. This coefficient of determination, however, applies to $\ln Y_t$ as a linear function of time, and the variable Y_t as a function of time will not have the same fit.

You must exercise care and judgment in generating forecasts from any of these models because the estimated trends may not continue indefinitely into the future. Special care needs to be taken with the quadratic and exponential models, even though they may fit the series very closely over the range of time analyzed. For example, the forecast values from the quadratic and exponential models of the series in Table 9.3 will be increasing at an increasing rate. Should economic and business conditions change, forecasts generated from such models could become very inaccurate.

One popular alternative is to estimate a time-series model that is sigmoid in shape. That is, the time series either increases at an increasing rate initially but then increases at a decreasing rate while approaching some maximum, or the series decreases at an increasing rate initially but then decreases at a decreasing rate while approaching some minimum. When the series Y_t is a proportion, the **logistic model** can be used:

Table 9.3 Net Annual Sales, XYZ Corporation

Time	Y_t (in millions)	$\ln Y_t$
1	$29.5	3.38
2	30.6	3.42
3	32.5	3.48
4	34.3	3.54
5	36.3	3.59
6	38.3	3.69
7	40.4	3.70
8	43.4	3.77
9	46.1	3.83
10	49.2	3.90
11	52.6	3.96
12	56.8	4.04
13	61.6	4.12
14	67.9	4.22
15	73.8	4.30
16	80.6	4.39
17	88.6	4.48
18	97.6	4.58
19	106.4	4.67
20	116.7	4.76
21	124.1	4.82
22	134.3	4.90
23	148.3	5.00
24	158.5	5.07
25	170.6	5.14
26	183.5	5.21

Logistic-trend model:

$$\ln\left[\frac{Y_t}{1 - Y_t}\right] = \beta_0 + \beta_1 t + \varepsilon_t$$

where Y_t is a proportion.

The logistic model may be very useful in forecasting a proportion. As an example, Y_t may be the proportion of repeat sales to customers, or Y_t may be market share, or any other series that can be measured as a proportion.[1]

---

1. In case Y_t is binary, $Y_t = 1$ if an event occurred in time t, the model is called a **binomial logit** model and can be estimated by maximum likelihood (ML). That is not likely to be a problem because computer programs are commonly available to do ML estimation. The logistic model can also be extended to the case of many independent variables.

ECONOMIC SCENE: *Cable-Television Subscriptions Slip*

During the early 1980s, Cinemax, Home Box Office, and Showtime cable television subscriptions were increasing at an increasing rate. The pay channels grew dizzyingly because viewers liked watching uncut movies before they appeared on the networks. But by 1990, subscription levels were increasing slowly at HBO and Showtime, and were relatively constant at Cinemax and the Movie Channel. Some recent trends are shown in Figure 9.2. Even though these series are short, a sigmoid shape is evident. Forecasts based on linear or increasing trends would have been too optimistic.

The number of homes buying pay-television channels, as a percentage of cable subscribers, is shrinking. "We are a maturing business," acknowledged Michael

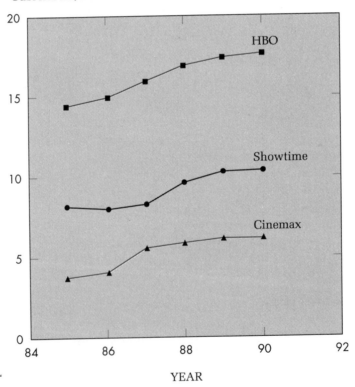

Source: Cable companies, as cited in the Los Angeles *Times,* December 9, 1990.

Figure 9.2   **Pay-television cable subscriptions:** Cable-television subscriptions between 1985 and 1990 increased at an increasing rate initially but continued to increase, though at a decreasing rate, toward the end of the decade. These series all seem to follow a sigmoid shape, and so a linear or strictly increasing predicted trend would lead to serious forecasting error.

Fuchs, chairman of HBO.* "It now is flat enough that the industry is finally getting concerned."

The primary change that has occurred in this market is that pay-television is now competing with videocassette recordings. Videocassette recorders, which were in only 5 percent of homes in the early 1980s, were in more than 70 percent of homes by 1990. Only the Disney Channel has been able to swim against the tide. It had only 12 percent market share in 1980, and so Disney still has a way to go before it reaches saturation.

*As reported by John Lippman in the *Los Angeles Times,* December 9, 1990.

9.3 Detrending a Time Series

We have just looked at several time-series models that could be used to detrend a series. Why should a series be detrended? One reason is to isolate cyclical or seasonal variation so as to understand and predict their influence on the series. Another reason is to transform the series so that it can be analyzed using an autoregressive model (to be considered later in this chapter). A third reason is to help judge whether the trend is linear or nonlinear.

One way to detrend a series is to fit a trend model so that predicted values $\hat{Y}_t$ can be made for each period t. Then a detrended series can be formed such as

$$y_t = Y_t - \hat{Y}_t$$

The transformed series y_t can then be analyzed, devoid of trend.

Another way to detrend a series is to use **differencing:**

> *Differencing of order d:*
> $$\Delta Y_t = Y_t - Y_{t-1}$$
> $$\Delta^2 Y_t = \Delta Y_t - \Delta Y_{t-1}$$
> $$\vdots$$
> $$\Delta^d Y_t = \Delta^{d-1} Y_t - \Delta^{d-1} Y_{t-1}$$

First differences are formed as

$$\Delta Y_t = Y_t - Y_{t-1}$$

Second differences are formed as

$$\Delta^2 Y_t = \Delta Y_t - \Delta Y_{t-1}$$

The differencing procedure can continue to construct differences of order d,

$$\Delta^d Y_t = \Delta^{d-1} Y_t - \Delta^{d-1} Y_{t-1}$$

Differencing is usually a very effective way to obtain a **stationary** series:

> **Stationary series:** *A series in which the covariances of Y_t with Y_{t-k} depend on the time interval (lag length k) and not on time itself—both the mean and variance of the series are time invariant.*

Stationarity, the property of a series being stationary, means:

- **The mean of the series is constant across time.** A series with trend should be detrended before fitting an autoregressive model.
- **The variance of the series is constant across time.** Correction for heteroscedasticity should be made before differencing. A simple transformation like taking logs may work.
- **The autocorrelations of the series depend only on the difference between the time points and not on the time period itself.** Seasonal differencing may be required to achieve stationarity.

Autocorrelation of Y_t with Y_{t-k} measures the correlation of values of the series with lagged values of the series having lag length k. Formulas for estimating autocorrelations are presented later in this chapter. For now it is sufficient to know that a stationary series is devoid of trend. Thus a series with a trend cannot be stationary. Usually $d = 1$ or $d = 2$ is sufficient to detrend an original time series and generate a new stationary series.

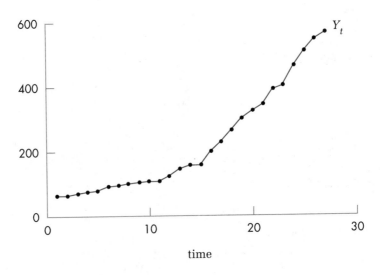

Figure 9.3 **Gross U.S. business savings:** This series shows how annual gross U.S. business savings have changed over a twenty-seven-year period. The trend does not appear to be linear.

Table 9.4 Gross Business Savings over Time

Year (t)	Y_t	Y_{t-1}	ΔY_t	ΔY_{t-1}	$\Delta^2 Y_t$
1	60.3	—	—	—	—
2	62.0	60.3	1.7	—	—
3	69.3	62.0	7.3	1.7	5.6
4	73.3	69.3	4.0	7.3	– 3.3
5	79.3	73.3	6.0	4.0	2.0
6	88.7	79.3	9.4	6.0	3.4
7	95.6	88.7	6.9	9.4	– 2.5
8	98.6	95.6	3.0	6.9	– 3.9
9	103.3	98.6	4.7	3.0	1.7
10	106.7	103.3	3.4	4.7	– 1.3
11	106.7	106.7	0.0	3.4	– 3.4
12	124.3	106.7	17.6	0.0	17.6
13	142.0	124.3	17.7	17.6	0.1
14	155.0	142.0	13.0	17.7	– 4.7
15	157.6	155.0	2.6	13.0	– 10.4
16	198.9	157.6	41.3	2.6	38.7
17	225.6	198.9	26.7	41.3	– 14.6
18	263.8	225.6	38.2	26.7	11.5
19	298.8	263.8	35.0	38.2	– 3.2
20	327.7	298.8	28.9	35.0	– 6.1
21	341.5	327.7	13.8	28.9	– 15.1
22	391.1	341.5	49.6	13.8	35.8
23	403.2	391.1	12.1	49.6	– 37.5
24	461.6	403.2	58.4	12.1	46.3
25	506.1	461.6	44.5	58.4	– 13.9
26	544.5	506.1	38.4	44.5	– 6.1
27	564.2	544.5	19.7	38.4	– 18.7

Source: *Survey of Current Business* (Washington, D.C.: U.S. Department of Commerce, 1987).

To see how differencing works, let's use the data on annual gross business savings in the United States, reported in Table 9.4. The first column lists the survey year or observation index t. The second column lists the level of savings Y_t in each year. The third column lists the one-period lagged values Y_{t-1} of Y_t. The fourth column lists the first differences, $\Delta Y_t = Y_t - Y_{t-1}$. The fifth column lists the one-period lagged values ΔY_{t-1} of ΔY_t. The sixth column lists the second differences, $\Delta^2 Y_t$, computed from the difference $\Delta Y_t - \Delta Y_{t-1}$. You could continue this differencing to calculate third differences and so on, as far as necessary.

The original series is plotted over time in Figure 9.3. This series has a distinctive upward trend that appears to be nonlinear. A plot of the first differences ΔY_t is shown in

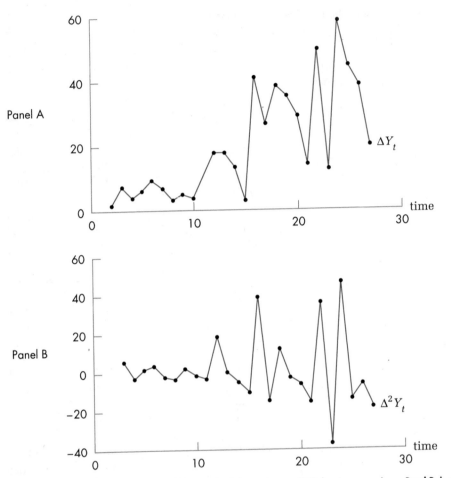

Figure 9.4 **Panel A** A plot of the first differences of the series on U. S. business savings. **Panel B** A plot of the second differences of the series on U.S. business savings.

Panel A of Figure 9.4. A trend still appears in the first differences, and that is an indication that the trend in Y_t is nonlinear. A plot of the second differences $\Delta^2 Y_t$ is shown in Panel B of Figure 9.4. You can see that no apparent trend lies in the series of second differences.

Examining the first differences, we noticed that the trend in the original series is nonlinear. One reasonable model specification to fit the trend is Y_t as a quadratic function of time. Regression yields:

$$\hat{Y}_t = 84.169 - 7.628t + 0.961t^2 \quad R^2 = 0.995$$
$$\phantom{\hat{Y}_t = }(10.827) \ (-5.962) \ (21.670)$$

where the t-ratios are in parentheses.

9.4 Autoregressive Forecasting Models

Lagged values of the time series can be used as independent variables in a regression model. The advantage of such a model is that we need know only past values of Y_t to prepare forecasts. The **autoregressive model** takes the form:

Autoregressive model AR(p):

$$Y_t = \beta_0 + \beta_1 Y_{t-1} + \beta_2 Y_{t-2} + \cdots + \beta_p Y_{t-p} + \varepsilon_t$$

where Y_{t-p} is the lagged value of Y_t at time $(t - p)$.

The **order** of the autoregressive model is p, and the model is denoted $AR(p)$.

One problem with this model is that because the independent variables are previous values of Y_t, the errors ε_t are no longer independent between periods. This condition causes a loss of efficiency—the estimators are no longer minimum-variance estimators. The loss of efficiency is negligible, however, if the sample is large.

Another problem with this model is that if Y_t has a trend, so too will Y_{t-1}, Y_{t-2}, and so on, and multicollinearity will appear. Therefore, when estimating an AR model, be sure the series is devoid of trend. In fact, the more stringent condition of stationarity is required.

When the order of the autoregressive model is $p = 1$, we have an $AR(1)$ model:

$$Y_t = \beta_0 + \beta_1 Y_{t-1} + \varepsilon_t$$

The estimate $\hat{\beta}_1$ is called the **estimated partial autocorrelation coefficient of lag 1.** Similarly, an $AR(2)$ model is represented by

$$Y_t = \beta_0 + \beta_1 Y_{t-1} + \beta_2 Y_{t-2} + \varepsilon_t$$

The estimate $\hat{\beta}_2$ is the **estimated partial autocorrelation coefficient of lag 2.** Care must be taken in interpreting the $AR(2)$ model because now $\hat{\beta}_1$ from the $AR(2)$ model does *not* represent a partial autocorrelation coefficient. In general, however, to get an estimate of the **partial autocorrelation coefficient of lag k,** perform regression using the model

$$Y_t = \beta_0 + \beta_1 Y_{t-1} + \beta_2 Y_{t-2} + \cdots + \beta_k Y_k + \varepsilon_t$$

Thus a repetitive procedure can be used to estimate partial autocorrelation coefficients. Start by estimating an $AR(1)$ model so that its $\hat{\beta}_1$ can be used as an estimate of the partial autocorrelation coefficient of lag 1. Next, estimate an $AR(2)$ model so that its $\hat{\beta}_2$ can be used as an estimate of the partial autocorrelation coefficient of lag 2. Continue to increase the order of the model incrementally, and each time the last $\hat{\beta}_k$ generated is an estimate of

Table 9.5 Monthly Newspaper Subscriptions

Month	Subscriptions (1,000s)
1	50.8
2	50.3
3	50.2
4	48.7
5	48.5
6	48.1
7	50.1
8	48.7
9	49.2
10	51.1
11	50.8
12	52.8
13	53.0
14	51.8
15	53.6
16	53.1
17	51.6
18	50.8
19	50.6
20	49.7
21	49.7
22	50.3
23	49.9
24	51.8
25	51.0

the partial autocorrelation coefficient of lag k.[2] Like other correlation coefficients, these should have values that lie in the range between -1 and $+1$.

At each step, with a large sample, you can use a rule-of-thumb test to see if any $\hat{\beta}_k$ is significantly different from zero. With a large sample of size T, the test of a null hypothesis H_0 that the true value is zero is

$$\text{Reject } H_0 \colon \beta_k = 0 \text{ if } |\,\hat{\beta}_k\,| > 2/\sqrt{T}$$

If the null is rejected, we are 95 percent confident that the true partial autocorrelation

---

2. Some computer programs generate the estimates of the partial autocorrelation coefficients without having to use this stepwise procedure, but they do not use least-squares regression. See the optional section on *ARIMA* models toward the end of this chapter.

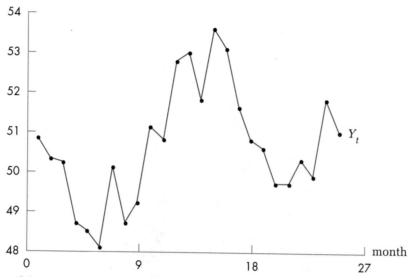

Figure 9.5 A plot of newspaper subscriptions in a city that has a stable population so that the series is devoid of trend.

coefficient β_k is nonzero. If the null is not rejected, we have support for $\beta_k = 0$.

This application of the t-test is useful for selecting p, the order of the model. You could estimate an $AR(1)$ model, then an $AR(2)$ model, and so on, until the last partial autocorrelation coefficient failed to pass the rule-of-thumb test.[3] In practice, keep the order of the model as small as is reasonable.

As an example of estimating an autoregressive model, consider the series in Table 9.5. Let's suppose this series is the number of newspaper subscriptions in a city with a stable population. This assumption suggests that the series is likely to be devoid of trend. The series in Table 9.5 is plotted in Figure 9.5. You'll see no evidence of trend. An estimated $AR(1)$ model is

$$\hat{Y}_t = 14.441 + 0.715Y_{t-1}$$
$$(1.909) \quad (4.787)$$

The t-ratios are in parentheses. The estimated partial autocorrelation coefficient of lag 1 is $\hat{\beta}_1 = 0.715$, and it is statistically significant. An $AR(2)$ model estimated for this series is

$$\hat{Y}_t = 12.761 + 0.639Y_{t-1} + 0.110Y_{t-2}$$
$$(1.495) \quad (2.873) \qquad (0.487)$$

The estimated partial autocorrelation coefficient of lag 2 is $\hat{\beta}_2 = 0.110$, but it is not statistically significant. Therefore, we can use the $AR(1)$ model to generate forecasts.

---

3. The best way to determine p is to look for a sharp "cutting off" after lag p in the sample autocorrelation function. This subject is discussed later in this chapter. Another way to test if p is sufficiently great is to apply the Durbin-Watson test of serial correlation in the residuals, as detailed in the appendix to Chapter 8.

DENNIS THE MENACE

"SEE? YESTERDAY AND TOMORROW ARE
JUST A COUPLE OF TODAYS."

Dennis the Menace® used by permission of Hank Ketcham and © by North America Syndicate.

The forecasting model becomes

$$Y_f = 14.441 + 0.715Y_{f-1}$$

where $f = T + 1$, $T + 2$, and so on. Because $T = 25$ and $Y_{25} = 51.0$, a one-period-ahead forecast is

$$Y_{26} = 14.441 + 0.715Y_{25} = 50.906$$

A two-period-ahead forecast is

$$Y_{27} = 14.441 + 0.715Y_{26} = 50.839$$

because Y_{26} is the previous forecast. You could continue to generate forecasts using previous forecasts for as far ahead as you wish. Dennis has the right idea in the cartoon.

9.5 Seasonal Adjustment Using Dummy Variables

One way of capturing the effect of seasonal variation in a series is to use dummy variables. Dummy variables can be used to measure additive deviations from a trend value. As an illustration, suppose you have time-series data on quarterly sales of a product. This model might be used to control for seasonal variation:

$$Y_t = \beta_0 + \beta_1 t + \beta_2 Q_2 + \beta_3 Q_3 + \beta_4 Q_4 + \varepsilon_t$$

where

t = time measured in number of quarters from a beginning period
Q_2 = 1 for the second quarter
Q_3 = 1 for the third quarter
Q_4 = 1 for the fourth quarter

The variable t will capture any linear trend in sales as time passes, and the quarterly dummies capture any systematic seasonal shift in sales from quarter to quarter. Figure 9.6 illustrates a possible outcome for this model. Notice that in models of this type with m mutually exclusive and exhaustive categories that could be represented by dummy variables, only $(m - 1)$ dummy variables are included in the regression. The intercept β_0 holds for the excluded category. If all m categories were to be represented by m dummy variables, a mistake called the **dummy variable trap,** the normal equations would not be independent unless the model were estimated without a constant term.

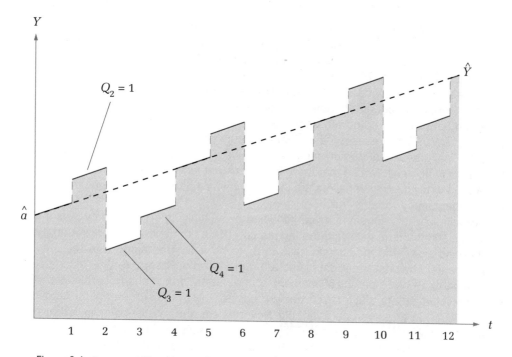

Figure 9.6 **Dummy variables and seasonal variation:** In the model

$$\hat{Y}_t = \hat{\alpha} + \hat{\beta}_1 t + \hat{\beta}_2 Q_2 + \hat{\beta}_3 Q_3 + \hat{\beta}_4 Q_4$$

$\hat{\beta}_1$ is an estimate for the time trend, $\hat{\alpha}$ is the intercept for the first season, $\hat{\alpha} + \hat{\beta}_2$ is the intercept for the second season ($Q_2 = 1$), $\hat{\alpha} + \hat{\beta}_3$ is the intercept for the third season ($Q_3 = 1$), and $\hat{\alpha} + \hat{\beta}_4$ is the intercept for the fourth season ($Q_4 = 1$).

AN APPLICATION: *Demand for Certificates of Deposit*

In a study of the demand for certificates of deposit held by the public, monthly observations were used to estimate this equation:*

$$\frac{CD_t - \beta_0 CD_{t-1}}{PI_t} = \beta_1 RCD_t + \beta_2 RTB_t + \beta_3 RBaa_t + \beta_4 (RBaa_t - RCP_t) + \sum_{j=1}^{12} \alpha_j M_j + \varepsilon_t$$

where

CD_t = monthly volume of negotiable certificates of deposit
PI_t = personal income
RCD_t = interest rate on certificates of deposit
RTB_t = interest rate on Treasury bills
$RBaa_t$ = interest rate on corporate bonds
RCP_t = interest rate on commercial paper
M_j = 1 for the jth month with j = 1 for January through j = 12 for December, zero otherwise

This demand relationship says that the difference between the current month's volume of certificates of deposit (CD_t) and some fraction β_0 of last month's volume (CD_{t-1}), as a proportion of current personal income (PI_t), is a linear function of a set of explanatory variables. They include the interest rate on certificates of deposit (RCD_t) as a measure of own price and the interest rates on Treasury bills (RTB_t) and corporate bonds ($RBaa_t$) as prices of competing financial assets. Also included was the difference between the corporate-bond rate and the rate on prime commercial paper ($RBaa_t - RCP_t$), representing the difference between long- and short-term interest rates. Finally, seasonal dummy variables (M_j) were included to control for seasonal variation in demand. Notice that there is no constant term in the equation. When all twelve monthly dummy variables are included, the constant term must be omitted to avoid the dummy variable trap.

To estimate this equation, it was modified by multiplying both sides by personal income, and the term involving the lagged certificates of deposit was moved to the right-hand side. This modification allows β_0 to be estimated along with the other coefficients. The parameter estimates are reproduced in Table 9.6. This estimated equation explained nearly 100 percent of the variation in monthly certificates of deposit volume (CD_t), a fit that was helped considerably by the inclusion of the lagged term (CD_{t-1}) as an explanatory variable. Nevertheless, the t-statistics indicate that all estimated coefficients were statistically significant using the rule of thumb.

The negative signs of the coefficients on the interest rates on T-bills and corporate bonds confirm that they are market substitutes for certificates of deposit, and the positive sign of the interest rate for certificates of deposit conforms to an expectation that quantity demanded should increase with its interest rate. The positive sign of the coefficient for the ($RBaa_t - RCP_t$) variable indicates that a long-term investment like a

---

*This application has been adapted from R. Pindyck and S. Roberts, "Optimal Policies for Monetary Control," *Annals of Economic and Social Measurement*, January 1974, as reported in R. S. Pindyck and D. L. Rubinfeld, *Econometric Models and Economic Forecasts*, 3d ed. (McGraw-Hill, 1991), pp. 108–9.

Table 9.6 Regression Results for CD Demand

Variable	Coefficient	Estimate	t-statistic
CD_{t-1}	β_0	0.72947	14.610
$RCD_t \cdot PI_t$	β_1	0.00225	6.903
$RTP_t \cdot PI_t$	β_2	-0.00150	-2.667
$RBaa_t \cdot PI_t$	β_3	-0.00128	-2.453
$(RBaa_t - RCP_t) \cdot PI_t$	β_4	0.00154	2.929
Monthly Indicators:			
$M_1 \cdot PI_t$	α_1	0.01057	2.886
$M_2 \cdot PI_t$	α_2	0.00977	2.768
$M_3 \cdot PI_t$	α_3	0.00974	2.279
$M_4 \cdot PI_t$	α_4	0.00916	2.607
$M_5 \cdot PI_t$	α_5	0.00952	2.656
$M_6 \cdot PI_t$	α_6	0.00971	2.659
$M_7 \cdot PI_t$	α_7	0.00163	3.137
$M_8 \cdot PI_t$	α_8	0.01208	3.265
$M_9 \cdot PI_t$	α_9	0.01113	2.986
$M_{10} \cdot PI_t$	α_{10}	0.01179	3.167
$M_{11} \cdot PI_t$	α_{11}	0.01117	3.016
$M_{12} \cdot PI_t$	α_{12}	0.01147	3.086

Source: R. S. Pindyck and D. L. Rubinfeld, *Econometric Models and Economic Forecasts,* 3d ed. (McGraw-Hill, 1991), p. 109.

certificate of deposit becomes more attractive as the difference between long- and short-term rates increases. The seasonal variation is quite important. The peak in the demand for public certificates of deposit occurs in August, falling off through December and beyond, with a low occurring in July.

9.6   Cycles and Leading Indicators

Cycles are associated with upswings and downswings in a series that cannot be explained by trend and seasonal variation. Cycles are far from regular or consistent, but each cycle can be divided into four phases, as shown in Figure 9.7. This series follows a cycle of expansion, reaching a peak and then contracting until a trough is reached. Then the cycle continues through another four phases.

Many business and economic time series are influenced by the cyclical fluctuations in national output and general economic activity. Not all series go up or down at the same time, however; some reach a trough and go up and reach a peak and go down before others. Economists, businesspeople, and government officials are interested in predicting turning points in the economy or in important time series:

> **Turning point:** *A turning point occurs when a time series that has been rising begins to fall, or vice versa.*

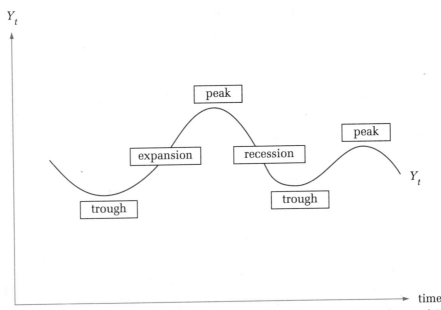

Figure 9.7 **Four phases of a cycle:** A peak in the cycle is followed by a recession, and a trough is followed by expansion. These four phases may be repeated over and over if the period is lengthy and the series is cyclical.

Turning points and cycles can sometimes be predicted by using leading indicators.

Because **leading indicators** begin to move upward or downward before major changes in the level of economic activity, they may be used to predict upturns and downturns in economic activity. **Coincident indicators** tend to move with the general level of activity. **Lagging indicators** measure reactions to change that persist after major swings in economic activity have taken place. Coincident and lagging indicators may be used to confirm changes in the direction of business activity. Indicators were originally proposed as a means for predicting changes in the business cycle, but they can be useful indicators of changes even outside a business cycle.

Several indicators were selected and classified by the National Bureau of Economic Research, starting in 1938. The NBER has since expanded the list, and other organizations have assembled other indexes. In 1977, the NBER listed 62 series as leading indicators of business-cycle peaks and 47 series as leading indicators of business-cycle troughs. Twenty-three were classified as coincident indicators, 18 were listed as lagging indicators of cycle peaks, and 40 were listed as lagging indicators of cycle troughs. All the indicators are classified into seven categories of economic processes: employment and unemployment (18 series); production and income (10 series); consumption (13 series); fixed capital investment (18 series); inventories (9 series); prices, costs, and profits (9 series); and money and credit (26 series). Leading indicators include series on job vacancies, consumption, residential construction, stock prices, money supply, and interest rates. Lagging indicators include series on duration of unemployment, unit labor costs, outstanding debt, unfilled orders, and velocity of money. All the main U.S. indicators and various composite indexes are published monthly.

ECONOMIC SCENE: *The New XLI*

The index of leading indicators is familiar to many business-cycle observers. Developed in 1937 at the National Bureau of Economic Research by Wesley Mitchell and Arthur F. Burns, the index is an average of several economic variables chosen for their ability to anticipate expansions and contractions.

In 1990, a new experimental leading index called the XLI was being applied. The XLI is the result of sophisticated statistical research conducted by James Stock and Mark Watson, econometricians working under the auspices of the NBER. Their index is much like the official index but presumably benefits from the extensive databases and number-crunching capability available today.

The official index of leading indicators includes eleven variables: hours worked in manufacturing, initial claims for unemployment insurance, manufacturers' new orders for consumer goods and materials, vendors' performance, contracts and orders for plant and equipment, building permits, changes in unfilled orders, changes in sensitive-materials prices, the money supply, and an index of consumer expectations. The XLI is a weighted average of only seven variables: building permits, unfilled orders, and index of workers employed part time, a trade-weighted U.S. exchange rate, the yield on ten-year Treasury bonds, the spread between interest rates on six-month commercial paper and six-month Treasury bills, and the spread between interest rates on ten-year and one-year Treasury bonds and bills.

The predictions made from the XLI are not always the same as those indicated by the official index. One reason is the XLI's greater reliance on financial variables. Another is that the XLI is more sensitive to global changes. Which index will prove the better forecasting tool remains to be seen. Stock and Watson may want to go back to their computers to make some alterations in the XLI—that is why "experimental" is the first name of the new index.

As you might expect, indicators are imperfect predictors. A stock-market index might *lead* the business cycle about 60 percent of the time and *lag* the cycle about 40 percent of the time. And the length of the leads and the lags are not regular. This behavior makes interpreting indicators difficult; their irregularity causes forecasters to avoid concentrating on just a few. They usually work with many indicators or a composite index. But experience indicates that even a composite index may generate many false signals. Frequently, by the time leading indicators have been consistently predicting a change in economic activity, that change can be confirmed by coincident and lagging indicators, and might have become obvious without the formal indicators.

Nevertheless, if you want to forecast a series Y_t using a leading indicator from the previous period X_{t-1}, the model to estimate is

$$Y_t = \beta_0 + \beta_1 X_{t-1} + \varepsilon_t$$

The forecasting model becomes

$$Y_{t+1} = \hat{\beta}_0 + \hat{\beta}_1 X_t$$

Given the current value of the indicator, X_t, you can now forecast one period ahead to get Y_{t+1}.

AN APPLICATION: *Eats Like a Hog**

Large corn crops lead to lower corn prices, which in turn make hog production more profitable, leading to increased hog production. Thus it seems reasonable to guess that corn production might be a leading indicator of hog production. The annual production of corn and hogs for the period 1971 to 1985 is reproduced in Table 9.7. Using the lagged value of corn production as a leading indicator, least-squares regression yields:

$$\hat{Y}_t = 57,517.752 + 1.360X_{t-1} \quad R^2 = 0.334$$
$$(6.464) \quad (2.453)$$

where *t*-ratios appear in parentheses. Although the overall goodness of fit is not very good, using corn production as a leading indicator works quite well, as indicated by the *t*-ratio.

When the lagged value of hog production is used alone as a predictor, regression yields:

$$\hat{Y}_t = 34,152.858 + 0.565Y_{t-1} \quad R^2 = 0.341$$
$$(1.893) \quad (2.493)$$

Table 9.7 Annual U.S. Corn and Hog Production

Y_t = hog production (thousands)
X_t = corn production (millions of bushels)

Year	t	Y_t	X_t
1971	1	86,667	5,641.0
1972	2	78,759	5,573.0
1973	3	72,264	5,647.0
1974	4	77,071	4,663.6
1975	5	64,926	5,797.0
1976	6	70,454	6,266.4
1977	7	74,019	6,425.5
1978	8	74,139	7,086.7
1979	9	85,425	7,938.8
1980	10	91,882	6,644.8
1981	11	87,850	8,201.6
1982	12	79,328	8,235.1
1983	13	84,762	4,174.7
1984	14	82,478	7,656.2
1985	15	81,974	8,865.0

Source: Nicholas R. Farnum and LaVerne W. Stanton, *Quantitative Forecasting Methods* (PWS-Kent, 1989), p. 417.

---

*This application was adapted from the *Survey of Current Business*, as seen in N. R. Farnum and L. W. Stanton, *Quantitative Forecasting Methods* (PWS-Kent, 1980), p. 417.

This result suggests that Y_{t-1} can be used to capture a trend and X_{t-1} can be used to capture the cycle. When both lagged variables are used, regression yields:

$$\hat{Y}_t = 25{,}320.968 + 0.495Y_{t-1} + 2.689X_{t-1} \quad R^2 = 0.546$$
$$\phantom{\hat{Y}_t = 25{,}320.968 +} (1.569) \quad (2.267) \qquad (2.228)$$

Again, *t*-ratios are in parentheses. Both lagged variables have estimated coefficients that are fairly precise. This final equation looks like a better forecasting model.

9.7 Econometric Forecasting Models

An econometric forecasting model might consist of one equation or several. This single-equation model has been used to forecast quarterly automobile production:[4]

$$\hat{Y} = -22{,}302 + 12.9X_1 - 97.8X_2 - 19.9X_3 + 230X_4 + 6.0X_5$$

where

$$X_1 = \text{real disposable income}$$
$$X_2 = \text{prime interest rate}$$
$$X_3 = \text{inventory--sales ratio}$$
$$X_4 = \text{index of auto sales}$$
$$X_5 = \text{index of nonauto prices}$$

To forecast the quantity of autos produced in a quarter, you insert values for X_1, X_2, X_3, X_4, and X_5 into the equation. Of course, you will probably have to forecast the values of the explanatory variables to do so.

Multiequation models are used by government and industry to capture the relationships among sectors of the economy. Several very complex multiequation models of the national economy are used to forecast aggregate output and employment, prices, wages, and interest rates. Some of these models are composed of hundreds of equations and hundreds of explanatory variables. Some of the best known of the complex econometric forecasting models are estimated and used by the Bureau of Economic Analysis, Chase Econometrics, Data Resources, Inc., and the Wharton Model.

Consider this example of a simultaneous national-income model:

$$C_t = a_0 + a_1 Y_t + \varepsilon_{1t}$$
$$I_t = b_0 + b_1 P_{t-1} + \varepsilon_{2t}$$
$$T_t = c_0 + c_1 GNP_t + \varepsilon_{3t}$$
$$P_t = d_0 + d_1 Y_t + d_2 I_{t-1} + \varepsilon_{4t}$$
$$GNP_t = C_t + I_t + G_t$$
$$Y_t = GNP_t - I_t$$

---

4. E. Harris, "Forecasting Automobile Output," *Federal Reserve Bank of New York Quarterly Review* (Winter 1985–86).

where C is consumption, I investment, Y disposable income, GNP gross national product, G government expenditures on goods and services, T taxes, and P profits. This example departs from the convention of using Greek letters to denote the parameters to be estimated. The first four equations are *structural* equations and are subject to stochastic error. The last two equations are *identities* that must be satisfied exactly and hence have no error terms. The identity equations link the structural equations logically.

The variables can also be classified. The variables C_t, I_t, T_t, and P_t are *endogenous* because they are determined by the system. The variables P_{t-1} and I_{t-1} are *predetermined* at time t because they have already occurred. The variable G_t is *exogenous* in this model because its value is determined outside the system by government policy.

Once the parameters of this system are estimated, it can be used to predict (forecast) values for the endogenous variables, given values for the exogenous and predetermined variables. And the forecasts will satisfy the logical requirements of the identity equations if the model is estimated simultaneously.

9.8 Forecast Errors

Forecast error arises from several sources. The first is random variation in any dependent variable. The second is random variation in the parameter estimates. Third, some explanatory variables will be subject to random variation if they are also stochastic. Fourth, the model may be misspecified. Thus, whenever you generate a point estimate to be used for your forecast, it is certain to be wrong.

To see how the various sources of forecast error contribute to the total error, suppose that you use an assumed value of X, denoted X_0, to forecast Y from a simple regression equation. A **point** forecast is given by

$$\hat{Y}_0 = \hat{\alpha} + \hat{\beta}X_0$$

A point forecast predicts a single number given an assumed value of X_0 of the explanatory variable. The random error in the stochastic regression model guarantees, however, that point forecasts will deviate from the actual outcome even if the true model is known with certainty. Additional forecast error is introduced because the regression parameters must be estimated, and even unbiased estimates will not be equal to the true parameters. Therefore, **interval forecasts** are used to predict a range of values within which, with some probability, the value of the dependent variable will lie.

To fix ideas, let's look at the simple linear regression model

$$Y_t = \alpha + \beta X_t + \varepsilon_t$$

Coefficient estimates $\hat{\alpha}$ and $\hat{\beta}$ are obtained by least squares. Then, given an assumed value of X_0 for the explanatory variable, the point forecast is $\hat{Y}_0$. The forecast error is $(Y_0 - \hat{Y}_0)$. The variance of the forecast error is composed of two parts. The first is due to the variance of the error term, σ^2, and would occur even if α and β were known. The second part results from the variance of the prediction $\hat{Y}_0$ about its mean $E(\hat{Y}_0)$ and is

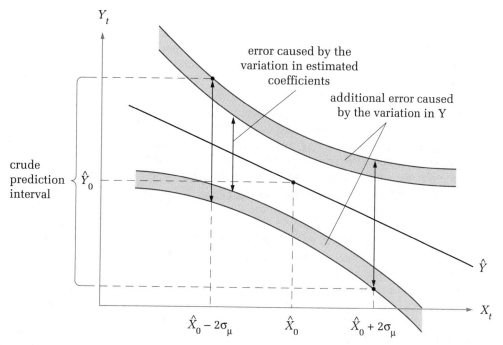

Figure 9.8 **A crude prediction interval when X is stochastic:** The prediction interval caused by the variation in $\hat{\alpha}$ and $\hat{\beta}$ plus the prediction interval caused by the variation in Y are determined for two values of X, $\hat{X}_0 + 2\sigma_\mu$ and $\hat{X}_0 - 2\sigma_\mu$, where σ_μ is the standard deviation of the random error associated with predicting X. The prediction interval for Y_0 around point estimate $\hat{Y}_0$ is estimated as the union of those two intervals.

caused by using $\hat{\alpha}$ and $\hat{\beta}$ in place of their unknown true values.[5] Further error is caused when the explanatory variables are stochastic so that those variables are also guesses or forecasts.

Figure 9.8 illustrates how a prediction *interval* might be obtained. The predicted value for X_0 is chosen as $\hat{X}_0$. Then an interval, say of two standard deviations of X_0, is chosen around $\hat{X}_0$:

$$\hat{X}_0 \pm 2\sigma_\mu$$

At each of these points is a prediction interval caused by the variation in $\hat{\alpha}$ and $\hat{\beta}$ plus the variation in Y. The union of these two intervals gives an estimate of the range of likely outcomes for Y when X is predicted by $X = \hat{X}_0$.

---

5. The variance of the forecast error is

$$\sigma_F^2 = \sigma^2 + \sigma^2 \left[\frac{1}{T} + \frac{(X_0 - \bar{X})^2}{\Sigma(X_i - \bar{X})^2} \right]$$

The variance of the forecast error can be estimated by replacing σ^2 with its estimate S^2. The forecast error is smallest for $X_0 = \bar{X}$ because then $(X_0 - \bar{X})^2 = 0$. Notice also that the larger T is initially and the greater the variance in X, the smaller the forecast error.

ECONOMIC SCENE: *Other Forecasting Methods*

Besides econometric model forecasts and time-series forecasts, other methods of forecasting can reduce uncertainty. These other methods may be useful when we have few historical data to rely upon. **Analogy forecasting** looks for similar situations to predict outcomes. The introduction of a new product may follow a traditional sales life cycle that can be used to predict the future. **Scenario forecasting** is an attempt to identify a logical sequence of events so as to make predictions. A decline in the rate of increase in the supply of money is expected to cause an increase in interest rates and in general inflation. The higher interest rates may attract more foreign investment, the inflation may reduce the demand for domestic goods, and so on. **Barometric forecasting** looks for leading indicators that can be used to predict changes in a dependent variable. A decrease in the prime interest rate may precede a decrease in mortgage interest rates, causing an eventual increase in the demand for housing.

Still other forecasts rely on "expert" opinion. The **single-genius method** of forecasting merely asks the best available expert a question like, "If this, then what?" or "What do you think will happen to that in the next period?" Rather than rely on one person's opinion, **committee forecasting** asks a group of experts to express a collective opinion. But committees are often dominated by one or two strong personalities, and a committee forecast may be little more reliable than that expressed by one expert. To compensate for the dominance tendency of committee forecasts, **mean forecasts** may be used, weighting the opinion of everyone on a panel equally. Similarly, **median forecasts** may be developed by placing more weight on the opinions expressed most convincingly or most often.

A more complex panel method eliminates the problem of dominance but allows the stronger arguments to influence the panelists. When using this forecasting technique, the **Delphi method,*** experts are polled, then their opinions are shared with the other panelists. A revised poll is taken and revised opinions are shared. The procedure is repeated until little change appears in any of the opinions. Then a mean or median forecast is constructed. Experiments with the Delphi method indicate several tendencies. First, opinions are likely to converge. Second, extreme views are most likely to change. Third is a tendency toward the median rather than the true outcome. Fourth, expert panels perform no better than generalist panels. Fifth, a Delphi panel is more likely to converge toward the truth than a panel involved in face-to-face discussion. The Delphi method can be quite costly to conduct, but survey methods can be quite costly also. Moreover, the Delphi method may be the only way of arriving at remotely reliable forecasts about events that depend on technological or political change.

Experience with widely varied techniques have led forecasters to the conclusion that no one method is best. And composite forecasts usually perform better than those derived from any one method. Thus, quantitative analysis and forecasts built from econometric models should always be tempered by logic, expert opinion, and sound judgment.

---

*The Oracle at Delphi is famed for its ambiguous predictions.

Even more forecast error is introduced whenever the model used is improperly specified so that it does not accurately represent the true model. It is usually difficult to measure the forecast error when using a misspecified model. Nevertheless we must keep this source of error always in mind, especially when specifying the model to be estimated. But even if you are sure that the original model was properly specified, other things do not remain constant, and the original model may no longer be appropriate for the present or the future. Structural changes do take place in any economic system.

These basic concepts apply to the multivariate regression model as well. Forecast error is caused by four things: (1) variation in Y; (2) variation in coefficient estimates; (3) variation in actual values of explanatory variables from their predicted values; and (4) model misspecification. The forecast error is smallest at the point of the means; it becomes larger and larger for values of the explanatory variables further from their means.

9.9 Distributed-Lag Models*

Some time may elapse before people react to change. Delays between a change in a stimulus and the response may be captured by using lagged explanatory variables, which are particularly useful in forecasting because they are predetermined. Lagged variables are not subject to random variation.

A simple example of a model using a lagged explanatory variable is demand as a function of advertising in this period and last period:

$$Y_t = \alpha + \beta_0 X_t + \beta_1 X_{t-1} + \varepsilon_t$$

where Y_t measures demand, and X_t and X_{t-1} measure advertising expenditures in period t and period $t - 1$. It is also possible to include other explanatory variables, which may or may not be lagged.

More generally, suppose we allow the effect of the explanatory variable to be distributed over several periods. The **distributed-lag model** is

$$Y_t = \alpha + \beta_0 X_t + \beta_1 X_{t-1} + \cdots + \beta_k X_{t-k} + \varepsilon_t$$

where the subscripts indicate the length of the lag. This distributed-lag model explains the current value of Y as a function of the current and past values of X. In most economic applications we expect the influence of X to diminish with time, making the magnitude of the betas smaller as the length of the lag increases. If the adjustment occurs quickly, one or two lags may be enough. If the adjustment is instantaneous, no lags are required and we can use the simple regression model.

The distributed-lag model has a number of problems. First, multicollinearity is likely to appear between the lagged variables. Second, we have no guarantee that the estimated

---

*This section is more advanced than others in the book and may be skipped without loss of continuity.

GLOBAL PERSPECTIVE: *World Copper Supply*

Supply equations for primary copper were estimated for the four principal producing countries and the rest of the world.* In this study the empirical model is based on an assumption of price-taking behavior. Producers in the United States estimate a long-run price they believe to be sustainable. They then decide on the amount of copper to produce at the long-run price. The rest of the world operates similarly, except that price is a free market price determined at the London Metal Exchange.

The U.S. producer price has often been well below the world price. A large difference between the two prices indicates that the U.S. market is out of long-run equilibrium and that the U.S. price will adjust. Adjustment is slow because it takes a long time to develop new copper mines, and sometimes even closing old mines takes time. Supply thus changes slowly and price differences persist over fairly long periods.

The long-run supply curve in each country was specified as

$$S_t^* = \alpha + \beta p_t$$

where S_t^* is desired supply that depends on price p_t at time t. Because it takes time to adjust the short-run supply, we can assume that the change in supply between two periods is a fraction λ of the desired change in supply,[†]

$$S_t - S_{t-1} = \lambda(S_t^* - S_{t-1})$$

Substitution for S_t^* yields

$$S_t = \lambda\alpha + \lambda\beta p_t + (1 - \lambda)S_{t-1}$$

This is the equation to be estimated. The short-run effect of a price change on actual supply is given by $\Delta S_t/\Delta p_t = \lambda\beta$. The long-run effect is given by $\Delta S_t^*/\Delta p_t = \beta$. If adjustments take place slowly so that λ is small, the long-run effect can be much larger than the short-run effect, and short-run supply is less elastic than long-run supply.

This empirical model was estimated using twenty annual observations. The estimated supply curves for the United States, Chile, Canada, Zambia, and the rest of the world (ROW) are summarized in Table 9.8. United States supply adjusts slowly, as indicated by the

Table 9.8 Equations for Estimated Copper Supply

Variable	Coefficient	U.S.	Chile	Canada	Zambia	ROW
Constant	$\lambda\alpha$	−160.04	−54.43	−43.73	−69.19	−28.44
Price	$\lambda\beta$	14.27	2.74	3.13	0.13[a]	0.22
Past supply	$(1-\lambda)$	0.73	0.95	0.99	1.10[b]	0.88

[a]Not significantly different from zero.   [b]Not significantly different from unity.

Source: F. M. Fisher, P. H. Cootner, and M. N. Baily, "An Econometric Model of the World Copper Industry," *Bell Journal of Economics and Management Science* (Autumn 1972).

*F. M. Fisher, P. H. Cootner, and M. N. Baily, "An Econometric Model of the World Copper Industry," *Bell Journal of Economics and Management Science* (Autumn 1972). Copyright 1972. Reprinted by permission of RAND.

†The Greek letter lambda (λ) is pronounced "lamb-duh."

coefficient on lagged supply, $(1 - \lambda) = 0.73$, and about 27 percent of the gap between desired production and actual production is closed each year. At the point where the sample means meet, the price-elasticity estimates were 0.45 for the short run and 1.67 for the long run.

For the other countries the speed of adjustment is even lower. The estimated elasticities for Chile were 0.11 for the short run and 0.40 for the long run, considerably less than the U.S. elasticities. For Canada, the estimated elasticities were 0.19 for the short run and 14.84 for the long run. For Zambia, the estimated short-run elasticity was 0.07, and the estimated long-run elasticity was huge. These elasticities indicate that the long-run supply curves for Canada and Zambia are nearly flat, evidence of a constant-cost industry in those countries. In contrast, the U.S. estimates indicate an increasing long-run industry supply curve, which we can interpret as evidence of an increasing-cost copper industry in the United States. The estimates for the rest of the world indicate a speed of adjustment of about 12 percent. The elasticities for the rest of the world were estimated as 0.20 for the short run and 1.68 for the long run.

coefficients will decrease as the length of the lag increases. Third, a severe loss of degrees of freedom may occur when many lagged variables are present. These problems motivate the following geometric-lag structure.

The **Koyck distributed-lag model** assumes that the coefficients decline geometrically so that

$$\beta_j = w^j \beta_0$$

where j is the length of the lag, $j = 0, 1, \ldots, \infty$. A weight w^j is attached to each explanatory variable. The Koyck lag model can be written as

$$Y_t = \alpha + \beta_0(X_t + wX_{t-1} + w^2X_{t-2} + w^3X_{t-3} + \cdots) + \varepsilon_t$$

where $0 < w < 1$, so that the weights of the lagged explanatory variables decline with time: $1 > w > w^2 > w^3$, and so on. The model is difficult to estimate in this form, but a simple transformation will convert the model into one that is linear in the coefficients. First, notice that

$$Y_{t-1} = \alpha + \beta_0(X_{t-1} + wX_{t-2} + w^2X_{t-3} + w^3X_{t-4} + \cdots) + \varepsilon_{t-1}$$

When this expression is multiplied by w and then subtracted from Y_t, the **Koyck model** becomes

$$Y_t - wY_{t-1} = \alpha(1 - w) + \beta_0X_t + v_t$$

where $v_t = \varepsilon_t - w\varepsilon_{t-1}$. By rearranging the terms, we find that

$$Y_t = \alpha(1 - w) + wY_{t-1} + \beta_0X_t + v_t$$

In this form the model is linear in the coefficients and can be estimated by least squares. Least-squares estimation applied directly to the Koyck model, however, results in biased and inconsistent estimates because Y_{t-1} is correlated with v_t.[6]

---

6. The implied autocorrelation is difficult to detect because the Durbin-Watson d-statistic will *always* be close to 2 whenever a lagged value of the dependent variable is used as a regressor. Therefore, the use of the Durbin-Watson test for autocorrelation is *not* valid when Y_{t-1} is used as an explanatory variable.

Consistent estimates can be generated if an instrumental variable is used in place of Y_{t-1}. One good instrument is X_{t-1} because it is predetermined but is correlated with Y_{t-1}. When X_{t-1} is used as an instrument, the Koyck model becomes

$$Y_t = \alpha(1 - w) + wX_{t-1} + \beta_0 X_t + v_t$$

This last version is quite easy to estimate.

9.10 $MA(q)$, $ARMA(p, q)$, and $ARIMA(p, d, q)$ Models*

The autoregressive model of order p, the $AR(p)$ model, specified the current value of a series, Y_t, as a function of p-lagged values of the series plus an error,

$$Y_t = \beta_0 + \beta_1 Y_{t-1} + \beta_2 Y_{t-2} + \cdots + \beta_p Y_{t-p} + \varepsilon_t$$

This is called a *purely* autoregressive model.

Instead of depending on past values of the series, Y_t may be most influenced by recent "shocks" to the series, which are captured by the random error. Then it would be reasonable to express the series as a weighted average of the errors from period to period. Because the series is moving, this model is called a **moving-average model:**[7]

> ***Moving-average model MA(q):***
>
> $$Y_t = \theta_0 + \varepsilon_t - \theta_1 \varepsilon_{t-1} - \theta_2 \varepsilon_{t-2} - \cdots - \theta_q \varepsilon_{t-q}$$
>
> *where ε_{t-q} is the lagged value of the shock (random error) at time $(t - q)$.*

The parameters of the model that need to be estimated are denoted by the Greek letter theta (θ). The mean of the $MA(q)$ series is equal to the constant term θ_0, and the signs attached to the other parameters are taken, by convention, to be negative. The order of this moving-average model is q, and the model is denoted by $MA(q)$. The $MA(1)$ model is

$$Y_t = \theta_0 + \varepsilon_t - \theta_1 \varepsilon_{t-1}$$

Similarly, the $MA(2)$ model is

$$Y_t = \theta_0 + \varepsilon_t - \theta_1 \varepsilon_{t-1} - \theta_2 \varepsilon_{t-2}$$

Any $MA(q)$ model must be subjected to a constraint that

$$\theta_1 + \theta_2 + \cdots + \theta_q < 1.$$

When this constraint is satisfied, along with some other conditions, the $MA(q)$ model can be inverted and written as an $AR(\infty)$ model.[8] A natural question to ask is: If MA models

---

* This section is advanced and may be skipped without loss of continuity.

7. Don't confuse this model with using moving averages of the series itself. Moving averages can also be constructed as an average of recent *values* of a series, but here we are using a weighted average of recent *shocks* to the series.

are just AR models in disguise, why not just use an AR model? The answer is parsimony, meaning that fewer parameters need to be estimated. It is more efficient to estimate a small MA model than an AR model with many parameters.

A *mixed AR* and *MA* model is also possible. The reason for adopting this model is again parsimony, this time in the number of parameters to be estimated. When autoregression and moving-average terms are mixed in the model, it is called an **ARMA** **model**:

ARMA(p, q) model:

$$Y_t = \beta_1 Y_{t-1} + \beta_2 Y_{t-2} + \cdots + \beta_p Y_{t-p}$$
$$+ \theta_0 + \varepsilon_t - \theta_1 \varepsilon_{t-1} - \theta_2 \varepsilon_{t-2} - \cdots - \theta_q \varepsilon_{t-q}$$

where we find p lagged terms from Y_t and q lagged terms from ε_t plus a constant.

By convention, the constant term is denoted θ_0 rather than β_0. The $ARMA$ models are required to be both stationary and invertible. Because of these restrictions, the $ARMA$ model is usually estimated by maximum likelihood, but that is no problem because computer routines are available.[9] The principal drawback of such estimating is that large sample sizes, say fifty or more, must be used.

Because of the stationarity requirement, and when differencing is used to detrend a series, the **autoregressive-integrated–moving-average model** has been developed:

ARIMA(p, d, q) model:

$$y_t = \beta_1 y_{t-1} + \beta_2 y_{t-2} + \cdots + \beta_p y_{t-p}$$
$$+ \theta_0 + \varepsilon_t - \theta_1 \varepsilon_{t-1} - \theta_2 \varepsilon_{t-2} - \cdots - \theta_q \varepsilon_{t-q}$$

where $y_t = \Delta^d Y_t$ is the differenced series from the original series that has been differenced d times to make it stationary.

Estimating is easy because computer routines require only that you specify the number of lags p in y_t, the number of times d the original series has been differenced, and the number of lags q in the error term ε_t.

The choice of (p, d, q) should be parsimonious—they should kept as small as possible and still generate a good fit. The fit is better for big values for p and q than for small values, however, and so a trade-off between fit and parsimony is always necessary.

---

8. When the AR model is stationary, then the MA model is "invertible"—it can be inverted to obtain its corresponding AR model. A proof of this assertion is beyond our scope here, but you might want to consult the citations at the end of this chapter.

9. Maximum-likelihood estimating works with a specific error distribution chosen by the analyst. A normal distribution is the one most often used, and then we compute the parameter values that are most likely to have generated the sample. That is, the estimated parameters are the ones most likely to have generated the observed sample, given the assumed error distribution of the specified equation to be estimated. For further details you might wish to consult one of the more advanced econometrics texts cited in Chapter 8.

How are the values for p, d, and q to be chosen? First, you choose d by evaluating the original series Y_t and look for a trend. If there is a trend, then evaluate the first differences for a trend. If you find a trend in the first differences, then evaluate the second differences for a trend. Continue until no trend is evident and d is fixed as the number of differences required to detrend the original series. Frequently it is sufficient just to plot Y_t, ΔY_t, $\Delta^2 Y_t$, and so on until no further trend is evident. Usually a value of d not greater than $d = 2$ will suffice. Be careful to avoid "overdifferencing" a series, because that inflates the variance of the differenced series and creates unstable models.

If you have chosen the correct d, the sample correlation coefficient between the dependent variable and the lagged values of the dependent variable should approach zero as the number of lags increases. The *sample* autocorrelation coefficient of lag 1 is

$$r_1 = \frac{\Sigma(Y_{t-1} - \bar{Y})(Y_t - \bar{Y})}{\Sigma(Y_t - \bar{Y})^2}$$

where $\bar{Y} = \Sigma Y_t/T$ and T is the sample size. The *sample* autocorrelation coefficient of lag 2 is

$$r_2 = \frac{\Sigma(Y_{t-2} - \bar{Y})(Y_t - \bar{Y})}{\Sigma(Y_t - \bar{Y})^2}$$

Similarly, the **sample autocorrelation coefficient of lag k** is

$$r_k = \frac{\Sigma(Y_{t-k} - \bar{Y})(Y_t - \bar{Y})}{\Sigma(Y_t - \bar{Y})^2}$$

These sample autocorrelation coefficients are fairly good estimators of their theoretical values as long as T is large and much bigger than lag-length k. The graph of the autocorrelation coefficients is called the sample **autocorrelation function (ACF).**

If a series is devoid of trend and has random errors, its sample autocorrelation coefficients should all be close to zero. When a series has trend, the sample auto-correlation coefficients are likely to be large and positive for short lags, decreasing slowly as the lag increases. When a series has seasonal movement, the sample auto-correlation coefficients are likely to be large at the lag length that corresponds to the length of the cycle. When a series is stationary but has positively correlated errors, low-order autocorrelation coefficients are likely to be large, but the sample autocorrelation coefficients are likely to damp out rapidly as lag length increases. If the original series is not stationary, usually choosing $d \leq 2$ is sufficient to obtain a stationary series by differ-encing. Thus a practical way of choosing d is to keep differencing the series until the *ACF* appears either to *decay* slowly or to *cut off*. By "decay" we mean that the r_j coefficients get smaller quickly—the *ACF* appears to "die off." By "cut off" we mean that the r_j coefficients drop close to zero in a steplike way.

Next, you have to choose p and q. Estimate an $ARIMA(0, d, 0)$ model and evaluate the results. Once again you will look at the sample autocorrelation coefficients, but now you will be using the series $y_t = \Delta^d Y_t$. The computer program will calculate these for you.

You will also have to look at the **partial autocorrelation coefficients:**[10]

> **Partial autocorrelation coefficients:** *Partial autocorrelation coefficients are the sample correlation coefficients between ε_t and ε_{t-k} when the other residuals have been held constant.*

Computer programs that estimate *ARIMA* models routinely generate a table or a graph of the partial autocorrelation coefficients along with the autocorrelation coefficients. The graph of the partial autocorrelation coefficients is called the sample **partial autocorrelation function (*PACF*).**

After you estimate the *ARIMA*(0, *d*, 0) model, look at the *ACF* and *PACF* generated by the computer program. The last lag before the *PACF* tends to zero is typically a good value for *p*, and the last lag before the *ACF* tends to zero is a good value for *q*.

Next you should see if you can get by with a pure *AR*(*p*) or pure *MA*(*q*) procedure. A stationary *AR*(*p*) procedure gives rise to an *ACF* that *decays* slowly while its *PACF cuts off* sharply after lag *p*. A stationary *MA*(*q*) procedure usually has an *ACF* that *cuts off* sharply after lag *q* while its *PACF decays*. If neither of these patterns appears, then a *mixed ARMA*(*p*, *q*) model is indicated. When estimating a mixed model, two more rules are helpful:

- The *ACF* should decay after lag $q - p$ if $q \geq p$, but the *ACF* should drop off at the beginning if $q < p$.
- The *PACF* should decay after lag $p - q$ if $p \geq q$, but it should decay from the beginning if $p < q$.

These rules have been written from statisticians' experience with theoretical simulations and practice in estimating mixed models. After determining (*p*, *d*, *q*) and estimating the *ARIMA* model, it can be used for forecasting.

The details needed for an *ARIMA* forecast can be illustrated with an *ARIMA*(1, 1, 1) model. The *ARIMA*(1, 1, 1) model, which uses first differences, is

$$y_t = \beta_1 y_{t-1} + \theta_0 + \varepsilon_t - \theta_1 \varepsilon_{t-1}$$

where $y_t = Y_t - Y_{t-1}$. Thus the original series is

$$Y_t - Y_{t-1} = \beta_1 (Y_{t-1} - Y_{t-2}) + \theta_0 + \varepsilon_t - \theta_1 \varepsilon_{t-1}$$

When solved for Y_t the model is

$$Y_t = \theta_0 + (1 + \beta_1) Y_{t-1} + \beta_1 Y_{t-2} + \varepsilon_t - \theta_1 \varepsilon_{t-1}$$

Once the parameter estimates $\hat{\theta}_0$, $\hat{\beta}_1$, and $\hat{\theta}_1$ have been obtained, a one-period-ahead forecast (time $t + 1$) is

$$\hat{Y}_{t+1} = \hat{\theta}_0 + (1 + \hat{\beta}_1) Y_t + \hat{\beta}_1 Y_{t-1} - \hat{\theta}_1 \hat{\varepsilon}_t$$

---

10. These are the same partial autocorrelation coefficients discussed previously in the section on autoregressive models.

AN APPLICATION: *An ARIMA Forecasting Model**

Suppose a manufacturer of computer printers collected weekly data on shipments of its product over a 78-week period, as reported in Table 9.9. To identify a suitable *ARIMA* model, you must first determine d, the required number of differences, in order to make the series stationary. Table 9.10 reports the sample autocorrelation and partial autocorrelation coefficients for this series. No trend is evident because r_1 is close to zero, and so no differencing is necessary and $d = 0$ can be chosen.

To see if a pure $AR(p)$ or a pure $MA(q)$ model is sufficient, we look at the *ACF* and *PACF* for patterns of decay and cutoffs. From Table 9.10 you can see that the *ACF* does

Table 9.9   Printers Shipped per Week, January 1987 to June 1988

Week t	Y_t	Week t	Y_t	Week t	Y_t
1	105	27	99	53	99
2	85	28	86	54	100
3	106	29	84	55	116
4	88	30	90	56	93
5	96	31	92	57	107
6	97	32	94	58	100
7	99	33	90	59	96
8	93	34	98	60	114
9	86	35	100	61	92
10	107	36	91	62	119
11	92	37	99	63	94
12	92	38	91	64	113
13	93	39	102	65	112
14	87	40	91	66	105
15	90	41	101	67	113
16	92	42	92	68	114
17	92	43	107	69	95
18	90	44	92	70	108
19	93	45	107	71	104
20	93	46	103	72	96
21	93	47	114	73	97
22	92	48	97	74	96
23	90	49	112	75	98
24	99	50	112	76	98
25	84	51	96	77	98
26	80	52	117	78	99

Source: Nicholas R. Farnum and LaVerne W. Stanton, *Quantitative Fore-casting Methods* (PWS-Kent, 1989), p. 473.

*This application was drawn from N. R. Farnum and L. W. Stanton, *Quantitative Forecasting Methods* (PWS-Kent, 1989), p. 473.

Table 9.10 ACF and PACF for Printers-Shipped Series

Lag k	Autocorrelation Coefficient	Partial Autocorrelation Coefficient
1	0.139	0.139
2	0.553	0.544
3	0.480	0.535
4	0.320	0.148
5	0.431	-0.030
6	0.263	-0.213
7	0.324	-0.128
8	0.306	0.096
9	0.163	-0.008
10	0.356	0.160
11	0.185	0.145
12	0.253	0.072
13	0.261	-0.002
14	0.131	-0.229
15	0.256	-0.199

Source: Nicholas R. Farnum and LaVerne W. Stanton, *Quantitative Forecasting Methods* (PWS-Kent, 1989), p. 474.

not die out or decay, and so a mixed-model ARIMA(p, 0, q) is indicated. Because the ACF drops off at its beginning (r_1 is close to zero), p should be less than q. Because the PACF cuts off after lag $k = 3$, the value of q should be $k = 3$ or less. A good start, therefore, is an ARIMA(1, 0, 2) model. If that doesn't work well, the next choices would be an ARIMA(1, 0, 3) model and then an ARIMA(2, 0, 3) model.

When estimated using *Minitab,* a computer program available on most mainframes and personal computers, the ARIMA(1, 0, 2) estimate is

$$\hat{Y}_t = 0.9011Y_{t-1} + 9.7277 + \varepsilon_t - 1.3995\varepsilon_{t-1} + 0.9645\varepsilon_{t-2}$$
$$(0.0524) \quad (0.3613) \quad (0.0409) \quad (0.0428)$$

where the standard errors are in parentheses. When the ACF and PACF of this model were examined, none of the sample autocorrelation coefficients were statistically different from zero, and so no further model estimation seemed to be necessary.

A forecast for period $t = 79$ becomes

$$\hat{Y}_{79} = 0.9011Y_{78} + 9.7277 + \hat{\varepsilon}_{79} - 1.3995\hat{\varepsilon}_{78} + 0.9645\hat{\varepsilon}_{77}$$

Using $E(\varepsilon_t) = 0$ for $\hat{\varepsilon}_{79} = 0$, and substituting Y_{78} from Table 9.8, along with the estimates $\hat{\varepsilon}_{78} = 1.3898$ and $\hat{\varepsilon}_{77} = 3.0977$ from the computer program, the forecast for Y_t for the period $t = 79$ is:

$$\hat{Y}_{79} = 0.9011(99) + 9.7277 + 0 - 1.3995(1.3898) + 0.9645(3.0997) = 99.98$$

For the period $t = 80$, the forecast is

$$\hat{Y}_{80} = 0.9011\hat{Y}_{79} + 9.7277 + \hat{\varepsilon}_{80} - 1.3995\hat{\varepsilon}_{79} + 0.9645\hat{\varepsilon}_{78}$$

After substitution we have

$$\hat{Y}_{80} = 0.9011(99.98) + 9.7277 + 0 - 0 + 0.9645(1.3898) = 101.16$$

The forecast for period $t = 81$ is

$$\hat{Y}_{81} = 0.9011\hat{Y}_{80} + 9.7277 + \hat{\varepsilon}_{81} - 1.3995\hat{\varepsilon}_{80} + 0.9645\hat{\varepsilon}_{79}$$

After substitution we have

$$\hat{Y}_{81} = 0.9011(101.16) + 9.7277 + 0 - 0 + 0 = 100.88$$

Subsequent forecasts will depend on only their immediately preceding forecast.

where $\hat{\varepsilon}_t$ is the computer's estimate of ε_t. A two-period-ahead forecast (time $t + 2$) is

$$\hat{Y}_{t+2} = \hat{\theta}_0 + (1 + \hat{\beta}_1)\hat{Y}_{t+1} + \hat{\beta}_1 Y_t$$

where the error term is replaced by its expected value of zero and Y_{t+1} is replaced by its forecast $\hat{Y}_{t+1}$. The three-period-ahead forecast (time $t + 3$) is

$$\hat{Y}_{t+3} = \hat{\theta}_0 + (1 + \hat{\beta}_1)\hat{Y}_{t+2} + \hat{\beta}_1\hat{Y}_{t+1}$$

This and all subsequent forecasts depend on only two immediately preceding forecasts.

Summary

Forecasters separate the sources of variation in a time series into a trend, seasonal, cyclical, and random components. Additive models express the series as the sum of the four components. Multiplicative models express the series as a product of the four components.

The trend in a series can be linear or nonlinear. A linear-trend model is the easiest to estimate, but it can be dangerous to forecast from a linear model if the trend is nonlinear. Therefore, the polynomial, exponential, and logistic trend models are used to capture nonlinear trends, but nonlinear models too can generate bad forecasts if they are the wrong specification.

A series can be detrended by subtracting the trend component in each period from the actual value of the series in each period. Another way to obtain a detrended series is to use differencing. Usually, first differencing or second differencing is sufficient to detrend a series.

The autoregressive model of order p, the $AR(p)$ model, specifies the value of the series to be a linear function of p-lagged values of the series. The $AR(p)$ model can be estimated by least-squares regression, and it is a useful but somewhat mechanical forecasting technique.

Seasonal variation in a series can be captured by using dummy variables for each season. Either the constant term or one of the seasonal-dummy variables must be excluded as an independent variable to avoid perfect multicollinearity.

Cyclical variation in a series can be captured by using leading indicators. A leading indicator precedes the cycle, and so leading indicators can be excellent forecasting variables and sometimes can be used to forecast turning points. The lag length between a leading indicator and a dependent variable is not always constant, though, and that is a source of forecasting error.

Econometric forecasting models may be made up of one equation or several. In a simultaneous system of equations, one or more dependent variables are functions of other variables that are endogenous to the system. Other explanatory variables include pre-determined or exogenous variables. The system may also include identity equations that define relationships between variables in a logical way. Multiequation models are used to capture the relationships among sectors of the economy in order to enhance the models' forecasting ability.

Point forecasts invariably being wrong, interval forecasting is a better way. A point forecast predicts one value for a dependent variable from values of the explanatory variables. An interval forecast uses estimates of forecast error to generate an interval within which the actual future value of the dependent variable is likely to fall. The precision of the interval forecast is influenced by random variation in the dependent variable, any random variation in independent variables, random variation in parameter estimates, and improper specification of the model. Forecast errors can be substantial, particularly when you are forecasting beyond the range of the original data, and so forecasts should always be tempered by good judgment.

A distributed-lag model uses an explanatory variable along with lagged values of the explanatory variable as independent variables. Because of the potential for multicol-linearity and the loss of degrees of freedom when many lags of the same variable are present, the Koyck distributed-lag model assumes that the coefficients decline geometrically. The dependent variable in the Koyck model becomes a linear function of its lagged value and the independent variable. To estimate the Koyck model, use an instrumental variable in place of the lagged value of the dependent variable.

When a series is expressed as a weighted average of q past shocks to the series, it is called a moving-average model of order q and is denoted by $MA(q)$. When the moving average is mixed with an $AR(p)$ procedure, the model is denoted $ARMA(p, q)$. When a series has been detrended by differencing, it is called an $ARIMA(p, d, q)$ model, where d is the number of times the original series was differenced. The objective in estimating such mixed models is to estimate as few parameters as possible while obtaining a good fit, and so the order of such models should be kept as small as possible.

Further Readings

Three excellent texts are

- Nicholas R. Farnum and LaVerne W. Stanton, *Quantitative Forecasting Methods* (PWS-Kent, 1989).
- C. W. J. Granger, *Forecasting in Business and Economics,* 2d ed. (Academic Press, 1989).

- R. S. Pindyck and D. L. Rubinfeld, *Economic Models and Economic Forecasts,* 3d ed. (McGraw-Hill, 1991).

For the original work on the *ARMA* and *ARIMA* models, see

- G. E. P. Box and G. M. Jenkins, *Time Series Analysis, Forecasting and Control* (Holden-Day, 1970).

This author provides a very readable and complete *ARIMA* presentation:

- A. Pankratz, *Forecasting with Univariate Box-Jenkins Methods* (Wiley, 1983).

Practice Problems

1. What are the four major components in a time series?
2. Graph the four components in the additive time-series decomposition of Table 9.1.
3. From this information on net earnings over $T = 16$ time periods:

Time (t)	Net Earnings (Y_t), in Millions
1	182
2	187
3	211
4	237
5	276
6	301
7	316
8	332
9	400
10	460
11	510
12	575
13	640
14	668
15	777
16	866

(a) Graph this series over time.
(b) Estimate a linear time-trend model.
(c) Estimate a quadratic time-trend model, using a computer program.
(d) Estimate an exponential time-trend model.
(e) Which model do you prefer, and why?

4. For the time series on net earnings of the preceding problem:
   (a) Calculate and plot the series ΔY_t, then judge whether or not this series has trend.
   (b) Calculate and plot the series $\Delta^2 Y_t$. What can you say about this series?
5. When an autoregressive model $AR(2)$ is estimated from the time series of problem 3, the results are (t-ratios are in parentheses):

$$\hat{Y}_t = 0.845 + 0.888Y_{t-1} + 2.454Y_{t-2} \quad R^2 = 0.991$$
$$\phantom{\hat{Y}_t = 0.845 + } (3.098) \qquad\ (0.776)$$

   (a) What do the estimated coefficients indicate about the trend in the original series?
   (b) Is it really legitimate to estimate an AR model using this original series? Why or why not?
   (c) You have at least two ways of detrending the original series. Differencing is one way. What is an alternative?
   (d) After taking first differences, $y_t = \Delta Y_t$, specify a new $AR(1)$ model, using first differences.
   (e) If you have a regression program, estimate the new model.
6. What are the four major sources of forecasting error?
7. If an $MA(q)$ model can be expressed equivalently as an $AR(\infty)$ model, what is the reason for estimating the $MA(q)$ model?
8. Given data on new-car sales (Y) by a dealer and the number of full-page ads (X) for a six-month period:

t	Y	X
1	10	0
2	10	1
3	15	2
4	20	2
5	30	3
6	40	4

   (a) Graph the scatterplot of Y as a function of X.
   (b) Fit the model $Y = \alpha + \beta X + \varepsilon$ by least squares and graph the resulting equation on the scatterplot.
   (c) Using a computer program, fit the model $Y = \alpha + \beta_1 X_1 + \beta_2 X_2 + \varepsilon$, where $X_1 = X$ and $X_2 = X^2$, then graph the resulting equation on the same scatterplot.
   (d) Fit the model $\ln Y = \alpha - (\beta/X) + \varepsilon$, where $\ln$ denotes a natural logarithm. Notice that $Y = \exp[\alpha - (\beta/X) + \varepsilon]$ and graph your estimated equation on the scatterplot.
   (e) State the summary statistics for all three equations.
   (f) Which model do you prefer, and why?

9. Suppose you had a time series on the number of skis sold per month over a sixteen-year period. Economic theory tells us that the demand for skis is a function of ski price, the price of complements like lift tickets, and consumers' income. The demand for skis also increases in winter. Specify a regression equation that could be used for forecasting—an equation that controls for seasonal demand.

10. Suppose you have estimated an $ARIMA(1, 0, 1)$ model from $T = 99$ observations. The estimated model is:

$$\hat{Y}_t = Y_{t-1} + \varepsilon_t + 0.5\varepsilon_{t-1}$$

Given that $Y_{99} = 27$, $\hat{Y}_{99} = 27.5$, $\varepsilon_{99} = 0.5$:
(a) Calculate a forecast for Y_{100}.
(b) Calculate a forecast for Y_{101}.

Technology, Production, and Cost

I n a private-ownership economy, decisions arrived at by firms can be examined by extending the theory of choice. The theory of the firm deals with output supply and input demand decisions and the influence those decisions have on markets and social welfare. Before we look at various market structures to see how they work, however, we need to understand how the costs of production can be measured.

This section is divided into two chapters. In Chapter 10, we look at how technology constrains firms in their ways of transforming inputs into outputs. The production function is applied to see how inputs can be used in the most technologically efficient way and to see how technical progress influences production. In Chapter 11, we transform the production function into cost functions. We study the behavior of cost in both the short and long runs. How can a firm identify the cost-minimizing input mix? How can it identify the optimal scale of operation and the best number of plants to operate? How should the firm measure costs, and how can it estimate its cost function? The answers to these and other questions are crucial if a firm is to maximize profit and if the economy is to operate efficiently.

Chapter

10

Technology and Production

S tudying production is the first step in forming a theory of the firm. Decisions on output supply and input demand made by firms depend crucially on technology, which dictates how inputs can be combined and what the resulting level of output will be if inputs are used efficiently. We must know how inputs are transformed into output—the production transformation—if we would understand how the costs of production and revenue vary with changes in outputs and variable inputs. To maximize profit, a firm needs to know how costs and revenues vary with inputs and outputs.

387 ▶

Our approach to the theory of the firm roughly parallels that taken in developing a theory of consumer choice. Technology's role is like that of consumer preference. Firms combine inputs to produce output, and consumers combine goods to produce utility. Firms attempt to minimize expenditure on inputs for any level of output, and consumers attempt to maximize utility for any level of expenditure on goods. We applied the theory of consumer choice in studying the demand for goods and the supply of inputs. And we use the theory of the firm to study the supply of goods and the demand for inputs.

Production decisions are meant to make the most efficient use of inputs: land, labor of all types, physical capital, raw materials, and entrepreneurial ability. Current technology constrains input combinations to those which are consistent with that technology. Not all input combinations are efficient, because technology always permits production of some good using more inputs than necessary. Once an input bundle is being used efficiently, though, output may increase only if technology changes or if more inputs are available.

At the Graduate School of Business

10.1 Technology as a Constraint

The current state of knowledge imposes a technological constraint on the production of any good. Applying known technology, the firm may combine inputs to transform them into a good. If the inputs are not used efficiently, the firm will not be producing as much as it could.

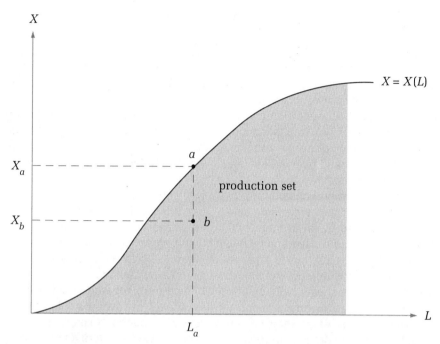

Figure 10.1 **Production with a single input:** Technology dictates the maximum level of output of X that can be produced with any quantity of input L. If the input is not used optimally given current technology, output will be lower than that which is technologically optimal.

To fix this idea, let's assume a simple form of production in which one good is being produced by one variable input. For the moment we ignore effects of any fixed inputs. A person might be gathering mushrooms in a forest or digging for clams on a beach. The quantity of the good produced is denoted by X, and the variable input is labor time, denoted L. One possible set of input and output combinations is illustrated by Figure 10.1. The available technology, which here includes the physiology of the human body, is constant. The technologically *feasible* set of all input and output combinations is called a **production set.**[1] As long as technology remains constant, any specified level of the input can be used in only one technologically efficient way. At any level of input use, the technologically *efficient* use of that input results in maximum output. The maximum level of output for a given level of the input falls on the *boundary* of the production set. In Figure 10.1, when L_a unit of labor is used efficiently the resulting level of output is X_a. A smaller level of output such as X_b is feasible but not efficient.

The boundary of the production set, denoted $X = X(L)$, is called a **production function.** This production function must pass through the origin because something

---

1. See Ronald W. Shephard, *Theory of Cost and Production Functions* (Princeton University Press, 1970) for a more formal and general definition of the production function.

ECONOMIC SCENE: *Productivity in Waste Processing**

The scrap and waste materials industry processes materials from scrap copper and gold to rags and fur cuttings, but most of its output is ferrous scrap metal and wastepaper. Scrap ferrous-metal processors and dealers collect junked autos and equipment, steel from destroyed buildings, and waste from metalworking industries. Scrap steel has become a primary feedstock for iron and steel manufacturing and foundry operations. Wastepaper processors collect used paper products such as newspapers, computer paper, and corrugated boxes. About one-third of the approximately 600 paper and pulp mills in the United States use processed wastepaper as their primary feedstock.

Since 1982, improvements in processing technology and machinery have resulted in dramatic gains in productivity. From 1982 to 1987, output per hour of all persons increased by an average of 5.2 percent per year. Output increases of 7.1 percent outweighed an average increase of 1.8 percent in hours worked.

The basic equipment used in processing ferrous scrap are shears, balers, shredders, crushers, briquetters, and blockbusters. The combination of equipment used has changed dramatically, with emphasis shifting from sheared to shredded scrap. Shredders are more expensive to operate than shears, but average output per worker hour is much higher. At the same time the industry has been installing higher-capacity equipment that can process ferrous steel twice as fast as before. Other changes in handling and transporting processed scrap have helped increase labor productivity.

Advances in automation and material handling have also been made in wastepaper processing. New paper balers automatically bind bundles that are easily handled by fewer workers.

These productivity improvements in the scrap and waste-materials industry were made possible by a growing demand for recycled products. The increase in demand made possible the use of more capital-intensive production methods. At the same time, technological advances in both the production of recycled material and uses for that material have reduced average costs.

---

* Based on Mark S. Sieling, "Productivity in Scrap and Waste Materials Processing," *Monthly Labor Review,* 113 (4) (April 1990), pp. 30–37.

---

cannot be produced from nothing. The shape of the production function is determined by the technology available. Thus the behavior of output as the input changes is determined by available technology.

A firm is operating in a technologically inefficient manner if it does not operate on the boundary of the production set. Point **b** in Figure 10.1 represents an inefficient use of the input. If a firm does not use inputs in a technologically efficient way, the costs of production will be greater than necessary in a real sense and, unless the inputs are free, also in a monetary sense. For any level of input usage, a technologically inefficient firm will produce less than an efficient firm, and the inefficient firm will soon find itself at a disadvantage in producing the good. Therefore, many firms hire engineers to identify the most technologically efficient production processes possible, and firms hire managers to organize the inputs into the most technologically efficient production activities possible.

Most production processes are irreversible. Once the inputs have been transformed into some good or service, you cannot recover the inputs in their original form. Labor time used up is gone forever. Other inputs, however, may be recovered by some form of recycling, as old newspaper can be recycled into usable paper products. But for the most part you cannot run the production process in reverse to recover all inputs in their original form.

10.2 Technological Efficiency and Isoquants

In the real world, production usually requires several inputs. The concept of a production function applies equally well when there are several inputs:

> **Production function:** *The production function is the maximum level of output that is attainable as a function of all inputs under current technology.*

When the firm uses L units of labor and K units of capital, the production function can be expressed symbolically as $X = X(L, K)$. The production function indicates the *maximum* output attainable when the firm uses L units of labor and K units of capital per unit of time. It becomes increasingly awkward to represent the production function graphically when the number of inputs increases, and so we concentrate mostly on the two-input case. The principles we will arrive at can be extended to the many-input case, however.

One way to represent a production function is by identifying production activities. A **production activity** is a technological relationship between the level of output and input levels, in which all inputs remain in fixed proportion to one another. An assembly line is a good way to think of a production activity.

Suppose we have just two inputs—capital and labor—and one activity requiring a constant capital–labor ratio. Suppose you are operating an assembly line that requires two units of labor for each unit of capital. Furthermore, let's suppose the input bundle $\mathbf{A} = \{L = 4, K = 2\}$ can be transformed into $X = 100$ units of output. Suppose also that the present technology is such that the level of output always increases at a constant rate when the inputs change. Four possible input bundles and the resulting levels of output for this activity are given in this schedule:

Activity 1		
L	K	X
4	2	100
8	4	200
12	6	300
16	8	400

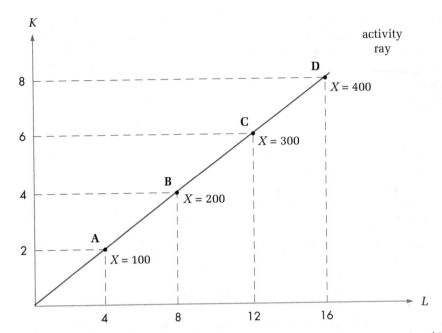

Figure 10.2 **A single production activity:** Available technology dictates that the two inputs L and K be combined in the fixed proportion of two units of L for one unit of K. This ratio defines an activity ray in input space. The resulting levels of output for alternative input bundles can be identified along the ray.

Figure 10.2 illustrates this production activity as a ray in input space along with the levels of output resulting from the different input bundles along the ray. The level of output for each input bundle represents the greatest level of output possible under current technology. Notice that the inputs are used in the fixed proportion of one unit of capital to two units of labor. The ray defined by the fixed proportion is called an **activity ray** or **production process.**

What happens when the firm has an input bundle that does not lie on the activity ray? Figure 10.3 illustrates such a case for the previous example when the firm has input bundle $C = \{L = 8, K = 2\}$ that does not lie on the activity ray. Nevertheless, as long as extra amounts of an input can be set aside, the firm can achieve an input combination required by the activity. Here, the firm sets aside 4 units of labor and uses bundle **A** to produce $X = 100$ units of output. Therefore, any input bundle along the L-shaped curve, labeled $X = 100$ in Figure 10.3, can be used to produce 100 units of output. Likewise, any input bundle along the L-shaped curve labeled $X = 200$ can be used to produce 200 units of output.

Input combinations that result in the same level of output are called **isoquants:**

> **Isoquant:** *An isoquant is a graph of all input bundles that result in the same level of output.*

Isoquant means "equal quantity." Isoquants are similar to the indifference curves of consumer preference. Because each indifference curve represents a constant level of

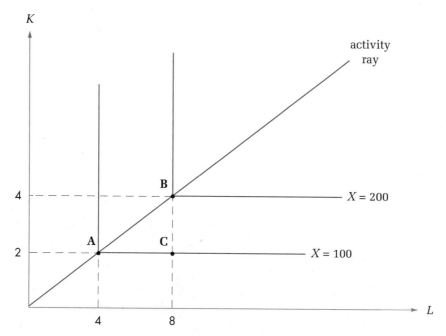

Figure 10.3 **L-shaped isoquants:** When the firm has more of an input than is required by the production activity, extra quantities of that input can be set aside to achieve the required input combination. In the two-input case with one activity, the resulting isoquants are therefore L-shaped.

preference called utility, indifference curves could be called isoutility curves. Consumer preference determines the shape and position of each indifference curve, and technology determines the shape and position of each isoquant. The primary difference between indifference curves and isoquants is that utility is an ordinal measure, but quantity is cardinal. In Figure 10.3, a movement from bundle **A,** where $X = 100$, to bundle **B,** where $X = 200$, represents a doubling of output.

Not all isoquants are L-shaped because not all production functions mandate that inputs be used in fixed proportions (one activity). Technology may permit more than one activity. Suppose that in the preceding example a second activity that is more capital intensive becomes feasible. The second activity may be a separate assembly line using more automated equipment but less labor than the first. Suppose this second activity results in:

Activity 2		
L	K	X
2	4	100
4	8	200
6	12	300
8	16	400

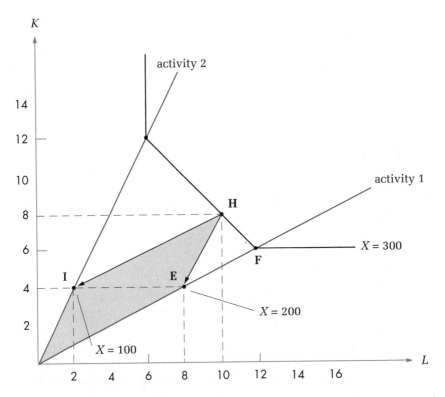

Figure 10.4 **An isoquant for independent activities:** Assuming that the two available activities can be operated simultaneously but independently, the isoquant $X = 300$ represents the various input bundles that can be used to produce 300 units of output. For instance, input bundle **H** can be allocated as bundle **E** to the first activity and as bundle **I** to the second.

This activity is illustrated in Figure 10.4 along with the first. The availability of the second activity permits the use of more capital and less labor to produce any given level of output. Hence, capital can be substituted for labor.

Now suppose the firm wants to produce $X = 300$ units of output. This output could be produced with bundle **F** by assigning $L = 12$ and $K = 6$ to activity 1. Alternatively, output $X = 300$ could be produced with bundle **G** by assigning $L = 6$ and $K = 12$ to activity 2. But can the firm produce $X = 300$ with a bundle like **H** where $L = 10$ and $K = 8$? The answer is yes if the firm can operate both activities simultaneously but independently. To see how, take $L = 8$ units of labor and $K = 4$ units of capital from bundle **H** and form bundle **E**. Bundle **E** is consistent with the fixed proportions required by activity 1 and results in $X = 200$ units. Now, take the remaining $L = 2$ units of labor and

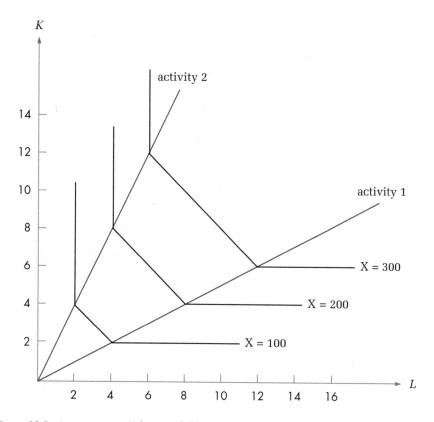

Figure 10.5 **An isoquant map:** When available technology permits only two activities that can be operated independently, the isoquants are composed of piecewise linear segments.

the remaining $K = 4$ units of capital from bundle **H** to form bundle **I**. Bundle **I** is consistent with the fixed proportions required by activity 2 and results in $X = 100$ units. Therefore, by dividing bundle **H** into two bundles **E** and **I** that are consistent with the two activities, the firm can produce a total of $X = 300$ units with bundle **H**. The efficient allocation of bundle **H** to the two activities is indicated by bundles **E** and **I** in Figure 10.4.

Similarly, any bundle on the straight-line segment drawn between bundles **F** and **G** can be allocated between the two activities to produce $X = 300$ units of output. The resulting isoquant is composed of piecewise linear segments. The isoquant represents the technologically efficient input combinations that can be used to produce $X = 300$ units. Given the available technology represented by the two activities, the production function $X = X(L, K)$ can be represented by an isoquant for every level of output. Figure 10.5 illustrates three isoquants for the two assumed activities.

10.3 Technological Dominance and Efficiency

Having more than one production activity enables the firm to substitute one input for the other. Only technologically efficient activities are considered because they dominate inefficient activities. No reasonable and rational production manager would knowingly choose an inefficient activity. To see how this ability affects the production function, let's introduce a third activity.

The introduction of a third activity is illustrated by Figure 10.6. If activity 3 requires bundle **D** to produce, say, $X = 200$ units of output, this third activity will be technologically inefficient and will never be used. Technologically inefficient activities can be dropped from the representation of this production function. Alternatively, if activity 3 requires bundle **E** to produce $X = 200$ units of output, the new activity *dominates* the adjacent activities. The new isoquant for $X = 200$ then becomes L-shaped and replaces the old isoquant because fewer of both inputs can be used to produce the same level of output. Whenever the new activity requires an input bundle below a shaded triangle like that shown in Figure 10.6, the new activity will dominate one or both of the old adjacent activities.

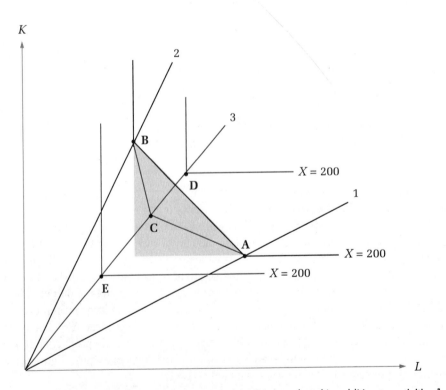

Figure 10.6 **Technological efficiency and dominance:** Activity 3 is introduced in addition to activities 1 and 2. If activity 3 permits use of an input bundle like **C** in the shaded triangle, adjacent activities 1 and 3 add the line segment **AC** to the isoquant, adjacent activities 3 and 2 add the line segment **CB** to the isoquant, and segment **AB** is removed from the isoquant. The new activity 3 neither dominates (as it would at **E**) nor is dominated by (as it is at **D**) the existing activities.

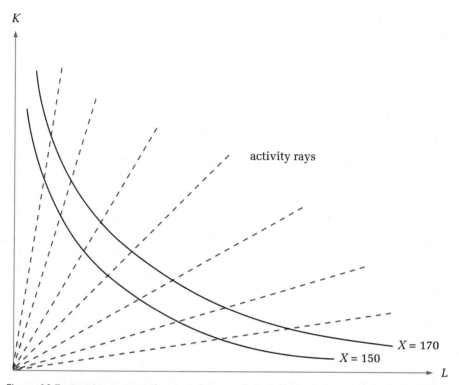

Figure 10.7 **Smooth isoquants:** When an infinite number of production activities are permitted by the technology so that continuous-input substitution is possible, the isoquants of the production function become smoothly convex.

Another possibility is available where the third activity is neither dominated by nor dominant over adjacent activities. This case too is illustrated in Figure 10.6, when bundle **C** is required to produce $X = 200$ when activity 3 is used alone. Notice that **C** falls within the shaded triangle between adjacent activities 1 and 2. Now activities 1 and 2 will never be used simultaneously because activity 3 can be used to produce $X = 200$ at **C** using fewer inputs. Moreover, a new edge between **A** and **C** is added to the isoquant. Likewise, a new edge between **C** and **B** is added because activities 3 and 2 can be operated simultaneously and independently. In summary, only efficient production activities will be considered.[2] All dominated activities are dropped from consideration because they are technologically inefficient.

Available technology may permit many efficient activities. Each activity contributes a different possibility for input substitution because the input ratios differ. Each combination of adjacent efficient activities adds linear segments to the isoquants. As the number of technologically efficient activities increases without limit, the linear segments of the isoquants shrink to points and each isoquant becomes smooth. Figure 10.8 shows two such isoquants, along with a few representative activities.

---

2. The horizontal and vertical segments of the new isoquants remain technologically efficient as long as free disposal of inputs is permitted.

We now have two versions of production technology. The case with a *finite* number of efficient activities is called the **linear model.** In the linear model, the production function can be described by isoquants composed of linear segments that remain parallel between adjacent rays. The rate of input substitution is constant between adjacent rays in the linear

AN APPLICATION: *Plotting Isoquants*

Graphic contour plots are often used to study both physical and economic relationships. Data from a corn fertility study were used to estimate and study the properties of a production function $Y = Y(N, K)$ where Y is the yield of corn in bushels per acre.* The inputs nitrogen (N) and potassium (P) are both measured in lb/acre. Various input combinations were used and the resulting yield was recorded for 212 observations. Because this was a controlled experiment, other inputs that might influence yield are assumed to be constant. The experimental results were used to generate the statistics in Table 10.1. These are the mean values of yield in the production of corn for the experimental combinations of the input amounts.

If these statistics were used to plot the production function $Y = Y(N, K)$, the surface would be distorted and irregular. Table 10.1 reveals several missing points or holes in the surface. Additional variation in yield was undoubtedly caused by factors that were outside the experimenters' control. Nevertheless, a great deal can be learned from the data about this production function.

The analysts tried several techniques to interpolate, refine, and smooth the data and improve the visual clarity of the plotted production function. By assuming that the

Table 10.1 Corn Yield, in Bushels per Acre

Potassium (K)	Nitrogen (N)					
	75	131	187	243	299	355
388	78	153		184	172	189
357		144	167	166		175
325	90	141	184	192	178	170
294	103	148	185	179	181	175
262	109	152	167	186	168	182
231	112	150	172	186	181	176
199	88	164	193	161	170	164
168	97	157	155		150	

Source: Ted F. Bay and Richard A. Schoney, "Data Analysis with Computer Graphics: Production Functions," *American Journal of Agricultural Economics*, 64(2) (May 1982), p. 290.

*Ted F. Bay and Richard A. Schoney, "Data Analysis with Computer Graphics: Production Functions," *American Journal of Agricultural Economics*, 64(2) (May 1982).

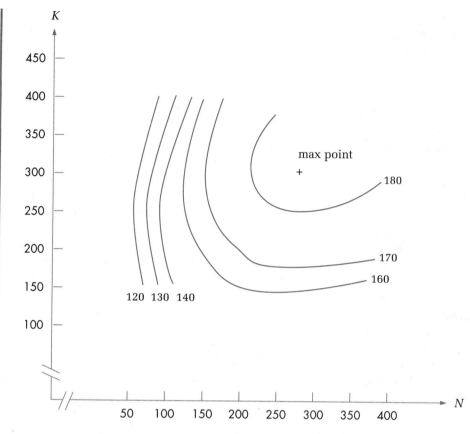

Source: T. F. Bay and R. A. Schoney, "Data Analysis with Computer Graphics: Production Functions," *American Journal of Agricultural Economics*, 64(2)(May 1982).

Figure 10.8 **Isoquant plot of an estimated production function:** The contours represent equal yield combinations of the two inputs from least-squares estimates of the production function $Y = Y(N, K)$.

production function was smooth, they were able to estimate several versions by least-squares regression. The version that fit the data best was

$$\ln Y = -8.306 + 1.766 \ln N + 2.96 \ln K - 0.276(\ln N)^2 - 0.372(\ln K)^2 + 0.2349(\ln N)(\ln K)$$

This equation explained 72.1 percent of the variation in the dependent variable, and all the estimated coefficients were statistically significant according to standard tests. An isoquant map was then generated by plotting the input combinations that yielded several levels of output. That isoquant map is reproduced as Figure 10.7. The yield reaches a maximum of 181 bushels per acre. The isoquants of this estimated production function represent technologically efficient input combinations at the different levels of output.

model. The case with an *infinite* number of efficient activities is called the **smooth model.** In the smooth model, the production function can be described by isoquants that are strictly convex so that the rate of input substitution changes continuously as the input ratio changes.[3]

10.4 What Happens in the Short Run?

All firms operate in the short run and plan for the long run. Economists define the **short run** as any period when technology is constant and at least one input is fixed. Input proportions must vary in the short run if the output level changes because the firm must use alternative production activities to change its output level. If only one activity is available, the level of output is determined uniquely by the fixed input. Thus, in the short run, the firm must switch from one production activity to another as it combines variable inputs with fixed inputs.

To keep things simple, we concentrate first on the smooth model, in which the production function has an infinite number of activities. Furthermore, we concentrate on just two inputs to illustrate principles graphically. The capital input is chosen as the fixed input because its acquisition usually is lumpy. A firm usually needs much planning and preparation to acquire more plant and equipment. Labor services, however, are usually quite variable. The firm can change the labor input by overtime or "undertime" and new hires or layoffs.

An isoquant map for a smooth production function $X = X(L, K)$ is illustrated by Figure 10.9. This case has no free disposal of inputs, and so the isoquants may bend inward as shown. As the firm combines the variable input with fixed capital to change the level of output, it must move among such input bundles as **A, B, C,** and **D.** Notice that input proportions vary as the firm moves from one ray to the next.

As labor increases, output can be graphed as a function of labor, creating a (short-run) **total product curve:**

> **Total product (TP) curve:** *A total product curve is a graph of maximum output as a function of a variable input when other inputs remain constant.*

The *TP* curve is sometimes referred to as a short-run production function. In the two-input case with labor and capital, we may denote the *TP* curve by $X = X(L; K)$. As shown in Figure 10.9, output is a function of labor, given capital. The shape of the *TP* curve is determined by the underlying technology.

Two ways of measuring the productivity of the variable input are very helpful in characterizing the total product curve and the underlying technology: the **average** and **marginal** products of an input.

---

3. "Strictly convex" means that a linear combination of two input bundles yields greater output than the least productive bundle. This is the same definition of convexity as that used in describing indifference curves.

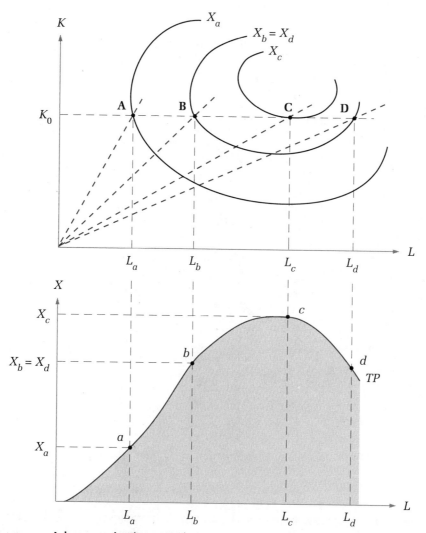

Figure 10.9 **A short-run total product curve:** This short-run total product (*TP*) curve graphs output as a function of the variable input labor, given that capital is fixed at K_0. Notice that variable input proportions are required as the firm increases labor relative to fixed capital.

> **Average product (AP):** *The average product of an input is the total product divided by the quantity of the input required.*

In producing good X, the average product of labor is

$$AP_L = \frac{X}{L}$$

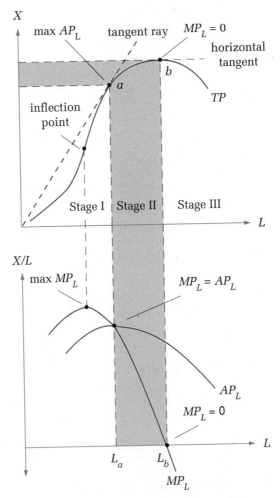

Figure 10.10   **The stages of production:** Stage I is the stage of increasing average product of the variable input. Stage II is the stage of diminishing average product when the marginal product remains positive. Stage III is the stage of zero or negative marginal product.

Figure 10.10 illustrates the graph of an AP_L curve for a specific TP curve. Average product is equal to the ratio of total product divided by the variable input at any point along the TP curve. Starting at the origin, the ratio X/L increases until point **a** is reached. Average product is at a maximum at point **a,** where a ray through the origin is tangent to the TP curve. Moving beyond point **a,** the ratio X/L diminishes as the variable input L increases, even though output X may continue to increase. This TP curve exhibits increasing average product of labor initially, but eventually the average product diminishes. The corresponding AP curve is mound shaped and reaches a maximum at the point along the TP curve where the ray is tangent to the curve.

The **marginal product** of an input is the change in output due to an incremental change in the input, while other inputs are held constant.

> **Marginal product (MP):** *Marginal product of an input is the change in output divided by the incremental change in the input as that input changes alone.*

The marginal product of labor can be measured by the slope of the *TP* curve,

$$MP_L = \frac{\Delta X}{\Delta L}$$

Geometrically, the MP_L at any point on the *TP* curve is the slope of the line tangent to the *TP* curve at that point. As illustrated by Figure 10.10, the MP_L increases until the inflection point along the *TP* curve. The inflection point occurs where the *TP* curve ceases to increase at an increasing rate and begins to increase at a decreasing rate. Beyond the inflection point, marginal productivity of labor diminishes. The MP_L is greater than the AP_L until point *a* is reached. At this point, where AP_L is at a maximum, the average and marginal products are equal. Beyond the point where AP_L is at a maximum, the MP_L continues to diminish. Moreover, the MP_L is less than AP_L beyond point *a* because the AP_L is diminishing. As always, when the marginal is above the average, the average will rise, and when the marginal is below the average, the average will fall.

As the labor input is increased beyond point *a*, the point of maximum AP_L, eventually point *b* will be reached. Output is at a maximum at point *b*, and marginal product is zero, $MP_L = 0$. Marginal product becomes negative beyond *b* as output falls in the absence of free disposal of the variable input.

It is useful to divide the *TP* curve into three **stages of production,** as illustrated by Figure 10.10. **Stage I** is the stage of increasing average product. The transition point between stages I and II occurs where $AP_L = MP_L$ and AP_L is at a maximum. **Stage II** is the stage of diminishing average product and positive marginal product. The transition point between stages II and III occurs where $MP_L = 0$ and output is at a maximum. **Stage III** is the stage of zero or negative marginal product.

The output elasticity of an input is the percentage change in output divided by the percentage change in the input. The output elasticity of labor is

$$\eta_L = \frac{\%\Delta \text{ in } X}{\%\Delta \text{ in } L}$$

As before, we can measure the ratio of percentage changes by the ratios of proportionate changes, and so[4]

$$\eta_L = \frac{\Delta X/X}{\Delta L/L} = \frac{\Delta X/\Delta L}{X/L} = \frac{MP_L}{AP_L}$$

That is, the output elasticity of labor is equal to the ratio of MP_L to the AP_L. At the transition point between stages I and II, the output elasticity for labor equals unity, and it approaches zero as you approach stage III.

---

4. Similarly, the output elasticity of capital is $\eta_K = MP_K/AP_K$.

AN APPLICATION: *A Multiplant Firm*

Suppose Steelcase has two plants producing ergonomic chairs for computer workstations. The two plants are geographically close and their labor pool is the same. One plant, though, is more modern than the other, and each plant's different production technologies and capital equipment causes labor to have different marginal product curves in each plant. Assume that in the short run labor service is a variable input in both operations. Capital inputs are fixed. The management problem is to allocate the labor service between the two operations so that total product is maximized.

Because input proportions vary in the short run, we can expect diminishing marginal product of labor services in both plants. The two marginal product curves can be drawn back to back in Figure 10.11. Labor services allocated to plant 1 are denoted L_1, and those allocated to plant 2 are denoted L_2. The total amount of labor is $L_1 + L_2 = L$. The problem is to allocate L units of labor between the two operations in the optimal way.

Suppose management tries allocating L_1^b units of labor to plant 1 and L_2^c units to plant 2. The marginal product of labor in plant 1 is indicated by point **b** on the MP_1 curve, and the marginal product of labor in plant 2 is indicated by point **c** on the MP_2 curve. For this initial allocation, the marginal product in plant 2 is greater than that in plant 1. This imbalance implies that ΔL units can be withdrawn from plant 1 and assigned to plant 2, increasing the marginal contribution of labor in plant 1 more than the decrease in marginal contribution in plant 2. The decrease in output in plant 1 will be less than the increase in plant 2. In general, as long as the marginal product of an

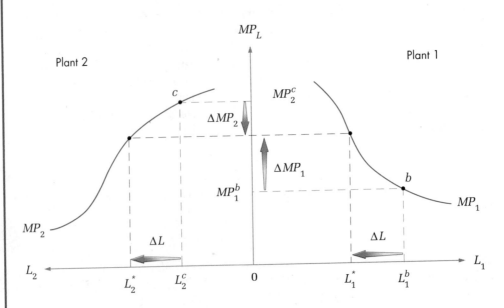

Figure 10.11   **A multiplant firm:** Management will maximize output by allocating the variable input labor in the most technologically efficient manner by assigning labor to the two plants so that the marginal product of labor is the same in both plants.

input in one use exceeds the marginal product of that input in another use, managers can increase production by reallocating some of the input to the use with the higher marginal product. Optimal allocation of the input thus requires that its marginal product be equal in all uses.

In the Figure 10.11 example, the optimal allocation is L_1^* units to plant 1 and L_2^* units to plant 2 because the marginal products of labor will be equal in the two uses. Any other allocation results in inequality of the MP_L between the two uses and lower total output. Thus the firm can maximize output by knowing how the marginal product of labor varies among alternative uses and allocating that labor to equalize the marginal products.

Recognize too that the stages in production may change when the underlying conditions change. Because any *TP* curve graphs output as a function of a variable input, given that other inputs and technology remain constant, a new *TP* curve results every time one of the fixed inputs or technology changes. Figure 10.12 illustrates such a shift in a *TP*

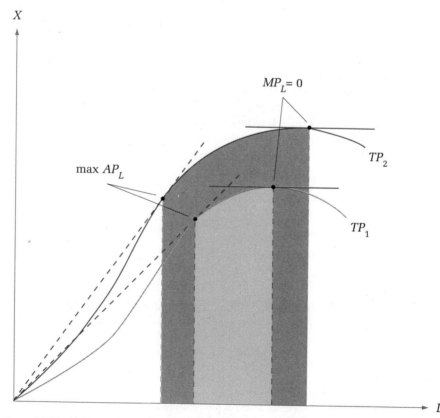

Figure 10.12 **Shifts in a *TP* curve:** The *TP* curve graphs output as a function of one variable input—in this case, labor. The *TP* curve will shift when conditions change, say by changing the level of a fixed input—in this case, capital. When the *TP* curve shifts, the transition points among the three stages of production may also change.

curve. Here the fixed-input capital increases, causing a shift in the TP curve from TP_1 to TP_2. Notice that when the TP curve shifts, the transition points between the stages of production may also change.

10.5 Diminishing Returns and Efficiency

In the short run, as an input changes, output may increase initially at an increasing rate, but eventually it will increase at a decreasing rate. This eventual diminishing productivity of a variable input in the short run is known as **diminishing returns.** Consider the successive addition of variable labor inputs using a machine to form steel fenders for automobiles. One person may be able to run the machine, but it is frequently more efficient to have two persons work together, increasing average productivity. That is, the average output per worker may be higher with two workers cooperating to move the steel in and out of the machine. But adding a third worker may not further increase average product even though total product may increase. When the extra output produced by the new worker is smaller than the extra output produced by the preceding worker, the rate of increase in output diminishes. In other words, the marginal product of labor falls. Eventually, the marginal product will be below the average product and the latter will diminish. In fact, continuing to add workers need not increase total product. Very soon, so many people will be working on the one machine that some will have to step aside so that the others can work. If those workers do not step aside, total product will begin to fall when marginal product becomes negative.

This property of total product curves so pervades the real world that eventual diminishing productivity is described as a law. Input proportions must vary as variable inputs are combined with at least one fixed input; the empirical phenomenon of diminishing productivity is called the **law of variable proportions:**

> **Law of variable proportions:** *Diminishing productivity of variable inputs will occur eventually as successive increases in variable inputs are combined with fixed inputs.*

The diminishing average product of a variable input in the short run is a consequence of the law of variable proportions.[5] Every total-product curve must exhibit diminishing productivity somewhere.

Although not every TP curve has all three stages of production, the law of variable proportions (diminishing returns) says that every TP curve must somewhere have a stage

---

5. Some economists argue that, like the "law" of diminishing utility, the law of diminishing productivity is not really a law of nature but a hypothesis about short-run production functions. George Stigler argues in *The Theory of Price*, however, that a sufficient proof of the law of variable proportions is that the whole world cannot be fed by crops grown in one flowerpot. I can think of no exception to the law of variable proportions, and challenge you to find one. The same cannot be said of diminishing marginal utility because it is so subjective.

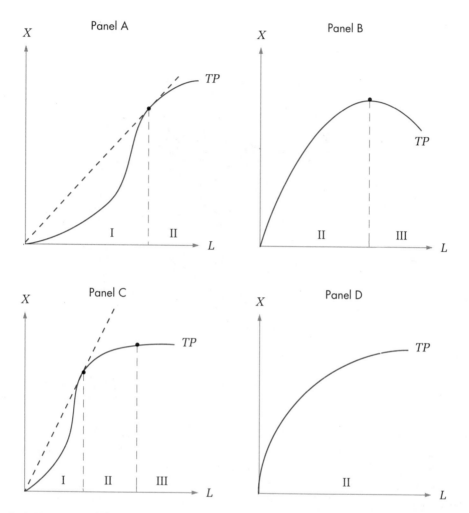

Figure 10.13 **Possible *TP* curves: Panel A** A *TP* curve with stages I and II. **Panel B** A *TP* curve with stages II and III. **Panel C** A *TP* curve with stages I, II, and III. **Panel D** A *TP* curve with stage II everywhere.

II. Some production functions have *TP* curves that have only stages I and II, and some have only stages II and III. Some production functions have *TP* curves that exhibit all three stages, and some have only stage II everywhere. The various possibilities are illustrated in Figure 10.13. All the *TP* curves have a stage of diminishing average product and positive marginal product of the variable input.

Stage III is technologically inefficient because output either decreases or remains constant when one input increases alone. No manager will knowingly move into stage III unless forced to do so, because marginal product is either negative or zero in that region. Thus, stage III for any input is technologically inefficient, and all production will take place where marginal products are nonnegative. The region of positive marginal products is called the **economic region of production.** The economic region is illustrated for the

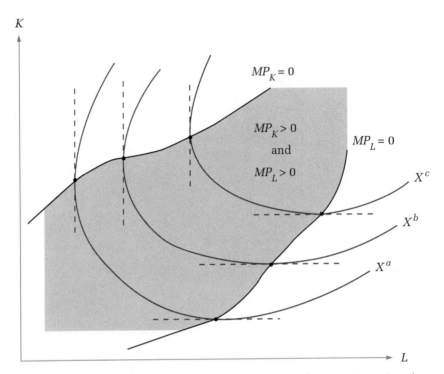

Figure 10.14 **The economic region:** All production will take place in the economic region where marginal products are nonnegative, the area between the ridgelines $MP_K = 0$ and $MP_L = 0$.

two-input case by Figure 10.14. **Ridgelines** are said to occur whenever output is at a maximum with respect to one input alone. Thus, a ridgeline occurs for any input combination that yields $MP_L = 0$. Beyond this ridgeline the isoquants bend inward and the marginal product of labor becomes negative. Likewise, another ridgeline occurs for the input combinations that yield $MP_K = 0$. Again, along this ridgeline the isoquants bend inward and the marginal product of capital becomes negative. The economic region where both marginal products are positive simultaneously, $MP_L > 0$ and $MP_K > 0$, lies between the ridgelines.[6]

10.6 Back to the Future—Efficient Input Substitution

In the long run all inputs are variable, and available technology determines the ability to substitute between inputs. Movement along any isoquant requires that one input be substituted for another while output remains constant. The slope of an isoquant may be used to measure the rate of input substitution at a point on the isoquant. Because this rate

---

6. Although it is true that a stage III for labor lies beyond the ridgeline $MP_L = 0$ and a stage III for capital lies beyond the ridgeline $MP_K = 0$, do not make the mistake of assuming that stage III for labor is stage I for capital, or that stage III for capital is stage I for labor, for neither is necessarily true.

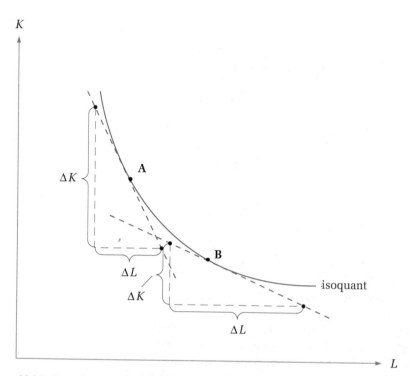

Figure 10.15 **Marginal rate of technical substitution:** The $MRTS_{LK}$ can be measured by the negative of the slope $\Delta K / \Delta L$ of a line tangent to a point along an isoquant. Convexity of the curve implies a diminishing MRTS as the firm uses more L relative to K.

of substitution is determined by technology, it is called the **marginal rate of technical substitution:**

> **Marginal rate of technical substitution (MRTS):** *The* MRTS *measures the quantity of one input that can be substituted for another while remaining on the same isoquant in the economic region.*

Notice the similarity between the $MRTS$ and the MRS of consumer choice. The MRS measures the rate of substitution between goods that keeps utility constant, and the MRS may be measured by the negative of the slope of an indifference curve. Likewise, the $MRTS$ may be measured by the negative of the slope of an isoquant:

$$MRTS_{LK} = -\frac{\Delta K}{\Delta L} > 0$$

where $\Delta K / \Delta L$ is the slope of an isoquant at a point. The slope of the isoquant is negative, but the marginal rate of technical substitution will be positive in the economic region.

Measurement of the marginal rate of technical substitution using the slopes of tangent lines is illustrated in Figure 10.15. At **A**, the slope of the tangent line measures the quantity of K that must be given up when an extra unit of L is used near **A** to maintain constant output. At **B**, the slope measures the reduction in K as L is substituted for K near point **B**. Notice that the $MRTS_{LK}$ is smaller near **B** than near **A** because of the isoquant's convexity. That is, the $MRTS_{LK}$ diminishes as the firm substitutes L for K. A diminishing marginal rate of technical substitution of labor for capital implies that it becomes harder and harder to substitute labor for capital as more labor is used relative to capital when output remains constant.[7]

Movement along any isoquant within the economic region requires substituting one input for another. Along any isoquant the change in total product is zero, and so the MP_L multiplied by the change in L added to the MP_K multiplied by the change in K must be zero,

$$MP_L \Delta L + MP_K \Delta K = 0$$

Rearranging the terms leads to

$$\frac{MP_L}{MP_K} = - \frac{\Delta K}{\Delta L}$$

The right-hand side of this equation is the marginal rate of technical substitution, and so the marginal rate of input substitution equals the ratio of marginal products, $MRTS_{LK} = MP_L/MP_K$. In the economic region this rate of substitution must be positive, $MRTS > 0$. Just as we measured the MRS of consumer choice by the ratio of marginal utilities, we can measure the $MRTS$ in production by the ratio of marginal products.

The $MRTS$ provides us with a measure for the ability to substitute one input for another. But like all measures of slope, the $MRTS$ is not invariant to changes in the scales of measurement. Therefore, it is useful to have a measure of the substitutability of inputs that is invariant to the scales of measurement. Such a measure is provided by an elasticity:

> **Elasticity of substitution:** *The elasticity of substitution is the percentage change in the input ratio divided by the percentage change in the marginal rate of technical substitution.*

The elasticity of substitution, denoted here by the Greek letter σ, is measured at any point along an isoquant by

$$\sigma = \frac{\%\Delta \text{ in } K/L}{\%\Delta \text{ in } MRTS_{LK}}$$

when L and K are the two inputs. This pure number characterizes the curvature of an isoquant at a point. Substitution elasticities are frequently reported in empirical

---

7. For the linear-activity model, isoquants are composed of parallel linear segments between adjacent activity rays. Thus, the $MRTS$ remains constant between adjacent rays. The $MRTS_{LK}$ diminishes sectionally, however, as the ratio of capital to labor falls from one cone determined by adjacent rays to the next cone determined by the next pair of adjacent rays.

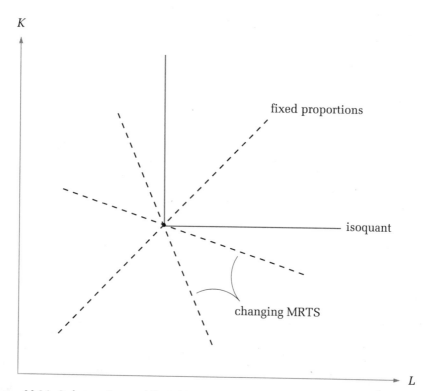

Figure 10.16 **Perfect complements:** When the two inputs are perfect complements, no substitution is possible and the substitution elasticity is $\sigma = 0$.

investigations of production functions; such elasticities provide important clues to a firm's ability to substitute between inputs and, hence, whether the costs of production will be affected a lot or a little when input prices change.

Two polar cases illustrate how the elasticity of substitution can be used to characterize a production function. First, for one activity resulting in L-shaped isoquants, the inputs must be combined in fixed proportion. As illustrated by Figure 10.16, no substitution is possible when the inputs are *perfect complements*, the K/L ratio remains constant, and $\sigma = 0$. Second, for an infinite number of activities when inputs are perfect substitutes everywhere, the isoquants are composed of parallel straight lines. As illustrated by Figure 10.17, the *MRTS* remains constant everywhere along all isoquants. The elasticity of substitution is $\sigma = \infty$ because the *MRTS* remains constant for an infinite number of possible input ratios.

Most production functions have isoquants with substitution elasticities between $\sigma = 0$ and $\sigma = \infty$. A big elasticity implies that two inputs are close substitutes and their isoquants are nearly straight lines. A small elasticity between two inputs implies that the inputs are close complements—it is difficult to substitute one input for the other—and the isoquants are highly convex.

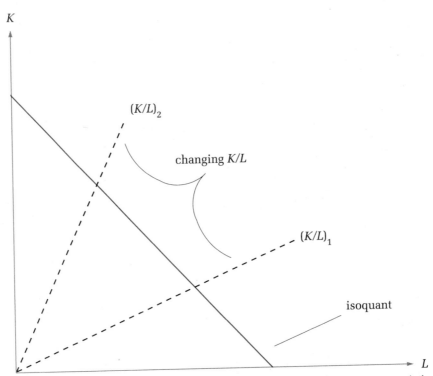

Figure 10.17   **Perfect substitutes:** When the two inputs are perfect substitutes, any input ratio is feasible but the *MRTS* remains constant. The substitution elasticity is σ = ∞.

Some actual estimates on the elasticity of substitution for capital and labor by industry are reported in Table 10.2. These elasticities, calculated from U.S. and Japanese data during the 1950s, are for the prevailing production technology of that decade. The elasticity of σ = 1.71 in the petroleum and natural-gas industry indicates that capital and labor were relatively good substitutes, but in the electric-power industry the elasticity of σ = 0.82 shows that capital and labor were relatively poor substitutes. The lowest elasticity was found in the apparel industry, where machines were poor substitutes for human labor; the highest was in the transport industry. It is easy to add more seats to a plane or bus, transporting more passengers (output) with less labor input. In general, the ability to substitute capital for labor in all industries at this level of aggregation was extensive during the 1950s.

10.7 Returns to Scale in the Long Run

Another useful way of characterizing the production function is to describe how output changes as the firm moves along an activity ray. As the firm moves, all inputs are variable but remain in fixed proportion. When all inputs are variable, economists describe the situation as occurring in the *long run*. In contrast, in the *short run*, at least one input

Table 10.2 Substitution Elasticities for Capital and Labor for Selected Industries in the 1950s

Industry	Estimated Elasticity (σ)
Transportation	1.74
Petroleum and natural gas	1.71
Metal mining	1.41
Printing and publishing	1.21
Agriculture	1.20
Nonmetallic minerals	1.18
Paper	1.14
Trade	1.12
Nonferrous metals	1.10
Coal	1.08
Transport equipment	1.04
Petroleum products	1.04
Iron and steel	1.00
Rubber	0.98
Shipbuilding	0.97
Fishing	0.94
Coal mining	0.93
Machining	0.93
Processed food	0.93
Electric power	0.82
Lumber	0.84
Grain mills	0.81
Textiles	0.80
Leather products	0.72
Apparel	0.42

Source: K. J. Arrow, H. B. Chenery, B. S. Minhas, and R. M. Solow, "Capital–Labor Substitution and Economic Efficiency," *Review of Economics and Statistics* (August 1961), p. 240. Reprinted by permission of Elsevier Science Publishers.

is fixed. No specific time interval is implied here. Whether a time interval is short run or long run depends on the situation and the kind of choices being made. For instance, the firm usually finds itself faced with a fixed capital input over fairly long intervals. Even if the firm decides to expand its physical plant, by the time land is purchased, the blueprints made, environmental impact reports filed, permits obtained, the land graded, the building constructed, and machines installed, the physical plant may be ready to use only after two or three years. And yet economists would describe the intervening period as a short-run situation because one input is fixed. Beyond that interval, the condition is a long run because all inputs including physical capital are variable.

Now let's consider how output might vary as the firm moves along an activity ray. All inputs are variable but remain in fixed proportion to one another, but the firm is still

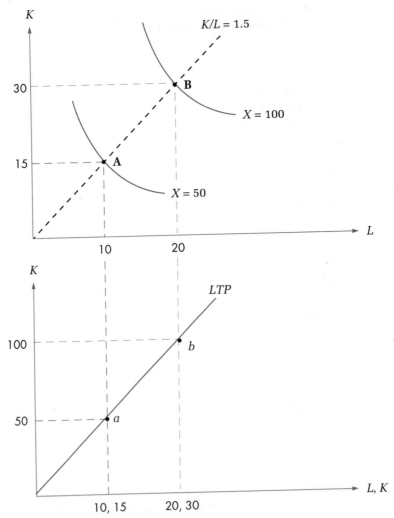

Figure 10.18   **Constant returns to scale:** This long-run total product curve has constant slope. As the firm moves along the activity ray, a doubling of both inputs leads to a doubling of output.

constrained by available technology. One possible case is illustrated by Figure 10.18. As the firm moves from bundle **A** to bundle **B**, both inputs have doubled and the resulting level of output has also doubled. If output is graphed as a function of one of the inputs when all inputs vary but remain in fixed proportion, the result is a **long-run total-product** (*LTP*) curve:

> **Long-run total product:** The long-run total-product curve graphs output as a function of all inputs, given fixed input proportions.

In the example illustrated by Figure 10.18, output doubles when all inputs are doubled. Here the production function $X = X(L, K)$ is said to exhibit **constant returns to scale:**

> **Constant returns to scale:** *Constant returns to scale occur when output changes by the* same *multiple quantity as the multiple of all inputs.*

When we see two inputs, if both inputs are scaled by some amount $\lambda > 0$, constant returns to scale imply that

$$X(\lambda L, \lambda K) = \lambda X(L, K)$$

That is, if both inputs are *scaled* by λ so that λL and λK are used in production, the result is λX. Notice that the long-run total product curve graphs as a straight line through the origin under constant returns to scale.

Another possibility is illustrated by Figure 10.19. Here, when both inputs are doubled, output is less than doubled. The resulting *LTP* curve increases at a *decreasing* rate, and the production function is said to exhibit **decreasing returns to scale:**

> **Decreasing returns to scale:** *Decreasing returns to scale occur when output changes by a* smaller *multiple amount than the multiple of all inputs.*

Decreasing returns to scale imply that

$$X(\lambda L, \lambda K) < \lambda X(L, K)$$

That is, if both inputs are *scaled* by λ so that λL and λK are used in production, the resulting level of output is *less* than λX.

A final possibility is illustrated by Figure 10.20. When both inputs are doubled, output is more than doubled. The resulting *LTP* curve increases at an *increasing* rate, and the production function is said to exhibit **increasing returns to scale:**

> **Increasing returns to scale:** *Increasing returns to scale occur when output changes by a* larger *multiple amount than the multiple of all inputs.*

Increasing returns to scale imply that

$$X(\lambda L, \lambda K) > \lambda X(L, K)$$

That is, if both inputs are *scaled* by λ so that λL and λK are used in production, the resulting level of output is *greater* than λX.[8]

---

8. Any production function $X(L, K)$ is said to be **homogeneous of degree** m if for any scalar λ,

$$\lambda^m X(L, K) = X(\lambda L, \lambda K)$$

When $m = 1$, constant returns to scale prevail and the production function is said to be **linearly homogeneous.** When $m > 1$, we find increasing returns to scale. When $m < 1$, we see decreasing returns to scale. With a homogeneous function, returns to scale remain unchanged along any activity ray.

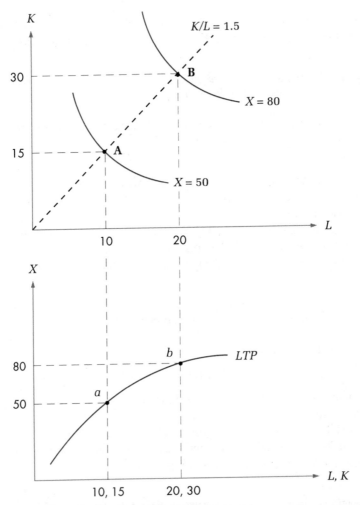

Figure 10.19   **Decreasing returns to scale:** This long-run total product curve increases at a decreasing rate. As the firm moves along the activity ray, a doubling of both inputs leads to a smaller increase in output.

Of the three possible cases, constant returns to scale seem to be the most natural and the most likely. The reason is that the firm can theoretically *replicate* a production activity, thereby doubling its output when all inputs are doubled. If two identical assembly plants can be operated simultaneously, then the firm will experience constant returns to scale until it covers the globe with identical assembly plants. Increasing returns to scale are most likely to be observed over some initial range of expansion of inputs and output. One frequently cited example of increasing returns to scale is an oil pipeline. When the diameter of a pipe is doubled, twice as much material is used but the cross-section of the pipe is quadrupled. The larger pipe has the potential of carrying four times the volume of oil. But this example of increasing returns to scale cannot be extended too far because the

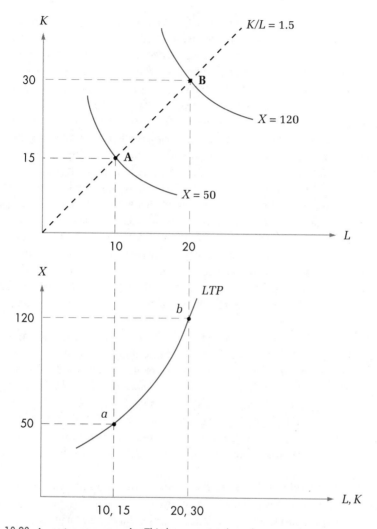

Figure 10.20 **Increasing returns to scale:** This long-run total product curve increases at an increasing rate. As the firm moves along the activity ray, a doubling of both inputs leads to a larger increase in output.

pipe will eventually become structurally unsound and collapse under its own weight unless the amount of material used more than doubles.

These observations are borne out by empirical evidence.[9] Examples of production functions having constant returns to scale are numerous. Although we may find many

---

9. See, for example, Edward M. Miller, "The Extent of Economies of Scale," *Southern Economic Journal,* 44(3) (January 1978). This study covers 448 American industries. Also see John R. Moroney, "Cobb-Douglas Production Functions and Returns to Scale in U.S. Manufacturing Industry," *Western Economic Journal,* 6(1) (December 1967).

examples of increasing returns to scale, older firms have usually increased their scale of operations so that further increasing returns to scale are small. Evidence of decreasing returns to scale is somewhat uncommon, probably because firms take action to avoid moving into the region of their production functions where decreasing returns to scale occur. Studying the banking industry, for instance, we find that large banks have avoided decreasing returns to scale by opening new small branches rather than increasing the scale at a central location. Nevertheless, all managers need to recognize and estimate returns to scale in order to judge any consequences of increasing their firm's scale of operation.

The two basic models of technology are the linear model and the smooth model. The linear model is *always* characterized by constant returns to scale everywhere because of the assumptions that activities could be operated simultaneously and independently and that adding input bundles results in a level of output that is the sum of their independent outputs. Thus replication of activities is always theoretically possible, isoquants remain parallel between adjacent activity rays, and constant returns to scale are found everywhere.[10] The smooth model though, may be characterized by increasing, constant, or decreasing returns to scale, and the type of returns to scale may change along a ray.[11] Figure 10.21 illustrates a case in which initially a firm's production process exhibits increasing returns to scale but, as the firm moves along the ray, eventually decreasing returns to scale begin.

Take care not to confuse diminishing productivity in the short run with returns to scale in the long run. Such a confusion is easy because diminishing productivity is sometimes referred to as *diminishing returns.* Diminishing returns is a short-run technological phenomenon caused by using more and more of a variable input when there is at least one other fixed input—input proportions vary. Returns to scale though, are long-run technological phenomena that occur when all inputs are variable but remain in fixed proportion. A production function may have increasing, constant, or decreasing returns to scale, but every production function must exhibit diminishing returns eventually in the short run.

Consider the Cobb-Douglas production function shown in Figure 10.22. This type of function was used in the first comprehensive study of manufacturing industries in the United States.[12] The Cobb-Douglas production function takes the form

$$X = \alpha L^\beta K^{1-\beta}$$

10. These characteristics of the linear model permit us to use a technique called linear programming when working with the linear model. For the smooth model, calculus can be used as a tool of analysis and optimization. Which is appropriate, the linear or smooth model, depends on the underlying technological constraints.

11. Unless the function is homogeneous.

12. See Paul H. Douglas, *The Theory of Wages* (Macmillan, 1924), pp. 132–135, and C. W. Cobb and P. H. Douglas, "A Theory of Production," *American Economic Review* (March, supplement), 1928. Charles W. Cobb was a mathematician at Amherst. Paul H. Douglas was an economist at the University of Chicago before he was reduced to being a U.S. Senator from Illinois. Stigler says of the Cobb-Douglas production function: "It is now customary in economics to deny its validity and then to proceed to use it as an excellent approximation" (*The Theory of Price,* 4th ed. [Macmillan, 1987], p. 153).

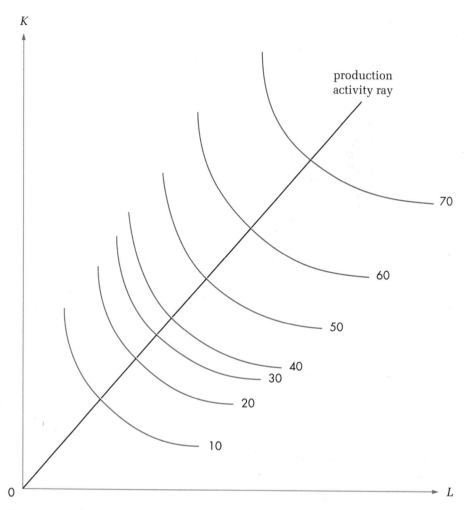

Figure 10.21 **Changing returns to scale:** This firm experiences increasing returns to scale from the origin to 40 units of output, but decreasing returns to scale begin after 40 units of output.

where $\alpha > 0$ and $0 \leq \beta \leq 1$. Figure 10.22 is a graph of the Cobb-Douglas when $\alpha = 1$ and $\beta = 1/2$ so that $X = \sqrt{LK}$. As you can see, this production function has constant returns to scale because output increases at a constant rate when input proportions are fixed. Yet any *TP* curve for the Cobb-Douglas, like the one shown by the shaded slice when $K = 20$, exhibits diminishing productivity of the variable input. Output increases at a decreasing rate in the short run. In fact, all Cobb-Douglas production functions have constant returns to scale everywhere because $\beta + (1 - \beta) = 1$, and they have diminishing marginal and average products everywhere because $0 < \beta < 1$. All isoquants, like the one for $X = 10$ in Figure 10.22, are convex because the *MRTS* diminishes.

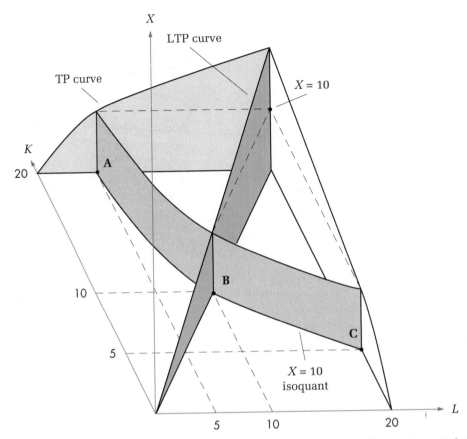

Figure 10.22 **Cobb-Douglas production function:** The Cobb-Douglas production function $X = \alpha L^\beta K^{1-\beta}$ has constant returns to scale everywhere, yet average and marginal products diminish everywhere and the isoquants are convex. This Cobb-Douglas is graphed for $\alpha = 1$ and $\beta = 1/2$ so that $X = \sqrt{LK}$.

10.8 Empirical Production Functions

One of the most appealing functional forms for estimating production functions is the cubic. The *cubic* function for the two-input case is:

$$X = \alpha + \beta_1 LK + \beta_2 L^2 K + \beta_3 LK^2 + \beta_4 L^2 K^2 + \beta_5 L^3 K + \beta_6 LK^3$$

The cubic is appealing because it can capture increasing and then decreasing returns to scale. Therefore it is fairly flexible in approximating most technologies. Another appeal is that it can be estimated by least-squares regression if you have enough observations.

Another fairly flexible form for the production function starts with the simplifying assumption that the elasticity of substitution is constant. Such functions are called constant elasticity of substitution (CES) production functions. The formula for the CES function with two inputs is

$$X = \alpha \left[\beta L^{\frac{\sigma-1}{\sigma}} + (1 - \beta)K^{\frac{\sigma-1}{\sigma}} \right]^{\frac{\sigma}{\sigma-1}}$$

with $\alpha > 0$ and $0 < \beta < 1$. The parameter σ is the elasticity of substitution. Although the CES may seem complicated at first glance, it is important because it is frequently applied in empirical work and can be used to generate other special types of production functions.

For example, the CES production function with inputs L and K has these marginal products:

$$MP_L = (\beta/\alpha^\rho)(X/L)^{\rho+1}$$
$$MP_K = [(1 - \beta)/\alpha^\rho](X/K)^{\rho+1}$$

where ρ is defined by the substitution elasticity $\sigma = 1/(1 + \rho)$. When $\sigma = 1$ (and $\rho = 0$), the CES becomes Cobb-Douglas $X = \alpha L^\beta K^{1-\beta}$ with:

$$MP_L = \alpha\beta L^{\beta-1}K^{1-\beta}$$
$$MP_K = \alpha(1 - \beta)L^\beta K^{-\beta}$$

These marginal products never reach zero but decline steadily as long as $0 < \beta < 1$ when the other input is fixed. Thus, stage II is everywhere. Yet this Cobb-Douglas has constant returns everywhere because $\beta + (1 - \beta) = 1$.

For the CES function, the elasticity of substitution may lie anywhere between 0 and ∞. When σ approaches zero, the inputs become perfect complements and the isoquants become L-shaped. When σ approaches infinity, the inputs are perfect substitutes and the isoquants become downward-sloping straight lines. When σ approaches unity, the isoquants graph as rectangular hyperbolas, and the production function is Cobb-Douglas.[13]

A variant of the Cobb-Douglas function used in many studies is the multiplicative power function. In the two-input case, this variant is

$$X = \alpha L^{\beta_1}K^{\beta_2}$$

One of the advantages of this function is that it is linear in logarithms,

$$\ln X = \ln \alpha + \beta_1 \ln L + \beta_2 \ln K$$

Thus, this type of model can easily be estimated by least-squares regression. Returns to scale are calculated by summing the exponents. If $\beta_1 + \beta_2 = 1$, then the returns to scale are constant. If $\beta_1 + \beta_2 > 1$, then returns to scale are increasing. If $\beta_1 + \beta_2 < 1$, then the returns to scale are decreasing.

In their original study, Cobb and Douglas used time-series data on the U.S. manufacturing sector from 1899 to 1922. Their original specification constrained the sum of the coefficients to be equal to unity, $\beta_1 + \beta_2 = 1$. Thus, the original Cobb-Douglas function

---

13. Strictly speaking, the formula for the CES cannot be used when $\sigma = 1$ because of division by zero. By applying L'Hopital's rule, however, we reduce the CES to the Cobb-Douglas.

was constrained to exhibit constant returns to scale. The estimated equation for American manufacturing as a whole was

$$X = 1.01L^{0.75}K^{0.25}$$

where output and both inputs were indexes based on the year 1899. This equation explained about 94 percent of the variation in output.

In a subsequent extension of their seminal work, Cobb and Douglas revised their measures of output and the inputs to remove any secular trend. They measured each variable as a percentage of its overall trend value. They also dropped the condition that the sum of the exponents must equal unity. The new estimate was

$$X = 0.84L^{0.63}K^{0.30}$$

Although the sum of the exponents is slightly less than 1, the difference was not statistically significant. Thus, the new estimate did not contradict their original hypothesis of constant returns to scale.

Another study by Moroney used the Cobb-Douglas variant to estimate production functions for eighteen U.S. manufacturing industries.[14] In this study the equation to be estimated was

$$\log V = \log \alpha + \beta_1 \log L_1 + \beta_2 \log L_2 + \beta_3 \log K + \varepsilon$$

where V is value added, L_1 is production labor time, L_2 is nonproduction labor time, K is gross capital stock, and ε is a random error. The results of Moroney's regression analyses are reproduced in Table 10.3. The results indicate fairly good fits, the signs of the coefficients are as expected, except for nonproduction labor in the rubber and plastics industry. Overall, we see much evidence of constant returns to scale. Only five industries show evidence that returns to scale are not constant, and in each of those the sum of the coefficients is greater than unity, indicating some increasing returns to scale.

Moroney also employed a second test that supported the seemingly widespread occurrence of constant returns to scale. If increasing returns to scale are important in any industry, then all plants should be uniformly large to take advantage of the returns to scale. But if decreasing returns to scale are important, then all plants should be uniformly small. When Moroney looked at plant size in each industry, he found widely ranging plant sizes. This result provides additional evidence of nearly constant returns to scale in the industries examined at the time of the study.

Most industry studies have found nearly constant returns to scale, with some important exceptions. Marc Nerlove found a returns-to-scale exponent of 1.53 in the electric-power industry, indicating substantial increasing returns to scale. This industry is regulated as a public utility because the substantial scale economies, along with large plant sizes relative to the market, usually indicate extensive monopoly power.

---

14. John R. Moroney, "Cobb-Douglas Production Functions and Returns to Scale in U.S. Manufacturing Industry," *Western Economics Journal,* 6(1) (December 1967).

Table 10.3 Output Elasticities in Selected U.S. Industries, 1957

Industry	Number of Observations	Production Labor (L_1)	Non-production Labor (L_2)	Gross Capital (K)	Returns to Scale	R^2
Furniture	22	0.8015 (0.1855)	0.1026 (0.1026)	0.2046 (0.1534)	1.1087[a] (0.0508)	.966
Chemicals	32	0.5534 (0.1247)	0.3363 (0.1016)	0.2002 (0.0932)	1.0900[a] (0.0601)	.970
Printing etc.	17	0.0454 (0.1709)	0.5741 (0.1920)	0.4590 (0.0556)	1.0786[a] (0.0317)	.989
Food and beverages	41	0.4388 (0.1279)	0.0761 (0.0375)	0.5553 (0.1210)	1.0702[a] (0.0213)	.986
Rubber and plastics	16	1.0332 (0.2057)	−0.4575[?] (0.1457)	0.4807 (0.1053)	1.0563 (0.0414)	.991
Apparel	24	0.4370 (0.0861)	0.4765 (0.0930)	0.1276 (0.0893)	1.0412 (0.0374)	.982
Instruments	11	0.8186 (0.2059)	0.0198 (0.1681)	0.2056 (0.1520)	1.0442 (0.0244)	.997
Lumber	23	0.5039 (0.1247)	0.1453 (0.1016)	0.3917 (0.0932)	1.0409 (0.0601)	.951
Leather	11	0.4412 (0.2010)	0.5227 (0.3149)	0.0760 (0.1492)	1.0399 (0.0392)	.990
Stone, clay, etc.	26	0.0316 (0.2245)	0.3659 (0.2010)	0.6317 (0.1054)	1.0292 (0.0454)	.961
Fabricated metals	33	0.5117 (0.0938)	0.3646 (0.0920)	0.1511 (0.0743)	1.0274[a] (0.0159)	.995
Electrical machinery	25	0.4291 (0.1922)	0.2290 (0.1294)	0.3680 (0.1187)	1.0261 (0.0364)	.983
Transportation equipment	29	0.7488 (0.1257)	0.0410 (0.0881)	0.2335 (0.0697)	1.0234 (0.0391)	.972
Nonelectrical machinery	30	0.2278 (0.1837)	0.3887 (0.2054)	0.4038 (0.1283)	1.0204 (0.0312)	.980
Textiles	21	0.5488 (0.2157)	0.3346 (0.0858)	0.1206 (0.1733)	1.0041 (0.0236)	.991
Paper and pulp	30	0.3667 (0.0943)	0.1872 (0.0703)	0.4205 (0.0446)	0.9844 (0.0189)	.990
Primary metals	29	0.0773 (0.1884)	0.5088 (0.1643)	0.3715 (0.1026)	0.9576 (0.0345)	.969
Petroleum and coal	17	0.5462 (0.2221)	0.0931 (0.1685)	0.3078 (0.1116)	0.9471 (0.0449)	.983

[a]Significantly greater than unity at 5 percent. [?]Questionable estimate; (estimated standard errors in parentheses).

Source: John R. Moroney, "Cobb-Douglas Production Functions and Returns to Scale in U.S. Manufacturing Industry," *Western Economics Journal,* 6(1) (December 1967).

AN APPLICATION: *Managerial Efficiency in Baseball*

The performance of managers in professional baseball contributes very substantially to producing won games. The output (win percentage) of major-league baseball teams and the inputs (players' skill) can be unambiguously measured, and the production function can be simply specified. In one study, a team's percentage of wins was specified as a function of the team's hitting and pitching performance.*

Teams play a constant number of games during their regular season, and the quality of those games can be measured by each team's percentage of wins (W). Winning is a function of the team's hitting performance (H) and pitching performance (P). Another input, the team's fielding performance, was not used because it does not differ significantly among teams. The production function was specified as Cobb-Douglas,

$$W = \alpha H^\beta P^{1-\beta}$$

Managers are responsible for transforming inputs H and P into output W, and they make technical and strategic decisions that affect the outcome of the games. A primary goal of the manager is to achieve technological efficiency—getting the most out of the available team roster. To remove the effect of variation among teams in players' talent in this empirical study, the production function is divided by output to obtain:

$$1 = \alpha h^\beta p^{1-\beta}$$

where $h = H/W$ and $p = P/W$ are the new measures for the hitting and pitching inputs.† This isoquant has been referred to as the *frontier unit isoquant* because it indicates the most efficient use of the inputs required to attain any given win percentage.

The unit isoquant is illustrated in Figure 10.23, where **A** represents actual performance and **B** represents the most technologically efficient performance. If all managers were efficient in using their players, each manager would be on the unit isoquant. That is, for any fixed-input proportion represented by a ray, a perfectly efficient manager could attain the team's win percentage by an input use at bundle **B** along the unit isoquant. A less efficient manager would require more of both inputs, say at **A**, to achieve the same win percentage. That is, managers who fail to attain the maximum output possible for their team roster require greater quantities of inputs than is indicated by the frontier isoquant. Managerial performance relative to potential performance can be measured by the distance from the origin to **A** divided by the distance from the origin to **B**. Simple geometry then indicates that relative managerial efficiency is $E = W/W^*$ where $0 \le E \le 1$.

Empirical estimates of the frontier unit isoquant for each of the major leagues and for each of the years 1961 to 1980 were calculated in this study. The estimating technique required that all observations of inputs per unit of output lie on or above the unit isoquant. The method minimized the sum of squared deviations from the observa-

---

*This account is based on Philip K. Porter and Gerald W. Skully, "Measuring Managerial Efficiency: The Case of Baseball," *Southern Economic Journal*, 48(3) (January 1982).

†This transformed production function has normalized output equal to 1, and the unit isoquant is $p = ah^\sigma$, where $a = \alpha^{1/(\beta-1)}$ and $\sigma = \beta/(\beta-1)$ is the substitution elasticity between pitching and hitting.

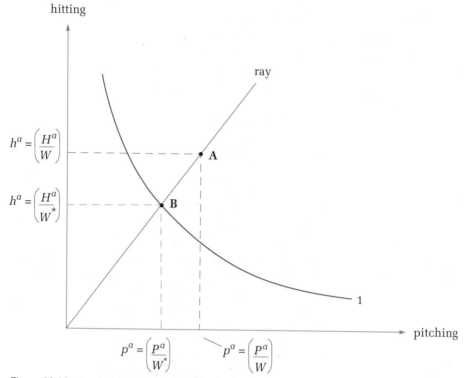

Figure 10.23 Managerial efficiency in baseball: The frontier unit isoquant represents the most efficient use of any input ratio along any ray. A manager attaining perfect efficiency of any input combination would attain a point like **B** along the unit isoquant. A less efficient manager would have to use a bundle like **A** to attain the same winning percentage.

tions to the isoquant along rays to the origin. In short, the unit isoquant was estimated as the frontier of all outcomes. Managers were then ranked by their average lifetime efficiency. Over the period of study, Earl Weaver's average performance was greatest (0.987). The second most efficient manager was Sparky Anderson (0.961). Walter Alston was third (0.945), and Billy Martin was tenth (0.912). Leo Durocher, who had 24 years of experience—more than any other manager in the sample—was twenty-fourth (0.856) out of the 28 managers ranked.

This study also reported an estimate on another type of production function, the annual efficiency by manager as a function of years of experience (Y) and a dummy variable (D). The dummy variable is $D = 0$ if the manager was with his original team, and $D = 1$ if the manager changed teams. The equation, estimated by least-squares regression, is

$$E = 0.8923 + 0.00828Y - 0.0033Y^2 - 0.0514D$$

This equation indicates that managerial performance increases at a decreasing rate, reaching a maximum of 94.4 percent after 12.5 years of experience. Lower efficiency is correlated with switching teams, but it is not clear whether the switch caused the lower efficiency or, the more likely possibility, lower efficiency caused the switch.

10.9 Technical Progress

Technical progress is technological change that leaves inputs more productive because better production techniques are developed. Graphically, the effect of technical progress can be illustrated on an isoquant diagram, where the isoquants are shifting toward the origin as technology changes. For any activity, fewer inputs are needed to produce any specified output.

One way to include technical progress is to represent the production function for some good X as

$$X_t = A(t)X(L, K)$$

where $A(t)$ represents the influence of technology. Frequently, the variable t is taken to be time. That is, the change in $A(t)$ as time passes, represents technical progress. We would expect that $\Delta A/\Delta t > 0$, so that the inputs become more productive in time. This form of technical progress is **neutral,** in that it affects all inputs equally. The influence of neutral technological change is illustrated by Figure 10.24. Technical progress implies that any given isoquant will shift toward the origin as fewer inputs are needed to produce that level of output. The form of technological change in this production function is said to be *neutral* because it leaves the slopes of isoquants constant along rays. We will see later that neutral technological change leaves the input proportions unchanged for any set of input prices because the $MRTS$ remains constant along each ray. Thus, this technological change is

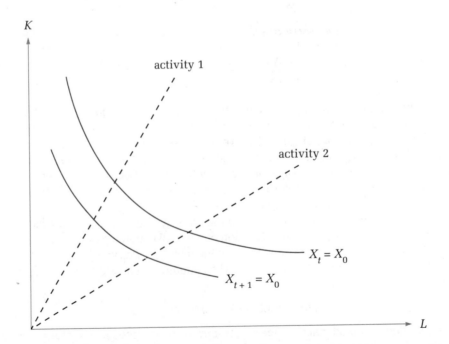

Figure 10.24 **Neutral technological change:** A change in technology between time t and $t + 1$ shifts the isoquant toward the origin. Fewer inputs are needed to produce the same level of output. The technological change is neutral if the isoquants remain parallel along activity rays.

neutral in its effect on input ratios.[15] Neutral technological change does not by itself cause one input to be substituted for another, and therefore is neutral in its effect in saving labor, capital, and other inputs.

Technical progress may not be neutral. When technical progress is **capital augmenting,** the production function may be written $X_t = X[L, A(t)K]$. Capital-augmenting technical progress tends to be labor saving as increasingly productive capital is substituted for labor. When technical progress is **labor augmenting,** the production function may be written $X_t = X[A(t)L, K]$. Labor-augmenting technical progress tends to be capital saving as increasingly productive labor is substituted for capital. Actually, all three types of technical progress can occur simultaneously.

The change in output with respect to time is $\Delta X/\Delta t$, and we expect that growth will be positive so that $\Delta X/\Delta t > 0$. If we divide this expression by X, we get

$$\frac{\Delta X/\Delta t}{X} = G_x$$

which is the geometric rate of growth of X per unit of time. It can be shown that[16]

$$G_x = G_A + \eta_L G_L + \eta_K G_K$$

where η_L and η_K are the elasticities of output with respect to the inputs L and K. An output elasticity of an input is given by the percentage of change in output divided by the percentage of change in the input. The terms G_L and G_K are the geometric rates of growth in L and K, and the term G_A is the geometric growth rate in technology. By rearranging the terms in the equation, we see that the rate of technical growth is

$$G_A = G_x - \eta_L G_L - \eta_K G_K$$

By broadly classifying inputs into labor and capital, R. M. Solow was able to calculate that the rate of growth in real output in the United States was about 2.75 percent per year between 1909 and 1949.[17] The growth in labor was 1.00 percent per year and the growth in capital was 1.75 percent per year. Solow's estimates of the elasticities of output with respect to L and K were 0.65 and 0.35. By substituting these values into the growth-rate formula, we obtain

$$G_A = 2.75 - 0.65(1.00) - 0.35(1.75) = 1.4875$$

Thus technology advanced at an approximate annual rate of 1.5 percent over the study period. More than half the growth in real output from 1909 to 1949 can be attributed to technical change rather than to growth in the factors of production.

Technical progress and the resulting shifts in the production function are not random; they are affected by the economic environment. Technical progress can be divided into three steps: invention, innovation, and the spread of innovation. *Invention* is the discovery

---

15. Actually, all marginal products increase by the same proportion.

16. See Walter Nicholson, *Microeconomic Theory: Basic Principles and Extensions,* 4th ed. (Dryden Press, 1989), ch. 10, pp. 293–297.

17. R. M. Solow, "Technical Change and the Aggregate Production Function," *Review of Economics and Statistics,* 39 (August 1957).

ECONOMIC SCENE: *Innovation in Japan and the United States*

We distinguish two types of innovation. **Product innovation** results in new and improved products, such as a color-fixing detergent or a faster computer chip. **Process innovation** results in new and improved production processes, such as employing robotics in production.

Interestingly, Japanese firms devote about two-thirds of their research-and-development budgets to process innovation and American firms only about one-third. Table 10.4 summarizes some recent evidence for 100 Japanese and American firms. The table lists the percentage of cost of developing and introducing a new product for each of six stages in innovation. The Japanese devoted almost twice as much of their budgets as the United States did to tooling and facilities, a category that includes manufacturing equipment. In contrast, the United States devoted almost twice as much as the Japanese did to marketing and startup.

American emphasis has been on innovating products rather than process, a trend most evident in industrial robotics. George C. Devol was an engineer who held one of the first patents on industrial robots. Devol's 1954 patent was sold in 1961, but American firms were slow to use robotics. In the meantime, robotics technology began to be transferred to Japan, which made improvements and reduced the cost of robotics. By 1983, the Japanese were the undisputed leaders in industrial robotics, both in using robots in production and selling them in the international market. Robotics is just one instance in which Americans have developed state-of-the-art products only to have them manufactured more cheaply by other countries.

American firms seem to emphasize finance, marketing, and pure research more than manufacturing. Jobs in manufacturing pay less than in those other areas. The best engineering talent has been drawn into research and design rather than production, and the best managerial talent has been drawn into finance and marketing rather than manufacturing. This balance contrasts sharply with such countries as Japan and Germany. Many observers believe that the United States must return to an emphasis on manufacturing if it is to regain its once dominant position.

Table 10.4 Distribution of Innovation Cost for 100 Firms, 1985

Stage of Innovation	Japan	United States
Applied research	14%	18%
Product development	7	8
Prototype or pilot plant	16	17
Tooling and facilities	44	23
Manufacturing startup	10	17
Marketing startup	8	17

Source: E. Mansfield, "Industrial Innovation in Japan and the United States," *Science* (September 30, 1988). Copyright 1972. Reprinted by permission of RAND.

of a new productive technique. *Innovation* is the first commercial application of the technique. The *spread of innovation* is the adoption and dispersion of the technology across the economy. All are influenced by the economic environment, and most are subject to some control.

Invention is never wholly accidental. Even Newton had to have the prerequisite knowledge to interpret the evidence when the fabled apple bounced off his head. Invention is related to existing knowledge and research. Hence, society can influence the rate of invention by education and research.

Innovation partly arises from the desire to reduce the costs of production. Highly competitive industries are more likely to adopt new technologies than industries insulated from competition. Generally, innovation's spread with time follows a sigmoid-shaped learning curve—innovation shows a slow initial rate of adoption followed by a period of rapid adoption that tapers off as the economy becomes saturated with the innovation. Innovation spreads as influenced by the costs and risks associated with adopting new technology as well as the attitudes of those who make the decisions. The big question is how the economic environment affects the rate at which innovation spreads.

Recent evidence on technological change and labor productivity indicates that the rate at which productivity is growing in private business has slowed. Consider these estimates:

Annual Rates of Growth in Private Business, 1948 to 1979, in Percentages

Period	1948–1957	1957–1968	1968–1973	1973–1976
Technological change	1.90	1.85	1.50	0.34
Labor productivity	3.11	2.76	2.31	0.85

Source: E. F. Denison, *Accounting for Slower Economic Growth: The United States in the 1970s* (Brookings Institution, 1979).

These statistics show a declining rate of growth in technical progress and in labor productivity. Other researchers argue that the slowdown is a myth and that U.S. productivity has been relatively constant in the postwar period.

Changes in productivity growth deeply interest business and society as a whole. What accounts for this decline? How can it be changed? Explanations have ranged from lagging innovation to conjectures that Americans have become lazy. Zvi Griliches reports lack of evidence that the recent decline in productivity can be blamed on a decline in research and development (R&D) expenditures.[18] Nadiri and Schankerman argue that only one-fourth of the slowdown from 1965 to 1973 and 1973 to 1978 can be attributed to changes in factor prices and R&D.[19] Christainsen and Haveman conclude that federal regulations

---

18. Z. Griliches, "R&D and the Production Slowdown," *American Economic Review,* 70(2) (May 1980).

19. M. I. Nadiri and M. A. Schankerman, "Technical Change, Returns to Scale, and the Production Slowdown," *American Economic Review,* 71(2) (May 1981).

are responsible for 12 to 21 percent of the slowed growth in labor productivity in U.S. manufacturing during 1973 to 1977 compared to 1959 to 1965, and decreases in the capital-to-labor ratio are responsible for 15 percent of the slowdown.[20] Significantly, D. M. Gordon concludes that 87.5 percent of the slowdown between 1954 to 1973 and 1974 to 1978 was caused by decreases in effective bureaucratic control at the corporate level.[21] The suggestion is that ineffective management of resources may be mostly responsible for the slowdown in real growth in the U.S. economy.

20. G. B. Christainsen and R. H. Haveman, "Public Regulations and the Slowdown in Productivity Growth," *American Economic Review,* 71(2) (May 1981).

21. David M. Gordon, "Capital-Labor Conflict and the Productivity Slowdown," *American Economic Review,* 71(2) (May 1981).

GLOBAL PERSPECTIVE: *Soviet Production*

A production function for Soviet industry has been estimated using data from 1955 through 1969.* After several versions of the constant elasticity of substitution (CES) function were estimated, the best exhibited constant returns to scale and included three inputs: labor (L), capital (K), and raw materials (R):

$$X = \alpha e^{\beta_0 t}[\beta_1 L^{-\rho} + \beta_2 K^{-\rho} + \beta_3 R^{-\rho}]^{-1/\rho}$$

where $\beta_0 > 0$, $\beta_1 \geq 0$, $\beta_2 \geq 0$, $\beta_3 = 1 - \beta_1 - \beta_2$, $0 \leq \beta_1 + \beta_2 \leq 1$ and $\rho \geq -1$. The parameter ρ is called the *substitution parameter* because it is related to the (pairwise) elasticity of input substitution σ by this equation:

$$\sigma = 1/(\rho + 1)$$

In this function the term $e^{\beta_0 t}$ allows for neutral technological change over time t, β_0 measures a constant rate of increase in the logarithm of output over time, and e denotes an exponential.

The dependent variable X is measured by gross output in year t deflated by the Soviet price index in industry with 1960 as the base year. Capital is measured as average fixed assets in industry in constant prices. Likewise, raw-material purchases are deflated to real terms. Labor is measured as annual worker hours. A nonlinear regression procedure generated these parameter estimates:

$$\hat{\beta}_0 = 0.0408$$
$$\hat{\beta}_1 = 0.6798$$
$$\hat{\beta}_2 = 0.0210$$
$$\hat{\beta}_3 = 0.2992$$
$$\hat{\sigma} = 0.2771$$

Common statistical tests indicated that the only coefficient not statistically different from zero was that for capital. The proportion of the variation in the dependent variable explained by these estimates was 0.9994, a very good overall fit.

* Padma Desai, "The Production Function and Technological Change in Postwar Soviet Industry: A Reexamination," *American Economic Review* (June 1976).

Several inferences can be drawn from these results. First, the CES production function with constant returns to scale adequately represented Soviet industry between 1955 and 1969. Second, an estimated elasticity of substitution of approximately 0.28 for each pair of inputs is significantly less than unity. The inputs thus were not close substitutes. Third, the technological-change parameter (β_0), estimated to be 0.0408, is greater than the value 0.023 for American manufacturing over a comparable period. The indicated rate of technological change is about 4 percent, nearly twice the American growth rate over the same period. This figure is consistent with the view that Soviet technology was "catching up." At the same time the low substitution elasticity, along with labor scarcity in the Soviet economy, implies that their rate of growth will begin to slow beyond the time frame of the study. This prediction conforms to what has happened in the Soviet economy since the early 1970s.[†] The recent stagnation was partly caused by their inability to develop new technology. It is likely, however, that lack of effective incentives to achieve production efficiency contributed more to that stagnation.

In a separate study, production functions for five major branches of Soviet industry and pooled data from 1961, 1970, and 1974 were used to estimate CES production functions for the fuel industry, machine building and metal working, chemicals, light industry, and food processing. In addition, data from 1961–1974 and 1975–1987 periods were used to estimate aggregate CES functions for total industry.[‡] Only two factor inputs were used in this study, employment and capital stock, along with a time trend. The estimated equations suggest constant to slight decreasing returns to scale in the machine building and metal working, chemicals, and light industry branches. Significant decreasing returns to scale were evident in food processing, and significant increasing returns to scale were evident in the fuel industry. The estimated returns to scale were nearly equal to those in similar American branches. This finding implies that the degree of returns to scale in an industry is mainly independent of the prevailing economic system and is chiefly determined by technology—a result that we would expect.

This study also supports the appropriateness of using the CES specification for estimation because the estimates were all quite precise according to standard statistical tests. The estimated elasticities of substitution between labor and capital ranged from a high of 1.01 in machine building and metal working to a low of 0.68 in food processing. These are somewhat higher than the estimates from the other study in which three inputs were used. Nevertheless, these relatively low elasticities, especially in food processing, indicate likely slow growth in sectors of the Soviet economy that have shortages of labor.

In the study of separate branches, the estimated rate of technical progress was fastest at 3.77 percent in machine building and metal working. This branch of Soviet industry is the most progressive, and it includes the production of semiconductors, integrated circuits, optical-electronics, communications equipment, and computers. When the aggregated data for the two periods 1961–1974 and 1975–1987 were used, the estimated rate of technical progress was 2.8 percent for the earlier period falling to -0.3 percent for the later period. This confirms our previous conclusion that the Soviet economy had stagnated during the 1980s.

[†]See Gur Ofer, "Soviet Economic Growth: 1928–1985," *Journal of Economic Literature*, 25(4) (December 1987).

[‡]Erkin Bairam, "Elasticity of Substitution, Technical Progress and Returns to Scale in Branches of Soviet Industry: A New CES Production Function Approach," *Journal of Applied Econometrics*, 6(1) (January-March 1991).

10.10 A Multiproduct Firm

Many firms produce more than one product at one plant. An office-furniture manufacturing plant may produce desks, tables, chairs, and files at the same facility, and an automobile plant may produce both cars and trucks. Managers of such production facilities must make decisions about how to use available stocks of the factors of production. One objective is to allocate inputs among competing uses in the most technologically efficient way.

Take Steelcase, Inc., the world's largest producer of steel office furniture. In its beginning, this Grand Rapids, Michigan, company produced steel safes, and that's where the company got its name. Today Steelcase produces desks, tables, files, and chairs in many styles. Modular workstations and ergonomic posture chairs are among its more recent products.

In the early 1960s, Steelcase responded to changing market demand by locating an assembly plant in southern California not far from Disneyland. Not only was demand increasing in the western part of the United States, it was increasing in the Pacific-rim countries and South America. Steelcase was also beginning to import more and more cold-rolled and sheet steel from Japan. Prefabricated parts and some raw materials were shipped by rail to California from the main plant in Michigan. Local suppliers were found to provide other raw materials and parts.

In the early 1970s, Steelcase implemented a materials-requirement planning system to project the need for parts and raw materials for assembling final products. Weekly production schedules based on customers' orders and planned replenishment of product inventories are disaggregated to piece parts and other material needed to meet planned production. Combined with a just-in-time program for production and inventory control, the company strove to minimize its need for inventories and to eliminate production delays. Ideally, customer orders are filled as demanded, and any slack in production capacity is used to replenish inventory.

Once the required stocks of the factors of production are on hand, the problem is to make most efficient use of those inputs. Production to meet customers' orders is set first, and then other available input stocks are allocated to producing final goods for inventory and piece parts to be used later. That is, the production manager needs to know how to allocate available inputs to achieve the production targets that will satisfy customers' orders while maximizing production of other goods.

To illustrate how such decisions can be made, let's simplify by considering only two goods and two inputs. Good X might be production of desks and good Y might be production of chairs. Producing each good requires two inputs, L and K. The labor and capital allocated to producing X are denoted L_X and K_X. Likewise, the labor and capital allocated to producing Y are denoted L_Y and K_Y. Given technology, the isoquants for good X can be identified by finding the allocations of labor and capital where the production function $X = X(L_X, K_X)$ generates fixed levels of output. Similarly, isoquants for Y can be identified for fixed levels of $Y = Y(L_Y, K_Y)$. Production efficiency occurs when a fixed quantity of resources has been allocated so that production of one good cannot be increased without decreasing production of the other good.

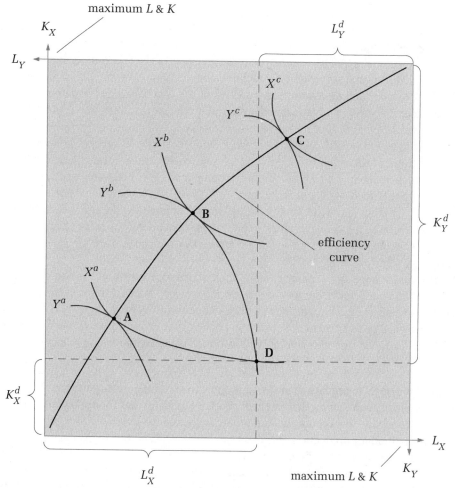

Figure 10.25 **Efficient production of two products with two inputs:** The Edgeworth-Bowley box is constructed by superimposing the two isoquant maps so that their axes intersect at the maximum amounts of the two inputs L and K. Production efficiency occurs along the curve where the X isoquants are tangent to the Y isoquants. That is, technological efficiency in joint production requires that the $MRTS$ in producing X be equal to the $MRTS$ in producing Y. The manager should allocate inputs so that the ratios of marginal products among all inputs are the same in all uses.

This concept of production efficiency can be illustrated by an Edgeworth-Bowley box diagram, analogous to the Edgeworth box used in the context of bilateral pure exchange. Now, however, we are analyzing the production of two goods from two inputs rather than the generation of welfare from the consumption of two goods.

Figure 10.25 illustrates the construction of an **Edgeworth-Bowley box.** The production function for good X has an origin in the lower left-hand corner and is described by the X isoquants. The production function for good Y has an origin in the upper right-hand corner and is described by the Y isoquants. The axes of the two isoquant diagrams intersect at the points of total available stocks of L and K. Hence, the width of the box is determined by the stock of labor services and the height of the box is determined by the stock of available capital services. Each point inside the box represents an allocation of the total stocks of labor and capital to the production of the two goods. For instance, at point **D**, L_X^d units of L and K_X^d units of K are allocated to producing X. Likewise, at point **D**, L_Y^d units of L and K_Y^d units of K are allocated to producing Y.

At **D**, the allocation of L and K results in X^a units of X and Y^b units of Y being produced. But this allocation is not efficient because reallocation of the inputs to point **A** results in an increase in Y to Y^a and X remains constant at X^a. Likewise, reallocation of the inputs from **D** to **B** results in an increase in X to X^b, and Y remains constant at Y^b. Notice that at a point like **A, B,** or **C,** any reallocation of inputs will cause a decrease in production of one of the goods in order to increase production of the other good. Thus, efficient allocations of L and K are identified where the X isoquants are tangent to the Y isoquants.

The efficient allocations of inputs identify an **efficiency curve** in the two-input case. The firm is on its efficiency curve when producing two goods when the isoquants are tangent to one another. The tangency of isoquants in the Edgeworth-Bowley box implies that the marginal rate of technical substitution of labor for capital in producing X must be equal to the marginal rate of technical substitution of labor for capital in producing Y,

$$MRTS_X = MRTS_Y$$

Because the *MRTS* in producing any good is equal to the ratio of marginal products, production efficiency requires that the firm allocate inputs so that the ratio of marginal products, MP_L/MP_K, will be the same in producing X and Y.

This condition for production efficiency can be generalized to the many-inputs, many-outputs case. A manager will be optimizing the use of inputs in the most technologically efficient way when inputs are allocated among alternative uses so that the ratios of marginal products of all inputs are equal in producing every good. That the concept of the marginal rate of technical substitution is important is clear. Managers must have some idea of the labor time required to substitute for machine time used to produce a good without reducing output. This knowledge is essential for the efficient operation of a multiproduct plant.[22]

The consequences of allocative efficiency and inefficiency of inputs can be explored with a **production possibilities curve** which plots the output combinations resulting from the efficient use of inputs as the firm moves along its efficiency curve. Figure 10.26 illustrates how the production possibilities curve is constructed from the information in

---

22. Failure to achieve allocative efficiency in production has been called "*X*-inefficiency." See Harvey Leibenstein, "Allocative Efficiency vs. X-Efficiency," *American Economic Review,* 56(3) (June 1966). Inefficient uses of available inputs cause the cost of producing any amount of a good to be greater than necessary.

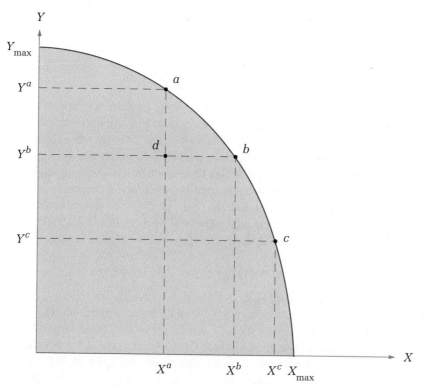

Figure 10.26 **Production possibilities in the two-product case:** In the two-good case, production possibilities are represented by the shaded area. Given fixed stocks of inputs, the production possibilities curve is the frontier of the set of production possibilities. All output combinations along the curve allocate the inputs between the two uses to achieve production efficiency.

Figure 10.25. At input allocation **A** on the efficiency curve, the production levels of the two goods are X^a and Y^a. Those amounts are plotted in Figure 10.26. Similarly, the production levels of the two goods at **B** and **C** along the efficiency curve of Figure 10.25 are plotted in Figure 10.26. When all such efficient production possibilities are plotted, the result is the production-possibilities curve. Other output combinations like X^a and Y^b at **D** in Figure 10.25 are feasible, but such combinations do not lie on the efficiency curve. Thus, the input allocation **D** results in output levels X^a and Y^b at point d in Figure 10.26. As you see, the output combination at d lies below the production possibilities curve. Such output levels are feasible but are not efficient.

For a firm like Steelcase to achieve its maximum production possibilities, it must be able to judge the marginal products of all inputs for all outputs. The firm therefore employs industrial engineers and other specialists to measure the productivity of inputs, particularly labor time, to ensure that inputs are being used in the most technologically efficient way.

The production possibilities curve is also called a **transformation** curve. Recall from Chapter 2 that the marginal rate of transformation of good X from good Y, when all inputs are being used efficiently, is

$$MRT_{XY} = -\frac{\Delta Y}{\Delta X}$$

The "bulge" in the production possibilities curve reflects an increasing opportunity cost for producing more X. That is, increasingly larger reductions in Y are necessary to produce X as the firm moves along the production possibilities curve. Two reasons explain the bulge in the production possibilities curve. The most pervasive reason is the different input ratios required by the different production functions when inputs are being used efficiently, but decreasing returns to scale can also contribute to the bulge. In contrast, if each good is produced under constant returns to scale and each production function uses inputs in equal proportions, then the transformation curve will be a straight line. Alternatively, significant increasing returns to scale might cause the curve to bulge inward.

10.11 Linear Programming and Efficiency*

Linear programming (LP) is a practical technique for solving any optimization problem that has a linear objective function with linear constraints. Originally developed by the Russian mathematician L. V. Kantorovich in 1939, and extended by U.S. mathematician George Dantzig in 1947 for the U.S. Air Force, LP has found many applications.[23] The objective function to be maximized or minimized might be revenue or net revenue, cost or expenditure, output or a variable input. Constraints may be equality or inequality constraints that usually define how inputs must be combined to transform them into an output according to the available technology. Therefore, LP can be applied naturally to problems where the underlying technology is linear. But LP can be extended to other problems as well. A smooth isoquant may be approximated by a *piecewise linear relation* and then fitted into the LP mold. As we proceed, we will have several occasions to apply LP to various important problems in managerial economics. In this chapter, however, we focus on describing the problem of *technological efficiency* as an LP problem.

Techniques for finding the optimal solution to an LP problem usually involve systematically searching for the optimal solution from a finite set of feasible solutions by some iterative technique. One such technique is the **simplex** method. Computers are usually used because computations can be quite tedious. Computer programs to find LP solutions are now so common that LP has become an important management tool. Our interest, however, is in the economic interpretation of LP problems and their solutions rather than the solution method. Thus, we concentrate on LP problems that can be solved graphically.

The most direct way to illustrate is by an explicit example. Consider a firm producing one good from two production activities under a linear technology. Two inputs are available

---

*This section is optional and may be skipped without loss of continuity.

23. George B. Dantzig, *Linear Programming and Extensions* (Princeton University Press, 1963).

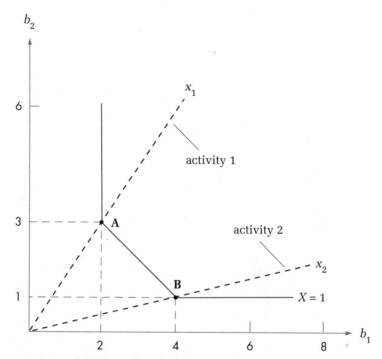

Figure 10.27 **A linear technology:** This production function has two inputs b_1 and b_2 and two activities. Activity 1 requires that $b_2/b_1 = 3/2$. Activity 2 requires that $b_2/b_1 = 1/4$. The $X = 1$ isoquant shows the combinations of b_1 and b_2 that can be used to produce one unit of output.

in fixed amounts b_1 and b_2. The output produced by activity 1 is x_1, and the output produced by activity 2 is x_2. Total output is $x_1 + x_2 = X$.

Suppose each unit of x_1 produced requires 2 units of b_1 and 3 units of b_2. Activity 1 thus requires that the ratio of b_2 to b_1 be 3/2, as shown in Figure 10.27. Suppose the available technology also requires that each unit of x_2 produced requires 4 units of b_1 and 1 unit of b_2. Thus, activity 2 requires that the ratio of b_2 to b_1 be 1/4, as shown in Figure 10.27. It is easy to see that the firm could produce $X = 1$ unit of output if it allocated 2 units of b_1 and 3 units of b_2 (bundle **A**) to producing x_1. The firm could produce $X = 1$ unit of output if it allocated 1 unit of b_1 and 4 units of b_2 (bundle **B**) to producing x_2. Thus, bundles **A** and **B** become the vertices of the unit isoquant, $X = 1$. Any other isoquant can now be identified because constant returns to scale occur under a linear technology.

Suppose $b_1 = 40$ and $b_2 = 30$. The firm can use less by setting aside extra units of each input, but it cannot use more. The objective is to find the isoquant furthest from the origin without using more than 40 units of b_1 or more than 30 units of b_2. The LP problem for this example is:

$$\begin{aligned} \text{maximize} \quad & x_1 + x_2 = X \\ \text{subject to} \quad & 2x_1 + 4x_2 \le 40 \\ & 3x_1 + x_2 \le 30 \\ \text{and} \quad & x_1 \ge 0, \, x_2 \ge 0 \end{aligned}$$

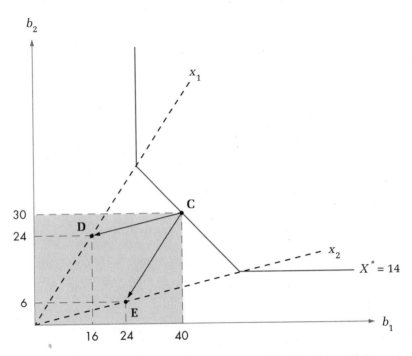

Figure 10.28 **Optimal output and resource allocation:** Under the linear technology with $2x_1 + 4x_2 \le 40$ and $3x_1 + x_2 \le 30$, the maximum level of output is $X^* = 14$. The shaded area represents feasible input allocations. The available bundle **C** should be allocated as **D** to activity 1 and **E** to activity 2 in order to use the inputs in the most technologically efficient way.

The two nonnegativity constraints are required to rule out negative production quantities for each activity. Figure 10.28 illustrates the feasible input allocations as the shaded area determined by $b_1 \le 40$ and $b_2 \le 30$. The firm's objective is to maximize $x_1 + x_2 = X$. It turns out that maximum output, denoted by X^*, is $X^* = 14$. This level of output can be identified from the geometry of this problem because of the constant returns to scale— the $X^* = 14$ isoquant is 14 times as far from the origin as the $X = 1$ isoquant. To achieve this level of output, 16 units of b_1 and 24 units of b_2 must be allocated to activity 1 to produce $x_1 = 8$, and 24 units of b_1 and 6 units of b_2 must be allocated to activity 2 to produce $x_2 = 6$. But how do you find x_1^* and x_2^*? Even finding x_1^* and x_2^* from a graph like Figure 10.28 is awkward.

The answers can be found by solving the LP problem directly. Graphically, the solution is shown in Figure 10.29. First, the boundary equations for both resource constraints are plotted. These constraints, along with the nonnegativity constraints, identify the feasible combinations of x_1 and x_2, shown as the shaded region. The outer edge of this region is the frontier of the production possibilities set. Second, the objective function is plotted for any feasible combination of x_1 and x_2, usually starting at $x_1 = 0$ and $x_2 = 0$ for a maximization problem. The $X = 0$ isoquant is shown in Figure 10.29. This objective function can be pushed outward parallel to itself as long as at least one point remains in the feasible set. As you can see in Figure 10.29, that occurs at the corner point

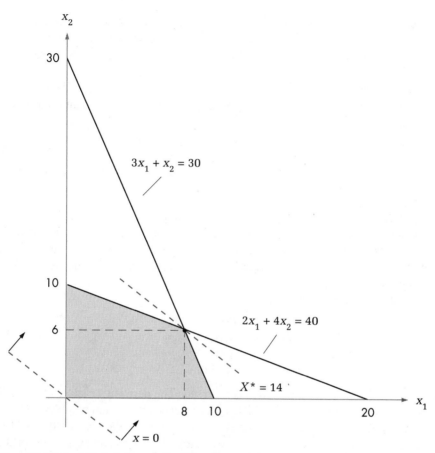

Figure 10.29 **A graphical solution to an LP problem:** To maximize $x_1 + x_2 = X$ subject to the constraints:

$$2x_1 + 4x_2 \leq 40$$
$$3x_1 + \ x_2 \leq 30$$

along with nonnegativity constraints for x_1 and x_2, the solution is $x_1 = 8$ and $x_2 = 6$, yielding $X^* = 14$.

$x_1 = 8$ and $x_2 = 6$, where the boundary equations intersect. Activity 1 produces $x_1 = 8$ units of X and activity 2 produces $x_2 = 6$ units of X.[24]

Now that we have found x_1^* and x_2^*, how do we allocate the available resources b_1 and b_2 to the two activities? Well, looking back at Figure 10.28, activity 1 requires $2x_1^* = 16$ units of b_1 and $3x_1^* = 24$ units of b_2. Similarly, activity 2 requires $4x_2^* = 24$ units of b_1 and $x_2^* = 6$ units of b_2. These are the technologically efficient allocations that maximize output under the assumed linear technology.

---

24. The simplex method works by systematically comparing the results of one feasible corner point to the next adjacent feasible corner point. The method always moves toward the optimal solution. The search will stop in a finite number of steps because the number of feasible corner points is finite.

Of course, graphical solutions are often impractical if not impossible. Computer-based solutions, however, are easy once the problem has been formulated correctly. The challenge is to formulate it correctly and then, after finding a solution, to interpret the results.

Every LP problem has a corresponding LP problem called its **dual.** The original LP problem is referred to as the **primal.** For the two-activity, two-constraint problem the primal was:

$$\text{maximize} \quad c_1 x_1 + c_2 x_2 = X$$
$$\text{subject to} \quad a_{11} x_1 + a_{12} x_2 \leq b_1$$
$$a_{21} x_1 + a_{22} x_2 \leq b_2$$
$$\text{and} \quad x_1 \geq 0, x_2 \geq 0$$

where $c_1 = 1$, $c_2 = 1$, $a_{11} = 2$, $a_{12} = 4$, $b_1 = 40$, $a_{21} = 3$, $a_{22} = 1$, and $b_2 = 30$. The x_j are the decision variables of this primal problem. The c_j measure the change in X that results from a unit increase in each x_j. The b_i are the quantities of the resources that are available for allocation. Each technological coefficient a_{ij} measures the quantity of b_i that is required by each unit of x_j.

The dual to this primal problem is:

$$\text{minimize} \quad b_1 y_1 + b_2 y_2 = W$$
$$\text{subject to} \quad a_{11} y_1 + a_{21} y_2 \geq c_1$$
$$a_{12} y_1 + a_{22} y_2 \geq c_2$$
$$\text{and} \quad y_1 \geq 0, y_2 \geq 0$$

Notice that the direction of optimization is reversed. The decision variables of the dual, the y_i, are called **dual variables,** multipliers, or shadow prices. You will be able to see why in a moment. The coefficients in the objective function of the dual are the right-hand-side values of the constraints of the primal. Similarly, the right-hand-side values of the dual constraints are the objective function coefficients from the primal. The a_{ij} coefficients of the primal become the a_{ji} coefficients of the dual. For each "less than or equal to" constraint in the primal, the corresponding dual variable must have a nonnegativity constraint. For each nonnegativity constraint in the primal, the corresponding constraint in the dual must be a "greater than or equal to" constraint.

A basic theorem of linear programming states that a solution to the primal LP problem exists if and only if its dual LP problem has a solution. Moreover, the optimal values of their objective functions are the same, $X^* = W^*$. Each dual variable is important because it measures the marginal contribution to the primal's objective due to a one-unit increase in the right-hand side of its corresponding constraint,

$$\frac{\Delta X^*}{\Delta b_i} = y_i^*$$

Thus, the dual variable y_i measures the marginal productivity of resource b_i. Dual variables may be referred to as **shadow prices** because they measure the real value or marginal contribution of each resource to the objective. Dual variables may be referred to as **multipliers** because, at the optimum, when the available resources are multiplied by their respective dual variables, the sum of those products yields the optimum value of the LP problem.

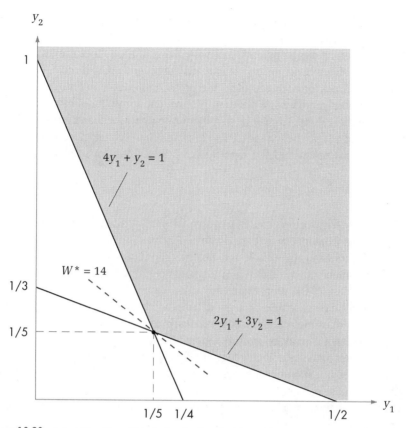

Figure 10.30 **A dual-LP problem:** This is the dual to the LP problem of Figure 10.28. Notice that the optimal value $W^* = 14$ of the dual is equal to the optimal value $X^* = 14$ of its primal. The optimal values of the dual variables $y_1^* = 1/5$ and $y_2^* = 1/5$ measure the marginal products of resources b_1 and b_2 of the primal.

Let's look at the dual to the numerical LP example of this section:

$$\begin{aligned} \text{minimize} \quad & 40y_1 + 30y_2 = W \\ \text{subject to} \quad & 2y_1 + 3y_2 \geq 1 \\ & 4y_1 + 1y_2 \geq 1 \\ \text{and} \quad & y_1 \geq 0, \ y_2 \geq 0 \end{aligned}$$

The boundary equations and the feasible set are illustrated in Figure 10.30. The feasible set is shaded. Because this dual is a minimization problem, the objective function is shifted as close to the origin as feasible. The optimal values of the dual variables are $y_1^* = 1/5$ and $y_2^* = 1/5$. When multiplied by the resource levels $b_1 = 40$ and $b_2 = 30$, the dual variables yield

$$40y_1^* + 30y_2^* = 14$$

Thus, the primal and dual have the same optimal values for their objective functions. The dual variables are the marginal products of the inputs, and so an extra unit of b_1 would increase X^* by $y_1^* = 1/5$ unit approximately. Likewise, an extra unit of b_2 would increase

X^* by $y_2^* = 1/5$ unit approximately. This firm would be willing to pay as much as 1/5 the value of one unit of X to obtain an extra unit of b_1 or b_2.

Linear programming can be extended in many ways. If the c_j coefficients are equal to output price, the problem becomes one of maximizing revenue. Or, if the c_j measure the net contribution to profit for each unit of x_j, the problem is converted into one of maximizing profit. If each x_j represents a different product and c_j measures its contribution to net revenue, then the LP problem is one of maximizing profit for a multiproduct firm. Activity analysis and LP can be extended also to multiplant technologies. The availability of computer programs has made LP a valuable and practical tool for many managerial decisions.

Summary

A production activity, or process, is the technological relationship between the production of a good from inputs that are combined in fixed proportions. The collection of all the activities describes the available technology. The technologically feasible set of all input and output combinations is called a production set. The production function describes the boundary of the production set.

An activity can be represented by a ray determined by a fixed input ratio. If inputs are substitutable, more than one activity will be available to the firm. When activities are independent, the activities may be operated simultaneously without affecting the production rates of other activities. Technological efficiency of an activity means that no other activities alone or in combination can produce the same level of output by using fewer inputs. Technologically inefficient activities are said to be dominated by technologically efficient activities. The two basic production models are the linear model and the smooth model.

The linear model is described by a finite number of technologically efficient activities. Isoquants in the linear model are composed of linear segments between the activity rays. Inputs are combined along one ray or between adjacent rays. The linear segments of isoquants between rays remain parallel to each other. The linear model is always characterized by constant returns to scale.

The smooth model is described by an infinite number of technologically efficient activities. Inputs are smoothly and continuously substitutable, and isoquants are convex. The marginal rate of technical substitution between two inputs, as measured by the negative of the slope of the isoquant, diminishes smoothly as one input is substituted for another along the isoquant. The smooth model may be subject to decreasing, constant, or increasing returns to scale.

The elasticity of substitution is defined as the percentage change in the input ratio divided by the percentage change in the marginal rate of technical substitution. The substitution elasticity characterizes the curvature of the isoquants. When the elasticity of substitution is zero, the inputs are perfect complements. When the elasticity of substitution equals infinity, the inputs are perfect substitutes. Most production functions have isoquants where the substitution elasticities between inputs lie somewhere between zero and infinity.

In the short run at least one input is fixed so that input proportions must vary as output varies. The average product of an input is defined as the total product divided by the quantity of the input. Marginal product of an input is the change in total product divided by the incremental change in the input as other inputs are held constant. The law of diminishing returns, also known as the law of variable proportions, says that diminishing productivity of a variable input will eventually occur as successive increases of that input are combined with at least one fixed input. Thus, the average and marginal products of any input will fall eventually as output increases in the short run.

The total product curve is a short-run production function and expresses output as a function of one variable input. Three potential stages in production can be identified along a total product curve. Stage I has increasing average productivity of the variable input. Stage II has diminishing average productivity and positive marginal productivity of the variable input. Stage III has zero or negative marginal productivity of the variable input. Not every total product curve has all three stages, but all total product curves have a stage II somewhere. Any stage III is technologically inefficient because of the zero or negative marginal product. Thus, all efficient production will take place within the economic region determined by nonnegative marginal products of all inputs. Within the economic region, the technical rate of substitution equals the ratio of marginal products.

In multiplant firms, management will maximize output by allocating a variable input so that its marginal product is the same in all uses. Management will be using inputs in the most technologically efficient way when the technical rate of substitution among all inputs is the same in the production of all goods. In this way the firm will produce along its transformation curve, the frontier of the production possibilities set.

The marginal rate of transformation measures the cost of producing more of one good in terms of another good. The marginal rate of transformation can be measured by the negative of the slope of the production possibilities curve. A diminishing marginal rate of transformation is expected when input proportions are different in the production of the two goods. Decreasing returns to scale can also contribute to the characteristic bulge in the transformation curve.

The powerful optimizing tool called linear programming can be applied when the technology is linear. Every linear programming problem, the primal, has a related linear programming problem, its dual. The dual to the dual is the primal. The dual variables are called multipliers or shadow prices, and their economic interpretation makes them marginal values because they measure the change in the optimal value of the primal's objective function given a one-unit increase in the right-hand side of the constraint corresponding to the dual variable. Linear programming has many practical and theoretical applications that are relevant to managerial decision making and economic analysis.

Further Readings

For a general presentation of production in the theory of the firm, see

- Arthur A. Thompson, Jr., *Economics of the Firm: Theory and Practice,* 4th ed. (Prentice-Hall, 1985).

The role of technology is pursued in these publications:

- Robert M. Solow, "Technical Change and the Aggregate Production Function," *Review of Economics and Statistics* (August 1957).
- Kenneth J. Arrow, "The Economic Implications of Learning by Doing," *Review of Economic Studies,* 29 (June 1963).
- Devendra Sahal, *Patterns of Technological Innovation* (Addison-Wesley, 1981).

Solow is another recipient of the Nobel Prize in Economics—mostly because of his work in analyzing the role of technological change in economic growth.

For more applications of production functions, see

- P. H. Douglas, "Are There Laws of Production?" *American Economic Review,* 38 (March 1948).
- George J. Stigler, "The Economics of Scale," *Journal of Law and Economics,* 1 (October 1958).
- K. J. Arrow, H. B. Chenery, B. S. Minhas, and R. M. Solow, "Capital-Labor Substitution and Economic Efficiency," *Review of Economics and Statistics* (August 1961).
- A. Zellner, J. Kmenta, and J. Dreze, "Specification and Estimation of Cobb-Douglas Production Function Models," *Econometrica* (October 1966).

The seminal work on linear programming was

- George B. Dantzig, *Linear Programming and Extensions* (Princeton University Press, 1963).

For two easier articles on using LP in economic analysis, see

- Robert Dorfman, "Mathematical, or Linear Programming: A Mathematical Approach," *American Economic Review,* 43 (December 1953).
- William J. Baumol, "Activity Analysis in One Lesson," *American Economic Review,* 48 (December 1958).

The next book demonstrates the widely varied LP applications in the theory of the firm as well as the theory of consumer choice:

- Daniel C. Vandermeulen, *Linear Economic Theory* (Prentice-Hall, 1971).

Practice Problems

1. Compare the indifference curves of consumer preference to the isoquants of production transformations. How are they similar and how do they differ?
2. Determine which of these production functions have increasing, constant, or decreasing returns to scale:
   (a) $X = 5L + 20K + 4R$
   (b) $X = L^{0.25}K^{0.75}$
   (c) $X = 0.25L^{0.3}K^{0.6}R^{0.2}$
3. Suppose b_1 is table tops, b_2 is end panels, b_3 is back panels, and b_4 is legs. Ignoring other inputs, write the equation for the production function for assembling these parts into tables.

4. Sketch the $X = 1$ isoquant for each of these production functions:
   (a) $X = \sqrt{LK}$ (b) $X = LK^2$
   (c) $X = L + K$ (d) $X = \text{minimum}[L, K]$

   Then, for each production function, comment on: diminishing marginal rate of technical substitution (convexity); diminishing returns to inputs (the law of variable proportions); and returns to scale.

5. Gathering mushrooms in a forest requires only labor input. The number of mushrooms gathered per hour is given by

$$X = 100\sqrt{L}$$

   where L is labor per hour:
   (a) Graph this production function.
   (b) What is the average product of labor?
   (c) The marginal product of labor is

$$MP_L = \frac{\Delta X}{\Delta L} = \frac{50}{\sqrt{L}}$$

   Graph the average product and marginal product curve on the same graph.

6. For the Cobb-Douglas production function

$$X = \alpha L^\beta K^{(1-\beta)}$$

   with MRTS given by

$$MRTS = \frac{\beta}{1-\beta}\left(\frac{K}{L}\right)$$

   Show that the elasticity of input substitution is $\sigma = 1$.

7. Draw at least three activity rays for a linear model, then show how a short-run total product curve is found from an isoquant map.

8. Draw a series of isoquants for the smooth model under an assumption of free disposal. Hold one input constant and illustrate how the TP curve becomes horizontal when the MP of a variable input reaches zero.

9. Construct a smooth TP curve that has all three stages of production. Identify the inflection point where MP is at a maximum. Identify the point where $AP = MP$. Identify the point where $MP = 0$. Graph the corresponding AP and MP curves and identify the stages of production.

10. Given the production function $X = \sqrt{LK}$ in a situation where $K = 4$:
    (a) Graph the TP curve.
    (b) Graph the AP and MP curves.
    (c) Identify stage II.

11. If a variable input is used beyond the point on a TP curve where diminishing productivity sets in, does this usage indicate an inefficient use of the input? Does this description hold true over the whole range of the variable input?

12. Can average product be rising while marginal product is falling? Explain.

13. Explain the differences in these four principles:
    (a) Diminishing returns
    (b) Decreasing returns to scale
    (c) Diminishing rate of technical substitution
    (d) Diminishing rate of product transformation

14. Suppose labor, capital, and energy inputs must be combined in fixed proportions. Will the returns to scale therefore be constant? Explain.

15. In a study of Indian manufacturing industries, V. N. Murti and V. K. Sastri ("Production Functions for Indian Industry," *Econometrica* [April 1957]) estimated production functions for two industries. They specified Cobb-Douglas type functions for output (Q) as a log-linear function of labor (L) and capital (K),

$$\ln Q = \beta_0 + \beta_1 \ln L + \beta_2 \ln K + \varepsilon$$

where ε is a random error term. These estimates were obtained for two industries (standard errors in parentheses):

Industry	β_0	β_1	β_2	R^2
Cotton ($N = 125$):	0.97	0.92 (0.03)	0.12 (0.04)	0.98
Sugar ($N = 26$):	2.70	0.59 (0.14)	0.33 (0.17)	0.80

Does a log-linear function seem justified in this case? What economic significance does the sum of the estimated coefficients β_1 and β_2 have?

16. In a study of Bell Canada (A. R. Dobell et al., "Telephone Communications in Canada," *Bell Journal of Economics and Management Science* [Spring 1972]) this production function was estimated

$$V = 0.56L^{0.705}K^{0.405}T^{0.010}$$

where V is the value added ($1,000), L is labor-hours (millions), K is net capital stock ($1,000), and T is a proxy for technological change (measured as the percentage of toll calls dialed by the customer). All coefficients were statistically significant, and the coefficient of determination was $R^2 = 0.998$:
   (a) Does this production function exhibit increasing, constant, or decreasing returns to scale? How can you tell?
   (b) Is this function characterized by diminishing marginal productivity for labor and capital?

17. Suppose you could use two Cobb-Douglas production functions (1 and 2) to produce the same good:

$$Q_1 = L_1^{2/3}K_1^{1/3} \qquad Q_2 = L_2^{1/2}K_2^{1/2}$$

If you have 100 units of capital and 105 units of labor, demonstrate that $L_1 = 67$, $K_1 = 47$, $L_2 = 38$, and $K_2 = 53$ will maximize output. Show your work.

18. Suppose a firm produces two goods, X and Y, using two inputs, L and K. If the marginal rate of technical substitution of capital for labor is currently such that $MRTS_X > MRTS_Y$, explain how the firm can reallocate inputs to increase the production of one or both goods.

19. Show that the production possibilities curve is a straight line for a firm producing two goods with two inputs under constant returns to scale if both production functions use the same factor intensities.

20. Show that the production possibilities curve has the characteristic bulge under decreasing returns to scale even if the factor intensities are the same in producing two goods.

21. For a firm producing two goods with two inputs, what happens to its production possibilities curve if a technological advance is made in producing one of the goods?

22. Given the linear production function having three activities:

Activity 1			Activity 2			Activity 3		
L	K	X	L	K	X	L	K	X
3	5	10	4	4	10	5	3	10
6	10	20	8	8	20	10	6	20
12	20	40	16	16	40	20	12	40

(a) With free disposal assumed, graph the isoquants for $X = 10, 20, 40$.

(b) From the isoquant map, construct the TP curve as a function of the labor input when $K = 12$. (Hint: The properties of fixed proportions and constant returns to scale can be used to identify the input combinations and resulting levels of X.)

(c) What would happen to the shape of the isoquants and to the TP curve if the second activity became slightly more efficient in use of inputs?

23. Given this LP problem:

$$\text{maximize} \quad x_1 + x_2 + x_3 = X$$
$$\text{subject to} \quad x_1 + 2x_2 + 5x_3 \le 5 \quad \text{(capital)}$$
$$4x_1 + 2x_2 + x_3 \le 8 \quad \text{(labor)}$$
$$\text{and} \quad x_1 \ge 0, x_2 \ge 0, x_3 \ge 0$$

(a) Graph the three activity rays.

(b) Graph the $X = 1$ isoquant. Then find the $X = 2, 3, 4$ isoquants.

(c) Identify the feasible set.

(d) Identify the maximum level of output.

(e) Identify the input allocations to the activities.

(f) Identify the optimal production rates for each activity.

24. Formulate the dual LP problem for the LP problem of the preceding question. Solve this dual graphically, then interpret the optimal values of the dual variables.

Measuring the Costs of Production

With rare exceptions, managerial decisions require us to consider how costs vary with production, for both profit-maximizing and nonprofit firms. Managers face the task of finding the cost-minimizing input combinations at every level of output. Therefore, they must measure how costs will vary as output changes. For the profit-maximizing firm, this measure allows the manager to find the profit-maximizing level of output. For the firm that wishes to produce at the lowest possible unit cost, the measure allows the manager to find the most efficient plant size.

A decision to increase output requires increased use of inputs. The quantities of the inputs required depend on the underlying technology, the production function. Once the technological optimizing problem has been solved, the lowest cost of producing each level of output can be determined. Cost is found by multiplying the quantities of the inputs required by their prices. In turn, which input bundle yields the lowest cost of production depends on input prices. Our objective in this chapter is to see how cost is influenced by the production function, changes in technology, changes in input prices, and changes in output. We start by considering how to measure costs.

11.1 Measuring Costs as Opportunity Costs

How should the firm's costs be measured? The measures for some costs are obvious—the wages paid to workers, current payments made for raw materials, and rents paid for equipment and real estate. But what if the firm already owns some equipment and doesn't have to pay for it? And what if some raw materials are left over from preceding production runs? How should we treat such previous expenditures?

The proper way to measure costs for economic analysis is to use *opportunity costs,* those associated with opportunities that are forgone by not using the resources in their highest-valued use. The opportunity cost of an input may not equal its *historical cost,* which is the amount the firm actually paid for the input. If an input was acquired in the past, its historical cost becomes a **sunk cost,** an expenditure that has already been made and cannot be recovered. Sunk costs may even include a contractual agreement to spend money in the future. Unless the contract can be renegotiated or the firm plans to declare bankruptcy, such a future commitment is a sunk cost. When Apple Computer started developing the Macintosh, it had planned to use a highly automated production plant. The plant started operating early in 1984. Within eight months, automated equipment that had cost about $7 million was removed because Apple was unable to make the equipment work as intended. This expenditure was a sunk cost and had no influence on subsequent production decisions. Because sunk costs cannot be recovered, they should be ignored when making economic decisions.

Opportunity costs may or may not be measured appropriately by accounting costs. Because accountants construct a firm's financial statements and keep track of assets and liabilities in order to evaluate past performance, accounting costs tend to be backward-looking. Managers, on the other hand, need to be forward-looking, and so they need to look at present and future opportunity costs when making decisions for today and for tomorrow.

Accounting costs frequently differ from economic costs. Both accountants and economists include current outlays, called *explicit costs,* in measuring the costs of production.

Explicit costs include current wages, payments for raw materials, and rents on property and equipment. These explicit costs are opportunity costs if the input prices used are market prices. Accountants and economists measure *implicit* costs in different ways, however.

When an accountant estimates the cost of capital equipment or real property that the firm owns, a depreciation rule is applied. Tax rules dictate formulas that can be used to calculate depreciation allowances based on the historical cost of the capital. Depreciation rules are unlikely to reflect the actual wear and tear on the equipment. When the rules for depreciation were changed in 1986, actual wear and tear on equipment remained unchanged but accounting costs did change. Moreover, when the calculation is based on the historical cost of the capital, depreciation is even more unlikely to measure the capital's opportunity cost. In fact, the market value of owned real assets may be increasing while it is being depreciated by the accountant.

As another example of how economic costs differ from accounting cost, consider the payments made to an owner who manages his or her own business. A managerial salary may be paid and recorded as an accounting cost. That salary though, may not accurately measure the owner's opportunity cost as a manager, the salary that could be earned by selling the managerial service in the market. That opportunity cost may be substantially different from the accounting entry.

11.2 Costs in the Short Run

In the short run, technology is constant and at least one input is fixed. To keep things simple, we look at an example with two inputs, labor and capital. As before, labor is denoted L, which measures the flow of labor services per unit of time. Capital is denoted K, which measures the flow of capital services per unit of time. The price of labor services is denoted w, the market wage rate. The price of capital services is denoted r, the market rental rate. We assume that the prices of inputs are determined exogenously in input markets. Firms can buy or sell input services at prevailing rental rates, and so input prices measure the opportunity costs of the inputs.

In the short run, **total cost** is the sum of variable and fixed cost,

$$TC = VC + FC$$

If labor is the variable input, the variable cost is $VC = wL$, where w is the price of labor. With capital as the fixed input, the fixed cost is $FC = rK$, where r is the price of capital services and K is a constant flow of services generated by the fixed stock of capital. The model is easily generalized to the case with many inputs. In the short run, variable inputs might include the different types of labor services, raw materials, and equipment. Fixed inputs might include land, physical plant, heavy machinery, and even managerial talent. Technology remains constant, but the behavior of short-run costs can be analyzed with comparative static analysis to see how alternative technologies affect the costs of production.

What is the smallest quantity of a variable input required in combination with fixed inputs to produce a specified level of output? The answer is found by analyzing the total product curve, $X = X(L)$. Any stage III is eliminated as technologically inefficient, and then the TP curve is inverted to get $L = L(X)$, the **input requirement curve:**

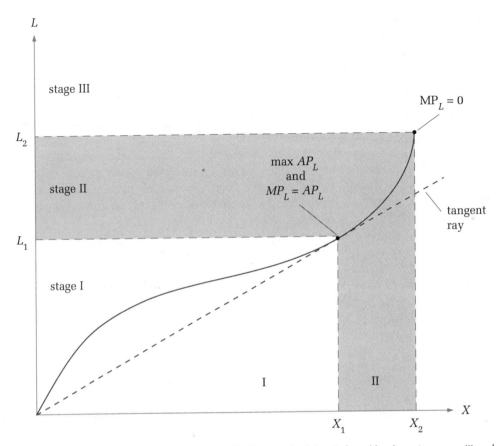

Figure 11.1 **Variable-input requirement curve:** The *IR* curve for labor is found by dropping stage III and then plotting the amount of labor required as a function of output. The shape of the curve is determined by technology.

> **Input requirement (IR) curve:** *An input requirement (IR) curve plots the minimal quantity of a variable input required as a function of output when other inputs remain constant.*

The nexus between the technological relationships of production and cost as a function of output is the variable input requirement curve. The *IR* curve indicates the minimum amount of the variable input required to produce any level of output in the short run. Graphically, constructing an *IR* curve amounts to rotating the axes of a *TP* curve and dropping stage III.

Figure 11.1 illustrates a typical *IR* curve for labor. You might wish to compare this curve with the *TP* curve of Chapter 10. Notice that the stages of production remain unaltered. The shape of the *IR* curve is determined by the shape of the *TP* curve, which is determined by technology. The transition point between stages I and II occurs where the ray is tangent to the curve. There AP_L equals MP_L, where AP_L is at a maximum. The transition point between stages II and III occurs where $MP_L = 0$. The *IR* curve stops

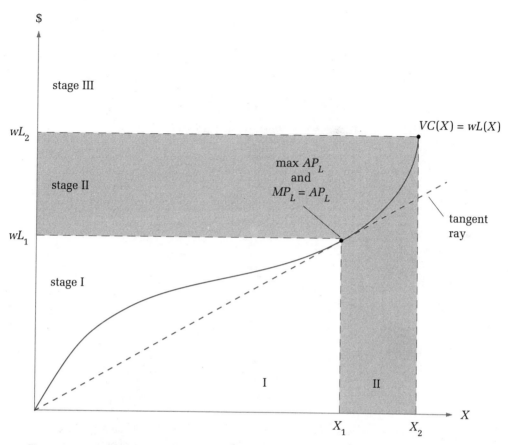

Figure 11.2 **Variable cost and output:** At any level of output X, variable cost is determined by multiplying the amount of the variable input required by its price. The shape of the VC curve is determined by technology.

where $MP_L = 0$ because maximum output has been reached, and so the IR curve does not extend into stage III.

Of course, not all IR curves will have all three stages because not all TP curves have all three stages. But all IR curves will be curving upward over some range because of the law of variable proportions—diminishing productivity of the variable input will occur over some range in the short run. Thus all IR curves will have a stage II even though some may not have stage I.

We are now ready to convert the IR curve into a variable-cost curve. Because variable cost is $VC = wL$ and L is a function of X, we can write

$$VC(X) = wL(X)$$

where $L(X)$ is the IR curve. That is, variable cost as a function of output is equal to the price of the variable input multiplied by the quantity of the input required as a function of output.

Figure 11.2 shows a variable-cost curve constructed from the IR curve of Figure 11.1. At any level of output X, variable cost is determined by multiplying the quantity of

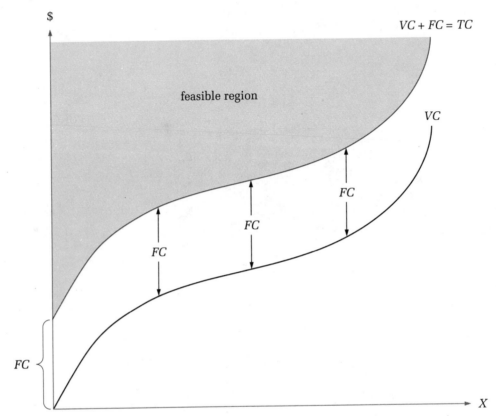

Figure 11.3 **Total cost and output:** In the short run, total cost as a function of output is equal to variable cost plus fixed cost. The slopes of the TC and VC curves are equal because they differ only by a constant, FC.

the variable input required by the input's price. For example, at $X = X_1$ the variable cost is $VC_1 = wL_1$, and at $X = X_2$ the variable cost is $VC_2 = wL_2$. The VC curve differs from the IR curve only in vertical scale. The shape of the VC curve and the transition points between the stages of production are determined by technology. Graphically, the VC curve has the same shape as the IR curve from which it was constructed.

Total cost is the sum of variable and fixed costs, $TC = VC + FC$. Graphically, FC is added to VC at every level of output, as illustrated by Figure 11.3. Because the FC curve adds zero slope, the slopes of the VC and TC curves are equal.

11.3 Average and Marginal Costs

Variable cost per unit of output is called **average variable cost:**

Average variable cost (AVC): *Average variable cost is variable cost per unit of output.*

Average variable cost is measured by variable cost divided by the quantity of output,

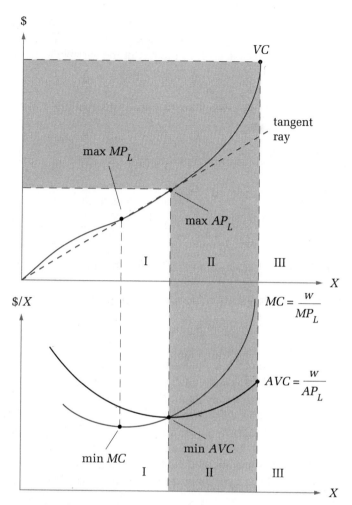

Figure 11.4 **Marginal and average variable costs:** AVC diminishes in stage I due to increasing average productivity, and AVC increases in stage II due to diminishing average productivity. When AVC is falling, MC lies below AVC. When AVC is rising, MC lies above AVC. At the transition between stages I and II AVC and MC are equal because $AP_L = MP_L$ there. As MC approaches III, it becomes infinitely large because MP_L approaches zero.

$$AVC = \frac{VC}{X}$$

Because $VC = wL(X)$ and $AP_L = X/L$, average variable cost is also equal to the variable-input price divided by the average product of the variable input,

$$AVC = \frac{w}{AP_L}$$

Therefore, an inverse relationship connects AVC and AP_L.

Figure 11.4 illustrates the relation between VC and AVC and the stages of production. In stage I, AVC diminishes because of the increasing average productivity of the variable input. At the transition point between stages I and II, AVC reaches a minimum because the average product of the variable input is at a maximum. Within stage II, AVC increases because of the diminishing average product of the variable input. Whenever the firm experiences increasing and then decreasing productivity of a variable input as output increases, AVC curves are U-shaped.

The extra cost associated with an additional unit of output is called **marginal cost:**

> **Marginal cost (MC):** *Marginal cost is the change in cost divided by an incremental change in output.*

Marginal cost can be measured by the slope of a line tangent to the VC curve,

$$MC = \frac{\Delta VC}{\Delta X}$$

Marginal cost is also equal to the slope of the TC curve because VC and TC differ only by a constant.

Marginal cost is inversely related to the marginal product of the variable input because

$$MC = \frac{\Delta wL}{\Delta X} = w\frac{\Delta L}{\Delta X} = \frac{w}{MP_L}$$

Thus MC is equal to the price of labor divided by the marginal product of labor when labor is the variable input. Figure 11.4 illustrates the relation between the MC curve and the VC and AVC curve. The MC lies below the AVC when the average is falling—the marginal draws the average down in stage I. The MC lies above the AVC when the average is rising—the marginal draws the average up in stage II. Of course, MC is equal to AVC at the transition point between stages I and II because marginal and average product are equal there. As output approaches its maximum, the marginal cost of production becomes infinitely large as the marginal product of the variable input approaches zero.

Figure 11.5 illustrates two related ways of measuring total variable cost. In panel A, the variable cost at any level of output, say X_1, is equal to the average variable cost multiplied by the level of output. The variable cost of producing any level of output is equal to the area of a rectangle defined by a point along the AVC curve. In panel B, an alternative way of measuring total variable cost is shown using the MC curve. Because marginal cost measures the cost of producing each extra unit, if we add up the cost of each ΔX unit produced, we get total variable cost:

$$VC(X) = MC(X)\Delta X + MC(X - \Delta X)\Delta X + \cdots + MC(0)\Delta X$$

where $MC(X)$ is the marginal cost of the last unit, $MC(X - \Delta X)$ is the marginal cost of the next-to-last unit, and so on. Each term in this equation represents the area of a rectangle with height $MC(X)$ and base ΔX. The sum of these rectangles provides us with a measure of the area under the MC curve. The area under the MC curve up to any level of output is therefore equal to the total variable cost of producing that level of output.

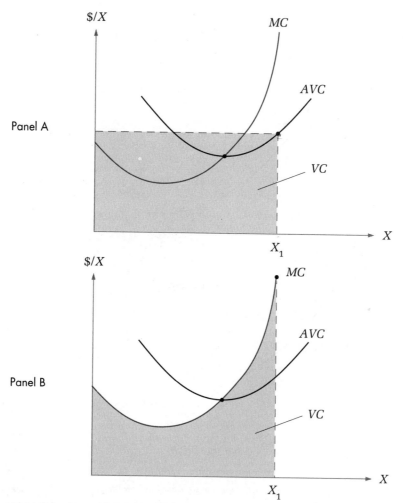

Figure 11.5 **Marginal and total variable costs: Panel A** Total variable cost at any level of output, say X_1, is equal to the average variable cost multiplied by the number of units. **Panel B** Total variable cost at any level of output, say X_1, is equal to the area under the MC curve up to that level of output.

Average fixed cost (**AFC**) is fixed cost per unit of output,

$$AFC = \frac{FC}{X}$$

Because an ever-increasing quantity of output is being divided into fixed cost, AFC must decline continuously, which is called "spreading the fixed cost." The AFC curve graphs as a rectangular hyperbola, as shown in Figure 11.6.

Total **average cost** (**AC**) is found by dividing total cost by output or adding AFC to AVC,

$$AC = \frac{TC}{X} = A\overset{\vee}{F}C + AFC$$

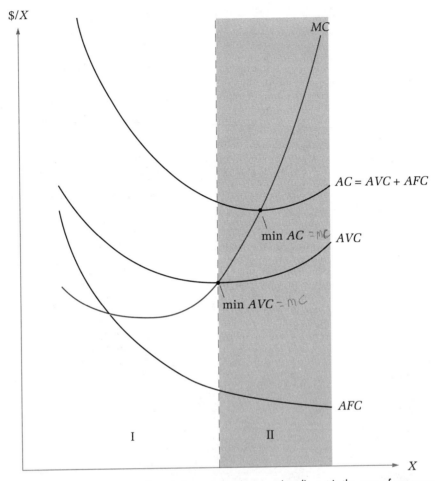

Figure 11.6 **Short-run average- and marginal-cost curves:** Average (total) cost is the sum of average variable and fixed costs. The marginal cost curve cuts the average cost curves from below at their minimum values. The AVC is at a minimum at the transition point between stage I and II, but AC reaches a minimum within stage II.

Curve AC will be U-shaped but will reach a minimum within stage II. Figure 11.6 illustrates the relation between the short-run average and marginal cost curves. The AC curve reaches a minimum within stage II because AFC is falling faster than AVC is rising at the transition point between stages I and II. Eventually the increasing marginal cost will cause AVC to increase faster than the decrease in AFC, thereby causing AC to rise. Thus, the AC curve will be U-shaped even when stage II is everywhere.

11.4 Short-run Changes in Input Prices

So far we have assumed that input prices are determined exogenously and remain constant. We continue to assume for the time being that input prices are exogenous, but we can analyze what happens to the cost curve when input prices change. Let's separate

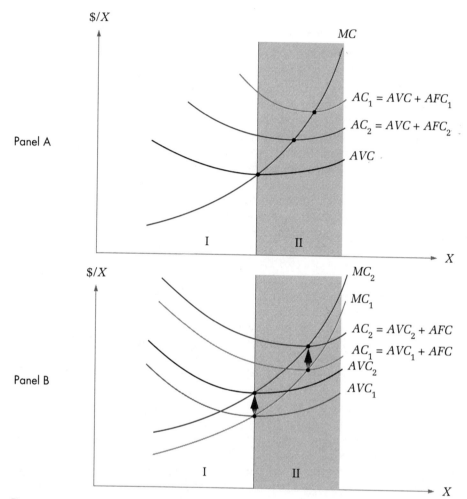

Figure 11.7 **Changes in input prices: Panel A** The price of the fixed input decreases. **Panel B** The price of the variable input increases.

our analysis into a change in the price of a fixed input and then look at what happens when the price of a variable input changes. Prices of fixed inputs are, like all other prices, determined by opportunity cost. Thus the price of the services of a fixed stock of capital is the market rental rate for those services.

Suppose a technological advance is made that can be acquired only by acquiring new capital because that technology is embodied in the new capital. This limitation could easily lead to a decrease in the opportunity cost and, hence, the price of old capital. How does this decrease in the price of old capital affect the average and marginal cost curves?

Average variable cost is not affected by the change in the price of the fixed input because the shape and position of the AVC curve is determined by current technology and the price of the variable input. As shown in panel A of Figure 11.7, the AVC curve remains unchanged. Likewise, the MC curve is determined solely by the shape and position of the VC curve, and so the MC curve too is not affected by the change in price

GLOBAL PERSPECTIVE: *Unit Labor Cost in Korea and the United States*

Output per hour of labor, or **labor productivity,** is the oldest measure of factor productivity used in analyzing production. Labor productivity is especially important because per capita real income cannot improve—and thus a nation's standard of living cannot rise—without an increase in per capita production.

Unit labor cost, the average cost of labor, measures the cost of labor per unit of output. Thus, unit labor cost is inversely related to labor productivity. Unit labor costs fall as labor productivity rises, and vice versa. Because labor is hired for a wage, requiring more labor time to produce each unit of output will raise labor costs per unit of output, and vice versa.

Recently, productivity in American labor has been questioned because of the loss in domestic employment that followed growth in imports of foreign-produced goods. Higher productivity, we are told, can offset the Third World's labor cost advantage.

As we have seen, increases in labor productivity do lead to decreased costs of production, and decreased unit labor costs lead to increased per capita income. But can the United States realistically expect to stem the import tide with growth in productivity? Walter Russel Mead argues that productivity in newly industrializing countries is growing so rapidly that the United States would be hard pressed to match their growth rates.* Korea, whose economic prowess frightens even the Japanese, saw worker productivity increase at an average of nearly 5 percent per year from 1973 to 1983. America's productivity growth averaged 1/3 of 1 percent over the same period.

When companies decide where to build a new factory, they are not interested in labor productivity itself but in the "dollar productivity" of labor. Nor are they directly interested in output per hour. Companies are interested, however, in output per dollar of labor cost. For Korea in 1983, workers earned about $1.29 per hour and produced $4.20 worth of goods. The dollar productivity in Korea, then, was about $3—a dollar of labor cost generated about $3 in revenue. In America, the cost of labor was $12.26 an hour, and one hour of labor produced roughly $23. The dollar productivity in America, then, was about $2 worth of output for each $1 cost of labor. This differential means that even if the United States were to match Korea's rate of productivity growth, the United States would still lose ground.

Suppose output per hour per worker increases 5 percent in both countries while wages remain constant. Output per unit of labor in Korea would rise by 21¢ while the U.S. gained $1.15. This figure looks good until we consider dollar productivity. With the 5 percent increase, $1 of labor cost in Korea would produce $3.42 worth of goods, up 17¢. In America, that same $1 of labor cost yields $1.97 in revenue, up only 7¢. To keep from losing more competitive ground to Korea, American productivity must grow faster than the Korean. If Korean growth remains at 5 percent, America will need 8 percent productivity growth just to stay even. That improvement is extremely unlikely.

Wages are not, of course, likely to remain constant. Moreover, they are likely to increase more rapidly in Korea than in the United States as their standard of living increases. A rise in Korean wages to $2 per hour, or a drop in American wages to $5.50 per hour, would have established equality in dollar productivity in 1983. It is also unlikely that Korea will be able to sustain its 5 percent growth in productivity. Nevertheless, America must do better than its less than 1 percent growth if it expects to slow the exodus of manufacturing jobs.

* Walter Russel Mead, "U.S. Productivity Becomes an Hourly Problem of Pay," *Los Angeles Times,* April 1987.

of the fixed input. The total AC curve, however, is the sum of AVC and AFC, and the AFC curve is affected by the change in price of capital. When the price of capital decreases, the AC curve will shift down, say, from AC_1 to AC_2. The new AC curve will reach a minimum when it intersects the MC curve as shown. The stages in production remain unaltered because they are determined solely by current technology. Of course, if the firm adopts the new technology by acquiring new capital, then all the cost curves will shift—but that is a long-run event.

Turning now to changes in the price of a variable input, let's assume that the wage rate has increased because of a new collective-bargaining agreement. An increase in the price of labor will affect the VC curve and hence the AVC and MC curves. But the stages in production remain unaltered because technology does not change in the short run. As shown in panel B of Figure 11.7, the AVC and MC curves shift upward as the price of labor increases. Because it is important later when we identify the profit maximizing supply decision of the firm, realize that the transition point between stages I and II is not influenced by a change in the price of any variable input. Moreover, the level of output where $MC = AVC$ remains the same because that is determined where $MP = AP$.

In the first case, where the price of capital decreased alone, economic profit will increase at every level of output. The firm will evaluate how the costs of production would behave under the new technology, and if the costs of production fall more under the new technology than they did under the old technology, the firm may invest in acquiring new capital. But that is a long-run decision that will involve comparing the present values of economic profits over time as well as the risks associated with the alternatives. Nevertheless, the firm is likely to change its input mix because of the change in relative prices.

In the second case, where the price of labor increases alone, economic profit will decrease in the short run. In the long run the firm may be able to do better by substituting other inputs, including capital for labor. Changes in input prices usually cause an eventual substitution toward inputs whose relative prices fall, from inputs whose relative prices rise.

11.5 Back to the Future—Part II: Minimizing Long-run Cost

In the long run all inputs are variable, and so a plant of any size is possible. One problem the firm faces is to choose the input mixture that minimizes cost at any level of output. That is, the firm always desires to produce every level of output at the lowest possible cost. Cost minimization is required if the firm is to maximize profit, and minimizing cost is desirable even for the nonprofit firm. To minimize cost at any level of output, the firm must use inputs in the most technologically efficient way and must choose the input combination that is least expensive.

In the two-input case, combinations of inputs that require the same level of expenditure are called **isocost lines.**

Isocost line: *An isocost line identifies input combinations that yield equal total cost.*

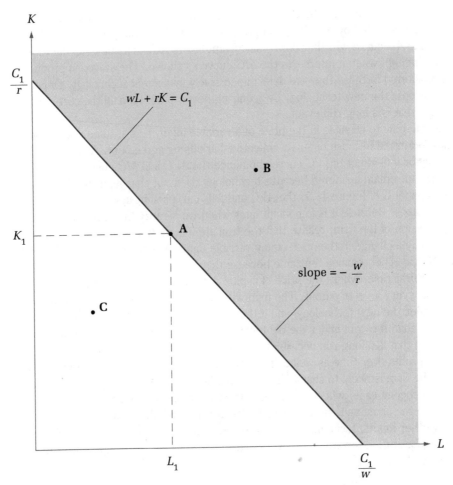

Figure 11.8   **An isocost line:** Given input prices w and r, the cost of any input bundle like **A** is determined by

$$wL_1 + rK_1 = C_1$$

The isocost line

$$wL + rK = C_1$$

identifies other combinations of L and K that require the same level of expenditure C_1. Bundles like **B** cost more, and bundles like **C** cost less.

Isocost lines are similar to the budget lines of the consumer, and isocost lines are the budget lines for the firm. Cost—total expenditure—is constant along an isocost line. With two inputs L and K, total cost is

$$wL + rK = C$$

At some level of expenditure, say $C = C_1$, the isocost line is

$$wL + rK = C_1$$

This equation is shown in Figure 11.8. If only L is purchased with expenditure $C = C_1$,

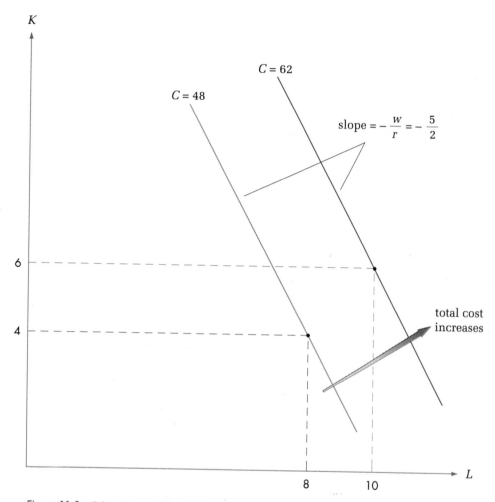

Figure 11.9 **Shifts in the isocost line:** Given that $w = 5$ and $r = 2$, the slope of the isocost lines remains equal at $-w/r = -5/2$. Isocost lines farther from the origin represent greater total cost, and isocost lines closer to the origin represent smaller total cost.

the maximum of L that can be purchased is C_1/w. If only K is purchased with $C = C_1$, the quantity of K that can be bought is C_1/r. Connecting these two points by a straight line yields the isocost line for $C = C_1$. Any bundle like **A** that lies on the isocost line results in the same total cost. Bundles like **B** above the isocost line cost more, and bundles like **C** below the isocost line cost less. Isocost lines can be found for those input bundles as well, however, and each isocost line represents a different level of total cost.

When graphed with K on the vertical axis, the slope of any isocost line is the negative of the input price ratio, $-w/r$. The slope of an isocost line measures the rate of exchange of capital for labor that will keep cost constant. Isocost lines remain parallel as long as input prices remain constant. Figure 11.9 shows how isocost lines shift as the level of total expenditure changes. Isocost lines farther from the origin represent greater total cost, and isocost lines closer to the origin represent smaller total cost.

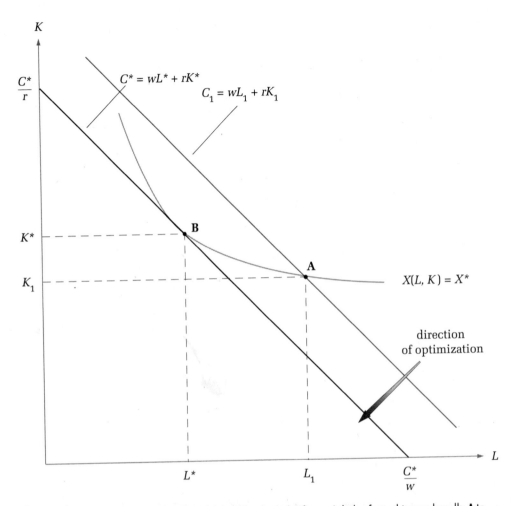

Figure 11.10   **Minimizing expenditure:** In the short run, the firm might be forced to use bundle **A** to produce X^* units of output. The cost of X^* at **A** is $C_1 = wL_1 + rK_1$. In the long run, X^* units of output can be produced at lowest total cost by using bundle **B** where the isocost line is tangent to the $X = X^*$ isoquant. The cost of X^* at **B** is $C^* = wL^* + rK^*$.

When all inputs are variable, one problem facing the firm is to choose the input mixture that minimizes the total cost of producing a specific level of output. This is the **cost minimization problem.**

Suppose the firm wants to produce $X = X^*$ units of output. As illustrated by Figure 11.10, the input bundles that yield X^* can be identified by the isoquant $X(L, K) = X^*$. Bundle **A** is one input combination that can produce X^* units by using $L = L_1$ and $K = K_1$. The total cost of producing X^* units by using **A** is given by the isocost line C_1 that passes through **A**. However, X^* units can be produced at a lower total cost by substituting K for L and moving to an input bundle like **B** that is closer to the origin. At **B** the isocost line is tangent to the isocost line C^*, where $L = L^*$ and $K = K^*$, and so the firm cannot reduce the cost of producing X^* units any further.

Given technology, the firm should choose an input bundle that minimizes the total cost of producing any level of output:

> **Minimizing cost**
>
> $$\text{minimize} \quad C = wL + rK$$
> $$\text{subject to} \quad X(L, K) = X^*$$

Graphically, the solution is given by the input bundle where an isocost line is tangent to the isoquant. The tangency conditions for long-run cost minimization can be expressed by two equations:

> **Tangency conditions for minimizing cost:**
> (1) The MRTS must equal the price ratio, $MRTS_{LK} = w/r.$
> (2) Technological optimization has occurred, $X(L, K) = X^*.$

The first equation is satisfied when the slope of the isoquant is equal to the slope of the isocost line. The second equation is satisfied when the firm uses the inputs in the most technologically efficient way to produce the desired level of output. A simultaneous solution to the two equations yields the cost-minimizing quantities of L and K.[1]

A numerical example illustrates how the tangency conditions for minimizing cost can be applied. Suppose the production function is Cobb-Douglas, and $X(L, K) = \sqrt{LK}$. Suppose also $w = \$8$ and $r = \$18$, and so the isocost line is $8L + 18K = C$. If the firm wants to produce $X = 6$ units of output, the cost-minimizing problem is

$$\text{minimize} \quad 8L + 18K = C$$
$$\text{subject to} \quad \sqrt{LK} = 6$$

Tangency requires that $MRTS_{LK} = w/r$ and $\sqrt{LK} = 6$. Recall that $MRTS_{LK} = MP_L/MP_K$. Thus, for this Cobb-Douglas function, $MRTS_{LK} = K/L$. Substituting known values into the tangency equations yields:

$$\frac{K}{L} = \frac{8}{18} \quad \text{and} \quad \sqrt{LK} = 6$$

A little algebra yields:

$$18K = 8L \quad \text{and} \quad LK = 36$$

The simultaneous solution to these two equations yields $L^* = 9$ and $K^* = 4$. Thus, the lowest cost of producing $X = 6$ units is

$$C^* = 8L^* + 18K^* = 144$$

The isocost line $C^* = 144$ will be tangent to the $X = 6$ isoquant at $L^* = 9$ and $K^* = 4$. You might wish to graph the isocost line and the isoquant to verify this result.

---

1. The dual to the constrained cost-minimizing problem subject to an output constraint is an output-maximizing problem subject to an expenditure constraint. The optimal values for L and K are the same as the optimal values obtained from the cost-minimizing problem. The primal cost-minimizing and the dual-output maximizing problem have the same solution values for L and K.

11.6 Expansion and Long-run Cost

As the firm changes the level of output in the long run, it will choose a cost-minimizing input bundle at each level of output. As shown in Figure 11.11, the firm will choose input bundles where the isoquants are tangent to isocost lines in order to minimize cost at each level of output. This path is called the **expansion path (EP)**. The *EP* is analogous to the income-expansion path of the consumer.

Cost is minimized in the long run along the *EP* curve. For the example in Figure 11.11, the lowest cost as a function of X is $C^*(X)$. As output changes from X_1 to X_2 to X_3,

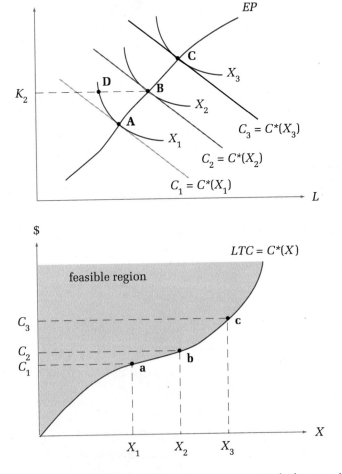

Figure 11.11 **Expansion and long-run cost:** As the firm increases output in the long run, it expands along path *EP*, where the isoquants are tangent to isocost lines. The level of expenditure required to produce each level of output identifies the long-run total cost (*LTC*) curve.

AN APPLICATION: *Bell-System Expansion Path*

A production function was estimated for the Bell System using annual data from the post-war period.* This specification was used:

$$\ln X = \beta_0 + \beta_1 \ln K + \beta_2 \ln L + \beta_3 \ln K \ln L$$

The marginal products are:

$$MP_L = \frac{X}{L}(\beta_2 + \beta_3 \ln K)$$

$$MP_K = \frac{X}{K}(\beta_1 + \beta_3 \ln L)$$

The ratio of marginal products yields the marginal rate of technical substitution of capital for labor,

$$MRTS_{LK} = \frac{K(\beta_2 + \beta_3 \ln K)}{L(\beta_1 + \beta_3 \ln L)}$$

For this production function, the elasticity of substitution is

$$\sigma = \frac{\beta_1 + \beta_2 + \beta_3 \ln KL}{\beta_1 + \beta_2 + \beta_3 \ln KL + 2\beta_3}$$

This substitution elasticity varies with the values of L and K.

Estimating by regression was used to generate this equation

$$\widehat{\ln X} = 69.8541 - 6.40795 \ln K - 10.5900 \ln L + 1.09574 (\ln K \ln L)$$

where

X = net value added of output deflated to exclude effects of inflation.
K = net capital stock deflated.
L = labor input, in millions of worker hours.

Standard statistical tests indicated that all estimated coefficients are statistically different from zero. More than 99 percent of the variation in the dependent variable was explained by the fitted production function.

The marginal products and the substitution elasticities were computed for each of the survey years and are reproduced in Table 11.1. That the estimated marginal productivity of labor was negative until 1952 indicates that the Bell System was operating outside the economic region. Why, then, didn't the company reduce its workforce? The author of this study records the partial explanation that the Bell System began postwar production with a highly labor-intensive structure. A shortage of telephone equipment was so severe that it took many years of strong capital growth to catch up. This shortage of capital persisted until 1955. The Bell System was forced to operate off the optimal expansion path until then. The relatively small but growing

---

* H. D. Vinod, "Non-homogeneous Production Functions and Applications to Telecommunications," *Bell Journal of Economics and Management Science* (Autumn 1972), pp. 531–543. Copyright 1972. Reprinted by permission of RAND.

Table 11.1 Substitution Elasticity for Bell System

Year	MP_k	MP_L	σ
1947	0.158	−1.451	0.098
1948	0.154	−1.087	0.165
1949	0.148	−0.807	0.205
1950	0.155	−0.677	0.227
1951	0.176	−0.620	0.248
1952	0.181	−0.300	0.286
1953	0.179	0.028	0.317
1954	0.178	0.273	0.336
1955	0.184	0.618	0.358
1956	0.193	0.981	0.383
1957	0.190	1.396	0.393
1958	0.181	1.868	0.402
1959	0.183	2.374	0.410
1960	0.185	2.853	0.418
1961	0.183	3.404	0.427
1962	0.183	4.057	0.437
1963	0.184	4.681	0.447
1964	0.194	5.382	0.460
1965	0.200	6.182	0.476
1966	0.226	7.108	0.487
1967	0.236	8.199	0.496
1968	0.256	9.092	0.504
1969	0.285	10.185	0.517
1970	0.294	11.222	0.529

Source: H. D. Vinod, "Non-homogeneous Production Functions and Applications to Telecommunications," *Bell Journal of Economics and Management Science* (Autumn 1972).

substitution elasticity indicates that capital and labor were imperfect substitutes but in time became better substitutes.

A plot of the *estimated* isoquants and the *actual* expansion path is shown in Figure 11.12. The theoretically *optimal* expansion path, the cost-minimizing capital–labor ratio, $(K/L)_{opt}$, requires that the $MRTS_{LK}$ be equal to the price ratio w/r:

$$\left(\frac{K}{L}\right)_{opt} = MRTS_{LK} = \frac{w}{r}$$

Substituting the *MRTS* and simple algebra reveals that

$$\left(\frac{K}{L}\right)_{opt} = \frac{w(\beta_1 + \beta_3 \ln L)}{r(\beta_2 + \beta_3 \ln K)}$$

The coefficient estimates for the production function, actual input prices, and actual

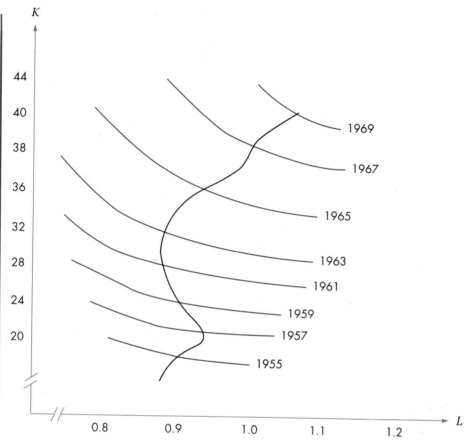

Source: H. D. Vinod, "Non-homogeneous Production Functions and Applications to Telecommunications," *Bell Journal of Economics and Management Science* (Autumn 1974), p. 540. Copyright 1972. Reprinted by permission of RAND.

Figure 11.12 **Estimated isoquants and an actual expansion path:** The isoquants were plotted for an estimated production function and superimposed on the actual expansion path for the Bell System.

input values for selected survey years can be substituted into this equation. The resulting estimated optimal input ratios are compared to the actual ratios from 1960 to 1970 in Table 11.2. The *actual* capital–labor ratio is seen to be *smaller* than the estimated *optimal* cost-minimizing ratio. The difference between the actual and optimal ratios suggests that the Bell System was not choosing the cost-minimizing input bundles over this period. The Bell System was using too little capital relative to labor.

Vinod stressed that these results were preliminary, and commented that the difference between the actual and the estimated optimal expansion paths may be due to the absence of any statistical control for technical change. Nevertheless, the estimation indicates that the Bell System was not "overcapitalized" during this period. That the Bell System was moving slowly toward the optimal path indicates slow postwar recovery from the severe shortage of capital.

Table 11.2 Capital–Labor Ratios for the Bell System

Year	Actual	Optimal
1960	29.17	50.99
1961	31.20	47.52
1962	33.27	44.97
1963	35.09	42.77
1964	36.23	44.92
1965	37.80	45.67
1966	37.97	49.50
1967	39.76	50.69
1968	40.16	50.88
1969	40.13	57.11
1970	41.47	59.44

Source: H. D. Vinod, "Non-homogeneous Production Functions and Applications to Telecommunications," Bell Journal of Economics and Management Science (Autumn 1972). Copyright 1972. Reprinted by permission of Rand.

minimum cost changes from C_1 to C_2 to C_3. When $C^*(X)$ is graphed, the resulting curve is called a **long-run total-cost curve:**

> **Long-run total cost (LTC):** *The* LTC *curve graphs minimum cost as a function of output in the long run.*

The *LTC* curve cannot be negatively sloped because the *EP* must lie within the economic region where all marginal products are nonnegative.

In the short run, it is highly unlikely that the firm will be on its expansion path. Suppose the firm is initially on the expansion path at **B** in Figure 11.11 and is producing $X = X_2$ units of output. At **B** the level of capital is K_2. Now suppose sales fall to X_1. If the firm responds by decreasing output to X_1, it will be forced to use input bundle **D** if capital is fixed at K_2. The firm will be forced off its expansion path, and the short-run cost of producing X_1 units will be greater than in the long run. For the long run, the firm will plan to adjust if it expects to be producing X_1 units in the future.

All firms are forced to operate in the short run and some inputs will be fixed. For that reason the *LTC* curve is called a planning curve; it indicates where the firm plans to be along its expansion path when it has time to adjust its scale of operation to long-run changes in output.

11.7 Shepherd's Lemma and Input Demand*

When input prices change, the expansion path shifts. At each point along any expansion path, we know that

$$\frac{w}{r} = MRTS_{LK} = -\frac{\Delta K}{\Delta L}$$

the input price ratio is equal to the marginal rate of technical substitution. By multiplying both sides of this equation by r and ΔL, we get

$$w\Delta L + r\Delta K = 0$$

Now consider the change in cost when the wage rate changes alone,

$$\Delta C = L\Delta w + w\Delta L + r\Delta K$$

The first term is the change in cost due to a change in w; the second is the change in cost due to a change in L; and the third is the change in cost due to a change in K. Because the sum of the last two terms is zero when the firm is minimizing long-run cost, we have $\Delta C = L\Delta w$. The variable L is the derived demand for labor services, and so

$$L = \frac{\Delta C}{\Delta w}$$

which is called **Shepherd's lemma.**[2] This lemma holds only if inputs change optimally so that the firm remains on the cost-minimizing expansion path:

> **Shepherd's lemma:** *For the cost-minimizing firm, the derived demand for any input is equal to the change in total cost due to a small change in that input's price alone.*

Shepherd's lemma can be used to measure how a LAC curve will shift for a change in input price. Using the lemma, where X is the quantity of output,

$$\frac{\Delta LAC}{\Delta w} = \frac{L}{X} = \frac{1}{AP_L}$$

Thus the shift in the LAC curve for a one-unit change in the wage rate is equal to unity divided by the average product of labor along the expansion path. Similarly, the shift in the LAC curve for a one-unit change in the rental rate of capital is equal to the inverse of the average product of capital.

---

* This section can be skipped without loss of continuity.

2. $\partial C/\partial w = L(w, r, X)$ and $\partial C/\partial r = K(w, r, X)$ are the factor-demand equations for a change in each input price.

11.8 Short- and Long-run Costs Compared

In the long run, as illustrated by Figure 11.13, the firm should move along an expansion path that minimizes the total cost of production. In the short run, however, the firm must combine labor with fixed capital as output changes. It is forced to choose more costly input bundles in the short run. At one level of output, short- and long-run costs are the same—where the firm would choose the level of capital in the long run that it is constrained to use in the short run.

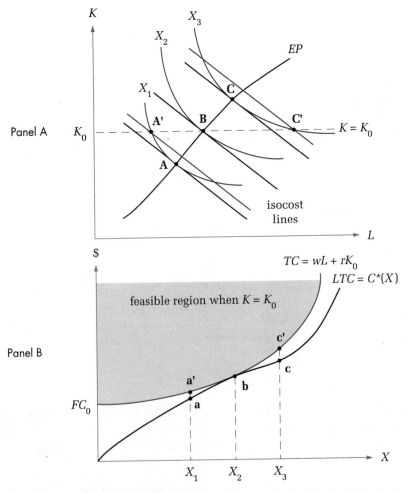

Figure 11.13 **Short- and long-run costs: Panel A** In the short run, capital is fixed at K_0, but in the long run the firm will move along path EP. Long-run cost is lower than short-run cost at every level of output but one. **Panel B** When capital is fixed at K_0, the corresponding short-run TC curve is the sum of variable and fixed costs. This TC curve lies everywhere above the LTC curve except for one point.

In the short run, the level of capital determines fixed cost. When the variable cost is added to the fixed cost, the resulting short-run total-cost curve lies everywhere above the *LTC* curve except for one point. As shown in Figure 11.13, the short-run *TC* and the *LTC* are equal at the level of output where the firm would choose the level of fixed capital in the long run that it is forced to use in the short run.

In general, the short-run *TC* curve for every scale of operations is determined by the level of the fixed input. Each short-run *TC* curve has one point in common with the *LTC* curve. At any other input bundle in the short run, short-run cost is greater than long-run cost; this condition applies in every scale of operation. Therefore, the *LTC* curve is the **envelope curve** of the short-run *TC* curve, as shown in Figure 11.14.

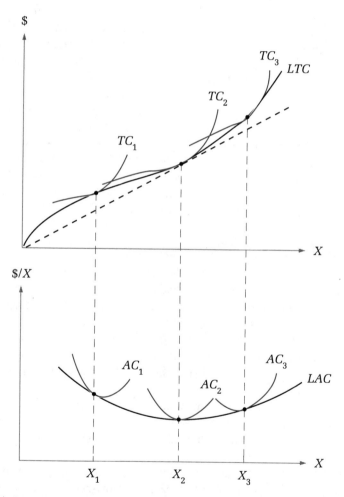

Figure 11.14 **Long-run cost curves as envelope curves:** Each short-run cost curve shares one point with the long-run cost curve. Everywhere else, short-run costs are greater than long-run costs. Thus the long-run cost curve is the envelope of the short-run cost curves.

Average and marginal costs can be measured in the long run just as they were in the short run. Long-run average cost is defined as

$$LAC = \frac{LTC}{X}$$

Long-run average cost (LAC) is long-run total cost per unit of output. Long-run marginal cost is

$$LMC = \frac{\Delta LTC}{\Delta X}$$

Long-run marginal cost (LMC) is the change in long-run total cost divided by an incremental change in output as the firm moves along its expansion path. The LMC measures the extra cost associated with producing an extra unit of output for the cost-minimizing firm in the long run. The LMC can be measured by the slope of the LTC curve. The relation between average and marginal costs in the long run is the same as in the short run. Average cost falls whenever the marginal is below the average, and the average cost rises whenever the marginal is above the average.

The relation between the short-run and long-run average and marginal cost curves is a bit more complex. A system of cost curves is illustrated in Figure 11.15. Each MC curve cuts its corresponding AC curve from below at the minimum average cost. Each AC curve shares one point with the LAC curve. At the point where $AC = LMC$, we have $MC = LMC$. The short-run MC curves are steeper than the LMC at any level of output because the firm has more flexible use of inputs in the long run. In the long run the firm can always do at least as well as in any short-run situation. In the short run, the law of variable proportions causes cost to rise faster than in the long run.

11.9 Scale Effects and Economies of Size

Industrial engineers refer to the LAC curve as the *planning curve.* Engineers and managers examine the technology available and develop isoquants for each output. Given forecasts of the input price ratio, the optimal expansion path is identified and the corresponding LTC curve is established. Then the LAC curve can be used to determine which level of output generates lowest unit cost. Minimizing LAC, however, may not generate the profit-maximizing level of output. But once the LAC curve is known, managers can plan which plant size will yield the lowest unit cost of production for *any* desired level of output.

When all inputs are varied, the firm's scale of plant changes. More of all inputs makes the scale larger, less of all inputs makes the scale smaller. The effect of plant size on the costs of production is called a **scale effect.** Scale effects show up in the shape of the LAC curve.

Figure 11.16 illustrates two cases. In panel A are decreasing average costs as the size of the plant increases. For the smaller plant size, the short-run cost curves AC_1 and MC_1 hold. For the larger plant size, the short-run cost curves AC_2 and MC_2 hold. As the firm increases its plant size, it moves along the LAC curve. **Economies of scale** are said to occur when the average costs fall as the scale is increased. In contrast, panel B shows

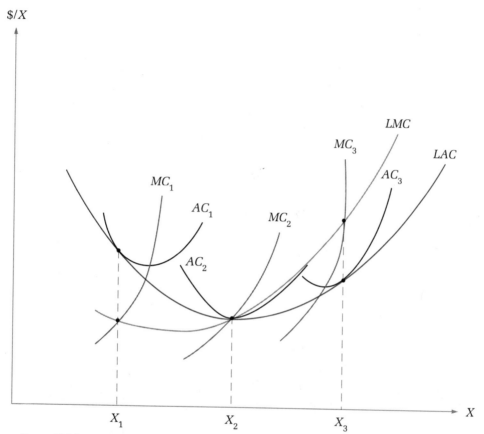

Figure 11.15 **A system of average and marginal cost curves:** Each short-run MC curve intersects the LMC curve at a level where short-run AC equals LAC. Which short-run AC curve confronts the firm depends on the scale of operations—the level of the fixed input.

increasing average costs as the size of the plant increases. **Diseconomies of scale** are said to occur when average costs rise as the scale of operations increases. Take care not to confuse *economies* of scale with *returns* to scale. Recall that *returns* to scale describes a production function as the firm moves along a ray with fixed input proportions. But scale effects describe how cost changes as the firm moves along an expansion path as it minimizes long-run cost. The expansion path need not coincide with a ray. Although returns to scale influence how cost changes in the long run, then, returns to scale are not the sole determinants of scale effects on long-run cost.[3]

---

3. In one case returns to scale and economies of scale are the same—when the production function has isoquants that remain parallel along rays, homothetic production functions. For these functions any expansion path will coincide with a ray through the origin, and increasing returns to scale implies economies of scale, decreasing returns to scale implies diseconomies of scale, and constant returns to scale implies constant long-run average cost.

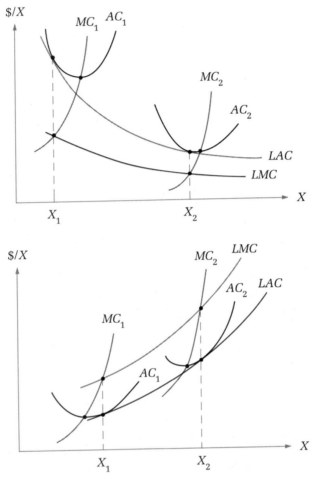

Figure 11.16 **Scale effects:** **Panel A** Decreasing average costs due to economies of scale. **Panel B** Increasing average costs due to diseconomies of scale.

The degree of economies or diseconomies of scale can be defined using the relation between long-run average and marginal costs. The **degree of scale economies (DSE)** at a given level of output is

$$DSE = \frac{LAC}{LMC}$$

Scale economies are locally increasing, constant, or decreasing as DSE is greater than, equal to, or less than unity. When LMC is below LAC, so that the LAC curve is falling and $DSE > 1$, the result is local economies of scale. When LMC is above LAC so that $DSE < 1$, the LAC curve is rising, and we see local diseconomies of scale. This measure of scale economies is also applicable to the multiproduct firm—just think of output as a bundle of outputs and cost as a function of that bundle.

Economies of scale may be experienced because of increasing possibilities in the division and specialization of labor. Workers in a small plant typically perform several tasks. Such a worker may not be equally proficient in all tasks, and time may be lost in changing from one task to another. In a large plant workers may specialize in the task at which they are most proficient. Specialization may eliminate time lost in changing tasks. Such specialization frequently reduces the average cost of production.

Economies of scale may be experienced because of enhanced ability to use a more efficient production activity. Technology remains constant, but large firms may be able to utilize production activities different from those appropriate to small firms. For large plant sizes, mass-production techniques may become feasible. As the firm uses a more capital-intensive production activity, average cost per unit may be substantially lower than is possible with a smaller plant. In July 1988, IBM introduced powerful new mainframe computers. An IBM official said the new S-series models provided a 20 to 50 percent increase in computer power over the older E-series at prices that were 9 to 12 percent higher. Among the new models was the 600S, which IBM said was the fastest general computer in the industry at that time: it could handle 130 to 140 million instructions per second. That compared to just 1 million per second for a typical mainframe of the 1970s. The price of the new 600S was $12.4 million. Not every firm could afford that, but large firms could accomplish 59 percent more work for a 12 percent increase in outlay. Large firms needing this computer power should be able to reduce the number of people needed to manage data and also cut the average cost of manufacturing. It would not be cost effective for smaller firms to switch to this alternative production activity.

Economies of scale may be reinforced by increasing returns to scale, or economies of scale may be thwarted by decreasing returns to scale. Also, increasing returns to scale may be thwarted by diseconomies of scale. One important source of diseconomies of scale is the increased complexity in managing resources as plant size increases. The increased complexity of coordination and control may decrease production efficiency. As plant size increases, decision making must be delegated and more resources must be devoted to coordination and control. Effective communication becomes increasingly difficult as the number of managers increases. To the extent that these difficulties reduce production efficiency, the average cost of production will increase as plant size increases.

These considerations suggest that the LAC curve will be U-shaped, as shown in Figure 11.17. A small plant results in a short-run AC curve like AC_1. As output increases from X_1 to X_2, a larger plant should be used to achieve AC_2 so that X_2 units can be produced at a lower cost per unit. The most efficient plant size results in AC_3, where LAC is at a minimum. Per unit cost is lowest at X_3 units. Beyond the plant size associated with AC_3, diseconomies of scale cause the LAC curve to turn upward.

As we will see, firms do not automatically choose the most efficient plant size. Rather, most choose the level of output that will maximize profit and then choose the plant size to produce that profit-maximizing output at the lowest unit cost. In fact, the firm must choose the most efficient scale at any level of output or it will not be able to maximize profit. If X_2 units in Figure 11.17 is the profit-maximizing level of output, the firm must choose a plant size that yields AC_2 to achieve LAC_2 in order to realize those profits.

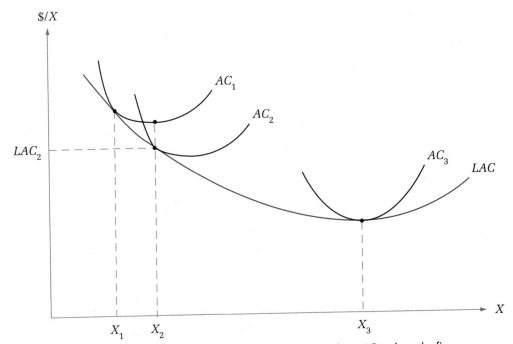

Figure 11.17 **Efficient plant size:** The most efficient plant size results in AC_3, where the firm can produce X_3 units of output at the lowest unit cost in the long run. But if the firm wishes to produce X_2 units of output, the appropriate plant size results in AC_2, where the AC curve is tangent to the LAC curve. Any other plant size, say one yielding AC_1, results in a larger average cost for producing X_2 units.

11.10 Number of Plants in an Industry

How many plants can survive in an industry depends on the relation between economies of scale and the industry demand curve. Consider the case illustrated by Figure 11.18, where the industry demand is labeled D. Given current technology and input prices, the industry has room for only two single-plant firms if the market price is p_0. At p_0 the quantity demanded is X_0 units. If each plant produces $X = X_1$ units using scale AC_1, where LAC is lowest, market demand will be met and the price is just equal to unit cost. At that price, any other plant size would result in unit cost greater than price, and the firm would operate at a loss.

Of course, market price need not be equal to p_0. But whatever the price, the position of the market demand curve relative to the LAC curve influences the number of plants in the industry. The scale of operation at which LAC is lowest when industry demand is satisfied by identical-sized firms is called the **minimum efficient scale (MES)**. If market demand shifts to the right in Figure 11.18, the number of plants that may be supported will increase. If the market demand shrinks, then the number of plants in the industry is likely to decrease. What do you think will happen if the LAC curve is declining over the whole range of market demand?

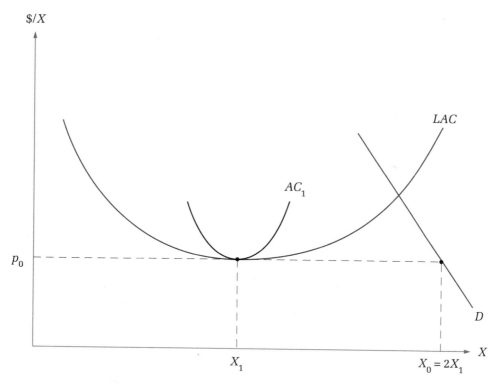

Figure 11.18 **Industry demand and the number of plants:** At price p_0 the industry demand is X_0. This industry will support only two single-plant firms, each producing $X = X_1$ units, when each firm chooses a scale that results in minimum unit cost in the long run.

ECONOMIC SCENE: *Trucking Along after Regulatory Reform*

Economists have argued that federal control of the trucking industry has produced costs and prices higher than they would have been without regulation. Because the industry has been considered competitive, removing regulatory constraints should lead to reduced costs and lower prices. Few economists therefore doubted the desirability of the Motor Carrier Act of 1980 that deregulated the trucking industry.

    The effects of deregulation on the cost of production in the trucking industry have been studied by John Ying, who estimated long-run cost functions using cross-sectional data for 1975, 1980, and 1984.* A cost function was estimated from each of these data sets. Cost was specified as a function of input prices, output, and a collection of operating characteristics. Factor prices included those for fuel, purchased transportation, labor, and capital. Output was measured by revenue ton-miles. Operating characteristics included average length of haul, average load, average shipment size, and average cargo loss. The research strategy was to see what happened to the representative firm between 1975 and 1980, and then between 1980

---

* John S. Ying, "Regulatory Reform and Technical Change: New Evidence of Scale Economies in Trucking," *Southern Economic Journal* 56(4) (April 1990), pp. 996–1005.

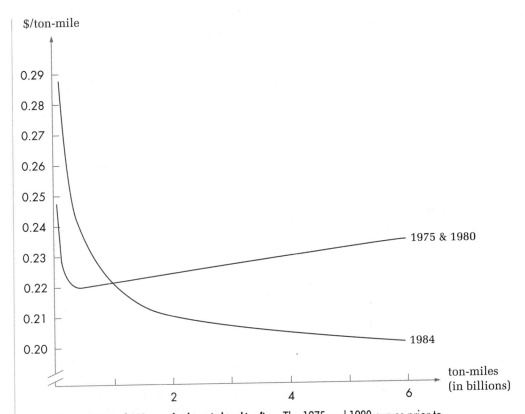

Figure 11.19 **Estimated *LAC* curves for the typical trucking firm:** The 1975 and 1980 curves prior to deregulation exhibited mild diseconomies of scale. By 1984, after deregulation, the *LAC* curve exhibited fairly strong economies of scale.

and 1984. Because no major technological changes have come along in this time, differences in cost can be attributed to deregulation.

The estimated cost curves for 1975 and 1980 showed mild diseconomies of scale, but constant long-run average costs could not be ruled out. By 1984, however, fairly strong economies of scale were evident, along with a declining *LAC* curve. To evaluate the possible consequences of these findings, Ying plotted the *LAC* curves estimated to have been appropriate for 1975, 1980, and 1984. Those curves are illustrated by Figure 11.19. The 1975 and 1980 curves are approximately identical and are shown by one curve.

The minimum efficient scale in 1980 was estimated to be about 215 million ton-miles of output at an average cost of just under 22¢/ton-mile. The total output in the United States in that year was about 97 billion ton-miles. This figure suggests that the number of identical efficient trucking companies that could have served this market was more than 450. This estimate suggests that the market structure is highly competitive.

By 1984, however, the *LAC* curve was declining over the entire range of industry output. The largest firm in the sample, Consolidated Freighting, had an output of more than 6.5 billion ton-miles in that year, but that was less than 15 percent of the industry output of 96 billion ton-miles. This ratio suggests that scale economies have not yet been exhausted and an oligopolistic market structure may form in time. Such a change in the structure of the trucking industry indicates that the largest carriers are likely to expand further in an effort to cut costs, and smaller firms will be squeezed out of the industry.

11.11 Economies of Scope

When the cost of producing two products in combination is less than the total cost of producing each product separately, the condition is called **economies of scope.** Cost is $C(X_1, X_2) < C(X_1, 0) + C(0, X_2)$, where $C(X_1, 0)$ is the cost of producing X_1 units of the first good alone, $C(0, X_2)$ is the cost of producing X_2 units of the second good alone, and $C(X_1, X_2)$ is the cost of producing X_1 and X_2 units jointly. This idea of economies of scope has been described as "subadditivity of costs."[4] The notion of economies of scope has been applied mostly to the firm that produces several goods, the multiproduct firm, but it appears that the theory is equally applicable to the firm that produces one good at several plants, the multiplant firm.

Economies of scope might arise in the multiproduct firm when the goods being produced are complements in production. Producing one good may generate a byproduct that can be sold separately or used as an input in producing another good. Cogeneration of electrical power and steam is one example. When producing electricity creates steam, that steam can be converted into heat that can be sold or converted into energy for use elsewhere.

Economies of scope may arise in the multiplant firm by reducing transportation cost or sharing advertising or research-and-development costs. Such costs are external to the plant operation, but would be larger if borne by separate plants because of unnecessary duplication. Such specialized services as purchasing, market research, personnel services, and marketing may lead to economies of scope when centralized and shared by many plants producing one or more goods.

To measure the degree of economies of scope, this formula is used:

$$S = \frac{C(X_1, 0) + C(0, X_2) - C(X_1, X_2)}{C(X_1, X_2)}$$

If economies of scope are present, S will be greater than zero because then $C(X_1, X_2)$ will be less than the total cost of producing each good alone, $C(X_1, 0) + C(0, X_2)$. Thus S measures the percentage of reduction in cost as a result of joint production.

---

4. William J. Baumol, "Scale Economies, Average Cost, and Profitability of Marginal Cost Pricing," in R. E. Grieson, ed., *Essays in Urban Economics and Public Finance in Honor of William S. Vickrey* (D. C. Heath, 1975), pp. 43–57. See also John C. Panzar and Robert D. Willig, "Economies of Scale and Economies of Scope in Multi-product Output Production," Bell Laboratories Economic Decision Paper No. 33, 1975.

11.12 External Economies and Diseconomies

So far we have assumed that input prices remained constant. When we analyze a large firm or the industry as a whole, however, the assumption of fixed input prices may not hold in the long run. Each firm's cost curve *shifts* when input prices change.

When input prices rise as production increases, the cost curves shift up and the firm is said to be experiencing **pecuniary diseconomies.** That would result when one large firm or the industry expands and thereby bids up the price of some factor of production. When input prices fall as production increases, the cost curves shift down, and the firm is said to be experiencing **pecuniary economies.** This condition may occur as the firm increases production, enabling it to use quantity discounts offered by suppliers of materials used in production.

Other external economies and diseconomies are associated with the entire industry. The three possible industry cost conditions are: increasing, decreasing, and constant. In an **increasing-cost industry,** the cost curves of each firm rise as industry production increases. Each firm and the industry are said to be experiencing **external diseconomies.** External diseconomies are usually caused by pecuniary diseconomies. External diseconomies are common in such extractive industries as mining, fishing, lumbering, and agriculture. As the fishing industry expands, fish become scarcer and reproduce at a slower rate; boats have to travel farther to extract the same yield than they had to before. In contrast, in a **decreasing-cost industry,** each firm's cost curves fall as industry production increases. Each firm is said to be experiencing **external economies.** As a practical matter, external economies are rare, but with some notable exceptions. In mining, the industry's growth and expansion enhanced the construction of railroads—a much cheaper form of transportation than trucking. In the oil-extraction industry, large pipelines and giant tankers became cost effective only with huge volumes of production. Thus an industry's expansion enables all firms in the industry to use less costly production methods. Finally, when the firms' cost curves are not affected by changes in industry output, the industry is called a **constant-cost industry.**

AN APPLICATION: *The Beer Industry*

The beer industry has seen a dramatic reduction in both the number of firms and the number of plants brewing and bottling beer, as shown by the data in Table 11.3. The brewing industry has evolved from many small local or regional breweries to dominance by a few relatively large firms. The reasons for this change have been analyzed by Kenneth Elzinga and others.*

---

* Kenneth Elzinga, "The Beer Industry," in *The Structure of American Industry,* 6th ed., Walter Adams, ed. (Macmillan, 1982). See also Ira Horowitz and Ann R. Horowitz, "Firms in a Declining Market: The Brewing Case," *Journal of Industrial Economics,* 13(2) (March 1965); Thomas F. Hogarty and Kenneth G. Elzinga, "The Demand for Beer," *Review of Economics and Statistics,* 59(2) (May 1972), pp. 195–198; Victor J. Tremblay, "Scale Economies, Technological Change, and Firm-Cost Asymmetries in the U.S. Brewing Industry," *Quarterly Review of Economics and Business,* 27(2) (Summer 1987), pp. 71–86.

Table 11.3 Breweries and Brewery Firms in the United States

Year	Plants	Firms
1947	465	404
1954	310	263
1958	252	211
1963	211	171
1967	154	125
1972	131	108
1976	94	49

Source: Charles F. Keithahn, "The Brewing Industry," *Staff Report of the Bureau of Economics,* U.S. Federal Trade Commission, 1978.

The decline in the number of plants and firms is partly explained by changing demand conditions. First came a shift toward home consumption of beer sold in disposable bottles or cans. This change in consumption patterns led to extra costs in bottling and pasteurizing in production. Keg beer does not require pasteurization when it is kept chilled continuously. Second came a change toward widely varied types and sizes of containers to meet varying customer preferences. Both of these changes favor large operations that use mechanized and automated equipment. At the same time, per capita beer consumption increased from 15 gallons per year in 1958 to 16.7 gallons per year by 1968 as brewers responded to the changes in consumer tastes toward beer that was light in color and lower in calories. The change in demand in favor of light beers put many of the smaller breweries specializing in stronger-flavored and stouter beers at a disadvantage.

Dramatic changes in technology also favored large-scale production operations. In 1965, the typical closing line that caps or seals containers could move about 500 bottles or 900 cans per minute. The speed of that line increased to about 750 bottles or 1,200 cans a minute. As technology changed, the minimum efficient size of the brewery increased dramatically, and many obsolete plants were closed. In 1987, for example, one firm closed an obsolete plant in the Northwest and transferred its production of Lucky beer to a more modern plant elsewhere. The old plant was sold, disassembled, and shipped to the People's Republic of China.

Significant increases in the size of the individual plant were accompanied by increased economies in operations at the firm level. One economy came from lower advertising cost per unit of production. Another came in complying with state and federal regulations and paying fixed fees that are less costly per unit for the large firm. It has been estimated that by 1977 a firm needed three to four plants to exhaust available multiplant economies and thus minimize average cost, and that each plant would be capable of producing 4 to 5 million barrels per year.† At that rate a firm with four plants would have been able to supply nearly the entire 1977 market.

Figure 11.20 illustrates what happened between 1947 and 1977. The cost curve SAC_{47-62} represents the minimum efficient plant size compared to its LAC_{47-62} curve, as determined by 1947 to 1962 technology. The position of the SAC led the Horowitzes to predict in 1965 that the smaller breweries would be abandoned or merged into larger, more efficient plants to take advantage of economies in advertising, transportation, and more efficient production methods. Technical change caused a downward shift in the long-run cost to LAC_{77}, as estimated by Scherer for 1977. The SAC_{77} corresponds to the plant size producing 5 million barrels per year. The 1977 curves indicate that economies of scale were still left in the industry. Mergers continued into the 1980s, accompanied by a decrease in the real price of beer. By 1982, 67 firms were producing malt beverages, including beer, but 86 percent of the industry

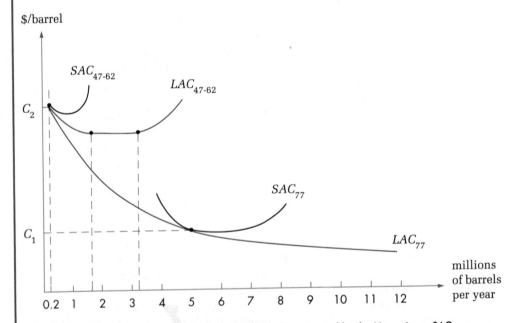

Figure 11.20 **Plant and firm sizes in the brewing industry:** As estimated by the Horowitzes, SAC_{47-62} shows the minimum efficient plant size compared to the LAC_{47-62} for the period 1947 to 1962. Technical changes by 1977 shifted the cost curves to those like SAC_{77} and LAC_{77}, as estimated by Scherer.

---

† Frederick M. Scherer, as cited by Charles F. Keithahn, *The Brewing Industry,* Staff Report of the Bureau of Economics, U.S. Federal Trade Commission, December 1978, pp. 34–37.

output was produced by the four largest firms.‡ Victor Tremblay concluded that the significant scale economies achieved during the 1950s were not exploited until the 1960s because of deficient market demand and excess capacity in most firms. Tremblay argues that the rise in industrial concentration was inevitable because of the scale increasing technological change.

‡ U.S. Bureau of the Census, *1982 Census of Manufactures: Concentration Ratios in Manufacturing,* MC 82-S-7 Subject Series, U.S. Government Printing Office, April 1986.

11.13 Input Prices, Technology, and the Input Ratio

Given input prices, the long-run cost curve is derived along an expansion path where the ratio of marginal products is equal to the input price ratio. At each level of output, the cost-minimizing input ratio is determined. If input prices change, the slope of the isocost line changes and the firm adjusts the input ratio. The firm finds itself on a new path of expansion, and the result is a new set of cost curves.

The sensitivity of cost to changes in the input price ratio depends on the substitutability of inputs. The more easily inputs can be substituted, the smaller the influence on cost. In Chapter 10, the elasticity of substitution was defined as

$$\sigma = \frac{\%\Delta \text{ in } K/L}{\%\Delta \text{ in } MRTS_{LK}}$$

when K and L are the two inputs. In the long run the firm that minimizes cost chooses K and L, so that $MRTS_{LK} = w/r$. Therefore, for the cost-minimizing firm in the long run, the elasticity of substitution may be measured by

$$\sigma = \frac{\%\Delta \text{ in } K/L}{\%\Delta \text{ in } w/r} = \frac{\dfrac{\Delta(K/L)}{K/L}}{\dfrac{\Delta(w/r)}{w/r}}$$

A large σ means that the inputs are close substitutes, a big change will occur in the input ratio for a small change in relative prices, and a small increase will come in the cost of producing any level of output.

Some production operations are much more capital intensive than others. One explanation is that capital has relatively high productivity. An alternative explanation is that labor is relatively expensive. Figure 11.21 illustrates the two possibilities. In panel A, two isocost lines are shown. For any given level of output the firm will choose a more capital-intensive production process when the price of labor is high relative to capital. The relatively higher price of labor $(w/r)_2 > (w/r)_1$, causes the cost-minimizing firm to choose

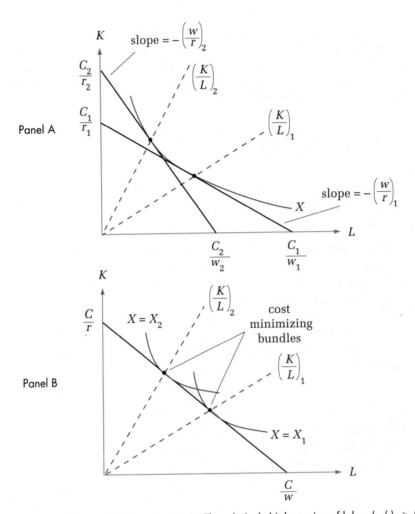

Figure 11.21 **Different capital-labor ratios: Panel A** The relatively higher price of labor $(w/r)_2 > (w/r)_1$ causes the firm to choose a more capital-intensive production activity. **Panel B** The technology represented by $X = X_2$ has a higher productivity of capital relative to labor, and so the firm chooses a production activity that is more capital intensive for any set of input prices.

$(K/L)_2$ over $(K/L)_1$. In panel B, two technologies are represented by the isoquants $X = X_1$ and $X = X_2$. Capital is more productive than labor for the second technology. If one firm uses the technology represented by X_1, and a second firm uses that represented by X_2, they will have different capital–labor ratios when they face the same set of relative input prices.

ECONOMIC SCENE: *You Need a New Cost System When . . .*

It's obvious that a company needs reliable information on product costs to make smart decisions. How do you know if your cost system is doing the job? The question is asked by Robin Cooper, who recently offered some answers.* It's time to redesign your cost system when, for instance, the manufacturing manager wants to drop a product that seems to generate the biggest profit. Changes are needed because this product costs more than your costing system reflects. Another indicator of an obsolete system appears when divisions or departments develop their own systems. A company system can make winners into losers and vice versa. Frustrated divisions, then, may initiate their own methods for costing products in order to guide them to use inputs efficiently. Other indicators of obsolete cost systems include instances in which profit margins are hard to explain, when hard-to-make products show big profits, when the accounting department spends a lot of time on special projects, when your profit margin appears to be large but no other firms want to compete, when customers don't complain about price increases, when the results of bids are hard to explain, when vendors' bids are lower than expected, and when reported costs change because of new financial regulations.

An effective cost system should measure the opportunity costs of all inputs. But a once-good cost system can become obsolete in several ways. One manufacturer introduced automation but didn't change its cost system to reflect the new technology. The company continued to allocate overhead by direct labor costs. But products made on the new machines consumed little direct labor, and so very little overhead was attributed to those products. The costs of items that consumed more direct labor were overestimated. Any time you see changed use of support functions, changes in technology, or changes in input proportions, examine the cost function.

A system can become obsolete when change appears in the competitive environment or in market strategy. When competition is stiff, companies need more accurate costs than ever because profit margins will be thin. When competition is intense, competitors are more likely to take advantage of poor pricing decisions. Moreover, most cost systems are designed with a particular production method in mind. If a firm makes a strategic decision to market in a low-volume niche, the cost system should be revised to reflect the lower-volume production. When bundled products are unbundled, allocating joint costs becomes more complex. One firm had been allocating all overhead costs to one of two bundled products. Because the products were being produced in a fixed proportion, allocating all overhead to one or the other made no difference. But when the firm unbundled the products and began to produce them in variable proportion, it failed to change its overhead allocation. One product was priced too high because all overhead was allocated to it. Over several years the company put little effort into that product line because the measured profit margin was small. As a consequence, this company missed a very attractive market opportunity.

---

* Robin Cooper, "You Need a New Cost System When . . . ," *Harvard Business Review* (January-February 1989).

These examples emphasize that you must continually monitor your cost system. The presence of symptoms doesn't make your system obsolete. A product may have a very low profit margin because your cost system is obsolete—or because a competitor has engaged in an aggressive market-penetration strategy that is cutting into your sales. But because production and market conditions rarely remain static for long, managers should evaluate their systems frequently.

THE FAR SIDE   By GARY LARSON

"Well, shoot. I just can't figure it out. I'm movin' over 500 doughnuts a day, but I'm still just barely squeakin' by."

THE FAR SIDE COPYRIGHT 1987 and 1991 UNIVERSAL PRESS SYNDICATE. Reprinted with permission.

11.14 Statistical Analysis of Cost

If the average cost curve for each plant and firm in each market were known, management would be able to identify the optimal scale of operation to minimize the cost of producing any level of output. As I mentioned, the engineering technique is one way to establish the cost curve from the production function. Frequently, however, sufficient engineering data are not readily available, particularly to an analyst not working for the firm. Analysts then fall back on statistical techniques to estimate the cost curves.

The statistical approach proceeds from a data base consisting of time-series, cross-section, or pooled observations. If your data consist of input and output quantities, you can estimate the production function and convert it into a cost function using input prices. In practice, however, good data on the input–output relationship are not available at the firm level, and if it were you could use the engineering technique in the first place. Fortunately, good data on input *prices* are usually available from accounting records or surveys. Because cost is a function of output and input prices, the cost function can be estimated directly. Once the cost function is estimated, the duality between the cost and production functions can be exploited to obtain estimates on returns to scale and input substitution elasticities if desired.[5]

With a sufficiently large number of observations, we can apply regression analysis to estimate a cost equation as a function of output. The cost measure should include all costs that are caused by production of the good—that is, costs that vary with output. Costs that are incurred but not yet paid for should be matched with the goods that cause the obligation. Fixed costs or external costs that do not vary with the level of production should be treated separately because the goal is to measure cost as a function of output.

The first step in directly estimating a cost function is to specify the equation to be estimated. A *linear* specification may provide an adequate fit over the range of your data:

$$C = a + bQ + \sum_{i=1}^{m} c_i Z_i$$

where C refers to total variable cost, Q is the quantity of output, and the Z_i are measures of all other variables that might affect output. These other variables might include input prices, plant size, size of production lot, measures of technological change, or anything else that changed and may have affected the cost of production. Including these other variables in the empirical model controls for their influence on cost and makes the model more compatible with the theoretical model that holds input prices, technology, and other factors constant.

The intercept should not be interpreted as fixed cost because such costs are not included in the cost measure. Rather, we should interpret it as capturing the effects of omitted variables. Even if fixed costs were included in the dependent variable, the intercept usually lies beyond the range of the data, and extending the regression equation beyond the range of the data is likely to result in significant error in prediction.

Although the linear model may sometimes fit the data fairly well, it is not very satisfactory because it constrains the estimated marginal cost to be constant. Better specifications would be the quadratic or cubic functions. Let's assume that input prices,

---

5. Just as the cost function can be derived from the production function, the production function can be derived from the cost function. That is, for every production function $X = X(z_1, z_2, \ldots, z_m)$, where the z's are the inputs, there is a corresponding cost function $C = C(X, w_1, w_2, \ldots, w_m)$, where the w's are the input prices, and vice versa. This relation between cost and output is called **duality**.

technology, and anything else that might influence cost remain constant so that their influence is captured in the intercept term. Then the *quadratic* specification,

$$C = a + bQ + cQ^2$$

and the *cubic* specification,

$$C = a + bQ + cQ^2 + dQ^3$$

both permit changing marginal costs. Figure 11.22 illustrates reasonable average and marginal cost curves for the quadratic (panel A) and cubic (panel B) cost curves.

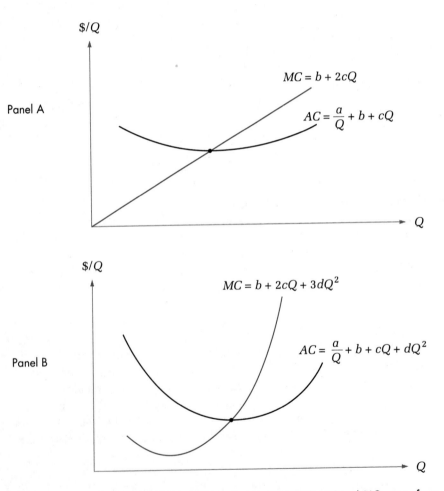

Figure 11.22   **Average and marginal costs for different cost curves: Panel A** The AC and MC curves for a quadratic cost curve when cost increases at an increasing rate. **Panel B** The AC and MC curves for a cubic cost curve when cost increases initially at a decreasing rate.

11.15 Empirical Long-run Cost Functions

One goal in estimating a long-run cost function is to determine the existence and extent of any economies of scale. In the long run all inputs are variable, input prices are likely to change, and technical progress may occur. The longer the time, the more things are likely to change, and so using time-series data usually involves more complexity than using cross-section data. Thus, paradoxically, cross-section data are usually used to estimate long-run cost curves. Data are gathered for plants of several sizes at one specified time, and cost is regressed on output and other explanatory variables. Input prices usually are included because factor prices tend to vary by region and hence by plant. When we use time-series data, we need to control for changes in technology and inflation as well as changes in factor prices.

Regardless of the type of data we use, average cost will be systematically overstated if firms do not all operate efficiently. A basic assumption in the theoretical model is that firms choose the most efficient scale so as to minimize cost. But when some inputs are lumpy, the firm may produce at points along a short-run *AC* curve that are not tangent to the *LAC* curve. As illustrated by Figure 11.23, the data points lie above the true envelope curve. The resulting estimated *LAC* curve lies everywhere above the theoretically attainable *LAC* curve.

Even more important is the potential for distorting the estimate of any economies or diseconomies of scale. If small firms are likely to produce at a point above the *LAC* curve

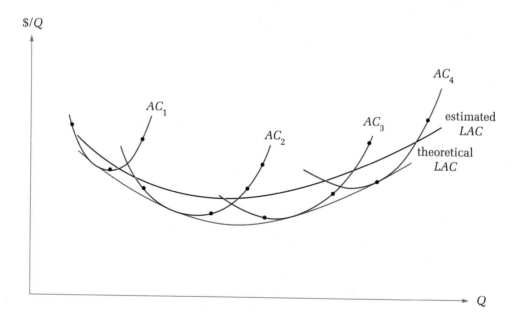

Figure 11.23 **Bias in estimating the *LAC* curve:** When firms are not operating at points of tangency of short-run AC curves to the LAC curve, the estimated LAC curve will lie above the true envelope curve.

Table 11.4 Average Cost for Selected Electric Companies

Company	Output, million kwh		$ cost/1,000 kwh	
	1955	1970	1955	1970
Newport Electric	68	50	11.69	10.75
Community Public Service	63	183	8.73	7.03
United Gas Improvement	235	467	10.39	8.44
St. Joseph Light & Power	253	938	8.03	5.45
Iowa Southern Utilities	299	1,328	11.36	6.07
Missouri Public Service	209	1,886	9.26	5.47
Rochester Gas & Electric	1,156	2,020	7.66	8.89
Iowa Electric Light & Power	1,166	2,445	7.37	5.37
Central La. Gas & Electric	353	2,689	7.53	5.54
Wisconsin Public Service	1,122	3,571	6.90	6.02
Atlantic City Electric	1,291	4,187	7.96	7.00
Central Illinois Public Services	2,304	5,316	5.48	4.43
Kansas Gas & Electric	1,668	5,785	5.08	3.36
Northern Indiana Public Service	1,137	6,837	7.01	4.96
Indianapolis Power & Light	2,341	7,484	5.51	3.94
Oklahoma Gas & Electric	2,353	10,149	4.94	3.01
Niagara Mohawk Power	8,787	11,667	5.47	6.40
Potomac Electric Power	3,538	13,846	6.79	6.95
Gulf States Utilities	2,507	17,875	3.85	3.27
Virginia Electric Power	5,277	23,217	6.12	4.85
Consolidated Edison	14,359	29,613	9.71	8.43
Detroit Edison	11,796	30,958	6.19	6.05
Duke Power	9,956	34,212	4.51	4.84
Commonwealth Edison	19,170	46,871	7.10	5.43
Southern	13,702	53,918	4.74	4.30

Source: L. R. Christensen and W. H. Greene, "Economies of Scale in U.S. Electric Power Generation," *Journal of Political Economy*, 84(4) (August 1976), p. 672. Reprinted by permission of the University of Chicago Press.

when the *LAC* is falling, then the estimated economies of scale will look greater than they really are because the estimated *LAC* curve will have a steeper slope than the true envelope curve. Or perhaps smaller, high-cost firms leave the industry so that their performance is not included in the data. This sample selection process will result in an underestimate of the potential scale economies.

In spite of these difficulties, econometricians have been fairly successful in estimating long-run cost curves. Lauritis R. Christensen and William H. Greene estimated long-run cost curves for generating electricity. They used cross-section data on average cost for several firms for 1955 and for 1970. That data set is reproduced in Table 11.4. Because it was important to separate the decrease in cost caused by technological change from any economies of scale, they estimated two long-run cost functions, one for 1955 and another for 1970. They used a number of functional forms, but the simplest was:

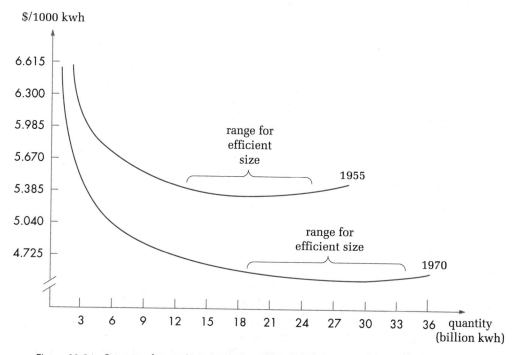

$/1000 kwh

range for
efficient
size

1955

range for
efficient size

1970

3 6 9 12 15 18 21 24 27 30 33 36 quantity
(billion kwh)

Figure 11.24 **Economies of size in the power industry, 1955 and 1970:** Estimates for LAC curves for the electrical-power industry by Christensen and Greene indicate a downward shift between 1955 and 1970. The range of output for the efficient plant size also increased.

$$\ln C = \alpha + \beta_Q \ln Q + \beta_L \ln P_L + \beta_K \ln P_K + \beta_F \ln P_F$$

where P_L, P_K, and P_F are the prices of labor, capital, and fuel inputs. This functional form implies that the underlying production function is of the Cobb-Douglas variety.

After estimating a long-run cost equation for each year, the analysts plotted an average cost curve for each of the two periods. The curves are reproduced in Figure 11.24. The average cost curve shifted downward significantly from 1955 to 1970, a trend attributable to technological advance in the industry. Notice that the shape of each curve indicates substantial economies of scale at lower production rates, but the curves flatten out rapidly. This shape is fairly typical of estimated long-run AVC curves. One reason is that firms usually do not expand beyond the range of current economies of scale, giving us no data to reveal diseconomies of scale even if they are present.

Christensen and Greene also found that most firms were operating at a scale *smaller* than the most efficient one, but that more firms were operating in the efficient range in 1970 than in 1955. In 1955, 118 of 124 firms producing about 75 percent of industry capacity were operating below the minimally efficient scale. In 1970, 97 of 144 firms producing about 45 percent of industry output were operating below the minimum. This proportion indicates a significant potential for cost reduction if all firms were to use more efficient plant sizes. One explanation for firms operating at a scale smaller than the most efficient one is the lumpiness of investment in capital for generating power. Let us put this study in perspective: the authors estimated that the cost of production in 1970 would have been $175.1 million less if all power had been produced at the point of minimum average cost.

The preceding empirical study of long-run cost curves is just one of hundreds of studies that have been conducted. One survey by A. A. Walters, conducted prior to 1963, reports relatively flat *LAC* curves for most manufacturing industries in the United States.[6] In another study that includes international comparisons between 1965 and 1967, F. M. Scherer reports that long-run cost curves are similar across countries and that the *LAC* curves are relatively flat.[7] It appears that the most typical shape of the *LAC* curve is one that falls steeply but reaches a level of minimum efficient scale for plant sizes at fairly low production levels and then remains flat for larger production levels. Thus the most typical *LAC* curve is "knee-shaped," like those shown in Figure 11.24.

Several industries do have significant economies of scale. These are usually extractive industries or those usually classified as public utilities or, in some countries, as nationalized industries. Some selected examples of the results from United States cost studies are reported in Table 11.5. Four studies on the rail-transport industry are included. George Borts found increasing costs in the eastern region, but he found decreasing or constant costs in the South and West. Zvi Griliches found that decreasing costs are not prevalent in the East or among the bigger railroads. Theodore Keeler found constant returns to firm size but substantial unexploited economies of traffic density (excess capacity). Douglas Caves *et al.,* found sizable returns to scale when changes in output were accompanied by changes in haul and trip length. The other studies summarized in Table 11.5 report on varied results from various industries.

---

6. A. A. Walters, "Production and Cost Functions," *Econometrica,* 31(1–2) (January-April 1963), pp. 1–66.
7. F. M. Scherer et al., *The Economics of Multi-plant Operations: An International Comparison Study* (Harvard University Press, 1975).

Table 11.5 Results from Cost Studies for Selected U.S. Industries

Industry	Author	Results
Rail transport	Borts (1960)	Increasing costs in eastern region; decreasing costs in South and West.
Rail transport	Griliches (1972)	Constant or mildly increasing returns to scale.
Rail transport	Keeler (1974)	Constant returns to firm size but substantial unexplained economies of traffic density.
Rail transport	Caves et al. (1981)	Returns to scale are sizable if output changes are accompanied by changes in haul and trip length.
Electricity	Nerlove (1961)	Increasing returns to scale at firm level: *LAC* declines but shows signs of increasing eventually.
Hospitals	Feldstein (1968)	*LAC* shallow U-shape with minimum at 310 beds (medium size).

Airlines, local	Eads et al.	Slightly increasing economies of scale.
Refuse collection	Stevens (1978)	Economies of scale in small cities, up to 20,000 population; all economies exhausted and constant returns to scale for cities over 50,000 population.
Brewing	Scherer (1978)	Declining *LAC* up to 18 million barrels per year.
Brewing	Tremblay (1987)	Scale increasing; technical change; reduced unit cost of production.
Shipping	Jansson et al. (1978)	Economies of scale in hauling but not in handling.
Sewage disposal	Knapp (1978)	Significant economies of scale up to 10 million gallons per day.
Cement	Norman (1979)	Substantial economies of scale.
Automotive	Friedlander et al. (1983)	No general economies of scale in industry, but increasing returns and economies of multiple production for General Motors.
Chemical processing	Lieberman (1987)	Scale economies resulting in large plant sizes over time caused by technical change.
Police protection	Gyapong et al. (1988)	No significant scale economies, but some economies of joint production.

Sources: George H. Borts, "The Estimation of Rail Cost Functions," *Econometrica*, 28(1) (January 1980), pp. 108–131; Zvi Griliches, "Cost Allocation in Railroad Regulation," *Bell Journal of Economics and Management Science*, 3(1) (Spring 1972), pp. 26–41; Theodore E. Keeler, "Railroad Costs, Returns to Scale, and Excess Capacity," *Review of Economics and Statistics*, 56(2) (May 1974), pp. 201–208; Douglas W. Caves, Laurits R. Christensen, and Joseph A. Swanson, "Productivity Growth, Scale Economies, and Capacity Utilization in U.S. Railroads, 1955–74," *American Economic Review*, 71(5) (December 1981), pp. 994–1002; Marc Nerlove, "Returns to Scale in Electricity Supply," in *Measurement in Economics in Memory of Yehuda Grunfeld*, Carl F. Christ et al., eds. (Stanford University Press, 1963), pp. 167–198; M. Feldstein, *Economic Analysis for Health Service Efficiency* (Markham, 1968); George Eads, Marc Nerlove, and William Raduchel, "A Long-run Cost Function for the Local Service Airline Industry: An Experiment in Non-linear Estimation," *Review of Economics and Statistics*, 51(3) (August 1969), pp. 258–270; Barbara J. Stevens, "Scale, Market Structure, and the Cost of Refuse Collection," *Review of Economics and Statistics*, 60(3) (August 1978), pp. 438–448; Frederick M. Scherer, as cited by C. F. Kethahn, *The Brewing Industry*, Staff Report of the Bureau of Economics, U.S. Federal Trade Commission, Washington, D.C., 1978; Victor J. Tremblay, "Scale Economies, Technological Change, and Firm-Cost Asymmetries in the U.S. Brewing Industry," *Quarterly Journal of Economics and Business*, 27(2) (Summer 1987), pp. 71–86; J. Jansson and D. Schneerson, "Economies of Scale of General Cargo Ships," *Review of Economics and Statistics* (May 1987); M. R. J. Knapp, "Economies of Scale in Sewage Purification and Disposal," *Journal of Industrial Economics*, 27(2) (December 1978), pp. 163–183; G. Norman, "Economies of Scale in the Cement Industry," *Journal of Industrial Economics* (June 1979); Ann F. Friedlander, Clifford Winston, and Kung Wang, "Costs, Technology, and Productivity in the U.S. Automotive Industry," *Bell Journal of Economics*, 14(1) (Spring 1983), pp. 1–20; Marvin B. Lieberman, "Market Growth, Economies of Scale and Plant Size in the Chemical Processing Industries," *Journal of Industrial Economics*, 36(2) (December 1987), pp. 175–191; Anthony O. Gyapong and Kwabena Gyimah-Brempong, "Factor Substitution, Price Elasticity of Factor Demand and Returns to Scale in Police Production: Evidence from Michigan," *Southern Economic Journal*, 54(4) (April 1988), pp. 863–878.

AN APPLICATION: *Police Protection in Michigan*

Providing public safety is labor intensive—personnel cost accounts for 50 to 70 percent of total. Increases in police wages, together with declining public-sector subsidies, have been squeezing city budgets. One way to reduce cost is factor substitution—using civilian employees in administration and using patrol cars and other equipment in place of police officers.

In a recent study using data from police departments in Michigan, Anthony Gyapong and Kwabena Gyimah-Brempong have attempted to answer these questions.* To what extent are civilian employees and capital inputs substitutes or complements to police personnel in production? How price elastic is the demand for these factors of production? Can unit cost be reduced by consolidating police operations in a metropolitan area? Are economies of scope possible in police production?

The analysts were able to divide output into seven measures: personal crimes (murder, rape, and assault), robbery, burglary, larceny, motor-vehicle theft, arson, and nonarrest outputs. Nonarrest outputs were assumed to be proportional to population, so that population could be used as a proxy for that output. Inputs included police officers, civilian employees, and a composite of capital inputs. The analysts estimated a seven-output and three-input translog cost function,†

$$\ln C = \alpha_0 + \sum_{i=1}^{7} \alpha_i \ln Q_i + \sum_{j=1}^{3} \beta_j \ln w_j + \frac{1}{2}\left[\sum_{i=1}^{7} \sum_{j=1}^{7} \alpha_{ij} \ln Q_i \ln Q_j \right]$$

$$+ \frac{1}{2}\left[\sum_{k=1}^{3} \sum_{j=1}^{3} \beta_{jk} \ln w_j \ln w_k \right] + \sum_{i=1}^{7} \sum_{j=1}^{3} \delta_{ij} \ln Q_i \ln w_j + \varepsilon$$

where $\alpha_{ij} = \alpha_{ji}$, $\beta_{jk} = \beta_{kj}$, $\Sigma\beta_j = 1$, $\Sigma\beta_{jk} = 0$ and $\Sigma\delta_{ij} = 0$ were imposed as restrictions. The term ε is a random error. The Q_i and Q_j are outputs, and the w_j and w_k are input prices. The Greek letters indicate coefficients to be estimated. The cost-share equations for inputs Z_j can be shown to be‡

$$S_j = \beta_j + \sum_{k=1}^{3} \beta_{jk} \ln w_j \ln w_k + \sum_{i=1}^{7} \delta_{ij} \ln Q_i + v$$

for each of the inputs. The term v is a random error. Relative shares depend on factor prices and outputs.

---

* Anthony O. Gyapong and Kwabena Gyimah-Brempong, "Factor Substitution, Price Elasticity of Factor Demand and Returns to Scale in Police Production: Evidence from Michigan," *Southern Economic Journal*, 54(4) (April 1988), pp. 863–878.

† The translog (transcendental logarithmic) cost function is a local, second-order approximation to any specification of a cost function. In general, the expansion path is unconstrained by the translog form. For these reasons the translog is being used with increasing frequency in empirical cost studies.

‡ $S_j = \partial \ln C/\partial \ln w_j = w_j C_j/C$ is the proportion (share) of total cost on the jth input because $w_j Q_j$ is the expenditure on the jth input. Shephard's lemma states that the demand equations are $\partial C/\partial w_j = Z_j$.

The final model to be estimated consisted of the cost equation plus two share equations. One share equation was deleted from the estimate because the share equations must sum to unity. The number of coefficients to be estimated was 55, too numerous to be reported here. The model was estimated, however, using cross-section data from 130 Michigan state municipal police departments for the years 1984 to 1985. The model performed quite well, explaining more than 96 percent of the variation for the cost equation and 21.7 percent and 11.8 percent for the police and civilian share equations. A hypothesis that the cost function was of the Cobb-Douglas type was rejected. The researchers proceeded to calculate the own- and cross-price elasticities of input demands. The calculated price elasticities are:

	Police	Civilian	Capital
Police	0.0917	0.7211	0.1891
	(0.0239)	(0.0001)	(0.0229)
Civilian	0.0596	0.4548	−0.1295
	(0.0343)	(0.3326)	(0.3384)
Capital	0.0321	−0.2658	0.0216
	(0.1352)	(0.1652)	(0.2101)

Notes: Calculated at the means. Standard errors in parentheses.

The own-price elasticities (the diagonal elements in the table) are all positive, in accordance with the sign convention, but the own-price coefficients are all negative, as demand theory predicts. The cross-price elasticities between police and civilian and between police and capital are positive, and so these inputs are substitutes. The civilian input and capital are complements, however, because that cross-elasticity is negative. Hence, the increased use of capital equipment should boost the employment of civilian employees while both substitute for police personnel. The own-price elasticities are largest for civilian and smallest for capital, suggesting greater potential for substitution using civilian employees. The demands for all three inputs, though, are inelastic, suggesting that total cost will rise faster than increases in the demand for law enforcement in spite of the input-substitution possibilities.

The researchers reported some slight evidence of increasing returns to scale, but the returns-to-scale effect was not statistically different from zero. Little is to be gained then, by consolidating municipal police departments.

The analysts looked next for economies of scope, which apply when the cost of jointly producing two or more goods is less than the cost of producing the outputs separately. Statistically significant economies of scope were found for all but five of the twenty-one output pairs, meaning that extensive interproduct complementarity occurs in police production. Most often, joint production of the seven outputs decreases the cost of production. Specialization in producing the seven outputs will increase the cost of production in most cases, suggesting that police officers should be trained and deployed as generalists rather than as specialists.

11.16 Linear Technology and Cost*

Long-run cost minimization for a linear technology is illustrated in Figure 11.25. In this illustration we see four activities. Two isoquants are shown. To minimize the cost of producing any level of output, say $X = 10$, the firm chooses the input bundle for which the isocost line just touches the isoquant. If the input prices are $w = 4$ and $r = 2$, the isocost line will have slope $-w/r = -2$. The cost-minimizing input bundle for this example is $L = 4$ and $K = 6$, and total cost is $C^* = 4L + 2K = 28$. The firm will be able to minimize total cost by using only one activity.

As output changes with constant input prices, the cost-minimizing expansion path coincides with an activity ray. If the isocost lines happen to have the same slope as linear segments of the isoquants, we find no unique expansion path because the cost-minimizing input bundles are in the cone defined by the two adjacent rays. Either way, however, cost has one value for every level of output.

Linear technologies are characterized by constant returns to scale everywhere, and so proportionate increases in all inputs will result in an increase in output by the same proportion. Thus as the firm increases output along an expansion path, cost will increase at a constant rate. Thus, the LTC curve is a straight line through the origin for the linear model. Moreover, the LAC curve graphs as a horizontal line, and every firm size generates the same average cost in the long run.

In the short run, however, the firm is forced to use other activities when output changes. For the example in Figure 11.25, let's assume that capital is fixed at $K = 6$. When the variable input increases from $L = 0$ to $L = 1$ with capital fixed at $K = 6$, the level of output increases linearly from $X = 0$ to $X = 5$, and the most capital-intensive activity is being used. Between $L = 1$ and $L = 4$, the level of output increases from $X = 5$ to $X = 10$ as the firm moves to the next activity. Likewise, between $L = 4$ and $L = 9$, output increases from $X = 10$ to $X = 15$, and between $L = 9$ and $L = 18$, output increases from $X = 15$ to $X = 20$. Output reaches a maximum of $X = 20$ at $L = 18$ when $K = 6$ for this example, and the most labor-intensive activity is used alone. Thus, the total product curve is composed of several linear segments, as summarized in the table.

L	$X(L;\ K=6)$	MP_L
$0 \leq L \leq 1$	$X = 5L$	5
$1 \leq L \leq 4$	$X = \frac{5}{3}L + \frac{10}{3}$	$\frac{5}{3}$
$4 \leq L \leq 9$	$X = L + 6$	1
$9 \leq L \leq 18$	$X = \frac{5}{9}L + 10$	$\frac{5}{9}$
$18 \leq L \leq \infty$	$X = 20$	0

---

* This section can be skipped without loss of continuity.

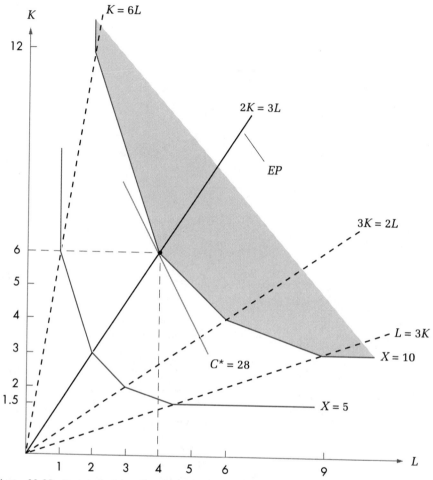

Figure 11.25 **Linear technology and minimizing long-run cost:** When input prices are $w = 4$ and $r = 2$, the isocost line will be tangent to the $X = 10$ isoquant, where $L = 4$ and $K = 6$. Minimum total cost is $C^* = 4L + 2K = 28$.

To find the input requirements for L as a function of X, get all necessary information in the preceding table. Because the technology is linear, the output is

$$X = MP_L L + MP_K K$$

The input requirement for L as a function of X given K is

$$L = \frac{X}{MP_L} - \frac{MP_K}{MP_L}K$$

After eliminating the stage of zero marginal product of labor, we have, from the preceding table:

X	L(X)	MP_L	MP_K
$0 \leq X \leq 5$	$\frac{1}{5}X$	5	0
$5 \leq X \leq 10$	$\frac{3}{5}X - 2$	$\frac{5}{3}$	$\frac{5}{9}$
$10 \leq X \leq 15$	$X - 6$	1	1
$15 \leq X \leq 20$	$\frac{9}{5}X - 18$	$\frac{5}{9}$	$\frac{5}{3}$

Thus, variable cost is given by

$$VC = wL = w\left(\frac{X}{MP_L} - \frac{MP_K}{MP_L}K\right)$$

Suppose now that the input prices are $w = 20$ and $r = 10$. The VC, FC, TC, MC, and AC relations are summarized below:

X	VC	TC	MC	AC
$0 \leq X \leq 5$	$4X$	$4X + 60$	4	$4 + 60/X$
$5 \leq X \leq 10$	$12X - 40$	$12X + 20$	12	$12 + 20/X$
$10 \leq X \leq 15$	$20X - 120$	$20X - 60$	20	$20 - 60/X$
$15 \leq X \leq 20$	$36X - 360$	$36X - 300$	36	$36 - 300/X$

These cost-curve segments are graphed in Figure 11.26. The slope of the VC curve measures marginal cost over each output range, and so the MC curve graphs as a step function. As you can see in the graph, AC falls when MC is below AC, and AC rises when MC is above AC.

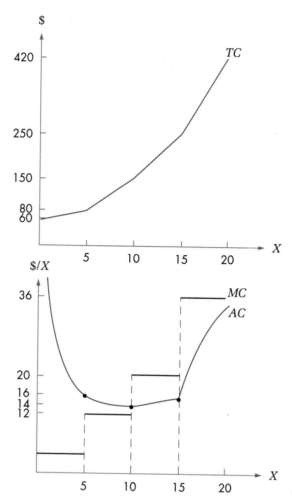

Figure 11.26 **Linear technology and short-run cost curves:** When capital is fixed, *TC* is found by adding *VC* and *FC*. The slope of the *TC* curve is marginal cost, and so the *MC* curve graphs as a step function for the linear technology.

Summary

The economic cost of any input is the payment that the resource would receive in its best alternative employment opportunity—its opportunity cost. Economic cost is likely to differ from accounting cost measures. Therefore, accounting profit and economic profit are measured differently.

Short-run variable cost as a function of output is found by multiplying prices of variable inputs by the amounts of the input required as output varies. The shape of a variable cost curve is dictated by the technology that determines the shape of the input requirement curve. Total cost is the sum of variable and fixed costs in the short run.

Average variable cost equals the price of the variable input divided by its average product, dictating an inverse relationship between average variable cost and average product. Similarly, marginal cost is equal to the price of the variable input divided by its marginal product. Diminishing productivity of a variable input will cause the average and marginal costs to increase eventually as output increases.

In the long run, all inputs are variable. With constant technology and fixed input prices, the firm will minimize the cost of producing any level of output by choosing the input bundle where the isocost line is tangent to the desired isoquant. Thus, long-run cost minimization requires that the ratio of the marginal products between all pairs of inputs be equal to the ratio of their prices. As output varies, the cost-minimizing firm moves along an expansion path, where the isocost lines are tangent to isoquants. Long-run cost is the minimum expenditure required to produce any level of output. The long-run total cost curve is the envelope curve of all short-run total cost curves.

Diseconomies of scale refers to cases in which the long-run average cost rises as output increases. Economies of scale describes cases wherein the long-run average cost falls as output increases. Economies and diseconomies of scale are influenced by returns to scale in production, but they are not exactly the same unless the expansion path coincides with an activity ray. One important source of diseconomies of scale is the increased complexity of managing resources as the scale of operations increases.

The number of plants in an industry depends on the extent of the economies of scale relative to industry demand. The most efficient plant size occurs where *LAC* is smallest. If diseconomies of scale occur at low levels of output relative to market demand, the industry will tend to be composed of many plants. But if economies of scale extend up to or beyond the range of market demand, the industry will support only one plant if lowest unit-production cost is to be achieved.

Economies of scope describes cases in which the firm produces several goods at a lower cost than if they were produced by separate firms. Economies of scope may also arise in multiplant production operations. Pecuniary economies or diseconomies arise when input prices vary as a consequence of output changes. Such external economies or diseconomies are associated with the entire industry.

Technology is an important determinant of how costs behave as output changes. The sensitivity of costs to changes in input prices depends on the ease with which inputs are substituted. For the cost-minimizing firm, the elasticity of input substitution can be measured by dividing the percentage of change in the input ratio by the percentage of change in the input price ratio. Productivity-enhancing changes in technology have been an important source of unit-cost reduction.

Cost as a function of output can be found from the production function if input prices are known. But if sufficient engineering information is unknown, and given a sufficiently large number of observations, regression techniques can be used to estimate cost equations. As usual, carefully specifying the functional form to be estimated is important to avoid specification error. The duality between cost and production functions makes the choice of functional form even more important. Other sources of bias should be considered also. One empirical specification frequently used is the translog cost curve, which serves as an approximation to any underlying cost function.

When the underlying technology is linear, long-run total cost increases at a constant rate as output increases. This relation is a consequence of constant returns to scale, and the long-run average and marginal costs are constant and equal to each other. In the short run, input proportions must vary even for the linear model. Marginal cost increases sectionally and graphs as a step function for the linear model in the short run.

Further Readings

Most of the references in Chapter 10 are relevant. You might also wish to consult

- Jacob Viner, "Cost Curves and Supply Curves," in G. J. Stigler and K. E. Boulding, eds., *Readings in Price Theory* (R. D. Irwin, 1952).
- C. E. Ferguson, *The Neoclassical Theory of Production and Distribution,* ch. 6 (Cambridge University Press, 1969).

On statistical cost analysis and surveys of empirical findings, see

- Joe S. Bain, "Economies of Scale, Concentration and Entry," *American Economic Review,* 44 (March 1954).
- A. A. Walters, "Production and Cost Functions: An Econometric Survey," *Econometrica,* 31 (1–2) (January–April 1963).
- F. M. Scherer, *Industrial Market Structure and Economic Performance,* 2d ed. (Rand McNally, 1980).

On the relatively new topic of the economies of scope, see

- John C. Panzar and Robert D. Willig, "Economies of Scale and Economies of Scope in Multi-Output Production Functions," Bell Laboratories Economic Decisions Paper No. 33, 1975.
- William J. Baumol, "Scale Economies, Average Cost, and the Profitability of Marginal Cost Pricing," in R. E. Grieson, ed., *Essays in Urban Economics and Public Finance in Honor of William S. Vickrey* (D. C. Heath, 1975).
- David Teece, "Economies of Scope and the Scope of Enterprise," *Journal of Economic Behavior and Organization,* 1 (September 1980).
- John C. Panzar and Robert D. Willig, "Economies of Scope," *American Economic Review,* 71(2) (May 1981).
- William J. Baumol, John C. Panzar, and Robert D. Willig, *Contestable Markets and the Theory of Industry Structure* (Harcourt Brace Jovanovich, 1982).

On using the translog cost function in empirical cost studies, see

- Lauritis R. Christensen, Dale W. Jorgenson, and Lawrence J. Lau, "Transcendental Logarithmic Production Frontiers," *Review of Economics and Statistics* (February 1973).

The linear model in this chapter is mostly suggestive. Activity analysis can be extended to multiplant and multiproduct technologies. The references in Chapter 10 are relevant, but you might also wish to look at

- Thomas H. Vernon, "The Theory of the Firm: A Comparison of Marginal Analysis and Linear Programming," *Southern Economic Journal* (January 1966).

Practice Problems

1. Explain why accounting costs often differ from economic costs.
2. Show graphically and explain how the stages in production can be transferred from a smooth total product curve to short-run total, average variable, and marginal cost curves as a function of output.
3. Given the production function $X = \sqrt{LK}$, assume that $w = \$1$, $r = \$4$, and $K = 1$ in the short run:
   (a) Derive the marginal and average product curves for labor, then identify any stages of production.
   (b) Derive the input requirement curve $L = L(X)$.
   (c) Derive the variable cost and total cost curve.
   (d) Derive the average variable, average total, and marginal cost curves.
4. Explain the relation between AVC and AP_L. Similarly, explain the relation between MC and MP_L.
5. Compare the effects on the short-run average and marginal cost curve of: (a) a change in the price of a fixed input, and (b) a change in the price of a variable input. How are the stages in production affected in each case?
6. Traditional breakeven analysis takes a linear revenue curve that starts at the origin and superimposes it on a graph of a linear total cost function that starts at fixed cost. The breakeven point occurs where revenue equals total cost. Economists have strong reservations about using this type of breakeven analysis. Why?
7. In a case with only two inputs, where the inputs are perfect substitutes (the $MRTS$ is constant), show on a graph that the cost-minimizing input ratio may require us to use only capital or only labor.
8. Explain why costs are minimized for a given level of output when $MP_L/MP_K = w/r$.
9. Suppose a firm's production function requires a fixed capital-to-labor ratio of 1 unit of capital to 2 workers to produce 10 units of output using a linear technology. The price of labor services is $w = \$3$ and the rental rate of capital is $r = \$1$:
   (a) Identify this firm's long-run expansion path.
   (b) Calculate the firm's long-run total and average cost curves.

(c) Now suppose capital is fixed at $K = 10$, and calculate the firm's short-run total and average cost curves.

(d) Graph the firm's short-run marginal cost curve when $K = 10$.

10. The table gives average cost as a function of output for four scales of operation.

Output	Scale 1	Scale 2	Scale 3	Scale 4
1	100	130	140	160
2	50	60	80	130
3	40	45	60	110
4	35	35	45	90
5	40	30	35	70
6	45	25	25	60
7	50	30	20	50
8	60	40	15	40
9	80	55	20	35
10	100	75	30	30
11	120	95	50	40
12	150	125	80	55

(a) Plot the short-run AC curve for each plant, then approximate the firm's long-run AC curve.

(b) Is it possible to determine the firm's optimum level of output and optimum scale of operations?

11. If input prices remain constant and if the production function has constant returns to scale everywhere, what will be the shape of the firm's long-run average cost curve? Explain.

12. Given the long-run total cost curve

$$LTC = 2X^3 - 12X^2 + 30X$$

where the long-run marginal cost curve is

$$LMC = 6X^2 - 24X + 30$$

(a) Plot the LTC curve on a graph.

(b) Find the LAC curve and plot the LAC and LMC curves on a new graph.

(c) What is the level of output where $LAC = LMC$?

(d) Identify the ranges of output where the firm experiences economies and diseconomies of scale.

13. Given the production function $X = \sqrt{LK}$, assume that $w = \$1$ and $r = \$1$. Treat capital as a parameter and find the short-run total and average cost curves for $K = 1$, $K = 4$, and $K = 9$. Graph each of these cost curves. Find and graph the long-run total and average cost curves to see that they are envelope curves.

14. Explain the difference between returns to scale and economies of scale. Under what special circumstance are they equivalent?

15. Explain the difference between economies of scale and economies of scope.

16. Explain the difference between internal economies and external economies.

17. Consider two firms that are producing along the same long-run expansion path. The only difference between the firms is that firm A has a *smaller* elasticity of substitution than firm B. If wages increase, will firm A experience a larger or smaller increase in total cost than firm B? Why?

18. As a nonprofit institution, why should a hospital care about theoretical cost models?

19. At any moment in time a firm is operating out of a given plant and only short-run costs can be observed. What, then, is the relevance of long-run costs from the manager's point of view?

20. Public utilities have been described as "natural monopolies" because they are usually characterized by significant economies of scale. Explain how economies of scale might cause the natural evolution of an industry into one that supports only one firm.

21. Public utilities may be regulated by setting a "fair rate of return" on capital invest-ment. The effect of such regulation is to decrease the cost of capital services relative to the cost of labor services. What effect does this regulation have on the K/L ratio? How does such rate-of-return regulation affect long-run costs?

22. X-inefficiency has been described as the technologically inefficient use of inputs. How will X-inefficiency influence a firm's estimated average cost curve?

23. Illustrate on a graph how technical progress might affect the firm's cost curve in both the short and long runs.

24. Suppose a company can produce one good in the amount $X_1 = 1,000$ and a second good in the amount $X_2 = 500$ at a total cost of $15,000, but if $X_1 = 1,000$ were produced alone the cost would be $12,000, and if $X_2 = 500$ were produced alone the cost would be $6,000. What is the degree of economies of scope? What is the percentage of saving from joint production?

25. Costs external to the operation of a plant may affect the optimal scale of operation. Suppose average transportation cost increases as output increases. Add average transportation cost to a typically shaped AC curve to show how the optimal scale is smaller when transportation cost is included. Would this addition tend to increase or decrease the number of plants in the industry?

26. Given the data on tomato production (Q) as a function of a fertilizer input (F) as shown in the table at the top of the following page. Least-squares regression of Q on F as a cubic function without an intercept will yield:

$$Q = 20.934F + 44.706F^2 - 4.483F^3$$
$$(11.322) \qquad (4.828) \qquad (0.493)$$

where the estimated standard errors are in parentheses.

(a) Given the estimated production function, derive the average and marginal product equations for fertilizer.

(b) Given that the price of fertilizer is $120 per unit, calculate the average variable and marginal costs as a function of output, listing the results in a table; then plot the AVC and MC curves from the information.

Q	F
55	1.0
110	1.5
181	2.0
259	2.5
345	3.0
433	3.0
520	3.5
602	4.0
675	4.0
763	4.5
780	5.0
804	5.5
805	6.0
381	6.0
500	6.0
723	6.5
758	7.0
400	3.5
581	4.5

27. Give some illustrations of situations in which you think the linear model might be a useful way to analyze the behavior of cost. Consider the problems incurred when strong economies of scale are present.

28. A mining company operates two mines producing the same type of ore. Let x_1 denote the days per week of production from mine 1, and let x_2 denote the days per week of production from mine 2. After it is mined the ore is graded into three grades: high, medium, and low. Management determines that the cost of operating both mines is

$$C = \$10,000x_1 + \$5,000x_2$$

The firm wishes to minimize the total cost of production subject to these constraints, which have been determined by technological and contractual requirements:

$$
\begin{aligned}
6x_1 + 2x_2 &\geq 24 \quad \text{(high-grade)} \\
2x_1 + 2x_2 &\geq 16 \quad \text{(medium-grade)} \\
4x_1 + 12x_2 &\geq 24 \quad \text{(low-grade)} \\
x_1 &\leq 7 \quad \text{(days per week)} \\
x_2 &\leq 7 \quad \text{(days per week)}
\end{aligned}
$$

The firm's objective is to determine how many days a week to operate each mine under current conditions.

Set up the linear programming problem by graphing the constraints and identifying the feasible set. Then determine the cost-minimizing values of x_1 and x_2 by graphing the optimal isocost line. What is the lowest operating cost per week?

Chapter 11 Appendix: *The Calculus of Costs*

In the smooth model, where isoquants are strictly convex and diminishing marginal productivity holds, calculus can be applied to the firm's optimal input decision making. With two inputs, Z_1 and Z_2, and given the available technology, the production function may be written

$$X = X(Z_1, Z_2)$$

The production function represents the maximum attainable output for any input combination, assuming that the technological optimization problem has been solved. The marginal product of input Z_j will be denoted

$$X_j(Z_1, Z_2) = \partial X/\partial Z_j$$

Given input prices w_1 and w_2, the total cost (expenditure) is given by

$$C = w_1 Z_1 + w_2 Z_2$$

Maximizing Output

Let's start by looking at the firm's constrained output-maximizing problem. The firm wants to maximize output subject to the constraint that total expenditure on the inputs is constant. That is, the firm wants to attain the highest isoquant, given that it must be on a specified isocost line:

$$\begin{aligned} \text{maximize} \quad & X(Z_1, Z_2) = X \\ \text{subject to} \quad & w_1 Z_1 + w_2 Z_2 = C^*, \qquad Z_1 \geq 0, Z_2 \geq 0 \end{aligned}$$

where C^* is the fixed level of expenditure. With an interior solution, both inputs will be chosen in positive quantities, and the Lagrangian is

$$L_1 = X(Z_1, Z_2) + \varphi(C^* - w_1 Z_1 - w_2 Z_2)$$

where φ is the Lagrange multiplier. Notice the similarity of this expression to that of the consumer's utility-maximizing problem (see Chapter 5 appendix).

The first-order conditions for an interior solution are:

$$\begin{aligned} X_1(Z_1, Z_2) &= \varphi w_1 \\ X_2(Z_1, Z_2) &= \varphi w_2 \\ w_1 Z_1 + w_2 Z_2 &= C^* \end{aligned}$$

where $X_j(Z_1, Z_2)$ denotes the marginal product MP_j. The second-order condition requires convexity of the isoquant curve tangent to the isocost line.

The solution to the first-order conditions yields the output-maximizing amounts Z_1^* and Z_2^* as well as φ^*. The first-order conditions require that:

$$\frac{MP_1}{MP_2} = \frac{w_1}{w_2}$$
$$w_1 Z_1 + w_2 Z_2 = C^*$$

The first equation states that the ratio of marginal products (the marginal rate of technical substitution) must equal the ratio of input prices. The second equation states that expenditure equals the specified level of cost. Together the two equations require tangency of the isoquant to the isocost line. Once Z_1^* and Z_2^* have been determined, the optimal level of output is given by $X^* = X(Z_1^*, Z_2^*)$.

Minimizing Cost

Alternatively, let's suppose that the firm wants to produce a predetermined level of output X^*. (This might be the profit-maximizing level of output.) The new problem is to minimize cost for that level of output:

$$\text{minimize} \quad w_1 Z_1 + w_2 Z_2 = C$$
$$\text{subject to} \quad X(Z_1, Z_2) = X^*, \quad Z_1 \geq 0, \, Z_2 \geq 0$$

With an interior solution, both inputs are chosen in positive quantities, and the new Lagrangian is

$$L_2 = w_1 Z_1 + w_2 Z_2 + \lambda[X^* - X(Z_1, Z_2)]$$

where λ is the Lagrange multiplier.

The first-order conditions for an interior solution are:

$$w_1 = \lambda X_1(Z_1, Z_2)$$
$$w_2 = \lambda X_2(Z_1, Z_2)$$
$$X^* = X(Z_1, Z_2)$$

where $X_j(Z_1, Z_2) = MP_j$ denotes the marginal product of Z_j. The second-order condition requires convexity of the isoquant curve tangent to the isocost line.

The solution to the first-order conditions yields the cost-minimizing amounts Z_1^* and Z_2^* as well as λ^*. The first-order conditions require that:

$$\frac{MP_1}{MP_2} = \frac{w_1}{w_2}$$
$$X(Z_1, Z_2) = X^*$$

The first equation states that the ratio of marginal products (the marginal rate of technical substitution) must equal the ratio of input prices. This is the same requirement derived from the output-maximizing problem. The second equation states that the inputs used in production must yield the chosen level of output. As before, the two equations require tangency of the isoquant to the isocost line. Once Z_1^* and Z_2^* have been determined, the lowest possible cost of producing X^* is given by $C^* = w_1 Z_1^* + w_2 Z_2^*$.

Long-run Cost as the Envelope of Short-run Costs

Because the first-order conditions depend only on input prices, output, and technology, the input requirements functions

$$Z_1 = Z_1(w_1, w_2, X)$$
$$Z_2 = Z_2(w_1, w_2, X)$$

exist for a specified production function. (The multiplier λ is also a function of prices and output.) Once Z_1 and Z_2 are determined, the required level of expenditure is known.

Thus, long-run cost is

$$C = C(w_1, w_2, X) = w_1 Z_1(w_1, w_2, X) + w_2 Z_2(w_1, w_2, X)$$

Given input prices, long-run total cost is $C = C(X)$ as the firm moves along an expansion path.

In the short run when the second input is the fixed input, marginal cost is given by

$$MC = \frac{\partial C}{\partial X} = w_1 \frac{\partial Z_1}{\partial X} = \frac{w_1}{MP_1}$$

because $\partial Z_2/\partial X = 0$. That is, short-run marginal cost is equal to the first input's price divided by its marginal product. The first-order conditions require that $w_1 = \lambda MP_1$, and so substitution into the MC equation results in

$$MC = \lambda$$

The multiplier λ is marginal cost.

Fixed cost is a function of the level of the fixed input,

$$FC(Z_2) = w_2 Z_2$$

The short-run cost-minimizing problem is

$$\text{minimize} \quad w_1 Z_1 + FC(Z_2) = C$$
$$\text{subject to} \quad X(Z_1, Z_2) = X^*, \quad Z_1 \geq 0, Z_2 \geq 0$$

The firm wants to minimize cost at any specified level of output X^*. The Lagrangian for this short-run cost-minimizing problem is

$$L_3 = w_1 Z_1 + FC(Z_2) + \lambda[X^* - X(Z_1, Z_2)]$$

Short-run total cost is given by

$$C = C(w_1, X, Z_2)$$

Marginal cost is given by

$$MC = \frac{\partial C}{\partial X} = \lambda(w_1, X, Z_2)$$

total cost and marginal cost are functions of the variable input price, output, and the level of the fixed input. Suppose now that the second input is allowed to adjust. The first-order conditions require that

$$\frac{\partial L_3}{\partial Z_2} = \frac{\partial FC}{\partial Z_2} + \lambda \frac{\partial X}{\partial Z_2} = 0$$

If we solve this equation along with $C = C(w_1, X, Z_2)$, we obtain an envelope of a family of short-run cost curves. The envelope curve $C = C(X)$ is the long-run cost curve.

Market Structure and the Price System

T he decisions of profit-maximizing firms influence allocation of resources, distribution of income, and national welfare in our economy. The behavior of firms depends crucially on how a market is structured. In Chapter 12 we look at pure and perfect competition. Perfect competition guarantees that resources will be used efficiently and that the gross national product of the economy will be at a maximum. You will learn that all firms produce at lowest unit cost, all inputs are paid according to their marginal contribution to output, and the gains from exchange are maximized under perfect competition. We turn to a study of monopoly behavior in Chapter 13. Topics include pure monopoly, monopolistic competition, and dominant-firm models. We present the important new model of contestable markets. Chapter 14 continues as we examine oligopolistic competition and collusive behavior. The predominant characteristic of oligopoly, strategic behavior, is examined using game theory.

In Chapter 15, we look at how firms set prices. What is cost-plus pricing? Are other pricing techniques better? What about price and quality, and pricing and advertising? We will see how a firm might increase profit by price discrimination, and how to set the optimal price of an intermediate good. At every juncture we ask how the firm's behavior affects consumers and society at large. In Chapter 16 we look at government regulation and antitrust. We examine protective regulation, including regulation of pollution, regulation of natural monopolies, mergers, and monopoly pricing practices.

Chapter

Purely Competitive Market Behavior

In this chapter we continue studying production decisions by looking at the nature of firms, their motives, and their behavior. The behavior of a firm depends on its market environment and its organization. We concentrate first on a competitive market environment in which large numbers of buyers and sellers exchange the same good. Other forms of market structure are examined in subsequent chapters.

Recall that **pure** competition exists when many small buyers and sellers trade a homogeneous product. There is no product differentiation among firms. Because so many small buyers and sellers are active, no buyer or seller can separately influence market price. Pure competition guarantees price-taking behavior. Market price is determined by the forces of demand and supply in the market, and buyers and sellers reactto that price. If any seller tries to sell above the market price, all buyers will turn to other sellers. Moreover, any seller can sell as much as it wishes at the market price, and so no one finds any advantage in selling below the market price. The competitive firm thus reacts to the market price by deciding how much to produce at that price. We also defined **perfect** competition as pure competition with two additional characteristics—perfect mobility of resources and perfect knowledge about the market.

We begin this chapter by examining the behavior of profit-maximizing, price-taking firms in the short run. You will learn that the supply curve for such a firm coincides with its marginal cost curve above its average variable cost curve. We then derive the short-run input demand for a variable input. The demand for inputs is derived from the firm's input requirements as it maximizes profits. After looking at the short run, we turn to the long run. You will learn that the long-run competitive equilibrium is characterized by zero economic profit and minimum average costs for all firms. Finally, you will also learn that perfect competition, without externalities and public goods, guarantees that national output will be maximized.

12.1 Maximizing Short-run Profit

Although pure competition guarantees price-taking behavior, sellers act as price takers in other circumstances. A large, dominant firm may be active along with numerous very small firms in an industry. The firms in the competitive fringe will act as price takers, but the industry is not purely competitive. Such a model is examined in Chapter 13. Even if only two firms are producing an identical product, if one insists on charging a fixed price, the other firm will face a demand curve like that illustrated in Figure 12.1. If p_0 is the fixed price charged by the first firm, the other firm's average revenue curve is perfectly inelastic at higher prices because quantity demanded is zero. This firm's average revenue curve is perfectly elastic at price p_0 up to quantity Q_0 because the firm can sell as much as it wants up to quantity Q_0 at that price. Below the fixed price the firm faces the market demand. Thus the model of the price-taking firm is broader in scope than the model of pure competition might suggest. Any firm that views price as independent of its output is a price-taking firm.

Because the price-taking firm views price as fixed, its average revenue is equal to price, $AR = p$, and the firm's demand curve is perfectly elastic and graphs as a horizontal line when quantity is on the horizontal axis. Total revenue is price multiplied by quantity, $TR = pX$, where X denotes the quantity demanded and sold. Thus the firm's total revenue curve graphs as a straight line through the origin, and the slope of the TR curve is equal to price. Marginal revenue thus equals price, $MR = p$. For the price-taking firm, then, marginal revenue and average revenue both equal price, $MR = AR = p$.

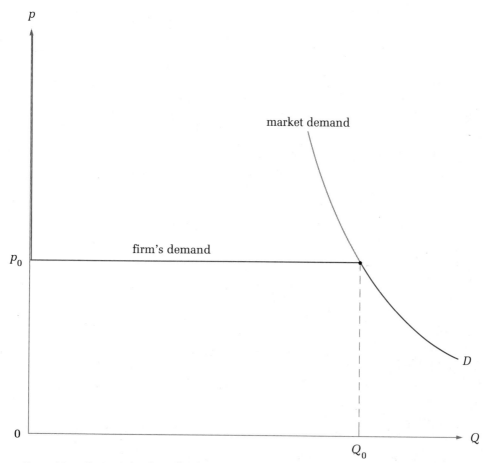

Figure 12.1 **The price-taking firm:** The demand curve for the price-taking firm is perfectly inelastic at $Q = 0$ for any price above $p = p_0$. The firm's demand curve is perfectly elastic at the market price $p = p_0$. For prices below $p = p_0$ and quantities above Q_0, the firm's demand curve coincides with the market demand curve.

Profit (π) as a function of output is found by subtracting cost from revenue,

$$\pi(X) = TR(X) - TC(X)$$

Figure 12.2 illustrates the relation between profit and output in the short run. At the origin, where $X = 0$, the firm incurs a loss equal to fixed cost. As output increases, a breakeven point is reached at point **a.** Profit becomes positive beyond point **a,** reaches a maximum, and then begins to decrease. A second breakeven point occurs at point **b,** beyond which profit once more turns negative.

The firm will maximize profit at the level of output $X = X^*$, where the slope of the profit curve is zero, $\Delta\pi/\Delta X = 0$. Because profit is revenue less cost, $\pi = TR - TC$, the

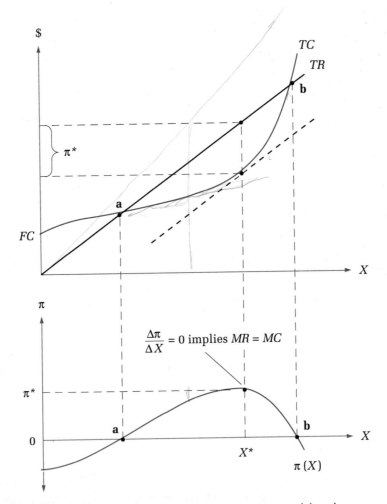

Figure 12.2   **Profit and output:** Profit increases, reaches a maximum, and then decreases as output increases. Profit is maximized at $X = X^*$, where $MR = MC$.

slope of the profit curve, **marginal profit,** is equal to marginal revenue less marginal cost:

$$\frac{\Delta \pi}{\Delta X} = MR - MC$$

Therefore, when the firm maximizes profit where the slope of the profit curve is zero, marginal revenue will be equal to marginal cost, $MR = MC$.

Finding the profit-maximizing level of output is based on common sense. As illustrated by Figure 12.2, when the slope of the revenue curve is greater than that of the cost curve, $MR > MC$, revenue is increasing faster than cost as output increases. Any manager would agree to increase output if that contributed extra revenue greater than the extra cost required. Likewise, when the slope of the revenue curve is less than that of the cost

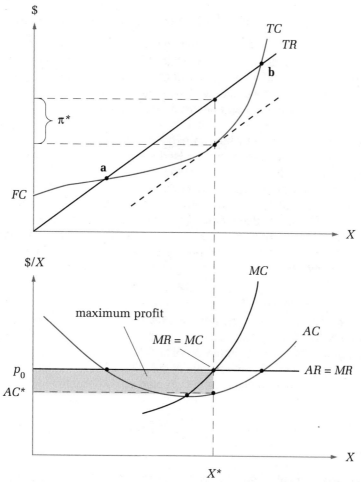

Figure 12.3 **Maximizing profit:** The firm maximizes profit at $X = X^*$, where $MR = MC$. Maximum profit π^* equals the area of the rectangle found by multiplying output X^* by the difference between price and average cost at X^*.

curve, $MR < MC$, revenue is increasing more slowly than cost as output increases. Again, any manager would agree to decrease output if the decrease in revenue were less than the decrease in cost. The firm would then increase output whenever $MR > MC$, and it would decrease output whenever $MR < MC$. And profit would be maximized where $MR = MC$.

In analyzing the price-taking firm's behavior, it is useful to view profit maximizing in terms of the average and marginal curves. Total profit equals unit profit, average revenue less average cost, multiplied by the number of units produced and sold. As Figure 12.3 illustrates, profit is maximized at $X = X^*$, where $MR = MC$. Maximum profit equals the area of the rectangle found by multiplying output X^* by the difference between average revenue and average cost at X^*.

AN APPLICATION: *Hedging and the Competitive Firm*

Duncan Holthausen extended the competitive model to decisions by risk-averse, competitive firms facing price uncertainty.* In this model firms can fix the price at which output is sold in the future by forward contracts. A forward contract is similar to a futures contract except that we find no formal market like that for futures market. A forward contract is a personal agreement between a buyer and a seller fixing the future price.

Recall that a hedge occurs when an economic agent simultaneously sells in a futures market and buys in the spot market. Hedging is possible with forward contracts in the same way as with futures contracts. Assume that the competitive firm faces an uncertain market price for its output X. The price may be treated as a random variable, and the probability that price equals p_i can be represented by a probability distribution $f(p_i)$. Output can be produced at a cost $C(X)$ with $MC > 0$. Output can be sold in the future at a random price p_i or sold forward at a specified price c. The quantity of output hedged forward is denoted H, and the portion of total output not hedged is $(X - H)$.

Profit is given by

$$\pi_i = p_i(X - H) + cH - C(X)$$

The uncertain revenue $p_i(X - H)$ depends on the random price p_i, and revenue obtained with certainty (cH) depends on forward price c and amount hedged H. If all output is hedged so that $H = X$, profit will not be a function of the uncertain price. The firm can avoid any uncertainty in revenue by hedging its entire output.

The firm is assumed to maximize the expected utility of profit

$$\max E\,[U(\pi_i] = \sum_{i=1}^{n} U[p_i(X - H) + cH - C(X)]\,f(p_i)$$

Maximizing expected utility requires the firm to set X and H so that both the marginal *expected* utility of profit with respect to X is equal to zero and the marginal *expected* utility of profit with respect to H is equal to zero simultaneously:

$$\sum_{i=1}^{n} MU(\pi_i)\,[p_i - MC(X)]\,f(p_i) = 0$$

$$\sum_{i=1}^{n} MU(\pi_i)\,[c - p_i]\,f(p_i) = 0$$

where $MU(\pi_i)$ is the marginal utility of profit. These two equations can be combined to eliminate the price term p_i, resulting in

---

*Duncan M. Holthausen, "Hedging and the Competitive Firm and Price Uncertainty," *American Economic Review* (December 1979).

$$[c - MC(X)] \sum_{i=1}^{n} MU(\pi_i)f(p_i) = 0$$

The term $[c - MC(X)]$ has been moved outside the summation because neither c nor $MC(X)$ depends on the uncertain price.

This combined condition holds true only if $MC(X) = c$ because $MU(\pi_i)$ is positive. The firm therefore chooses X so that marginal cost equals the certain forward price. Moreover, differences in risk aversion or price expectations do not affect production decisions. The ability to hedge mitigates any effect that price uncertainty might have on production decisions. The optimal amount to be hedged, however, remains to be determined.

Hedging will occur when the forward price is less than the expected price. The expected market price is

$$E(p_i) = \sum_{i=1}^{n} p_i f(p_i)$$

In a typical case, the forward price is less than the expected price, $c < E(p_i)$, because the firm is willing to pay to avoid price uncertainty on the units hedged. The difference between the expected price and the forward price is the premium paid by the hedger.

The condition of zero expected marginal utility of profit with respect to the amount hedged, H, can be written in terms of expected value:

$$E\{MU(\pi_i)[c - p_i]\} = E[MU(\pi_i)] E\{[c - p_i]\} + Cov[MU(\pi_i), -p_i] = 0$$

This equation follows from a well-known rule of elementary statistics.† The term $Cov[MU(\pi_i), -p_i]$ is the covariance between the random variables $MU(\pi_i)$ and $-p_i$. This covariance must be positive because increases in price reduce $-p_i$ and also reduce $MU(\pi_i)$ because of risk aversion. Recall that risk aversion requires diminishing marginal utility. Because $MU(\pi_i) > 0$, and $Cov[MU(\pi_i), -p_i] > 0$, the term $E\{[c - p_i]\}$ must be negative for maximizing expected utility. Taking the expected value of this last term results in

$$E\{[c - p_i]\} = c - E(p) < 0$$

Thus, the forward price c must be less than the expected price $E(p_i)$, and the requirement that $c < E(p_i)$ and $H < X$ go hand in hand. If the forward price is less than the expected price, the units hedged will be less than total production.

The conclusions are intuitively appealing. The risk-averse, competitive firm is willing to trade off higher expected profit for lower certain profit. When the forward price is less than the expected price, some but not all of the output is hedged. The number of units hedged depends on the degree of risk aversion, but total production is not affected by the price uncertainty.‡

---

†If x and y are random variables, then $E(xy) = E(x)E(y) + Cov(x, y)$.
‡This conclusion depends on the assumption that only prices are uncertain, and so the analysis holds for the firm that has control of its output. If output uncertainty also applies, the optimizing conditions will change.

12.2 The Shutdown Rule and Supply

We have no guarantee that profits will be positive. What should the firm do if revenue is everywhere below cost? Suppose the best that a firm can do is to produce a level of output at which $TR = \$100$ and $TC = \$120$. The loss is $20 per period. Should this firm shut down and go out of business? The answer depends on whether or not revenue covers variable cost. If fixed cost is $FC = \$50$, then this firm does *worse* by shutting down because the firm's short-run loss is only $20 if it continues to produce. This firm's variable cost is $70, and revenue exceeds variable cost. Thus by producing where $MR = MC$, even though revenue is less than total cost, the firm minimizes its loss in the short run as long as revenue exceeds variable cost.

Figure 12.4 illustrates a case in which the firm is indifferent to producing X^*, where $MR = MC$, or to produce $X = 0$. At $X = X^*$, loss is minimized, and the loss is just equal to fixed cost. Thus the best the firm can do in this short-run situation is to incur a loss equal to FC, because FC is unavoidable in the short run.

Whenever price is below minimum average variable cost, the firm should definitely shut down to avoid losses greater than FC. Whenever price is above minimum average variable cost, the firm should produce $X = X^*$, where $MR = MC$. Profit will be negative when price is between AC and AVC, but the firm will minimize its loss by producing where $MR = MC$.

The profit-maximizing rule can now be stated formally:

> **Maximizing profit:** *Set output so that marginal revenue is equal to marginal cost if price is at least equal to average variable cost. If price is below average variable cost, the firm should shut down to minimize the loss.*

GLOBAL PERSPECTIVE: *Mexico Hedges Oil Price**

Mexico picked up an additional profit of about $125 million by selling 100 million barrels of oil at a guaranteed forward price. The trades took place in December 1990 and January 1991 and took advantage of higher oil prices prevailing at that time. Some traders expected those higher prices to continue or to go even higher because of the Persian Gulf crisis.

The price hedge guaranteed that Mexico would receive $17 a barrel for low-quality oil that had been selling for much less. "This is something that worked. It was a great trade," a well-placed Wall Street source was reported to say. "It's just the type of hedging that a producing government should be doing."

A price hedge gives both the buyer and seller insurance against future price fluctuations. Other oil-producing nations, including members of the Organization of Petroleum Exporting Countries (OPEC), were then expected to use price hedging. By using commodities trading to fix prices months in advance, producing nations could set a floor for oil prices around the world. "This will have a very arresting effect on senior management at other major oil countries,"

---

*This account is based on an article by Mark Potts and Thomas W. Lipman of the *Washington Post*, "Mexico 'Hedges' for Oil Guaranties," *Los Angeles Times*, March 31, 1991.

said Daniel Yergin, president of Cambridge Energy Research Associates in Boston. "Instead of . . . assuming an oil price and plugging it into your budget, what [the Mexicans] have done [has] gone much further than that. . . . Up until now, they've always struggled with what assumption to use in their budget on price. Now they don't have to do that."

Because Mexican crude oil is of lower quality, its spot price was about $4 less than the world market price for high-quality crude. At the time of the hedge, Mexican crude was selling for $15.76 a barrel. With the $17 guaranteed price, Mexico would get an extra $1.24 a barrel when its oil was delivered. Mexico was able to negotiate the $17 futures price because some buyers believed that oil prices would rise. If the world price did rise before the delivery date, Mexico would have forfeited additional revenue. At the time of the trade, however, Mexico received a higher price than the current spot price, thereby establishing a floor on the revenue they would receive in the future.

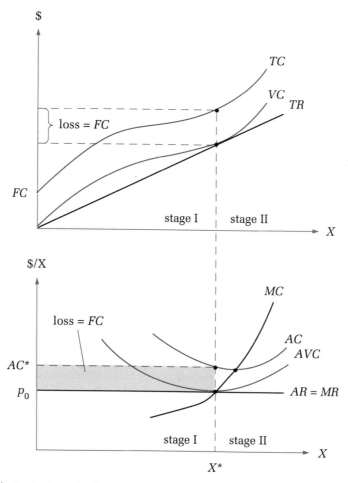

Figure 12.4 **The shutdown rule:** If price is just equal to minimum AVC, the firm will be indifferent to producing $X = X^*$ and $X = 0$. The firm will shut down, produce $X = 0$, and will incur a short-run loss equal to FC if $p < AVC$.

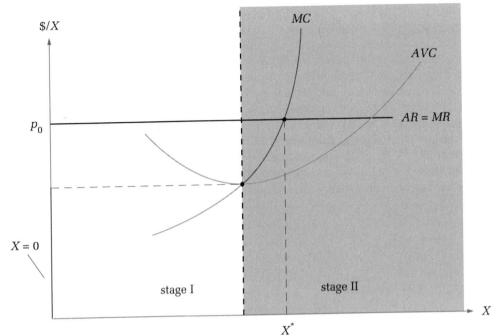

Figure 12.5 **Marginal cost and supply:** Because the price-taking firm sets MC equal to price in order to maximize profit but shuts down when price is below AVC, the firm's supply curve coincides with the MC curve in stage II. In stage II, diminishing productivity causes increasing marginal cost, and the supply curve will have positive slope.

This short-run profit-maximizing rule is applicable to all firms, not just price-taking firms. For the price-taking firm, however, the shutdown point coincides with the transition point between stages I and II, where AVC is at a minimum.

As the price-taking firm reacts to price changes, the profit-maximizing quantity supplied coincides with the MC curve above the AVC curve. As shown in Figure 12.5, the firm will shut down if price is below AVC. The MC curve within stage II becomes the firm's supply curve. Whatever the market price p, the firm will choose a level of output X, where $p = MC(X)$ within stage II:

> **Short-run Supply Curve:** *The supply curve for the profit-maximizing, price-taking firm coincides with its short-run marginal cost curve above its average variable cost curve.*

The equation $p = MC(X)$ is the *inverse* supply curve, supply price as a function of output. The supply curve $X = X(p)$ can be found by solving for X. Suppose $VC = 2X^2$, so that $MC = 4X$. Because price equals marginal revenue for the price-taking firm, the firm will set $p = MC$ to maximize profit. Substituting for MC yields the inverse supply curve $p = 4X$. Solving for X yields supply curve $X = p/4$.

12.3 Changes in Factor Prices

How is supply affected by changes in factor prices? The answer depends on whether the input is fixed or variable. The case of a change in the price of a *fixed* input is easy to analyze. Nothing happens to the supply curve in the short run because fixed cost is irrelevant to the supply decision. Changes in the price of a fixed input do not influence the variable and marginal costs, making no change in the shutdown point. Profit will be affected, however, but in a way that does not affect the supply decision in the short run.

Changes in the price of a *variable* input do affect the marginal and variable costs. Figure 12.6 illustrates the case in which input price increases. The AVC and MC curves shift upward as the price of the variable input increases. The shapes of these cost curves are not affected because that depends on technology. The shutdown point shifts upward, but the stages in production do not change. At any price, say $p = p_0$, supply decreases. Thus the increase in the price of a variable input leads to a decrease in supply.

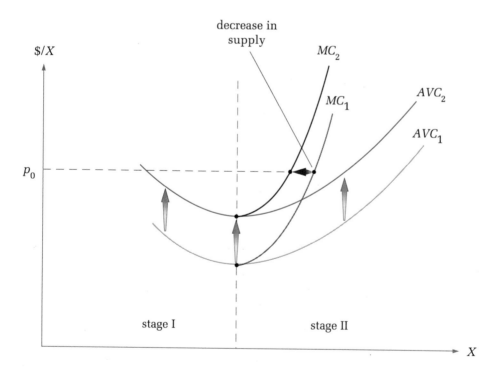

Figure 12.6 **Changes in marginal cost and supply:** As the price of a variable input increases, average variable and marginal costs increase. The shapes of the cost curves do not change because that depends on technology—the stages of production do not depend on prices. As marginal cost increases, supply decreases at every price.

12.4 Derived Input Demand

Once the level of output has been set by the firm, the amount of a variable input required can be determined from the input requirement curve. Thus, if $X = X^*$ maximizes output, the profit-maximizing demand for labor will be $L^* = L(X^*)$. The demand for a variable input is derived from that input's contribution to profit. An input contributes to profit through the revenue derived from the sale of output generated by input.

Recall that the input requirement curve for labor is found by inverting the total product curve $X(L)$. This *TP* curve can be converted into revenue as a function of labor by multiplying $X(L)$ by output price,

$$R(L) = p_X X(L)$$

A typical $R(L)$ curve is shown in Figure 12.7. The shape of this revenue curve is dictated by the shape of the *TP* curve $X(L)$ because output price p_X is fixed. The stages in production are determined by the underlying technology.

The extra revenue generated by using an extra unit of the input measures the value of that input in production. Thus, the slope of the $R(L)$ curve measures labor's marginal contribution to revenue. This measure of marginal revenue is called **marginal revenue product:**

> **Marginal revenue product (MRP):** *Marginal revenue product is the change in revenue divided by the incremental change in the variable input as that input changes alone.*

The marginal revenue product of labor can be measured by the slope of the revenue curve $R(L)$,

$$MRP_L = \frac{\Delta R}{\Delta L}$$

For the price-taking firm, the change in revenue is given by $\Delta R = p_X \Delta X$ because price is fixed. In this case the slope of the revenue curve is $p_X \Delta X / \Delta L$, or $p_X MP_L$. It is easy to see that the *MRP* of labor measures the *value* of the marginal product of labor:

> **Value of the marginal product (VMP):** *The value of the marginal product is the marginal product of a variable input multiplied by the fixed price of the good being produced.*

The *VMP* is just a special case of the *MRP* for the price-taking firm. Because output price is constant, the *VMP* of labor is

$$VMP_L = p_X MP_L$$

That is, the marginal product of labor is valued by the price of the product being produced by the incremental unit of labor.

The relation between the *VMP* curve and the revenue curve is shown in Figure 12.7. The *VMP* curve is mound-shaped, following the shape of the *MP* curve. Maximum *VMP* occurs where *MP* is at a maximum. The *VMP* diminishes when diminishing marginal

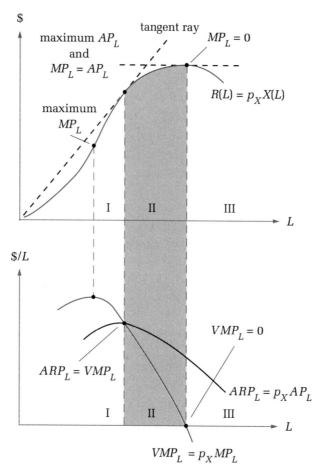

Figure 12.7 **Revenue and a variable input:** Revenue as a function of labor has the same shape as the underlying *TP* curve. Likewise, the value of the marginal product curve has the same shape as the *MP* curve, and the average revenue product curve has the same shape as the *AP* curve. The shapes of the curves are determined solely by technology when product price remains constant.

productivity sets in. The *VMP* equals zero at the transition point between stages II and III because $MP = 0$ at that point. The *VMP* is negative within stage III because *MP* is negative.

It is also useful to measure the **average revenue product** of a variable input:

> ***Average revenue product (ARP):*** *Average revenue product is revenue per unit of a variable input.*

The average revenue product of labor is

$$ARP_L = \frac{R(L)}{L} = \frac{p_X X(L)}{L} = p_X AP_L$$

Because revenue is price multiplied by output, the ARP of labor equals the average product multiplied by output price. The ARP curve is shown in Figure 12.7. In stage I, the ARP curve increases because of increasing average productivity. Maximum ARP occurs at the transition point between stages I and II, where AP is at a maximum. Within stage II and beyond, the ARP curve has negative slope because of diminishing average productivity.

Cost may also be viewed as a function of the variable input. Variable cost is $VC = wL$, where w is the wage rate. Total cost as a function of L, denoted $C(L)$, has the same slope as the VC curve because they differ only by fixed cost. The slope of the $C(L)$ curve measures the marginal cost of an extra unit of labor. To avoid confusion with the marginal cost of output, the marginal cost of a factor of production is called **marginal factor cost:**

> **Marginal factor cost (MFC):** *Marginal factor cost is the change in cost divided by the incremental change in a variable input, holding other inputs constant.*

The marginal factor cost of labor is

$$MFC_L = \frac{\Delta C(L)}{\Delta L} = \frac{\Delta wL}{\Delta L} = w$$

when the wage rate is fixed. When an input has a constant price, its marginal factor cost is equal to its price.

Revenue and cost have been expressed as functions of the variable input, so that profit too may be expressed as a function of the input,

$$\pi(L) = R(L) - C(L)$$

Maximizing profit requires that $\Delta\pi/\Delta L = 0$. Because profit is revenue less cost, the slope of this profit curve is equal to VMP minus MFC:

$$\frac{\Delta\pi}{\Delta L} = VMP - MFC$$

Thus, when the firm maximizes profit by setting L so that $\Delta\pi/\Delta L = 0$, the value of the marginal product will be equal to marginal factor cost.

Finding the profit-maximizing derived demand for labor is illustrated in Figure 12.8. The market-determined wage rate fixes the MFC of labor. The firm then demands $L = L^*$ units of labor, where $VMP = w$. For any wage rate above ARP, revenue will not cover the variable cost of production, and the firm will shut down and demand $L = 0$ units of labor. For any positive wage rate below maximum ARP, the derived demand for labor coincides with the VMP curve.

The profit-maximizing rule for choosing a variable input is:

> **Derived input demand:** *Choose a variable input so that the value of its marginal product is equal to its marginal factor cost as long as average revenue product is at least as great as the input's price. If the input's price is greater than average revenue product, then shut down to minimize the short-run loss.*

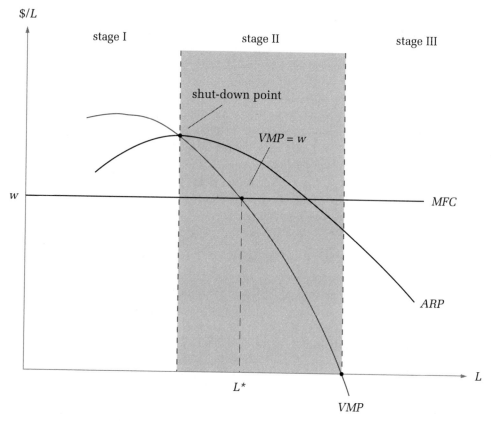

Figure 12.8 **Variable input demand:** The profit-maximizing, price-taking firm demands $L = L^*$ units of labor, where $VMP = MFC$. If the input price w is greater than ARP, the firm will shut down to minimize the short-run loss. Thus, the derived demand-for-labor curve coincides with the VMP curve within stage II.

Thus the price-taking firm will set $VMP_L = w$. Because the VMP_L is a function of L, we can find the demand-for-labor curve $L = L(w)$.

©Mell Lazarus. By permission of Mell Lazarus and Creators Syndicate.

A simple numerical example will demonstrate. Consider a TP curve $X = 2\sqrt{L}$, where $MP_L = 1\sqrt{L}$. If the market price of the good being produced is $p_X = 16$, the value of marginal product curve is $VMP_L = 16/\sqrt{L}$. Now suppose the wage rate is $w = 8$. To maximize profit, the firm should set $VMP = w$. Substitution yields $16/\sqrt{L} = 8$, so that the demand for labor is $L^* = 4$. This choice can be reconciled with the profit-maximizing level of output. The input requirement curve is $L = X^2/4$, and so the VC curve becomes $VC = wL = 2X^2$, and marginal cost is $MC = 4X$. When the firm sets $p = MC$, the profit-maximizing output is seen to be $X^* = 4$. When the input requirement curve is evaluated at X^*, we get $L^* = L(X^*) = 4$. Thus you get L^* when $L(X)$ is evaluated at X^*, and you get X^* when $X(L)$ is evaluated at L^*. Now, to find the demand-for-labor curve, set $VMP = w$ and solve for $L = L(w)$. Substitution yields $16/\sqrt{L} = w$, and so $L = 256/w^2$ is the derived demand for L as a function of w, given $p = 16$. The TP curve for this example has stage II everywhere, and so we need not worry about the shutdown point.

12.5 Short-run Market Supply and Determining Price

To derive a market supply curve, let's start by assuming no changes in input prices caused by all firms changing their levels of production. This assumption is justified if the competitive industry is only one small user of each of the inputs whose prices are determined in competitive markets also. In the short run, then, the **market supply curve,** or **industry supply curve,** is the sum of all the individual firms' supply curves:

$$S(p) = \sum_{j=1}^{m} X_j(p)$$

Geometrically, the industry supply curve is the horizontal sum of all firms' supply curves. To fix this idea, let's take a simple case of two firms, $m = 2$, as illustrated by Figure 12.9. The first firm's supply curve is $X_1(p)$, which coincides with its MC curve above its AVC curve. Likewise, the second firm's supply curve is $X_2(p)$, which coincides with its MC curve above its AVC curve. If these are the only two firms in the industry, the market supply at any price is the sum of the quantities supplied by the two firms, $S(p) = X_1(p) + X_2(p)$.

To reinforce this idea, consider the case of $m = 100$ identical firms. Assuming identical

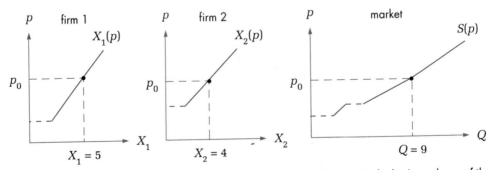

Figure 12.9 **Short-run market supply:** The market, or industry supply curve is the horizontal sum of the firms' supply curves. At p_0, for instance, the first firm supplies 5 units and the second firm supplies 4 units, and so industry supply is 9 units.

firms simplifies the analysis. Suppose each firm has a marginal cost curve $MC = 4X$. When the market price is $p = 16$, each firm will set output at $X = 4$ to maximize its profit, where $p = MC$. The industry will supply 400 units when $p = 16$, and each of the 100 firms will supply 4 units. Because the supply curve of each firm is $X = p/4$, the market supply is

$$Q = S(p) = \sum_{j=1}^{100} X_j(p) = 25p$$

Thus, assuming no externalities, all 100 supply curves $X = p/4$ may be added together to get market supply.

The price-taking firm reacts to market price. But how is market price determined? Well, the answer is simple: Market price is determined by the forces of demand and supply in the market. As shown in Figure 12.10, market price is determined where the quantity demanded equals quantity supplied, and the market is in equilibrium. When price is above the equilibrium price, a surplus of goods in the market will force price to fall. When price is below the equilibrium price, a shortage of goods will allow firms to raise their price. In equilibrium, each firm reacts to that price and sets its output to maximize profit. In so doing, the total quantity of output produced by all firms is just sufficient to meet total quantity demanded at that price, and there is no pressure for price to change as long as market conditions remain static. The firm represented in Figure 12.10 just happens to earn a positive profit, but some firms may suffer a loss at the market price. But as long as the sum of the output by all firms in the industry is just sufficient to meet market demand, the market is in equilibrium in the short run—after all, market supply coincides with the horizontal sum of their MC curves, and they all set output so that price equals marginal cost.

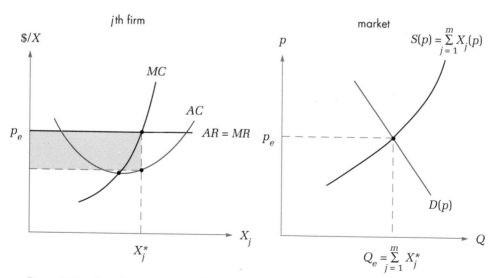

Figure 12.10 **Determining market price:** Market price is determined where the quantity demanded equals the quantity supplied in the market. Each price-taking firm reacts to market price and sets its output to maximize profit. The sum of the quantities supplied by the firms in the industry is just sufficient to meet market demand. The firm shown just happens to earn a profit.

AN APPLICATION: *Short-Run Influence of License Fees*

Suppose government decides to impose a license fee on construction contractors. The fee is meant to gain revenue for financing such public services as parks and roads. A license to practice an occupation or activity is a fixed input, and so the fee causes an increase in fixed cost.

Figure 12.11 shows what would happen to a firm that earns a profit before the fee. The AVC and MC curves are not affected by changes in fixed cost, but the AC curve shifts upward as fixed cost increases. In this illustration the fee is greater than the profit prior to the fee. After the fee, the firm experiences a short-run loss. Supply is not affected, however, because MR and MC are not affected by the fee. Changes in fixed cost do not affect short-run supply. In the long run, however, the firm will make some adjustments, perhaps by leaving the industry.

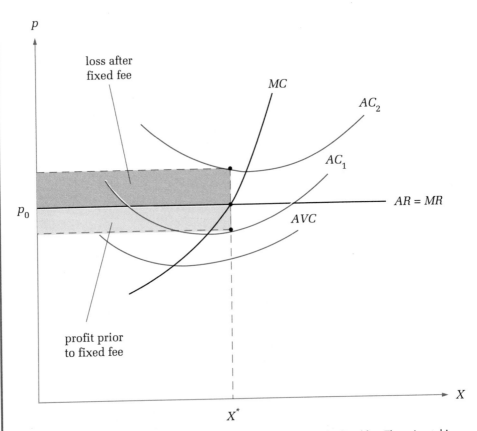

Figure 12.11 **Increase in a license fee:** This firm earns a profit prior to the fixed fee. The price-taking firm sets output so that p = MC. The AVC and MC curves are not affected by the license fee, but AFC and AC are increased. The fee in this illustration is greater than the profit prior to the fee, and so the firm experiences a short-run loss. Supply is not affected by changes in fixed cost.

12.6 Long-run Output Supply with No Entry

In the long run all inputs are variable. The profit-maximizing, price-taking firm will set output so that long-run marginal cost equals price. The *LMC* curve therefore traces out the quantity supplied as a function of price. Because all costs are variable, the firm should shut down if price is less than average cost.

Figure 12.12 illustrates the long-run decision. The firm sets output where $p = LMC$ to maximize profit. When price falls below the *LAC* curve, the firm should shut down and divest itself of all assets. The long-run supply curve coincides with the *LMC* curve above the *LAC* curve. To achieve maximum profit, the firm chooses a scale of operation that enables it to achieve the lowest possible cost of production at the profit-maximizing level of output. We will see, however, that when entry and exit are possible, firms may not change their plant size immediately. In the long run the effects of entry on price need to be determined while firms decide on the optimal scale of plant.

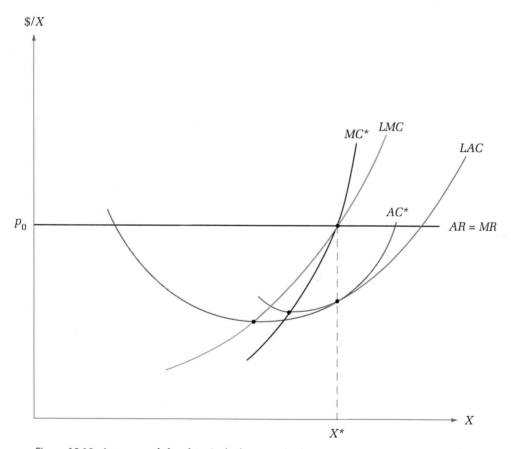

Figure 12.12 **Long-run supply for a firm:** In the long run the firm sets output at X*, where $MR \stackrel{.}{=} LMC$. The firm's long-run supply curve coincides with the LMC curve above the LAC curve. To produce X*, the firm chooses a scale of operation, that results in short-run cost curves AC* and MC*. Thus, in the long run, p = MC = LMC.

12.7 Long-run Input Demand

In the long run the firm will adjust the variable inputs so that the ratio of marginal products equals the price ratio of all pairs of inputs. For labor and capital, minimizing cost requires that $MP_L/MP_K = w/r$ for any level of output. At the same time the firm chooses a level of output that maximizes profit. Thus when an input price changes, the firm moves to a new expansion path and adjusts output along the new path.

Figure 12.13 illustrates the adjustment for a fall in the wage rate. The original input bundle is **A** along the expansion path EP_1. Holding expenditure constant, the firm moves to bundle **B**. The movement from **A** to **B** can be decomposed into a substitution effect from **A** to **C** and an expenditure effect from **C** to **B**. The expenditure effect is analogous to a price-induced income effect. When the expenditure effect reinforces the inverse substitution effect, the quantity of labor demanded will be inversely related to its wage

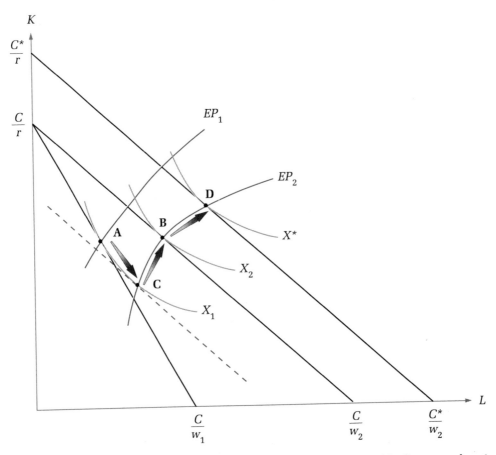

Figure 12.13 **Long-run input adjustments:** As the wage rate falls from w_1 to w_2, the firm moves from **A** to **B** when expenditure remains constant. This movement from **A** to **B** can be decomposed into a substitution effect from **A** to **C** and an expenditure effect from **C** to **B**. The firm then moves from **B** to **D** as it further adjusts output to maximize profit.

rate if cost is held constant. But the level of output will not remain at X_2, and cost will change.

A new long-run cost curve is associated with the new expansion path EP_2. The firm will choose a new level of output X^*, where LMC equals price p_x. Although X^* is shown to be greater than X_2 in Figure 12.13, it is possible that X^* will be less than X_2. The movement from bundle **B** to the final bundle demanded, **D,** is caused by the firm's adjustment of output and expenditure to maximize profit. The main question is whether or not the quantity of labor demanded is inversely related to its wage rate—does bundle **D** lie to the right of bundle **A?**

If bundle **D** lies to the right of bundle **A,** then more labor will be demanded when its price falls, and the long-run demand curve for labor will have negative slope. Figure 12.14

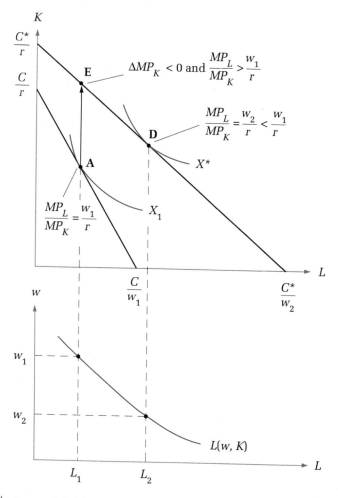

Figure 12.14 **Long-run derived demand for labor:** If an increase in capital alone causes an increase in the marginal product of labor, then the long-run derived demand curve for labor must have negative slope.

shows a negatively sloped demand for labor curve. One condition does ensure this result: The long-run demand curve for labor will have negative slope if the marginal product of labor *increases* when *capital* increases.[1] It seems reasonable that labor will become more productive when more capital is available, and so the condition does not seem overly restrictive.

To see how this condition works, consider bundle **E** in Figure 12.14. From **A** to **E**, capital has increased while labor has remained constant, and diminishing productivity implies that MP_K must fall. At the same time the MP_L at **E** is larger than at **A** by the assumed condition that increases in capital augment the productivity of labor. Thus the ratio MP_L/MP_K is *larger* at **E** than at **A**. But the new profit-maximizing bundle **D** must have a ratio MP_L/MP_K that is *smaller* than at **A** because the ratio w/r is smaller. Thus a bundle like **E** cannot maximize profit, and the new bundle **D** must lie to the right of **A** and **E**, and the demand-for-labor curve will have negative slope.[2]

12.8 Long-run Competitive Equilibrium

In the long run firms are able to adjust their fixed inputs—plant size, capital equipment, or whatever. The firm will choose output so that price equals *LMC,* and thereby identify the optimal scale of plant. But additional adjustments will occur with the entry and exit of firms or the opening or closing of plants. When a firm experiences losses in the long run, the firm will close unprofitable plants and may eventually *exit* from the industry. Similarly, when firms in the industry are making profits so that they are experiencing returns above their opportunity costs, they can open other plants while other firms are attracted into the industry.

Entry to the industry will occur when positive profits are present *unless* **barriers to entry** are present. Barriers to entry may include such things as licenses or other legal restrictions on the number of firms in the industry. But no barriers are erected to entry under perfect competition, and profits will signal movement of resources into the industry as new firms enter or present firms build new plants.

We needn't expect all firms to be profitable in the short run. Unprofitable firms will adjust their production activities to use inputs more efficiently if possible. If not possible, they leave the industry in the long run. If some firms continue to make a profit, new firms will be attracted to the industry. As these adjustments occur the industry supply curve will shift and market price will change.

---

1. This statement implies that labor is a "normal" input; that is, parallel movements in any isocost line result in tangencies with isoquants along positively sloped paths. This property amounts to a convexity property for the isoquants that is ensured when $\Delta MRTS/\Delta L < 0$.
2. See C. E. Ferguson, "Production, Prices and the Theory of Jointly Derived Input Demand Functions," *Economica,* 33 (1966), for a demonstration that factor demand curves must be negatively sloped for more than one variable input.

AN APPLICATION: *Long-run Influence of License Fees*

In the short run the only consequence of assessing the firm a license fee is to reduce profit. No short-run effect touches supply and market price. But in the long run all costs are variable. The model of a competitive, long-run equilibrium can be used to trace the consequences of a license fee.

Let's suppose the industry is in long-run equilibrium before the fee is imposed. As shown in Figure 12.15, the industry is in equilibrium at price p_1 and quantity Q_1. All firms earn zero economic profit. A license fee increases average cost from LAC_1 to LAC_2 as firms adjust their input combination. All firms now experience a short-run loss, but in the long run some will leave the industry. As exit occurs, market supply will shrink to, say, S_2, where price is just sufficient to cover long-run average cost once more. The new equilibrium results in a higher market price and lower industry output than before the fee was imposed.

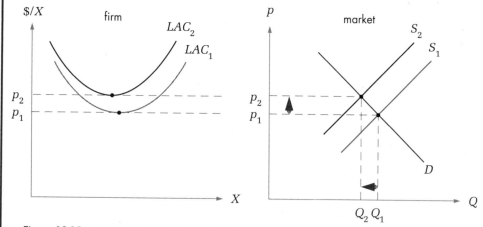

Figure 12.15 **Long-run influence of a license fee:** An increase in a license fee causes an increase in every firm's LAC curve. As firms adjust their input mixture, all firms become unprofitable, and so some firms must leave the industry. The industry supply curve will shift from S_1 to S_2. Market price will increase until all remaining firms once more earn zero economic profit. In the end, industry output will be less than before the fee increase.

A **perfectly competitive industry** has no barriers to entry or exit, and resources can move freely into or out of the industry. Free entry implies that positive economic profits will be short lived. Because costs include opportunity costs of capital and entrepreneurship, positive profits will induce new capital and entrepreneurial services to enter the industry. As more firms enter, industry supply increases, causing a decrease in market price. This sequence will continue until economic profits are zero. Alternatively,

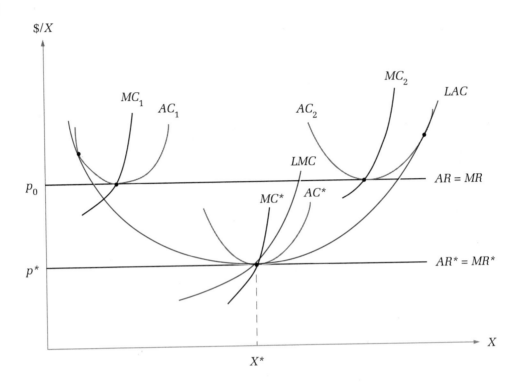

Figure 12.16   **Economies of scale and competitive equilibrium:** When price is p_0, firm 1 can earn a temporary profit by increasing its scale, and firm 2 can earn a temporary profit by decreasing its scale. But positive profits signal entry, and industry supply will increase. Eventually, price falls to p^* and all firms produce $X = X^*$, where $p^* = AC^* = MC^* = LAC = MC$, and all profits are zero.

losses will induce firms and resources to leave the industry, causing market supply to shrink and market price to rise.

Not only does the competitive model result in zero economic profits in the long run, it also implies that each firm will choose a scale of operation and a level of output that results in minimal long-run average cost. To see this effect, consider Figure 12.16. Firm 1 can earn a temporary profit by *increasing* its scale. Firm 2 can earn a temporary profit by *decreasing* its scale. New firms, to earn a profit, will choose a scale between those of firms 1 and 2. As a consequence, market supply increases, causing price to fall. All firms are forced to take advantage of any economies of scale to remain competitive. Perfect knowledge implies that all firms can use the most efficient technology, and so when confronted with competitive input markets, all firms will have identical long-run cost curves. Eventually, all firms will wind up with short-run cost curves AC^* and MC^*. Market price will be p^*, where $LMC = LAC$. In summary, the long-run competitive equilibrium is characterized by zero economic profit and minimal average cost for all firms.

ECONOMIC SCENE: *St. Benedict's Quits the Egg Business*

The monks of St. Benedict's monastery in Colorado recently quit the egg business.*
They went into the egg business in 1967, quickly discovering that they couldn't control
their own price. They faced vigorous competition from California producers; when the
monks raised their price, California producers would ship their eggs to Colorado,
forcing price back down. If the monks had not had competition from California, it would
have come from somewhere else. You can ship a dozen eggs across the country for
about 2¢, making a national market for eggs.

Over the decade after 1967, the cost of chicken feed more than doubled, to about
$200 per ton. Feed is a large part of the cost of producing eggs. The increase forced
the price of eggs up nationwide, but costs had risen even more. Figure 12.17 illustrates what happened. When the price of chicken feed rose, the marginal cost curve
shifted upward for all firms and industry supply decreased. The market price of eggs
rose in response to the decrease in supply, but the price increase was less than the
increase in marginal cost. The monks were caught in a price squeeze.

The monks then looked for ways of reducing the feed used to produce eggs. Older
hens were retired to the soup pot earlier because they were larger and ate more feed.
This change in production method was matched throughout the industry. It was
reported to take 7.9 pounds of grain to produce a dozen eggs in 1976, but that cost was

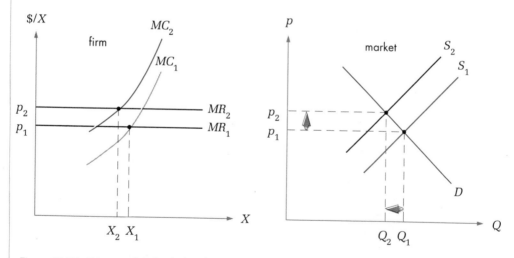

Figure 12.17 **Rising cost of chicken feed:** When the price of chicken feed rose, it increased the
marginal cost of producing eggs from MC_1 to MC_2. Industry supply decreased from S_1 to S_2,
causing the egg price to rise. But the increase in egg price is less than the increase in marginal
cost.

---

*This application is based on an article by Timothy Tregarthen, "The Monks of St. Benedict's Getting
Out of the Egg Business," *The Margin*, 4(1) (September/October, 1988).

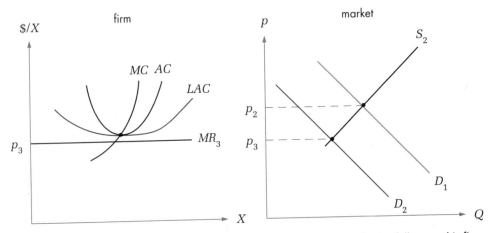

Figure 12.18   **Falling demand and the exit cue:** When demand falls to D_2 and price falls to p_3 this firm can no longer cover long-run average cost. This firm will leave the industry.

cut to 6.0 pounds by 1980. At the same time egg producers confronted slumping demand.

Changing consumers' preferences and habits of eating dramatically reduced demand. This decrease in demand was reflected as the price of eggs fell in spite of rising costs. In 1984, the wholesale price of eggs averaged 72.3¢ a dozen. By summer 1987, the price had fallen below 50¢. What happened next is illustrated by Figure 12.18. When demand fell to D_2, and price fell below minimum long-run average cost, the monastery quit the egg business.

"We weren't losing money in the financial sense," Fr. Joseph said. "After all, we don't have to pay for labor. But we had reached a point that we were going to have to replace our equipment. We considered doing that, but finally we decided that we wanted something where we had a little more control. We had started an experiment the year before with selling cookies, and that had been a success. We decided that devoting our time and energy to other enterprises would pay off better than the egg business."† The phrase *opportunity cost* isn't part of Fr. Joseph's vocabulary, but the idea certainly is part of his thinking.

Other producers tried other means of coping with rising costs and falling demand. Some tried advertising to reduce national competition. Others were able to take advantage of scale economies unattractive to the monks. But even some of the larger producers left the industry.

The monks sold 200,000 ounces of cookies in 1987. Fr. Joseph commented, "It was easy to get started, and it would be easy to get out if we needed to." Getting out of the egg business has produced another benefit. "The chickens didn't stop laying eggs on Sunday, but now we can take Sundays off." Using their leisure time in producing eggs was certainly a real cost of doing business.

---

†As quoted by Tregarthen, "Monks of St. Benedict's," p. 15.

12.9 Long-run Industry Supply

Entry and exit of firms are crucial in defining long-run industry supply. The **long-run industry supply curve** connects the long-run equilibrium price-quantity pairs after all demand-induced changes have occurred.

To keep things simple, let's continue to assume that input prices remain constant. In the long run the competitive model implies that each firm has zero economic profit and chooses a scale minimizing LAC. Figure 12.19 shows each firm producing X_j^* units of output because the market price is p_1. The initial long-run supply curve $S_1(p)$ is the horizontal sum of the firms' short-run MC curves.

Now, suppose demand increases to D_2. Initially, market price will increase to p_2 and firms increase their output to maximize profits. In the short run, output for each firm increases to $X = X_2$, and each firm enjoys short-run profits shown by the shaded area in Figure 12.19. The positive profits also induce entry into the industry, however, and so industry output will increase. As new firms enter the industry the market supply curve shifts to the right. New firms continue to enter until industry supply increases to S_2, where price is at its original level, p_1. All firms, old and new, produce X_j^* units once more, where $p = LMC = LAC$. Price p_1 is established as the long-run equilibrium price in the industry because there is no pressure for further change. Minimum LAC and zero profits for all firms are established once again.

The long-run price and output combinations determine the long-run supply curve, $LS(p)$, for the industry. Here input prices were constant, the $LS(p)$ curve is horizontal. An industry with a *horizontal* long-run supply curve is called a **constant cost industry**.

The assumption of constant input prices may not be very realistic in an expanding industry. Resource prices are likely to be bid upward to attract resources from other

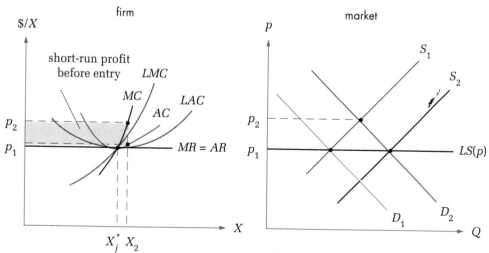

Figure 12.19 **Constant-cost industry:** An increase in demand to D_2 causes an increase in price initially. Without entry, the increase in price would cause an increase in profits, but new firms enter the industry. Entry occurs until price falls back to its initial level. This long-run industry supply curve $LS(p)$ is horizontal.

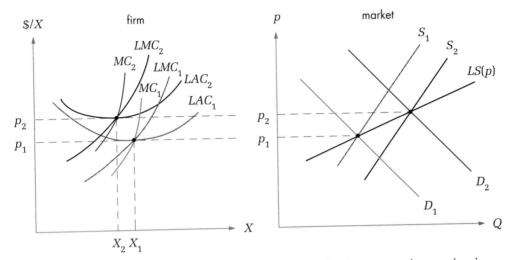

Figure 12.20   **An increasing-cost industry:** An increase in demand to D_2 causes an increase in price initially. The increase in price causes a temporary increase in profits, and new firms enter the industry. The increased competition for scarce resources bids input prices upward, and the costs of production increase, leading to an increase in both short-run and long-run costs at every level of output. The industry expands with the entry of new firms, but each firm may produce less than before. The long-run industry supply curve $LS(p)$ has positive slope because of the increase in costs.

sectors of the economy. Looking at Figure 12.20, suppose demand increases from D_1 to D_2, causing an initial increase in output price. As output price increases, positive profits induce expansion in old firms and entry by new firms, and supply will increase, damping the initial increase in price. But will market price fall back to its original level? Not if the industry expansion causes a rise in input prices, because that causes an increase in the average and marginal cost curves. The industry will reach a new equilibrium, at which market price is just sufficient to cover the higher long-run average cost. As shown in Figure 12.20, the new equilibrium price p_2 is greater than before the increase in demand. Once again each firm in the industry, including new entrants, produces at minimum average cost and has zero profit, but the average cost of production has increased.

When the long-run industry supply curve $LS(p)$ reflects an increasing price required to cover increasing average cost, the industry is called an **increasing cost industry.** A firm facing a *positively* sloped long-run industry supply curve is said to be experiencing external or **pecuniary diseconomies.** Such pecuniary effects are not the same as the economies or diseconomies of scale that describe movements along a given LAC curve.

A third possibility gives the long-run industry supply curve *negative* slope. If increases in demand lead to decreases in input prices, the industry is called a **decreasing-cost industry.** Each firm faces **pecuniary economies.** Decreasing input prices are possible if economies of scale are achieved in producing inputs. Quantity discounts frequently reflect such economies of scale.

AN APPLICATION: *Dairy Price Supports**

Milk prices have been supported by a variety of government actions. In 1922, dairy cooperatives were exempted from antitrust actions against producer organizations that restricted production to push prices upward. In 1935, the U.S. Department of Agriculture (USDA) was empowered to enforce payment of established minimum prices to farmers. Since 1949, the federal government has supported the price of milk directly by guaranteeing to purchase all milk that cannot be sold in the market at the established support price. The price of milk is maintained by Commodity Credit Corporation (CCC) purchases of dairy products. Prices are also supported indirectly by food stamps, import restrictions on dairy products, and government purchases of milk for school lunch programs. Food disbursements to the poor and elderly typically include flour, rice, butter, cheese, honey, and powdered milk.

From 1977 through 1979, net CCC expenditures on dairy production averaged about $500 million annually. In 1980, the value of purchases began to increase dramatically. In the 1983 fiscal year, CCC purchases and storage costs exceeded $2.7 billion. This dramatic increase was unchecked because, unlike other price-support programs, the dairy program placed virtually no restrictions on the volume of milk that a farmer could market at the support price. A steady increase in milk production between 1970 and 1983 is partially attributable to a 1.9 percent annual increase in average productivity of dairy cows. But the cost of the program also increased because the program's incentives caused output to grow faster than demand.

Consider the model illustrated by Figure 12.21 to see how the price-support

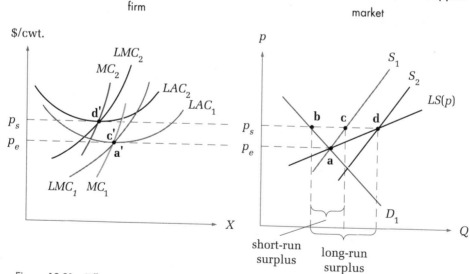

Figure 12.21 **Milk price-support program:** Competitive equilibrium in the industry occurs at point *a* and each firm produces at point *a'*. With a price support, p_s, each firm moves to point *c'* in the short run. Subsequent entry forces all firms to point *d'* in the long run as resource prices increase, and the industry supply occurs at point *d*, given the support price p_s.

---

*This account is based on Michael T. Belgonia, "The Dairy Price Support Program: A Study of Misdirected Economic Incentives," *Federal Reserve Bank of St. Louis*, February 1984.

program affects the milk market. Without a support price, the long-run market equilibrium occurs at point *a*, where supply equals demand. Given a support price p_s above p_e, however, both consumers and producers modify their behavior. At the support price, quantity demanded falls to point *b* and quantity supplied rises to point *c*. The result is a short-run milk surplus.

The support price greater than the equilibrium price p_e yields higher returns to the producers of milk, upsetting the long-run equilibrium for each firm at point *a'*. Old firms move to point *c'* in the short run. But in the long run, entry of new firms occurs because they are attracted by the positive economic profits. This short-run expansion of old firms and the long-run entry of new firms bid up the prices of scarce resources: dairy cows, feed, tractors, and land. As the input prices increase, marginal and average costs increase. At point *d'*, all firms are at a new long-run equilibrium and economic profits equal zero once again. Industry supply, however, is greater that it was before. Because of the industry's expansion and increasing costs, the industry quantity supplied occurs at point *d* along the long-run industry supply curve $LS(p)$. The result is a long-run surplus that is greater than the short-run surplus. The surplus would not appear without the support price.

Who benefits from this program? Farm owners benefit from price supports even though economic profits are still zero because the values of inputs (including the entrepreneurial input and the farmer's time and land) have increased. The suppliers of all inputs used in the dairy industry have benefited from the program. Thus, as you'd expect, both input suppliers and farm owners oppose any reductions in price supports because that would reduce their wealth.

In November 1983, the support price of milk was reduced from $13.10 per hundredweight (cwt.) to $12.60 by imposing a 50¢ fee on all milk produced. The fee was intended to reduce the growing volume of surplus production. Instead, in 1984 the quantity produced by the typical firm increased. Does this result represent a failure of the competitive model to predict accurately? As a consequence of the production increase that followed the fee, an effort to further reduce the support with another 50¢ fee was defeated in Congress.

As shown in Figure 12.22, historical data suggest that dairy farmers responded to the price support in 1980 by producing at point *b* rather than at point *a*. Reducing the price support from $13.10 to $12.60 should reverse the long-run adjustments illustrated previously. Instead, the typical dairy farmer produced at point *c*, and market surpluses increased rather than decreased. A short-run adjustment downward along the MC_{1980} curve was thwarted by a dramatic decrease in the price of feed caused by stocks of grain swollen by unexpectedly good weather and price supports for grain. The subsequent shifts in the MC and AC curves by 1984 resulted in increased production. Thus, the increase in the market surplus was not a failure of the model to predict a reversal; rather, it was caused by an exogenous decrease in the costs of production and insufficient time for the market to adjust to the reduction in the price support.

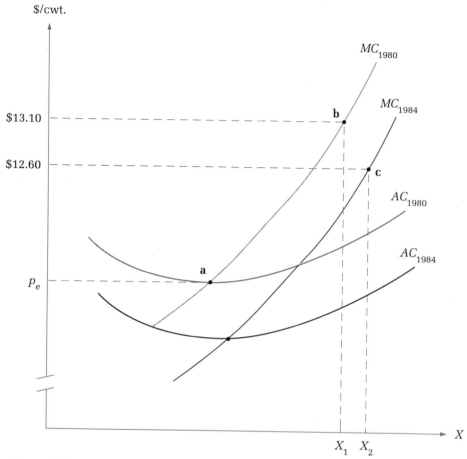

Figure 12.22 **Dairy-farm changes suggested by data:** In 1980, farmers produced at point *b* in response to the price support at $13.10—a short-run response. In 1984, after the price support was reduced to $12.60, a typical farm produced at point *c*. The net *increase* in production from X_1 to X_2, which is contrary to that predicted by the long-run competitive model, is explained by a dramatic decrease in the price of grain that led to a shift in the cost curves.

12.10 General Competitive Equilibrium and Efficiency

The welfare of everyone is affected by efficient use of resources and efficient distribution of the income produced. Under some conditions, pure competition guarantees an efficient outcome. Understanding efficiency and the conditions that guarantee the efficiency of competitive markets will identify departures from pure competition and other market imperfections that affect social welfare. Simultaneously, insights can be gained on when, how, and why social interference in the market may be beneficial.

Even though every economy is continually in flux, useful comparisons can be made between alternative states of general equilibrium. An economy is in general equilibrium when all output markets and all input markets are cleared. **General equilibrium analysis** focuses on the economy in its entirety. When the economy is in general equilibrium, we can ask whether or not that outcome is efficient. Furthermore, we can ask whether or not that outcome is equitable.

As you might expect, general equilibrium analysis would be quite complicated without simplifying assumptions. With such assumptions, however, the analysis becomes quite manageable. You already have all the tools necessary, but it's necessary to put everything together. First, let's assume that all markets are purely and perfectly competitive. (We'll look at monopoly behavior and other market imperfections later on.) Second, let's assume that no externalities occur in consumption or production. That is, no pollution affects the air or water in consumption or production—at least none whose cost is not borne by its creator. Third, let's assume no public goods. This idealized society needs no national defense or national health programs. Finally, let's assume a private-ownership economy.

To keep the model simple, we look at the smallest number of goods and consumers that we possibly can, but we need at least two consumers, two goods, and two inputs.[3] Figure 12.23 shows the production possibilities for the economy as a whole. To be on the production possibilities curve, inputs must be used efficiently. That is, the production possibilities curve is derived under the conditions that the marginal rates of input substitution must be equal in the production of two goods X and Y, $MRTS_X = MRTS_Y$. Pure competition forces firms to use inputs efficiently and so the economy will be on its production possibilities curve at a point such as B.

Recall that the marginal rate of product transformation (MRT), measured by the slope of the production possibilities curve, is the opportunity cost of producing more X in terms of Y. Given output prices, the **gross national product** of the economy is $GNP = p_X Q_X + p_Y Q_Y$, the money value of all goods produced. The GNP is maximized for a given set of output prices when the GNP line is tangent to the production possibilities curve. The price ratio therefore must be equal to the MRT when GNP is at a maximum, $MRT_{XY} = p_X/p_Y$. But how are the prices determined?

Equilibrium prices are determined where all markets are cleared. The consumers' utility-maximizing demands are just satisfied by the profit-maximizing supplies of X and Y. When the economy is producing X_e and Y_e units of the two goods, an Edgeworth box is established under the production possibilities curve, as shown by the shaded rectangle in Figure 12.24. Efficiency in consumption requires determining an output allocation along the contract curve. Otherwise the allocation would not be Pareto optimal, and one consumer could be made better off without making the other consumer worse off. In addition, for a set of prices p_X and p_Y to generate equilibrium, both markets must be cleared. Both markets will be cleared at the trading bundle T^*, where both consumers' indifference curves are tangent with one another and with a common budget line. The slope of the common budget line must be equal to that of the GNP line as long as

---

3. Some interesting lessons can be learned by looking at a Robinson Crusoe economy (before Friday arrived) with just one consumer-producer, with one variable input—labor time, but that would ignore the issues of efficiency in exchange and input allocation.

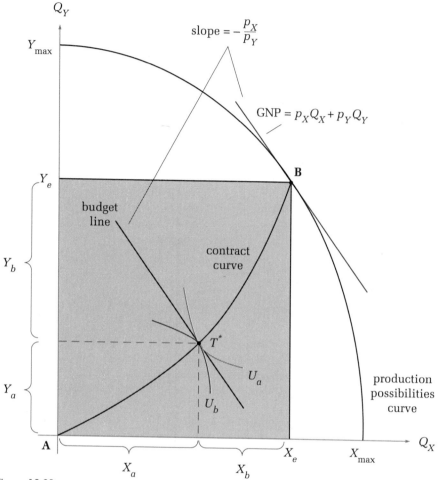

Figure 12.23 **Equilibrium in exchange and production:** In a general equilibrium: (1) the slope of the GNP line is equal to the slope of the production possibilities curve, so that $MRT_{XY} = p_X/p_Y$; and (2) the slopes of the indifference curves are equal to the slope of the budget line, so that $MRS_{XY} = p_X/p_Y$.

everyone pays the same price for any given product. Thus, to qualify for general equilibrium, the *MRS* for both consumers must equal the *MRT* for the economy, and both the *MRS* and the *MRT* must equal the price ratio p_x/p_Y. Otherwise, the quantity demanded will not be equal to the quantity supplied in one or both product markets.

The *conditions* for general equilibrium for a competitive economy under private ownership of the factors of production can now be summarized:

1. The distribution of output must be such that the marginal rates of commodity substitution between any pair of goods is the same for all consumers, $MRS_{XY} = p_x/p_Y$.

2. The allocation of resources must be such that the marginal rate of technical input substitution between any pair of inputs is the same for all producers, $MRTS_{LK} = w/r$.

3. All output and input markets must be cleared.
4. The marginal rate of product transformation must be equal to the marginal rate of substitution, $MRT_{XY} = MRS_{XY}$.

Prices will adjust until these conditions are satisfied. The existence of general competitive equilibrium depends on establishing relative output and input prices that satisfy all these conditions simultaneously.[4] Maximizing profit guarantees selection of an output combination on the production possibilities curve. If prices do not clear all markets, prices adjust until all markets are cleared.

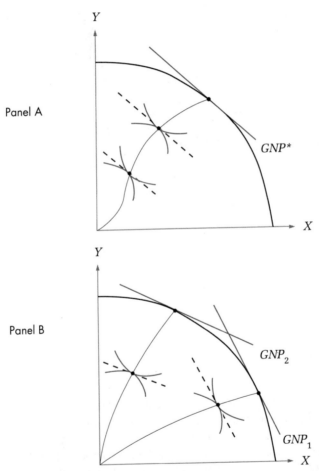

Figure 12.24   **Multiple equilibria: Panel A** There is only one general equilibrium GNP but two income distributions along the contract curve. **Panel B** There are two general equilibrium GNP values and two income distributions on two contract curves.

4. The first completely acceptable proof of the existence of general competitive equilibrium was presented by Kenneth J. Arrow and Gerard Debreu, "Existence of an Equilibrium for a Competitive Economy," *Econometrica,* 22 (1954). The proof was later simplified by Debreu in *Theory of Value* (John Wiley, 1959). The conditions are actually more general than those imposed to simplify the presentation in this chapter.

GLOBAL PERSPECTIVE: *Steel Exit Barriers**

Once upon a time the steel industry in the United States was described as oligopolistic. Since 1960, however, the steel industry has become much more competitive, for two reasons. First is the rise of minimills. Integrated mills, which produce steel from iron ore, are the traditional steel industry, but the minimills, which produce steel products by recycling scrap, are relative newcomers. Minimills increased their market share from about 3 percent in 1960 to 18 percent in 1985. Second is the new competition from imports, particularly from Japan. Countries like Japan experienced phenomenal growth in steel consumption after World War II. Their steel industries were able to build new plants using the latest technology. Higher productivity combined with lower wage rates reduced the unit cost of labor below U.S. levels. The result of the rise in minimills and foreign competition was a decline in market share of the integrated steel mills in the United States from more than 90 percent in 1960 to less than 65 percent in the 1980s.

At the same time the growth in demand for steel slowed in the United States. The increased use of such substitutes as aluminum, plastics, and composites in consumer goods, particularly cars, has reduced the U.S. economy's need for steel. Given the slow growth in market demand and increased supplies from imports and recycled steel, the dominance of the integrated mill has waned. The industry is more competitive than ever before.

The contraction of the industry led to several plant closings and exit by firms from the industry. From its height in the early 1970s of approximately 155 million tons, annual raw-steel capacity has fallen to about 112 million tons. But that contraction has taken a long time, even though profit rates have been subnormal for many years. Firms appear to be clinging tenaciously to excess capacity as though demand might miraculously increase. Why are the integrated firms delaying plant closings?

Our competitive model predicts that, for an industry facing an inward-shifting demand curve, high-cost plants will be closed and unprofitable firms will leave the industry in the long run. In the short run, though, a firm will continue to produce as long as variable costs are covered. Because most production involves fixed costs, the decision to close a plant usually will involve a period of operation and disinvestment before shutdown. The optimal closing time will not occur until the return to continued operation of capital equals the return that could be earned on the salvage value. That is, the firm will continue to operate at a loss as long as the return to fixed capital is greater than the opportunity cost of capital that can be salvaged.

Other factors also affect the timing of a plant's closing. Low or negative salvage value will extend the time before exit. The firm may also face labor-related closing expenses, such as severance pay, early retirement pay, and pensions. Thus, in a contracting industry with durable and specific capital and high closing costs, firms will delay closing plants. In such an industry, like the steel industry, capacity will contract slowly and plants will close in bunches during downturns in demand that lower revenues. The slow shutdown rate, however, is optimal in that resources are always being utilized in their highest return activity.

Is public policy needed to slow down or speed up plant closings? At least three public programs have affected the U.S. industry by altering the cost of closing plants. First, the Pension Benefit Guaranty Corporation insures pension benefits. This coverage encourages firms to close earlier than otherwise because they can declare bankruptcy and let the

---

*Based on Mary E. Deily, "Exit Barriers in the Steel Industry," *Economic Review,* 24(1) (Quarter 1, 1988), Federal Reserve Bank of Cleveland, pp. 10–17.

insurance assume responsibility for the firms' pension liabilities. Second, the five-year Voluntary Restraint Agreements that the Reagan administration negotiated with several steel-exporting countries tends to delay plant closings if protection causes revenues to rise in the short run. Third, and the most misguided public policy, is the Steel Import Stabilization Act of 1984 that requires the industry to reinvest its net cash flow from steel back into steel plants. This directive forces investment in steel-producing plants that may never yield an adequate return.

The *consequences* of general competitive equilibrium are:

1. The price of any good will be equal to its marginal cost.
2. The price of any input will be equal to its value of marginal product.
3. The price of any asset will be equal to its discounted present value.
4. In the long run, with free entry, the price of any good or asset will be equal to its long-run average cost.
5. In the long run, with free entry, economic profits are zero.

Now do you see why perfect competition is so attractive? Perfect competition, without externalities and public goods, guarantees that *GNP* will be maximized in such a way that every resource will be paid in accordance with its contribution to *GNP.* Both production and consumption efficiency are achieved. And, because economic profits are zero, the *GNP* will be distributed completely to the owners of the resources. No undistributed economic profits or any other gains are to be made given current technology and initial distribution of wealth. Of course, because perfect competition is rare, we usually have to settle for effective competition. Moreover, we have no guarantee that general equilibrium is efficient in the presence of monopoly power, externalities in consumption or production, or public goods.

12.11 Income Distribution and Equilibrium*

Finding an equilibrium point along a production possibilities curve and an equilibrium distribution of that total output along the contract curve is not necessarily unique. Two examples are illustrated by Figure 12.24. First, more than one distribution of equilibrium output may be consistent with general equilibrium. As shown in panel A, more than one income distribution can be associated with a single equilibrium point along the production possibilities curve. Second, more than one contract curve may have income distributions consistent with general equilibrium. As shown in panel B, two points along the production possibilities curve have budget lines with slopes equal to corresponding *GNP* lines. Which point along the production possibilities curve in panel B, or which income distribution along the contract curve in panel A, are socially optimal cannot be determined from efficiency criteria. Nor will some point along the production possibilities curve, or some income distribution that is deemed socially optimal, be selected necessarily under perfect competition.

---

*This section is optional and may be skipped without loss of continuity.

Under pure competition, every input is paid a price equal to the value of its marginal product. Therefore, if all persons have identical tastes in consumption of goods and leisure, and if all are endowed with the same human capital and other assets, then all income produced in a competitive economy will be distributed equally. Some people have a stronger preference for leisure than others, however. Some are endowed with more productive human capital than others. Some have invested more heavily in their own human capital. Some are endowed with handicaps. Some have saved more in the past. Some have inherited wealth. All these conditions influence the competitive outcome.

These considerations lead us to conclude that the distribution of income among members of society is determined by many factors quite independent of efficiency in production and exchange and the determination of prices that clear all markets. Although every competitive equilibrium is efficient in the sense of Pareto optimality, some Pareto optimal states may be undesirable on equity grounds.

But any Pareto optimal state can be achieved through the competitive mechanism. This remarkable result is called the **unbiasedness property** of competitive equilibrium. To see how this property works, suppose the economy settles on a distribution of income in general equilibrium. That result depended on the initial endowment of all consumers. Now suppose society decides that a different distribution of income would be more equitable. If the initial endowments are changed just right, the desired distribution can be achieved through competition.

Summary

Competition is *pure* when many small buyers and sellers trade a homogeneous good. A purely competitive firm is a price-taking firm because no one firm can perceptibly influence market price. *Perfect* competition is pure competition when perfect mobility of resources and perfect knowledge about the market are also present. Easy entry and exit guarantee zero economic profits in all perfectly competitive markets. *Effective* competition may occur when the market outcome is close to that which occurs under perfect competition.

Output supply is determined from the firm's desire to maximize profit. The profit-maximizing, price-taking firm will choose a level of output at which marginal cost equals output price. Thus the firm's short-run supply curve coincides with its marginal cost curve above its average variable cost curve. Input demand is also derived from the firm's desire to maximize profit. The profit-maximizing, price-taking firm will choose a variable input at which marginal factor cost equals the value of the marginal product. Thus the firm's short-run derived demand curve for the input coincides with the input's value of marginal product curve.

The market supply curve is the short-run industry supply curve, and market supply is the sum of all the individual firms' supply curves. Thus, market supply is the horizontal sum of all the firms' *MC* curves. In the long run, along with scale adjustments, entry and exit also occur. Firms adjust their scale or exit from the industry in response to negative short-run profits. In response to short-run positive profits, firms adjust their scale and other firms enter the industry. Ultimately all firms in a competitive industry will be producing at minimum long-run average cost and zero economic profit.

In the long run all inputs are variable and the profit-maximizing firm will set output so that long-run marginal cost equals price. In the long run firms choose inputs to minimize cost at any level of output. Thus the technical rate of substitution between each pair of inputs will be equal to their price ratio.

Long-run industry supply reflects long-run industry price and quantities after all demand-induced changes have occurred. The long-run industry supply curve reflects pecuniary, or external, effects on input prices caused by changes in demand. A constant-cost industry has a horizontal long-run supply curve. An increasing-cost industry has a positively sloped long-run supply curve. A decreasing-cost industry has a negatively sloped long-run supply curve.

The phrase general competitive equilibrium identifies a set of prices for all inputs and outputs such that all markets are cleared under conditions of price-taking, profit-maximizing behavior of all firms, utility-maximizing behavior by all consumers, and private ownership of the factors of production. Thus, quantity demanded must equal quantity supplied in every market. In exchange, the *MRS* between any pair of goods must be the same for all consumers—Pareto efficiency occurs in exchange. In production, the *MRTS* between any pair of inputs must be the same for all firms—Pareto efficiency in production. Finally, the production bundle chosen along the production possibilities frontier must have an *MRT* equal to the *MRS*. When these conditions are satisfied, the economy will be on the boundary of its production possibilities set—*GNP* will be maximized. All firms will be using resources efficiently, will be producing at the lowest possible long-run unit cost, and will be experiencing zero economic profit if entry is free. All inputs will be paid a price equal to their values of marginal products. The resulting distribution of income is efficient but not necessarily equitable.

A competitive general equilibrium is not necessarily unique even though all achieve efficiency. One general equilibrium might be more desirable than another because it is more equitable, but such choices require value judgments. If society selects one general equilibrium as more desirable, it can always be achieved by appropriate redistribution of consumer endowments (wealth) without loss in efficiency.

Further Readings

Two articles worth reading on the firm are

- Ronald H. Coase, "The Nature of the Firm," *Economica,* 4 (November 1937).
- Armen Alchian and Harold Demesetz, "Production, Information Costs, and Economic Organization," *American Economic Review,* 62 (December 1972).

For an excellent article on the meaning of competition, see

- Paul J. McNulty, "Economic Theory and the Meaning of Competition," *Quarterly Journal of Economics* (November 1968).

A classic reference work on supply is

- Jacob Viner, "Cost Curves and Supply Curves," in *Readings in Price Theory,* G. J. Stigler and K. E. Boulding, ed. (Richard D. Irwin, 1952).

On factor demand curves, see

- C. E. Ferguson, "Production, Prices and the Theory of Jointly Derived Input Demand Functions," *Econometrica*, 33 (1966).

Proofs on the existence of general competitive equilibrium are offered by

- Kenneth J. Arrow and Gerard Debreu, "Existence of an Equilibrium for a Competitive Economy," *Econometrica*, 22 (1954).
- David Gale, "The Law of Supply and Demand," *Mathematica Scandinavia*, 3 (1955).
- Gerard Debreu, *Theory of Value* (John Wiley 1959).
- Lionel W. McKinzie, "On the Existence of a General Equilibrium for a Competitive Market," *Econometrica*, 27 (1959).

The first completely acceptable proof of a general competitive equilibrium was presented by Arrow and Debreu (1954) and was later simplified by Debreu (1959). The conditions of the proof are actually more general than those imposed to simplify the presentation in this chapter.

Practice Problems

1. Show how we can find the short-run supply curve for a price-taking firm under the assumption of profit maximization. Explain the "shutdown" rule and its relevancy in the search for the supply curve.

2. Let the demand curve for a competitive industry be given by:

$$D(p) = 100 - 5p$$

Assume that $X = \sqrt{LK}$ and $K = 1$ for each of 10 firms in the industry, and assume that input prices are $w = \$1$ and $r = \$2$.

(a) Determine the short-run total, average, average variable, and marginal cost curves.

(b) Determine the short-run industry supply curve, and determine the short-run equilibrium price and quantity for the industry.

(c) Calculate short-run profits for each firm.

3. The short-run production function is $X = 2\sqrt{L}$ and marginal product is $MP = 1/\sqrt{L}$. When market price is $p = \$16$, plot revenue as a function of L and, on a separate graph, plot ARP and VMP.

4. Under profit maximization, show how the value of the marginal product curve becomes the input demand curve for a price-taking firm.

5. An increase in productivity is expected to affect the demand for a variable input. What predictions can be made about employment and factor price?

6. The Visions company tints car windows and receives $150 for each car tinted. This firm believes that its production function is

$$Q = 3.8L - 0.75L^2$$

where Q is the number of cars tinted per day, and L is the number of workers per day. Thus the marginal product of each worker is

$$MP_L = 3.8 - 1.5L$$

The Visions company pays each worker $120 per day.

(a) How many workers should be hired?

(b) How many cars should be tinted each day?

7. The production function is $X = \sqrt{LK}$, where L is labor and K is capital. Given $w = \$1$, $r = \$4$, and $K = 1$:

(a) Derive the firm's short-run supply curve for X.

(b) Derive the firm's short-run demand curve for L if the output price is $p = \$3$.

8. In a competitive industry, suppose every firm faces an identical cost curve, where

$$TC = 200 + 10X + 2X^2$$

so that marginal cost to each firm is

$$MC = 10 + 4X$$

The industry demand curve is

$$Q_X = D(p) = 800 - 8p$$

Using the competitive model, if this industry is in long-run equilibrium:

(a) Find the level of output produced by each firm.

(b) Find the industry price.

(c) Find industry output.

(d) Determine the number of single-plant firms in this industry.

9. Much unease has been expressed about U.S. managers' emphasis on short-run profits. How would you structure an incentive system to encourage managers to maximize long-run profits?

10. Suppose energy and labor are two variable inputs. Use an isoquant diagram to explain a firm's reaction to an increase in energy price. In the diagram, identify the substitution effect, the expenditure effect, and the profit-maximizing effect on the demand for labor as the energy price increases. What happens to this firm's expansion path?

11. Given constant returns to scale everywhere, find the long-run supply curve for the profit-maximizing, price-taking firm. Is one unique scale of operation most efficient?

12. In long-run competitive equilibrium with identical firms, price equals average cost and firms earn zero profit. Why would a manager want to produce in the long run if total revenue is just equal to total cost?

13. Describe the long-run equilibrium for a competitive firm and industry. Now suppose demand decreases, but the government forbids exit. Sketch out the adjustments by a representative firm and the industry.

14. Suppose a sales tax is placed on a good sold in a competitive industry. How will the sales tax affect equilibrium price? How will the tax affect a typical firm?

15. Can you think of any condition facing firms in a competitive industry that might lead naturally to a pure monopoly?

16. Assume that a good X is produced with an input L according to a production function $X = X(L)$ that is subject to diminishing productivity (a Robinson-Crusoe economy). The consumer (Robinson) maximizes utility, given by $U = U(X, \ell)$ where ℓ denotes leisure time. Profit is $\pi = pX - wL$.

(a) State the consumer's budget constraint and budget line.
(b) With labor time on the horizontal axis, graph this economy's production function.
(c) Recall that labor time and leisure time can be measured along the same axis. Show the consumer's optimal indifference curve U^* on the same graph as the production function.
(d) On the same graph, draw the budget line for a competitive equilibrium. Determine the real wage rate w/p and the real profit π/p in equilibrium.
(e) State the conditions for a competitive equilibrium in this economy.

17. Within the context of a bilateral model of pure exchange, what must conditions be to have an equilibrium?

18. What conditions must be satisfied for a general equilibrium in production? Illustrate the conditions for the two-input, two-output case with a box diagram.

19. Show that the production possibilities curve for the economy is a straight line under constant returns to scale in producing X and Y if both production functions have the same factor intensities.

20. Show that the production possibilities curve for the economy is convex under decreasing returns to scale in producing X and Y even if the factor intensities are the same.

21. How does attaining Pareto optimality through competition depend upon the distribution of wealth?

Chapter 12 Appendix: *The Calculus of Maximizing Profit*

Profit as a function of output is

$$\pi(X) = R(X) - C(X)$$

where $R(X)$ is total revenue and $C(X)$ is total cost. For the price-taking firm, revenue is given by

$$R(X) = p_X X$$

Thus, marginal revenue is given by

$$MR_X = \frac{\partial R}{\partial X} = p_X$$

To find the profit-maximizing level of output, differentiate the profit function with respect to output. The first-order condition is

$$\frac{\partial \pi}{\partial X} = \frac{\partial R}{\partial X} - \frac{\partial C}{\partial X} = MR_X - MC_X = 0$$

Thus, marginal revenue must be equal to marginal cost, whether the firm operates in a competitive market or not. The second-order condition is

$$\frac{\partial^2 \pi}{\partial X^2} < 0$$

This expression implies that the marginal cost curve cuts the marginal revenue curve from below at the profit-maximizing level of output. Because $MR_X = p_X$ for the competitive firm, profit is maximized, where

$$p_X = MC_X$$

This statement implies that the competitive firm treats its marginal cost curve as its supply curve, supplying output so that the marginal cost of producing each output level always equals price.

Derived input demand can be examined by expressing profit as a function of the inputs. With Z_1 and Z_2 as the inputs, profit is

$$\pi = p_X X(Z_1, Z_2) - w_1 Z_1 - w_2 Z_2$$

where $X(Z_1, Z_2)$ is the production function, and w_1 and w_2 are the input prices. No constraint is needed because the production function summarizes available technology. The first-order conditions are:

$$\frac{\partial \pi}{\partial Z_1} = p_X \frac{\partial X}{\partial Z_1} - w_1 = 0$$

$$\frac{\partial \pi}{\partial Z_2} = p_X \frac{\partial X}{\partial Z_2} - w_2 = 0$$

where

$$\frac{\partial X}{\partial Z_1} = MP_1 \quad \text{and} \quad \frac{\partial X}{\partial Z_2} = MP_2$$

Thus, the first-order conditions imply that the value of the marginal product of each input must be equal to the input's price:

$$VMP_1 = p_X MP_1 = w_1$$

$$VMP_2 = p_X MP_2 = w_2$$

The optimal input combination is found by solving the first-order conditions for Z_1^* and Z_2^*. Maximum profit is computed by evaluating the production function at the optimal input combination, $X^* = X(Z_1^*, Z_2^*)$.

Maximizing Short-run Profit

The short-run profit function for the competitive firm is

$$\pi = p_X X - w_1 Z_1 - FC$$

where FC is given by $FC = w_2 Z_2$. The first-order condition is

$$\frac{\partial \pi}{\partial Z_1} = p_X \frac{\partial X}{\partial Z_1} - w_1 = 0$$

In other words, the value of the marginal product of the variable input must be equal to the price of the variable input,

$$VMP_1 = p_X MP_1 = w_1$$

Because $MC = w_1/MP_1$, this equation may be written

$$p_X = \frac{w}{MP_1} = MC(X^*)$$

In other words, price equals marginal cost when the firm is maximizing profit. Moreover, the value of the marginal product must be equal to the variable input's price. Diminishing marginal productivity implies that the VMP curve has negative slope and that the MC curve has positive slope. The firm will shut down whenever output price is below average variable cost. The shutdown rule guarantees that the second-order condition will be satisfied when $p_X = MC(X^*)$. That is, the marginal cost curve will cut the marginal revenue curve from below whenever price is above average variable cost.

As output price changes, the competitive firm reacts by setting output where $p_X = MC(X^*)$. Thus the profit-maximizing level of output X^* is traced out along the MC curve as price varies. To see how the short-run supply might be derived directly, we can express profit as a function of output, parametric prices, fixed inputs, and technology:

$$\pi = \pi(X; p_X, w_1, w_2, Z_2)$$

Maximizing profit requires that

$$\frac{\partial \pi}{\partial X} = 0$$

this first-order equation yields an implicit function for X in terms of p_X, and so if the profit function $\pi(X)$ has negative second derivative, an explicit function $X^*(p_X)$ is the firm's supply curve. This supply curve is the inverse of the firm's marginal cost curve,

$$X^*(p_X) = MC^{-1}$$

Monopoly and Monopolistic Competition

Price-taking behavior is ensured by the form of market structure called perfect competition. More usual forms of market structure result in the ability to influence price. Once a *seller* has some control over price, that seller is described as having some **monopoly** power. Once a *buyer* has some control over price, that buyer is described as having some **monopsony** power. If only one seller is involved, it is called a **pure monopoly.** If we have only one buyer, it is called a **pure monopsonist.** The extent of the ability to influence price depends on the structure of the market. Market structure is described by the number of buyers and sellers in the market, the ease of entry and exit, the degree of product differentiation, and whether or not agents in the industry have any interdependence in making decisions.

Our primary focus in this chapter is monopoly behavior. We start by looking at **pure monopoly** and construct that model. We then examine the social costs of monopoly power, and we assemble some ways of measuring extent of monopoly power. The most frequent forms of market structure lie between the extremes of perfect competition and pure monopoly. **Monopolistic competition** departs from the model of perfect competition only in that firms produce close but not perfect substitutes. Other topics include the case in which the monopolist cannot exercise monopoly power—contestable markets.

Employment and resource prices are also affected by the exercise of monopoly power. We therefore examine the demand of a monopoly for inputs and the supply of outputs by a monopsony. Applications include regulating monopoly behavior in resource markets and efficient use of resources.

13.1 Pure Monopoly and Monopoly Pricing

A **pure monopoly** occurs when an industry consists of only one firm, so that the product being produced is unique. In contrast with price-taking behavior of the competitive firm, a pure monopolist is a **price-setting** firm.

The pure monopolist has the power to set output and price simultaneously. But the monopolist cannot set price independently of output because the monopolist is constrained by market demand. The demand curve facing the monopolist is the market demand curve, $Q = D(p)$. Price and output are inversely related to each other because $Q = D(p)$ has negative slope. A monopoly firm cannot charge just any old price, because demand is determined by consumers.

The price the monopolist can charge is determined by the inverse market demand curve $D^{-1} = p(Q)$. Graphically, this AR curve coincides with the market demand curve. Total revenue becomes $TR = p(Q)Q$, where Q is the quantity produced and sold. Typical TR and AR curves are illustrated in Figure 13.1. A falling average revenue curve usually implies a mound-shaped TR curve. Because price falls as output increases, the slope of the TR curve decreases. In contrast, a price-taking firm has a TR curve that graphs as a straight line.

Recall that marginal revenue is the change in TR with respect to an incremental change in output, $MR = \Delta TR/\Delta Q$. Marginal revenue is given by[1]

$$MR = p + \frac{\Delta p}{\Delta Q} Q$$

where $\Delta p/\Delta Q$ is the slope of the average revenue curve. Because $\Delta p/\Delta Q$ is negative, the MR curve lies everywhere below the AR curve, as shown in Figure 13.1. The MR curve *must* lie everywhere below the AR curve because AR is falling.

Recall that MR is also given by

$$MR = p\left[1 - \frac{1}{\eta}\right]$$

---

1. $\partial TR/\partial Q = \partial(pQ)/\partial Q = p + Q(\partial p/\partial Q)$

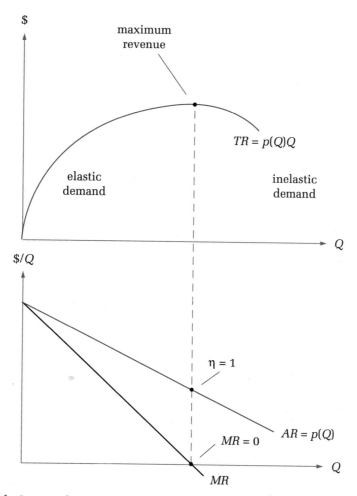

Figure 13.1 **Revenue and pure monopoly:** The monopolist's demand curve—its average revenue curve—coincides with the market demand curve, which is elastic when marginal revenue is positive.

where η is the elasticity of demand. The MR is positive when demand is elastic ($\eta > 1$), and negative when demand is inelastic ($1 > \eta > 0$). When total revenue is at a maximum, demand has unitary elasticity and $MR = 0$. A monopolist will never choose to produce in the inelastic range of the AR curve because, as shown by Figure 13.1, MR is negative when demand is inelastic.

For the monopolist the rule for maximizing profit is the same as the rule for the price-taking firm: Set output so that marginal revenue is equal to marginal cost if price is at least equal to average variable cost; however, if price is below average variable cost, the firm should shut down to minimize the loss. Because the monopolist is not a price-taking firm, though, AR and MR are not equal to each other. The monopolist sets output *and* price

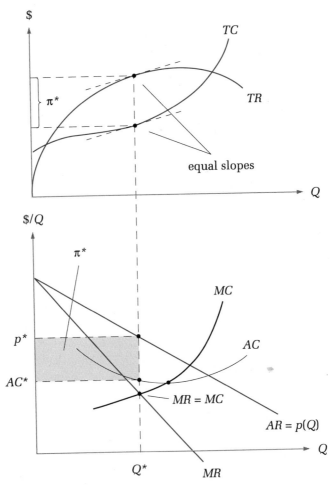

Figure 13.2 **Profit-maximizing price:** The monopolist sets output at Q*, where MR = MC. Price is set at p* so that Q* units can be sold.

simultaneously to maximize profit. A typical case is illustrated by Figure 13.2. The firm sets output at Q^*, where $MR = MC$. Price is set so that Q^* units can be sold. This analysis applies to both the short run and the long. The only difference is that in the long run all costs are variable. Either way, the firm should shut down if price is less than average variable cost.

We need no separate model for the industry for the pure monopoly, because the firm is the industry. Also notice another difference between the monopoly model and pure competition: no monopoly supply curve. The supply decision is one of choosing output and price simultaneously—a supply point.

How can the firm's manager find the correct price and output in practice? Frequently managers have only limited knowledge of their firm's average revenue (demand) curve.

Moreover, they may know their firm's marginal cost only over a limited range of output. A rule of thumb is needed that can more easily be applied in practice.

We know how MR is related to elasticity, $MR = p[1 - 1/\eta]$. Now, if MC is known, we can set MR equal to MC:

$$p\left[1 - \frac{1}{\eta}\right] = MC$$

This expression, which is a condition for maximizing profit, can be rearranged to yield

$$\frac{p - MC}{p} = \frac{1}{\eta}$$

The left-hand side is the markup over marginal cost as a fraction of price. Equivalently, this equation can be rearranged to express price directly as a markup over marginal cost. The result is this rule of thumb:

Profit-maximizing price:

$$p = \frac{MC}{1 - 1/\eta}$$

For example, if the elasticity of demand is $\eta = 2$ and the marginal cost is $9, price should be $9/(1 - 1/2) = $18 per unit. Thus, if marginal cost and price elasticity are known, we can apply the rule of thumb to check whether a specific output level and price maximize profit.

If the firm is not a pure monopoly but still has some market power in setting price, the rule of thumb can still be applied by using the elasticity of demand for the firm rather than the elasticity of market demand. It is harder to determine the elasticity for a firm, though, because the firm must consider how its competitors will react to price changes. Nevertheless, given an estimate of the firm's elasticity of demand, the profit-maximizing markup too can be estimated. Notice that if the firm's demand is highly elastic, the mark-up will be small. Indeed, the markup for the competitive firm is zero, because $p = MC$ when profit is maximized. If the firm has considerable market power, the difference between price and marginal cost may be quite large.

13.2 Long-run Equilibrium

Long-run equilibrium occurs where long-run marginal cost is equal to marginal revenue. As Figure 13.3 shows, the firm sets price at p^* to sell Q^* units. Average cost at Q^*, denoted LAC^*, is achieved by choosing the scale of operation that results in the short-run curves AC^* and MC^*. The important result is that average cost incurred at Q^* is greater than minimal LAC. Unlike a competitive industry, no guarantee is given that output will be produced at lowest average cost in the long run. Moreover, positive profits may come in the long run under monopoly.

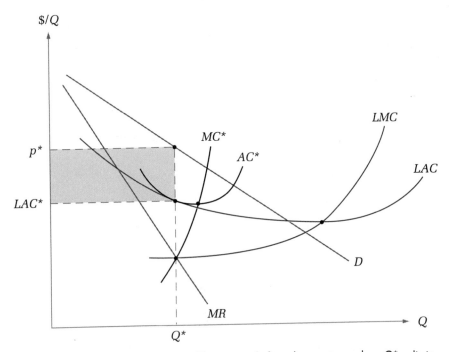

Figure 13.3 **Long-run monopoly equilibrium:** The monopoly firm chooses to produce Q^* units to maximize long-run profit. The firm chooses a scale represented by the short-run cost curves AC^* and MC^*. It is unlikely that the long-run average cost will be minimized.

Exercising monopoly power has a social cost. As shown in Figure 13.4, the monopolist will choose price at p^* and output at Q^* so that MR equals LMC. At that level of output, price is greater than marginal cost. This gap between price and marginal cost creates a welfare loss due to socially inefficient use of resources. Output is inefficiently low, and price is inefficiently high.

To see why output is inefficiently low, notice that at output level Q^*, the marginal value (price) of an extra unit of output is greater than marginal cost. A social gain can be made by producing an extra unit of output. When price exceeds marginal cost, a competitive firm will always choose to produce more, because the gain in revenue exceeds the marginal cost, and pure competition results in a price equal to marginal cost. But a monopolist must reduce price to sell more. Once the monopolist reaches the point where $MR = LMC$, further increases in price will reduce profit. Under monopoly, the industry reaches an equilibrium, where $MR = LMC$ and $p > LMC$, rather than the socially optimal equilibrium, where $p = LMC$. The social gains from producing beyond Q^* are sacrificed, yielding a deadweight loss.

What happens if a competitive industry becomes a monopoly? Figure 13.5 shows the case in which competitive firms in an industry are operating in the long run. Each competitive firm chooses a scale resulting in AC^* and MC^*. Competitive industry supply is

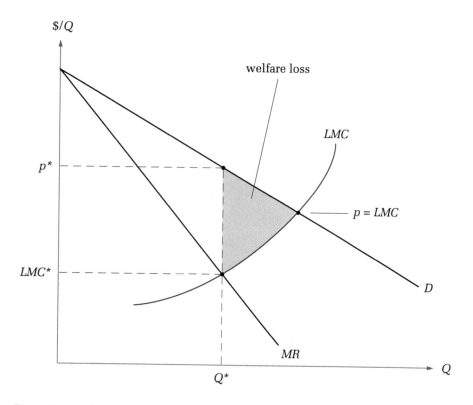

Figure 13.4 **Welfare loss of monopoly:** A monopolist produces $Q = Q^*$, where $MR = LMC$ and $p > LMC$. The social gains if production were increased to the point where $p = LMC$ are lost. A deadweight loss occurs, and too few resources are used in producing the good.

the horizontal sum of the individual firm's marginal cost curves, $\Sigma MC^{-1}(p)$, when there are, say, n firms. The long-run equilibrium price is established as p_c where the market clears. Under competition, there is no deadweight loss and profit is zero in the long run. Now, if these competitive firms were combined into one multiplant monopoly, the new monopoly firm would no longer operate n plants. The reason is that, with reduced output, average costs would be higher if all the original plants were operated at lower production rates. The monopoly firm would no longer be operating each plant at its lowest average cost. Thus the monopolist will operate fewer plants, say $k < n$ of them, to maximize profit by selling a total level of output Q_m, where $LMC = MR_m$. The monopolist's average cost at the new equilibrium is equal to the competitive price, but the monopoly price is greater than the competitive price, $p_m > p_c$, and output is lower, $Q_m < Q_c$. The monopolist chooses the number of plants k, so that ΣMC^* now crosses the monopolist's marginal revenue curve MR_m, where marginal revenue equals long-run marginal cost. A deadweight loss is created because the monopolist produces fewer units than are socially optimal. Monopoly profits are gained because the monopoly price p_m is greater than average cost.

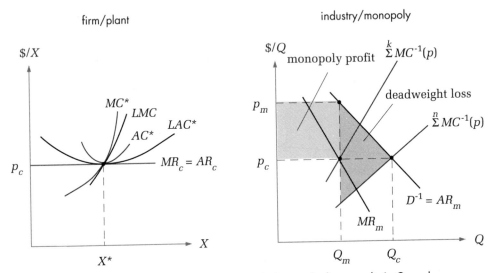

Figure 13.5 **Monopoly vs. competition:** A competitive industry of n firms results in Q_c and p_c. Converting this industry into a multiplant monopoly results in $k < n$ plants, supplying $Q_m < Q_c$. The monopoly price is $p_m > p_c$, and a monopoly profit is extracted from the consumer surplus. A deadweight loss is created because the monopoly price is too high and the quantity produced is too low.

GLOBAL PERSPECTIVE: *British Telecom*

British Telecom, Britain's monopolist telephone operator, was privatized in 1984. At that time the government gave the firm's new shareholders solid assurance that no other big changes would be made for at least seven years. The time is up.

In 1991, only British Telecom and Mercury were allowed to sell fixed-line telephone calls in Britain. Other companies were not allowed to build private networks of their own. They must lease lines from British Telecom or Mercury instead. Under one proposal for change, any company will be allowed to provide telephone services. British Telecom would be required to connect all new newcomers to its network.

The easiest way to build a private network is to install two-way satellite dishes known as VSATs, or "very small aperture terminals." Only one-way VSATs were allowed in 1991, and only seven companies may sell VSAT services. Once these restrictions go, VSATs should prove popular. After America's "open-sky" policy began in 1981, the use of VSATs grew to 30,000 ten years later. That compares to a measly 600 in heavily regulated Europe.

Deregulation can engender competition only if companies take advantage of changes in the rules. Luckily, plenty are ready to do so. America's Baby Bells have already snapped up most of Britain's new cable-television franchises. Cable-television firms are restricted to using Mercury or British Telecom switches, but once they are allowed to do their own switching, many will offer telephone services too. British Waterways is talking to U.S. Sprint about laying cables along canals. Big telecommunications firms like GTE and Millicom, and equipment manufacturers like GEC and Siemens, may also be interested in taking up licenses in a deregulated Britain. But the lack of immediate competition poses a problem for government.

As long as British Telecom controls access to most customers, it can exercise monopoly power to keep prices high.

The best remedy may be to break up British Telecom into separate long-distance and local companies. The alternative of just requiring access to lines already in service is likely to emulate the American experience in the early 1970s. America let new long-distance operators connect with AT&T, the country's largest telephone monopoly. This marriage didn't work well, for AT&T retained much power, and dozens of private antitrust suits were filed accusing it of unfair interconnect practices and predatory pricing. Eventually, in 1983, the Justice Department used antitrust law to break up AT&T. The result was a long-distance and international carrier, still called AT&T, and the Baby Bells, the seven regional carriers. Since then, many new entrants have come along, and much more competition, in the long-distance telephone market. The table makes some comparisons for 1989.

	Employees per 10,000 lines	Revenue per employee
Pacific Telesis (United States)	48	$147,000
NYNEX (United States)	53	166,000
STET (Italy)	59	129,000
Telepona (Spain)	60	105,000
British Telecom (Britain)	98	97,000

Source: The Economist, March 2, 1991.

13.3 Rent-Seeking Behavior

When we see the potential for profit, we expect any individual to spend up to the full value of the expected profit to gain that profit. After all, economic profit is the return above all opportunity costs. The behavior individuals engage in to earn payments in excess of opportunity costs is called **rent seeking**. What is economic rent?

> **Economic rent:** Economic rent is a payment to a resource in excess of its opportunity cost.

Originally, *economic rent* described the payment to land that was in fixed supply. When the supply of land is perfectly inelastic, any payment at all exceeds that which is required to supply the land, and the total payment is economic rent. For all resources, the economic rent is equal to the sellers' surplus.

In the short run any payment to such a reproducible input as physical or human capital in excess of its opportunity cost is called a **quasi-rent:**

> **Quasi-rent:** Quasi-rent consists of short-run payments to any input in excess of its opportunity cost.

It is quasi-rents that drive the competitive model toward its long-run equilibrium, where economic profits are zero, and hence zero economic rents. Quasi-rents arise naturally in the price system through shifts in demand and supply curves. The pursuit of quasi-rents is the equivalent of profit seeking, and in a perfectly competitive environment all quasi-rents are fully dissipated. Under competition, rent seeking induces entry and exit and other long-run adjustments that result in zero long-run profits. Under monopoly, rent seeking is just as pervasive even though the consequences are different.

Rents can be contrived by monopoly power or government action. Monopoly rent equals the economic profit gained by the monopolist. Why, then, should we distinguish between rent seeking and profit seeking? A simple example will illustrate:[2] Suppose a king decides to grant a monopoly right to sell playing cards. As a consequence of the artificial scarcity the king creates, monopoly rents will come about in the form of a transfer from consumers of playing cards to the monopolist. Thus, aspiring monopolists will seek the king's favor. If no real resources are used to compete for the king's favor, the rents become monopoly profit. But if the winning monopolist uses real resources to acquire the right to the monopoly, monopoly profit is reduced and the rent remains unchanged. Consider the incipient monopolist who hires a lawyer to lobby the king for the monopoly right. From a social point of view, this activity creates no value.

By permission of Johnny Hart and Creators Syndicate, Inc.

---

2. See Robert D. Tollison, "Rent Seeking: A Survey," *Kyklos,* 35 (1982).

AN APPLICATION: *Computing the Total Cost of Monopoly*

Richard Posner suggests a way of computing the social cost of monopoly.* He assumes that each firm has marginal costs that are approximately constant, as shown in Figure 13.6, and that each firm's average revenue curve is linear. Given a linear average revenue curve and constant marginal cost, the deadweight loss can easily be calculated. For instance, in Figure 13.6, profits are given by $\pi = Q_m \Delta p$ and the deadweight loss is given by $D = (\Delta p \Delta Q)/2 = \pi/2$ because $Q_m = \Delta Q$. In Table 13.1, Posner's estimates of the deadweight losses due to monopoly power are presented. Two categories of industries are represented. In the first, government regulation has forced price above competitive levels. The second category is for some private—mainly international—cartels that attempt to emulate monopoly behavior. Posner concludes that these estimates, crude as they are, indicate substantial social costs due to monopoly behavior. In a pathbreaking study, Arnold Harberger estimated the welfare loss due to monopoly misallocation of resources to be less than one-tenth of 1 percent of U.S. national income, but his estimate of the dollar loss in 1954 dollars was

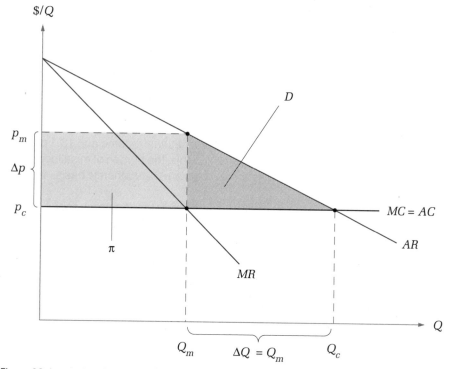

Figure 13.6 **Estimate of deadweight loss:** Assuming linear AR curves and constant MC curves for firms having monopoly power, the deadweight loss D is sometimes called the "welfare triangle." Notice that when average revenue is linear, $D = \pi/2$.

* Richard A. Posner, "The Social Costs of Monopoly and Regulation," *Journal of Political Economy,* 83(4) (1975), pp. 807–827; and *Antitrust Law* (University of Chicago Press, 1976).

Table 13.1 **Social Costs of Monopoly Power**

Industry	Price increase (Δp) (as % of marginal cost)	Deadweight loss (D) (as % of industry sales)
Regulated industries		
Physician's services	40	14
Eyeglasses	34	13
Milk	11	5
Motor carriers	62	19
Oil	66	20
Airlines	66	20
Cartelized industries		
Nitrogen	75	21
Sugar	30	12
Rubber	100	25
Electric bulbs	37	14
Copper	31	12
Cast-iron pipe	39	14

Source: Richard A. Posner, *Antitrust Law* (University of Chicago Press, 1976), p. 254. Reprinted by permission of the University of Chicago Press.

81 million.† Harberger's calculations were based on assumptions of unitary elasticity of demand, constant long-run costs, and other assumptions that tended to inflate his estimates. Other studies of the U.S. economy estimate that the deadweight loss due to monopoly power ranges between 0.07 percent of national income and 13.1 percent.‡ Even if the higher estimates are overstated by double, the burden of misallocation has been significant in total dollars. These social costs are the economic basis of antitrust policy.

Posner argues that the deadweight loss understates the total social costs of monopoly because of rent-seeking behavior. He states:§

> The existence of an opportunity to obtain monopoly profits will attract resources into efforts to obtain monopolies, and the opportunity costs of those resources are social costs of monopoly too (Tullock 1967). Theft provides an instructive analogy. The transfer of wealth from victims to thief involves no artificial limitation of output, but it does not follow that the social cost is zero.

It is the opportunity for such transfers, Posner suggests, that draws resources to thieving and in turn to protection against theft. The resources consumed are the social

---

† Arnold C. Harberger, "Monopoly and Resource Allocation," *American Economic Review: Papers and Proceedings* (May 1954), pp. 77–87.

‡ For a survey of some estimates of welfare loss due to market power, see William G. Shephard, *The Economics of Industrial Organization,* 2nd ed. (Prentice-Hall, 1985), p. 137.

§ Posner, *Antitrust Law* (1975), pp. 807–827.

costs of theft. When a thief steels three radios from a home and destroys one by dropping it, the broken radio, Posner says, is like a deadweight loss. He claims, however, that the total social loss is greater than the deadweight loss even though two radios have been transferred elsewhere. It is greater because resources will be diverted to replacing or recovering the three radios, and because the theft activity is nonproductive. Similarly, when monopoly is achieved by bribery, the bribe is a pure transfer that shifts part of the monopoly profit to officials receiving the bribe and draws real resources into the activity of becoming an official who can receive bribes.

If the cost of gaining a monopoly is exactly equal to the expected profit of being a monopolist, and if the costs of getting the monopoly have no socially valuable by-products, then the monopoly profits should be added to the deadweight loss to find the total cost of monopoly. If these conditions are true, then the deadweight losses of Table 13.1 should be tripled, because $\pi + D = 3\pi/2 = 3D$, to get measures of the total social losses due to those monopolies.

The activity of wasting resources in striving for artificially contrived transfers is called **rent seeking:**

> **Rent seeking:** *Rent seeking is the expenditure of scarce resources to capture an artificially created transfer.*

Rent-seeking costs should be added to the welfare triangle in calculating the total social cost of monopoly.

Any sensible would-be monopolist would be willing to pay an amount up to its expected monopoly profit to get economic rent from monopoly pricing. As we have seen, monopoly pricing creates a deadweight loss. But an even greater waste may be transfers to bureaucrats whose only function is to receive them, and who would otherwise have to find economically useful employment. Or hiring lawyers (and economists) to lobby the government.

The expression "rent seeking" was coined by Anne Kruger, formerly of the World Bank, in 1974. Her target was the monopoly profit created when governments use quotas to restrict the supply of imports or foreign exchange. Jagdish Bhagwati has refined the idea to **directly unproductive profitseeking (DUP).**[3] His DUP includes rent seeking of the sort analyzed by Anne Kruger and also lobbying to get a bigger share of government spending or to reduce a group's tax burden; it also includes transfers associated with government regulation. A manufacturer of seatbelts will spend money supporting their mandatory use. Bribery is a form of DUP. The cost of rent seeking also arises from the need of governments and rent seekers to disguise their sharing of rents. One example is the European Community's common agricultural policy (CAP), whose aim is to keep small farmers in business. Simple subsidies could do the same, but that would be visible. A deliberately opaque system of farm support is used instead to dupe the public. Any inefficiencies created by this deception should also be counted as DUP.

---

3. Jagdish Bhagwati, "Directly Unproductive Profit-Seeking Activities," *Journal of Political Economy,* 90 (October 1982).

13.4 Monopolistic Competition

In the model of perfect competition we assumed that each of the several small firms produced a homogeneous product. What happens when such firms differentiate their products? In fact, this form of market structure is very common. At least in sheer numbers of firms, the industries where firms produce close but not perfect substitutes make up a significant part of our economic environment.

Edward Chamberlin (1933) called this form of market structure **monopolistic competition:**

> **Monopolistic competition:** *Monopolistic competition is an industry structure wherein several firms produce slightly differentiated products but otherwise have the same characteristics as perfectly competitive firms.*

Like perfect competition, each firm acts independently. And like perfect competition, entry and exit are easy. Product differentiation is the one characteristic that differentiates monopolistic competition from perfect competition.

Product differentiation is caused by advertising, packaging, product design, type of service, geographic location, slight differences in quality, and other attributes that alter consumers' perceptions of the products. Product differentiation is a source of monopoly power because it permits a firm to raise its price without losing all its sales. Some consumers will continue to purchase the good at a higher price because they prefer it to others. Price reductions lead to increased sales, though, because the product is a close substitute for others. Thus the average revenue curve facing the monopolistically competitive firm is highly but not perfectly elastic.

The short-run, profit-maximizing, monopolistically competitive firm sets output where $MR = MC$—just like any other profit-maximizing firm. The firm will shut down if revenue is less than variable cost. But if revenue covers fixed cost, profit may be positive, zero, or negative.

In the long run monopolistic competition is subject to shifting revenue curves when entry or exit take place and market shares change. Increased product differentiation also shifts the position of the firm's average revenue curve as consumers react to product changes. This shift in the firm's demand causes a change in the firm's demand elasticity and market share. Any positive profits provide a signal to potential entrants. As new firms enter the industry, the market shares of original firms are likely to shrink and each firm's demand curve becomes more elastic. The opposite reactions will occur in response to negative profits. Also, increased product differentiation is likely to shift the position of the firm's cost curves, reflecting an increase in the cost of producing and marketing the good. Moreover, resource prices may be bid upward as new firms enter the industry. The cost curves therefore shift upward with entry and increased product differentiation. At the same time the firm will be choosing an optimal scale, but any substantial economies of scale are inconsistent with the existence of many small firms.

With these adjustments in mind, the long-run equilibrium for the firm under monopolistic competition is illustrated by Figure 13.7. Changes in product differentiation shift the firm's cost curves, and entry and exit shift the firm's AR curve until AR is tangent to the

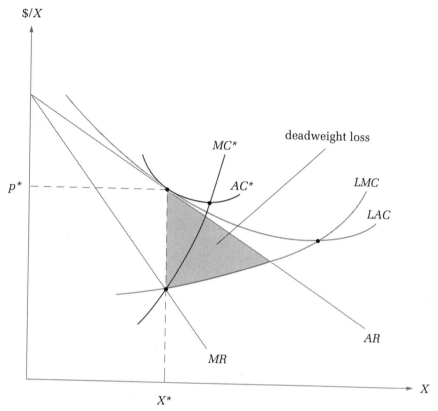

Figure 13.7 **Monopolistic competition:** In the long run the firm produces X^* units, where $LMC = MR$, and chooses a scale so that $MC^* = MR$. Economic profits are zero because $AR = LAC$, but the scale chosen does *not* result in minimal LAC. Price exceeds marginal cost, leaving a deadweight loss equal to the shaded area.

LAC curve. Product differentiation causes the firm's AR curve to be less than perfectly elastic. The firm is forced to choose a scale along the LAC curve at which economic profits are zero. As a consequence, profits for each firm under monopolistic competition in the long run are zero. In contrast with the competitive model, however, the long-run equilibrium under monopolistic competition never yields minimal average cost.

Excess capacity is defined as a firm's ability to reduce average cost by expanding output. The excess occurs under monopolistic competition because firms do not choose a scale that results in minimal LAC. Thus the value to consumers of additional units of output exceeds the marginal cost of producing those units, creating a deadweight loss, as illustrated in Figure 13.7. This loss is a measure of the welfare loss that occurs because price exceeds marginal cost.

Should monopolistic competition therefore be banned or regulated? Probably not. The primary source of the inefficiency costs of monopolistic competition is the monopoly power arising from product differentiation. This inefficiency must be balanced against the gains from product diversity. People who buy Supercuts would not feel better off if they

AN APPLICATION: *Advertising and Monopolistic Competition*

Advertising is frequently used to differentiate a product in order to gain some monopoly power. Such selling is called **persuasive advertising.** How does persuasive advertising affect pricing strategy? And what are the social costs of such pricing practices?

Figure 13.8 illustrates what happens when a purely competitive firm differentiates its product with persuasive advertising and thereby becomes monopolistically competitive. Initially, let's assume that the industry is in competitive long-run equilibrium so that the firm produces X_c units at price p_c and the firm's economic profits are zero. Advertising that differentiates the product causes the firm's demand curve to be less than perfectly elastic, as in AR_m. We now have monopolistic competition. The advertising expenditure causes the average cost curve to shift from AC_c to AC_m. This now monopolistically competitive firm maximizes profits where $MR_m = MC$ at quantity X_m

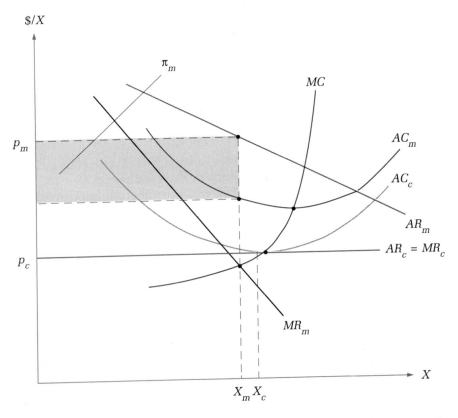

Figure 13.8 **Persuasive advertising and price:** Without advertising to differentiate the product, the producer of good X is competitive and economic profit is zero. Advertising that differentiates the product causes the firm's AR curve to change to AR_m, but average cost shifts to AC_m. This monopolistically competitive firm maximizes profits when price is p_m.

and price p_m. Price will surely rise and the firm will earn a quasi-rent. That is, short-run profits will be generated, and the remainder of the increase in economic rent will be transferred in the form of advertising costs.

To evaluate the welfare consequences of persuasive advertising, we need to look at what happens in the long run. Figure 13.9 illustrates the long-run result. The short-run profits will attract new entrants, shrinking each firm's market share. A new equilibrium will be established in the long run where the AR_m curve is tangent to the LAC_m curve. The welfare loss can be measured by the area between the average revenue and marginal cost curves over the change in output. This welfare loss is created partly from the decrease in quantity and partly from the shift in the cost curve. The loss is associated with the actions of just one firm in this now monopolistically competitive industry.

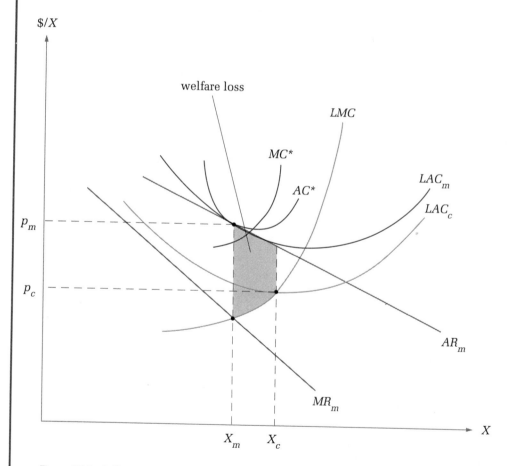

Figure 13.9 **Welfare cost of persuasive advertising:** In the long run the entry of firms and changing market shares under monopolistic competition will cause economic profit to shrink to zero once more. Price will be higher at p_m and quantity lower at X_m compared to the competitive solution. A welfare loss is created partly from the decrease in quantity and partly from the increase in cost.

had to go to a regular barbershop, and vice versa. Most consumers value the ability to choose among differentiated products. Although differentiation increases the cost of production and reduces the elasticity of each firm's demand, resulting in excess capacity and deadweight loss, the degree of monopoly power is usually small. Thus the excess capacity should be small, and the deadweight loss should be small too. The gains from product diversity are probably large enough to outweigh the welfare losses resulting from downward-sloping AR curves. And yet one must wonder sometimes if having the vastly varied brands of cereal on the supermarket shelves is really worth it.

13.5 The Dominant-Firm Model

Consider an industry composed of many relatively small firms and one large firm, all producing the same product. An example might be AT&T and its rivals in the interstate telecommunications industry. Other examples of dominant firms that have a fringe of smaller competitors, at least for some historical periods, are ALCOA in aluminum, IBM in mainframe computers, Xerox in photocopy machines, and Kodak in cameras and film. Though not technically a pure monopoly, the potential for monopoly power is there when one firm is dominant and a competitive fringe is active.

The basic operational assumption is that, without regulation, the dominant firm can set price and allow minor firms to sell all they can at that price. The minor firms act as price takers, and the dominant firm sells the remaining part of market demand after the minor firms decide on their output levels. Each minor firm ignores the effects of its actions on industry price and on decisions by all other firms in the industry. Therefore, each minor firm is like a competitive firm because each has an insignificant influence on the market.

Figure 13.10 illustrates the dominant-firm model. The industry demand curve is D. The supply by the minor firms is the sum of their individual supply curves, ΣX_j. This curve is *not* the market supply curve. Rather, curve ΣX_j indicates the part of the market supplied by the minor firms. At any price, each minor firm sets its output so that price equals its marginal cost. The dominant firm supplies the remainder between market demand and the quantity supplied by the minor firms. Therefore, the dominant firm's average revenue curve AR_d is found by subtracting the quantity supplied by the minor firms from market demand.

At or above price p_0, the minor firms supply all the quantity demanded. At prices below p_0, the minor firms supply the part of the market demand determined by their marginal cost curves. The dominant firm supplies the remainder. Confronted with cost curves AC_d and MC_d, the dominant firm sets price at p^*, where $MR_d = MC_d$, and sets its output at Q^*. The minor firms view price p^* as constant to them and collectively supply Q_m units. Total quantity supplied is $Q_m + Q^*$ and equals quantity demanded Q_d, and the market is in equilibrium at price p^*.

This solution is stable in the short run. If the price set by the dominant firm results in economic profits for the minor firms, however, new firms have an incentive for entry. Moreover, minor firms will want to expand if there are economies of scale. Expansion or entry causes the minor firms' supply to increase, and the dominant firm's AR curve will

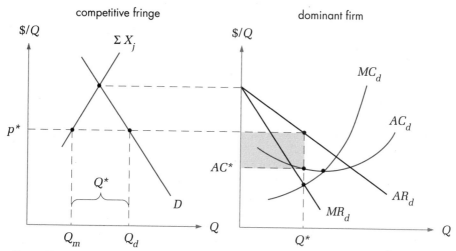

Figure 13.10 **An industry with a dominant firm:** The industry demand is D, and supply by the minor firms is ΣX_j. The dominant firm's average revenue curve is AR_d, which is found by subtracting from market demand the quantity supplied by the rest of the market. The dominant firm sets price at p^*, where its marginal revenue equals its marginal cost. The minor firms on the competitive fringe take price p^* as constant and collectively supply Q_m units. Market demand is met because $Q_m + Q^* = Q_d$.

shift to the left. The dominant firm's share of the market and profits will shrink unless the expansion and entry of minor firms is limited.

A **limit price** discourages or prevents entry. Firms that can practice limit pricing give up short-run profits to increase long-run profits. When a firm considers limit pricing, it should compare the present value of expected profits without limit pricing to the present value of expected profits with limit pricing.

The feasibility of pricing to limit expansion and entry depends on the long-run cost curves facing the firms. As a first possibility, if diseconomies of scale are present, smaller firms will have a higher profit per unit than larger firms. The dominant firm can then discourage entry only by setting price below average cost. Because this practice leads to long-run losses, the industry is likely to evolve toward a more competitive structure.

A second possibility is that neither economies nor diseconomies of scale prevail over the whole range of market demand. To discourage entry then, the dominant firm will have to set price equal to *LAC*. If minimal *LAC* occurs within the range of market demand, the industry is likely to evolve into a structure that supports only a few relatively large firms. If the *LAC* curve is flat over a wide range of output, then the dominant firm will be able to discourage entry by threatening to set price below *LAC*. This dominant firm might capture short-run profits by setting price above *LAC* and then punishing minor firms with price cuts whenever they attempt to expand or enter. Such action creates instability, providing an incentive for merger or collusion. As before, the industry is likely to evolve into a more balanced oligopolistic structure, with only a few firms.

History is replete with examples of dominant firms that eventually lost market share.

The U.S. Steel Corporation was a dominant firm in its industry, but its share of the market has declined steadily from the 75 percent share it held in 1903. In 1920, U.S. Steel controlled 50 percent of its market, and its share continued to decline to less than 25 percent during the 1960s. In another industry, American Can controlled 90 percent of the tin-can market in 1901. The company's share fell to 40 percent by 1960. Few firms have managed to retain dominance. General Motors held 55 to 45 percent share of the domestic automobile market, but its share has been falling since Ford Motor Company increased its market share in the late 1980s. Of course, all domestic auto manufacturers have faced stiff competition from foreign imports.

A third possibility is that substantial economies of scale can be had. Then, aggressive pricing by the dominant firm will eliminate minor firms. This is the classic natural-monopoly setting.

13.6 Measuring Monopoly Power

The extreme forms of market structure are perfect competition and pure monopoly. Within this spectrum lie other forms of market structure, such as monopolistic competition, the dominant-firm model, and oligopoly. At one extreme, the perfectly competitive firm views its AR curve as determined by market price, so that $MR = AR$. At the other extreme, the pure monopolist views its AR curve as coincident with market demand, so that $MR < AR$. In the real world most forms of market structure fall between the two extremes. Hence, most firms possess some market power.

Monopoly power is the ability to set price above marginal cost. The gap between price and marginal cost depends on the elasticity of the firm's demand curve. Four things determine the firm's elasticity of demand. First is the *elasticity of market demand*. The market demand limits the potential for monopoly power because the firm's demand will be at least as elastic as market demand. Second is the *number of firms* in the market. If it has many firms, all about the same size, it is unlikely that any one firm by itself will significantly influence the market. Moreover, collusion is unlikely with many firms because of the increased transaction costs. Third is *rivalry* among firms. If only a few firms are present but each is aggressive in trying to capture market share, no one firm will be able to raise price significantly. Fourth is the *potential for entry*. Even if the market has only one firm, if other firms can enter easily, the incumbent firm will not be able to enjoy large monopoly profits for very long. Such firms may be forced to price low to deter entry. How can we measure the extent of monopoly power? Several alternatives are available.

A widely used measure of monopoly power is the Lerner monopoly index:[4]

> *Lerner monopoly index:*
>
> $$L = \frac{p - MC}{p}$$

4. Abba P. Lerner, "The Concept of Monopoly and the Measurement of Monopoly Power," *Review of Economic Studies,* 1 (June 1934), pp. 157–175.

Any firm possessing monopoly power faces a downward-sloping AR curve. If such firms set price and output so that $MR = MC$, price will be greater than MC because $p = AR$ and $AR > MR$. Under pure competition, where $p = AR = MR$ because the firm's demand curve is perfectly elastic, the Lerner index becomes $L = 0$. But when monopoly power is present and $p = AR > MR$, the Lerner index becomes greater as the difference between price and marginal cost grows. Thus, other things being equal, the Lerner index becomes larger as the firm's demand curve becomes less elastic.

Problems can arise in applying the Lerner index. For one, marginal cost is often difficult to measure, and so average variable cost is often used in place of MC. It would be even better to use MR in place of MC because profit-maximizing firms set $MR = MC$. For another problem, if the firm sets price below the profit-maximizing price, the potential for monopoly power will not be reflected in the index. And some firms have good reasons for not establishing a short-run profit-maximizing price. An example is a dominant firm setting a limit price or a contestable market, which we examine in the next section.

A second and related approach to measuring monopoly power concentrates on demand elasticities. Notice that the price-markup equation is the same as the Lerner index:

$$L = \frac{p - MC}{p} = \frac{1}{\eta}$$

where η is the own-price elasticity of demand. No markup appears under pure competition because the firm's demand curve is perfectly elastic and $p = MC$. But the markup becomes greater as demand becomes less elastic. Thus, demand elasticity can be used as an index to the degree of competitiveness—a firm is *more* competitive as its average revenue curve becomes *more* elastic. The firm's demand elasticity can also be difficult to measure, however.

A third measure of monopoly power concentrates on the uniqueness of the product. A pure monopolist produces a unique product with no close substitutes. A competitive firm produces a homogeneous product. The cross-elasticity of demand provides a measure of market substitutability of products. Big cross-price elasticities indicate that goods are close substitutes.

A fourth approach focuses on the conclusion that, in the long run, perfectly competitive firms earn zero economic profits but monopolistic firms may earn positive economic profits. Economic profits in the long run indicate the presence and exercise of monopoly power. This observation gives rise to the Bain index:

> **Bain monopoly index:** *Accounting profit less an imputed return on owner's investment.*

The Bain index uses the divergence between price and average cost to measure monopoly power. This measure is an attempt to index economic profit.[5] The imputed return is

---

5. Empirical studies have presented evidence that firm size tends to be positively related to high profit rates. See, for instance, Marshal Hall and Leonard Weiss, "Firm Size and Profitability," *Review of Economics and Statistics* (August 1967), pp. 319–331, and James Koch, *Industrial Organization and Prices* (Prentice Hall, 1974), p. 134.

calculated by multiplying the investment by an interest rate for capital funds requiring the same degree of risk. One problem with applying the Bain index is that it requires actual measurement of *all* costs. Such measurement can be difficult using standard accounting data. Another problem is the focus on profit. Profit depends on average cost relative to price, and a firm with much monopoly power may have low economic profit. Yet that same firm may cause considerable deadweight loss due to monopoly pricing.

A fifth measure of monopoly power is provided by concentration ratios. The **market concentration ratio** is defined as the percentage of total industry sales, output, employment, value added, or assets associated with the largest firms ranked in order of market shares. The four-firm concentration ratio, the one most frequently used, is the percentage of industry sales associated with the four largest firms. For example, in 1982 the four-firm concentration ratio for the U.S. automotive industry was 92 percent, with 254 firms. In the aircraft industry, the four-firm concentration ratio was 64 percent, with 139 firms. For ready-mixed concrete, the four-firm concentration ratio was 6 percent, with 8,163 firms.[6]

A sixth index of monopoly power uses the market shares of all firms in the market:

> **Herfindahl monopoly index:**
>
> $$H = \sum_{i=1}^{n} S_i^2$$
>
> where S_i is the market share of the ith firm in a market of n firms.

In pure monopoly, $H = 1$. The Herfindahl index *decreases* as the number of firms increases. When the industry is highly atomistic, the H index is very close to zero. The H index also *rises* as market shares become more unequal because squaring the market shares weights the values for larger firms more heavily.

The Herfindahl index is used by the U.S. Department of Justice in evaluating how mergers influence concentration of industry. When two firms merge, the change in the H index is

$$\Delta H = (S_1 + S_2)^2 - S_1^2 - S_2^2 = 2S_1 S_2$$

where S_1 and S_2 are the shares of the two firms. Suppose the index is originally $H = 0.5$. Now suppose one firm with a 20 percent share merges with a second firm with a 10 percent share. The change in the H index is

$$\Delta H = 2S_1 S_2 = 2(0.2)(0.1) = 0.04$$

The new index will be $H + \Delta H = 0.54$. The increase in market concentration would be 8 percent.

---

6. U.S. Department of Commerce, "Concentration Ratios in Manufacturing," *1982 Census of Manufactures,* MC 82–S7.

AN APPLICATION: *A Case of Beer*

Rising concentration in an industry may be the result of economies of scale that permit lower prices, but concentration may create market power that leads to higher prices. In studying the brewing industry, William Lynk concluded that rising concentration led to lower prices as well as higher industry output.[*] In a subsequent study, Victor Tremblay criticized Lynk's research.[†] Tremblay argued that several important variables, especially advertising, were omitted from Lynk's analysis. This omission matters because advertising influences costs and supply as well as demand. Tremblay contends that prices will not necessarily fall as industry output increases, because a simultaneous decrease in supply may counter the increase in demand. In short, Tremblay implies that Lynk's demand curve was unidentified and misspecified.

Tremblay estimated this reduced-form price equation:

$$\hat{P} = -4.26 + 0.0042A_F - 0.000005A_I + 0.00011A_O - 0.00082Q_I - 0.00016Q_O$$
$$- 0.0039M + 0.00093N - 0.007Y + 3.57D_N + 0.0052\hat{C} - 0.018R + 2.18D_P$$

where:

P = a firm's wholesale price per barrel of beer

A_F = the quantity of the firm's advertising per brand

A_I = the quantity of advertising per brand from three dominant rivals *inside* the firm's strategic group

A_O = the quantity of advertising per brand from all firms *outside* the firm's strategic group

Q_I = the quantity of output from the three dominant rivals *inside* the firm's strategic group

Q_O = the quantity of output from all firms *outside* the firm's strategic group

M = the quantity of beer imports

N = the size of the primary drinking-age population (ages 20 to 44)

Y = per capita income

D_N = 1 if the firm is a national rather than a regional producer, else $D_N = 0$

$\hat{C}$ = the estimated marginal cost of production

R = a ratio measuring the market share of the five largest firms

D_P = 1 if price was computed by dividing total revenue by quantity, else $D_P = 0$

The sample used to estimate this equation covered 22 firms over 28 years between 1950 and 1977. This pooled data set included 316 observations. The estimated

---

[*] William J. Lynk, "Interpreting Rising Concentration: The Case of Beer," *Journal of Business,* 57(1) (1984), pp. 43–55.

[†] Victor J. Tremblay, "A Reappraisal of Interpreting Rising Concentration: The Case of Beer," *Journal of Business,* 58(4) (1985), pp. 419–431.

coefficients were statistically significant except those for A_O, Q_O, D_N and R. The variables A_I and A_O were included to control for variation in the "quality" of advertising. The beer industry can be separated into national and regional strategic groups. The variables Q_I and Q_O were included to control for differences in competitiveness inside and outside of each firm's strategic group. The variable M is included to control for competition from imports. The dummy variable D_N was included to control for differences in demand between national and regional producers, and the dummy variable D_P was included to control for any error in measurement associated with measuring price by dividing total revenue by physical output for a few firms for which price was unobservable. The variable C was estimated from a separate equation because the marginal cost for each firm was unobservable. The results imply that advertising significantly affects price. Marginal cost has a positive significant influence. The concentration ratio R is not statistically significant but has a negative coefficient.

Between 1950 and 1971, concentration and advertising expenditures rose and costs fell in the brewing industry. Tremblay found that even though rising concentration did not directly put upward pressure on prices, increases in advertising were sufficient to keep prices from falling in the wake of falling costs during this period. Tremblay concludes that these results provide evidence that the rising concentration, economies of size, and advertising expenditures in the brewing industry generated higher wholesale beer prices between 1950 and 1971.

Lynk disagrees with Tremblay's interpretation.‡ In a rebuttal, Lynk argues that a change in wholesale price does not require a change in retail price, because increased advertising by wholesalers has historically led to lower retail margins. Lynk also says his estimate of the effect of concentration is biased upward but is more negative than Tremblay's estimate. Lynk states that this difference resulted because Tremblay confused a shift in the prices of all grades of beer with a shift in the mix of beer toward higher-priced premium brands. Thus, Lynk disagrees with Tremblay's findings and concludes that his findings of increased concentration causing lower prices and higher output are still valid.

---

‡ William J. Lynk, "The Price of Beer Revisited," *Journal of Business,* 58(4) (1985), pp. 433–437.

Both the Herfindahl index and concentration ratios tend to *understate* monopoly power when the market is defined as including products that are close substitutes. On the other hand, these two indexes *overstate* monopoly power when close substitutes are excluded from the defined market. Another problem in using these indexes is that market concentration may be necessary for exercising monopoly power, but high concentration is not sufficient. Nevertheless, concentration ratios indicate the potential for monopoly power.

All measures of monopoly power are flawed in some way. Interestingly, however, empirical comparisons indicate high correlations between the alternative measures. For instance, the Herfindahl index correlates highly with market-concentration ratios, and both are correlated highly with high profit rates. This correlation affords some reassurance to economists and policy makers who use such measures of monopoly power.

13.7 Contestable Markets

Even when only one firm is in a market, that firm may behave as if it were competitive. This behavior may occur when there is competition *for* a market even though competition is absent *within* the market. Consider an airline route between two small cities. Traffic may not be adequate for more than one airline company to provide service between the cities, and one airline may establish what appears to be a monopoly. Can that company charge monopoly fares? Many other airlines could establish service if it became profitable. Entry is easy because the cost of airplanes is not specific to any route. Moreover, even if at first traffic is adequate to support two airlines, exit is easy if demand should fall because either firm could switch its airplanes to other routes with little expense, or the airplanes could be sold or leased in a well-developed international market.

Markets in which entry and exit are easy are said to be **contestable:**[7]

> ***Perfectly contestable market:*** *Without sunk costs and entry barriers, and with some lag in incumbents' ability to react to pricing initiatives of entrants, even markets with a lone incumbent will behave as if they were perfectly competitive.*

When no sunk costs are present, firms can exit from the market without losing any investment in capital specific to that market and valueless elsewhere. When markets are perfectly contestable, incumbent firms are not able to charge a price higher than marginal cost. If any incumbent attempts to charge a price above marginal cost, a rival firm will enter the market, charging a lower price to capture the market. The lag in the response by incumbents is required, for otherwise the incumbent could drop price to marginal cost to ensure against loss of the market. Even without the lag, however, if such sunk costs are zero, contestability will keep the price equal to marginal cost and all that will change is the name of the carrier. The outcome is the same as under perfect competition.

Most markets are not perfectly contestable, however, because some sunk costs will be present. These costs mean that entrants put those costs at risk when they enter the market. As a result, incumbent firms have an advantage and can charge a price higher than marginal cost. But a market will be highly contestable if sunk costs are low. Moreover, the market is more contestable as the lag in response by the incumbent firms lengthens. The essential concept in contestability is that entrants can engage in "hit-and-run" entry in response to profit opportunities.

---

7. Contestability theory is presented by William J. Baumol, John C. Panzar, Jr., and Robert D. Willig, *Contestable Markets and the Theory of Industrial Structure* (Harcourt Brace Jovanovich, 1982). This relatively new idea has its critics. See, for instance, Marius Schwartz and Robert J. Reynolds, "Contestability: An Uprising in the Theory of Industrial Structure: Comment," *American Economic Review*, 73 (June 1983), pp. 488–490, and Marius Schwartz, "The Nature and Scope of Contestability Theory," *Oxford Economic Papers*, 38 (supplement 1986), pp. 37–57.

AN APPLICATION: *Rural Banking Markets*

Collusion among firms is more likely in a concentrated industry. Increased concentration, therefore, should be positively correlated with profits. And yet, studies investigating bank market structure have not always found a positive correlation between concentration and profits. One explanation for the absence of such correlation is that some banking markets are contestable.

One recent study on rural banking was performed by Gary Whalen.* He estimated these profitability functions for 159 rural banks in Ohio from 1979 to 1981:

$$Profit = f(ActComp, PotComp, MrtShare, Risk, Controls)$$

where

Profit = a measure of profitability, the after-tax rate of return on equity

ActComp = a proxy for actual competition, the number of actual competitors in each market

PotComp = a proxy for potential competition, the number of potential competitors legally permitted to bank in each market

MrtShare = a measure of risk faced by each bank, the standard deviation of return on equity

Controls = a vector of additional control variables

The additional control variables included bank size, whether the bank was a subsidiary, average per capita personal income of each local market, per capita personal income growth, and membership in the Federal Reserve System. The equation was estimated by two-stage least squares as part of a simultaneous system. Table 13.2

Table 13.2 Rural Bank Profitability Equations

Variable	Version 1	Version 2
ActComp	0.007936 (0.05)	−0.520134 (−1.79)
PotComp	−0.158830 (−1.30)	−0.801043 (−2.46)
MrkShare	0.035831 (1.43)	0.035265 (1.43)
Risk	−0.087202 (−3.00)	−0.803704 (−2.80)
Act·Pot		−0.111721 (2.13)

Note: t-statistics in parentheses.
Source: Gary Whalen, "Actual Competition, Potential Competition, and Bank Profitability in Rural Markets," *Economic Review*, 24(3), Federal Reserve Bank of Cleveland, 1988.

---

* Gary Whalen, "Actual Competition, Potential Competition, and Bank Profitability in Rural Markets," *Economic Review*, 24(3), Federal Reserve Bank of Cleveland, 1988.

reports on the estimated coefficients for two versions of the profit function.

The results tend to support the notion that rural bank markets are contestable. The actual competition proxy is insignificant in the first specification, but ActComp becomes significantly negative when an interaction variable is included. The potential competition proxy is negative and significant, supporting the hypothesis that potential competition reduces bank profitability. The actual or potential competition interaction variable, *Act·Pot,* has a positive, significant coefficient. This finding supports the view that the negative marginal influence of extra actual competitors declines as the number of potential competitors increases. Similarly, the larger the number of actual competitors in a market, the smaller the negative marginal effect of additional potential competitors.

ECONOMIC SCENE: *Air Wars*

Providing scheduled air transportation has been cited as an example of a contestable market. Even though only one or a few firms may provide transportation from one city-pair to another, firms can switch to other city-pairs with ease and little cost. Many of the conventional measures of monopoly power are at odds with the notion that the airlines industry is competitive. For instance, a consumer would not view going from city A to city C as a close substitute for going from city A to city B. The result is high concentration measures over both routes when the routes are used to define the relevant markets. From a sample of 5,023 city-pair markets, Bailey, Graham, and Kaplan found that the Herfindahl index was 0.78—a value more than four times that the Department of Justice considered "highly concentrated."[*]

Similarly, when Texas International merged with National Airlines, both serving the Houston–New Orleans market, the two-firm concentration ratio increased from 51 to 75 percent. In the past, such extensive market domination would have been grounds for opposing the merger. But the Civil Aeronautics Board decided to support the merger because the routes were contestable. Elizebeth Bailey points out that eleven other carriers had the capacity to contest the routes.[†] After the merger, in spite of the large size of the newly merged firm, a small regional carrier, Southwest Airlines, entered the market and captured a 25 percent market share.

On December 31, 1984, the authority of the Civil Aeronautics Board was transferred to the Department of Transportation. On February 28, 1986, Texas Air Corporation filed an application to acquire Eastern Airlines. Texas Air also operated New York Air and Continental Airlines. At the time of the merger application, Texas Air was the third largest carrier. It was widely perceived that Texas Air's motivation was to transform Eastern from a high-cost, low-productivity carrier into a low-cost competitor in an era of deregulation. In the end Eastern didn't succeed in remaining a viable competitor, but at the time the proposed merger had the potential to profoundly affect fares

---

[*] Elizebeth E. Bailey, Daniel R. Gordon, and Daniel P. Kaplan, *Deregulating the Airlines* (MIT Press, 1985).

[†] Elizebeth E. Bailey, "Contestability and the Design of Regulatory and Antitrust Policy," *American Economic Review,* 71 (May 1981), pp. 178–183.

nationally if Texas Air were to successfully reduce costs. Moreover, the potential for financial gain to Texas Air was substantial.

Other airlines frequently oppose proposed mergers. The intensity of their opposition can reveal how the industry views a merger's influence on competition. If a merger is considered cost reducing, with resultant downward pressure on prices, rivals will oppose it. On the other hand, if the merger is thought to be anticompetitive, resulting in higher prices and reduced output, rivals will benefit and will favor the merger. In the Texas Air–Eastern combination, other carriers large and small were against the merger.

To determine how the Texas Air–Eastern merger would influence competitiveness in the industry, George W. Douglas looked at the announcement's effect on the stock prices of airlines.‡ Douglas reasoned that if financial markets efficiently incorporate news into current stock prices, that suggests a way to distinguish between procompetitive and anticompetitive mergers. If stock prices fall for rival firms, the market has perceived the merger as procompetitive—the expected fall in product price and increased output causing a reduction in profits. If stock prices rise for rival firms, the market has perceived the merger as anticompetitive—the expected prices and profits increasing in the industry. To screen out any other influences on stock prices, Douglas estimated each stock's "Beta"—the regression coefficient of the return of a stock relative to the return to the market as a whole. By multiplying a stock's Beta by the percentage of change in the composite index of all stocks, Douglas was able to calculate the statistically expected change in each stock's price.

The Texas Air–Eastern merger was announced on Monday, February 24, 1986. Between Friday, February 21 and Friday, February 28, Eastern's stock rose 31 percent and Texas Air's by 67 percent. At first glance these large increases seem to indicate that the merger would be anticompetitive, but much of the observed increase was expected to occur without the merger. Moreover, analyzing rivals' stock prices after adjusting for normal predicted change suggests a different conclusion. The Beta values of the rivals' stocks are listed in Table 13.3. Profits of the three other carriers at the top of the list—Delta, People Express, and Presidential—would be most susceptible to competition from a more efficient Eastern. The three carriers least affected—PSA, Pan Am, and American—faced little direct competition from Texas Air or Eastern or were already in competition with low-cost Continental. At the bottom of the list—American West, Alaska, Southwest, Midway, Aloha, and Western—lies a group whose value might be enhanced because of the prospect of their acquisition. The stock for TWA also increased that week because of its impending acquisition of Ozark. In summary, when the Beta values for these assets as predicted to change due to the merger are compared to the Beta values as they would normally change, that comparison suggests that the proposed merger was widely perceived as procompetitive.

‡ George W. Douglas, "The Importance of Entry Conditions: Texas Air's Acquisition of Eastern Airlines," in *The Antitrust Revolution*, John E. Kwoka, Jr. and Lawrence J. White, ed. (Scott, Foresman, 1989), pp. 99–119.

Table 13.3 Beta Values of Airline Stock

Carrier	Beta (4/4/86)	Normal % change[a]	Predicted % change due to merger
Texas Air	1.35	+1.39	+66.25
Eastern	1.10	+1.13	+30.24
Other carriers			
Delta	1.15	+1.18	−11.04
People Express	1.30	+1.34	−4.99
Presidential	1.00	+1.03	−3.20
Northwest	1.15	+1.18	−2.91
United	1.35	+1.39	−2.85
US Air	1.35	+1.39	−2.73
Piedmont	1.25	+1.28	−2.52
Republic	1.10	+1.13	−1.93
Ozark	1.35	+1.39	−1.39
PSA	1.20	+1.23	+0.14
Pan Am	0.95	+0.98	+0.52
American	1.35	+1.39	+0.29
American West	1.00[b]	+1.03	+5.16
Alaska	1.00	+1.03	+7.14
Southwest	1.35	+1.39	+7.65
Midway	1.00[b]	+1.03	+8.06
Trans World	1.00[b]	+1.03	+15.64
Aloha	1.00[b]	+1.03	+17.49
Western	1.40	+1.44	+17.96

[a]Beta times the percentage change in the New York Stock Exchange Composite Index.
[b]Not available; assumed equal to 1.00.
Source: George W. Douglas, "The Importance of Entry Conditions: Texas Air's Acquisition of Eastern Airlines," in *The Antitrust Revolution,* John E. Kwoka, Jr., and Lawrence J. White, eds. (Scott, Foresman, 1989), p. 103. Reprinted by permission of HarperCollins Publishers.

13.8 Monopoly Demand for Inputs

In the long run, any profit-maximizing firm chooses a level of output at which $MR = LMC$. At the same time the firm chooses an input combination that allows it to produce the profit-maximizing level of output, and so the profit-maximizing firm must choose inputs so that the marginal rate of technical substitution equals the ratio of input prices. The isocost line tangent to the profit-maximizing isoquant identifies the optimal input mix. In this way the optimal scale is identified as well as the optimal input mix.

Long-run cost minimizing requires that the ratio of marginal product to input price be equal for all pairs of inputs. For labor and capital the condition is

$$\frac{MP_L}{w} = \frac{MP_K}{r}$$

Recall that $MC = w/MP_L$. It is also true that $MC = r/MP_K$ when K is treated as the variable input. Because the firm chooses a scale such that $MR = LMC = MC$, the firm demands inputs and supplies output so that

$$\frac{MP_L}{w} = \frac{MP_K}{r} = \frac{1}{MC} = \frac{1}{MR}$$

The only difference in this condition between a monopoly firm and a competitive firm is that we have no assurance the monopolist will choose a scale that results in lowest unit production cost.

In the short run the monopolist will choose a variable input at which the extra revenue generated from production is equal to the extra cost of the input. That is, the marginal revenue product will equal the marginal factor cost. Recall that marginal revenue product of labor is $MRP_L = \Delta R/\Delta L$. The extra revenue comes from producing an extra

AN APPLICATION: *The A-J Effect*

Because of practical problems in measuring normal profit, regulatory commissions frequently set prices of public utilities so that the firm earns a "fair" rate of return on invested capital. Regulators usually restrict the rate base to the physical plant and equipment used in production. This restriction produces a bias toward choosing inputs that qualify for inclusion in the rate base. This bias is called the Averch-Johnson or A-J effect.*

To keep things simple, let's lump all capital used into the rate base. If the rental rate of capital services is r dollars per year extending into the indefinite future, the discounted present value of the capital is $DPV = r/i$, when i is the discounting interest rate. The total value of K units of capital services per year is Kr/i. Then, if the allowed rate of return is ρ, the allowed profit for the firm is $\rho Kr/i$.

Notice that when the public utility rents an extra unit of capital services, both the rental cost r and the rate base increase. An extra unit of capital increases cost by r dollars and revenues by $\rho r/i$. And the increase in revenue will be greater than the increase in cost as long as $\rho > i$. Thus, when only capital is included in the rate base, rate-of-return regulation works like a decrease in the effective price of capital. This form of regulation causes substitution of capital for other inputs which is called the A-J effect.

The A-J effect is illustrated by Figure 13.11. The bias toward more capital-intensive production causes the firm to choose bundle **B** rather than **A** to produce the indicated

* H. Averch and L. L. Johnson, "Behavior of the Firm under Regulatory Constraint," *American Economic Review,* 52 (December 1962), pp. 1053–1069.

level of output. The firm does so because it considers the effective price of capital to be lower than capital's market price, for capital is being subsidized. The firm behaves as if its isocost line were steeper than that determined by market prices for capital and labor. The actual price of capital hasn't changed, however, but the firm has been motivated to choose a different and more costly input bundle. As the costs of production increase because of the A-J effect, the *LAC* curve will rise. As a consequence, output price will increase from p_1 to p_2. At the same time output will fall from X_1 to X_2. The A-J effect of causing the use of an inefficient input combination moves the public utility away from the competitive solution approximated by regulated average cost pricing.

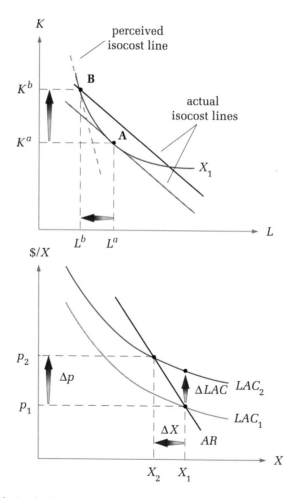

Figure 13.11 **The Averch-Johnson (A-J) effect:** Including only capital in the rate base causes the regulated monopolist to choose bundle **B** rather than **A.** Total cost is higher at every level of output, and so the regulated price must be higher.

unit of output, $\Delta R / \Delta X$, and the extra output comes from using an extra unit of labor, $\Delta X / \Delta L$. Thus, the marginal revenue product of labor is

$$MRP_L = \frac{\Delta R}{\Delta X} \cdot \frac{\Delta X}{\Delta L} = MR_X MP_L$$

The MRP_L is equal to the MR of output multiplied by the MP of labor.

The monopolist will choose a variable input so that its MRP is equal to its marginal factor cost as long as the ARP of the input is at least equal to its wage rate:

> **Monopoly input demand:** *Choose a variable input so that the marginal revenue product is equal to marginal factor cost as long as average revenue product is at least as great as the input's price. If the input's price is greater than average revenue product, then shut down to minimize the short-run loss.*

This is almost the same rule as for the competitive firm. The difference is that, for the monopolist, marginal revenue is less than output price. For the monopolist, MRP falls for two reasons: the decline in MR and the decline in MP.

For the price-taking firm the VMP has negative slope, caused by diminishing productivity alone because price is fixed. For the monopolist the MRP has negative slope because of diminishing productivity and falling marginal revenue. The diminishing productivity of the variable input is reinforced by declining marginal revenue. Thus the stages in production cannot be used to identify the shutdown point for the monopolist.

13.9 Pure Monopsony

So far we have focused on the selling side of a market, but now we turn to the buying side. A single buyer in a market is called a **pure monopsonist**. A firm that is the only buyer of labor in a local market is a monopsonist, but that same firm may sell the good produced in a competitive product market. In contrast, a firm might be a pure monopolist in the product market but face a competitive resource market. Thus, we distinguish between any firm's selling and buying characteristics.

As the only buyer, a pure monopsonist faces an upward-sloping supply curve for the resource. The monopsonist must pay a higher price for the input to obtain greater quantities. Consider a monopsonist's market for labor services. The wage rate measures the **average cost of labor** or ALC_L. The marginal cost of labor is no longer equal to the wage rate if the supply curve (ALC) has positive slope. Rather, the MFC is greater than the ALC because the firm must pay the higher wage to all units hired, not just the last unit.

More formally, the MFC of labor is given by

$$MFC_L = w + L\frac{\Delta w}{\Delta L}$$

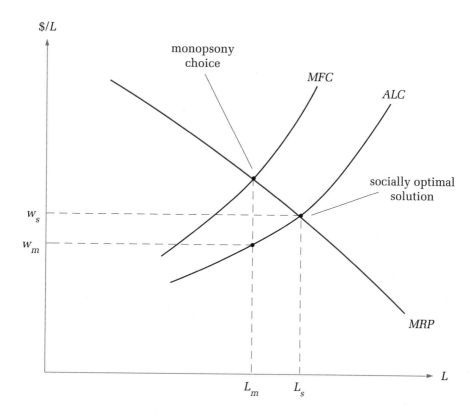

Figure 13.12 **Monopsony market for labor:** A monopsony buyer of labor views the market supply curve as its ALC curve. When the supply-of-labor curve has positive slope, the monopsonist's MFC curve lies everywhere above the ALC curve. To maximize profit, the monopsonist demands labor of L_m, where MRP = MFC and will pay a wage rate w_m. In contrast, the socially optimal wage rate would be w_s, where the MRP curve crosses the ALC curve. The level of employment is higher at the socially optimal solution.

where $\Delta w / \Delta L$ is the slope of the ALC curve. The marginal cost of labor equals the wage rate plus the increase in wages paid to labor.

A typical monopsony market for labor is illustrated by Figure 13.12. The ALC curve coincides with the labor supply curve because the firm is the only buyer. The MFC curve lies above the ALC curve everywhere, drawing that average upward. Maximized profit occurs where the MRP curve crosses the MFC curve, and the monopsonist chooses L_m units of labor and pays a wage rate w_m.

If the labor market were competitive, the wage rate would be w_s where the MRP curve crosses the ALC curve. Thus, monopsony results in a lower wage rate and a lower level of employment than would occur if the labor market were competitive.

"Not only do we honor our pharoah, but they say it has created fifty thousand new jobs."

Drawing by Dana Fradon.

Pure monopsony is not too common. A historical example is the building of pyramids, as illustrated by Dana Fradon's cartoon. The classic case is the company town, in which the mining firm owns the mine and all other places of employment. Any person who wishes to work for wages must work for the mining firm. Most cases are not so extreme, and yet monopsony power does exist. Consider the only hospital in a geographic region. Pediatric nurses, if they wish to remain in that occupation and live in that community, have little choice but to work for the only hospital. Monopsony power also ruled in organized baseball before free agency was implemented in the mid-1970s. Before free agency, players could play only for the team that "owned" the rights to the player's baseball talents. No player could move to another team without a formal trade—selling the rights to the player's talents to another team. Players had the option of playing for the salary negotiated with his team's owner or leaving baseball.[8]

---

8. Since free agency, free agents have claimed that the owners collude with one another on salary offers. In 1989, an arbiter awarded about $10 million to a player to compensate for damage due to owners' collusion during the 1986 season. See "Collusion Award Exceeds $10 Million," *The New York Times,* September 1, 1989.

AN APPLICATION: *Monopsony and Minimum Wages*

In a competitive labor market the effects of a minimum wage above the equilibrium wage create unemployment. The result may differ, however, when the buyer of labor has monopsony power. Of the three possible cases, two are illustrated by Figure 13.13.

In panel A the minimum wage is set above the monopsony wage but below the level where demand crosses supply. The effective labor supply curve is perfectly elastic at the minimum wage until it intersects the old supply curve. The marginal cost of labor equals the minimum wage until the wage must be bid up along the old supply curve. At

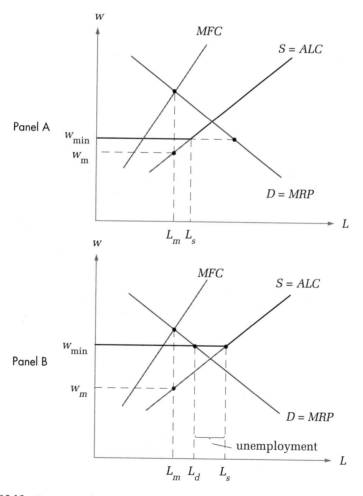

Figure 13.13 **Monopsony and minimum wages: Panel A** The minimum wage rate is below the socially optimal wage. Employment increases. **Panel B** The minimum wage rate is above the socially optimal wage but below the level at which MFC = MRP. Employment increases but unemployment is present.

the minimum wage the quantity of labor supplied increases from L_m to L_s. Because quantity demanded exceeds quantity supplied, there is no unemployment.

In panel B the minimum wage is set above the level at which *ALC* equals *MRP.* The quantity of labor supplied is now greater than the quantity demanded, and so some measured unemployment remains. Nevertheless, overall employment is greater than before the minimum wage was imposed.

A third condition would occur if the minimum wage were set above the level at which *MFC = MRP.* In that position, which is to be avoided, the level of employment would fall below that under monopsony. Ideally, the minimum wage would be set close to the market clearing wage so that the deadweight loss would be small.

What determines the degree of monopsony power? That power depends on the elasticity of supply, the number of buyers in the market, and the ways in which those buyers interact. A monopsonist benefits because the supply curve for the service of an input being bought has positive slope: the marginal expenditure exceeds average expenditure. As shown in Figure 13.12, the *MFC* curve of labor is above the *AFC* curve. The buyer has more monopsony power as the difference between the marginal expenditure and the average expenditure grows. That difference will be greater as the supply curve becomes *less* elastic. Thus, if supply is highly elastic, monopsony power is small.

The *number of buyers* in the market is an important determinant of monopsony power. When there are many buyers the supply curve facing each buyer will be highly elastic because one buyer has little influence over price. When the number of buyers is very large, each buyer acts as a price taker and the market is highly competitive. But with only a few buyers, each faces a positively sloped, less elastic supply curve. Then too, with only a few buyers the potential for *interaction among buyers* increases. Rather than compete with other buyers, the buyers might collude or behave strategically to keep price low.

Monopsony power results in a lower input price than would occur in a competitive market. The difference in price, which depends on the elasticity of supply η_s, provides us with a way of measuring the extent of monopsony power:

> **Monopsony index:**
>
> $$M = \frac{MFC - w}{w} = \frac{1}{\eta_s}$$

Monopsony power is the ability to pay a price below the marginal factor cost of an input. Hence the input price will be less than the input's *MRP* because the profit-maximizing demand is determined where *MFC = MRP.* The monopsony index measures the percentage of markdown ascribed to monopsony power. The size of the markdown is inversely proportional to the elasticity of supply facing the buyer. The index equals zero if *MFC = w,* as it is under competition. The index increases as the difference between

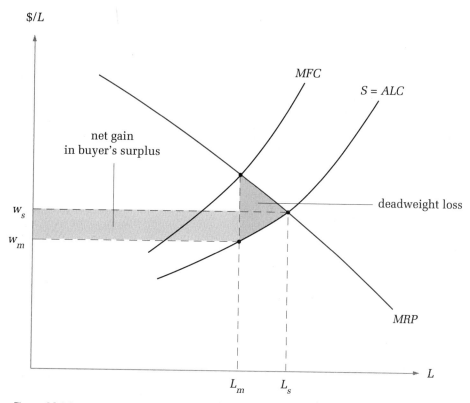

Figure 13.14 **Deadweight loss from monopsony:** The monopsonist pays a price w_m for L_m units. The monopsony price and quantity are lower than the socially optimal price and quantity. A change appears in both buyer (consumer) surplus and seller (producer) surplus. Part of the loss in seller surplus is transferred to the monopsonist for a net gain in buyer surplus, but part of the loss in seller surplus becomes a deadweight loss.

marginal value and price grows, and the index increases as the supply curve becomes less elastic.

Monopsony power results in a lower price paid and a lower level of employment than would otherwise occur. Therefore the monopsonist is better off and the seller is worse off. But how is aggregate social welfare affected? The answer is found by comparing the changes in consumer and producer surpluses that occur. Figure 13.14, illustrating a labor market, is the same as the preceding diagram except for the indicated changes in welfare. The price decrease from w_c to w_m causes an increase in buyer surplus larger than the decrease in seller surplus. Only part of the decrease in seller surplus is transferred as a net gain in buyer surplus to the monopsonist. The remainder of the decrease in seller surplus becomes a deadweight loss to society. Even if the monopsonist's gains were redistributed to the suppliers, an aggregate loss would occur because the level of employment is lower than it would be in a competitive market.

13.10 Bilateral Monopoly

A bilateral monopoly consists of just one seller and one buyer. Consider a union facing a monopsonistic employer. Though in general the input can be any resource or intermediate good used in producing the good sold by the monopsonist, both buyer and seller of the input are assumed to be profit maximizers.

Let Z denote the intermediate good or labor input, as shown in Figure 13.15. The average revenue product curve for input Z is given by ARP_m, where the subscript stands for monopsonist. The monopsonist's marginal revenue product curve is MRP_m. The MRP_m

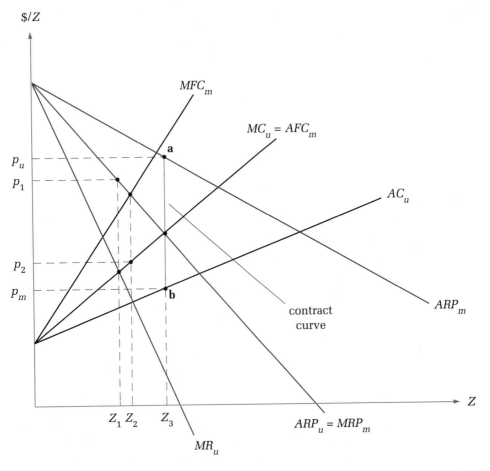

Figure 13.15 **Bilateral monopoly:** Neither the outcome (Z_2) of a monopsonist facing a competitive seller of the input, nor the outcome (Z_1) of a monopoly seller, say a labor union, facing a competitive input buyer, will occur. Rather, the bilateral monopoly output level will be Z_3 units, with price established somewhere between p_m, the minimum price achieved when the monopsonist dominates the negotiation, and p_u, the maximum price achieved when the seller dominates the negotiation. This level of output will maximize joint profits.

coincides with the monopoly seller's average revenue product curve, labeled AR_u. The subscript stands for union or "upstream" monopoly. The curve labeled MR_u is marginal to AR_u and MR_u represents the marginal revenue associated with selling Z to a "downstream" firm that *does not have* monopsony power.

Turning to the cost curves, AC_u is the upstream monopolist's average cost of supplying Z, and MC_u is that supplier's marginal cost. If the supplier were to behave like a competitive firm, MC_u would correspond to the supply curve. Thus, when the monopsonist buys Z from a competitive firm, the monopsonist's average factor cost curve AFC_m coincides with the supply curve MC_u, and the monopsonistic buyer's marginal factor cost curve will be the MFC_m.

At this juncture it may be tempting to conclude that the monopoly seller wants a price p_1 to sell quantity Z_1, where $MR_u = MC_u$. But that arrangement occurs only when the monopolist faces a competitive buyer. Likewise, if the seller behaves competitively, its supply curve will correspond to MC_u and the lone buyer will want the standard monopsony solution, buying quantity Z_2, where $MRP_m = MFC_m$, and price will be p_2. We cannot, however, assume competitive behavior on the part of either firm when we see a bilateral monopoly. Neither the pure monopoly nor the pure monopsony solution is relevant because each entails competitive behavior on one side of the market. That is not a characteristic of bilateral monopoly, and so neither firm can choose those earlier solutions.[9]

A profit incentive encourages cooperation between the two parties under bilateral monopoly. An incentive to pursue joint maximizing of profit arises because profits are not maximized for either firm at Z_1 or Z_2. Such cooperation may take the form of vertical integration or bargaining. Integrated profits would be maximized where the marginal revenue product of the input is equal to its marginal cost. For Figure 13.15, this crossing occurs at Z_3 units.

Suppose, however, that the parties do not integrate but engage in negotiation. Again, a union might be negotiating a labor contract with a monopsonistic employer.[10] Each party wishes to maximize its profit subject to the constraint that the other party will participate in the exchange. Without assuming competitive behavior for either party, let's examine two extreme examples.

First, let's suppose the seller dominates the negotiations. The seller wishes to maximize profit, but the buyer must be willing to negotiate. Thus profit will be maximized for the monopolistic seller, but will be zero for the monopsonistic buyer. The price that exhausts the buyer's profit is given by p_u, where the price desired by the upstream seller equals the buyer's ARP_m.

9. For more on this point and a more formal rendering of the simultaneous profit-maximizing behavior under bilateral monopoly, see Roger D. Blair, Daniel L. Kaseman, and Richard E. Ronono, "A Pedagogical Treatment of Bilateral Monopoly," *Southern Economic Journal*, 55(4) (April 1989), pp. 831–841.

10. Indeed, unionism has been described as the rise of a "countervailing power" opposing the monopsony power of big business. See John Kenneth Galbraith, "Countervailing Power," *American Economic Review* (May 1954).

Second, let's suppose the buyer dominates the negotiations. The buyer wishes to maximize profit, but the seller must be willing to negotiate. Thus profit will be maximized for the buyer, but zero for the seller. The price that exhausts the seller's profit is given by p_m, where the price desired by the monopsonistic buyer equals the seller's AC_u.

Regardless of which firm dominates the negotiations, the same quantity is chosen, the one that maximizes joint profits. The only thing that differs is the price of the input and the division of the profit. Thus, the vertical line drawn between points **a** and **b** identifies a vertical contract curve—price is negotiable but quantity is not. Neither party need ever experience negative profit, and so the contract curve will never extend below point **b** or above point **a**. The joint profit-maximizing quantity Z_3 will be agreed upon, and determining price is a means for dividing the joint profits.

Summary

A firm having monopoly power is a price-setting firm. Because its average revenue curve slopes downward, it chooses a combination of price and output that maximizes profit. The monopolist sets price and output so that marginal revenue equals marginal cost, as long as price is not less than average variable cost. Unlike the competitive firm, a monopoly firm is not forced to choose a scale minimizing long-run cost. Moreover, zero economic profit is not ensured, because entry is restricted when monopoly power is active.

Under monopoly pricing, output is inefficiently low and price is inefficiently high because the monopoly price will exceed marginal cost. A deadweight loss results from exercising monopoly power, and too few resources are used to produce the good. The deadweight loss understates the social cost of monopoly if rent-seeking behavior leads to a socially wasteful use of other resources. An upper bound on the total social losses due to monopoly equals monopoly profit plus the deadweight loss.

Monopolistic competition arises when several small firms produce slightly differentiated products. Product differentiation gives each firm some control over price, and each firm's average revenue curve is no longer perfectly elastic. In contrast with perfect competition, monopolistic competition never yields minimum average cost. Price exceeds marginal cost, and a deadweight loss occurs. The gains from product diversity, however, may be large enough to outweigh any welfare losses. Moreover, this form of market structure may be one of "workable" competition.

In the dominant-firm model, the industry has many small firms and one large firm producing a homogeneous product. The potential for monopoly power is present if the large firm dominates the market. Minor firms act as price takers, reacting to the price set by the dominant firm, and the dominant firm sells the remaining part of market demand. Such markets tend to be unstable if they have the potential for entry or expansion. To maintain dominance the firm must be able to limit entry and expansion.

Monopoly power is the ability to set price above marginal cost. A frequently used measure of monopoly power, the Lerner index, measures the difference between price and marginal cost as a proportion of price. The Lerner index equals zero when price equals marginal cost, and the index becomes larger as the difference between price and marginal cost increases. Another frequently used index is the Herfindahl, which equals the sum of the squares of the market shares of all firms in the relevant market. The Herfindahl index decreases as the number of firms increases, but the index rises as the shares become more unequal for a fixed number of firms. Other indicators of the potential for monopoly power are elasticity of demand, number of firms, extent and nature of rivalry, and potential for entry.

Markets in which entry and exit are easy are contestable. A monopoly firm may behave as if it were competitive if the market is contestable. With no entry barriers, and with some lag in the response of incumbent firms to pricing initiatives by entrants, price will be forced to be equal to average and marginal cost in the long run.

Monopsony is monopoly power when buying an input. The input supply curve facing a monopsonist measures average factor cost. The marginal factor cost is greater than average factor cost because the input supply curve has positive slope. The monopsonist chooses a level of input use so that its marginal revenue product equals marginal factor cost. As a result, both the level of employment and the input price are lower than they would be if the market were competitive. One measure of the extent of monopsony power is the difference between the marginal factor cost and the input price—a monopsony index analogous to the Lerner index. The departure from competitive input pricing also causes a deadweight loss. Minimum-wage legislation can help mitigate the welfare loss due to monopsony power in a labor market. The competitive solution may also be approximated for a bilateral monopoly.

Further Readings

For a comprehensive treatment of the various forms of market structure, see

- F. M. Scherer, *Industrial Market Structure and Economic Performance,* 2d ed. (Rand McNally, 1980).

For a survey of some issues on rent-seeking behavior, see

- Robert D. Tollison, "Rent Seeking: A Survey," *Kyklos,* 35 (1982), pp. 575–601.

The citation in the Posner quotation in this chapter is from

- Gordon Tullock, "The Welfare Costs of Tariffs, Monopolies, and Theft," *Western Economic Journal,* 5 (June 1967), pp. 224–232.

The model of contestable markets is covered thoroughly in

- W. J. Baumol, J. C. Panzar, and R. D. Willig, *Contestable Markets and the Theory of Industrial Structure* (Harcourt Brace Jovanovich, 1982).

These publications have historical importance:

- Joan Robinson, *The Economics of Imperfect Competition* (Macmillan, 1933).
- Edward Hastings Chamberlin, *The Theory of Monopolistic Competition* (Harvard University Press, 1933).

Practice Problems

1. If the demand curve is linear, average revenue can be expressed as

$$p = a - bQ, \; b > 0$$

   (a) Show that MR can be calculated from $MR = a - 2bQ$
   (b) Show that $Q = a/2b$ when the price elasticity of demand is unitary.
   (c) Plot any related linear AR and MR curves on a graph, then identify the elastic and inelastic ranges on both curves.

2. The Laser Corporation is the sole producer of a type of printer. The market demand for this printer is

$$Q_d = 8,800 - 2p$$

   where Q_d is quantity demanded per month. The firm's marginal cost function is

$$MC = 300 + 40Q$$

   where Q is quantity per month.
   (a) What is the firm's marginal revenue function?
   (b) How many printers should be produced and sold each month?
   (c) What will be the firm's maximum profit?

3. Consider a monopoly firm with fixed but no variable costs. What would be the firm's profit-maximizing price? What elasticity of demand would you expect at that price?

4. Suppose a firm has a revenue function given by:

$$TR(Q) = 12Q - Q^2$$

   The firm's cost function is

$$TC(Q) = \frac{Q^3}{3} - 3Q^2 + 12Q$$

   Marginal revenue and marginal cost are then given by:

$$MR = 12 - 2Q \qquad MC = Q^2 - 6Q + 12$$

   (a) Plot TR and TC as a function of Q. On a separate graph, plot profit as a function of Q.
   (b) Find the equation for AR, then plot AR, MR, and MC on a graph.
   (c) Find the profit-maximizing level of output, Q^*, and mark that output on the graph of part (b).
   (d) Find the optimal price, and identify that price on the graph of part (b).

5. Suppose a monopolist has an average revenue curve given by

$$p = 50 - 5Q$$

   and has constant marginal and average costs given by $MC = AC = 10$:
   (a) Calculate the profit-maximizing output Q^* and price p^* for this firm.
   (b) What is the price elasticity of demand, η, at the monopoly price?
   (c) Calculate the deadweight loss due to monopoly pricing.

6. An opportunity cost is associated with producing more of any good. That is, producing more of one good means that we must produce less of other goods with the same resources. Why would it be desirable, then, to increase a monopolist's output?

7. Draw a graph of a competitive industry in the long run. Suppose this industry is converted into a noncheating, market-sharing cartel. Indicate the cartel's total output, and identify the resulting deadweight loss. How is this case different from converting the industry into a monopoly?

8. If a firm sets its product's price at $1,000, it expects to earn $4 million in each of the next two years and $1 million for each of two subsequent years because other firms are expected to enter the industry. But the firm can discourage entry by setting price at $700 and earn expected profits of $2.5 million per year for the next four years.
   (a) If the relevant discounting interest rate is 5 percent, should this firm engage in limit pricing?
   (b) What if the discount rate is 10 percent?

9. Suppose a market is contestable with more than one identical firm. Assume that their average cost curves slope upward where they cross the industry demand curve. Illustrate graphically how price, output, average cost, and marginal cost are determined. How does this outcome compare to the competitive solution?

10. Calculate the 4-firm concentration ratio and the Herfindahl index for an industry composed of 10 firms, all sharing the market equally.

11. Calculate the 4-firm concentration ratio and the Herfindahl index for an industry composed of 10 firms having these market shares:

Firm	Market share
1	0.50
2	0.20
3	0.10
4	0.05
5	0.05
6	0.04
7	0.03
8	0.01
9	0.01
10	0.01

12. If two firms with market shares of 0.2 and 0.3 merge, what will happen to the Herfindahl index? What is the actual change in this index?

13. Suppose a monopoly faces a perfectly elastic labor supply curve and $MFC = 4$. Furthermore, suppose the firm's average revenue product curve is $ARP = 20 - L$, so that its marginal revenue product curve is $MRP = 20 - 2L$. What is the firm's profit-maximizing quantity of labor?

14. Compare and contrast the effects of a minimum-wage law in a labor market under competition and under monopsony. Consider both employment effects and changes in welfare.

15. If you could have a worldwide monopoly over water or diamonds, which would you rather have? Why?

Oligopoly and Game Theory

This chapter continues our look at the different forms of market structure. We have examined monopolistic competition and the dominant-firm models and the two extremes of pure competition and pure monopoly. The pure-monopoly and dominant-firm models have only one large firm. The pure-competition or monopolistic-competition models have many small firms. Under these forms of market structure, firms are characterized as making *tactical* decisions—deciding how to use and deploy resources. But when only a few large firms are in the industry, the form of market structure called oligopoly, firms also make *strategic* decisions—planning moves anticipating what a rival might do to achieve an objective.

A *strategy* is a plan, method, or series of maneuvers meant to gain a specific goal or result. Strategy is the science or art of combining or employing resources in planning or directing large operations. Strategic behavior arises under oligopoly because with only a few large firms an industry has a great deal of interdependence.

After describing oligopoly more carefully, we look at some oligopoly models that have historical and theoretical significance. Sweezy's kinked demand model is important because it emphasizes the price interdependence between oligopoly firms and how their behavior depends on anticipating rivals' responses. Cournot's duopoly model is important because it demonstrates the quantity interdependence between oligopoly firms with reactions to a rival's output decision. The Cournot model is also a useful way to introduce the concept of a Nash equilibrium—an equilibrium that occurs when you are doing the best that you can given what your rivals are doing while they are doing their best given what you are doing.

Why, in some industries, are prices often sticky? Or when prices change, why do firms seem to behave in concert with one another? Is that collusion? Are they trying to behave like a monopoly? Cournot's model and Sweezy's model also provide useful ways of showing why oligopoly firms are motivated to collude, implicitly or explicitly, in fixing price and sharing the market to increase profits and avoid destructive market wars. One form of formal collusion is the cartel. We look at two types: the profit-sharing cartel and the market-sharing cartel.

We then turn to game theory, perhaps the most promising "new" approach to the study of strategic decision making, and hence the study of oligopoly firms. Once we have examined oligopoly, you will have been introduced to all the primary forms of market structure. In Chapter 15, you will apply what you have learned to pricing decisions.

14.1 Oligopoly and Strategic Behavior

Under the form of industry structure known as oligopoly, the firms may be producing a homogeneous or differentiated product yet possess much monopoly power. Monopoly power arises when only a few firms are in the industry, regardless of the product. Oligopoly means "a few sellers":

> **Oligopoly:** *Oligopoly is an industry structure with a few relatively large firms.*

Because firms are few, each firm's actions affect other firms in the industry. In numbers of firms, oligopoly lies between monopoly and monopolistic competition, but analytically and conceptually, oligopoly is quite different because of the strategic interdependence. How few firms are needed for oligopoly? How many firms are needed to have competition or monopolistic competition? When an industry includes, say, fifty or more firms of approximately the same size, we are likely to have some form of competition. But we will find no magic number. The answer lies in their behavior, and whether or not an industry is oligopolistic becomes an empirical question. Does the behavior of firms exhibit strategic interdependence? If firms must consider rivals' reactions to any decision, and if interdependence between firms is so extensive that strategic behavior arises, then the industry is oligopolistic.

Oligopoly is present where each of a few relatively large firms has a significant share of the market, and entry is difficult because of large fixed costs for large-scale operations. We will see a great deal of interdependence among firms because of their size relative to the market and because they all produce close substitutes. Under an oligopoly market structure, firms rely on differences in price and product in making strategic decisions. Because price competition alone may lead to destructive price wars, oligopoly firms try to differentiate their products even when the good is physically identical for all firms. Product differentiation allows the firm to have a price different from that of a rival's close substitute.

Besides watching closely how consumers react to changes in price and quality, an oligopoly firm must anticipate how rival firms will react. The firm's decisions depend on how it *thinks* its rivals will react, and the outcome of such decisions will depend on how the rivals *do* react. Because rivals may react in many ways not contemplated, strategic decision making becomes very complex. Therefore, no one set of rules will identify equilibrium for the firm or industry, and no one oligopoly model will suffice. Rather, many oligopoly models are available, perhaps as many as there are oligopoly industries.

Managers must consider reactions by rival firms, and how to react to rivals' actions. One way to begin is to assume that any rival is as rational and intelligent as you are; then put yourself in the rival's place and consider how it would react.

ECONOMIC SCENE: *Cola Wars*

Pepsi-Cola and Coca-Cola sell syrup concentrate to local bottling companies. The bottlers add soda water and distribute the product to local retailers. Most bottlers are independently owned and are free to set the price of the final product. But both Pepsi and Coke also own bottling operations in some local markets. Coke controls firms that bottle 45 percent of the Coke sold in the United States. Pepsi controls 40 percent of the Pepsi sold in local markets. Both companies are aggressive in seeking to expand market share, and they have engaged in cutthroat pricing. Just before the Fourth of July, it seems like one and then the other offers deep price discounts to capture the seasonal increase in demand, and the firms have engaged in price warfare at other times too.

Why would two dominant firms engage in such behavior? Each firm must know that its rival will respond in kind to a price cut—why then would either firm cut price when it knows that will eventually reduce its profits? One possible answer is provided by the **Edgeworth duopoly model**. In Edgeworth's model, the market is composed of two identical firms. Neither firm can capture the entire market because of capacity limits. Capacity limits are quite reasonable in the bottling industry in the short run. To reflect the identical costs and capacity limits, we assume that marginal costs are

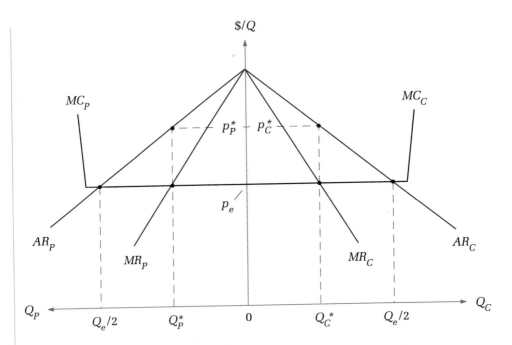

Figure 14.1 **Edgeworth duopoly:** Two identical firms share market demand equally. If one firm tries to capture market share by reducing its price, the other will follow suit. Price warfare forces price down to the competitive level at which price equals marginal cost. If the firms agree to keep price at the monopoly level where $MR = MC$, joint profits will be maximized. Whenever either firm cheats, price warfare ensues.

constant until capacity is reached, at which time each firm's marginal costs increase sharply, as shown in Figure 14.1.

Let's also assume that Coke and Pepsi are sufficiently close substitutes that they share market demand equally. Each firm has an average revenue curve that is one-half the market demand for cola soft drinks. In actuality, the combined market share of the two giants is only about 60 percent, and so the model abstracts from reality to simplify our analysis. Given the assumptions, the profit-maximizing price for Coke is p_C^* and for Pepsi is p_P^* in Figure 14.1. Without price competition, Coke produces and sells Q_C^* units, and Pepsi sells Q_P^* units.

Suppose one of the firms undercuts the price to capture market share, perhaps in response to an anticipated seasonal increase in market demand. Or perhaps Coke expects it will be able to increase its market share, thereby increasing its demand by reducing some of Pepsi's market share in response to a cut in Coke's price. Pepsi, however, is likely to respond in kind, cutting its price too. According to Edgeworth, this price-cutting scenario will continue until price falls to marginal cost. Consumers benefit because the competitive solution will be reached at $MC = p_e$ and total quantity is Q_e, with each firm supplying $Q_e/2$ units.

The story doesn't end here, however, because each firm will realize what has happened. Edgeworth suggested that one firm will now raise its price, hoping that its rival will act rationally and follow suit. If that happens, the market will move back to the monopoly solution once more. But if either firm cheats on the tacit agreement, another price war will break out. The Edgeworth model leads to a prediction that oligopoly will be characterized by periods of price stability and occasional price wars.

14.2 Model of Kinked Demand Curve

One model of oligopoly behavior predicts that price is likely to be "sticky" even amid changes in cost and technology. This explanation of price rigidity is called Sweezy's **kinked demand-curve model.**[1] Sweezy assumed that if an oligopolist were to *cut* its price, rivals would quickly match the price cut to protect their market shares. But if an oligopolist were to *raise* its price, rivals would *not* follow suit to increase their market shares. The oligopolist's demand curve would thus be more elastic for price increases than for price decreases. The oligopolist's AR curve would be relatively flat above the current price and relatively steep below that price. Sweezy's model is named after the kink in the firm's AR curve.

The kinked demand-curve model is illustrated by Figure 14.2. Marginal revenue is positive for output levels before X^* because the firm sees AR as elastic in that range. Beyond X^*, marginal revenue is negative if the AR curve is viewed as inelastic in that range. That curve has a gap occurring at the current level of output X^*.

The MC curve passes through the gap in the MR curve. If the MC curve were to cut the MR curve, a new optimal price and output combination would be established and the "kink" would occur at that new point. As shown, the current price and output will remain unchanged for large vertical shifts in the cost curves. Changes in cost brought by changes in technology or factor prices, particularly changes that reduce marginal cost, have no effect on output price. The optimal price also remains at p^* for a wide range of lateral shifts in the AR curve. The optimal level of output will change with shifts in the AR curve, but price remains unaffected until the MC curve cuts the shifting MR curve.

The primary flaw in the kinked demand-curve model is that it does not explain how price and output are determined initially. Additional criticism arises from an examination of industries, such as automobile, steel, and gasoline, in which firms have matched price increases.

Three significant predictions follow from the kinked demand model. First, oligopoly firms are reluctant to *raise* prices *independently* for fear of losing market share. Second, an oligopoly firm will also be reluctant to *cut* price *independently* unless it has a cost advantage because rivals will do the same and profits will fall. Third, the resulting price rigidity encourages nonprice competition, including product differentiation when possible. Even when products are highly differentiated, oligopolists tend to charge prices that are *comparable.*

---

1. Paul M. Sweezy, "Demand Conditions Under Oligopoly," *Journal of Political Economy,* 47 (August 1939), pp. 568–738. See also George J. Stigler, "The Kinky Oligopoly Demand Curve and Rigid Prices," *Journal of Political Economy,* 55 (October 1947), pp. 432–449.

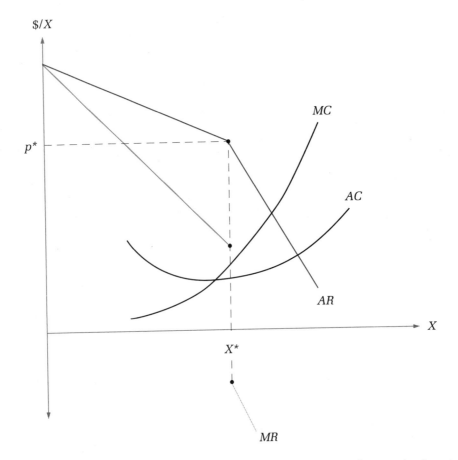

Figure 14.2 **The kinked demand-curve model:** If an oligopoly firm expects rivals to match price cuts but ignore price increases, the firm's demand curve will be elastic above the current price and inelastic below the current price. Thus, MR is negative beyond X*, and a gap occurs in the MR curve. Relatively large vertical shifts in the cost curves will then have no influence on price.

ECONOMIC SCENE: *Rival Brewers Foam*

The Anheuser-Busch Company holds roughly 42 percent of the U.S. beer market. Budweiser alone has 27 percent. Big as it is, Anheuser plans to get bigger, having set its sights on attaining 50 percent of the market by the mid-1990s. In August 1989, the company announced it would lower prices on all its brands to match price discounts as high as 25 percent given by rivals. This action would hurt its earnings for the rest of the year, but the company expected the move to increase its market share.

The Miller Brewing Company, Anheuser's closest rival, has a 21.8 percent share of the market. Adolph Coors Company, which recently agreed to buy the Stroh Brewery, will have an 18.7 percent share. And further consolidation seems likely.

Indeed, seemingly the only way to grow in such a market is to grab someone else's business.

Given Anheuser's strength, many analysts don't interpret its price-cutting move as a true reaction to competitive pricing. "I think they say that as a good excuse to implement a very calculated strategy," said Tom Pirco, the president of Bevmark Inc., an industry consulting firm.* "They saw the middle of the beer industry in disarray. When you have the enemy troops in disarray, the best thing to do is charge."

---

* As reported by N. R. Kleinfield of *The New York Times* in the *Orange County Register,* December 14, 1989.

14.3 Price Rigidity and Price Leadership

Under an oligopoly market structure, firms rely on differences in price and product in making strategic decisions. An oligopoly firm may be reluctant to *raise* price *independently,* though, for fear of losing market share. Moreover, an oligopoly firm will also be reluctant to *cut* price *independently* unless it has a cost advantage because rivals will do the same and profits will fall. Such wariness encourages nonprice competition, including product differentiation when possible. At times, though, all firms in an oligopoly industry are motivated to change price, as when they experience similar shifts in costs or demand. The problem becomes one of encouraging rivals to follow your lead, or deciding whether to follow a rival's lead. The two major forms of price leadership are **dominant firm** leadership and **barometric firm** leadership.

Recall that in the dominant-firm model one large firm or a cartel of firms dominates a competitive fringe of smaller firms. The dominant firm sets its preferred price and allows the fringe firms to sell all they want at that price. Then the dominant firm supplies a residual demand. Thus, the dominant firm acts as a price leader. The fringe firms' followership stems from implicit coercion and potential punishment from the dominant firm. Dominant-firm price leaders have included Alcoa, American Can, Birdseye, Coca-Cola, Exxon, Firestone, General Motors, International Paper, IBM, R. J. Reynolds, Sears, and United States Steel. Most of these firms have lost their position of dominance.

Barometric price leadership occurs when one firm announces price changes that are followed by other firms in the industry. The barometric price leader is not necessarily a dominant firm. Rather, interpretation of market conditions is left to one firm, which sets the price. All other firms follow the lead to avoid divisive economic warfare. Prior experience with volatile price fluctuations and cutthroat competition, or the desire to avoid the rigid price suggested by the kinked demand curve, may generate recognition that they will all be better off by following the leader.

One explanation for price leadership emphasizes the efficiency of the barometric firm. This **low-cost leadership model** is illustrated by Figure 14.3. Market demand is divided between the two firms and that determines their AR curves. The split depends on the prices being charged by both firms. The position of follower's demand curve AR_2 depends on the leader's price p_1^*. The position of the leader's demand curve, AR_1, depends on the

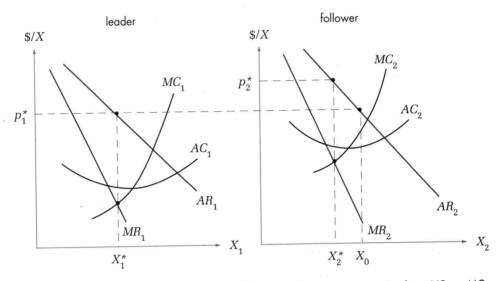

Figure 14.3 **Price leadership by a low-cost firm:** The low-cost firm sets price at p_1^*, where $MR_1 = MC_1$. The high-cost firm sets its output at X_0 even though it would prefer to produce X_2^* at price p_2^*. The high-cost firm follows the lead because the low-cost firm could reduce price below the minimum average cost of the high-cost firm.

follower's accepting price p_1^*. The low-cost firm sets price at p_1^* and produces X_1^* units to maximize its profits. The high-cost firm reacts to that price and produces X_0 units. The market clears because the total quantity supplied by both firms equals the market quantity demanded at price p_1^*. The high-cost firm would prefer price p_2^*, but then the low-cost firm could respond by reducing its price below the minimum average cost of the high-cost firm, which would cause a shift in AR_2 to the left, causing even greater losses for the high-cost firm. To avoid such a possibility, the high-cost firm passively and tacitly accepts the price set by the price leader.

Rarely is the price leader able to enforce its decision. In fact, the leader may be one of the smaller firms in the industry. Sometimes price leadership is conferred on a firm because other firms recognize its competence in judging market conditions. At other times the role of the leader changes from one firm to another. Price leadership in the copper industry has been exercised by Anaconda, Kennecott, and Phelps Dodge—the three largest firms. In the beer industry, Anheuser-Busch and Miller Brewing share the leadership.

Price leadership is not the only explanation for price conformity under oligopoly. Firms may in fact share technology, face common resource prices, and choose about the same scale of operations. Hence, such firms would have roughly equivalent cost structures, and they would react to changes in resource prices, technology, or market demand. They seem to conform without formal or informal agreement.

AN APPLICATION: *Price Leadership and Welfare Losses*

Estimates of the deadweight loss under a price-leadership model were made by Micha Gisser for 445 U.S. manufacturing industries.* Gisser's model is illustrated by Figure 14.4. Market demand is represented by the curve labeled *D*. Gisser assumes that the demand curve takes the form

$$D = kp^{-\eta_d}$$

where η_d is the price elasticity of demand. The supply of price takers, the competitive fringe, is given by

$$S_t = gp^{\eta_t}$$

where η_t is the price elasticity of supply for the price takers. The *aggregate* supply of the industry's dominant firm or a group of price leaders is

$$S_L = hMC_L^{\eta_L}$$

where MC_L is the marginal cost of the leaders, η_L is the elasticity of this aggregate supply curve, and *h* is a parameter.

The excess demand curve *E* facing the leaders is defined as *D* minus S_t, or

$$E = D - S_t$$

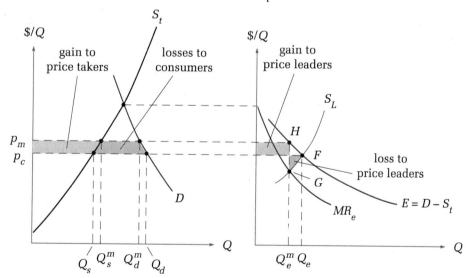

Figure 14.4 **Gains and losses due to price leadership:** Price leadership under collusion by the leaders results in a price increase from p_c to p_m. The deadweight loss to society is equal to the area of the *HGF* triangle.

* Micha Gisser, "Price Leadership and Welfare Losses in U.S. Manufacturing," *American Economic Review*, 74(4) (September 1986), pp. 756–767.

The elasticity of excess demand is given by

$$\eta_e = (D/E)(\eta_d) + (S_t/E)(\eta_t)$$

In an industry, each of the leading firms is confronted with an excess demand curve that it views as its demand curve. Suppose industry demand elasticity η_d is unitary, and suppose the leading firms collectively have supply elasticity η_t that is unitary. The elasticity of leaders' excess demand would be

$$\eta_e = (D/E)(+1) + (S_t/E)(+1)$$

Now if only one price-leading firm supplies $E = 10$ units out of a total industry output of $D = 100$, that firm's elasticity of excess demand will be

$$\eta_e = (100/10)(+1) + (90/10)(+1) = 19$$

If, however, a cartel of four identical firms is formed, with each supplying 10 units of the industry output of $D = 100$, the cartel's elasticity of excess demand will be

$$\eta_e = (100/40)(+1) + (60/40)(+1) = 4$$

The elasticities of excess demand facing one price-leading firm acting independently are quite different from the elasticity facing a group of colluding price-leading firms.

This difference in elasticity of excess demand when firms collude has significant implications about the price distortion that occurs. Profit maximization implies that

$$MR = p\left(1 - \frac{1}{\eta_e}\right)$$

Thus, the cartel of four firms just mentioned would have an MR of

$$MR = p\left(1 - \frac{1}{4}\right) = 0.75p$$

As the cartel tries to maximize profit, it operates where marginal cost is 75 percent of market price.

In Figure 14.4, the marginal revenue curve associated with the leaders' excess demand curve is labeled MR_e. If they collude to set a "monopoly" price at p_m, the quantity produced by the leaders will be Q_e^m. At price p_m, the price takers will supply Q_s^m units. The total market demand, Q_d^m, is met because $Q_s^m + Q_e^m = Q_d^m$. In contrast, a price p_c would prevail if the leaders were to behave competitively, and total quantity demanded would be Q_d, composed of Q_s from the fringe and Q_e units from the leaders' excess demand. The deadweight loss from the price distortion is given by the area of the triangle *HGF* in Figure 14.4. This deadweight loss to society is the loss to consumers plus the loss to the price leaders minus the gains to both price leaders and price takers.

To make numerical estimates of the losses due to price leadership, Gisser assigned values to the parameters of the demand and supply curves. He chose a unitary elastic demand as a reasonable value, allowing the supply elasticities to vary, but assumed that $\eta_L = \eta_t$. He normalized price and quantity under competition at $p_c = 1$ and $Q_c = 100$ percent. Given a concentration ratio denoted C, supply coefficients become $g = 100 - C$ and $h = C$. Gisser then calculated the percentage of dead-weight losses based on industry four-firm concentration ratios. This percentage was multiplied by each industry's total value of shipments to find a dollar value of dead-weight loss. Gisser concludes that 0.114 percent of *GNP* is an upper limit on the deadweight loss when the largest four firms act independently, but the deadweight loss can increase to 1.823 percent if they collude. A small percentage of *GNP* translates into a huge dollar loss. A loss of only 0.114 percent of *GNP*, for instance, was equal to about $2.16 billion at the time of this study.

Gisser next constructed a test of a hypothesis that leaders collude. He calculated economic profit for each industry, and he standardized profit by dividing by value added. This standardized profit measure was regressed on the four-firm concentration ratio, yielding the estimate

$$\hat{\pi} = 0.332 + 0.001C$$

Both coefficients were statistically significant. The estimated equation indicates that the profit measure is 33 percent of value added, and profit will rise by one-tenth of 1 percent per 1 percentage point rise in the concentration ratio. An increase in the concentration ratio of 10 percent would cause a 1 percent increase in profit over value added. This is a very small effect, and a prediction that is too small if the firms were colluding. Thus, little evidence of collusive behavior was found in this study.

ECONOMIC SCENE: *Media Signals*

In 1979, the four major companies selling lead additives for gasoline were charged with using the media to fix prices. The Federal Trade Commission alleged that DuPont, Ethyl, Nalco Chemical, and PPG Industries were coordinating prices by announcing any planned price change to the news media. In this way, reactions from the market and from rivals could be "tested," leaving time to modify the price change. The FTC claimed that eighteen lockstep price increases occurred over four years. DuPont argued that nine of the price changes were connected to changes in the price of lead and that six were price cuts.

The FTC proposed that each firm be prohibited from making advance announcements on price changes to anyone but its customers. The FTC case against sellers of lead additives was not the first of its kind. In 1972, the Justice Department charged General Motors and Ford Motor Company with "coordinated action" to eliminate discounts on fleet sales. The alleged mechanism for fixing prices was that the two companies signaled each other with press reports. This case was dismissed by a federal judge because the government had failed to prove conspiracy, even though no proof of conspiracy is necessary under FTC rules. All that is needed is that the practice be sufficiently anticompetitive.

14.4 The Cournot Model and Nash Equilibria

Of all the oligopoly models, Cournot's is both the first and the most famous.[2] Apart from its historical significance, the model provides a simple example for understanding important basic principles of oligopoly behavior. The Cournot model emphasizes the interdependence among firms in an industry. In its general form, where the number of firms can vary, the model approaches the two polar cases, pure monopoly and pure competition. The model also illustrates how an industry-wide cartel generates gains to every firm and why that cartel tends to be unstable. The model also illustrates a strategic situation in which each firm's choice is optimal given opponents' actions—a concept known as a Nash equilibrium.

Augustin Cournot described two proprietors selling water from one spring. With only two firms, the industry is a **duopoly.** Marginal cost for each firm was assumed to be zero—an assumption that is not unreasonable for firms selling access to the spring if the cost of extracting water is borne by the buyer. With zero marginal cost, each firm will maximize its profit by maximizing its revenue. The industry demand curve is assumed to be linear, $Q = a - bp$, in the Cournot duopoly model.

Let's denote the quantity sold by the first firm X_1 and the quantity sold by the second firm X_2. Industry output is $Q = X_1 + X_2$, and so market demand is

$$X_1 + X_2 = a - bp, \ a > 0, \ b > 0$$

Each firm wishes to set its output to maximize profit, and each sets its output where its marginal revenue equals its marginal cost. Because marginal cost is zero in the classical Cournot model, each firm sets output where marginal revenue equals zero.

Revenue to the first firm is $R_1 = pX_1$. Solving for industry price from the market demand equation and substituting that price equation into the first firm's revenue equation yields

$$R_1 = \left[\frac{a}{b} - \frac{X_1}{b} - \frac{X_2}{b} \right] X_1$$

Marginal revenue to the first firm is

$$MR_1 = \frac{a}{b} - \frac{2X_1}{b} - \frac{X_2}{b}$$

Because marginal cost is assumed to be zero, the first firm will set X_1 so that $MR_1 = 0$. Solving for X_1 results in

$$X_1 = \frac{1}{2} (a - X_2)$$

This equation is called the firm's **reaction function** because it determines how the firm

---

2. Augustin Cournot, *Researches into the Mathematical Principles and the Theory of Wealth* (1838), trans. Nathaniel T. Bacon (Macmillan, 1927).

reacts to the second firm's output. The decision of the first firm depends on what the second firm does. By the symmetry of the model, the second firm's reaction function is

$$X_2 = \frac{1}{2}(a - X_1)$$

The problem now is to find values of X_1 and X_2 that provide an equilibrium. The problem is complicated by the response when one firm sets its output—the other firm reacts. But then the first firm reacts to the second firm's output, and so on. Can we find some combination of X_1 and X_2 where the firms' actions are mutually consistent, in that neither firm will react further?

The search for such an equilibrium is assisted by the **Nash equilibrium** from game theory. Rather than require that a player's choice be optimal for all possible strategies chosen by opponents, we can require that a player's choice be optimal *given* that their opponent's choice is optimal. When both players' choices are optimal given their opponents' actions, neither player will have any reason to make another choice, and the process (game) is at an equilibrium:

> **Nash equilibrium:** *A pair of strategies is a Nash equilibrium when each player's choice is optimal given the opponents' actions.*

In a Nash equilibrium, you are doing the best you can given what your opponents are doing, and your opponents are doing the best they can given what you are doing.

A Nash equilibrium solution to the Cournot duopoly problem is illustrated by Figure 14.5, where both reaction functions are graphed: X_1 as a function of X_2; and X_2 as a function of X_1. The simultaneous solution to the two reaction functions is

$$X_1 = X_2 = a/3$$

This is a Nash equilibrium in the sense that neither firm has an incentive to change its output or price as long as it believes that the other firm will maintain its output at $a/3$.

To see how the Nash equilibrium was reached, consider this scenario. Suppose the first firm sets its output to maximize revenue without considering the other firm's output. The first firm initially views its demand curve as equal to market demand, $X_1 = Q = a - bp$. In other words, it acts as a monopoly, and the profit-maximizing level of output would be $X_1 = a/2$, where $MR_1 = 0$ when $X_2 = 0$. This "monopoly" will choose point (1) in Figure 14.5.

The second firm now reacts to the first firm's initial choice and takes the remainder of industry demand as its demand curve, $X_2 = (a/2) - bp$. The second firm maximizes its revenue by setting its output at $X_2 = a/4$, when $X_1 = a/2$, point (2) in Figure 14.5.

Now the first firm will adjust because its initial output no longer maximizes its revenue. If the first firm assumes that the second will maintain its output at $X_2 = a/4$, the demand curve facing the first firm becomes $X_1 = (3a/4) - bp$. The new revenue-maximizing output becomes $X_1 = 3a/8$. Therefore the first firm moves to point (3) in Figure 14.5.

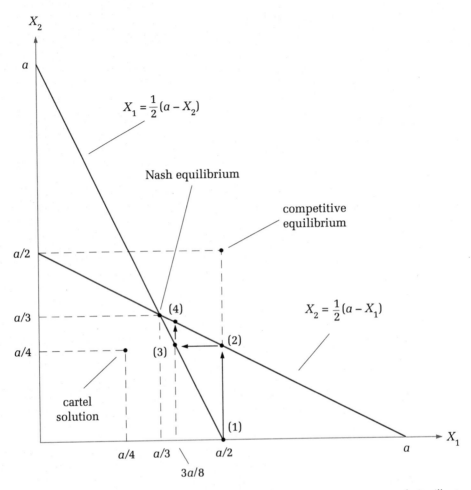

Figure 14.5 **Cournot duopoly reaction functions:** If the first firm tries to act as a monopoly, it will set output at point (1), where $X_1 = a/2$ and $X_2 = 0$. The second firm will then react by setting its output at point (2), where $X_2 = a/4$. The first firm will now react by setting its output at $X_1 = 3a/8$ at point (3). This adjustment will continue until a Nash equilibrium is reached at $X_1 = X_2 = a/3$.

Now it is the second firm's turn to adjust. The second firm reacts to the level of output $X_1 = 3a/8$, and it will move to point (4) in Figure 14.5. This adjustment will continue until the Nash equilibrium of $X_1 = X_2 = a/3$ is reached, where the two reaction functions intersect. No matter where we start, the Nash equilibrium will be reached.

The Cournot model can be extended to k firms in the industry. With k firms, industry output is given by

$$Q = \sum_{j=1}^{k} X_j$$

With equal marginal costs, the solution is symmetrical, so that

$$X_1 = X_2 = \cdots = X_k = Q/k$$

The reaction function for the first firm is

$$X_1 = \frac{1}{2}\left(a - \sum_{j=2}^{k} X_j\right)$$

The summation term is equal to industry output less X_1,

$$\sum_{j=2}^{k} X_j = Q - \frac{Q}{k} = (k - 1)\frac{Q}{k}$$

Substitution into the first firm's reaction function yields

$$\frac{Q}{k} = \frac{1}{2}\left[a - \frac{(k - 1)Q}{k}\right]$$

Solving for industry output yields

$$Q = \left(\frac{k}{k + 1}\right)a$$

Each firm produces Q/k units, and so

$$X_1 = X_2 = \cdots = X_k = \frac{Q}{k} = \frac{a}{k + 1}$$

In the monopoly case, where $k = 1$, the revenue-maximizing level of output is $a/2$. In the duopoly case, where $k = 2$, the revenue-maximizing level of output for each firm is $a/3$ and the industry produces $Q = 2a/3$. Under pure competition, where k is very large, industry output becomes $Q = a$, price will equal marginal cost, and each firm contributes a small amount to the industry output.

The realism of the Cournot model is strained by the assumption that each firm acts as if its rivals' outputs remain unchanged when the firm changes its own level of output. Nevertheless, it illustrates nicely the concept of a Nash equilibrium, which, however, is not necessarily stable.

In the Cournot duopoly case, both firms can gain by merging into a monopoly or by forming a cartel. As a monopoly or as a cartel, the industry output is set where industry revenue is maximized, and output becomes $Q = a/2$, with price determined by industry demand as $p = a/2b$. Total revenue is $pQ = a^2/4b$. Each of the two "firms" receives half the revenue. Without a cartel, the output of each firm is $a/3$, yielding an industry output of $Q = 2a/3$. At that output level, price becomes $p = a/3b$, and industry revenue is $2a^2/9b$. Each of the two firms, acting independently, receives an equal revenue of $a^2/9b$, less than $a^2/8b$, which each would receive under a profit-sharing cartel. Thus, each firm can increase its revenue by forming an industry-wide cartel.

A cartel, however, will be unstable because each firm can increase its profits if it cheats on the other firm *as long as* it assumes that the other firm will continue to produce where it is. Under a cartel, each firm contributes $a/4$ units to industry output of $a/2$ units. The cartel solution is indicated in Figure 14.5. If the first firm then cheats by producing on its reaction curve, it will produce $X_1 = 3a/8$ units because $X_2 = a/4$. We wind up back at point (3). The second firm now reacts to make itself better off, and the cartel breaks down.

The Nash equilibrium and the cartel solution to the Cournot duopoly problem can be compared to a competitive equilibrium. Under pure competition, both firms would earn zero profits, and so both set price equal to marginal cost. In the preceding example, marginal cost was assumed to be equal to zero, and so under competition each firm sets price equal to zero and produces $a/2$ units, as shown in Figure 14.5. The good is free except for the costs of extracting the water, and consumer surplus is maximized. The Cournot outcome, however, is better for the firms than perfect competition, but not as good as the outcome under collusion.

14.5 Strategic Price Competition

In the Cournot duopoly model the firms compete by setting quantities—a reasonable assumption when the firms sell a homogeneous product such as water. When the products of the firms in the industry are perfect substitutes, one price must prevail. Many oligopoly industry products, though, are differentiated. Product differentiation has many sources. Even physically identical goods can be differentiated at the point of purchase. Location, ease of parking, delivery service, variety of color, and return policy are just a few of the characteristics that can differentiate one good from an otherwise identical good. Once the goods become close but not perfect substitutes, their prices will vary also.

The Cournot model can be modified and applied to price competition. Suppose two firms have equal fixed costs of $FC = 20$ but zero marginal costs. Let's suppose they face similar demand curves:

$$X_1 = 24 - 2p_1 + p_2$$
$$X_2 = 24 + p_1 - 2p_2$$

In this example the own-price and cross-price effects are identical for both firms. Each firm's product is a market substitute for the other firm's product because the cross-price effects are positive.

Now let's assume that each firm sets its price, taking its competitor's price as a constant. The profit function for the first firm is

$$\pi_1 = p_1 X_1 - 20 = 24p_1 - 2p_1^2 + p_1 p_2 - 20$$

The profit-maximizing price for the first firm can be found by setting marginal profit equal to zero:

$$\frac{\Delta \pi_1}{\Delta p_1} = 24 - 4p_1 + p_2 = 0$$

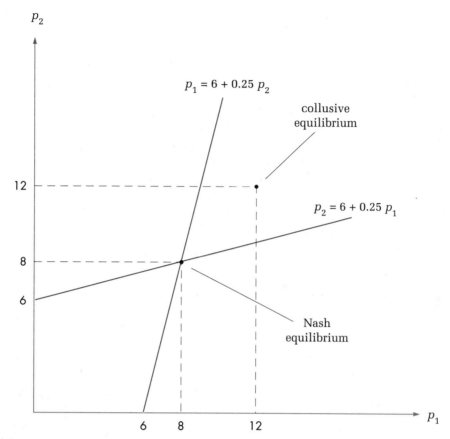

Figure 14.6 **Price-reaction curves:** For a duopoly under price competition, each firm reacts to the other's price. A Nash equilibrium occurs where neither firm will change its price given the other firm's price.

Therefore, in setting its price p_1 to maximize profit, the firm must react to p_2, the other firm's price. The *price-reaction* function for the first firm is

$$p_1 = 6 + 0.25p_2$$

Because of the symmetry in the profit functions, the price-reaction function for the second firm is

$$p_2 = 6 + 0.25p_1$$

These reaction curves are graphed in Figure 14.6. The Nash equilibrium occurs at $p_1 = p_2 = 8$ where the two curves intersect.

This is a Nash equilibrium because neither firm will change its price given the price of the other firm. The firms can do better, though, if they collude to maximize joint profit, given by

$$\pi = \pi_1 + \pi_2 = 48p - 2p^2 - 40$$

Marginal profit for the cartel is

$$\frac{\Delta\pi}{\Delta p} = 48 - 4p$$

Setting this expression equal to zero yields the cartel's profit-maximizing price of $p = 12$. As before, the collusive solution tends to be unstable if either firm reacts to the other firm's output because each firm can do better if it cheats.

14.6 The Cartel

A **cartel** is a collusive arrangement accomplished by formal agreement. The intent of any cartel is monopoly emulation. The two basic types are the profit-sharing cartel and the market-sharing cartel. In the **profit-sharing cartel,** members transfer control to a centralized organization that acts like a multiplant monopoly firm. Cartel policy results from negotiation and compromise, but a member's power is not necessarily proportional to its size. In the **market-sharing cartel,** members agree on market shares but do their own marketing. The market-sharing cartel is a more loosely formed organization in which each firm acts like a monopolist in its segment of the market.

The centralized **profit-sharing cartel** is illustrated by Figure 14.7. To keep the illustration simple, only two firms are producing a homogeneous product. The cartel is faced with a joint demand curve that is the industry demand if these are the only two firms in the industry. This curve is viewed as the cartel's AR curve, and an MR curve is marginal to the joint AR curve. The cartel's MC curve is determined by the horizontal summation of all firms' MC curves. The cartel maximizes profit where $MR = MC$ and output is Q^*. Price is set at p^* in accordance with the joint demand curve.

Once price and output have been set, the cartel must decide on the production levels and profit shares for the member firms. These must be settled in such a way that the sum of the members' outputs equals Q^*. One solution is for the firms to treat the cartel's MR at Q^* as each firm's marginal revenue. As illustrated by Figure 14.7, each firm's quota is set so that its MC equals MR^*. Each firm's share of the market is determined by its

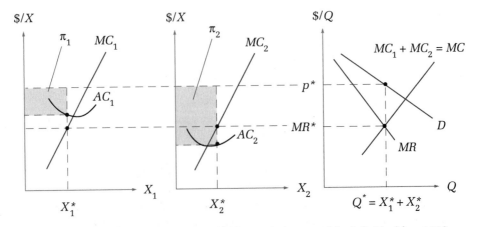

Figure 14.7 **Profit-sharing cartel:** The cartel's MC curve is the sum of the individual firms' MC curves. The joint demand curve is viewed as the cartel's AR curve, and MR is marginal to the joint demand curve. The cartel sets price at p* so that MR = MC. Each firm takes MR* as its marginal revenue curve and sets its output so that MR equals its MC curve.

proportionate contribution to marginal cost. Total cartel profit is the sum of members' profits. Under this arrangement, member firms frequently become discontented with their relative shares because low-cost firms may not be the largest ones in the cartel.

Member firms will also be motivated to cheat. Each firm can increase its profit if it produces more than its quota and sells at a price below the cartel price, as illustrated by Figure 14.8. As before, the cartel sets price at p_a, where $MR = MC$, and each firm's quota is set at X_j^a. Each firm's demand curve depends on the other firms' prices, and so the position of each firm's average revenue curve AR_j is influenced by the single cartel price p_a. Each firm's revenue is $p_a X_j^a$, and so its average revenue curve AR_j must pass through point a. Because the firm's marginal revenue curve MR_j lies below AR_j, the firm can increase its own profits by selling at price p_b and selling X_j^b units of output where $MR_j = MC_j$. This firm's profit-maximizing price is below the cartel's price. Thus each firm is motivated to reduce its price below the cartel price. The increased sales by the firm cause a reduction in cartel sales and shifts in the other firms' average revenue curves, and so small cheaters are less likely to be detected. Nevertheless, other members are motivated to do the same thing, and the gains from collusion will be dissipated as they do so.

The **market-sharing cartel** is the other form. Market-sharing agreements are more common than centralized, profit-sharing cartels because enforcement is easier. The market-sharing cartel is illustrated by Figure 14.9. Suppose two identical firms are in the market. The cartel's average revenue curve AR_{1+2} is the horizontal sum of the two firms' AR curves AR_1 and AR_2, and the cartel's marginal cost curve MC_{1+2} is the horizontal sum of the firms' MC curves MC_1 and MC_2. The cartel price, where $MR_{1+2} = MC_{1+2}$, is the same as each firm's profit-maximizing price, where $MR_j = MC_j$ for $j = 1, 2$. The

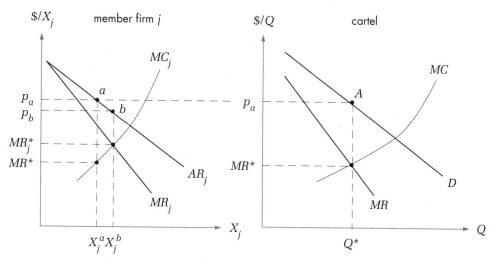

Figure 14.8 **Profit incentive to cheat:** The member firm has an average revenue curve that must pass through point a. This firm can increase its profits above its share of cartel profits by setting price at p_b, which is below the cartel price p_a. The increase in profit to the cheating firm occurs only if no other firms cut their price too, but all firms have the same price-cutting incentive.

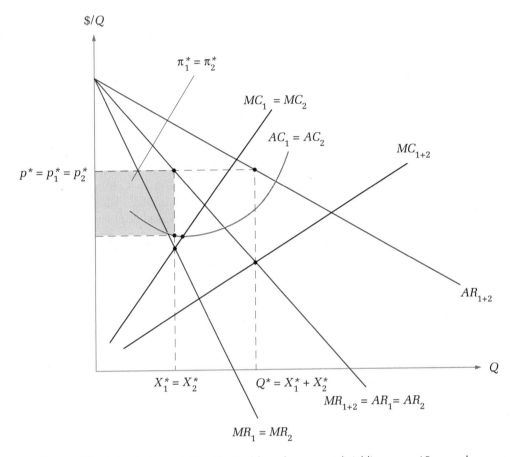

Figure 14.9 **Market-sharing cartel:** Two identical firms form a cartel yielding curve AR_{1+2} and marginal cost curve MC_{1+2}. The AR_{1+2} curve is the horizontal sum of AR_1 and AR_2, and the MC_{1+2} curve is the horizontal sum of MC_1 and MC_2. The cartel sets quantity at Q^*, where $MR_{1+2} = MC_{1+2}$, and sets price at p^*. Each firm, acting independently, sets output at X_i^* where $MR_i = MC_i$, and sets price at p_i^* for $i = 1, 2$. Here we find no advantage in belonging to this cartel.

collusive agreement confers no advantage except to prevent members from trying to increase market share by product differentiation.

More realistically, the costs of production are likely to be different for member firms. Then market sharing avoids transferring quotas from firms with high marginal costs to firms with lower marginal costs—a problem for the profit-sharing cartel. High-capacity firms receive larger market shares under market sharing. Market sharing may also be geographic, which may reduce transportation costs that might otherwise occur. Nevertheless, the cartel reduces the independence of member firms that may wish to differentiate their products and encroach upon others' markets.

Whatever the type of cartel, most collusive agreements in trade and manufacturing have been illegal in the United States since the Sherman Anti-Trust Act of 1890.

GLOBAL PERSPECTIVE: *OPEC*

Frequently, the world's oil supply has been threatened by conflict. In 1956, the Suez Canal was blocked. In 1967, Israel attacked Egypt's massing armies, and the Arabs tried to embargo supplies to America. Another Arab–Israeli conflict caused the "first" oil shock in 1973, and the Iranian revolution led to the second oil shock in 1979. When Iraq invaded Kuwait in 1990, oil prices jumped and the world economy again shuddered.

Producers have repeatedly tried to escape oil's volatility with monopolies and cartels. The greatest of these was the nineteenth-century monopoly, the Standard Oil Trust that was called the "seven sisters." The most recent cartel of oil producers is the Organization of Petroleum Exporting Countries (OPEC).

Membership in OPEC is voluntary. Currently it is composed of members from thirteen governments. As might be expected, each member has its own goals. Four members— Kuwait, Qatar, Saudi Arabia, and the United Arab Emirates—have large oil reserves. The remaining nine members—Algeria, Ecuador, Gabon, Indonesia, Iran, Iraq, Libya, Nigeria, and Venezuela—had relatively low reserves prior to 1987. Iraq, however, has claimed recoverable reserves of 100 billion barrels, second only to Saudi Arabias' 169.5 billion barrels and quadruple the U.S. proven reserve of 25.3 billion. Members of OPEC are not the only countries producing oil. In 1988, Abu Dhabi was ranked fifth in the world, with 92.2 billion barrels in reserve. The Soviet Union was sixth, with 59 billion barrels, but their reserves have been steadily decreasing. The United States was ranked eighth.

In 1989, the Middle East held about 65.3 percent of the world's oil reserves. Saudi Arabia held 25.4 percent, Iraq 9.8 percent, and Kuwait 9.5 percent. About 20.6 percent of the world's reserves were held by other Middle East countries. Members of OPEC with high reserves also have small populations and large per capital incomes, and are inclined to be long-run profit maximizers. Members with low reserves have large populations and low per capita incomes, and are interested in short-run profit maximizing. Because the long-run elasticity of demand exceeds the short-run elasticity at each price, the long-run profit maximizers want a lower price than the short-run profit maximizers. With these differences in goals, what holds OPEC together?

The organization is a market-sharing cartel. Members agree on quotas that are targeted to achieve a desired world price. In the late 1970s, OPEC members produced about two-thirds of the world output, and the cartel was strong. Incentives to cheat were present, but Saudi Arabia and its allies, principally Kuwait, could keep other members in line by threatening to dump oil onto the market to push price down and punish cheaters. Together, Saudi Arabia and Kuwait could flood the oil markets with 1 million additional barrels of oil merely by changing their definition of crude oil. Smaller members were not without power and influence, however. Iran, Iraq, and Libya, for instance, have had reputations for being militarily strong and politically unpredictable.

In the 1980s, the OPEC cartel was weakened because of new discoveries. By 1985, Mexico had become the world's fourth largest producer. Between 1980 and 1986, Britain and Norway nearly doubled their output. Discoveries in Angola, Argentina, Australia, Benin, Brazil, Cameroon, China, Colombia, Congo, Egypt, India, Malaysia, Oman, Peru, Syria, Tunisia, and Zaire made those countries at least self-sufficient in oil. Attempts by OPEC to expand its membership failed. Mexico and Egypt attend meetings but refuse membership. In 1986, Saudi Arabia tried to force Britain and Norway to join OPEC, but the effort failed. The cartel had lost its dominance.

Table 14.1 Top Ten Crude-Oil Producers for 1989

Company, country	Crude production (mb/d)	Years of reserves[a]
Aramco (Saudi Arabia)	5.34	132.2
Pemex (Mexico)	2.89	49.2
NIOC (Iran)	2.87	88.6
PDV (Venezuela)	1.99	81.5
Royal Dutch/Shell (Holland/UK)	1.85	14.0
Exxon (United States)	1.80	11.3
BP (United Kingdom)	1.41	13.7
KPC (Kuwait)	1.41	188.6
Sonatrack (Algeria)	1.22	20.6

[a]Based on 1989 output rates.
Source: Petroleum Intelligence Weekly, as cited in *The Economist,* January 12, 1991.

The organization has been ineffective in preventing cheating on quotas. In 1984, Iraq, Iran, and Libya began to barter for arms from the Soviet Union. Even Saudi Arabia bought U.S. Boeing 747s and French jet fighters with bartered oil. Moreover, as conservation practices around the world were adopted at the same time as non-OPEC production rose, price cutting within OPEC became widespread. By mid-1985, about 80 percent of OPEC's sales were discounted and quotas were flouted openly. Its ability to agree on and enforce quotas was further complicated by the Iran–Iraq war and later by Iraq's invasion of Kuwait.

The top ten producers of crude for 1989 are listed in Table 14.1. Before Iraq's tanks rolled into Kuwait, things were looking up for the oil industry, particularly in the Middle East. Consumption was growing at about 1.5 percent a year, and non-OPEC production had reached a plateau. Then, however, producers like Saudi Arabia and Venezuela, which increased their output in response to disruption in supply from Iraq and Kuwait, seemed unwilling to forgo much-needed revenue by cutting output back again. Kuwait and Iraq were desperate to regain their market shares. Discipline within OPEC was harder to enforce than ever. Most economists agree that without entry restrictions and effective sanctions against cheaters, OPEC will continue to be an ineffective emulator of a monopoly.

Exceptions include some joint agreements that apply to foreign markets, labor unions, agricultural co-ops, and organized sports. Before 1890, price fixing was common in many industries, and illegal collusive agreements have been discovered since. In 1951, four firms producing circuit breakers agreed to rotate sealed-bid business. General Electric was targeted to receive a 45 percent market share. Westinghouse was to receive 35 percent. Allis-Chalmers and Federal Pacific were to receive 10 percent each. Secret meetings were held about every two weeks, and decisions were based on the target shares. General Electric, Westinghouse, and Allis-Chalmers were formally charged with agreeing on price and market shares between July 1957 and May 1958, and the cartel dissolved in 1958 as the three firms became involved in vigorous price competition. In 1958, an attempt was made to reestablish the cartel, but that incarnation was short-lived.

In 1960, the Justice Department obtained indictments against 40 companies and 18 persons on charges of dividing the market and price fixing. Again the firms all produced circuit breakers and switchgears. In 1961, a U.S. district court levied fines of more than $1.9 million against 29 of those firms. The stated reasons for participating in the conspiracy were increased profits, personal reward, and less "worry" about competition.

For a cartel to last, it must be empowered to impose penalties on cheaters. The harsh penalties with which organized crime syndicates chastise dissident "families" is a classic example. Alternatively, a legal remedy must be provided under law. In some European nations where cartels are common, they are legal and enforced by contract law. But without effective enforcement, cartels are unstable because of the incentive to cheat.

ECONOMIC SCENE: *Of Computer Chips and Oranges*

A consortium of U.S. computer and semiconductor firms was proposed in 1989 to make state-of-the-art DRAM chips. Dynamic random access memory chips are expected to be essential for the next generation of supercomputers. The consortium, to be called U.S. Memories, would receive equity contributions from Advanced Micro Systems, Digital Equipment Corporation, Hewlett-Packard, IBM, Intel, LSI Logic, and National Semiconductor. The initial technology would be licensed from IBM, and each investor would be required to buy some fraction of the manufactured DRAMs.*

This would be a novel arrangement for U.S. industry. The consortium is intended to meet Japanese competition, but the new firm is impeded by U.S. antitrust laws. First, preliminary discussions about future investment plans among competitors may be illegal. Second, the new firm will be exposed to possible lawsuits and treble damages if the firm ventures into such related products as static RAMs. Third, the consortium's intent to build new facilities was a response to avoid antitrust action due to a cooperative contractual arrangement.

Law professor Thomas Jorde and business professor David Teece comment that a key reason for joining the consortium is that DRAMs are "technology drivers," creating new technology. Jorde and Teece argue that to imprison this technology for antitrust reasons is to hold hostage U.S. competitiveness. They say Congress should modify antitrust laws to ensure that consortiums like this one are legal. One proposal is that a certificate of exemption be issued by Justice or the Federal Trade Commission. When combined market shares of cooperating firms exceeded 20 percent, a consortium would be approved only if it improved competitive performance, if the combination fostered economies of scale, and if there was a demonstrable need for operational and strategic coordination.

The consortium is not without its opponents. T. J. Rodgers, one of Silicon Valley's best-known venture capitalists, said, "It's a dumb plan. Have you ever heard of an American consortium that helped us? If so, I'll take 50 Amtraks" (*The Los Angeles Times,* December 26, 1989). Of course, Rodgers was seeking a license to use the same IBM technology. Rodgers argued that concentrating a development effort in one

---

* This account is based on an opinion written by Thomas M. Jorde and David J. Teece, "To Keep U.S. in the Chips, Modify the Antitrust Laws," *The Los Angeles Times,* Monday, July 24, 1989, Part II.

large corporation isn't the right strategy for a battle that should be fought in guerrilla style.

Many computer firms were not interested from the beginning. Apple declined membership, saying that it wanted to spend its money on more important areas. Apple also said that its membership would not benefit Apple's customers.

Early in 1990, after seven months of hoopla, the consortium folded from lack of support and commitment by potential members. In January 1990, representatives from eleven electronics firms were asked to indicate how much money everyone was willing to contribute. "The room got real quiet real fast," said Sanford Kane, president of U.S. Memories (*The Los Angeles Times*, January 16, 1990). The demise of U.S. Memories demonstrates the penchant of American companies to think tactically rather than strategically. Whether U.S. companies will be able to respond individually to the Japanese challenge remains to be seen.

One cartel in the United States would make OPEC jealous, the citrus cartel.† The Navel Orange Administrative Committee (NOAC) is authorized by federal "marketing orders" dating back to the Great Depression and rests on a combination of *Grapes of Wrath* rhetoric and campaign contributions. Here's how they work: Federal law allows some farmers—say, California and Arizona orange growers—to establish a committee that will decide how much of the crop will be delivered to market. The rest is stored, processed, or left to rot.

The NOAC then allocates market shares to packers. The packers in turn divvy up business among the growers. Cartel decisions carry the force of law, and violators face criminal as well as civil penalties. One grower was sued by the USDA for giving oranges away.

Most growers support the system, believing that it makes farming less risky and perhaps more equitable. At least they vote for it every few years. Sunkist, the big cooperative, insists that the cartel is a blessing for everybody. One industry representative said that without the cartel, "those who will survive will be those who produce the best quality fruit, the greatest production per acre and the lowest cost." Imagine: Producers of crummy, expensive fruit would face ruin!

James Moody, a lawyer representing dissident growers, says the system works mainly for Sunkist, which dominates the NOAC. He also says it has helped kill off hundreds of small packing firms. Predictably, some packers ship black-market oranges when their quotas are filled. To thwart this subterfuge, each individual fruit will now be labeled, indicating its source and authorized sale. All the while, society devotes more resources to growing oranges than are warranted by demand.

---

† This account is based on Daniel Akst, "Citrus Cartel Would Make OPEC Jealous," *The Los Angeles Times*, January 8, 1991.

14.7 Game Theory and Strategic Decisions

Strategic decision making is an important part of business rivalry. A basic feature in such rivalries is that the final outcome depends primarily on the strategies, or lines of play, selected by adversaries. John von Neumann and Oskar Morgenstern (1944) called the models that deal with strategic decision making by adversaries **game theory.** The economic games that firms play can be either *cooperative* or *noncooperative.*

A game is **cooperative** if the players can negotiate and plan joint strategies. When preplay discussions and binding agreements are allowed, the game is cooperative. When more than two players take part, coalitions may be formed in cooperative games. An example of a cooperative game is several firms that negotiate a joint investment to come up with new technology that no firm would be able or willing to develop on its own. The previously discussed computer consortium may be viewed as a strategic response to a move made by the Japanese in the global computer market.

A game is **noncooperative** if the players independently determine their strategies even though they take each other's behavior into account. Binding contracts are not permitted in noncooperative games. In this chapter we consider mostly noncooperative games. In any game, however, the most important element is the assumption that all players act rationally and intelligently.

A **strategy** is a predetermined line of play that specifies completely how to respond to each possible circumstance at each stage in the game. Choosing a strategy commits a player to an entire sequence of moves contingent upon the moves of all players. One of the simplest games is the two-person zero-sum game. A **zero-sum** game occurs when gains by some players equal losses by other players so that the sum of losses and gains is zero. Chess is a two-person zero-sum game. In principle, a zero-sum game can be expressed in terms of the two strategies when only two players take part. Therefore, an entire chess game can be expressed by the two strategies adopted by the two players.

A payoff table lists the outcomes of the game as determined by the strategies of the two players. In a zero-sum game, the payoff table is determined for only one player because the payoffs for the second player are just the negative values of the payoffs to the first. Suppose two firms are each faced with a fixed advertising budget. Each firm considers advertising in two areas. Each can spend its entire budget in one area or divide its budget between the two. Each firm has these three strategies:

$$\text{Strategy } 1 = \text{spend in the first area}$$
$$\text{Strategy } 2 = \text{spend in the second area}$$
$$\text{Strategy } 3 = \text{spend in both areas}$$

Payoffs to the first firm, player I, expressed in percentage of gain in market share, are given in this payoff table:

Game 1: Gain to player I

		Player II		
	Strategies	1	2	3
Player I	1	0	1	2
	2	−2	0	−1
	3	2	4	3

The payoffs depend on the choices both players make.

How can you decide on the best strategy for playing this game? What is the game's most likely outcome? One rule would be to choose a strategy that is *at least as good as* any other strategy *regardless* of what an opponent does. For player I, you can see from the gains that strategy 1 dominates strategy 2 and strategy 3 dominates strategy 1. For player I, strategy 3 is called a dominant strategy. Similarly, player II discards strategy 2 because it is dominated by strategy 1, which has uniformly lower payoffs to player I. Thus, rows 1 and 2 and column 2 can be eliminated from consideration. The solution to game 1 becomes obvious because player I will always choose strategy 3, and player II will choose strategy 1 to minimize losses.

A **dominant strategy** is one that is optimal for a player no matter what an opponent does:

> **Dominant strategy:** *A dominant strategy is one that yields the best result no matter what an opponent does.*

In the preceding game, strategy 3 was the dominant one for player I. Once player II recognizes that, strategy 1 becomes the dominant one for player II. The **principle of dominance** says that no player will ever choose a strategy that yields worse results for every alternative a rival might choose:

> **Principle of dominance:** *No player will choose a strategy that yields worse results for all the rivals' alternatives.*

The principle of dominance is a useful way to reduce the size of a payoff table and sometimes leads to a solution. A dominant strategy equilibrium is a special case of a Nash equilibrium.

Not all games have dominance strategies. Consider this payoff table:

Game 2: Gain to player I

		Player II		
	Strategies	1	2	3
Player I	1	− 3	− 2	6
	2	2	0	2
	3	5	− 2	− 4

In game 2, neither player has a dominant strategy. Therefore, we need a more general solution concept; let's try to find a Nash equilibrium. One rule for selecting between alternatives that are not dominated is suggested by Morgenstern and Von Neumann:

> **Minimax criterion:** *Each player should make the best of the worst possible situation.*

Each player will try to minimize the maximum losses whenever this tactic will not give an advantage to the opponent. In game 2, player I should select the strategy with the maximum minimum payoff. Player II should select the strategy with the minimum maximum payoff because the payoffs are losses to player II. Player 1 first calculates the *minimum gain* from each strategy—these are -3, 0, and -4 respectively. Player I then chooses strategy 2 because that yields the maximum of the minimum gains, namely zero. Player I thereby ensures against any loss in this game. Likewise, player II first calculates the *maximum loss* for each strategy—these are 5, 0, and 6 respectively. Player II then identifies the minimum of the maximum losses, namely zero, and chooses strategy 2. Player II, therefore, also ensures against any loss in this game because player II's minimax payoff is zero.

When the maximin and minimax are equal, the game is said to have a "saddle point," a solution such that neither player has any motive to change strategies—a Nash equilibrium.

14.8 Mixed Strategies—Being Unpredictable

Not all games have a saddle point because the maximin for player I may not be equal to the minimax for player II. Consider this payoff table:

Game 3: Gain to player I

	Strategies	Player II 1	Player II 2	Player II 3
Player I	1	0	-2	2
	2	5	4	-3
	3	2	-3	-4

In this game the maximum of the minimum gains to player I, the maximin, has a value of -2 and occurs for strategy 1. The minimum of the maximum losses to player II, the minimax, has a value of 2 and occurs for strategy 3. Because the maximin does not equal the minimax, this game has no saddle point. Player II does best by choosing strategy 3 when player I chooses 1, but player I would anticipate this move and play 2 instead. But player I would anticipate this switch and play 2 instead. And then player II would switch to 3, causing player I to switch to 1 once more, and the cycle would start over.

Whenever a game does not have a saddle point, a player can take advantage of an opponent's strategy. The opponent then chooses appropriate counterstrategy, and so on, so that a stable solution is never reached. But what would happen if players disguised their choices from one another? Sometimes it pays to be unpredictable. As the cartoon by Modell suggests, the pencil salesman is likely to sell more pencils if he is seen to be irrational. But is being unpredictable irrational?

Game theory advises each player to randomize choices. When actually playing the game, each player must choose a pure strategy, but it can be chosen by a random device that hides its selection from any opponent:

> **Mixed strategy:** *A mixed strategy occurs by assigning probabilities of choosing the pure strategies.*

The probabilities are assigned to maximize the *expected* payoff of the game. Thanks to a result proved by Von Neumann and Morgenstern, known as the **minimax theorem,** every mixed strategy, two-person, zero-sum game is known to have a saddle point. A Nash equilibrium in mixed strategies occurs when each player chooses the optimal *frequency* for choosing strategies given the *frequencies* of choices made by opponents.

Let P_i be the probability (frequency) that player I will use strategy i, and let Q_j be the probability that player II chooses strategy j. Player I specifies a mixed strategy by assigning values to the P_i. Likewise, player II specifies a mixed strategy by assigning values to the Q_j. Each player wants to assign probabilities so that their *expected* payoff is maximized.

Consider game 3 above, which has no saddle point for pure strategies. It does, however, have some dominated strategies, and that will simplify the game. For player I, strategy 3 is dominated by 2, and so player I sets $P_3 = 0$ because strategy 3 should never be chosen under any circumstance. Because $P_1 + P_2 + P_3 = 1$ and $P_3 = 0$, we can see that $P_2 = 1 - P_1$. Likewise, for player II, strategy 1 is dominated by 2, and so player II sets $Q_1 = 0$.

Drawing by Modell; © 1971 The New Yorker Magazine, Inc.

The key idea is that player I should choose a mixed strategy so that player II is also willing to play a mixed strategy. The expected payoff to player II can be found for each of the remaining pure strategies of player II:

Pure Strategy by II	Expected Payoff to II
$Q_2 = 1$	$-[-2P_1 + 4P_2]$
$Q_3 = 1$	$-[2P_1 - 3P_2]$

The expected payoff equations to player II can be graphed as shown in Figure 14.10. The two equations cross at the minimax value of 2/11, where $P_1 = 7/11$ and $P_2 = 4/11$. Player

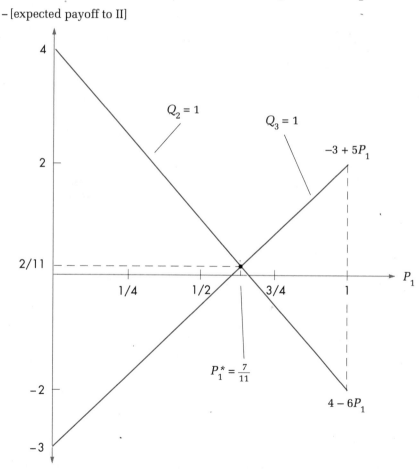

Figure 14.10 **Optimal mixed strategy:** The expected payoffs to player II are each graphed as a function of P_1 for each pure strategy available to player II. Player I then chooses $P_1 = 7/11$, according to the minimax rule, because this strategy makes player II indifferent between II's strategies and player II is willing to play a mixed strategy also.

I should choose strategy 1 with frequency 7/11, strategy 2 with frequency 4/11, and strategy 3 with frequency zero. By making these choices, player II will be indifferent between strategies 2 and 3.

Player II will not be choosing pure strategies. For any *mixed* strategy for player II, the expected payoff to player I is

$$Q_2(4 - 6P_1) + Q_3(-3 + 5P_1)$$

because $P_2 = 1 - P_1$ and $Q_1 = 0$. According to the minimax theorem, this formula must be equal to 2/11. We also know that $Q_2 + Q_3 = 1$. Simultaneous solution yields $Q_2 = 5/11$ and $Q_3 = 6/11$. Thus, the optimal mixed strategy for player I is $P_1 = 7/11$, $P_2 = 4/11$, and $P_3 = 0$, and the optimal mixed strategy for player II is $Q_1 = 0$, $Q_2 = 5/11$, and $Q_3 = 6/11$. For us, the important lesson in games of this type is that a mixed-strategy Nash equilibrium always exists.[3]

14.9 The Prisoners' Dilemma

Not all games are zero-sum games. A nonzero-sum game is one in which the gains of one player do not exactly offset the losses of other players. That is, the sum of all gains and losses of all players does not equal zero in a nonzero-sum game. The Nash equilibrium of a nonzero-sum game does not necessarily lead to a Pareto-efficient outcome. A classic example known as the prisoners' dilemma game will illustrate.

Butch Cassidy and the Sundance Kid are arrested for train robbery. Each is placed in a separate cell where they cannot communicate with each other. The authorities haven't enough evidence to convict them for train robbery unless they confess, but enough to convict them of possessing stolen property. Each prisoner is told that if you confess and your partner doesn't, you will receive a suspended sentence for turning state's evidence. But if you don't confess and your partner does, you will be sentenced to 25 years of hard labor. If you both confess, both of you will be sentenced to 20 years. If neither of you confesses, you will be sentenced to 5 years for possession of stolen property.

The payoff table looks as follows:

		Sundance	
		Confess	Don't Confess
Butch	Confess	(20, 20)	(0, 25)
	Don't Confess	(25, 0)	(5, 5)

The first number in each cell is the sentence Butch receives and the second number is the sentence Sundance receives. Both prisoners promptly confess and each receives 20 years in prison. Why? Because it is a dominant strategy for each to confess. If communication

---

3. It may happen that players select some strategy with probability 1, which is equivalent to a pure-strategy Nash equilibrium.

is permitted between the prisoners and an agreement is reached, however, perhaps neither would confess so that both would receive only a 5-year sentence. Even then the incentive would be strong to cheat by confessing unless an enforcement mechanism could be found.

The prisoners' dilemma applies to many kinds of real-world problems. In the political sphere, consider arms control. The best strategy is joint disarmament, but without a binding agreement or mutual trust, no country disarms and all are worse off. In the economic environment, the formation and instability of cartels is a good application for this type of game. When firms agree to act as a cartel, they do so to emulate a monopoly. Jointly, they achieve a higher profit if the cartel is successful. Yet the incentive is strong to cheat because each member can do better by itself *after* the cartel is formed.

14.10 Repeated Games and Tit for Tat

Firms operating in oligopolistic markets are often confronted with a prisoners' dilemma when making output and pricing decisions. And collusive agreements such as cartels tend to be unstable because it pays to cheat. But the prisoners' dilemma game is *static*—in the real world, firms play *repeated* games. In a repeated game, you could choose to punish your opponents for undesirable behavior. With each repetition of play in the game, players have the opportunity to establish reputations about their behavior. If a player punishes opponents whenever they act noncooperatively, and at the same time acts to cooperate, an environment of mutual cooperation may be established.

Let us reconsider the prisoners' dilemma game when the players make repeated decisions. Suppose each of two identical firms can charge a high price or a low price. If both firms charge a high price, they both make large profits. But if one firm charges a low price and the other charges a high price, the firm with the low price makes even greater profits but the one with the high price suffers a loss. On the other hand, if both charge a low price, they both make small but positive profits. The payoff table for this game is:

		Firm II	
		Low Price	High Price
Firm I	Low Price	(20, 20)	(80, −10)
	High Price	(−10, 80)	(60, 60)

In each cell the profit for firm I is listed first and the profit for firm II is listed second.

Now suppose each firm announces its pricing decision at the beginning of each round of play. One strategy would be to protect against a loss on each round by setting a low price. In that way you would earn a high profit if your rival set a high price and would ensure against a loss. If your rival did the same, you'd have the classical prisoners' dilemma because you would both wind up with low but positive profits.

But this game will be repeated, and so an alternative strategy might induce cooperation. After all, your opponent is not stupid. Both firms would be better off by cooperating and setting price at the higher level—as long as neither cheats. Therefore, an alternative strategy might be to set your price at the high level and leave it there as long as your rival does the same. But if your opponent cheats, then you lower your price in the next period. Recognizing that once you both set the low price you would be caught in the prisoners' dilemma, you raise your price in the subsequent round of play, expecting your opponent will do likewise. This strategy is called "tit for tat."

As you can see, the tit-for-tat strategy is only one of many that might be adopted. Robert Axelrod, however, asked game theorists to choose a strategy for playing this type of game an indefinite number of times.[4] He then played various strategies one against another in a computer simulation to see which one worked best on average. The best strategy, and also one of the simplest, was tit for tat.

Tit for tat does very well because it assumes that your rival is smart and motivated by profit. **Tit for tat** offers immediate punishment whenever your rival cheats, but it is also a forgiving strategy. Tit for tat fosters cooperation because your rival is rewarded for that cooperation.

The tit-for-tat strategy, though, breaks down with only a fixed number of repetitions. The reason is simple. You can gain even more by cheating on the last round. But your opponent sees this opportunity too, and so you both lose. You will then try to cheat on the next-to-last round. But your opponent will do the same. If no way can be found to foster cooperation on the last round, then no way will be found to foster cooperation on the next-to-last round, and so on. Thus the tit-for-tat strategy degenerates into a prisoners' dilemma on each round of play.

It has been argued that cartels and oligopoly firms use strategies like tit for tat.[5] If the game can be repeated an indefinite number of times, players can establish reputations, cheaters can be punished, and cooperation can be encouraged. Tit for tat and other cooperative strategies also help to explain why sticky prices and nonprice competition are characteristics of so many oligopoly markets.

14.11 Sequential Games and Moving First

In a sequential game, one player moves first. To see how sequential games may be represented, let's look at a game of entry deterrence. Suppose a monopolist is facing the potential entry of a rival into the industry. The potential entrant moves first by deciding whether or not to enter. The incumbent monopolist must decide to accommodate the new firm or to fight. This payoff tree represents the outcomes:

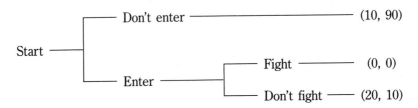

4. Robert Axelrod, *The Evolution of Cooperation* (Basic Books, 1984).

5. Robert Porter, "A Study of Cartel Stability: the Joint Executive Committee, 1880–1886," *Bell Journal of Economics,* 14(2) (Autumn 1983), pp. 301–325.

GLOBAL PERSPECTIVE: *Strategic Trade Policy*

International markets frequently are imperfectly competitive when a few large firms operate in an environment fraught with market interference and uncertainty. This observation, coupled with a new view that international trade is driven by economies of scale rather than comparative advantage, suggests that government policy can tilt oligopolistic competition to shift excess returns from foreign trade to domestic firms.

Let's look at an example provided by Paul Krugman, a professor of economics at MIT.* He starts his strategic trade policy argument by assuming that a world market as a whole has room for only one profitable entrant because of large economies of scale. If two firms enter they will both incur losses, but the first to become established earns economic profits that will not be competed away. In Krugman's example, two firms are capable of producing a 150-seat passenger aircraft. One firm is Boeing, located in America. The other firm is Airbus, located in Europe. To focus on rent seeking, Krugman assumes that neither America nor Europe has any domestic demand for the good, and so it is intended solely for export. Producer surplus can thus be identified with the national interest.

Each firm has the option of producing or not producing. Relevant payoff tables are represented in Table 14.2. Boeing's choices of producing (P) or not producing (N) are represented by upper-case letters, Airbus's corresponding choices by lower-case letters, p and n. In each cell the first number is Boeing's profit, the second number is Airbus's profit. The first game, with no subsidy, has no unique Nash equilibrium, but the game will have a unique outcome if one firm can move first. If Boeing can move first and commit itself to produce before Airbus's decision, with no government intervention, the outcome will be (P, n). Boeing will earn large profits while deterring entry by Airbus.

Europe's government can change this outcome by committing itself to a subsidy of 10 if Airbus produces the plane, regardless of what Boeing does. The new payoff table with the

Table 14.2 Hypothetical Payoffs for Strategic Trade

No-subsidy game:

		Airbus	
		p	n
Boeing	P	$(-5, -5)$	$(100, 0)$
	N	$(0, 100)$	$(0, 0)$

European-subsidy game:

		Airbus	
		p	n
Boeing	P	$(-5, 5)$	$(100, 0)$
	N	$(0, 110)$	$(0, 0)$

Source: Paul R. Krugman, "Is Free Trade Passé?" *Economic Perspectives*, 1(2) (Fall 1987).

---

* Paul R. Krugman, "Is Free Trade Passé?" *Economic Perspectives*, 1(2) (Fall 1987), pp. 131–144.

subsidy guarantees that Airbus will make a positive profit. The decision to produce dominates Airbus's alternative no matter what Boeing does. Thus even if Boeing has a first-mover advantage, Airbus will produce. Boeing now knows that even if it commits itself to production, Airbus will produce and Boeing will make losses. This condition reverses the original outcome to (N, p) instead of (P, n).

The surprising result is that a small subsidy raises Airbus's profits from 0 to 110. Of this, 100 represents a transfer of excess returns (profit) from America to Europe. In reality, of course, even the best-informed governments will not have the information required to construct such a payoff table. Krugman points out that uncertainty is a feature in most economic policy, but uncertainty is even more likely under oligopolistic competition. The reason is that economists do not have reliable models of how oligopolists behave. Even in simple games the outcomes depend on whether firms behave cooperatively or non-cooperatively, or whether firms commit or bluff, or whether a first mover has an advantage or disadvantage. Consider what might happen if America too offered a subsidy as an industrial policy. The rules of a real-world game may be so complex that the rules and outcomes are obscure even to the players themselves. Nevertheless, Krugman's example shows that strategic trade policy, under some circumstances, can raise the national welfare of one country at the expense of another.

The numbers in parentheses indicate the payoff to the rival first and the incumbent second. If the potential entrant doesn't enter, it gains (saves) 10 and the incumbent gains 90. If the first mover enters the market and the incumbent fights, both earn 0 payoff. But if the incumbent doesn't fight when entry occurs, the entrant receives 20 and the incumbent's profits fall to 10. The problem that the incumbent faces is that once entry occurs it is better off not to fight. A threat to fight will not work because that is an "empty threat" unless the incumbent is "crazy."

But suppose the incumbent purchases extra production capacity that reduces its profits by 10 if no entry occurs. The extra capacity allows the incumbent to fight more aggressively by increasing production, forcing price down, and to earn a profit even if the potential rival enters the market. The payoff tree becomes:

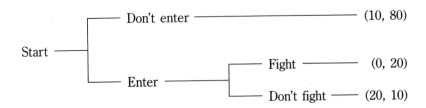

Now if the first mover enters the market and the incumbent fights, the new firm receives 0 and the incumbent receives 20. The fighting option is more viable, and the threat to the potential entrant is real. Entry will be deterred because the incumbent firm will always be better off if it fights. The extra capacity, though it reduces profits, ensures greater profit in perpetuity because of the entry deterrence.

What lessons are to be learned from this sequential game? First, you may gain an advantage by being a first mover. By moving first you may be able to limit your opponent's options. Second, you may find an advantage in making an irrevocable commitment. If, for example, the rival commits to entry *before* the incumbent develops a credible threat, the entrant has an advantage. If, on the other hand, the incumbent monopolist commits itself to fighting by developing a credible threat *before* the potential entrant acts, the monopolist has the advantage. Third, in some situations developing a reputation for an "irrational" response may be advantageous.[6] If the potential entrant believes the incumbent monopolist to be irrational, entry may be deterred even when the monopolist does not have the capacity to make the threat of fighting seem rational.

Summary

Oligopoly is the type of market structure composed of a few large sellers. Strategic behavior becomes important because each firm's actions affect other firms in the industry. Because no one set of rules describes all possible forms of strategic behavior, we have no single model of oligopoly.

One model of oligopoly behavior is Sweezy's kinked demand model, which predicts that oligopoly firms will be reluctant to change price independently for fear of starting a price war or of losing market share. This fear tends to encourage product differentiation and collusion. Because price fixing is illegal, price leadership and followership may arise.

Price rigidity is a characteristic that has been observed in many oligopolistic markets. Explanations concentrate on oligopoly firms' desire to avoid costly price wars. Price-leadership models such as the dominant firm help explain how oligopoly firms learn to change prices in concert without formal collusion. Collusive agreements to fix prices are illegal in the United States under the Sherman Anti-Trust Act.

Another famous oligopoly model is the Cournot, which illustrates a strategic situation wherein each firm's optimal output level depends on another firm's output. The model reaches an equilibrium if each firm reacts to the other firm's level of output—a Nash equilibrium. Cournot's model also illustrates how an industry-wide cartel generates gains to every firm and why that cartel is unstable. The Cournot model can also be modified and applied to price competition.

A cartel is a formal collusive arrangement. Whether a profit-sharing or a market-sharing cartel, the goal is to emulate monopoly behavior so that members become better off. But once the cartel is formed, each member can become even better off if it alone cheats. Thus, cartels are usually unstable.

Perhaps the most promising approach to the study of oligopoly is game theory. Games can be cooperative or noncooperative. A strategy specifies how to respond to each possible circumstance at each stage in play. A dominant strategy is one that is optimal no matter what an opponent does. If all players have dominant strategies, then the outcome of the game involves each player's choosing a dominant strategy. But not all games have dominant strategies, and then we look for a Nash equilibrium, which occurs when each

---

6. You can see an analogy here also to the threat of nuclear retaliation in response to a conventional attack.

player's choice is optimal given the opponent's actions. One rule that can be used to find a Nash equilibrium in a zero-sum game is the minimax criterion—each player makes the best of the worst possible situation.

The prisoners' dilemma arises when players, in making independent rational choices, fail to arrive at a Pareto-efficient equilibrium. This game applies to many real-world problems. In economics, the prisoners' dilemma game provides insights into cartel behavior.

The "tit-for-tat" strategy often works well in repeated games with an indefinite number of plays. Tit for tat does well because it assumes that your opponent is smart and rational, offers immediate punishment whenever your opponent makes a "bad" move, and fosters cooperation because "good" moves are rewarded. Tit for tat breaks down, however, when the number of moves is fixed, because players will cheat in the last period when no reprisal is possible.

Further Readings

On general oligopoly theory, see

- James Friedman, *Oligopoly Theory* (Cambridge University Press, 1983).

The pioneering work on the theory of games is

- John von Neumann and Oskar Morgenstern, *Theory of Games and Economic Behavior* (Princeton University Press, 1944).

For an extended discussion on the prisoners' dilemma and related games, see

- R. D. Luce and Howard Raiffa, *Games and Decisions* (John Wiley, 1957).

Research on game theory has not concentrated solely on oligopoly behavior. Game theory has found applications in the study of general equilibrium, public-utility pricing, allocating joint costs, externalities and public goods, strategy-proof voting mechanisms, and designing institutions and their stability properties. Although these topics are beyond the scope of this text, the interested reader might wish to start with this survey:

- Andrew Schotter and Gerhard Schodiane, "Economics and the Theory of Games: A Survey," *Journal of Economic Literature* (June 1980).

I also highly recommend these:

- Michael E. Porter, *Competitive Strategy* (Free Press, 1980).
- Guillermo Owen, *Game Theory* (Academic Press, 1982).
- David Kreps, Paul Milgrom, John Roberts, and Robert Wilson, "Rational Cooperation in the Finitely Repeated Prisoners' Dilemma," *Journal of Economic Theory*, 27 (1982, pp. 245–252).
- Morton D. Davis, *Game Theory: A Nontechnical Introduction* (Basic Books, 1983).
- James W. Friedman, *Game Theory with Applications to Economics* (Oxford University Press, 1986).

- David Kreps, *A Course in Microeconomic Theory* (Princeton University Press, 1990).
- Avinash K. Dixit and Barry J. Nalebuff, *Thinking Strategically* (W. W. Norton & Co., 1991).

Practice Problems

1. Within the context of Sweezy's kinked demand-curve model:
   (a) Show how an increase in technological efficiency or a decrease in variable input price may have no influence on output price.
   (b) Show how changes in market demand may have no effect on output price, even though output changes.
2. Why do some firms follow the price leadership of another firm? In your answer, consider the dominant-firm leadership and barometric-firm leadership models.
3. Discuss the possibility of empirical verification that a firm is monopolistically competitive or oligopolistic. Carefully consider the market characteristics under each form of market structure. How might it be possible to measure the various elements of market structure? What role might the various measures of monopoly power play in determining market structure?
4. Consider a Cournot duopoly in which the market price is determined by

$$p = 24 - X_1 - X_2$$

   so that $Q = 24 - p$ because $Q = X_1 + X_2$. Suppose the MR and MC curves for the first firm are:

$$MR_1 = 24 - 2X_1 - X_2 \text{ and } MC_1 = 8$$

   The MR and MC curves for the second firm are:

$$MR_2 = 24 - X_1 - 2X_2 \text{ and } MC_1 = 4$$

   Notice that the marginal costs for the firms are unequal.
   (a) Set $MR = MC$ for each firm to find the reaction functions for each.
   (b) Solve for the Cournot equilibrium levels of output.
   (c) Find market price at the equilibrium, then compute the revenues for each firm.
   (d) An obvious relation connects market shares and marginal costs. What is it?
5. Suppose two firms have complete information about market demand and each other's cost functions. The first firm's cost function is

$$C_1 = 6{,}000 + 16X_1$$

   The second firm's cost function is

$$C_2 = 9{,}000 + 10X_2$$

   Market demand is

$$Q = X_1 + X_2 = 1{,}000 - 10p$$

   so that the inverse demand function is

$$p = 100 - 0.1(X_1 + X_2)$$

(a) Determine the two firms' profit functions $\pi_1(X_1, X_2)$ and $\pi_2(X_1, X_2)$.

(b) Find the marginal profit functions for both firms, and find the Cournot equilibrium.

6. The classical prisoners' dilemma game results in a dominant-strategy Nash equilibrium that is Pareto inefficient. How would the outcome be altered if the two prisoners were allowed to retaliate after their prison terms? Could a Pareto-efficient outcome result?

7. What is a dominant strategy? Why is a dominant-strategy equilibrium stable?

8. What is a "tit-for-tat" strategy? Why is it a rational strategy for the indefinitely repeated prisoners' dilemma?

9. Many oligopoly firms compete over a long time. With a large number of repetitions, why don't collusive outcomes occur more often?

10. Many industries are plagued by overcapacity that far exceeds demand. This excess happens in industries wherein demand is volatile and unpredictable, but also in industries in which demand is stable. What factors lead to overcapacity?

11. What is meant by "first-mover advantage"? Give an example of a game with a first-mover advantage.

12. By eliminating dominated strategies, determine the optimal pure strategy for each player of a game having this payoff table:

		Player II		
Strategies		1	2	3
Player I	1	1	2	−3
	2	2	1	1
	3	0	−2	1

13. Find the Nash equilibrium, the saddle point, for this game. How much would you be willing to pay to play this game?

		Player II			
Strategies		1	2	3	4
Player I	1	−1	2	−3	0
	2	0	1	2	3
	3	−2	−3	4	−1

14. For this payoff table, use the graphical procedure to determine the optimal mixed strategy for each player:

			Player II	
	Strategies	1	2	3
Player I	1	1	3	4
	2	2	1	0

15. Consider this market demand schedule:

Price	Quantity
50¢	1,000
60¢	900

Two firms share this market, which is divided equally when the firms charge the same price:

(a) Formulate a payoff matrix in the pattern of the prisoners' dilemma if average cost is a constant 40¢.

(b) If the game is noncooperative, what is the market price and what is the profit to each firm?

(c) If the game is cooperative, what is the market price and what is the profit to each firm?

Chapter

15

Pricing Strategy and Practices

Deciding how to price products is among the manager's most important functions. Even in a purely competitive market where market conditions force the firm to act as a price taker, if its price is above the market price, sales will be lost until the firm adjusts, and if it sets price below the market price, revenue will be lost. Under other forms of market structure the consequences of wrong pricing can be even more severe.

Cost-plus pricing is used frequently, but is cost-plus pricing consistent with economic models of profit maximizing? Other questions arise about how to set the price of a new product, how to set price and quality jointly for new and evolving products, and how to set price and advertising expenditures.

If demand fluctuates, should the firm respond by changing price? If demand differs across markets, can and should the firm set different prices in those markets? And what are the welfare consequences of price discrimination? Other vital issues involve pricing intermediate goods that can be consumed as an input internally or sold to an external market. As for goods sold to retailers, can and should the supplier dictate a resale price to a retailer?

15.1 Cost-Plus Pricing

Cost-plus pricing, or **markup pricing,** is the method most frequently used. Typically, the firm estimates the average variable cost of producing and marketing a product, adds a charge for overhead, and then adds a markup. The cost-plus pricing formula is

$$\text{price} = \text{cost} \, (1 + \text{markup})$$

If the average total cost is $3 and the firm sets the markup at 20 percent, the price will be

$$\text{price} = \$3(1 + 0.2) = \$3.60$$

Cost-plus pricing has been criticized because it fails to consider demand conditions, it uses accounting costs rather than economic costs, and it emphasizes variable cost rather than marginal cost. If these criticisms are accurate, applying cost-plus pricing should lead to suboptimal price decisions. Why, then, do so many firms continue to use this technique?

ECONOMIC SCENE: *Apple Macintosh Plus What?*

The Mac SE with a 20MB (megabyte) hard drive was Apple's bestselling model in 1988. The SE can be broken down into six separate modules, plus a category for miscellaneous parts:*

- **Logic board:** The four Single Inline Memory Modules (SIMMs) cost about $120. The SE's custom gate-array chip costs around $15. Connectors and the four-layer board cost about $25, the Sony sound chip costs $1, the NCR SCSI controller costs $5. The Mac ROM chips cost $3 apiece. The 7.83 MHz 68000 chip costs only about $6. *Total cost:* less than $200.
- **Analog board:** The switching power supply is $15. Video circuiting totals about $13. The two-layer board is $4. *Total cost:* $32.
- **Display:** The estimated cost of the 9-inch black-and-white CRT is $9. The transformer costs about $4, and the cable harness runs $2. *Total cost:* $15.

---

* See Eric Winn, "How Much Does a Mac Cost?" *Macworld* (June 1988), pp. 114–117.

- **Disk drives:** At least one 3 1/2-inch floppy is included in every Mac, and one costs $50. The 20MB hard drive at $250 is the most expensive part of the SE. *Total cost:* $300.
- **Keyboard:** Key switches total about $15, and the Intel 8021 microprocessor costs $3. Other chips add about $2. The plastic housing runs about $5, not including the tooling for molds. *Total cost:* $25.
- **Mouse:** Channel detectors and the bus chips cost about $5, a small microprocessor costs $1. Plastic runs about $2. *Total cost:* $8.
- **Miscellaneous:** The SE case costs about $7. The fan costs $3. Add another $8 for cables, labels, knobs, screws, and the battery. *Total cost:* $18.

The total materials cost for the Mac SE was $598.

The suggested retail price was $3,698 for a Mac SE with 20MB internal drive and keyboard, and the average retail price was lower, at $2,971. The wholesale price to volume Apple dealers in a major city was around $2,137. The difference between what you paid and the price a dealer paid represented a 39 percent markup. The dealer must, of course, pay labor and overhead out of this markup.

Apple's annual report gives an idea about where revenues go. In 1987, about 14 percent was operating income and net profit. Figure 15.1 applies the percentages of the major expenditure areas to the average wholesale price of $2,137 for the Mac SE. Apple Computer makes roughly $298 for every SE sold. The total cost of production was about $1,839. The average dealer pays a 16.2 percent markup over the total cost and about 263 percent markup over the materials cost alone.

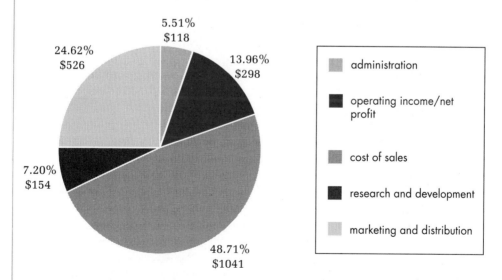

Figure 15.1 **Apple's revenue distribution:** The percentages for revenues for all Apple products were taken from Apple's 1987 annual report. Applying those percentages to the average wholesale price a dealer pays for an SE, $2,137, gives a rough estimate of markups and where SE revenues go.

Using average cost rather than marginal cost is wrong if the firm is maximizing short-run profit. But if the firm is operating in the long run close to minimal average cost, then the fully allocated average accounting costs may be close to marginal cost. How close depends on the methods used to assign prices to the variable inputs. If the costing method closely approximates the inputs' opportunity costs, and if the markup closely approximates the opportunity cost of owners' equity plus a return on any monopoly power, then markup pricing will closely approximate marginal cost pricing.

A big difference appears in the margins applied by firms using cost-plus pricing, implying that demand analysis does influence pricing. Studies indicate that most firms set markups according to differences in competitive pressure and demand elasticities. Moreover, the "list" price determined by a markup formula is frequently adjusted as market conditions vary. Adjustments are made with rebates, off-peak pricing, and other discounting methods. Thus, the list price can be adjusted to determine a price that reflects changes in demand elasticity.

With positive marginal cost, the profit-maximizing firm will choose a price along the elastic part of its AR curve, and so $\eta > 1$. Recall that the rule of thumb for the profit-maximizing price expressed as a markup over marginal cost is

$$p = \frac{MC}{1 - 1/\eta} = MC\left[\frac{\eta}{\eta - 1}\right]$$

When marginal cost is used in the cost-plus pricing formula, the price established is

$$p = MC\,(1 + \text{markup})$$

Setting these two price formulas equal to each other and dividing both sides by marginal cost yields

$$1 + \text{markup} = \frac{\eta}{\eta - 1}$$

Thus, the profit-maximizing markup is

$$\text{markup} = \left[\frac{\eta}{\eta - 1}\right] - 1$$

If $\eta = 2$, then the markup is 1 or 100 percent. If $\eta = 3$, then the markup is 1/2 or 50 percent. The profit-maximizing markup then is inversely related to the elasticity of demand. The optimal markup will be smaller as the demand grows more elastic. Therefore, the cost-plus formula will, if carefully applied, allow the firm to determine profit-maximizing price.

AN APPLICATION: *Pricing Textbooks*

Authors of textbooks are usually paid a royalty determined by multiplying the number of books sold by a fixed royalty percentage per book sold. Authors typically are placed under contract with a publisher after the publisher evaluates a prospectus, an outline, and several chapters. Upon signing a contract, the author may get an advance against future royalty payments. The publisher usually agrees to reimburse the author for expenses up to some maximum amount. Covered expenses usually include outlays for typing, photocopies, and postage. Once a draft of the remaining chapters is finished, the publisher has the book reviewed by several other experts and their comments are forwarded to the author. The author then revises the text before the book is put into production. The writing and revising take several months, and the initial production (editing, design, typesetting) takes several more. Then the author proofreads the galleys and, when the book is paged, prepares an index. The book then goes to final manufacturing (plating, printing, binding). The publisher usually retains all creative control over the physical properties of the book: size, typographic style, use of color, artwork, and cover. After production and manufacture, marketing takes several forms. Brochures are mailed to prospective users, and ads are placed in appropriate journals. Exhibition may occur at conferences, and sample books are given to all teachers who request examination copies. At this juncture all the author's costs are sunk costs. The publisher, however, will incur costs of paper, printing, binding, and distributing the book as well as payment of royalties.

The publisher's profits are given by*

$$\pi = pQ - \alpha pQ - C(Q) = (1 - \alpha)pQ - C(Q)$$

where α is the royalty rate and $C(Q)$ is the variable cost. The term αpQ equals total royalty payments. The publisher's *net marginal revenue, MR_n,* after deducting payments to the author, is

$$MR_n = (1 - \alpha)\left(p + Q\frac{\Delta p}{\Delta Q}\right)$$

Gross marginal revenue is

$$MR = p + Q\frac{\Delta p}{\Delta Q}$$

To maximize profits, the publisher will set price so that $MR_n = MC$.

Figure 15.2 illustrates the pricing problem under an assumption of constant marginal cost to the publisher. The publisher will maximize profits at quantity Q_P and price p_P, where $MR_n = MC$. The author's royalties, however, would be maximized at quantity Q_A and price p_A, where $MR = 0$. The author will always want a lower price and

---

* See Stephen K. Layson, "Is There a Conflict between Authors and Publishers over Book Prices?" *Southern Economic Journal,* 48(4) (April 1982), pp. 1057–1060.

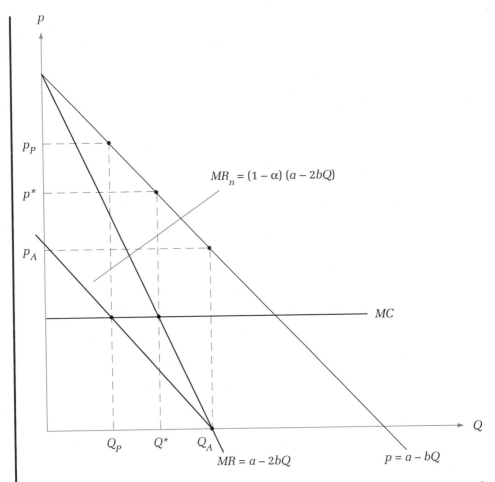

Figure 15.2 **Pricing textbooks:** The publisher sets price at p_P and quantity at Q_P to maximize profits net of royalties, where $MR_n = MC$, but the author prefers price p_A and quantity Q_A where $MR = 0$ and revenue is maximized. If the royalty rate α and the price are negotiable, however, equilibrium will occur at price p^* and quantity Q^*.

greater sales as long as the author's marginal cost is zero and the publisher's marginal cost is positive.

Thus far we have assumed that the royalty rate, α, is constant. That is not unreasonable because most textbook publishers offer a standard contract of 12 percent royalty on sales, less book returns. If the royalty rate is negotiable, though, the equilibrium price will settle at p^* and Q^*, where $MR = MC$. This bargain will be reached, because both publisher and author can be made better off by moving to p^* and Q^* from any other price-quantity combination, because the sum of profits plus royalties will be greatest where $MR = MC$. Bargaining will result in p^* and Q^*, however, only if both the royalty rate *and* price are negotiable. Usually, even when the author can bargain over the royalty rate, the publisher retains control over price. Then disagreement can arise over the price desired by the author and that set by the publisher.

15.2 New-Product Pricing

Pricing a new product, one that has not been sold in the market before, is more difficult than pricing current and evolving products. Pricing a new product is difficult because no empirical information is available to help guide your decision. Market research will be helpful, but often buyers' behavior cannot be predicted accurately until after the product has been introduced. Demand for the personal computer grew much faster than surveys had predicted. A more accurate forecast of demand might have encouraged firms to set higher initial prices to "skim the cream" off demand—the buyers willing to pay a higher price. Firms might then have been able to recover development costs more quickly. Alternatively, a lower "penetration" price might have been set to establish a broad market base initially. The higher quantity from a lower price could have discouraged potential entrants or resulted in lower average costs of production.

Price skimming is the practice of setting a high initial price to "skim" the demand by limiting demand by those buyers willing to pay the higher price. The idea is to maximize short-run profit. Initially, the firm introducing the new product has a monopoly, and the firm's average revenue curve coincides with the market demand curve. The firm sets price where marginal revenue equals marginal cost. Figure 15.3 illustrates how price skimming can be used to extract more of the consumer surplus and thereby increase profit. At the time the new product is introduced, demand is D_1. The product might be the Chikita personal computer produced by the Banana corporation. The monopolist sets the price of the Chikita at p_1, where $MR_1 = MC$. The quantity demanded is Q_1. These initial buyers will not be back in the market for another computer very soon, and so demand in

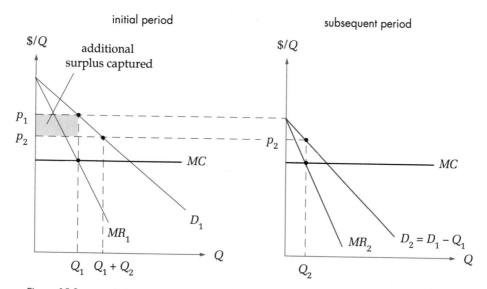

Figure 15.3 **Price skimming:** Total demand is D_1, but the monopolist segments the market into initial demand and subsequent demands. The first Q_1 units are sold at price p_1 and subsequent units are sold at a lower price, p_2. The additional consumer surplus captured occurs because the initial consumers are not willing or able to wait until price falls, or because consumers did not anticipate that price would fall.

the subsequent period will fall to $D_2 = D_1 - Q_1$. Now Banana sets the price of the Chikita at p_2, where $MR_2 = MC$. An additional Q_2 units are sold. If this firm had set price at p_2 initially, the total quantity demanded would have been $Q_1 + Q_2$ units. Total profit would have been lower by the difference in price, $p_1 - p_2$, multiplied by the number of units sold at the higher price, Q_2. This extra profit is the additional consumer surplus captured by the firm by price skimming.

Later, the market will evolve into an oligopoly unless it has barriers to entry. As the market becomes more competitive, the profits to each firm will shrink. Therefore the first firm to market may try to skim the market while it can by setting a high initial price. A second reason for charging a high initial price is to reduce the risk associated with committing resources to meet the higher quantity demanded at a lower price. The risk of new-product failure is notoriously high, and the firm may choose to wait and see if sufficient market demand is realized. In the long run the firm will change its price as market conditions are more accurately measured.

In two cases price skimming is consistent with long-run profit maximizing. First, if entry of rivals is impossible, the monopolist will maximize the expected present value of the new product by choosing the short-run profit-maximizing price. If entry can be discouraged by setting a limit price, the skimming price is the limit price. Second, if demand for the product is expected to be short-lived, then short-run profit maximizing will maximize expected present value. Fad items such as the "pet rock" or "I survived Hugo" T-shirts have temporary demand until the fad disappears. Emergencies may create a temporary demand for other items like bottled water and blankets after an earthquake or flood.

Another case of price skimming occurs when the firm expects consumers to relate price to product quality. Then the price may be higher or lower than the short-run profit-maximizing price, but price is high relative to average variable cost. The markup will be high because the firm believes the higher price will be perceived as a signal of a better-quality product. Quantity demanded will be higher as the demand shifts in response to the signal.

Penetration pricing occurs when price is set relatively low with the intent of establishing a broad market base. The idea is to ensure a larger market in subsequent

Doonesbury

BY GARRY TRUDEAU

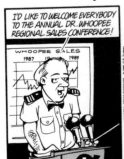

DOONESBURY COPYRIGHT 1989 G. B. Trudeau. Reprinted with permission of Universal Press Syndicate. All rights reserved.

periods. A low price may encourage consumers to try the new good as they search for products with the most desirable attributes. Penetration pricing is also used when entry of rivals is relatively easy. By establishing a broad market base the firm may expect to retain a greater market share after other firms enter the market. The relatively low penetration price may be a limit price that discourages entry by all but the most efficient firms. Successful penetration pricing may also yield scale economies due to large sales volume. Penetration pricing is usually consistent with long-run profit maximizing.

15.3 Price and Quality

The firm frequently has a choice about the quality embodied in its product. The choice may cover materials, design, and workmanship. A difference in quality differentiates the product from others. Typically, however, higher quality costs more. Thus the firm must choose the price–quality combination that is optimal.

Figure 15.4 illustrates the trade-offs between price and quality. The demand for the lower-quality product Q_1 is labeled D_1. If Q_1 is produced, the profit-maximizing firm will price this good at p_1^* to generate a profit of π_1^*. Alternatively, the firm could produce a higher-quality product Q_2 that has demand D_2. The demand for the higher-quality product is greater than for the lower-quality product, but the costs of production are greater, too. If Q_2 is produced, the profit-maximizing firm would set price at p_2^* to generate a profit of π_2^*. Now, by comparing the maximum profits from each good the firm can decide on the price–quality mix.

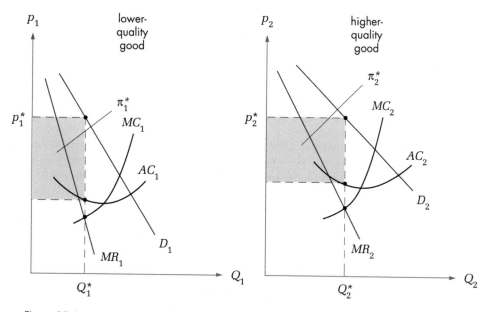

Figure 15.4 **Price and quality:** The firm should choose the price–quality combination that maximizes profit. Here the demand for Q_2 and the costs of producing Q_2 are greater than for Q_1. The profit π_2^* is greater than π_1^*, and so the firm should produce and sell Q_2^* units at price p_2^*.

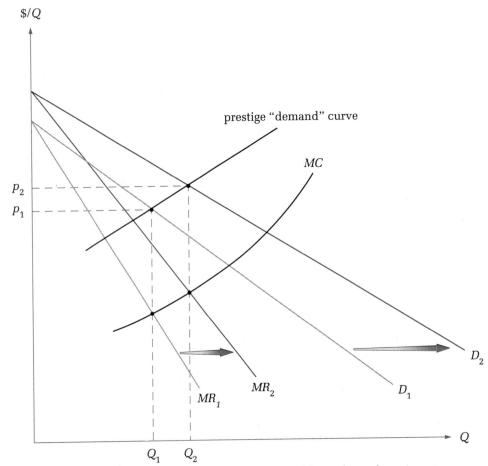

Figure 15.5 **Price as a quality signal:** Price is used as a signal for quality, and so price enters consumers' utility functions. Demand shifts to the right as preference changes because of the price increase, and so the firm should choose price p_2 rather than p_1.

Consumers may sometimes use price as a signal for the degree of quality embodied in a product—"You get what you pay for." This effect can be modeled by allowing price to enter directly into the consumer's utility function.[1] As the price varies, indifference

---

1. See, for instance, Peter J. Kalman, "Theory of Consumer Behavior When Prices Enter the Utility Function," *Econometrica*, 36 (July-October 1968), pp. 497–510, and Robert A. Pollack, "Price Dependent Preferences," *American Economic Review*, 67(2) (March 1977), pp. 64–75, for analyses of demand when prices enter into the utility function. Quality has also been treated as a characteristic in an activity-analysis model in Hayne E. Leland, "Quality Choice and Competition," *American Economic Review*, 67(2) (March 1977), pp. 127–137. Leland shows that Pareto optimality is achieved under competition, in that firms choose socially optimal levels of quality.

curves change and demand shifts. If demand increases as price increases, at least over some range of price, the firm needs to identify the optimal demand curve as a function of price. Figure 15.5 shows an increase in demand from D_1 to D_2 as price increases. Each demand curve reflects the quantity demanded as a function of price alone, and so separate demand curves are drawn for a specified set of consumer preferences. But if price is used as a signal for quality, then preferences change as price changes because the perceived attributes of the product change. Marketing analysts refer to the resulting price–quantity relationship when changes in quality are signaled by price as a "prestige demand curve." This special "demand" curve may be positively sloped because preferences change with changes in price.

15.4 Pricing and Advertising

When we derive a market demand curve, price is varied and all other things are held constant. Suppose instead that we vary advertising expenditures alone while holding price and all other things constant. Presumably, advertising influences demand by informing the consumer about the product and its availability, but advertising can also change consumers' preferences. When expressed as a function of advertising alone, demand will be equal to some constant, representing the effect of price and all other things being held constant, plus some function of advertising expenditures. Because advertising expenditures may affect demand more at initial levels and less and less at higher levels, quantity demanded as a function of advertising might be cubic,

$$Q = \alpha + \beta_1 A + \beta_2 A^2 + \beta_3 A^3$$

where A represents advertising expenditure. The β_1 and β_2 coefficients are expected to be positive and β_3 is expected to be negative. This cubic function is sigmoid in shape, like that shown in Figure 15.6. With historical experience, the firm or industry could estimate such a function by regression techniques.

As shown in Figure 15.6, successive increases in advertising expenditures are expected to shift demand to the right, but the successive shifts become smaller as advertising increases by equal increments. As advertising increases, total revenue increases also. The marginal revenue from advertising is expected to be positive but diminishing. At the same time, however, marginal costs of advertising are positive and increasing. Moreover, the firm will be experiencing increasing marginal production costs as output expands.

In the current period, advertising must be regarded as a fixed cost because expenditures are made in a previous period and are independent of current output and sales. Thus average advertising cost will graph as a rectangular hyperbola against output, and the marginal cost of advertising is zero in the current period. Figure 15.7 shows how the average advertising cost is determined by the profit-maximizing price-quantity decision. The firm sets price at p_1 to sell Q_1 units, where $MR = MC$, and average advertising cost is AAC_1.

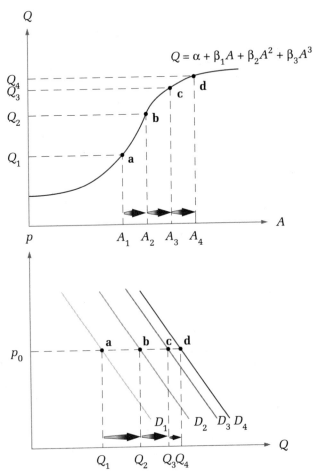

Figure 15.6 **Advertising and demand:** Quantity demanded as a function of advertising expenditures will eventually reflect diminishing returns to advertising. The shifts in demand become smaller and smaller for equal increases in advertising.

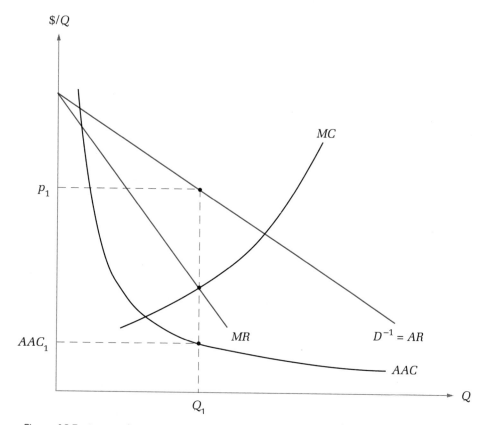

Figure 15.7 **Average advertising cost:** In the current period, previous advertising gives rise to the inverse demand curve *AR*. Average advertising cost graphs as a rectangular hyperbola *AAC*. The firm sets price at p_1 to sell Q_1 units, where marginal revenue equals marginal cost. At Q_1, the average advertising expenditure equals AAC_1.

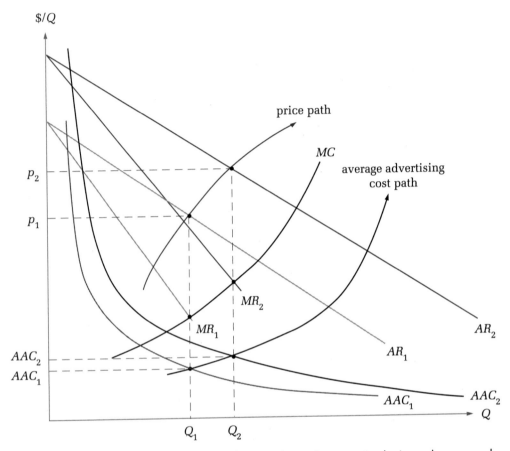

Figure 15.8 **Optimal paths and advertising:** Each demand curve has an optimal price and a measured level of advertising cost. As total advertising cost varies, demand shifts and an optimal path for price and a path for measured average advertising cost can be identified. The next step is to determine the optimal level of advertising.

A different level of advertising will cause a shift in the demand curve.[2] Figure 15.8 illustrates two average advertising cost curves and their corresponding demand and marginal revenue curves. For demand AR_1, the optimal price is p_1 and the measured average advertising cost is AAC_1. For demand AR_2, the optimal price is p_2 and the average advertising cost is AAC_2. Other levels of advertising will bring other optimal prices and measured average advertising costs. The locus of optimal prices, the price path, and the measured average advertising cost path can be plotted as a function of output. The shapes of the paths are determined by the diminishing returns to advertising. But what are the optimal levels of price, output, and advertising?

2. See N. S. Buchanan, "Advertising Expenditure: A Suggested Treatment," *Journal of Political Economy* (August 1942), pp. 537–557.

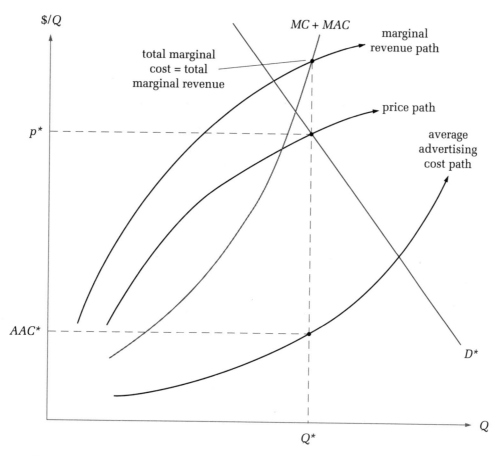

Figure 15.9 **Optimal price, demand, and advertising:** The firm adds marginal advertising cost (MAC) to marginal production cost (MC) to obtain MC + MAC. The optimal level of output Q* is identified where the marginal revenue path crosses the sum of MC and MAC. The optimal price p* occurs along the optimal price path at Q*. This point identifies the optimal level of advertising and the demand curve D*.

The average advertising cost path measures the average cost of advertising as output changes in response to changes in total advertising and price. Like any other rising average cost curve, the ACC curve has a corresponding marginal cost curve. That marginal advertising cost, denoted MAC, must be added to marginal production cost at every level of output. Total marginal cost from production and advertising is labeled $MC + MAC$ in Figure 15.9. Similarly, the price path is an average revenue path as demand shifts in response to advertising and the firm chooses the optimal price. Thus a marginal revenue path corresponds to the price path. The profit-maximizing level of output occurs where the marginal price path crosses the curve of the sum of the marginal costs. To sell output Q^*, the firm sets advertising expenditures so that AAC^* is obtained, generating optimal demand D^*. The optimal price p^* is identified where D^* cuts the price path at Q^*.

ECONOMIC SCENE: *"Where's the Beef?"*

Wendy's hamburger restaurants engaged in a highly successful advertising campaign in 1984.* Prior to the campaign, the market shares were 41.5 percent for McDonald's, 16.2 percent for Burger King, and 9.4 percent for Wendy's. Many other firms had the remainder of the market. By asking, "Where's the Beef?" Wendy's increased its market share to about 12 percent, generating an extra $494 million over Wendy's 1983 sales of $1.9 billion. Wendy's spent $73.5 million on advertising in 1984. Operating costs increased as well, but not as fast as revenues. McDonald's spent more than three times as much, and Burger King nearly twice as much. As a consequence, most of Wendy's gain in market share came from the rest of the market.

* See "The Fast-Food War: Big Mac under Attack," *Business Week* (January 30, 1984), pp. 44–46 and *The Wall Street Journal*, March 7, 1985, p. 35.

In summary, advertising is increased until its extra cost is just covered by the extra revenue generated by the increased demand from advertising. The model emphasizes that demand, and hence price, depends on advertising. The main drawback of the model, besides the problem of knowing demand as a function of advertising, is that rivals' reactions have been ignored. It is entirely feasible, in fact probable, that rivals will react in kind. Therefore the firm should also consider reactions by its rivals, particularly in oligopoly markets.

15.5 Peak-Load Pricing

Many businesses face demands that fluctuate with the seasons or the time of day. The demand for electricity reaches two peaks, one in late morning and the other in early evening, and is lowest after midnight. In many regions the demand for electricity is also seasonal because of air conditioning in summer. For natural gas, however, demand is greater during the cold winter days and long winter nights. Other products too have seasonal demands—some that might not be so obvious. The demand for office furniture is seasonal because it follows—with a lag—a seasonal supply of office buildings.

In all these cases demand fluctuates predictably as time passes. Thus, average and marginal revenues also fluctuate predictably. Moreover, cost differences occur between periods. Increases in production during peak demand periods lead to increases in marginal costs. Not only does the firm experience diminishing productivity, factor prices too may be bid up. An office-furniture manufacturer may have to pay overtime to meet its demand during the peak season.

Peak-load pricing is the practice of charging higher prices during peak demand periods. Telephone companies usually charge less for long-distance calls made in the evening. Vacation resorts frequently charge less during off-season periods.

Besides the shifting demand curve, another feature of peak-load pricing is a relatively constant marginal cost until "capacity" is reached. The firm operates at a scale that permits it to meet most fluctuations in demand without experiencing rapidly increasing

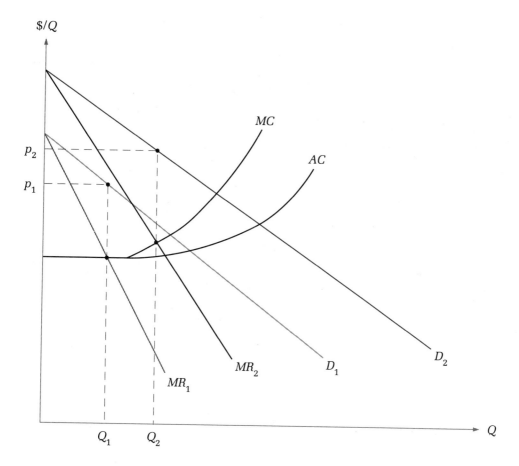

Figure 15.10 **Peak-load pricing:** Demand shifts from D_1 to D_2 during the peak demand period. The increase in price from p_1 to p_2 is attributed partly to the increase in demand and partly to the increase in marginal cost.

marginal cost. Beyond some level of output, however, marginal cost increases sharply. Figure 15.10 illustrates peak-load pricing. Demand shifts from D_1 to D_2 during peak demand. As demand shifts, the firm experiences an increase in its marginal cost. The optimal price increases from p_1 to p_2. The increase in price is caused partly by the increase in demand and partly by higher marginal cost.

AN APPLICATION: *Pricing Electricity*

Electric-utility companies favor peak-load pricing for the reason illustrated in Figure 15.11. The utility faces an off-peak demand of D_1 and a peak demand of D_2. If the regulators set price at p_1, where D_1 crosses the AC curve, the utility breaks even in the off-peak periods but suffers a loss in peak demand periods, when quantity demanded increases to Q_3. At Q_3, the average cost is greater than the price, p_1. The regulators could set a peak-demand price where AC crosses the D_2 curve to eliminate the loss. The utility prefers a peak-demand price of p_2, however, where the MC curve crosses the demand curve D_2 (marginal cost pricing) because then the utility enjoys a profit.

The increase in the average cost of providing electricity during peak-demand periods is not unrealistic. Many electric-power companies operate nuclear power plants or other technologically efficient methods until demand exceeds the capacity of such plants. The utility then switches to plants using older technologies and more costly production methods. Thus average cost can increase from 1¢ per kilowatt hour to as high as 12¢. As demand peaks, average cost goes up and returns go down.

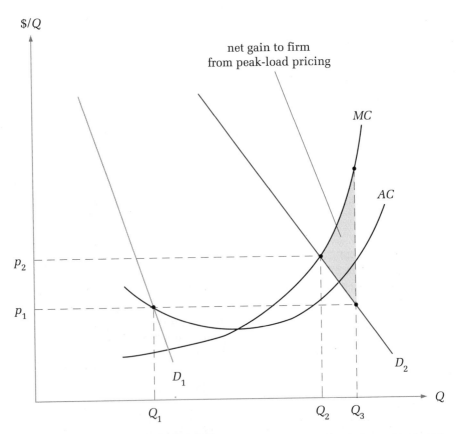

Figure 15.11 **Gains from peak-load pricing:** Off-peak demand is D_1 and peak demand is D_2. If the regulators set price at p_1, the firm breaks even in the off-peak period and suffers a loss in the peak period, when quantity demanded increases to Q_3. If the regulators set the price at p_2, where D_2 crosses the MC curve, a net gain accrues to the firm.

15.6 Capturing Consumer Surplus by Price Discrimination

Price discrimination is the act of charging different prices for an identical good produced under unchanging cost conditions. Price differences that are related to differences in the cost of supplying the product are *not* cases of price discrimination. Price discrimination is possible only when the seller has some monopoly power. Moreover, the seller must be able to prevent resale or else arbitrage will eliminate any ability to discriminate. Here are the three traditional classes of price discrimination.

Perfect price discrimination occurs when the monopolist sells each unit for the maximum price each consumer is willing to pay.

> **Perfect price discrimination:** *The price of each unit sold to each customer is set equal to each customer's marginal value of each unit.*

Perfect price discrimination is also called **first-degree price discrimination.** Without price discrimination, the ordinary monopolist views the inverse demand curve as its average revenue curve and sets price to sell the quantity at which $MR = MC$. This procedure is shown in Figure 15.12. At price p_m, the ordinary monopolist captures some of the consumer surplus in an amount greater than its loss in producer surplus at Q_m, but society has a deadweight loss. In contrast, the perfectly discriminating monopolist sells each successive unit for a different price along the market demand curve. The discriminating monopolist will continue to sell more and more as long as the price is greater than marginal cost, so that the last unit is sold at price p_d, where demand crosses the MC curve. By selling Q_d units at different prices, the perfect price discriminator is able to capture all the consumer surplus and adds to producer surplus as well. The deadweight loss has been eliminated, but all the social gains from producing where MC equals price have been captured by the monopolist.

Perfect price discrimination is nearly impossible in practice because the monopolist must be able to prevent resale. That tactic is impractical when dealing with many consumers. Any monopolist will be tempted to price discriminate, however, because that will increase profit. In contrast, the competitive firm is not tempted to price discriminate because it can sell all it can at the going market price and cannot charge more without losing all its customers.

A more usual form of price discrimination occurs when the monopolist charges one price for one block of goods and another price for another block. **Block pricing** occurs when the same customer is charged different prices for identical items.

> **Block pricing:** *The same customer pays a different price for different quantities of an identical good.*

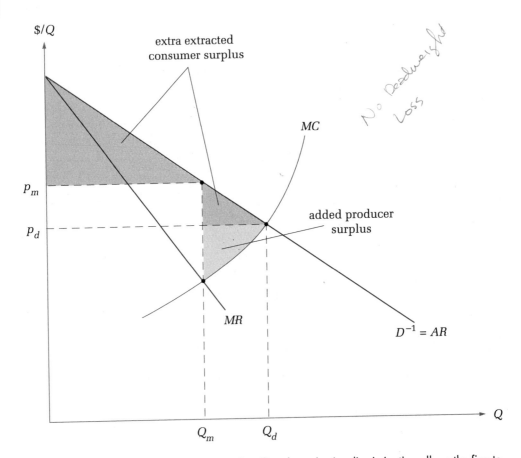

Figure 15.12 **Perfect price discrimination:** Perfect (first-degree) price discrimination allows the firm to extract all the consumer surplus. Without price discrimination, the monopolist charges p_m for Q_m units where $MR = MC$. With perfect price discrimination, the monopolist sells each unit for the maximum price each consumer is willing to pay, selling the last unit, Q_d, at price p_d. The monopolist captures all the consumer surplus and adds to producer surplus, and the deadweight loss of simple monopoly pricing has been eliminated.

Block pricing is also called **second-degree price discrimination.** This form of price discrimination is illustrated by Figure 15.13. Constant costs are assumed, for simplicity. The ordinary monopolist sets price at p_m and sells Q_m units. If, however, this monopolist can sell an extra ΔQ units by lowering price to p_d *and prevent resale,* then profits can be increased as long as p_d is greater than marginal cost.

Second-degree price discrimination is fairly common in pricing products supplied by public utilities. Natural-gas or electric-power distributors may set a higher price for consumption up to a specific amount and a lower price for all that is used over that amount. Clearly, revenue will be greater under block pricing unless the second block price

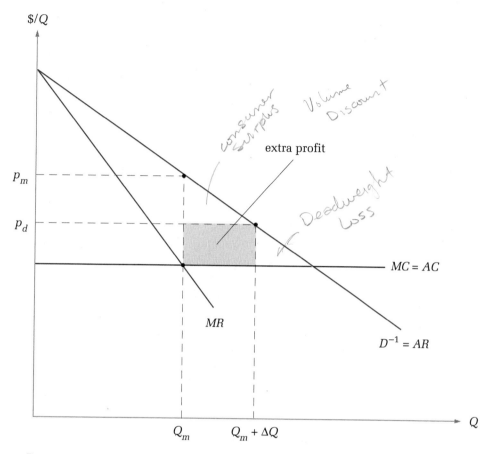

Figure 15.13 **Block price discrimination:** Block (second-degree) price discrimination occurs when the monopolist can sell an extra ΔQ units to any customer at a lower price p_d while preventing resale. Block pricing may often be feasible when perfect price discrimination is impractical.

is too high. The appearance of block pricing is sometimes an illusion, however. The difference in price charged for different levels of consumption may be caused by differences in costs. Gas and electric utilities incur transactions costs and setup costs for all customers whose reservation price exceeds the product price. Such lumpy, "quasi-fixed" costs vary as customers enter the market, but those costs remain fixed thereafter.

The commonest form of price discrimination occurs when a seller faces different groups of buyers having different demand curves. If these curves have different elasticities at any given price, it pays the firm to price discriminate, using **group price discrimination:**

> **Group price discrimination:** *Different prices are charged to different groups having different price elasticities of demand.*

Group price discrimination is also called **third-degree price discrimination.** In general, the firm should choose quantities so that marginal revenue is the same in all market groups.

Suppose a firm faces two markets. We are given the demand curve in market 1 as

$$X_1 = 60 - 4p$$

This expression yields an average revenue curve

$$AR_1 = 15 - 0.25X_1$$

The demand curve in market 2 is

$$X_2 = 100 - 10p$$

This curve yields an average revenue curve

$$AR_2 = 10 - 0.10X_2$$

These two average revenue curves are illustrated in Figure 15.14 along with their corresponding MR curves. Whenever average revenue is a straight line of the form $AR = a - bX$, marginal revenue is given by $MR = a - 2bX$. Therefore, the marginal revenue curves for the two groups are

$$MR_1 = 15 - 0.50X_1$$
$$MR_2 = 10 - 0.20X_2$$

Total market demand is the horizontal summation of the group demand curves, $Q = D(p) = X_1(p) + X_2(p)$, and so market demand is

$$Q = 160 - 14p$$

Thus the average revenue curve for the firm that cannot price discriminate is

$$AR = 11.429 - 0.0714Q$$

The total marginal revenue curve is

$$MR = 11.429 - 0.1428Q$$

To maximize profit, the nondiscriminating monopolist will set output and price so that $MR = MC$. To keep things simple, let's assume constant marginal cost of $MC = 2$. When $MR = MC$, the profit-maximizing output is $Q^* = 66$ and the price to both markets would be $6.71.

If the firm can prevent resale between the two markets, though, the firm can increase profits by price discrimination. Now the firm needs to set output in each market so that $MR_1 = MR_2 = MC$. But at the single price of $6.71, MR_2 is greater than MR_1. Profits can thus be increased by selling more to group 2 and less to group 1. Because $MC = 2$, setting MC equal to MR_1 results in

$$2 = 15 - 0.50X_1$$

The optimal quantity of X_1 is $X_1^* = 26$. Thus the group 1 price should be

$$p_1^* = 15 - 0.25X_1^* = \$8.25$$

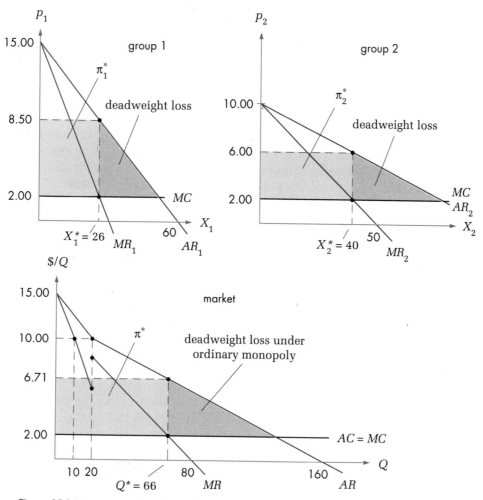

Figure 15.14 **Group price discrimination:** To maximize total profit using group (third-degree) price discrimination, this firm should set the price in each market so that marginal revenue equals marginal cost in each market. Price will be lower in the market having the more elastic demand curve.

Likewise, setting $MC = 2$ equal to MR_2 results in

$$2 = 10 - 0.20X_2$$

The optimal quantity of X_2 is $X_2^* = 40$. Thus the group 2 price should be

$$p_2^* = 10 - 0.10X_2^* = \$6.00$$

Total output will be $X_1^* + X_2^* = Q^* = 66$. Notice that price is *lower* in the market that has the *more* elastic demand.

As you can see in Figure 15.14, the total profit under group price discrimination is larger than under ordinary monopoly pricing. Without the ability to price discriminate, the ordinary monopolist would set price at $p = \$6.71$ in both markets. The deadweight loss would be equal to the area of the welfare triangle under the total market demand curve. In contrast, the ability to set prices differently for each group results in deadweight losses in each separate market, and the sum of those welfare losses is greater than the loss under ordinary monopoly pricing. An extra social cost is caused by group price discrimination. The reason for this extra welfare loss is pursued further in the next section.

We can now summarize the conditions necessary to make price discrimination possible. First, the seller must have some monopoly power. Second, resale of the good must not be possible. Finally, for group price discrimination, groups must be identifiable, with different demand elasticities between them. Examples of price discrimination abound. Restaurants offer senior-citizen discounts on meals. Amusement parks offer lower prices to children. Grocery stores redeem discount coupons rather than offer a lower price to all shoppers. Airlines charge less to travelers who make their reservations far in advance of their trips, and they charge less for standby travelers, too. Physicians charge low-income patients less. Goods for export may be sold for a lower price than the domestic price—a practice called dumping. An attempt to thwart dumping in America of Japanese small-business phone systems was made in November of 1989 by the U.S. International Trade Commission.[3] Extra duties—more than 100 percent—will be imposed on importers found dumping such products in the United States.

Some cases of price differences that may appear to be price discrimination are not. Some apparent price discrimination is illusory. Lower rates for off-peak long-distance telephone calls reflect lower opportunity costs for the seller. Quantity discounts on large purchases typically reflect lower transactions costs on such purchases. Lower prices for cash purchases on gasoline similarly reflect a lower transactions cost for the purchase. Price discrimination is not present when the price difference reflects differences in the cost of supplying the good.

Reprinted by permission of UFS, Inc.

---

3. *Los Angeles Times*, November 21, 1989.

15.7 Group Pricing, Welfare, and Profit

A simple geometric technique can be used to measure the welfare effects of third-degree price discrimination under linear demand.[4] Figure 15.15 illustrates the profit-maximizing solution for a monopolist who faces two independent linear demands. The demand and marginal revenue curves for group 1 are drawn with respect to the left-hand

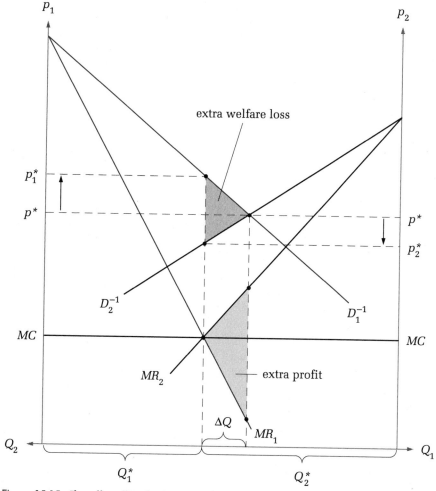

Figure 15.15 **The welfare effect of group price discrimination:** At the simple monopoly price p^*, MR_2 is greater than MR_1. But if the firm can price discriminate, profit will be maximized where $MR_1 = MR_2 = MC$. The group 1 price will be p_1^* and the group 2 price will be p_2^*. The profit gain equals the area between the two MR curves over the range ΔQ. The reduction in consumer surplus equals the area between the demand curves over range ΔQ. This change in consumer surplus comes from transferring ΔQ units from group 1 to group 2 even though group 1 values the good more than group 2.

4. See Stephan Layson, "Third-degree Price Discrimination, Welfare and Profits: A Geometrical Analysis," *American Economic Review*, 78(5) (December 1988), pp. 1131–1132.

ECONOMIC SCENE: *Who Wins with Price Matching?*

Big retailers increasingly are promising to match the lowest advertised price a shopper can find. The tactic was first used in the consumer-electronics, auto-supply, and general discount-store businesses, but it has spread. Late in 1988, Montgomery Ward expanded its price-matching policy from electronics and auto-supply departments to all items. In March 1989, Sears, Roebuck instituted a similar pledge. "We think it would be uncompetitive not to have a price-matching policy when many of our rivals do," said the vice president of marketing at Sears. (*The Wall Street Journal,* March 16, 1989)

Price-matching policies typically require shoppers to produce a competitor's ad showing a lower price for an identical item at the time of purchase or within 30 days of purchase. But retail-industry executives and consultants concede that few shoppers bother to collect on price guarantees. Ivan Png, a pricing specialist at the Graduate School of Management at the University of California at Los Angeles, said price matching gives merchants "a way to help keep prices a little higher for the loyal customers while giving a lower price" to new customers. "It's a way to make more money," he added. (*The Wall Street Journal,* March 16, 1989) Could price matching be a subtle way to price discriminate?

origin, and the demand and marginal revenue curves for group 2 are drawn with respect to the right-hand origin. The width of Figure 15.15 represents the total profit-maximizing level of output at the given marginal cost. The simple monopoly price would be p^* without group discrimination. As we saw in section 15.7 on group price discrimination and Figure 15.14, price p^* is established where MC equals aggregate MR. The aggregate MR curve, which is the horizontal sum of MR_1 and MR_2, crosses the MC curve at a level of output where AR_1 crosses AR_2.

At price p^*, $MR_2 > MR_1$, and so the price-discriminating monopolist will increase sales to group 2 and decrease sales to group 1. Profits are maximized where $MR_1 = MR_2 = MC$. Thus the price to group 1 will be p_1^*, and the price to group 2 will be p_2^*. The profit gain because of price discrimination is the additional revenue from increased sales to group 2 minus the revenue lost from reduced sales to group 1. The area of the triangle between the two marginal revenue curves is the profit gain from price discrimination. The reduction in consumer surplus due to discrimination is equal to the area of the triangle between the two demand curves. This change in welfare comes from transferring ΔQ units from group 1 to group 2 even though group 1 values the good more than group 2.

Notice that the heights of the two triangles are both ΔQ. But the base of the profit triangle is twice the base of the welfare-loss triangle because the MR curves are twice as steep as their demand curves. Thus the area of the profit triangle is twice the area of the loss triangle. The change in welfare is

$$\Delta W = \frac{-\Delta\pi}{2} = \frac{-(p_1^* - p_2^*)\Delta Q}{2}$$

The range ΔQ can be determined from the demand curves. Thus, when the demand curves are approximately linear over range ΔQ, this formula can be used to approximate the decrease in consumer surplus ascribable to group price discrimination alone.

15.8 Bundling and Tied Sales

Many firms bundle products together and set one price for the bundle. When the goods cannot be purchased separately, these are called **tied sales. Mixed bundling** occurs when the products can be purchased separately as well as in the package. Bundling is quite common. Computers and computer software are bundled—and after all, one will not work without the other. Season tickets are offered for theatrical events. Vacation package deals are offered that include transportation, lodging, and entertainment. The two main reasons for using tied sales are to reduce cost and to price discriminate.

Cost saving from bundling usually occurs in the marketing and distribution of the bundle. Six-packs are priced lower than six separate bottles or cans because a six-pack has to be handled only once compared to six times for the six cans. Computer software and hardware may be bundled to save marketing and advertising expenses as well as to reduce the consumer's search costs.

One of the more interesting reasons for bundling, however, is to price discriminate. A seller will be able to extract more of the consumer surplus by offering the bundle at a package price that is less than the expenditure on the same number of units when sold separately. Consider a good that sells for $3 per unit or bundled at two for $5. Some consumers will be willing to buy the package at $5 even though they would be willing to buy only one unit at $3. Why? Because their marginal value for the second unit is less than $3 but greater than $2. Total buyer expenditure is greater because more is bought at the bundled price than at the separate price. Why, for instance, does it cost $1.20 for an 8-oz. soft drink at a movie theater and $1.30 for the 12-oz. size? The vendor must believe that the marginal value of the extra 4 ounces to the average consumer is about 10¢ and the marginal cost of providing the extra four ounces is less than 10¢.

15.9 The Two-Part Tariff

Profit is largest under perfect price discrimination because the monopolist can extract all the buyers' surplus. But perfect price discrimination usually is prohibitively difficult to implement and so the monopolist looks for other alternatives, such as block pricing, group pricing, and bundling. Another pricing scheme, however, can be used to extract all the consumer surplus without engaging in perfect price discrimination.

A two-part pricing scheme called the **two-part tariff** occurs when a firm charges an initial fee in exchange for the right to purchase the good. The first part of the price is an "entry" fee. The second part is the regular price.

> **Two-part tariff:** *A two-part pricing scheme in which an initial "entry" fee must be paid in order to purchase the good.*

The firm that uses the two-part tariff must decide how much to charge for the entry fee and how much to charge per unit of the good. Consider the monopoly firm illustrated by Figure 15.16. In panel A, with no price discrimination, the firm sets price at p_m, so that $MR = MC$. If the firm can identify the consumer's surplus for each consumer at that price, it can extract each consumer's surplus by charging each consumer a tariff equal to

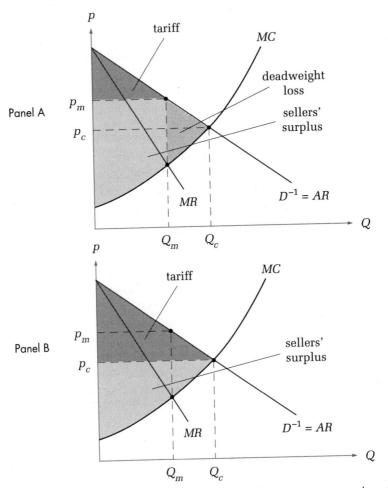

Figure 15.16 **Pricing with a two-part tariff: Panel A** If the monopolist sets price at p_m, where MR = MC, the firm can increase profit by charging a tariff equal to the buyers' surplus at price p_m. **Panel B** If the monopolist sets price at p_c, where AR = AC, the firm can charge a tariff equal to the buyers' surplus at price p_c. Although the sellers' surplus is less at p_c than at p_m, the extracted buyers' surplus is greater at p_c than at p_m. The net gain is equal to the deadweight loss that would occur at price p_m.

that consumer's surplus. The previous deadweight loss remains.

But the monopolist can increase profit even more under two-part pricing. As shown in panel B of Figure 15.16, if price is set at p_c, where $AR = MC$, and entry fees are set so that they yield the tariff equal to the total buyers' surplus at price p_c, the monopolist can extract all the social gains, including the old deadweight loss. With a perfect two-part tariff, all the social gains that arise from marginal cost pricing are transferred to the monopolist. This monopolist will set price at the competitive price p_c but will set entry fees for each consumer to extract each consumer's surplus.

ECONOMIC SCENE: *Mickey-Mouse Pricing?*

Disneyland has always used two-part tariff pricing since it opened in the mid-1950s. In the beginning, Disneyland charged a small fee for entry to the park and customers had to buy ride tickets or a book of ride tickets to get on the rides. The book had tickets for rides ranging from the cheaper to the more costly. The more costly tickets for the more popular rides were called "E tickets." The advantage to customers was that they didn't have to wait in separate lines to buy tickets for each ride. In June 1982, Disneyland implemented the single-ticket "passport" program and set general-admission prices at $12 for adults and $9 for children. In December 1989, Disneyland raised prices for the tenth time, setting ticket prices at $25.50 for adults and $20.50 for children. All the other major theme parks in Southern California—Knott's Berry Farm, Magic Mountain, Sea World, and Universal Studios—have single-entry prices also. Why? How should Disneyland decide what combination of entry fee and per-ride ticket to charge?

Let's assume that the cost of the number of rides is the same regardless of the number of riders. That is, the marginal cost of operating a ride is zero. Although this assumption is not completely realistic, the marginal cost for a last rider surely is very low. Under the assumption of zero marginal cost, if Disneyland were to allow free entry into the park and charge only a fee per ride, the profit-maximizing price would be where $MR = MC = 0$.* But Disneyland can also charge a fee for entering the theme park.

Panel A of Figure 15.17 illustrates how Disneyland can increase its profit by charging an entry fee. If the entry fee is set equal to the consumer surplus at the ride price of p_1 where $MR = MC$, profit will be increased by the amount of the consumer surplus. But this price will not maximize profit because fewer people will enter the park than would if the price were lower.

Panel B of Figure 15.17 shows how total revenue and profit are maximized when the ride price $p = 0$. With free rides, the quantity demanded for each ride will be greatest. Thus when marginal cost is zero, Disneyland can maximize profit by setting the entry fee equal to the area under this demand curve.

Of course, this illustration assumes that marginal cost is zero. Although that assumption may be reasonable for one ride, it is not likely to be true for the entire park. Disneyland has always taken pride in keeping the park clean—and that goal is likely to be increasingly costly as the park becomes more crowded. Not only that, but rides do not all have the same demands, and customers do not all have identical demands. Therefore the optimal entry fees to charge customers are not all the same. A high entry fee will discourage some customers. If, then, the customers who want to go on a lot of rides are also the ones willing to pay a higher entry fee, then a higher ride fee would be an indirect way of charging a higher total price. But that does not seem to happen. Disneyland discovered that, with low entry fees, many people would come to the park but would not all buy ride tickets. In fact, many of these customers did not fit the Disney "family" image. Teenagers and military personnel used the park as a hangout, discouraging families from coming to the park. Thus, by having a higher entry fee with "free" rides, Disney was able to discourage attendance by persons not

---

* Knott's Berry Farm, near Disneyland, actually pursued this pricing policy until it evolved into a theme park.

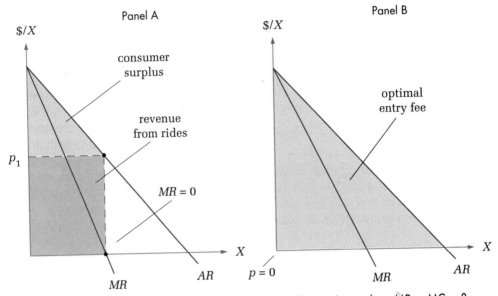

Figure 15.17   **Pricing rides at Disneyland: Panel A** When the ride price is p_1, where $MR = MC = 0$, profit equals the entry fee plus the revenue from the ride. **Panel B** When $MC = 0$, greater profit is made by setting the ride price to zero and setting the entry fee equal to the consumer surplus.

as interested in the rides and encourage attendance by those who wanted access to rides in an environment compatible with the Disney family theme.

Occasional price increases should come as no surprise because theme parks have increased admission prices 6 to 7 percent each year. In fact, Disneyland increased ticket prices every six to nine months after it introduced single-ticket pricing. Disneyland's attendance over recent years, however, has remained relatively constant at 13 million per year.

In January 1991, Disneyland also began to engage in group price discrimination. For the first time in its 35-year history, it cut its price at the admissions gate—but only to Southern California residents. Under the new program, any adult could buy up to five admissions tickets at $20 each (one price for children and adults), after presenting a driver's license or other identification that showed residency in zipcodes 90000 through 93599. Disney management must have believed that demand was less elastic for tourists than for local residents. Although temporary, the price cut for locals might help Disney officials determine how elastic local demand was to changes in price.

If all consumers have identical demand curves, implementing perfect two-part pricing is fairly easy. Consider the monopolist shown in Figure 15.18. The firm's average revenue curve coincides with the sum of the buyers' demand curves, $AR^{-1} = \Sigma d_j$. For customer j, the optimal entry fee is equal to that buyer's consumer surplus at price p_c. If T is the desired total tariff, then the tariff for customer j is $t_j = T/n$, where n is the total number

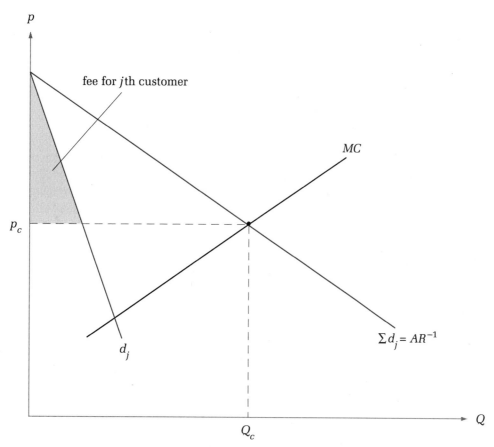

Figure 15.18 The entry fee for each customer: The entry fee for each customer that allows the monopolist to extract all the consumer surplus will be equal to each buyer's surplus. The optimal fee will be the same for all buyers only if all have identical demand curves.

of consumers. The optimal fee to each buyer will be the same if they have identical demand curves. The total tariff will be $T = \Sigma t_j$, but the t_j will be harder to find when consumers have different demands.

If groups of consumers have similar demands, then they can be charged the same fee: member restaurants offer discount prices to customers who pay a fee to join the Diner's Club. But if many consumers have diverse demands there may be no practical way to determine the optimal fees for every one. Two-part pricing can still be used, however, to increase profit in lieu of overt price discrimination. In the days of computer "punched cards," IBM required users of its computers to buy all their cards from IBM. This pricing strategy enabled IBM to charge different prices to different customers. Customers who used more cards paid more even though the price of the basic computer was the same to all customers. Thus IBM could effectively price discriminate by charging a low entry fee (the price for the computer), and then charging a price above marginal cost for the cards.

15.10 Transfer Pricing

When one division of a firm sells an intermediate product to another division of the same firm, **transfer pricing** occurs. Suppose division 1 makes an intermediate good that is used by division 2. Division 2 makes a final good. The problem is to determine optimal levels of production and prices for the goods. The price of the intermediate good charged by division 1 and paid by division 2 is called the *transfer price*. The problem is to set the transfer price to maximize the profit of the entire firm. We will look at three cases. The first occurs when no external market exists for the intermediate good. The second case occurs when there is a purely competitive external market. The third case occurs when an imperfectly competitive market appears for the intermediate good. To keep things simple, we assume that one unit of the intermediate good is always required to produce one unit of the final good, and so we can use Q to measure the quantity of either good.

Figure 15.19 illustrates the case with *no external market*. For the two operating divisions, the marginal costs are MC_1 and MC_2. Total marginal cost is the sum of the

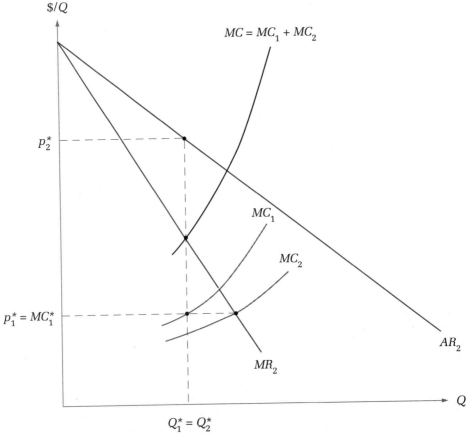

Figure 15.19 **Transfer pricing with no external market:** Division 1 produces the intermediate good, which is transferred to division 2. The firm sets price of the final good at p_2^*, where $MR_2 = MC$. The transfer price is set at $p_1^* = MC_1^*(Q_1^*)$.

marginal costs from each division, $MC = MC_1 + MC_2$. The inverse demand curve for the final good is the average revenue curve, AR_2. The profit-maximizing price for the final good is p_2^*, where MR_2 equals total marginal cost. The optimal levels of output are $Q_1^* = Q_2^*$. The transfer price for the intermediate good is set at p_1^*, so that the transfer price equals the marginal cost of the intermediate good. Thus division 1, which produces the intermediate good, acts like a price-taking firm. Total profit to the firm is maximized when marginal revenue from the final good is equal to the total marginal costs of production and when the transfer price is equal to the marginal cost of the intermediate good. The firm has identified the profit-maximizing levels of output for both the intermediate good and the final good.

Figure 15.20 illustrates a *perfectly competitive external market* for the intermediate

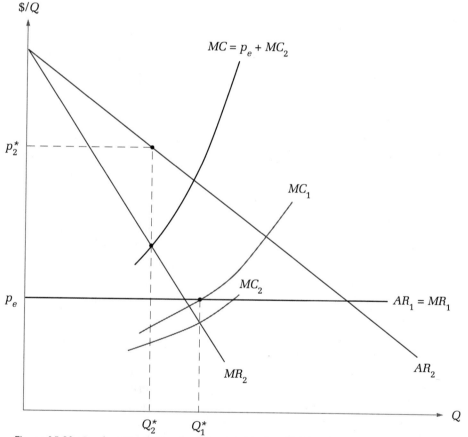

Figure 15.20 **Transfer pricing with a competitive external market:** Division 1 reacts to the market price p_e, which determines $AR_1 = MR_1$. The profit-maximizing level of output of the intermediate good is Q_1^*, where $p_e = MC_1$. Total marginal cost is $MC = p_e + MC_2$, and the firm sets the final good's price at p_2^* and produces Q_2^* units. In this case, because the quantity of the intermediate good Q_1 is greater than the amount used in producing Q_2, the firm sells $Q_1^* - Q_2^*$ units of Q_1 in the external market.

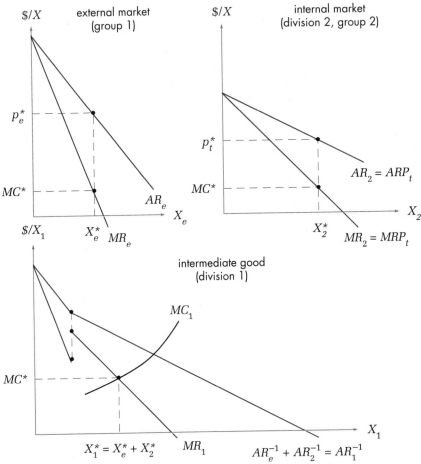

Figure 15.21   **Transfer pricing with monopoly power:** Demand for the intermediate good X_1 produced by division 1 is the sum of the external demand and the internal demand. The firm sets output where marginal revenue to division 1 equals marginal cost, $MR_1 = MC$. The firm maximizes profit by price discriminating between the two groups. The transfer price to division 2 is p_t^*, and the external price is p_e^*.

good. When the intermediate good is bought and sold in a competitive market, the firm will react to the market-determined price p_e. Thus, for the intermediate good, the average revenue and marginal revenue are equal to the market price, $AR_1 = MR_1 = p_e$. When an external market is available, the firm is no longer forced to produce all the intermediate good required to produce the final good. The firm can *buy* from the external market, or find it profitable to make more than it requires and *sell* the excess in the external market. The profit-maximizing level of the intermediate good is Q_1^*, where $MC_1 = MR_1$. The firm will produce Q_1^*, no matter what the output level of the final good turns out to be. Total marginal cost to the firm, therefore, will be $MC = p_e + MC_2$, because the marginal cost of the intermediate good to division 2 is equal to the market price, p_e. The firm then identifies the profit-maximizing price of the final good at p_2^*, where $MR_2 = MC$, and sets output at Q_2^*. In the case shown in Figure 15.19, division 1 produces more of the intermediate good than required by division 2, and the excess is sold in the intermediate market. If division 1 produced less than the amount required by division 2, the difference would be bought from the external market.

In the third case, where the firm has some *monopoly power in selling* the intermediate good in an external market, the pricing problem works just like third-degree price discrimination. Figure 15.21 illustrates this case. A demand for the intermediate good in the external market gives rise to average and marginal revenue curves, AR_e and MR_e. The firm can also transfer the good internally to division 2. The internal demand for the intermediate good is a derived demand for an input—derived from a desire to maximize profit from the final good, using the intermediate good as an input. Thus, the average revenue and marginal revenue curves for division 2 coincide with the average revenue product and marginal revenue product curves of the transferred good, $AR_2 = ARP_t$ and $MR_2 = MRP_t$. The total demand for the intermediate good facing division 1, the producer of the intermediate good X_1, is the horizontal summation of the external and internal demands, $AR_1^{-1} = AR_e^{-1} + AR_2^{-1}$. A corresponding marginal revenue curve facing division 1 is denoted MR_1.

Now, given the marginal cost curve for producing the intermediate good, the firm can identify the optimal level of division 1 output as X_1^*, where $MR_1 = MC_1$. Because of the two distinct demands for X_1, the firm can price discriminate between the two groups— the external and internal markets. The marginal cost of producing X_1^* units, MC^*, is set equal to the distinct marginal revenues in each market. The group 1 price, the external market price, is p_e^*. The group 2 price, the transfer price, is p_t^*. The firm sells X_e^* units to the external market and transfers X_i^* units internally to division 2. The total amount of the intermediate good produced is just sufficient to meet total demand for the intermediate good, $X_1^* = X_e^* + X_2^*$, and the firm maximizes profit.

15.11 Resale Price Maintenance

Resale price maintenance, or **fair trade,** is a supplier's practice in forbidding retailers to undercut a retail price floor. Enforcement takes the form of cutting off supplies to any retailer violating the price floor. The motivation by the manufacturer or wholesaler is to induce the retailer to provide better services and to prevent "unfair" trade by discount retailers. Without fair trade, customers would search for products at expensive showrooms but purchase the good from a discounter. Retailers offering the extra services would also be forced by competition to become discounters, and the nature of the product is changed. Resale price maintenance, however, is designed to encourage dealers to compete with each other by offering extra services.

Notice that the manufacturer does not benefit directly from resale price maintenance. The price floor determines a minimum retail price, whereas the manufacturer's price is a wholesale price. Fair trade, however, does affect the retailer directly. Once the wholesale price is given, retail price maintenance determines the maximum retail margin.

Figure 15.22 illustrates the procedure. For simplicity, suppose the retailer has no costs other than the wholesale price p_w. Given demand, competition forces each retailer to charge a price equal to marginal cost, and Q_1 units are sold in the market. Now suppose the manufacturer sets a fair-trade retail price of p_r. At this higher price, fewer units will be sold unless the retailers change their product by adding more services, thereby increasing the value of the good by, say, v dollars per unit. The dealers provide the additional service up to the point at which the marginal cost of providing those services equals the increase in price, $\Delta MC = \Delta p$. Why? Because competition forces them to

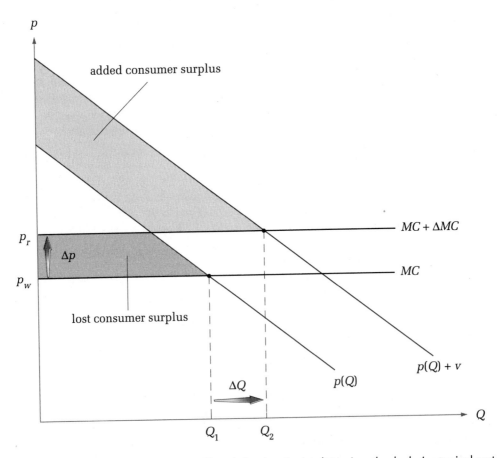

Figure 15.22   **Resale price maintenance:** The wholesale price p_w determines the dealer's marginal cost if there are no other costs. The market clears at Q_1 units sold. With the retail price fixed at a fair-trade price p_r, competition forces dealers to compete for customers by providing added services, which adds a value v to the demand price. Marginal cost increases by Δp because of the zero-profit condition for competitive retailers.

increase output until the new price p_r equals the new marginal cost. Dealer profits are zero once more.

The monopoly wholesaler uses resale price maintenance only if it expects its profits to be greater than before. In the example of Figure 15.22, p_w and Q_2 must be the profit-maximizing price and quantity for the wholesaler. If it were not, the wholesale price would change, and the outcome shown in Figure 15.22 would not be an equilibrium outcome. Notice also that, for this example, consumer surplus is greater than before.

The legal treatment of fair trade has a mixed history. In 1911, the Supreme Court declared resale price maintenance to be a per se violation of Section 1 of the Sherman Act. This decision placed fair trade in the same category as horizontal price fixing. But in 1937, the Miller-Tydings Act exempted fair trade from the Sherman Act at the discretion of the individual states. Then in 1975, the Consumer Goods Pricing Act returned the legal provision of resale price maintenance to where the Supreme Court had left it in 1937. In 1977, the Court declared fair-trade pricing practices to be subject to the "rule of reason" that only unreasonable acts in restraint of trade merited conviction under the Sherman Act. Currently, firms can set "suggested" resale prices, but those prices may not be enforced by any formal action or mechanism imposed on the retailer.

15.12   Pricing Joint Products*

Many firms produce and sell more than one product. Those products may be substitutes or complements in consumption. Thus, their demands are related, meaning that determining optimal prices requires determining how various price combinations affect joint revenues.

Pricing decisions are influenced by demand relations through their effect on marginal revenue. For a firm producing two products, X and Y, the marginal revenue functions are:

$$MR_X = \frac{\Delta TR}{\Delta X} = \frac{\Delta TR_X}{\Delta X} + \frac{\Delta TR_Y}{\Delta X}$$

$$MR_Y = \frac{\Delta TR}{\Delta Y} = \frac{\Delta TR_Y}{\Delta Y} + \frac{\Delta TR_X}{\Delta Y}$$

The marginal revenue of good X is the change in revenue directly associated with selling more X *plus* the change in revenue associated with selling Y when more X is sold. A similar statement can be made for the marginal revenue of Y. The second term on the right-hand side of each equation represents the cross-effects between the two products. These cross-marginal revenue terms can be positive or negative. A cross-marginal revenue term will be positive if one good is a market complement of the other, but the cross-marginal revenue will be negative if one good is a market substitute for the other.

Multiple products are also related through the production technology. Some goods may be produced in fixed proportion—mutton and wool, and beef and leather hides. Other

---

*This section and the next can be skipped without loss of continuity.

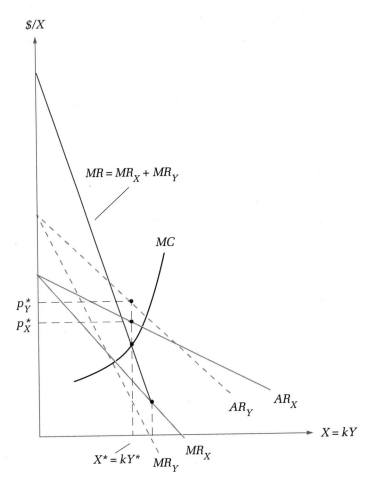

Figure 15.23   **Joint products produced in fixed proportion:** Total marginal revenue is the *vertical* sum of the marginal revenue curves for each product. The optimal level of output occurs where $MR = MC$. Prices are set at p_X^* and p_Y^* to sell the profit-maximizing levels of output.

goods may be produced in variable proportions—refining crude oil into different grades of gasoline and fuel oil. Some goods compete for resources, other goods are by-products.

Let's start with two goods produced in fixed proportion. When the technology dictates fixed output proportions, one set of cost curves describes the costs of production. These goods, however, have two marginal revenue curves, one for each good. Figure 15.23 illustrates two goods being produced in the fixed proportion $X = kY$, where $k > 0$. Total marginal revenue is the *vertical* sum of the separate marginal revenue curves because each unit of output provides revenues from both goods. Profit is maximized where total marginal revenue equals marginal cost. Prices are set to sell the optimal quantity of each good in accordance with its demand curve.

A complication arises when we find *negative* marginal revenue for one of the joint products, as shown in Figure 15.24. Here, MR_X is negative when total marginal revenue is

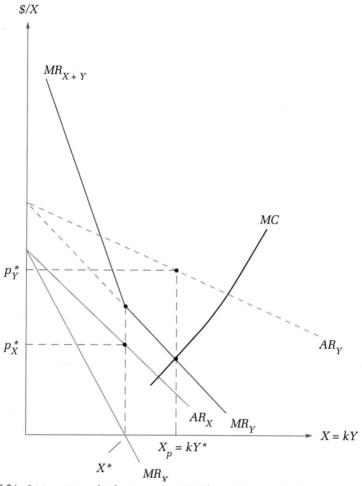

Figure 15.24 **Pricing a joint product having negative MR:** When a joint product has negative marginal revenue at the optimal output level, $MR < 0$ at X_p, set price so that $MR_X = 0$ to sell X^* units. The profit-maximizing prices are p_X^* and p_Y^*, and $X_p - X^*$ units must be withheld from the market.

equal to marginal cost. Negative marginal revenue means that sales of the good at that level reduce revenue. What should the firm do? Well, it should still produce both goods where MR_{X+Y} equals MC, but it should sell the amounts produced only if marginal revenue is positive. In this illustration, the amounts produced should be X_p and kY^*. The firm should sell Y^* units at price p_Y^*. But the firm should not sell X_p because $MR_X < 0$ at X_p units. The firm can increase revenue and profit by selling only X^* units where $MR_X = 0$. The amount $X_p - X^*$ must be withheld from the market in a way to avoid detracting from the demand for X. As long as disposing of the excess withheld is costless, the price at which $MR_X = 0$, p_X^*, will maximize the revenue from selling X. Selling all that is produced is pointless because demand for X is inelastic for prices below p_X^*.

15.13 Joint Pricing and Variable Output Proportions*

If all output demands are independent and if no interdependence appears in production, then each good can be treated separately. But joint production decisions are more complicated when output proportions are variable. The profit-maximizing output and input mix does not lend itself readily to graphic illustration, but the basic idea is demonstrated by Figure 15.25.[5] The concave curves are isocost curves that represent product-transformation curves for different levels of cost. These curves are concave because of the usual characteristic bulge in the underlying product-transformation curves, reflecting increasing opportunity costs for producing more of either good. The convex

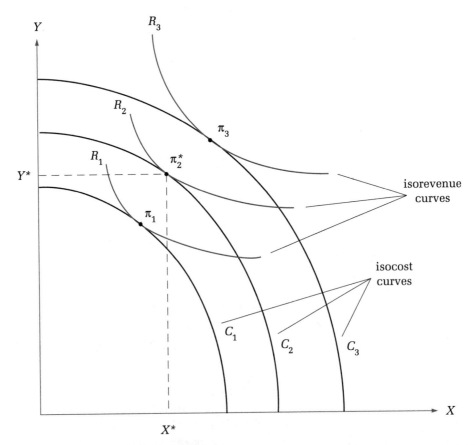

Figure 15.25 **Maximizing profit for joint products:** If the isocost curve C_2 and isorevenue curve R_2 yield maximum profit, then prices are set to sell X^* and Y^* units of the joint products.

---

*This section can be skipped without loss of continuity.

5. For a complete derivation, see, for instance, Kalman J. Cohen and Richard M. Cyert, *Theory of the Firm: Resource Allocation in a Market Economy,* 2nd ed. (Prentice-Hall, 1975), pp. 124–131. They assume a competitive environment, however, so that output prices remain fixed.

curves are isorevenue curves. Each isorevenue curve indicates output bundles that yield the same level of total revenue. Isorevenue curves are convex when marginal revenue falls with an increase in either good.[6]

At any given level of cost, the firm maximizes profit by choosing an output combination at which an isorevenue curve is tangent to the isocost curve. Tangency implies that the marginal costs of producing the products are proportionate to their marginal revenues, $MR_X/MR_Y = MC_X/MC_Y$. The firm must also identify the optimal levels of production and the optimal input mixes in producing both goods. The optimal output levels must be such that marginal revenue equals marginal cost for each good. The optimal input mix in producing each good must be such that the marginal product for each input equals its price. Moreover, the input mix must be such that the ratios of marginal revenue products equal the ratios of marginal factor costs. These conditions must hold when all inputs and all outputs are nonzero. But if a corner solution lies somewhere, the profit-maximizing conditions need to be modified. For instance, for any input not used, its marginal factor cost must be greater than its marginal revenue product. Likewise, an output will not be produced if its marginal cost is greater than its marginal revenue.

Summary

Cost-plus pricing—markup pricing—is the pricing method most frequently used by firms in the real world. Price is set equal to cost plus a markup over cost. The theoretically correct measure of cost to use is marginal cost. If the costing methods used closely approximate the opportunity costs for inputs, and if the markup used closely approximates owners' equity, then markup pricing will closely approximate marginal cost pricing. Also, markup pricing has been criticized for ignoring demand considerations. But if differences in demand are reflected in the markup used in the calculation, then markup pricing can be used to determine profit-maximizing prices.

Pricing a new product can be difficult because historical empirical information is not available. Price skimming is the strategy of setting a high initial price to skim the cream demand of those willing to pay a higher price. The idea is to maximize short-run profit. Penetration pricing is the strategy of setting a low initial price to establish a broad market base. Penetration pricing is usually consistent with long-run profit maximizing.

Quality is one way of differentiating a product from others. Differences in quality usually mean differences in the costs of production. Differences in quality also cause shifts in the product's demand curve. The firm should choose the price–quality combination that maximizes profit.

Advertising is another way of differentiating a product, but even informational advertising can shift the demand curve. We expect diminishing returns from advertising costs. Price and advertising should be set jointly to maximize profit. The problem is one of finding the optimal demand curve as a function of advertising while choosing the optimal price to maximize profit. Advertising is increased until its extra cost is just covered by the extra revenue generated by the increased demand created by advertising.

---

6. If both goods are sold in competitive markets, the isorevenue curves will graph as downward-sloping straight lines given by $p_X X + p_Y Y = R$, where prices are fixed in the markets.

Many firms face a demand curve that fluctuates regularly or differs across markets. Peak-load pricing is the practice of charging a higher price during peak demand periods. Price discrimination is the act of charging different prices for an identical good under unchanging cost conditions. Price discrimination, possible only when the seller has some monopoly power and only if the seller can prevent resale, has three basic forms.

Perfect price discrimination occurs when the price of each unit sold to each buyer is set equal to each buyer's marginal value. By selling each unit at the maximum price each buyer is willing to pay, the firm can extract all the consumer surplus under the demand curve.

Block pricing occurs when the same customer pays a different price for an identical good. Block pricing is an imperfect form of perfect price discrimination; it may be feasible when perfect price discrimination is impractical.

Group price discrimination occurs when different groups of buyers have different demand curves. The firm will set prices in the different markets so that marginal revenue is the same in all markets and equal to marginal cost. Price will be lower in markets having more elastic demand curves.

One way to engage in price discrimination is to implement a two-part tariff, which occurs when a firm charges an initial fee called an "entry fee" for the right to purchase the good. With a perfect two-part tariff, all the consumer surplus can be extracted by the monopolist. Thus, the two-part tariff can be viewed as a method for implementing perfect price discrimination. Usually, however, many customers have diverse demands, and a firm has no practical way of determining optimal fees for all buyers. Nevertheless, two-part pricing can be used imperfectly to approximate block pricing and thereby increase profit to the monopolist.

Transfer pricing occurs when one division of a firm sells an intermediate product to another division of the same firm. When the intermediate good has no external market, the firm first determines the optimal price and quantity for its final good and then sets the price of the transfer good equal to its marginal cost. When a competitive external market presents itself for the intermediate good, the firm reacts to the price determined in that market. It then determines the profit-maximizing price and output for the final good so that it can determine how much of the intermediate good to buy or sell. When the firm has some monopoly power in the external market, the total demand for the intermediate good is the sum of the internal and external demands. The firm sets final output where total marginal revenue equals marginal cost. Then the firm maximizes profit by price discriminating between the internal and external markets.

Resale price maintenance, or fair trade, occurs when a producer sets a price floor on a dealer's retail price. The wholesale price influences the dealer's marginal cost, and the dealer sets output where price equals marginal cost. With a retail price floor above marginal cost, the dealer is forced to compete for customers by adding an extra value to establish a new demand curve. Under competition, the increase in the wholesale price causes marginal cost to increase until profits are zero once more. Both output and price are greater than before, and so the producing firm enjoys an increase in profit.

When firms produce many products using many inputs, pricing those products becomes a complex problem. Product demands are related if the products are substitutes or complements in consumption. Input demands are related if the goods are jointly produced under the same technology. If two goods are produced in fixed proportions, total marginal revenue is the vertical sum of the goods' marginal revenue curves, and the firm should set output where total marginal revenue equals marginal cost as long as marginal revenue for each good remains positive. If one of these goods has negative marginal revenue, output is set where its marginal revenue is zero. The output of the other good is set where its marginal revenue equals marginal cost.

When two goods are produced in variable proportions, the firm should choose output levels so that the ratio of marginal costs is equal to the ratio of marginal revenues, and marginal revenue must be set equal to marginal cost for each good. The optimal input mix must be such that the ratio of marginal revenue products equals the ratio of marginal factor costs, and the marginal factor cost must be equal to each input's marginal revenue product. These conditions must be modified when corner solutions occur.

Further Readings

General issues in the firm's pricing behavior are covered in these publications:

- Fred J. Weston, "Pricing Behavior of Large Firms," *Western Economic Journal* (March 1972), pp. 1–18.
- Frederic M. Scherer, *Industrial Market Structure and Economic Performance*, 2nd ed. (Rand McNally, 1980).
- Vihala R. Rao, "Pricing Research in Marketing: The State of the Art," *Journal of Business* (January 1984), pp. 39–60.

Some specific issues in the pricing behavior of firms are covered by these authors:

- Joan Robinson, *The Economics of Imperfect Competition* (Macmillan, 1933).
- Jack Hirshleifer, "On the Economics of Transfer Pricing," *Journal of Business,* 29 (July 1956), pp. 172–184.
- L. Telser, "Why Do Manufacturers Want Fair Trade?" *Journal of Law and Economics,* 3 (1960), pp. 86–105.
- Phillip Areeda and Donald F. Turner, "Predatory Pricing and Related Practices under Section 2 of the Sherman Act," *Harvard Law Review,* 88 (February 1975), pp. 697–733.
- William J. Adams and Janet L. Yellen, "Commodity Bundling and the Burden of Monopoly," *Quarterly Journal of Economics,* 90 (May 1976), pp. 475–498.
- Richard Schmalensee, "Commodity Bundling by Single-Product Monopolies," *Journal of Law and Business,* 25 (April 1982), pp. 67–71.
- Mark R. Isaac and Vernon L. Smith, "In Search of Predatory Pricing," *Journal of Political Economy,* 94(2) (April 1986), pp. 266–296.

Practice Problems

1. Why is cost-plus pricing used so frequently? Does that use invalidate the use of economic models of profit maximizing? Explain.
2. If a firm sets price using a "cost-plus" formula, will profits always be positive? Why or why not?

3. Suppose a monopolistically competitive firm faces an average revenue curve given by

$$p = 100 - 3X + 4\sqrt{A}$$

where A represents advertising expenditure. The effect of advertising on price is $\Delta p / \Delta A = 2/\sqrt{A}$. The firm's total cost function is

$$C = 4X^2 + 10X + A$$

so that marginal cost is

$$MC = 8X + 10$$

Find the values of A, X, and p that maximize profit. The easy way to do this problem is to find π as a function of X and A and then use calculus to maximize π.

4. Graphically illustrate how price discrimination may make it possible for a monopolist to earn positive profits even though AC lies everywhere above AR.

5. Under what conditions is price discrimination possible?

6. Is peak-load pricing a form of price discrimination? Why or why not?

7. In third-degree price discrimination with two markets, show that demand is less elastic in the market where the higher price is charged if production costs are the same in both markets.

8. A firm exports a product to a foreign market and sells the product domestically. The domestic demand yields average revenue given by

$$p_d = 100 - 15Q$$

The foreign demand yields average revenue given by

$$p_f = 60 - 2.5Q$$

The firm has one plant with total production costs given by

$$C = 10,800 + 20Q + 0.1Q^2$$

that yields this marginal cost equation,

$$MC = 20 + 0.2Q$$

(a) What is the profit-maximizing level of output?

(b) How much should be sold to each market?

(c) What prices should be charged in each market?

9. A firm sells an intermediate product to two other firms. The two buyers have these inverse demand curves:

$$p_1 = 500 - 8X_1$$
$$p_2 = 400 - 5X_2$$

where $Q = X_1 + X_2$ is the total produced and sold. The seller's total cost curve is given by

$$TC = 10,000 + 20Q$$

(a) Determine the marginal revenue curves for each buyer (as a function of X_1 or X_2).

(b) Determine the profit-maximizing prices and quantities if the seller can price discriminate.

(c) Determine the profit-maximizing prices and quantities without price discrimination.

(d) Compare the seller's profits with and without price discrimination.

10. A firm has two divisions. Division 1 produces an intermediate good that can be used by division 2 in producing a final good. The intermediate good has a perfectly competitive external market, in which the price is $p_c = \$350$. The marginal costs for the two divisions are

$$MC_1 = 200 + 0.375Q$$
$$MC_2 = 100 + 0.50Q$$

The average revenue curve for the final good is

$$AR_2 = 1,000 - 0.625Q$$

(a) Determine the MR equations for divisions 1 and 2.

(b) Determine the optimal quantity Q_1^* for division 1.

(c) Determine the MC equation facing this firm.

(d) Determine the optimal quantity and price for the final good.

(e) What is the transfer price?

(f) How much of the intermediate good is bought or sold in the external market?

11. A firm has two divisions. Division 1 produces an intermediate good that can be used by division 2 in subsequent production. The intermediate good can be sold to an external market, and the firm has a monopoly in that market. Suppose the external demand gives rise to

$$AR_e = 1,200 - 0.8X_e$$

Moreover, the internal demand for the transfer good gives rise to

$$AR_2 = 1,000 - 0.625X_2$$

The marginal cost of producing the good by division 1 is given by

$$MC_1 = 200 + 0.375X_1$$

(a) Find the total average and the total marginal revenue curves AR_1 and MR_1 for division 1.

(b) Determine the profit-maximizing quantity X_1^*.

(c) Determine the profit-maximizing price p_e^* and quantity X_e^* to be sold externally.

(d) Determine the profit-maximizing transfer price p_t^* and quantity X_2^* to be transferred to division 2 for internal use.

12. Assume that a firm produces two products, X_1 and X_2, in fixed proportions $X_1 = X_2$. The average revenue curves are

$$p_1 = 60 - 0.05X_1$$
$$p_2 = 90 - 0.04X_2$$

The joint marginal cost curve is

$$MC = 25 + 0.07X$$

where $X = X_1 = X_2$.

(a) Determine and graph the marginal revenue curves for both products.
(b) Graph the *total* marginal revenue curve and the marginal cost curve on the same graph.
(c) Determine and identify the optimal level of output.
(d) Determine the optimal price for each product.
(e) Suppose the average revenue curve for X_2 changes to

$$p_2 = 144 - 0.05X_2$$

Determine and graph this new marginal revenue curve for X_2, along with the old marginal revenue curve for X_1.

(f) Determine and identify the new optimal level of output. How much of each good will be sold?
(g) Determine the new optimal price for each product.

Chapter

16

Government Regulation and Antitrust

In this chapter we investigate market imperfections and failures and attempts by society to make socially optimal corrections. First, we consider the rationale behind such protective regulations as safety standards and licenses. Second, we concentrate on how the environment is protected by regulation of activities that contribute to emissions of pollution. We then examine how the behavior of firms with monopoly power is regulated.

One form of market structure often evolves naturally into pure monopoly—natural monopoly. Natural monopolies arise because of substantial economies of scale over the entire range of market demand, enabling one large firm to supply the entire market at a lower average cost than a number of smaller firms can reach. Society can benefit from the lower unit costs of production if the potential for abuse of monopoly is thwarted. The question we face is how society can benefit from the economies of scale while avoiding high monopoly prices and huge deadweight losses.

We have seen that pure competition, with no externalities and public goods, guarantees that the resources available to society will be used efficiently. For that reason social policy's objective has been workable competition. Antitrust laws prohibit monopoly, attempts to monopolize, and conspiracies in restraint of trade. But antitrust policy is not static—every businessperson should be familiar with the major antitrust statutes and their evolving interpretation. We also briefly examine the legality of pricing practices that may create a monopoly. Every manager should be aware of the harsh penalties for engaging in these practices.

One route followed by an industry that is evolving into one in which firms are likely to acquire monopoly power is the mergers. As major firms merge, the industry becomes more concentrated. As firms acquire monopoly power and engage in monopolistic pricing, substantial deadweight losses may arise. Are mergers therefore always undesirable from a social point of view? After examining the potential effects of different kinds of mergers, we look at the current merger guidelines used by the U.S. Department of Justice (DOJ).

16.1 Protective Regulation

Some regulations arise because pressure groups lobby for protection from the actions of others. This political action results in laws that protect businesses from competition, protect workers against hazardous working conditions, and protect consumers from deceptive business practices. Such legal protections include licensing, patents, restrictions on some forms of price competition, prohibitions on deceptive advertising, restrictions on the free flow of international trade, occupational health and safety laws, prohibition of discrimination in employment, environmental regulation, and many others.

Many regulations create artificial market power; others mitigate the effects of market power.

A **certificate** of competency is required to practice in many professions. An accountant may become a certified public accountant (CPA) after passing a test. Lawyers have to pass a bar exam to practice law in most regions. These certificates are required beyond acquired formal education and experience.

A **license** is required to enter and remain in many businesses. A city may require a license for a firm that removes leaded paint from old buildings. To receive and retain the license, the firm may need to require its employees to receive specialized training. In general, building contractors must pass tests or demonstrate competency to obtain a contractor's license. Special licenses are also required to drive taxicabs, buses, and large trucks.

Sometimes, of course, it seems licensing and certification perform little beyond restricting supply, thereby increasing price. Examples include the strict limitations the American Medical Association attaches to admission to medical schools and its prohibitions on those who would employ paramedical personnel. Another example is the restrictively high qualifications to get into some craft unions. Even when the need for licensing and certification is clear, applying them reduces supply. The corresponding increases in price and profit motivate businesses and trade and professional associations to support regulation. In response to declining prices and profits in the 1980s because of deregulation, the American Truckers' Association wants to bring back regulation of the trucking industry.

A **patent** gives the right of exclusive use to an inventor for seventeen years. The patent holder can use the invention directly or grant a license to others in exchange for royalty payments. Granting a patent gives the inventor a monopoly for a limited period, during which it restricts entry; the result is a higher price for the product of the invention. The limited monopoly is granted to reward investors, encouraging both technical changes in production and development of new products. Nevertheless, the patent holder has the opportunity to establish a dominance in the industry that may last long after the patent expires.

Tariffs and **quotas** protect domestic firms from foreign competition. A tariff is a tax on imports that raises price directly; a quota limits supply and raises price indirectly.

Many regulations are designed to protect workers. Minimum-wage laws impose a floor on the wages paid to labor. To protect other workers' jobs, many states prohibit use of convict labor in manufacturing. The Equal Employment Opportunity Commission (EEOC) regulates hiring and firing practices to protect people from arbitrary or discriminatory practices. The Occupational Safety and Health Administration (OSHA) specifies safety standards in places of employment to protect workers from being exploited when they individually have little bargaining power in monopsonistic labor markets. When a worker operates machinery, OSHA may require safety restraints, without which workers' productivity is higher but risk of injury is greater. The employer's cost is higher with the OSHA regulation, and so without regulation the restraints probably would not be used.

Consumers too are protected by many regulations. Laws require mail-order businesses to fill orders within thirty days or give a refund. By law, warranties must be written in plain language so that the consumer can easily understand the coverage. Among others are truth-in-labeling laws, truth-in-lending laws, and laws that require warning of potential danger. Unsafe features are prohibited in some products, and other features are explicitly required. A power lawn mower must have an automatic shutoff device to stop the mower when unattended. The Consumer Product Safety Commission, established in 1972 to protect consumers against risk and injury, provides safety information and develops uniform safety standards.

16.2 Environmental Regulation

In 1970, the Environmental Protection Agency (EPA) was created to regulate activities that cause pollution or environmental degradation. Reflecting the public's increasing insistence on safety in the air we breathe and the water we drink, the EPA has become one of the most powerful federal regulatory agencies. Still, businesses persist in criticizing the EPA for imposing unreasonable standards.

Pollution is a negative externality—the act of creating pollution imposes a cost on another party that is not reflected in the price of the good. A negative externality occurs in our use of the internal-combustion engine because of the air pollution it creates. And yet banning these engines has, at least so far, been rejected as a solution, and we have

© Washington Post Writers Group. Reprinted with permission.

instead passed regulations attempting to reduce emissions. Apparently we are willing to accept some air pollution, balancing the cost of controlling emissions against the benefits from the use of polluting engines.

Because many externalities have the characteristics of public goods, the cost of the externalities is not reflected in market prices, a potential source of market inefficiency. To see why, let's consider our use of automobiles with internal-combustion engines. Figure 16.1 shows the market demand curve for automobile use, perhaps measured in miles driven. The inverse demand curve measures price—the marginal value—to consumers. With many independent suppliers, the inverse supply curve coincides with the sum of all firms' marginal cost curves. This market is in equilibrium at price p_0 and quantity Q_0.

Now let's assume that air pollution is proportionate to automobile use. Then, without technical change, pollution can be reduced only by cutting automobile use. We assume, therefore, that the **marginal external cost** (*MEC*) curve rises at a constant rate. When the *MEC* curve is added to the marginal cost of production *MC*, we obtain a **marginal social cost** (*MSC*) curve, $MSC = MEC + MC$. From a social point of view, the optimal price should be p^* and the quantity should be Q^*.

Because consumers do not pay for the pollution directly, and the cost of producing pollution is not included in the cost of producing the good, the market price is too low and the equilibrium quantity is too high. The social loss caused by this inefficiency can be found by summing the difference between marginal social cost and marginal value for all units of output that exceed the social optimum. In Figure 16.1, the social cost is equal to the shaded area between the *MSC* curve and the demand curve from Q^* to Q_0 units.

How can the inefficiency caused by the externality be corrected? With no change in the product being produced, the externality can be reduced only if less of the good is produced and used. Pollution can be reduced in three ways: set an emissions standard, impose an emissions fee, or establish transferable emissions permits. We consider each technique in turn.

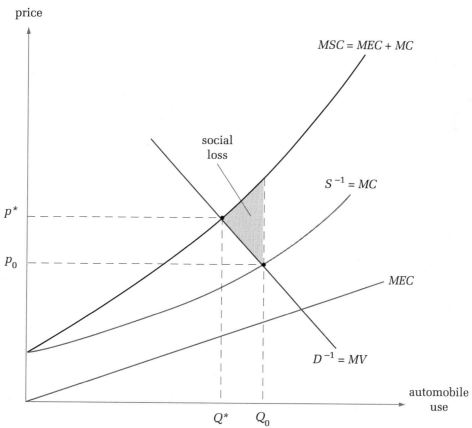

Figure 16.1 **Externalities and social loss:** This market is in equilibrium at p_0 and Q_0, where the demand curve intersects the supply curve. The social optimum occurs at p^* and Q^*, where the marginal social-cost curve intersects the marginal value curve. A social loss occurs that is equal to the area between the MSC curve and the MV curve from Q^* to Q_0 units.

An **emissions standard** sets a legal limit on how much pollution can be produced. If the standard is exceeded, a severe penalty is imposed. A producer may be fined or forced to stop production. But how can society determine the socially efficient level of pollution in order to establish the standard?

Figure 16.2 shows how the socially efficient level of pollution might be found. As more of the polluting good is consumed, the marginal social cost of emissions rises. The MSC curve has positive slope because of a realistic assumption that increased pollution has cumulatively bad affects. The curve labeled MCA is a **marginal cost of abatement.** Abatement is a reduction in emissions. Hence, the MCA curve has negative slope, reflecting an increasing marginal cost from reduced emissions, or extra levels of abatement. In other words, the MCA declines because the incremental cost of abatement falls to zero when there is no abatement. Given the MSC and MCA curves, the socially optimal level of emissions is E^*.

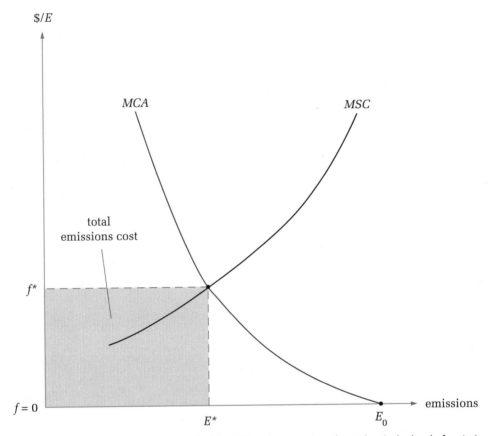

Figure 16.2 **Efficient emissions standard and fee:** When the emissions fee is $f = 0$, the level of emissions will be E_0. A socially efficient emissions standard occurs at E^*, where the marginal social cost (MSC) is equal to the marginal cost of abatement (MCA). A socially efficient fee is established as price f^*. The total cost to the industry of producing E^* units of emissions is equal to the shaded area.

An **emissions fee** is a charge levied on each unit of emissions. An emissions fee on producers will raise their average and marginal production costs, thereby reducing emissions. If an emissions fee of f^* is charged to every producer, the market will reduce its emissions to E^*, where the f^* is equal to the marginal cost of abatement. This relation suggests that establishing an emissions fee at f^* will result in the same level of pollution that results when an emissions standard is established at E^*. Will this result always occur, or does one method work better than the other?

Let's look at what happens when the regulator makes an error in setting the fee or the standard. Suppose the fee is set 20 percent too low or the standard is set 20 percent too high. Both situations result in a social loss because the level of emissions will be too high. But the extent of the loss from either error depends on the elasticities of the *MSC*

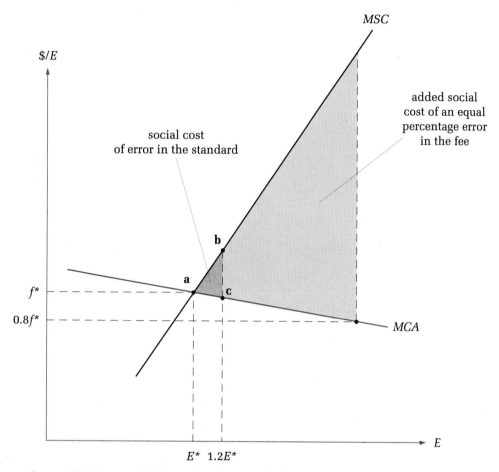

Figure 16.3 **Wrong standard and wrong fee:** Suppose that, because of uncertainty, the standard is set 20 percent too high or the fee 20 too low. The wrong standard here results in a smaller social loss than does the wrong fee because the MSC curve is steep and the MCA curve is nearly flat.

and *MCA* curves.

Figure 16.3 illustrates the case in which the *MSC* curve is very steep and the *MCA* curve is nearly flat. If the regulator sets the standard 20 percent too high, at $1.2E^*$ rather than at E^*, the social loss is equal to the area of the more darkly shaded triangle **abc.** If, on the other hand, the regulator sets the emissions fee 20 percent too low, at $0.8f^*$ rather than f^*, the social loss is even greater (equal to both shaded areas) because the *MSC* curve is steep but the *MCA* curve is nearly flat. The standard clearly seems to be preferred to the fee if the regulator is uncertain about their optimal values.

Alternatively, we will see an indication that a fee will work best if the *MSC* curve is nearly flat but the *MCA* curve is steep. Either way, however, the less efficient regulation may be better than doing nothing.

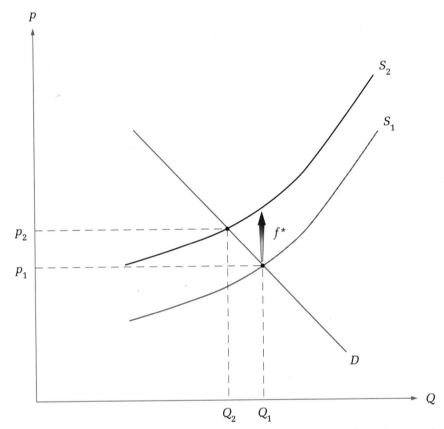

Figure 16.4 **Emissions fee and market supply:** If the socially optimal emissions fee is f^*, the market supply curve will shift from S_1 to S_2 because each firm's marginal cost increases by an amount equal to the fee. The new market price and quantity, p_2 and Q_2, generate the socially optimal level of pollution.

A stronger case can be made for using fees when polluters have different production processes and hence different abatement costs. As illustrated by Figure 16.4, if an emissions fee of f^* is charged for each unit produced, the supply curve will shift from S_1 to S_2. This change will reduce output to Q_2, which generates the socially optimal level of pollution E^*, even though each producer has different marginal costs of production.

Instead, if an equal standard were imposed on each producer, each would reduce output by the same amount. The result would be the same as imposing an equal emissions fee only if the producers have identical abatement costs. But if abatement costs differ between producers, one will be able to reduce emissions more cheaply than another. It stands to reason that the producer with the lower marginal abatement cost should reduce output more. An equal abatement standard prohibits that, however, and so equal standards cannot be socially optimal.

We have identified two problems with controlling pollution. First, a standard may work better than a fee when regulators err in setting the standard and fee. Second, a fee

GLOBAL PERSPECTIVE: *Increased Pollution and Awareness*

Why are we so disturbed about pollution when just a few years ago most of us had no such worry? Figure 16.5 shows why. Because of increased production and consumption over the years, uncontrolled emissions have increased. In earlier times, the world had fewer people, factories, and automobiles.

Not only have uncontrolled emissions grown, the marginal cost curve becomes steeper and steeper because of the cumulative effects of such pollution as hydrocarbons in the air, acid rain, and depletion of the ozone layer. Fortunately, we have recognized the increasing social costs and have begun to regulate emissions of pollution. The important questions now are how much pollution is tolerable and how to achieve reasonable limits.

One approach is being tried by the country that brought us the word *mariachi*, the revolutionary mural, and the margarita. Starting in March 1991, new *casetas de oxygiena* were

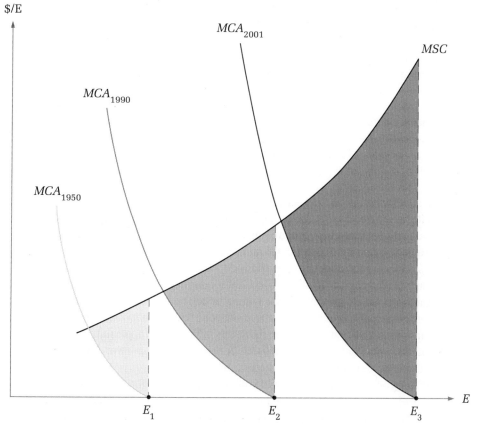

Figure 16.5 **Pollution and time:** The marginal cost of abating emissions has shifted over the years because uncontrolled emissions have increased with time. By 2001, the welfare loss from uncontrolled emissions of E_3 will be much larger than the uncontrolled emissions of E_1 back in 1950. Thus, if left uncontrolled, the social cost of emissions will be significantly larger in the future.

available in Mexico City. For about $2 a shot, people will be able to enter a booth and breathe pure oxygen for one minute.*

Why is Mexico City putting on this program? That city may well have the dirtiest air in the world. At 7,500 feet (2,300 meters) above sea level, a given volume of its air contains only about one-third as much oxygen as it would at sea level. Every day, cars and refineries spew out 1,200 tons of pollution. In winter, most is trapped by cold air that prevents the pollution from escaping over the surrounding mountains. Respiratory infections are the biggest cause of death in Mexico City. Perhaps the demand is there for more oxygen.

In the meantime, the United States is thinking about selling rights to pollute.† In the fight against acid rain that affects the Northeast and Canada, primarily caused by sulfur emissions from coal- and oil-burning electric power plants, the favored strategy has been to set limits on the quantity of sulfur that utilities are allowed to emit. Until now. Proposed legislation would allow companies to buy and sell the right to pollute. Government would sell a limited number of "rights," and a market for rights should then form and decide on the cheapest way to contain smokestack emissions. A utility that holds rights to pollute that it doesn't need can sell them to a company that needs them. This exchange will encourage producers with lower abatement costs to reduce pollution more than those with high costs. The limit on total emissions would then gradually be ratcheted down. One way to lower the limit would be for government to buy rights. Regulators could then control total emissions without interfering with the operation of firms.

---

* As reported in *The Economist*, February 16, 1991.

† As reported in *The New York Times*, May 17, 1989.

---

may work better when producers have different marginal costs of abatement. Fortunately, a market alternative to either a fee or a standard is available.

A **transferable emissions permit** grants the holder a right to produce pollution. Permits are distributed to all producers, and the number of permits is equal to the desired emissions standard. But producers are allowed to buy and sell permits.

If enough producers are involved, a market for permits will form. Any producer with high marginal cost for abatement will be willing to pay more for a permit than a producer with low marginal cost for abatement, and producers will begin to buy and sell permits. When the market for permits reaches equilibrium, the price of a permit will be equal to every producer's marginal cost of abatement. A producer with a lower *MCA* curve will reduce pollution more than those with higher *MCA* curves.

In summary, when information is incomplete, standards offer more certainty about emissions levels but will not be cost minimizing if producers have different abatement costs. In contrast, fees offer more certainty about achieving equal marginal costs of abatement between producers, but the level of abatement remains uncertain. Emissions permits, as a third alternative, create a market for the externalities of pollution. With a market for permits, the regulator has control over total emissions but without interfering with producers' cost-minimizing decisions.

16.3 Natural Monopoly and Regulating Public Utilities

Some production technologies give rise to substantial economies of scale. A declining long-run average cost curve means that a larger scale results in lower average and marginal production costs. Suppose the LAC curve facing the firms in an industry declines over a substantial range of market demand, as illustrated by Figure 16.6, with several small firms, each producing at a scale resulting in AC_j and MC_j. If these firms behave as price takers, short-run industry supply S is the horizontal sum of their marginal cost curves. The resulting competitive price is p_c. Any one of these firms can increase its scale and slide down the LAC curve, but the market will not support several large-scale firms. As some firms slide down the LAC curve by increasing the scale of operation, other firms are forced out of the market or combine with others. Monopoly power arises as the number of firms decreases. As rival firms compete for limited market demand, the market structure evolves away from competition toward monopoly. Eventually, this market has room for only one large firm because of the declining LAC over the entire range of market demand. That one firm has become a monopoly.

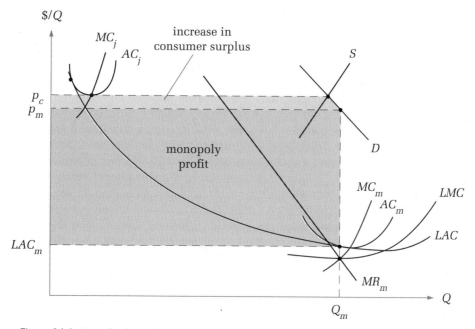

Figure 16.6 **Unregulated natural monopoly:** Several small firms producing at AC_j will evolve naturally into a monopoly firm producing at scale AC_m if the LAC falls over a substantial range of market demand. The natural monopolist experiences lower average cost but also enjoys monopolist profits. The resulting monopoly price might be lower than the purely competitive price, increasing consumer surplus.

AN APPLICATION: *Public Utilities Such as AT&T*

Most natural monopolies are regulated as public utilities. The reason is to achieve the greatest possible social benefit without having to subsidize the industry. Public utilities are either regulated by a government body that sets the price or output, or the firm is owned and operated by government. The privately owned and publicly regulated natural monopoly is the usual type in the United States. Nationalization and public ownership are more frequent in other countries, although Europe is moving toward privatization and regulation.

Privately owned natural monopolies are regulated to mitigate the social losses that arise from monopoly pricing. Price regulation is intended to approximate the competitive pricing solution, to eliminate monopoly profit, and to realize the available economies of scale. Consider the monopoly power possessed by a lone, unregulated telephone company. On the other hand, consider the waste in having many competitive firms erecting poles, stringing wires, providing maintenance, and so on, in one geographic area. A single public utility can string one set of wires, centralize operations, and avoid duplicating services.

Average cost pricing, the regulators' attempt to set price equal to *LAC,* is illustrated by Figure 16.7. An unregulated monopolist would set price equal to p^* and would produce Q^* units. Monopoly profits appear when price is greater than average cost at Q^*. If the regulators set price at p_r, where the market demand crosses the *LAC* curve, the public utility would produce Q_r units and no monopoly profit would appear. Though economic profit is zero, the utility earns normal profits because it covers all costs of production.

Recall that another outcome of pure competition is that price equals marginal cost. But for the natural monopoly, if regulators were to set price equal to marginal cost, where the demand crosses the *LMC* curve, the utility would experience a long-run loss. A subsidy would be required to keep the utility in business because price would be less than average cost. Thus, unless the demand curve just happens to cross the *LAC* curve at its lowest point, the efficiency condition requiring that price (marginal value) be equal to marginal cost will not be achieved by average cost pricing. Moreover, this efficiency condition will not be achieved by marginal cost pricing unless society is willing to subsidize the monopolist.

In practice, many public utilities are required to set prices in such a way that they will earn no more than a normal rate of return—the return they could have earned by investing the same amount of capital elsewhere at the same risk. A normal rate of return implies zero economic profit. One problem with rate-of-return regulation is that it does not address the efficiency issue directly. Although efficiency and zero profits are compatible under competition, efficiency is not ensured by zero profits under monopoly. The efficient level of output occurs where price equals marginal cost. Price will not equal marginal cost for the regulated monopolist, though, unless the demand curve cuts the *LAC* curve where *AC* equals *MC.*

Another problem with regulation is that it eliminates any incentive to adopt the most efficient method of production. If the utility must reduce price to match a reduction in average cost enabled by a new technology, the utility has no reason to use the new technology. In contrast, the competitive firm is forced to adopt the most efficient technology to remain competitive.

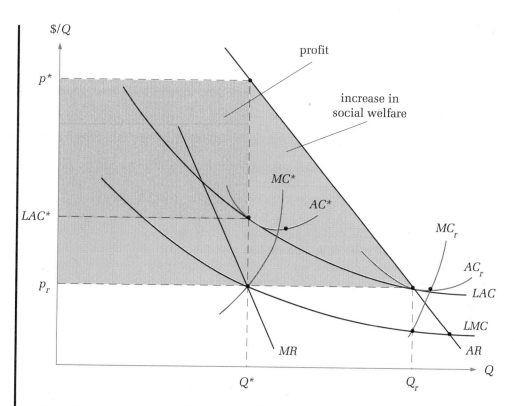

Figure 16.7 **Average cost pricing:** The unregulated monopoly would set price at p* and would produce at Q*. When regulators set price at p_r, the firm produces Q_r units, where p_r = LAC. When regulated by average cost pricing, the firm covers all the cost of production but earns zero economic profit.

These and other considerations led the Federal Communications Commission to modify its way of regulating AT&T. A new regulatory system that took effect July 1, 1989, sets upper and lower limits on prices and lets AT&T price its services within those limits. For nearly thirty years while AT&T was a monopoly, the FCC set all interstate phone-call prices at levels calculated to cover AT&T's actual cost plus an allowed profit rate, 12.2 percent at the time of this change in policy. Under the old system, AT&T had no motivation to adopt cost-reducing changes in production methods because price would be adjusted to keep the profit constant.

Under the new so-called rate-cap approach, also called incentive regulation, the better the utility performs the more it will benefit. Under the rate-cap approach, AT&T's long-distance prices may rise by no more than the annual rate of inflation minus 3 percent to allow for higher profits arising from improved technology. If the price index increases 5 percent, AT&T may raise price by no more than 2 percent. If the price index increases 2 percent, AT&T rates must drop 1 percent. Consumers benefit because price caps will be adjusted downward in real terms at a faster rate than could be achieved under the old regulations. If it can reduce production rates faster than the 3 percent differential, AT&T benefits. The FCC estimated the average annual gain in productivity to be about 2.5 percent, and so AT&T has to increase productivity by only 0.5 percent to earn extra profits. In a given year, however, AT&T must justify cutting price by more than 5 percent to prevent "predatory pricing"—setting price below actual costs to drive rivals out of the market. Because of its former monopoly status and still-dominant position in the $50-billion telecommunications market, only AT&T and the Baby Bell regional phone companies that were spun off from AT&T are currently subject to FCC regulation.

The market demand in Figure 16.6 coincides with this monopolist's average revenue curve, giving rise to the monopolist's marginal revenue curve, MR_m. The monopolist chooses output at Q_m and sets price at p_m to maximize profits where $MR_m = LMC$. The optimal scale is associated with the short-run cost curves AC_m and MC_m. No smaller firm can survive without the monopolist's consent because the monopolist can always reduce price below the average cost of any smaller firm.

A **natural monopoly** is said to be formed when economies of scale appear over a substantial range of market demand. One firm can supply the entire market at a price lower than the minimum short-run average cost of smaller firms. The lower price is permitted for a large firm because of the low average cost when the scale is large.

Natural monopolies usually have high fixed costs and low marginal costs. In the electric power industry, construction of a nuclear generation plant or hydroelectric dam is a substantial investment, but the marginal cost of electricity is low once the plant is built. New firms are unlikely to enter because of the huge initial investment required. The natural monopoly firm can thus charge a price that may yield large profits, but the resulting monopoly price p_m may be lower than the purely competitive price p_c. When price is lower and quantity greater under natural monopoly, consumer surplus increases. Moreover, producer surplus always increases under natural monopoly, as evidenced by the monopoly profit. Therefore a welfare gain has been achieved because of the evolution into a natural monopoly. And yet, further welfare gains are possible because the monopoly price is greater than average cost.

16.4 Antitrust and Monopoly Power

Monopoly power can arise in three ways. First, economies of scale interacting with the size of the market may dictate that only one firm or a few large firms can effectively serve the market. Second, mergers can lead to a single or dominant firm. Third, government regulations and restrictions can lead to monopoly. This third path to monopoly includes airline routes between some city-pairs prior to the late 1970s; taxicab, garbage-collection, and cable-television franchises in some cities; and the U.S. Postal Service's delivery of first-class mail. Even the government-created patent creates a property right that may lead to monopoly power. Inventions that have led to true monopolies are Polaroid's early patents on self-developing films, Xerox's early patents on photocopying, and pharmaceutical companies' patents on unique drugs.

Although regulation and government ownership have been the most frequent ways of dealing with monopoly in the United States, antitrust law too has been used to deal

---

AN APPLICATION: *The ALCOA Case*

The Court of Appeals held that ALCOA had monopolized the virgin aluminum ingot market. This decision by Judge Learned Hand in 1945 reversed an earlier decision by Judge Caffey in a district court.

The ALCOA monopoly arose from control of basic production processes secured by patents that had expired in 1909. The company also signed long-term contracts with companies that controlled essential raw materials. Even though these agreements were annulled by court decree in 1912, ALCOA maintained a monopoly position by increasing productive capacity and by restrictive pricing practices. A pattern of price discrimination and systematic market penetration coupled with economies of scale discouraged potential competitors.

It was ALCOA's claim that being the sole producer of virgin aluminum ingot in the United States did not constitute a monopoly because it faced competition from foreign producers, from secondary aluminum ingot produced from scrap, and from other materials that are substitutes for aluminum. The case was determined by considering market share.

The district court under Judge Caffey excluded the ingot that ALCOA produced for its own use in calculating market share. Judge Caffey's formula indicated that ALCOA controlled 33 percent of the market. Later, Judge Hand maintained that ingot produced for internal use had an effect on the market. The Court of Appeals concluded also that aluminum scrap should not be included in calculating market share because most secondary ingot had originally been produced by ALCOA. This definition of the market indicated that ALCOA controlled 90 percent of the market. The ALCOA decision was important because the Court emphasized market structure rather than abusive practices.

---

with monopoly power. Antitrust laws prohibit monopoly, attempts to monopolize, and conspiracies in restraint of trade. The **Sherman Anti-Trust Act** (1890) was the first major law directed toward checking monopoly power. Section 1 declares every contract, combination, or conspiracy in restraint of trade to be a felony. Section 2 states that persons who monopolize, or attempt to monopolize, or combine or conspire to monopolize, shall be guilty of a felony.

Antitrust prosecution was notably absent in the years immediately following the Sherman Act, and the first major wave of merger activity accelerated. Then in 1903, under Theodore Roosevelt's administration, the Antitrust Division of the Department of Justice was created. Subsequently, three major prosecutions were initiated. In the Standard Oil case (1911) and the American Tobacco case (1911), the Supreme Court enunciated the "rule of reason" that only *unreasonable* combinations in restraint of trade merited conviction under the Sherman Act. The rule of reason was given a narrow interpretation in the U.S. Steel case (1920), in which the Court said that the *intent* to monopolize was not a violation of the law because the firm had not achieved a monopoly, and the Court said that mere size was not an offense. The Court ruled that *potential* monopoly power was beside the point. Because of these and related decisions, few major antitrust prosecutions were initiated until 1937.

AN APPLICATION: *The Continental Can Case*

Whether or not a merger constitutes a substantial lessening of competition or a tendency toward monopoly depends crucially on the definition of the relevant market. In the Continental Can case (1964), the Supreme Court held illegal a merger between the second-largest manufacturer of metal containers, Continental Can, and the third-largest manufacturer of glass containers, Hazel Atlas. The raw materials and manufacturing methods of each company were quite different, but their products had many of the same uses. Other materials such as plastic, paperboard, and foil might also be used to produce containers, but beer breweries were the only industry to which both firms sold containers.

If the relevant market had been defined as including all types of containers, the share of the market would have been small and the merger would have been allowed. Paradoxically, if separate markets had been defined for every type of container, the merger would have been legal also, because it would not have increased concentration in those markets. The only way the merger could have been found to "substantially" lessen competition would be if metal and glass were considered the relevant market.

The Court commented that metal and glass containers were separate industries, but held that competition existed between the two firms. The Court decided that a relevant market includes physically different products whenever the "interchangeability of use" and the "cross-elasticity of demand" between them is substantial. Furthermore, the Court said that the effects of a merger must be examined "in each...economically significant submarket." In the words of the Court, "By the acquisition of Hazel-Atlas stock, Continental not only increased its own share more than 14 percent from 21.9 percent to 25 percent, but also reduced from five to four the most significant competitors who might threaten its dominant position."

The second and third major antitrust laws were the **Clayton Act** (1914) and the **Federal Trade Commission Act** (1914). The FTC Act made illegal all "unfair" methods of competition and provided an agency to resolve questions about the legitimacy of specified business practices. Section 2 of the Clayton Act declares unlawful any price discrimination that lessens competition or tends to create a monopoly. Section 3 declares illegal any exclusive dealing or tying contracts when the effect is to lessen competition or to tend to create a monopoly. Section 7 prohibits stock acquisitions that may substantially lessen competition or tend to create a monopoly. Labor was specifically exempted from the Clayton Act.

The appointment of Thurman Arnold in 1937 as head of the Antitrust Division began a period of more rigorous antitrust activity. Several cases initiated in the late 1930s became landmark decisions. A decision against Socony-Vacuum Oil (1940) said that any combination that had the effect of price fixing was illegal and no test of "reasonableness" would be applied to price fixing. Another decision against ALCOA (1945) directly reversed the rule of reason. The Court found ALCOA to be an illegal monopoly even though the firm had not engaged in unreasonable behavior. The ALCOA decision suggested that beyond some point mere size does become an offense.

The Celler-Kefauver Act (1950) dealt directly with controlling industry concentration. This act closed a loophole in the Clayton Act by applying the same provisions to asset acquisition that had previously applied only to stock acquisitions. Later, the Hart-Scott-Rodino Antitrust Improvement Act (1976) amended both the Sherman and Clayton acts to increase penalties and make mergers easier to attack.[1]

16.5 Mergers and Social Welfare

If major rival firms merge, industry concentration must rise, whether measured by concentration ratios or by the Herfindahl index. The increase in monopoly power may be both substantial and socially undesirable. On the other hand, mergers of small firms may permit the new firm to experience economies of scale, thereby reducing the costs of production. Or, as for an industry dominated by a large firm, the merged minor firms may become a more viable competitor. Other mergers may be designed to diversify the product line of a business, reducing risk to shareholders. Still other mergers may result in increased effectiveness to compete in international markets. Public policy therefore should be designed to prohibit only socially harmful mergers.

Mergers can be classified into three types. **Horizontal integration** is the merging of firms that produce the same product. **Vertical integration** merges a firm that produces an intermediate good or supplies raw material with another firm that uses that input. A **conglomerate merger** combines firms from unrelated industries.

The first of four major waves of merger activity in the United States occurred at the turn of the century. Corporate holding companies known as *trusts* consolidated control of several major industries: banking, oil, steel, railroads, and others. Most mergers during this wave were horizontal, forming firms like U.S. Steel and Standard Oil. A second wave came during the roaring twenties, ending with the Great Depression. Most of those mergers were vertical, a shift caused, at least partly, by the prohibition of monopolization by the Sherman Act of 1890 and the Clayton Act of 1914. The third big wave of merger activity began in the late 1950s and lasted through the early 1970s. Most of these combinations were conglomerate acquisitions. A fourth wave began in the early 1980s. All three types of mergers were common during this wave, but the most notorious trend was "corporate raiding" and the "hostile takeover." Undervalued corporations or firms with substantial holdings of cash were targets for acquisition by "raiders" who purchased controlling interest by creative financing. A raider typically sets up a new corporation on paper, makes an offer to purchase stock in a target company, and issues so-called junk bonds to pay for the acquisition. Once in control, raiders raise cash to finance the

---

1. See Richard A. Posner, *Antitrust Law* (University of Chicago Press, 1976), for a cogent argument that only Section 1 of the Sherman Act is needed to effectively pursue antitrust policy. In Chapter 9, "Toward Simplification of Antitrust Doctrine," Posner argues that redundant antitrust statutes stimulate an uncritical and unwise prohibitory scope of antitrust policy, and that Section 1 is itself sufficiently encompassing in its prohibition of antitrust practices.

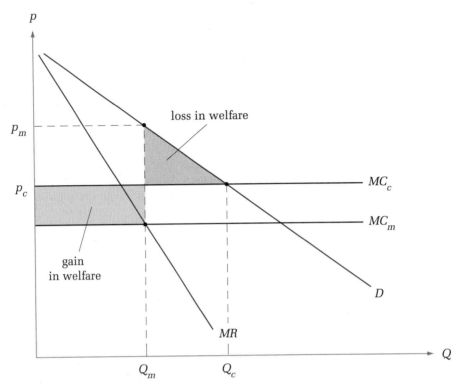

Figure 16.8 **Welfare change and a horizontal merger:** A merger that reduces competition and reduces marginal cost may result in a net welfare loss or a net welfare gain, depending on which area is larger.

transaction by selling assets of the acquired company. Although stockholders of the target firm frequently benefit from the sale of their stocks, managers may feel threatened and fight the takeover. Defenses include: "lollipops"—counteroffers to buy its own stock; "poison pills"—requirements to sell back the stock at a reduced price to the target company; and finding a "White Knight"—a buyer that the target company prefers to the raider. Between 1978 and 1983, more than 30 percent of the takeover attempts were met by hostile response by the target company.[2] The public reaction, however, indicates a belief that such takeovers generate net benefits to the economy from economies in production and distribution, shifting assets to higher valued uses, technology transfer, and improved management.

The welfare consequences of mergers are frequently ambiguous. Consider Figure 16.8, where the industry is initially competitive, with marginal cost curve MC_c. We assume constant marginal cost for simplicity. No producers' surplus is present before the merger because of the constant marginal cost, making the total social benefit from the

2. "The Market for Corporate Control," *Economic Report of the President,* 1985, ch. 6.

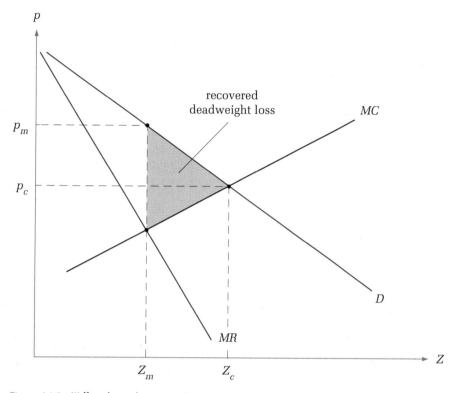

Figure 16.9 **Welfare change due to vertical integration:** A monopolist selling this input will set price at p_m, resulting in a deadweight loss. If this firm is acquired by the buyer, the buyer will want to maximize the sum of the seller's surplus and the buyer's surplus by producing Z_c units, and the deadweight loss will be eliminated.

competitive solution equal to the consumers' surplus at competitive price p_c. Now suppose mergers give rise to a monopoly but also result in reduced marginal cost MC_m. The monopoly firm sets price at p_m and sells Q_m units, causing a loss in welfare by the increase in price. But a gain in welfare also follows the fall in marginal cost. Whether or not a net gain or loss in welfare comes about depends on which area is larger.

Vertical mergers can also increase social welfare by *reducing* monopoly power, as Figure 16.9 illustrates. Suppose the seller of an input Z is a monopolist, who sets price at p_m, resulting in a deadweight loss. If the buyer of this input acquires the seller by vertical integration, the merged firm will want to maximize the sum of the former seller's surplus and the buyer's surplus. That maximizing is accomplished by producing Z_c units, and the deadweight loss is eliminated. The increased use of Z leads to increased production of the final good sold at a lower price. You might ask why the buyer doesn't "bribe" the seller to behave like a competitive firm. The reason is that effective enforcement is required to keep the seller from reneging on the agreement. Vertical integration, however, brings the two firms under one management.

GLOBAL PERSPECTIVE: *Bristol-Myers and Squibb*

Bristol-Myers, the largest U.S. pharmaceutical company (in 1988 revenues), and Squibb, the tenth-largest company, announced July 27, 1989, that they had agreed to a $12-billion stock-swap merger.* The deal would create the world's second-largest drug company. The two firms said they would be able to compete better in a worldwide market after the merger. The merger would bring diversity to Squibb, which is dominant in the hypertension drug market, and would add several developing products to Bristol-Myers, which produces consumer products, over-the-counter drugs, and cancer-fighting prescription drugs.

To discourage any hostile takeover attempts, Squibb granted Bristol-Myers the right to buy about 20 percent of Squibb's stock for a fixed price above the current market price. The firms also agreed to market each other's products immediately. That agreement was not contingent on the merger.

Industry analysts point out that it takes from eight to twelve years and more than $100 million to bring a new drug to market, and so merging with a company that has proven consumer products provides a source of steady earnings to pay for drug research. Moreover, the merging firms said they have a global strategy—they identify a "critical mass" of product diversification, marketing skill, and expertise in scientific research required to compete worldwide. Industry executives and other observers say small companies won't be able to compete in the evolving market. Thus, many similar mergers are expected to follow. But even with recent mergers and more to come, the new big companies will have relatively small market shares in the $127-billion global industry.

* *The Los Angeles Times*, Part IV, Friday, July 28, 1989.

16.6 The DOJ Merger Guidelines

The body of antitrust law remains fundamentally hostile to mergers between firms with significant market shares when entry is not easy. The Antitrust Division of the Department of Justice (DOJ) implemented *Merger Guidelines* in June 1982[3] that are intended to prevent the exercise or enhancement of market power that might arise as a consequence of a merger. The *Guidelines* address five crucial issues.

First, a market is defined as a product or product group sold by sellers who, if they acted in concert, could raise their prices by a significant amount for a significant period. A 5 percent increase in price sustained for one year is stated as the most likely guideline. The smallest group of sellers who could exercise market power is usually selected as the relevant market for the analysis.

Second, the *Guidelines* use a variation of the Herfindahl index to set acceptable limits for concentration. The **Herfindahl-Hirschman (HH) index** is computed by summing the *squared* market shares of all sellers in the market. The HH index measures the shares as percentages, giving a pure monopoly an HH index of 10,000. The *Guidelines* specify two

3. The 1982 *Guidelines* replaced others used since 1968.

ECONOMIC SCENE: *Coca-Cola and Dr Pepper**

Early in 1986, the Coca-Cola Company announced its intention to purchase the Dr Pepper Company. Later in that year, the FTC declared its opposition to the merger under Section 7 of the Clayton Act. Coca-Cola and Dr Pepper decided to contest the FTC's attempt to seek a preliminary injunction in District Court. On July 13, 1986, Judge Gerhard Gesell found in favor of the FTC. The proposed merger was effectively halted when Dr Pepper decided to withdraw from the acquisition. Most of the arguments advanced by both sides were structured by the DOJ *Merger Guidelines.*

The FTC argued that the relevant product markets were carbonated soft-drink concentrate and carbonated soft drinks. The relevant geographic markets were a national market *and* local metropolitan areas. The FTC claimed that pricing and marketing strategies were developed by considering the reactions of other carbonated soft-drink producers and not toward the sellers of other beverages. Coke argued that they competed against all other beverages. With respect to geography, the FTC claimed that the United States was one market and that imports were negligible. Furthermore, the FTC argued that because producers could charge different prices in different local areas, those local areas should be considered separate markets.

At the time of the proposed merger, Coca-Cola had a 37.4 percent market share of domestic retail sales and Dr Pepper had a 4.6 percent share. They were, respectively, the largest and fourth-largest firms in the industry. The second-largest firm was Pepsico, with a 28.9 percent share. The third-largest firm sold Seven-Up, which had a 4.6 percent market share. With the merger, the HH index for the national market would have risen by 341 points to 2,646—well above the guideline decision point. Moreover, the HH index would have risen by more than 100 points in more than two-thirds of the local areas for which data were available. In contrast, if all beverages in the United States were taken to be the relevant market, the post-merger HH index would have been 739, well below the guideline threshold.

The FTC argued that entry into the market was difficult because substantial sums are required for advertising and promotion of soft drinks. For instance, Coca-Cola planned to spend $44 million on first-year promotion of its new Cherry Coke alone. Moreover, such expenditures are very risky and are a "sunk" cost. Coca-Cola argued that even if the relevant market were defined only for concentrated soft drinks, entry was easy because no specialized resources were needed in production and no significant economies of scale arose. If entry was easy, then the high HH index was irrelevant because the market was contestable. The FTC countered that limited access to vendors and distributors deterred entry, stating that even a firm like Procter and Gamble, who owned Crush International, had not been able to make a dent in the market.

The antagonists also presented arguments about other market characteristics. The FTC said the merger would make coordinated behavior of all producers easier.

---

* This account is based on the analysis provided by Lawrence J. White, "Application of the Merger Guidelines: The Proposed Merger of Coca-Cola and Dr Pepper," in *The Antitrust Revolution,* John E. Kwoka, Jr. and Lawrence J. White, eds. (Scott, Foresman, 1989), pp. 80–98.

The direct competition between some brands would be eliminated. Furthermore, to the extent that Coca-Cola might consolidate its distribution through one local bottler, the smaller producers might find their volume insufficient to achieve adequate economies of scale. Being unable to piggyback on the bottling of large-volume producers might drive the smaller firms from the industry. Coca-Cola argued that the wide variety of product types and sizes made it impossible for any one firm to coordinate the behavior of other firms—only the merger of Coke and Pepsi would stifle competition. Coke also said that the stock prices of its rivals fell in response to the announcement of the intent to merge, indicating that the stock market believed the merger would be procompetitive. Last, Coca-Cola argued that the merger would permit efficiencies and reduce cost, that it could use its marketing skills to improve the Dr Pepper operation. The reduced costs of production would enhance competition and enable lower pricing. The FTC considered this argument irrelevant to the case.

Judge Gesell ruled that the relevant product market was concentrated soft drinks and that the relevant geographic markets were the entire United States and thirty-two significant population areas, markets that were highly concentrated. He said Dr Pepper had been one of the few effective competitors to Coke, and that Coke was now trying to buy out its competition. Judge Gesell said that other firms seeking to challenge the dominance of Coca-Cola and Pepsico would have great difficulty finding effective distribution and that entry was difficult. The merger would eliminate the direct rivalry between the first- and fourth-largest firms. Finally, he paid little attention to Coca-Cola's efficiency argument, and said the acquisition lacked any redeeming feature.

decision points using the HH index. If the post-merger index is below 1,000, the merger will usually not be challenged. If the post-merger index is above 1,800 and the merger would cause an increase in the index by 100 or more, the merger is likely to be challenged. When these two conditions are not met, other market characteristics are analyzed before a challenge is made.

Third, the *Guidelines* indicate that entry is an important element in analyzing the potential effect of a merger. They indicate that entry within two years of a significant price increase is a relevant threshold. Beyond that, the *Guidelines* do not specify any other quantitative definition of ease or difficulty of entry.

Fourth, the *Guidelines* discuss three other market characteristics that influence the ability of merging firms to coordinate their decisions: the level of concentration on the buyers' side of the market; the type of product, including quality and service components; and the past behavior of sellers in the relevant market. No quantitative measures are specified, however, and no mention is made about the relative importance of these three characteristics.

Fifth, the *Guidelines* indicate that any social loss resulting from increased monopoly power caused by a merger should be offset by cost efficiencies created by the merger. Past guidelines took a more skeptical view of promised reductions in costs.

16.7 Pricing Practices and the Law

Every manager should be aware of the legality of pricing practices. Penalties can be harsh for violating the law. In 1960, several electrical companies, including General Electric and Westinghouse, were fined $2 million for collusive price fixing. About $300 million in treble damages was paid to injured parties in addition to the fines. And seven managers went to prison.

Collusive agreements to fix prices are illegal under Section 1 of the Sherman Act. **Price fixing** is illegal per se, meaning that no defense is possible. Chief Justice Earl Warren said,[4]

> It has been held too often to require elaboration now that price fixing is contrary to the policy of competition underlying the Sherman Act and that its illegality does not depend on a showing of reasonableness, since it is conclusively presumed to be unreasonable. It makes no difference whether the motives of the participants are good or evil; whether the price fixing is accomplished by express contract or by some subtle means; whether the participants possess market control; whether the amount of interstate commerce affected is large or small; or whether the effect of the agreement is to raise or lower prices.

Price fixing also includes fixing quality, for limiting quality amounts to raising price. Similarly, market-sharing agreements may be interpreted as a mechanism for fixing prices. Price leadership and parallel pricing, however, are *not* considered price fixing as long as the firms act independently. But any evidence of meetings or communication of any kind may invite prosecution.

Price discrimination is illegal under Section 2 of the Clayton Act, as amended by the Robinson-Patman Act, whenever the effect is to lessen competition or to tend to create a monopoly. Two legal defenses may be raised against charges of price discrimination. First, price discrimination is legal when due to "differences in grade, quality or quantity," or where lower prices are due to "differences in cost of selling or transportation." Second, price discrimination is legal when lower prices are offered "in good faith to meet competition." Price discrimination may be permitted also if it causes no significant injury to competition, actual or potential. Senior discounts for meals and movies, and student discounts for bus rides, are not likely to lead to prosecution. Thus, a business may legally practice price discrimination unless that prevents entry into the industry.

Predatory pricing "for the purpose of destroying competition, or eliminating a competitor," is illegal under Section 3 of the Robinson-Patman Act. The aggressor firm need not set its price below the rival's price to be guilty of predatory pricing. Borden priced a product called ReaLemon about 25 percent *above* rivals' prices; it was able to take this step because of the ReaLemon brand name. Borden was found guilty of predatory pricing because the price–cost differentials pushed rivals' prices below their costs while

---

4. U.S. v. McKesson & Robbins, Inc., 351 U.S. 305, 309–310 (1956).

Borden continued to earn a profit. Borden's pricing practice was illegal because its intent was to destroy or eliminate competition.

Resale price maintenance, the practice of setting a price floor at the retail level, has been illegal since the "fair-trade" laws were repealed in 1975. The Miler-Tydings Resale Price Maintenance Act (1937) and the McGuire Act (1952) had exempted *vertical* price agreements between firms. Manufacturers of brand-name or trademarked products could set a price floor at the retail level. The idea was to prevent "cutthroat" competition and "unfair" pricing practices by discounters. Since repeal of the fair-trade laws, firms may no longer set minimum resale prices. They can, however, set "suggested" resale prices, but those prices may not be enforced by raising wholesale price, restricting supply, or any other mechanism.

In summary, it is illegal to have *horizontal* price agreements among rival firms and *vertical* price agreements between suppliers and resale firms. To avoid severe fines and possible jail time, managers should avoid *any* communication with other firms about pricing decisions.

AN APPLICATION: *The IBM Cases**

Several private antitrust suits seeking treble damages were filed against IBM for actions taken in the early 1970s. The basic issue in the related cases was the extent to which a dominant firm can protect itself from rivals. The plaintiffs alleged that IBM engaged in practices designed to maintain monopoly power. The IBM response was that its actions were evidence of competition.

In the 1960s, IBM was the dominant computer systems manufacturer, with about 70 percent of the market. The remaining 30 percent was divided among the "seven dwarfs"—Burroughs, Control Data, General Electric, Honeywell, NCR, RCA, Sperry Rand—and a number of smaller firms. At that time computers were sold or leased as complete systems. Individual components were not priced to meet competition but to maximize overall profit from the system. In the late 1960s, several companies developed tape and disk drives that would work with IBM units. These new products threatened IBM's dominance, because entry barriers were substantially lower for components than for complete systems.

According to economic theory, if the limit price on a component was below IBM's average variable cost, then IBM would leave that market unless it decided to engage in predatory pricing. If the limit price was above average variable cost, then IBM would set the price at that limit price to guard against entry. The results would be greater profits on central processing units (CPUs), reduced profits from peripheral equipment, and reduced total profits. An alternative strategy would be to tie products together to preclude purchasers of IBM CPUs from purchasing peripheral equipment from other companies.

* This application is based on Gerald W. Block, "Dominant Firm Response to Competitive Challenge: Peripheral Equipment Manufacturers' Suits Against IBM," in *The Antitrust Revolution,* John E. Kwoka, Jr. and Lawrence J. White, eds. (Scott, Foresman, 1989).

In early 1970, IBM designated peripheral competition as a key issue. In late 1970, IBM cut its price on a high-capacity disk drive by 26 percent. The new price was $1,000 for three drives—effectively setting the unit price at $333, which was below the breakeven rental price of $381 per month per drive. But the new price was available only to new customers. Only customers considering switching to a compatible product were eligible for the new price.

Competitors responded by cutting their prices too, and IBM convened a new study group to find a solution. The group recommended even more drastic price cuts—from 50 to 80 percent—on particularly vulnerable products. Management rejected this recommendation, however, and ordered the task force to devise a long-term lease plan as an alternative. A new plan would provide an excuse for cutting prices and a way to protect installed equipment from being replaced. The customer received an 8 percent discount for a one-year lease and a 16 percent discount for a two-year lease. Penalties for early termination were 2.5 times the monthly rental for a one-year lease and 5 times the rental for a two-year lease. The leases were available only on peripheral equipment and not on CPUs. Soon, IBM announced price increases on its CPUs. Little change was made in the price of the entire system. When the new leasing plan was announced, the stock of rival companies fell about 15 percent, and most continued to fall for the next two years. By 1972, new products being introduced by IBM included modified interfaces that required integrated components. The new technology further limited rivals' ability to compete with IBM.

Telex filed an antitrust suit, charging IBM with monopolizing and attempting to monopolize the market for peripheral equipment. Telex claimed that IBM had 90 percent of the relevant market, and that IBM's actions were designed to reduce or eliminate competition after evaluating competitors' capabilities. In a broader relevant market, IBM claimed its share had declined from 62 percent in 1952 to 35 percent in 1970. It also claimed that its actions were brought about by increased competitiveness in the industry. Filing a countersuit, IBM charged that Telex had stolen trade secrets, violated patent rights, and infringed on copyrighted manuals. In September 1973, both parties were found guilty of the respective charges. The net payment obligation from IBM to Telex was about $260 million.

An appeal to the Tenth Circuit Court reversed the award of damages from IBM to Telex, but the award from Telex to IBM was allowed to stand. Telex appealed to the U.S. Supreme Court, but both companies agreed to drop all litigation before a decision was announced. It seemed IBM had a lot to lose but nothing to gain by pursuing the case, because Telex would have been bankrupt if IBM had won, and so IBM would not have been able to collect.

Three West-Coast companies—CalComp, Memorex, and Transamerican Computer—decided to press their suits against IBM in spite of the Telex reversal. The CalComp case was the first to reach trial. CalComp used the basic Telex theory, but concentrated more on establishing the relevant market in a broader context, thereby avoiding the primary reason for the reversal of the Telex case. CalComp hired an economic consultant to determine IBM's market share. They argued that IBM's average share fell from 78.4 percent between 1961 and 1965 to 70.7 percent between 1966 and 1970. After CalComp rested its case, IBM moved for and received a directed verdict. The judge did not find an antitrust violation even while accepting CalComp's view of the facts.

In 1979, the Ninth Circuit Court upheld this IBM victory, concluding that because CalComp made no showing that IBM's prices were below marginal cost or average variable cost, IBM's actions could not be condemned. The court concluded that "IBM's price cuts were part of the competitive process..." and that "IBM...had the right to redesign its products to make them more attractive to buyers...and was under no duty to help CalComp or other peripheral equipment manufacturers survive or expand."

The Memorex and Transamerican cases went through separate trials. Both cases ended with deadlocked juries and with directed verdicts in favor of IBM. Thus, these judgments indicate that a plaintiff must overcome a presumption of competitive pricing to prove predatory pricing.

ECONOMIC SCENE: *College Price Fixing*

The image of the university as an altruistic institution searching for truth was tarnished by a Justice Department investigation into tuition fixing. Some forty of America's most prestigious schools were scrutinized for violations of the Sherman Act. According to the Justice Department, college tuition charges were suspiciously similar. College aid packages were also strikingly similar. These similarities might have been in part the result of annual meetings at which college administrators gathered to compare applicants and determine aid packages.

Similar tuition prices and aid packages do not necessarily imply collusion in price fixing. Price equality may be a consequence of strong competition. Only when collusion is present does the equality of prices alarm economists.

If all firms collude to raise price above the competitive equilibrium, an unjustifiable loss to society follows. But the Justice Department must show that the sharing of information is coupled with ability to fix price. The schools investigated must, therefore, comprise a market separate from state universities and other colleges.

A confidential document drafted at Wesleyan University lent credence to the charge of collusion. On March 4, 1988, to justify a tuition increase, the Wesleyan treasurer's office reported the percentage increases in tuition at six other schools.* Because the tuition increases cited *had not yet been released,* possession of that information suggests espionage or collusion.

As long as the Justice Department investigated tuition fixing and collusion in student financial aid, perhaps it should also investigate the National Collegiate Athletic Association. Ian Ayres, a law professor at Northwestern University, stated that "the NCAA openly engages in cartel-like collusion to suppress wages" (*New Republic,* October 16, 1989). Gary S. Becker, an economist at the University of Chicago,

---

* See Alexander Hollander Siegal, "College Price-fixing: Collusion and Monopoly in Academia," *Campus,* 1(1) (Spring 1990), p. 10.

described the NCAA's actions as "blatant restrictions on aid to student athletes" (*Business Week,* September 25, 1989). The probable existence of athletic cartels and student-housing monopolies are topics that could be added to the Justice Department's investigations.

Summary

Regulation arises when special-interest groups lobby to enact laws that serve them. Many regulations are motivated by a need to correct some market imperfection or to mitigate the presence of monopoly power. Some, though, cause market imperfections and create social losses.

One of the most important areas of regulation has grown out of increasing social awareness of the negative externalities from environmental pollution. If left unregulated in the absence of property rights to the externality, pollution has the potential for creating huge social losses. Corrections may take the form of emissions standards, fees, or transferable permits. Using transferable permits, when producers are numerous enough to ensure a competitive market for the permits, allows the regulator to control emissions while avoiding interference with cost minimizing by producers.

A natural monopoly occurs when economies of scale cause decreasing long-run average costs over a substantial range of market demand. One firm can supply the entire demand at a price lower than the minimum average costs of smaller firms. Natural monopolies are usually regulated as public utilities to mitigate the welfare losses of monopoly while taking advantage of the lower unit costs permitted by the economies of scale.

Antitrust laws prohibit monopoly, attempts to monopolize, and conspiracies in restraint of trade. Generally, the intent of antitrust laws has been to provide an environment favorable to competition. The Department of Justice is likely to challenge mergers that tend to reduce market competition. The DOJ uses formal guidelines to evaluate a merger's effect on market structure. The guidelines address five issues: the relevant market, industry concentration, ease of entry, potential for collusion, and social gains and losses.

Price discrimination is illegal under the Clayton Act, as amended by the Robinson-Patman Act, whenever it lessens competition or tends to create a monopoly. But price discrimination is defensible when cost differences are discernible. Moreover, price discrimination may be permitted when no significant injury is done to competition.

Predatory pricing for the purpose of destroying competition is illegal under the Robinson-Patman Act. The IBM cases, however, have demonstrated reluctance in the courts to prosecute price-cutting firms just because rivals suffered losses. Price reductions down to marginal cost are now viewed as consistent with competition. Limit pricing appears to be legal, but predatory pricing by setting price below marginal cost is likely to be found illegal.

Further Readings

For further discussion of emissions fees, pollution standards, and transferable permits, see

- William J. Baumol and Wallace E. Oates, *Economics, Environmental Policy, and the Quality of Life* (Prentice-Hall, 1979).

On the economic theory of regulation, see

- George Stigler, "The Theory of Economic Regulation," *Bell Journal of Economics and Management Science* (Spring 1971), pp. 3–21.
- Richard Posner, "Theories of Economic Regulation," *Bell Journal of Economics and Management Science* (Autumn 1974), pp. 335–358.

I also highly recommend this work:

- Robert H. Frank, *Choosing the Right Pond* (Oxford University Press, 1985).

Robert Frank looks at the consequences of people's feelings about where they stand on the economic totem pole and how their quest for status influences private transactions and underlies much of the regulatory apparatus seen in Western societies. For more on antitrust economics, these books are excellent reading:

- Sumner Marcus, *Competition and the Law* (Wadsworth, 1967).
- E. M. Singer, *Antitrust Economics: Selected Cases and Economic Models* (Prentice-Hall, 1968).
- J. E. Kwoka, Jr., and Lawrence J. White, eds., *The Antitrust Revolution* (Scott, Foresman, 1989).

Practice Problems

1. The social cost of pollution generated by the chemical industry (in billions of dollars) is

$$C = 3E + 3E^2$$

   where E is the quantity of polluting emissions (in thousands of tons). Thus the marginal social cost of emissions is

$$MSE = 3 + 6E$$

   The marginal cost of abatement (in billions of dollars) is

$$MCA = 7 - 4E$$

   (a) What is the socially optimal level of emissions?
   (b) What is the optimal emissions fee?

2. Compare and contrast these mechanisms for addressing pollution externalities under conditions of uncertainty: (a) an emissions standard, (b) an emissions fee, and (c) transferable emissions permits.

3. Graphically illustrate the natural monopoly case. Show the profit-maximizing price and output for the unregulated natural monopolist. On the same graph, identify the price

and output where $p = LMC$, a result guaranteed by perfect competition. Show the subsidy that would be required if the monopolist were forced to charge a price equal to long-run marginal cost.

4. Suppose the market demand curve for facing a public utility shifts to the right. At the same time, suppose the LAC curve shifts upward because of production inefficiencies. Show the price a regulatory agency might set, and indicate the quantity of services supplied, if the regulator does not detect the production inefficiencies.

5. Compare and contrast the effect on a monopolist's output and price decisions of a fixed tax per unit of output to a lump-sum tax levied without regard to output.

6. Compare the effect on a monopolist's output and price decisions of an ad valorem (value added) tax (a fixed percentage of price) to an excess-profits tax.

7. Suppose a natural monopolist operates in a contestable market. Illustrate graphically how price, output, average cost, and marginal cost are determined. Will this firm be able to sustain an economic profit?

8. Briefly explain the significance of each of these events:
   (a) The Supreme Court's enunciation of the "Rule of Reason."
   (b) The appointment of Thurman Arnold as head of the Antitrust Division.
   (c) The decision by Judge Hand against ALCOA in 1945.
   (d) The passage of the Celler-Kefauver Act (1950) and the Hart-Scott-Rodino Act (1976).
   (e) The decision by the Supreme Court against Continental Can (1964) under the Clayton Act.

9. Given an industry composed of ten firms with these market shares:

Firm	Market share (%)
1	20
2	18
3	15
4	10
5	8
6	8
7	6
8	5
9	5
10	5

   (a) Suppose the two largest firms have proposed a merger. Calculate the Herfindahl-Hirshman index before and after the merger. Is the Department of Justice likely to challenge this merger?
   (b) Suppose instead that the third- and fourth-largest firms propose to merge. Is that merger likely to be challenged by DOJ under its guidelines?

    (c) Suppose instead that two of the smallest firms wish to merge. Is that merger likely to be challenged under the DOJ guidelines?

    (d) What are some of the other things that the DOJ is likely to consider in making a decision about a proposed merger?

10. What is predatory pricing? How is it distinguished from rigorous price competition? How is it related to but different from limit pricing?

11. Under what conditions is price discrimination allowable?

Functions, Graphs, and Optimizing with Calculus

Functions and graphs communicate information. Many of the models in this book are illustrated graphically and are represented by functions. Some of the numerical examples require you to apply simple algebra. Other models and examples rely on the assumption that economic agents wish to optimize something. Consumers strive to maximize satisfaction. Firms try to minimize cost and maximize profit. Society wishes to use resources most efficiently and maximize real gross national product. This appendix is provided to help you more easily understand the presentations in this textbook. Even students who feel comfortable working with equations and graphs are likely to find a quick review helpful. Moreover, although the text does not rely on calculus-based models, understanding calculus can only facilitate understanding of models of economic optimization. For that reason, this appendix also briefly surveys some of the more popular optimization techniques using calculus.

Functions, Relations, and Graphs

A **function** is a mathematical relation for which the value of a dependent variable is determined from the values of one or more independent variables. A function may be expressed

$$y = f(x)$$

where y is the dependent variable and x is the independent variable. The functional relationship is read "y is a function of x." The symbol $f(x)$ is read "f of x." Another frequently used notation is $y = y(x)$, where $y(x)$ is the rule by which values of y are determined by the values of x.

Let's take the **linear** function

$$y = a + bx$$

as an illustration. In this case $f(x) = a + bx$, where a is called the **intercept** and b is called the **slope**. For example,

$$y = f(x) = -4 + 2x$$

yields one and only one value for y, determined by the function $f(x)$ for any value of x. This function is illustrated in Figure A.1. Because this function is linear, only two points need to be plotted so that a straight line can be drawn through them. An infinite number of

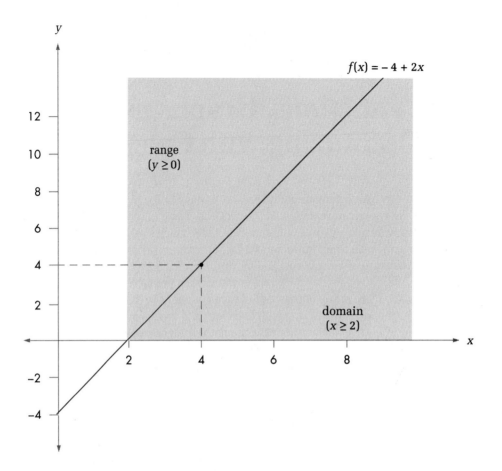

Figure A.1   **A linear function:** The linear function $y = -4 + 2x$ can be plotted by drawing a straight line between two points (x, y). For instance, $x = 0, y = -4$ and $x = 4, y = 4$ are two such points. If the domain is $x \geq 2$, then the range is $y \geq 0$.

possible values for x and y, however, satisfy the function $y = f(x)$, not just the two points chosen. Any pair will do to plot the function.

Frequently, it makes sense to restrict the values of the independent and dependent variables. For instance, negative values for price and quantity produced usually do not make sense. Permissible values of the independent variable are called the **domain** of the function. If the domain of the function $f(x) = -4 + 2x$ is restricted to be $x \geq 2$, then the function should be written

$$y = -4 + 2x \text{ for } x \geq 2$$

The permissible values for the dependent variable are called the **range** of the function. For our example, the range of y is $y \geq 0$. The domain and the resulting range are shaded in Figure A.1.

Other relations that are not functions can be defined by **sets**. The difference between a relation and a function is that a **relation** may have more than one value of y (the range) associated with any value of x in the domain of x. A **linear inequality** of the form

$$y \geq a + bx \text{ or } y \leq a + bx$$

is a relation that defines a set of points. The linear inequality

$$y \leq -1 + x \text{ for } x \geq 0$$

is illustrated by Figure A.2. The equality part of the equation is called the **boundary**. The **set** of permissible values of y given x in the domain of x is shown by the shaded area on the graph.

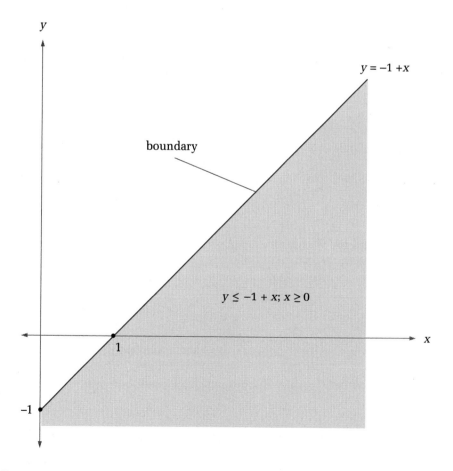

Figure A.2 **A linear inequality:** The set of points $y \leq -1 + x$ over the domain $x \geq 0$ is identified by the boundary equation and the shaded region.

Graphing Multivariate Functions

A function is a **multivariate function** when the dependent variable is related to more than one independent variable. The function

$$y = f(x_1, x_2)$$

relates y to x_1 and x_2. Graphing multivariate functions can be tricky because one dimension is required for each variable. The function $y = f(x_1, x_2)$ requires three dimensions unless the dimensionality is reduced by holding constant one variable. Two techniques can be used to reduce the number of dimensions.

The first technique is to plot y as a function of one independent variable alone while holding all others constant. The multivariate function

$$y = f(x_1, x_2) = 2x_1 + 3x_1x_2 + 6x_2$$

can be plotted as a function of x_1 alone, given x_2. When x_2 is held constant, we write

$$y = f(x_1; x_2)$$

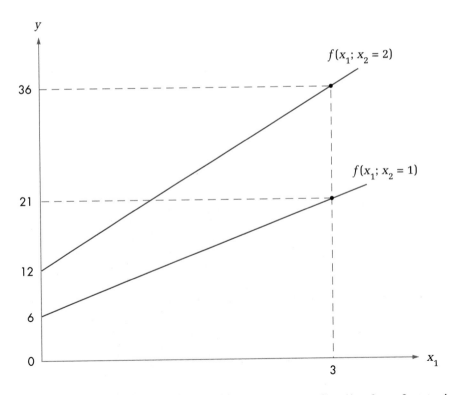

Figure A.3 **Graphing a multivariate function conditionally:** The function $y = f(x_1, x_2) = 2x_1 + 3x_1x_2 + 6x_2$ is graphed for $x_2 = 1$ and $x_2 = 2$.

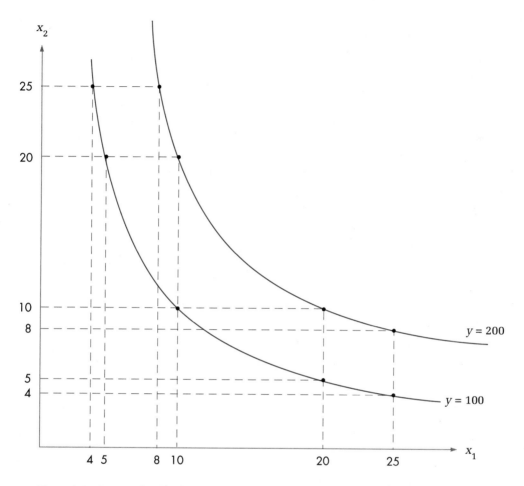

Figure A.4 **A contour plot:** The function $y = x_1 x_2$ is plotted for $y = 100$ and $y = 200$.

where the semicolon denotes the condition that x_2 is held constant. Then x_2 can be varied parametrically:

$$y = f(x_1; x_2 = 1) = 5x_1 + 6$$
$$y = f(x_1; x_2 = 2) = 8x_1 + 12$$

and so on. The function $y = f(x_1, x_2)$ can now be plotted by graph $y = f(x_1; x_2)$ as x_2 varies, as illustrated in Figure A.3. Alternatively, you could graph $y = f(x_2; x_1)$ as x_1 is varied parametrically.

The second technique treats the dependent variable parametrically. The resulting graph is called a **contour**. For instance, the function

$$y = f(x_1, x_2) = x_1 x_2$$

can be plotted by determining values of x_1 and x_2 that yield different fixed values of y. Figure A.4 illustrates a graph of $y = x_1 x_2$ for $y = 100$ and $y = 200$.

Systems of Equations

A **system** of equations consists of several equations with one or more independent variables. As an example, a system of two equations with one independent variable is

$$y = g(x) = 10/x \text{ for } x \geq 0$$
$$y = h(x) = 5x \text{ for } x \geq 0$$

A **solution** to this system, if a solution exists, is the set of x and y values that satisfies both equations simultaneously. The solution can be found by setting $g(x) = h(x)$ over the domain of x and then substituting the values of x found into either function to find corresponding values for y:

$$10/x = 5x$$

implies that $10 = 5x^2$. Thus $x = \sqrt{2}$ and $y = 7.071$ is the solution. This principle is illustrated in Figure A.5.

Systems of equations can be used to represent economic relations. To keep things simple, illustrations are frequently limited to systems of linear equations. Thus it is important to be able to find solutions to systems of linear equations in order to follow the illustrations. An example of a linear system with two equations and two variables is:

$$3x_1 + 2x_2 = 14$$
$$6x_1 - 2x_2 = 4$$

We can find a solution in several ways when it exists. One technique is **row operations**. Each equation is called a row. The three legitimate row operations are:

1. Any two rows can be interchanged.
2. Any row may be multiplied by a nonzero constant.
3. Any row can be added to another row.

The solution technique is to perform row operations until each row has only one of the independent variables. The solution can then be read from the right-hand side of the transformed equations.

For the preceding system, suppose we multiply the first equation by 1/3 to get

$$x_1 + \frac{2}{3}x_2 = \frac{14}{3}$$

Next, let's multiply this equation by -6 and add the resulting equation to the second equation to get

$$-6x_2 = -24$$

We have just eliminated x_1 from the second equation by substitution. Now we can multiply this transformed equation by $-1/6$ to obtain

$$x_2 = 4$$

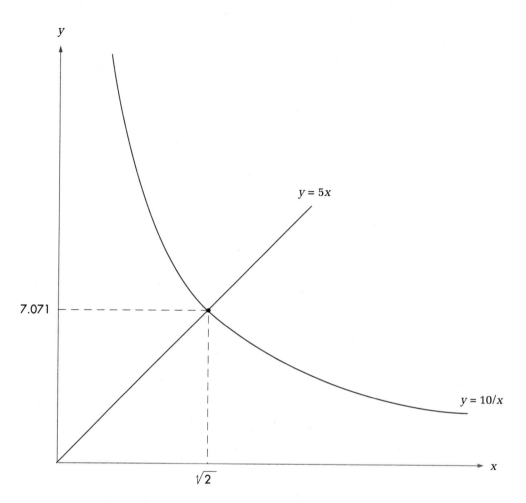

Figure A.5 **Solving a system of equations:** The solution to $y = 5x$ and $y = 10/x$ is $x = \sqrt{2}$, $y = 7.071$.

Next, this equation can be multiplied by $-2/3$ and added to the transformed first equation to get

$$x_1 = 2$$

The solution is $x_1 = 2$ and $x_2 = 4$.

In summary, the solution by row operations is to choose subsequent variables. After each variable's coefficient is forced to unity by scalar multiplication, we use it to eliminate that variable from the remaining equations. Row operations are continued until we find the final solution.

Nonlinear Functions

A general form of the **polynomial** class of functions is

$$y = f(x) = a_0 + a_1x + a_2x^2 + a_3x^3 + \cdots + a_nx^n$$

where a_0, a_1, ..., a_n are coefficients and n is a positive integer. The polynomial is **linear** when $n = 1$. When $n = 2$, the polynomial is **quadratic**. The general form of the quadratic is

$$y = a + bx + cx^2$$

The shape of the quadratic is determined by the coefficients, as illustrated by Figure A.6.

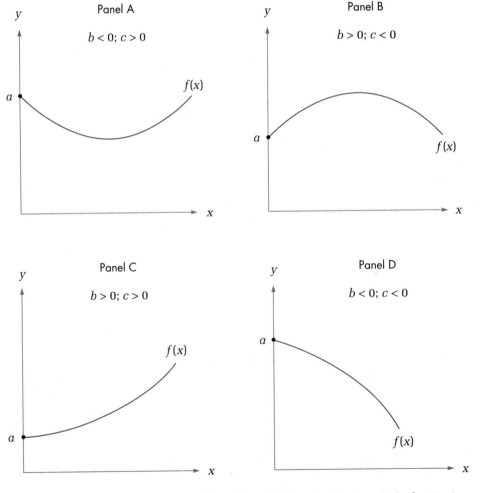

Figure A.6 **The quadratic function** $y = a + bx + cx^2$**: Panel A** When $b < 0$ and $c > 0$, the function is concave. **Panel B** When $b > 0$ and $c < 0$, the function is convex. **Panel C** When both b and c are positive, the function increases at an increasing rate. **Panel D** When both b and c are negative, the function decreases at an increasing rate.

When $n = 3$, the polynomial is **cubic**. The general form of the cubic is

$$y = a + bx + cx^2 + dx^3$$

The shape of the cubic function has many variations. The distinguishing characteristic about the shape of all cubic functions is that they change from being locally convex to locally concave or vice versa as x increases.

Two other nonlinear functions that are related to each other are the exponential and logarithmic functions. An **exponential** function has the form

$$y = f(x) = a^x$$

where a is a constant called the *base* and $a > 0$ and $a \neq 1$. The variable y increases as x increases if $a > 1$, and the variable y decreases as x increases if $a < 1$. The two variations are illustrated in Figure A.7. One of the most frequently used bases for the exponential is

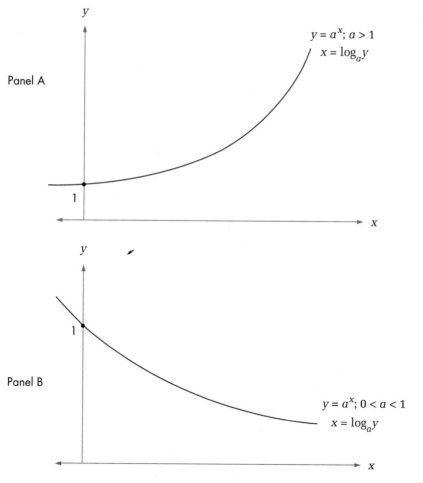

Figure A.7 **The exponential and logarithmic: Panel A** The exponential increases at an increasing rate when $a > 1$. **Panel B** The exponential decreases at a decreasing rate when $a < 1$.

the number e, defined as the limit of the expression $[1 - 1/n]^n$ as n approaches infinity, $e = 2.7182818\ldots$.

The **logarithmic** function has the form

$$x = \log_a y$$

where a is the base. The inverse of the logarithmic is the exponential. When the logarithm is taken to the base e, it is called the *natural* logarithm and is denoted by $\log_e y = \ln y$.

Any exponential can be expressed in terms of logarithms by taking the log of both sides of the equation. For example,

$$y = kb^{f(x)}$$

can be expressed as

$$\log_a y = \log_a k + f(x)\log_a b$$

If the base e is chosen, the function becomes

$$\ln y = \ln k + f(x)\ln b$$

It is frequently helpful to recognize that $\log_a(a) = 1$ and $\log_a(1) = 0$.

Establishing Functions

An easy way to establish functions through known points is to solve simultaneous equations. For any polynomial function, $(n + 1)$ known points on the function are substituted into the general form of the equation and the resulting $(n + 1)$ equations are solved simultaneously for the $(n + 1)$ coefficients $a_0, a_1, \ldots, a_n$.

Two points are required to establish a linear function. Suppose the two points (x, y) are $(2, 2)$ and $(4, 0)$. These points are substituted into the linear form $y = a + bx$ to get:

$$2 = a + b(2) = a + 2b$$
$$0 = a + b(4) = a + 4b$$

The simultaneous solution yields $a = 4$ and $b = -1$. Thus, the linear equation has been established as $y = 4 - x$.

Three points are required to establish a quadratic function. Suppose the three points (x, y) are $(1, 3)$, $(3, -1)$, and $(6, 8)$. Substitution into the general form of the quadratic $y = a + bx + cx^2$ yields:

$$3 = a + b(1) + c(1)^2 = a + b + c$$
$$-1 = a + b(3) + c(3)^2 = a + 3b + 9c$$
$$8 = a + b(6) + c(6)^2 = a + 6b + 36c$$

The solution is $a = 8$, $b = -6$, and $c = 1$, and so the function is $y = 8 - 6x + x^2$.

An exponential can be established through any two points except $x = 0$ and $y = 0$. The first step is to write the exponential as a logarithmic function. Second, the two points are substituted for x and y and the resulting equations are solved simultaneously. Suppose you wish to establish the equation $y = ke^{cx}$ and are given the two points (x, y) as $(1, 2)$ and $(4, 6)$. First, convert the equation to natural logs:

$$\ln y = \ln k + cx$$

because $\ln e = 1$. Substituting the two known points yields:

$$\ln(2) = \ln k + c(1)$$
$$\ln(6) = \ln k + c(4)$$

finding natural logs with a calculator yields:

$$0.69315 = \ln k + c$$
$$1.79176 = \ln k + 4c$$

Simultaneous solution yields $\ln k = 0.32695$ and $c = 0.36620$. The antilog of 0.32695 yields $k = 1.386$. Thus, the exponential has been established as[1]

$$y = 1.386e^{0.3662x}$$

Slopes and Derivatives

The **slope** of a function is the change in the dependent variable caused by an incremental change in an independent variable while other independent variables are held constant:

$$\text{slope} = \frac{\text{change in dependent variable}}{\text{change in independent variable}}$$

If the dependent variable is a linear function of the independent variable, then the slope can be measured uniquely by dividing the finite change in y by the finite change in x between any two points on the function. Thus the slope of the linear function $y = a + bx$ is

$$\frac{\Delta y}{\Delta x} = \frac{\text{finite change in } y}{\text{finite change in } x} = b$$

If the function is *not* linear, the ratio $\Delta y/\Delta x$ depends on the distance between the two points and the starting point. Consider the function $y = f(x)$ in Figure A.8. Given some finite change in x to $x + \Delta x$, the corresponding change in y is given by $\Delta y = f(x + \Delta x) - f(x)$. The ratio $\Delta y/\Delta x$ measures the slope of a secant line drawn between two points on the curve, say points a and b. Thus, this measure of the slope of a curved function depends on the size of the change in the independent variable.

An alternative measure of the slope of a curved function is given by the slope of a line tangent to a point determined by the value of the independent variable. To see how to find the slope of a tangent line, suppose Δx shrinks toward zero. As Δx approaches zero, the length of the secant line shrinks to a point. In the limit as Δx approaches zero, the secant

---

1. To establish a logarithmic function of the form $y = a\, ln(bx)$, let $a = 1/c$ and $b = 1/k$ and use the equivalent equation $x = ke^{cy}$. Now proceed as if establishing the exponential, but with x as the dependent variable and y as the independent variable. Once you have established k and c, they can be converted into a and b.

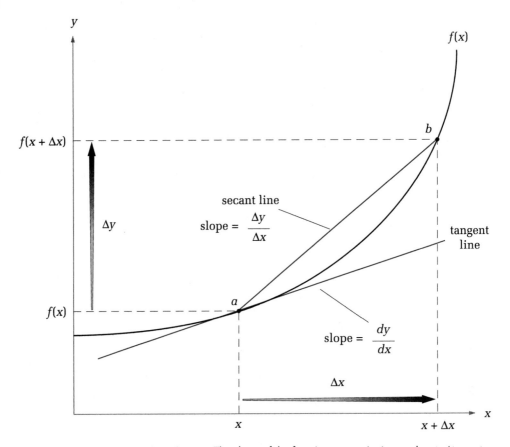

Figure A.8 **Slope of a nonlinear function:** The slope of the function at a point is equal to $\Delta y/\Delta x$ as Δx approaches zero. The slope of the tangent line is denoted dy/dx.

line coincides with the tangent line. The slope of a function as measured by the slope of a tangent line is called a **derivative** and is denoted

$$\frac{dy}{dx} = \lim_{\Delta x \to 0} \frac{\Delta y}{\Delta x}$$

Several rules have been developed for finding derivatives, some of them listed in Table A.1. The first rule says that the derivative of a constant is zero. The second rule says that the derivative of a power function $y = ax^n$ is

$$\frac{dy}{dx} = nax^{n-1}$$

For example, for the function

$$y = 5x^3$$
$$\frac{dy}{dx} = 15x^2$$

Table A.1 Rules for Differentiating Functions

Function	Derivative
1. constant: $y = a$	$\dfrac{dy}{dx} = 0$
2. power function: $y = ax^n$	$\dfrac{dy}{dx} = nax^{(n-1)}$
3. sums: $y = u + v$	$\dfrac{dy}{dx} = \dfrac{du}{dx} + \dfrac{dv}{dx}$
4. products: $y = uv$	$\dfrac{dy}{dx} = u\dfrac{dv}{dx} + v\dfrac{du}{dx}$
5. quotients: $y = u/v$	$\dfrac{dy}{dx} = \dfrac{v(du/dx) - u(dv/dx)}{v^2}$
6. chains: $y = y(u), u = u(x)$	$\dfrac{dy}{dx} = \dfrac{dy}{du} \cdot \dfrac{du}{dx}$
7. exponential (base e): $y = e^u, u = u(x)$	$\dfrac{dy}{dx} = e^u\dfrac{du}{dx}$
8. exponential (base a): $y = a^u, u = u(x)$	$\dfrac{dy}{dx} = a^u\dfrac{du}{dx} \ln a$
9. logarithmic (base e): $y = \ln u, u = u(x)$	$\dfrac{dy}{dx} = \dfrac{1}{u} \cdot \dfrac{du}{dx}$
10. logarithmic (base a): $y = \log_a u, u = u(x)$	$\dfrac{dy}{dx} = \dfrac{1}{u \ln a} \cdot \dfrac{du}{dx}$

Notice that you can find the slope of the tangent line to the function for any value of x because the slope is also a function of x. The remaining rules are presented without examples, but they can be applied straightforwardly.

The rules can be applied to find the derivative of a complex function. For the function

$$y = 10 - 6x + 2x^2$$

$$\frac{dy}{dx} = -6 + 4x$$

because $d(10)/dx = 0$, $d(-6x)/dx = -6$ and $d(2x^2)/dx = 4x$. Here we have used the first three rules.

Optimizing with Calculus

Sometimes we wish to maximize a function; at others we wish to minimize a function, as for instance, maximizing profit or minimizing cost. As shown in panel A of Figure A.9, a function reaches a **local maximum** at the value $x = x^*$ of the independent variable if the value of the dependent variable at x^* is greater than at adjacent points. Similarly, as shown in panel B of Figure A.9, a function reaches a **local minimum** at $x = x^*$ if the value of the dependent variable is lower at x^* than at any adjacent point. End points are *not* considered candidates for *local* maxima or minima.

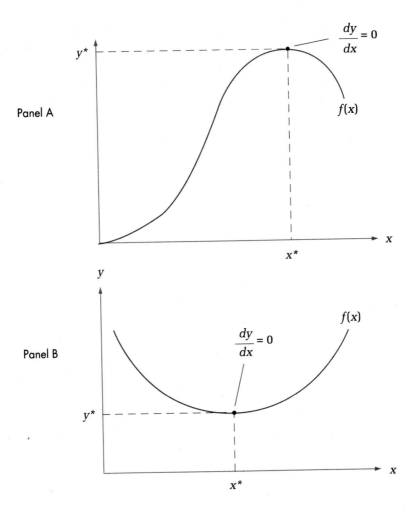

Figure A.9   **Optimizing with calculus: Panel A** The function reaches a local maximum at x^*, where $dy/dx = 0$ and $d^2y/dx^2 < 0$. **Panel B** The function reaches a local minimum at x^*, where $dy/dx = 0$ and $d^2y/dx^2 > 0$.

Values of the independent variable for which the slope of the function equals zero are called **critical points**. These values of x can be determined from the derivative by setting the derivative equal to zero and solving for x. Given the function

$$y = x^2 - 6x + 8$$

Setting the derivative equal to zero yields

$$\frac{dy}{dx} = 2x - 6 = 0$$

and $x = 3$ is the critical point. Critical points are designated by an asterisk, $x^* = 3$.

An interior local optimum must be a critical point. But not all critical points are a local optimum because some critical points may be points of *inflection* rather than a local optimum. Thus we need some way of ruling out inflection points. Moreover, we need some way to distinguish between a local maximum and minimum at critical points.

The **second derivative** of a function is the derivative of the first derivative,

$$\frac{d(dy/dx)}{dx} = \frac{d^2y}{dx^2}$$

To have an interior local optimum, the *first* derivative must be *zero* and the *second* derivative must be *nonzero*. Then the *sign* of the second derivative is used to determine whether we have a maximum or a minimum. If the second derivative is *negative*, we have a *maximum*. If the second derivative is *positive*, we have a *minimum*. If the second derivative is *zero*, some other information is required to determine the nature of the critical point.

For example, for this cubic function:

$$y = \frac{x^3}{3} - 4x^2 + 12x + 20 \quad \text{for } 0 \le x \le 10$$

$$\frac{dy}{dx} = x^2 - 8x + 12$$

$$\frac{d^2y}{dx^2} = 2x - 8$$

Setting the first derivative equal to zero to find the critical points,

$$x^2 - 8x + 12 = (x - 2)(x - 6) = 0$$

yields $x^* = 2$ and $x^* = 6$. The critical point $x^* = 2$ yields a local maximum because

$$2x^* - 8 = -4 < 0$$

The critical point $x^* = 6$ yields a local minimum because

$$2x^* - 8 = +4 > 0$$

Partial Derivatives

If the dependent variable is a function of more than one independent variable, but only one independent variable changes, the slope is called the **partial derivative**

$$\frac{\partial y}{\partial x_j} = \lim_{\Delta x_j \to 0} \frac{\Delta y}{\Delta x_j}$$

The symbol ∂ is read "partial change in." This notation implies that all other independent variables are being held constant. The rules of differentiation can be applied to functions of several variables. Consider the function

$$y = f(x_1, x_2) = 10x_1 + 2x_1^2 - x_1x_2 + 3x_2^2 + 6x_2$$

To find $\partial y/\partial x_1$, you must treat x_2 as a constant. Likewise, to find $\partial y/\partial x_2$, you must treat x_1 as a constant. Then the rules are applied straightforwardly:

$$\frac{\partial y}{\partial x_1} = 10 + 4x_1 - x_2$$

$$\frac{\partial y}{\partial x_2} = -x_1 + 6x_2 + 6$$

The partial derivative $\partial y/\partial x_1$ measures the change in y due to a change in x_1 alone—the *marginal* effect of a change in x_1. Likewise, the partial derivative $\partial y/\partial x_2$ measures the change in y due to a change in x_2 alone—the *marginal* effect of a change in x_2.

Suppose sales s of a product are related to price p, advertising a, and the number of sales personnel n, according to

$$s = (10,000 - 800p)n^{1/2}a^{1/2}$$

If $p = \$5$ and $a = \$10,000$, what is the effect of adding sales personnel? The marginal effect is described by the partial derivative

$$\frac{\partial s}{\partial n} = \frac{1}{2}a^{1/2}(10,000 - 800p)n^{-1/2}$$

$$= \frac{100}{2}(10,000 - 4,000)/\sqrt{n}$$

$$= \frac{300,000}{\sqrt{n}}$$

If we have $n = 100$ salespersons, then

$$\frac{\partial s}{\partial n} = \$30,000$$

For a one-unit increase in n, the approximate change in sales will be

$$\Delta s \cong \Delta n \frac{\partial s}{\partial n} = \$30,000$$

Multivariate Optimizing

The method for finding the optimizing values of the independent variables for a multivariate function is similar to optimizing a function of a single variable. The multivariate function to be maximized or minimized is

$$y = f(x_1, x_2, \ldots, x_n)$$

All first partial derivatives must equal zero simultaneously:

$$\frac{\partial y}{\partial x_1}(x_1^*, x_2^*, \ldots, x_n^*) = 0$$

$$\frac{\partial y}{\partial x_2}(x_1^*, x_2^*, \ldots, x_n^*) = 0$$

$$\vdots$$

$$\frac{\partial y}{\partial x_n}(x_1^*, x_2^*, \ldots, x_n^*) = 0$$

Second derivatives can then be used to determine if the critical point yields a maximum or a minimum, but the exact conditions are beyond the scope of this book. We assume then that any functions are "well behaved" in that the proper conditions hold.

Suppose we wish to maximize

$$y = -4x_1^2 + 4x_1x_2 - 2x_2^2 + 16x_1 - 12x_2$$

Setting the first partial derivatives equal to zero simultaneously:

$$\frac{\partial y}{\partial x_1} = -8x_1 + 4x_2 + 16 = 0$$

$$\frac{\partial y}{\partial x_2} = 4x_1 - 4x_2 - 12 = 0$$

Solving simultaneously yields $x_1^* = 1$ and $x_2^* = -2$.

Constrained Optimizing

Most problems in economic optimizing will be to maximize or minimize a function subject to one or more constraints. For instance, the consumer maximizes utility by consuming several goods, the purchase of which is constrained by the consumer's income. Consider a firm that wishes to minimize the cost of inputs used in producing a good, subject to a technological constraint that determines how the inputs can be transformed into the good being produced.

The technique considered here is the **Lagrangian multiplier method.**[2] Let's start with an objective function of two independent variables and one constraint. The problem is

$$\text{maximize } y = f(x_1, x_2)$$

$$\text{subject to } g(x_1, x_2) = 0$$

If the constraint is in the form $h(x_1, x_2) = b$, it must be converted to the form $g(x_1, x_2) = b - h(x_1, x_2) = 0$. The Lagrangian to be maximized is

$$F(x_1, x_2, \lambda) = f(x_1, x_2) + \lambda g(x_1, x_2)$$

---

2. When the constraints are linear and the objective function is nonlinear, a simple method of substitution can be used instead. Constraint equations are substituted into the objective function, converting the problem into an unconstrained problem in optimizing.

where λ is called the **Lagrangian multiplier**. Because the constraint equation $g(x_1, x_2)$ is equal to zero, adding the term $\lambda g(x_1, x_2)$ to the objective function $f(x_1, x_2)$ does not change its value. Now we are ready to proceed as before by setting all first partial derivatives equal to zero:

$$\frac{\partial F}{\partial x_1} = 0, \; \frac{\partial F}{\partial x_2} = 0, \; \frac{\partial F}{\partial \lambda} = 0$$

These three equations are solved simultaneously for the critical points x_1^*, x_2^* and λ^*.
For example, determine the critical points and the constrained maxima for

$$y = x_1^2 + 3x_1x_2 + x_2^2$$

subject to

$$x_1 + x_2 = 100$$

Putting the constraint into the form $100 - x_1 - x_2 = 0$, the Lagrangian is

$$F(x_1, x_2, \lambda) = x_1^2 + 3x_1x_2 + x_2^2 + \lambda(100 - x_1 - x_2)$$

The partial derivatives are:

$$\frac{\partial F}{\partial x_1} = 2x_1 + 3x_2 - \lambda = 0$$

$$\frac{\partial F}{\partial x_2} = 3x_1 + 2x_2 - \lambda = 0$$

$$\frac{\partial F}{\partial \lambda} = 100 - x_1 - x_2 = 0$$

The three equations are solved simultaneously for $x_1^* = 50$, $x_2^* = 50$ and $\lambda^* = 250$. The optimal value for the objective function is $y^* = 12,500$. It is easy to confirm that this is a maximum.

The Lagrangian multiplier λ indicates how y^* will change given a one-unit change in constant term b of the constraint. Thus,

$$\frac{\partial y^*}{\partial b} = \lambda^*$$

In the preceding example, $\lambda^* = 250$, and so an increase in the constant term from $b = 100$ to $b = 101$ will result in an approximate increase in the objective function value from $y^* = 12,500$ to $y^* + \Delta y^* = 12,750$.

The Lagrangian method can be extended to cases with several constraints. For example, to optimize the objective function

$$y = 2x_1x_2 - 3x_3^2$$

subject to

$$x_1 + x_2 + x_3 = 15 \text{ and } x_1 - x_3 = 4$$

The Lagrangian is

$$F(x_1, x_2, x_3, \lambda_1, \lambda_2) = 2x_1x_2 - 3x_3^2 + \lambda_1(15 - x_1 - x_2 - x_3) + \lambda_2(4 - x_1 + x_3)$$

There is one multiplier for each constraint. Equating the partial derivatives to zero results in:

$$\frac{\partial F}{\partial x_1} = 2x_2 - \lambda_1 - \lambda_2 \quad = 0$$

$$\frac{\partial F}{\partial x_2} = 2x_1 - \lambda_1 \quad\quad\quad = 0$$

$$\frac{\partial F}{\partial x_3} = -6x_3 - \lambda_1 + \lambda_2 \quad = 0$$

$$\frac{\partial F}{\partial \lambda_1} = x_1 + x_2 + x_3 - 15 = 0$$

$$\frac{\partial F}{\partial \lambda_2} = x_1 - x_3 - 4 \quad\quad = 0$$

The simultaneous solution is $x_1^* = 4.43$, $x_2^* = 10.14$, $x_3^* = 0.43$, $\lambda_1^* = 8.86$, and $\lambda_1^* = 11.42$. These critical values yield a constrained optimum of $y^* = 89.5$.

Statistical Tables

Table B.1 Percentiles of the *t* distribution

df	Pr[a] .80	.60	.40	.20	.10	.05	.02	.01
1	0.325	0.727	1.376	3.078	6.314	12.706	31.821	63.657
2	0.289	0.617	1.061	1.886	2.920	4.303	6.965	9.925
3	0.277	0.584	0.978	1.638	2.353	3.182	4.541	5.841
4	0.271	0.569	0.941	1.533	2.132	2.776	3.747	4.064
5	0.267	0.559	0.920	1.476	2.015	2.571	3.365	4.032
6	0.265	0.553	0.906	1.440	1.943	2.447	3.143	3.707
7	0.263	0.549	0.896	1.415	1.895	2.365	2.998	3.499
8	0.262	0.546	0.889	1.397	1.860	2.306	2.896	3.355
9	0.261	0.543	0.883	1.383	1.833	2.262	2.821	3.250
10	0.260	0.542	0.879	1.372	1.812	2.228	2.764	3.169
11	0.260	0.540	0.876	1.363	1.796	2.201	2.718	3.106
12	0.259	0.539	0.873	1.356	1.782	2.179	2.681	3.055
13	0.259	0.538	0.870	1.350	1.771	2.160	2.650	3.012
14	0.258	0.537	0.868	1.345	1.761	2.145	2.624	2.977
15	0.258	0.536	0.866	1.341	1.753	2.131	2.602	2.947
16	0.258	0.535	0.865	1.337	1.746	2.120	2.583	2.921
17	0.257	0.534	0.863	1.333	1.740	2.110	2.567	2.898
18	0.257	0.534	0.862	1.330	1.734	2.101	2.552	2.878
19	0.257	0.533	0.861	1.328	1.729	2.093	2.539	2.861
20	0.257	0.533	0.860	1.325	1.725	2.086	2.528	2.845
21	0.257	0.532	0.859	1.323	1.721	2.080	2.518	2.831
22	0.256	0.532	0.858	1.321	1.717	2.074	2.508	2.819
23	0.256	0.532	0.858	1.319	1.714	2.069	2.500	2.807
24	0.256	0.531	0.857	1.318	1.711	2.604	2.492	2.797
25	0.256	0.531	0.856	1.316	1.708	2.060	2.485	2.787
26	0.256	0.531	0.856	1.315	1.706	2.056	2.479	2.779
27	0.256	0.531	0.855	1.314	1.703	2.052	2.473	2.771
28	0.256	0.530	0.855	1.313	1.701	2.048	2.467	2.763
29	0.256	0.530	0.854	1.311	1.699	2.045	2.462	2.756
30	0.256	0.530	0.854	1.310	1.697	2.042	2.457	2.750
40	0.255	0.529	0.851	1.303	1.684	2.021	2.423	2.704
60	0.254	0.527	0.848	1.296	1.671	2.000	2.390	2.660
120	0.254	0.526	0.845	1.289	1.658	1.980	2.358	2.617
∞	0.253	0.524	0.842	1.282	1.645	1.960	2.326	2.576

[a]Pr represents the probability that the *t* value will exceed each number in the table in absolute value. This is appropriate for two-tailed tests. For one-tailed tests simply divide each probability in half. For example, 0.325 in row 1, column 1 tells us that the probability of *t* being less than −0.325 or greater than 0.325 is 0.8.

Source: Reprinted with permission of Haffner Press, a division of Macmillan Publishing Company, from *Statistical Methods for Research Workers*, 14th ed., by Ronald A. Fisher. Copyright © 1970 by University of Adelaide.

Table B.2 Durbin-Watson Test Values (Savin-White tables)

Durbin-Watson statistic: 1% significance points of d_L and d_U.

n	k=1 d_L	k=1 d_U	k=2 d_L	k=2 d_U	k=3 d_L	k=3 d_U	k=4 d_L	k=4 d_U	k=5 d_L	k=5 d_U	k=6 d_L	k=6 d_U	k=7 d_L	k=7 d_U	k=8 d_L	k=8 d_U	k=9 d_L	k=9 d_U	k=10 d_L	k=10 d_U
6	0.390	1.142	—	—	—	—	—	—	—	—	—	—	—	—	—	—	—	—	—	—
7	0.435	1.036	0.294	1.676	—	—	—	—	—	—	—	—	—	—	—	—	—	—	—	—
8	0.497	1.003	0.345	1.489	0.229	2.102	—	—	—	—	—	—	—	—	—	—	—	—	—	—
9	0.554	0.998	0.408	1.389	0.279	1.875	0.183	2.433	—	—	—	—	—	—	—	—	—	—	—	—
10	0.604	1.001	0.466	1.333	0.340	1.733	0.230	2.193	0.150	2.690	—	—	—	—	—	—	—	—	—	—
11	0.653	1.010	0.519	1.297	0.396	1.640	0.286	2.030	0.193	2.453	0.124	2.892	—	—	—	—	—	—	—	—
12	0.697	1.023	0.569	1.274	0.449	1.575	0.339	1.913	0.244	2.280	0.164	2.665	0.105	3.053	—	—	—	—	—	—
13	0.738	1.038	0.616	1.261	0.499	1.526	0.391	1.826	0.294	2.150	0.211	2.490	0.140	2.838	0.090	3.182	—	—	—	—
14	0.776	1.054	0.660	1.254	0.547	1.490	0.441	1.757	0.343	2.049	0.257	2.354	0.183	2.667	0.122	2.981	0.078	3.287	—	—
15	0.811	1.070	0.700	1.252	0.591	1.464	0.488	1.704	0.391	1.967	0.303	2.244	0.226	2.530	0.161	2.817	0.107	3.101	0.068	3.374
16	0.844	1.086	0.737	1.252	0.633	1.446	0.532	1.663	0.437	1.900	0.349	2.153	0.269	2.416	0.200	2.681	0.142	2.944	0.094	3.201
17	0.874	1.102	0.772	1.255	0.672	1.432	0.574	1.630	0.480	1.847	0.393	2.078	0.313	2.319	0.241	2.566	0.179	2.811	0.127	3.053
18	0.902	1.118	0.805	1.259	0.708	1.422	0.613	1.604	0.522	1.803	0.435	2.015	0.355	2.238	0.282	2.467	0.216	2.697	0.160	2.925
19	0.928	1.132	0.835	1.265	0.742	1.415	0.650	1.584	0.561	1.767	0.476	1.963	0.396	2.169	0.322	2.381	0.255	2.597	0.196	2.813
20	0.952	1.147	0.863	1.271	0.773	1.411	0.685	1.567	0.598	1.737	0.515	1.918	0.436	2.110	0.362	2.308	0.294	2.510	0.232	2.714
21	0.975	1.161	0.890	1.277	0.803	1.408	0.718	1.554	0.633	1.712	0.552	1.881	0.474	2.059	0.400	2.244	0.331	2.434	0.268	2.625
22	0.997	1.174	0.914	1.284	0.831	1.407	0.748	1.543	0.667	1.691	0.587	1.849	0.510	2.015	0.437	2.188	0.368	2.367	0.304	2.548
23	1.018	1.187	0.938	1.291	0.858	1.407	0.777	1.534	0.698	1.673	0.620	1.821	0.545	1.977	0.473	2.140	0.404	2.308	0.340	2.479
24	1.037	1.199	0.960	1.298	0.882	1.407	0.805	1.528	0.728	1.658	0.652	1.797	0.578	1.944	0.507	2.097	0.439	2.255	0.375	2.417
25	1.055	1.211	0.981	1.305	0.906	1.409	0.831	1.523	0.756	1.645	0.682	1.766	0.610	1.915	0.540	2.059	0.473	2.209	0.409	2.362
26	1.072	1.222	1.001	1.312	0.928	1.411	0.855	1.518	0.783	1.635	0.711	1.759	0.640	1.889	0.572	2.026	0.505	2.168	0.441	2.313
27	1.089	1.233	1.019	1.319	0.949	1.413	0.878	1.515	0.808	1.626	0.738	1.743	0.669	1.867	0.602	1.997	0.536	2.131	0.473	2.269
28	1.104	1.244	1.037	1.325	0.969	1.415	0.900	1.513	0.832	1.618	0.764	1.729	0.696	1.847	0.630	1.970	0.566	2.098	0.504	2.229
29	1.119	1.254	1.054	1.332	0.988	1.418	0.921	1.512	0.855	1.611	0.788	1.718	0.723	1.830	0.658	1.947	0.595	2.068	0.533	2.193
30	1.133	1.263	1.070	1.339	1.006	1.421	0.941	1.511	0.877	1.606	0.812	1.707	0.748	1.814	0.684	1.925	0.622	2.041	0.562	2.160
31	1.147	1.273	1.085	1.345	1.023	1.425	0.960	1.510	0.897	1.601	0.834	1.698	0.772	1.800	0.710	1.906	0.649	2.017	0.589	2.131
32	1.160	1.282	1.100	1.352	1.040	1.428	0.979	1.510	0.917	1.597	0.856	1.690	0.794	1.788	0.734	1.889	0.674	1.995	0.615	2.104
33	1.172	1.291	1.114	1.358	1.055	1.432	0.996	1.510	0.936	1.594	0.876	1.683	0.816	1.776	0.757	1.874	0.698	1.975	0.641	2.080
34	1.184	1.299	1.128	1.364	1.070	1.435	1.012	1.511	0.954	1.591	0.896	1.677	0.837	1.766	0.779	1.860	0.722	1.957	0.665	2.057
35	1.195	1.307	1.140	1.370	1.085	1.439	1.028	1.512	0.971	1.589	0.914	1.671	0.857	1.757	0.800	1.847	0.744	1.940	0.689	2.037
36	1.206	1.315	1.153	1.376	1.098	1.442	1.043	1.513	0.988	1.588	0.932	1.666	0.877	1.749	0.821	1.836	0.766	1.925	0.711	2.018
37	1.217	1.323	1.165	1.382	1.112	1.446	1.058	1.514	1.004	1.586	0.950	1.662	0.895	1.742	0.841	1.825	0.787	1.911	0.733	2.001
38	1.227	1.330	1.176	1.388	1.124	1.449	1.072	1.515	1.019	1.585	0.966	1.658	0.913	1.735	0.860	1.816	0.807	1.899	0.754	1.985
39	1.237	1.337	1.187	1.393	1.137	1.453	1.085	1.517	1.034	1.584	0.982	1.655	0.930	1.729	0.878	1.807	0.826	1.887	0.774	1.970
40	1.246	1.344	1.198	1.398	1.148	1.457	1.098	1.518	1.048	1.584	0.997	1.652	0.946	1.724	0.895	1.799	0.844	1.876	0.789	1.956
45	1.288	1.376	1.245	1.423	1.201	1.474	1.156	1.528	1.111	1.584	1.065	1.643	1.019	1.704	0.974	1.768	0.927	1.834	0.881	1.902
50	1.324	1.403	1.285	1.446	1.245	1.491	1.205	1.538	1.164	1.587	1.123	1.639	1.081	1.692	1.039	1.748	0.997	1.805	0.955	1.864
55	1.356	1.427	1.320	1.466	1.284	1.506	1.247	1.548	1.209	1.592	1.172	1.638	1.134	1.685	1.095	1.734	1.057	1.785	1.018	1.837
60	1.383	1.449	1.350	1.484	1.317	1.520	1.283	1.558	1.249	1.598	1.214	1.639	1.179	1.682	1.144	1.726	1.108	1.771	1.072	1.817
65	1.407	1.468	1.377	1.500	1.346	1.534	1.315	1.568	1.283	1.604	1.251	1.642	1.218	1.680	1.186	1.720	1.153	1.761	1.120	1.802
70	1.429	1.485	1.400	1.515	1.372	1.546	1.343	1.578	1.313	1.611	1.283	1.645	1.253	1.680	1.223	1.716	1.192	1.754	1.162	1.792
75	1.448	1.501	1.422	1.529	1.395	1.557	1.368	1.587	1.340	1.617	1.313	1.646	1.284	1.682	1.256	1.714	1.227	1.746	1.199	1.785
80	1.466	1.515	1.441	1.541	1.416	1.568	1.390	1.595	1.364	1.624	1.338	1.653	1.312	1.683	1.285	1.714	1.259	1.745	1.232	1.777
85	1.482	1.528	1.458	1.553	1.435	1.578	1.411	1.603	1.386	1.630	1.362	1.657	1.337	1.685	1.312	1.714	1.287	1.743	1.262	1.773
90	1.496	1.540	1.474	1.563	1.452	1.587	1.429	1.611	1.406	1.636	1.383	1.661	1.360	1.687	1.336	1.715	1.312	1.741	1.288	1.769
95	1.510	1.552	1.489	1.573	1.468	1.596	1.446	1.618	1.425	1.642	1.403	1.666	1.381	1.690	1.358	1.717	1.336	1.741	1.313	1.767
100	1.522	1.562	1.503	1.583	1.482	1.604	1.462	1.625	1.441	1.647	1.421	1.670	1.400	1.693	1.378	1.720	1.357	1.741	1.335	1.767
150	1.611	1.637	1.598	1.651	1.584	1.665	1.571	1.679	1.557	1.693	1.543	1.708	1.530	1.722	1.515	1.746	1.501	1.752	1.486	1.765
200	1.664	1.684	1.653	1.693	1.643	1.704	1.633	1.715	1.623	1.725	1.613	1.735	1.603	1.746	1.592	1.757	1.582	1.768	1.571	1.779

Note: k is the number of predictors excluding the constant.

n	k=11 d_L	k=11 d_U	k=12 d_L	k=12 d_U	k=13 d_L	k=13 d_U	k=14 d_L	k=14 d_U	k=15 d_L	k=15 d_U	k=16 d_L	k=16 d_U	k=17 d_L	k=17 d_U	k=18 d_L	k=18 d_U	k=19 d_L	k=19 d_U	k=20 d_L	k=20 d_U
16	0.060	3.446	—	—	—	—	—	—	—	—	—	—	—	—	—	—	—	—	—	—
17	0.084	3.286	0.053	3.506	—	—	—	—	—	—	—	—	—	—	—	—	—	—	—	—
18	0.113	3.146	0.075	3.358	0.047	3.557	—	—	—	—	—	—	—	—	—	—	—	—	—	—
19	0.145	3.023	0.102	3.227	0.067	3.420	0.043	3.601	—	—	—	—	—	—	—	—	—	—	—	—
20	0.178	2.914	0.131	3.109	0.092	3.297	0.061	3.474	0.038	3.639	—	—	—	—	—	—	—	—	—	—
21	0.212	2.817	0.162	3.004	0.119	3.185	0.084	3.358	0.055	3.521	0.035	3.671	—	—	—	—	—	—	—	—
22	0.246	2.729	0.194	2.909	0.148	3.084	0.109	3.252	0.077	3.412	0.050	3.562	0.032	3.700	—	—	—	—	—	—
23	0.281	2.651	0.227	2.822	0.178	2.991	0.136	3.155	0.100	3.311	0.070	3.459	0.046	3.597	0.029	3.725	—	—	—	—
24	0.315	2.580	0.260	2.744	0.209	2.906	0.165	3.065	0.125	3.218	0.092	3.363	0.065	3.501	0.043	3.629	0.027	3.747	—	—
25	0.348	2.517	0.292	2.674	0.240	2.829	0.194	2.982	0.152	3.131	0.116	3.274	0.085	3.410	0.060	3.538	0.039	3.657	0.025	3.766
26	0.381	2.460	0.324	2.610	0.272	2.758	0.224	2.906	0.180	3.050	0.141	3.191	0.107	3.325	0.079	3.452	0.055	3.572	0.036	3.682
27	0.413	2.409	0.356	2.552	0.303	2.694	0.253	2.836	0.208	2.976	0.167	3.113	0.131	3.245	0.100	3.371	0.073	3.490	0.051	3.602
28	0.444	2.363	0.387	2.499	0.333	2.635	0.283	2.772	0.237	2.907	0.194	3.040	0.156	3.169	0.122	3.294	0.093	3.412	0.068	3.524
29	0.474	2.321	0.417	2.451	0.363	2.582	0.313	2.713	0.266	2.843	0.222	2.972	0.182	3.098	0.146	3.220	0.114	3.338	0.087	3.450
30	0.503	2.283	0.447	2.407	0.393	2.533	0.342	2.659	0.294	2.785	0.249	2.909	0.208	3.032	0.171	3.152	0.137	3.267	0.107	3.379
31	0.531	2.248	0.475	2.367	0.422	2.487	0.371	2.609	0.322	2.730	0.277	2.851	0.234	2.970	0.196	3.087	0.160	3.201	0.128	3.311
32	0.558	2.216	0.503	2.330	0.450	2.446	0.399	2.563	0.350	2.680	0.304	2.797	0.261	2.912	0.221	3.026	0.184	3.137	0.151	3.246
33	0.585	2.187	0.530	2.296	0.477	2.408	0.426	2.520	0.377	2.633	0.331	2.746	0.287	2.858	0.246	2.969	0.209	3.078	0.174	3.184
34	0.610	2.160	0.556	2.266	0.503	2.373	0.452	2.481	0.404	2.590	0.357	2.699	0.313	2.808	0.272	2.915	0.233	3.022	0.197	3.126
35	0.634	2.136	0.581	2.237	0.529	2.340	0.478	2.444	0.430	2.550	0.383	2.655	0.339	2.761	0.297	2.865	0.257	2.969	0.221	3.071
36	0.658	2.113	0.605	2.210	0.554	2.310	0.504	2.410	0.455	2.512	0.409	2.614	0.364	2.717	0.322	2.818	0.282	2.919	0.244	3.019
37	0.680	2.092	0.628	2.186	0.578	2.282	0.528	2.379	0.480	2.477	0.434	2.576	0.389	2.675	0.347	2.774	0.306	2.872	0.268	2.969
38	0.702	2.073	0.651	2.164	0.601	2.256	0.552	2.350	0.504	2.445	0.458	2.540	0.414	2.637	0.371	2.733	0.330	2.828	0.291	2.923
39	0.723	2.055	0.673	2.143	0.623	2.232	0.575	2.323	0.528	2.414	0.482	2.507	0.438	2.600	0.395	2.694	0.354	2.787	0.315	2.879
40	0.744	2.039	0.694	2.123	0.645	2.210	0.597	2.297	0.551	2.386	0.505	2.476	0.461	2.566	0.418	2.657	0.377	2.748	0.338	2.838
45	0.835	1.972	0.790	2.044	0.744	2.118	0.700	2.193	0.655	2.269	0.612	2.346	0.570	2.424	0.528	2.503	0.488	2.582	0.448	2.661
50	0.913	1.925	0.871	1.987	0.829	2.051	0.787	2.116	0.746	2.182	0.705	2.250	0.665	2.318	0.625	2.387	0.586	2.456	0.548	2.526
55	0.979	1.891	0.940	1.945	0.902	2.002	0.863	2.059	0.825	2.117	0.786	2.176	0.748	2.237	0.711	2.298	0.674	2.359	0.637	2.421
60	1.037	1.865	1.001	1.914	0.965	1.964	0.929	2.015	0.893	2.067	0.857	2.120	0.822	2.173	0.786	2.227	0.751	2.283	0.716	2.338
65	1.087	1.845	1.053	1.889	1.020	1.934	0.986	1.980	0.953	2.027	0.919	2.075	0.886	2.123	0.852	2.172	0.819	2.221	0.786	2.272
70	1.131	1.831	1.099	1.870	1.068	1.911	1.037	1.953	1.005	1.995	0.974	2.038	0.943	2.082	0.911	2.127	0.880	2.172	0.849	2.217
75	1.170	1.819	1.141	1.856	1.111	1.893	1.082	1.931	1.052	1.970	1.023	2.009	0.993	2.049	0.964	2.090	0.934	2.131	0.905	2.172
80	1.205	1.810	1.177	1.844	1.150	1.878	1.122	1.913	1.094	1.949	1.066	1.984	1.039	2.022	1.011	2.057	0.983	2.097	0.955	2.135
85	1.236	1.803	1.210	1.834	1.184	1.866	1.158	1.898	1.132	1.931	1.106	1.965	1.080	1.999	1.053	2.033	1.027	2.068	1.000	2.104
90	1.264	1.798	1.240	1.827	1.215	1.856	1.191	1.886	1.166	1.917	1.141	1.948	1.116	1.979	1.091	2.012	1.066	2.044	1.041	2.077
95	1.290	1.793	1.267	1.821	1.244	1.848	1.221	1.876	1.197	1.905	1.174	1.934	1.150	1.963	1.126	1.993	1.102	2.023	1.079	2.054
100	1.314	1.790	1.292	1.816	1.270	1.841	1.248	1.868	1.225	1.895	1.203	1.922	1.181	1.949	1.158	1.977	1.136	2.006	1.113	2.034
150	1.473	1.783	1.458	1.799	1.444	1.814	1.429	1.830	1.414	1.847	1.400	1.863	1.385	1.880	1.370	1.897	1.355	1.913	1.340	1.931
200	1.561	1.791	1.550	1.801	1.539	1.813	1.528	1.824	1.518	1.836	1.507	1.847	1.495	1.860	1.484	1.871	1.474	1.883	1.462	1.896

Table B.2 (Continued) Durbin-Watson statistic: 5% significance points of d_L and d_U.

n	k = 1		k = 2		k = 3		k = 4		k = 5		k = 6		k = 7		k = 8		k = 9		k = 10	
	d_L	d_U	d_L	d_U	d_L	d_U	d_L	d_U	d_L	d_U	d_L	d_U	d_L	d_U	d_L	d_U	d_L	d_U	d_L	d_U
6	0.610	1.400	—	—	—	—	—	—	—	—	—	—	—	—	—	—	—	—	—	—
7	0.700	1.356	0.467	1.896	—	—	—	—	—	—	—	—	—	—	—	—	—	—	—	—
8	0.763	1.332	0.559	1.777	0.368	2.287	—	—	—	—	—	—	—	—	—	—	—	—	—	—
9	0.824	1.320	0.629	1.699	0.455	2.128	0.296	2.588	—	—	—	—	—	—	—	—	—	—	—	—
10	0.879	1.320	0.697	1.641	0.525	2.016	0.376	2.414	0.243	2.822	—	—	—	—	—	—	—	—	—	—
11	0.927	1.324	0.758	1.604	0.595	1.928	0.444	2.283	0.316	2.645	0.203	3.005	—	—	—	—	—	—	—	—
12	0.971	1.331	0.812	1.579	0.658	1.864	0.512	2.177	0.379	2.506	0.268	2.832	0.171	3.149	—	—	—	—	—	—
13	1.010	1.340	0.861	1.562	0.715	1.816	0.574	2.094	0.445	2.390	0.328	2.692	0.230	2.985	0.147	3.266	—	—	—	—
14	1.045	1.350	0.905	1.551	0.767	1.779	0.632	2.030	0.505	2.296	0.389	2.572	0.286	2.848	0.200	3.111	0.127	3.360	—	—
15	1.077	1.361	0.946	1.543	0.814	1.750	0.685	1.977	0.562	2.220	0.447	2.472	0.343	2.727	0.251	2.979	0.175	3.216	0.111	3.438
16	1.106	1.371	0.982	1.539	0.857	1.728	0.734	1.935	0.615	2.157	0.502	2.388	0.398	2.624	0.304	2.860	0.222	3.090	0.155	3.304
17	1.133	1.381	1.015	1.536	0.897	1.710	0.779	1.900	0.664	2.104	0.554	2.318	0.451	2.537	0.356	2.757	0.272	2.975	0.198	3.184
18	1.158	1.391	1.046	1.535	0.933	1.696	0.820	1.872	0.710	2.060	0.603	2.257	0.502	2.461	0.407	2.667	0.321	2.873	0.244	3.073
19	1.180	1.401	1.074	1.536	0.967	1.685	0.859	1.848	0.752	2.023	0.649	2.206	0.549	2.396	0.456	2.589	0.369	2.783	0.290	2.974
20	1.201	1.411	1.100	1.537	0.998	1.676	0.894	1.828	0.792	1.991	0.692	2.162	0.595	2.339	0.502	2.521	0.416	2.704	0.336	2.885
21	1.221	1.420	1.125	1.538	1.026	1.669	0.927	1.812	0.829	1.964	0.732	2.124	0.637	2.290	0.547	2.460	0.461	2.633	0.380	2.806
22	1.239	1.429	1.147	1.541	1.053	1.664	0.958	1.797	0.863	1.940	0.769	2.090	0.677	2.246	0.588	2.407	0.504	2.571	0.424	2.734
23	1.257	1.437	1.168	1.543	1.078	1.660	0.986	1.785	0.895	1.920	0.804	2.061	0.715	2.208	0.628	2.360	0.545	2.514	0.465	2.670
24	1.273	1.446	1.188	1.546	1.101	1.656	1.013	1.775	0.925	1.902	0.837	2.035	0.751	2.174	0.666	2.318	0.584	2.464	0.506	2.613
25	1.288	1.454	1.206	1.550	1.123	1.654	1.038	1.767	0.953	1.886	0.868	2.012	0.784	2.144	0.702	2.280	0.621	2.419	0.544	2.560
26	1.302	1.461	1.224	1.553	1.143	1.652	1.062	1.759	0.979	1.873	0.897	1.992	0.816	2.117	0.735	2.246	0.657	2.379	0.581	2.513
27	1.316	1.469	1.240	1.556	1.162	1.651	1.084	1.753	1.004	1.861	0.925	1.974	0.845	2.093	0.767	2.216	0.691	2.342	0.616	2.470
28	1.328	1.476	1.255	1.560	1.181	1.650	1.104	1.747	1.028	1.850	0.951	1.958	0.874	2.071	0.798	2.188	0.723	2.309	0.650	2.431
29	1.341	1.483	1.270	1.563	1.198	1.650	1.124	1.743	1.050	1.841	0.975	1.944	0.900	2.052	0.826	2.164	0.753	2.278	0.682	2.396
30	1.352	1.489	1.284	1.567	1.214	1.650	1.143	1.739	1.071	1.833	0.998	1.931	0.926	2.034	0.854	2.141	0.782	2.251	0.712	2.363
31	1.363	1.496	1.297	1.570	1.229	1.650	1.160	1.735	1.090	1.825	1.020	1.920	0.950	2.018	0.879	2.120	0.810	2.226	0.741	2.333
32	1.373	1.502	1.309	1.574	1.244	1.650	1.177	1.732	1.109	1.819	1.041	1.909	0.972	2.004	0.904	2.102	0.836	2.203	0.769	2.306
33	1.383	1.508	1.321	1.577	1.258	1.651	1.193	1.730	1.127	1.813	1.061	1.900	0.994	1.991	0.927	2.085	0.861	2.181	0.795	2.281
34	1.393	1.514	1.333	1.580	1.271	1.652	1.208	1.728	1.144	1.808	1.080	1.891	1.015	1.979	0.950	2.069	0.885	2.162	0.821	2.257
35	1.402	1.519	1.343	1.584	1.283	1.653	1.222	1.726	1.160	1.803	1.097	1.884	1.034	1.967	0.971	2.054	0.908	2.144	0.845	2.236
36	1.411	1.525	1.354	1.587	1.295	1.654	1.236	1.724	1.175	1.799	1.114	1.877	1.053	1.957	0.991	2.041	0.930	2.127	0.868	2.216
37	1.419	1.530	1.364	1.590	1.307	1.655	1.249	1.723	1.190	1.795	1.131	1.870	1.071	1.948	1.011	2.029	0.951	2.112	0.891	2.198
38	1.427	1.535	1.373	1.594	1.318	1.656	1.261	1.722	1.204	1.792	1.146	1.864	1.088	1.939	1.029	2.017	0.970	2.098	0.912	2.180
39	1.435	1.540	1.382	1.597	1.328	1.658	1.273	1.722	1.218	1.789	1.161	1.859	1.104	1.932	1.047	2.007	0.990	2.085	0.932	2.164
40	1.442	1.544	1.391	1.600	1.338	1.659	1.285	1.721	1.230	1.786	1.175	1.854	1.120	1.924	1.064	1.997	1.008	2.072	0.945	2.149
45	1.475	1.566	1.430	1.615	1.383	1.666	1.336	1.720	1.287	1.776	1.238	1.835	1.189	1.895	1.139	1.958	1.089	2.002	1.038	2.088
50	1.503	1.585	1.462	1.628	1.421	1.674	1.378	1.721	1.335	1.771	1.291	1.822	1.246	1.875	1.201	1.930	1.156	1.986	1.110	2.044
55	1.528	1.601	1.490	1.641	1.452	1.681	1.414	1.724	1.374	1.768	1.334	1.814	1.294	1.861	1.253	1.909	1.212	1.959	1.170	2.010
60	1.549	1.616	1.514	1.652	1.480	1.689	1.444	1.727	1.408	1.767	1.372	1.808	1.335	1.850	1.298	1.894	1.260	1.939	1.222	1.984
65	1.567	1.629	1.536	1.662	1.503	1.696	1.471	1.731	1.438	1.767	1.404	1.805	1.370	1.843	1.336	1.882	1.301	1.923	1.266	1.964
70	1.583	1.641	1.554	1.672	1.525	1.703	1.494	1.735	1.464	1.768	1.433	1.802	1.401	1.837	1.369	1.873	1.337	1.910	1.305	1.948
75	1.598	1.652	1.571	1.680	1.543	1.709	1.515	1.739	1.487	1.770	1.458	1.801	1.428	1.834	1.399	1.867	1.369	1.901	1.339	1.935
80	1.611	1.662	1.586	1.688	1.560	1.715	1.534	1.743	1.507	1.772	1.480	1.801	1.453	1.831	1.425	1.861	1.397	1.893	1.369	1.925
85	1.624	1.671	1.600	1.696	1.575	1.721	1.550	1.747	1.525	1.774	1.500	1.801	1.474	1.829	1.448	1.857	1.422	1.886	1.396	1.916
90	1.635	1.679	1.612	1.703	1.589	1.726	1.566	1.751	1.542	1.776	1.518	1.802	1.494	1.827	1.469	1.854	1.445	1.881	1.420	1.909
95	1.645	1.687	1.623	1.709	1.602	1.732	1.579	1.755	1.557	1.778	1.535	1.803	1.512	1.826	1.489	1.852	1.465	1.877	1.442	1.903
100	1.654	1.694	1.634	1.715	1.613	1.736	1.592	1.758	1.571	1.780	1.550	1.803	1.528	1.826	1.506	1.850	1.484	1.874	1.462	1.898
150	1.720	1.746	1.706	1.760	1.693	1.774	1.679	1.788	1.665	1.802	1.651	1.817	1.637	1.832	1.622	1.847	1.608	1.862	1.594	1.877
200	1.758	1.778	1.748	1.789	1.738	1.799	1.728	1.820	1.718	1.820	1.707	1.831	1.697	1.841	1.686	1.852	1.675	1.863	1.665	1.874

Note: k is the number of predictors excluding the constant.

n	k = 11 d_L	k = 11 d_U	k = 12 d_L	k = 12 d_U	k = 13 d_L	k = 13 d_U	k = 14 d_L	k = 14 d_U	k = 15 d_L	k = 15 d_U	k = 16 d_L	k = 16 d_U	k = 17 d_L	k = 17 d_U	k = 18 d_L	k = 18 d_U	k = 19 d_L	k = 19 d_U	k = 20 d_L	k = 20 d_U
16	0.098	3.503	—	—	—	—	—	—	—	—	—	—	—	—	—	—	—	—	—	—
17	0.138	3.378	0.087	3.557	—	—	—	—	—	—	—	—	—	—	—	—	—	—	—	—
18	0.177	3.265	0.123	3.441	0.078	3.603	—	—	—	—	—	—	—	—	—	—	—	—	—	—
19	0.220	3.159	0.160	3.335	0.111	3.496	0.070	3.642	—	—	—	—	—	—	—	—	—	—	—	—
20	0.263	3.063	0.200	3.234	0.145	3.395	0.100	3.542	0.063	3.676	—	—	—	—	—	—	—	—	—	—
21	0.307	2.976	0.240	3.141	0.182	3.300	0.132	3.448	0.091	3.583	0.058	3.705	—	—	—	—	—	—	—	—
22	0.349	2.897	0.281	3.057	0.220	3.211	0.166	3.358	0.120	3.495	0.083	3.619	0.052	3.731	—	—	—	—	—	—
23	0.391	2.826	0.322	2.979	0.259	3.128	0.202	3.272	0.153	3.409	0.110	3.535	0.076	3.650	0.048	3.753	—	—	—	—
24	0.431	2.761	0.362	2.908	0.297	3.053	0.239	3.193	0.186	3.327	0.141	3.454	0.101	3.572	0.070	3.678	0.044	3.773	—	—
25	0.470	2.702	0.400	2.844	0.335	2.983	0.275	3.119	0.221	3.251	0.172	3.376	0.130	3.494	0.094	3.604	0.065	3.702	0.041	3.790
26	0.508	2.649	0.438	2.784	0.373	2.919	0.312	3.051	0.256	3.179	0.205	3.303	0.160	3.420	0.120	3.531	0.087	3.632	0.060	3.724
27	0.544	2.600	0.475	2.730	0.409	2.859	0.348	2.987	0.291	3.112	0.238	3.233	0.191	3.349	0.149	3.460	0.112	3.563	0.081	3.658
28	0.578	2.555	0.510	2.680	0.445	2.805	0.383	2.928	0.325	3.050	0.271	3.168	0.222	3.283	0.178	3.392	0.138	3.495	0.104	3.592
29	0.612	2.515	0.544	2.634	0.479	2.755	0.418	2.874	0.359	2.992	0.305	3.107	0.254	3.219	0.208	3.327	0.166	3.431	0.129	3.528
30	0.643	2.477	0.577	2.592	0.512	2.708	0.451	2.823	0.392	2.937	0.337	3.050	0.286	3.160	0.238	3.266	0.195	3.368	0.156	3.465
31	0.674	2.443	0.608	2.553	0.545	2.665	0.484	2.776	0.425	2.887	0.370	2.996	0.317	3.103	0.269	3.208	0.224	3.309	0.183	3.406
32	0.703	2.411	0.638	2.517	0.576	2.625	0.515	2.733	0.457	2.840	0.401	2.946	0.349	3.050	0.299	3.153	0.253	3.252	0.211	3.348
33	0.731	2.382	0.668	2.484	0.606	2.588	0.546	2.692	0.488	2.796	0.432	2.899	0.379	3.000	0.329	3.100	0.283	3.198	0.239	3.293
34	0.758	2.355	0.695	2.454	0.634	2.554	0.575	2.654	0.518	2.754	0.462	2.854	0.409	2.954	0.359	3.051	0.312	3.147	0.267	3.240
35	0.783	2.330	0.722	2.425	0.662	2.521	0.604	2.619	0.547	2.716	0.492	2.813	0.439	2.910	0.388	3.005	0.340	3.099	0.295	3.190
36	0.808	2.306	0.748	2.398	0.689	2.492	0.631	2.586	0.575	2.680	0.520	2.774	0.467	2.868	0.417	2.961	0.369	3.053	0.323	3.142
37	0.831	2.285	0.772	2.374	0.714	2.464	0.657	2.555	0.602	2.646	0.548	2.738	0.495	2.829	0.445	2.920	0.397	3.009	0.351	3.097
38	0.854	2.265	0.796	2.351	0.739	2.438	0.683	2.526	0.628	2.614	0.575	2.703	0.522	2.792	0.472	2.880	0.424	2.968	0.378	3.054
39	0.875	2.246	0.819	2.329	0.763	2.413	0.707	2.499	0.653	2.585	0.600	2.671	0.549	2.757	0.499	2.843	0.451	2.929	0.404	3.013
40	0.896	2.228	0.840	2.309	0.785	2.391	0.731	2.473	0.678	2.557	0.626	2.641	0.575	2.724	0.525	2.808	0.477	2.892	0.430	2.974
45	0.988	2.156	0.938	2.225	0.887	2.296	0.838	2.367	0.788	2.439	0.740	2.512	0.692	2.586	0.644	2.659	0.598	2.733	0.553	2.807
50	1.064	2.103	1.019	2.163	0.973	2.225	0.927	2.287	0.882	2.350	0.836	2.414	0.792	2.479	0.747	2.544	0.703	2.610	0.660	2.675
55	1.129	2.062	1.087	2.116	1.045	2.170	1.003	2.225	0.961	2.281	0.919	2.338	0.877	2.396	0.836	2.454	0.795	2.512	0.754	2.571
60	1.184	2.031	1.145	2.079	1.106	2.127	1.068	2.177	1.029	2.227	0.990	2.278	0.951	2.330	0.913	2.382	0.874	2.434	0.836	2.487
65	1.231	2.006	1.195	2.049	1.160	2.093	1.124	2.138	1.088	2.183	1.052	2.229	1.016	2.276	0.980	2.323	0.944	2.371	0.908	2.419
70	1.272	1.986	1.239	2.026	1.206	2.066	1.172	2.106	1.139	2.148	1.105	2.189	1.072	2.232	1.038	2.275	1.005	2.318	0.971	2.362
75	1.308	1.970	1.277	2.006	1.247	2.043	1.215	2.080	1.184	2.118	1.153	2.156	1.121	2.195	1.090	2.235	1.058	2.275	1.027	2.315
80	1.340	1.957	1.311	1.991	1.283	2.024	1.253	2.059	1.224	2.093	1.195	2.129	1.165	2.165	1.136	2.201	1.106	2.238	1.076	2.275
85	1.369	1.946	1.342	1.977	1.315	2.009	1.287	2.040	1.260	2.073	1.232	2.105	1.205	2.139	1.177	2.172	1.149	2.206	1.121	2.241
90	1.395	1.937	1.369	1.966	1.344	1.995	1.318	2.025	1.292	2.055	1.266	2.085	1.240	2.116	1.213	2.148	1.187	2.179	1.160	2.211
95	1.418	1.929	1.394	1.956	1.370	1.984	1.345	2.012	1.321	2.040	1.296	2.068	1.271	2.097	1.247	2.126	1.222	2.156	1.197	2.186
100	1.434	1.923	1.416	1.948	1.393	1.974	1.371	2.000	1.347	2.026	1.324	2.053	1.301	2.080	1.277	2.108	1.253	2.135	1.229	2.164
150	1.579	1.892	1.564	1.908	1.550	1.924	1.535	1.940	1.519	1.956	1.504	1.972	1.489	1.989	1.474	2.006	1.458	2.023	1.443	2.040
200	1.654	1.885	1.643	1.896	1.632	1.908	1.621	1.919	1.610	1.931	1.599	1.943	1.588	1.955	1.576	1.967	1.565	1.979	1.554	1.991

Source: Reprinted by permission of The Econometric Society from *Econometrica*, Vol. 45, No. 8, 1977, pp. 1992–1995.

Solutions to Odd-Numbered Problems

Note: Most of these are partial solutions. The answers are intended to provide hints or final numerical check solutions. Ask students to be prepared to show all their work if asked to do these problems as homework assignments or in examinations.

Chapter 1 Check Solutions

1.1 (a) Normative, because of the word *poor*.
    (b) Normative, because of the word *good*.
    (c) Positive; the policy is established.
    (d) Positive; just count the number of winners and losers.

1.3 A legal rule that describes a condition of ownership. Without property rights that define the right to own, use, and sell things, contracts would not be enforceable and trade would be inhibited.

1.5 An externality in production occurs when production costs do not equal social costs in the supply of some good. One example is effluents dumped in a sewer without cost after being generated in a manufacturing operation. An externality in consumption occurs when the social cost of a good is different from the price of the good. An example is the noise pollution caused by playing a stereo set so loudly that it bothers your neighbor. Another example is the ambient smoke from a cigarette to a nonsmoker.

1.7 The merger should be judged on whether or not it is anticompetitive and whether or not cost savings will be passed along to the consumer. We consider these issues in more detail in Chapter 16.

Chapter 2 Check Solutions

2.1 Scarcity. Insatiable wants and limited resources.

2.3 Banana should specialize in products on which it has a comparative advantage. Thus it should not produce chips as long as some other firm has a comparative advantage unless it chooses to do so for strategic reasons—say, to protect a crucial supply of the component. If Banana has a comparative advantage over some range of producing chips, then it should produce chips until that advantage is dissipated by diminishing returns. At the level of production where it loses its comparative advantage, Banana should stop producing chips. If it needs more to produce its computers and other products, then it should buy them. If it produces more chips than it needs, then Banana should sell the excess. We consider these issues in more detail in the section on transfer pricing in Chapter 15.

2.5 Ms. Smith must have a comparative advantage in managing, and so that is the most efficient way to spend her time. The most efficient typist is Mr. Jones, because he has a comparative advantage in typing even though he is slower.

2.7 Assume that firms do the exporting and importing. Your diagram should look like Figures 2.7 and 2.8, with a foreign sector added, along with real flows for exports and imports between the foreign sector and firms along with corresponding money flows in the opposite direction.

Chapter 3 Check Solutions

3.1 (a) $\Delta Q/\Delta p = -5$
(b) $p(Q) = 20 - Q/5$
(c) $\Delta p/\Delta Q = -1/5$
(d) at the midpoint, where $Q = 5$ and $p = 10$

3.3 The variables should include the good's price, the prices of close substitutes and complements, and such proxies as age, education, and gender for unmeasurable tastes and preferences. Advertising expenditures might help explain changes in demand over time. Because demand changes as time passes, a measure of the number of potential buyers may help, too. In short, explanatory variables that influence individual choice and aggregate demand should be included in the demand equation.

3.5 (a) $p_1 = 2.5$ and $Q_1 = 750$
(b) $S_2(p) = 500 - 100(p - 2) = 300 + 100p$; $p_2 = 3.5$ and $Q_2 = 650$
(c) consumers' share $= \Delta p/\text{tax} = 1/2$ and producers' share $= 1 - (\Delta p/\text{tax}) = 1/2$, and so they pay 50 percent each.
(d)

$$D = \frac{\text{tax} \cdot (Q_1 - Q_2)}{2} = \frac{\$2 \cdot 100}{2} = \$100$$

3.7 America's welfare is reduced by the deadweight loss because the tax revenue transferred to America is less than the lost consumer surplus.

3.9 (a) $E_X = D_X - S_X = 100 - 5p_X + p_Y$
(b) $E_X(p_Y = 50) = 150 - 5p_X = 0$ implies $p_X = 30$
(c) $E_X(p_Y = 100) = 200 - 5p_X = 0$ implies $p_X = 40$
(d) In equilibrium, p_X increases as p_Y increases because good X is a market substitute for good Y. The increase in p_Y causes an increase in the demand for X, and that causes the equilibrium price of X to rise.

3.11 Your graph should look like Figure 3.22 of the text except that the demand for unskilled labor now shifts to the right when the skilled wage rises in response to the increase in demand for skilled workers. At the new equilibrium, there is unemployment in the unskilled market even though employed workers are paid the higher minimum wage. Skilled workers all gain because their wage rate and employment are higher than without the minimum wage.

Chapter 4 Check Solutions

4.1 (a) $R = pQ = 100p - 5p^2$ is maximized at $p = 10$.
(b) $\eta = 1$

4.3 $X = Q/10 = (1,000 - 10p)/10 = 100 - p$, and so $AR = p = 100 - X$ for each firm.

4.5 You must use the arc elasticity formula because the demand function is not known:

$$\text{arc } \eta = -\frac{\Delta Q}{\Delta p} \cdot \frac{\bar{p}}{\bar{Q}} = \frac{400}{10} \cdot \frac{90}{2,400} = 1.5 \text{ is elastic.}$$

4.7 (a)
$$\eta_{15} = 0.1 \, (15{,}000/2{,}000) = 0.75$$
$$\eta_{20} = 0.1 \, (20{,}000/2{,}500) = 0.80$$
$$\eta_{25} = 0.1 \, (25{,}000/3{,}000) = 0.83$$

(b) The proportion of income spent on this good gets larger as income increases.

(c) Yes, because the good is normal and income usually declines in a recession. Demand will decrease with decreasing income even though the response becomes smaller and smaller as income falls.

(d) A sustained inflation is likely to change the demand equation. For one thing, as other things change, the intercept in the Engel curve will decrease, causing the ratio M/Q to increase at every level of income, thereby increasing income elasticity.

4.9 The IBM PCs have plenty of substitutes: clones, Apples, AT&Ts, and other brands. Thus, even though the demand for IBMs might be less price elastic than that for other brands, the demand for IBMs will be sensitive to its own price. The market as a whole, however, has few close substitutes for PCs—calculators and mainframes are not good substitutes for a PC. Thus, market demand would be less price elastic than the demand for IBM PCs.

4.11 Other things have changed over the last half century, including the price of servants, the invention of time-saving substitutes, and attitudes.

4.13 Water is a necessity in both short run and long run. In contrast, movies are one form of entertainment. Consumers may persist in their moviegoing habits in the short run, but they will find substitutes in the long run.

4.15 Cross-elasticity is useful in determining the scope of the market. Although the manufacture of aluminum cans is a different industry than the making of waxed-paper containers, these products along with glass containers, tin cans, and plastic containers may all have relatively high positive cross-elasticities of demand. The relevant market may include competition among all these products.

4.17 $\overline{Q} = 34$, and so $\overline{\eta}_p = 1.2(8.1/34) = 0.286$ and $\overline{\eta}_M = 4.3(5.9/34) = 0.746$.

4.19 This linear supply curve is inelastic because it cuts the quantity axis before it cuts the price axis.

Chapter 5 Check Solutions

5.1 (a) slope $= -2$; the opportunity cost of one unit of X is 2 units of Y.

(b) slope $= -1$; now the opportunity cost of one unit of X is 1 unit of Y.

(c) $2(10) + 1(10) = 30 > 20$; $1(5) + 1(10) = 15 < 20$

5.3 When price increases by $3, the required compensating *increase* in income is $60. When the price decreases by $2, the required compensating *decrease* in income is $40.

5.5 His indifference curves are negatively sloped straight lines with $MRS = 1$. The two "goods" are perfect substitutes. These indifference curves are *not* consistent with those presented in the text because they are not strictly convex. This is not a problem because the two brands can be combined, for this consumer, into one good called beer.

5.7 At any bundle of X and Y with X on the horizontal axis, the indifference curves are steeper than before. Persuasive advertising changes the consumers' preferences, and so a whole new set of indifference curves arise.

Some advertising is intended to convey information and may affect choice though it does not affect preferences. For instance, if you do not know that you can buy a good at a lower price, you operate with the wrong budget line. Other advertising is intended to influence peoples' "good will" toward the firm and may not affect the demand for the good. For instance, such advertising might be designed to head off regulation—take the oil-producing companies' claims that they are environmentally responsible. Or such advertising might be intended to enhance a firm's ability to raise financial capital. It is possible, however, that such advertising may affect demand if consumers feel better about the product than before.

5.9 $X = X(p_X, p_Y, M) = M/2p_x$

5.11   The pure income effect occurs when the attainable set expands or contracts while price ratios remain constant. A price-induced income effect occurs when the attainable set expands or contracts because of the change in relative prices. The price-induced income effect is that part of the total effect of the price change not caused by the substitution effect.

5.13   A normal good will always have a negatively sloped demand curve because the always-inverse substitution effect will be reinforced by an inverse price-induced income effect. An inferior good will have a negatively sloped demand curve when the always-inverse substitution effect dominates a now-direct price-induced income effect.

5.15   Leisure time is sold, and so real income increases when the wage rate increases. The price-induced income effect is direct for any normal good that is sold. Because the substitution effect is always inverse, the two effects work in opposite directions for a normal good being sold. Thus, when the demand-for-leisure curve has positive slope, the wage-induced income effect must be direct and must dominate the inverse substitution effect.

5.17   The graph should look like Figure 5.38 in the text. Competitive equilibrium in both markets simultaneously requires that $MRS = p_X/p_Y$ for both consumers simultaneously. Each person's indifference curve at equilibrium must be tangent to the common budget line where it cuts the contract curve.

5.19 $WAI = 121.65$; $LPI = 100.27$; $PPI = 100.15$

5.21   (a) If the public utility wants to keep its rates current with the general level of prices, it can argue that its current rate should be adjusted by the increase in the CPI-U since 1978.

      (b) Multiply the 1980 home price by the change in the CPI and divide by the old CPI. Using the housing category alone might increase accuracy.

      (c) Divide current CPI into the CPI of two years ago.

      (d) Assuming that $3.35 was adequate in 1981, multiply that standard by the ratio of the current CPI divided by the 1981 CPI.

Chapter 6 Check Solutions

6.1   Because total earnings over a person's lifetime are not received in one lump sum at the beginning of that person's life, the airlines might argue that, over the person's expected working life they could pay the salary in periodic payments as if the person were working; or they could pay the present value of total earnings calculated at the market rate of interest. Some combination of the two alternatives, called a structured settlement, is also used frequently. Of course, choosing the appropriate discount rate is also an issue.

6.3   To increase present consumption by $1,100, this person must borrow that amount at 5 percent. Thus, the increase in future consumption will be reduced by $1,155. The increase in future consumption is:

$$\Delta C_2 = \Delta M_2 - (1 + i)\Delta C_1 = \$2,100 - \$1,155 = \$945$$

6.5   As the interest rate rises, the budget line becomes steeper because the opportunity cost of present consumption increases. The affordable set contracts for borrowers and expands for savers.

6.7   A lender who remains a lender after a fall in the interest rate is worse off.

6.9   (a) The indifference curves become steeper.

(b) The savings supply curve will shift to the left.

6.11 (a) The appropriate value to attach to the services of a durable good is its opportunity cost. The services of a house should be valued at the amount the consumer would be willing to pay to rent the house.

(b) A durable good should be purchased as long as the PV of its services is at least as great as its market price. If $NPV < 0$, then lease.

6.13 (a) Choose B because

$$NPV_a = (1{,}000/0.10) - 3{,}800 = 6{,}200$$

$$NPV_b = (1{,}400/0.10) - 7{,}000 = 7{,}000$$

(b) Choose A because

$$NPV_a = (1{,}000/0.15) - 3{,}800 = 2{,}867$$

$$NPV_b = (1{,}400/0.15) - 7{,}000 = 2{,}333$$

6.15 (a) The aggregate demand for a public good is the sum of all consumers' marginal values as measured by price, where

$$MV_1 = p_1 = 4 - 0.5X_1 \text{ and } MV_2 = p_2 = 12 - X_2$$

The inverse AD curve is

$$AD^{-1} = MV_1 + MV_2 = 16 - 1.5Q_d$$

This curve yields the aggregate demand as

$$Q_d = (16 - p)/1.5$$

(b) Optimal production occurs where quantity demanded equals quantity supplied,
$Q_d = Q_s = 6.4$

(c) $p_1 = 0.8; p_2 = 5.6$

(d) Market demand for a private good is the horizontal summation of the individual demands. As you can see when you graph market demand along with supply, the equilibrium price is above the first person's reservation price, and so only the second person will consume the good. The amount consumed is $X_2 = 6$ at price $p = 6$.

Chapter 7 Check Solutions

7.1   Information about the quality of American cars is asymmetric. If a high-quality import had not been available as a substitute, American manufacturers might have chosen to ignore the decrease in demand predicted when new-car "lemons" appeared. But with the substitute, some American manufacturers responded by improving quality. Asymmetric information remained, however, and so total demand remained depressed. Guaranties on new cars reduce the risk associated with getting a lemon. Not only does this tactic increase the demand for domestic cars that have the guaranties, it also tends to increase demand for all domestic cars.

7.3   The law of large numbers states that if an event occurs k times in n replications of an experiment, then k/n approaches the probability of the event as n gets large. When the law of large numbers does not apply, the expected value rule of choosing the action having the highest expected value might not be appropriate because the probabilities assigned are not verifiable by experiment. Then, if you can't establish the probabilities by logic, those probabilities are necessarily subjective. Hence, the decision will differ for every decision maker. In addition, and perhaps more important, when the decision will not be replicated many times, the possibility of large losses should be considered. But the expected value rule does not adjust for the risk associated with variation in the payoff.

7.5 Set $E[U(A)] = E[U(B)]$ to get $P = 5/9$. ($P = 0.555$ approximately.)

7.7 E(gamble) $= \$325$, and the risk-averse person will choose \$325 with certainty over any gamble having the same expected value. The expected value of a gamble is preferred to the gamble itself under risk aversion.

7.9 This person is risk averse, not a pessimist. For someone who is risk averse, the price has to be less than the expected value of the gamble.

7.11 (a) $E(T) = 50$
  (b) ΔU(win) $= 2/5$; ΔU(lose) $= -3/5$
  (c) Diminishing marginal utility of money appears, and so this person is risk averse.
  (d) This risk-averse person will not pay the lottery's expected value to play because the utility of the price is greater than the expected utility of the lottery.

7.13 (a) When $\beta = 2$, $\mu_j = 0.06 + 2(0.10 - 0.06) = 0.14$
  (b) When $\beta = 1$, $\mu_j = 0.06 + 1(0.10 - 0.06) = 0.10$
  (c) When $\beta = 1/2$, $\mu_j = 0.06 + 0.5(0.10 - 0.06) = 0.08$
  (d) When $\beta = 0$, $\mu_j = 0.06 + 0.0(0.10 - 0.06) = 0.06$
    The beta of an asset measures the change in μ_j relative to an incremental change in μ_m, and so the adjusted discounting interest rate is directly related to the market rate when beta is positive. This result also means that the price of an asset will be inversely related to its beta. When $\beta > 1$, the asset is riskier than the market as a whole. When $\beta < 1$, the asset is less risky than the market as a whole. If $\beta = 0$, then $\mu_j = c$, and the risk-adjustment factor is zero. It would be a mistake, however, to conclude that this asset has no risk. No firm can offer a risk-free asset. When the asset has zero covariance with the market, the beta of the asset will be zero. That condition doesn't imply no variation in the return to the asset; rather, zero covariance with the market as a whole means that the asset's returns are not correlated with the market's returns.

7.15 $E[U$(lottery)$] = 2$ and the certainty equivalent is $M = \$4$. The expected value of the lottery is E(lottery) $= \$12$. The player would receive \$12 if the lottery were replaced by its expected value. Thus, this person would be willing to pay \$8 to receive \$12 with certainty rather than take the gamble.

7.17 (a) A_1
  (b) The minimax regret is 1 and A_3 is indicated.
  (c) A_4 is indicated by the Laplace rule.

Chapter 8 Check Solutions

8.1 $\alpha > 0$ and $0 < \beta < 1$

8.3 $\hat{Y} = \hat{\alpha} + \hat{\beta}X = \bar{Y} - \hat{\beta}\bar{X} + \hat{\beta}X$, and so $\hat{Y} = \bar{Y}$ when $X = \bar{X}$.

8.5 This econometrician was trying to emphasize the drawbacks associated with losing degrees of freedom and was arguing that maximizing R^2 is not a good criterion for judging the validity of the estimated model. You can always increase R^2 by adding explanatory variables, even if they don't belong in the equation. In fact, if you engage in nonstochastic curve fitting, an $(n - 1)$

degree polynomial can be fitted to a sample of size n with perfect fit, but the explanatory variable may have no relation, causal or otherwise, with the dependent variable.

8.7 Perfect multicollinearity. Drop one of the variables.

8.9 Multicollinearity is clearly present between *GNP* and *CPI*, but both are properly included variables. In the fourth equation, all variables are deflated by the price index, and so both *GNP* and *CPI* remain in the equation, and it solves the multicollinearity problem in a way that avoids omitted-variables bias.

8.11 (a) 78.38 percent

(b) Using the rule of thumb for a two-sided test, the coefficients for X_2 and X_3 are statistically different from zero.

(c) \$3,469

8.13 (a) D_t, R_{t-1}, and t are predetermined, but R_t and I_t are probably endogenous if t refers to a survey year. (I_t might be exogenous if the observation period is short, like weekly data.)

(b) The demand equation is identified, but the supply equation is not identified unless I_t is exogenous.

8.15 (a) The first-differences model is

$$(Y_t - Y_{t-1}) = \beta(X_t - X_{t-1}) + (\varepsilon_t - \varepsilon_{t-1})$$

(b) First, the new error has constant variance and is independent of the explanatory variable $(X_t - X_{t-1})$. Second, the model must be estimated without an intercept to get $\hat{\beta}$. Then α is estimated for the original model, using the variable means: $\hat{\alpha} = \bar{Y} - \hat{\beta}\bar{X}$

8.17 For a two-sided test at a 10 percent level of significance with $n - 2 = 16$ degrees of freedom, the critical values from the table are $t_c = \pm 1.753$. The rejection region is outside of this interval. The test statistic is

$$t_0 = \frac{\hat{\beta}}{S_{\hat{\beta}}} = \frac{10.56}{5.16} = 2.047$$

which is in the right-hand side of the rejection region. Thus, the null is rejected, and the evidence lends support to the alternative hypothesis that $\beta \neq 0$. With this level of significance, there is only a 10 percent chance of wrongly rejecting the null. At a 5 percent level of significance the critical values are $t_c = \pm 2.131$, and so we cannot reject the null that $\beta = 0$ at the 5 percent level of significance.

8.19 The generalized-differences model is

$$(Y_t - \rho Y_{t-1}) = \alpha(1 - \rho) + \beta(X_t - \rho X_{t-1}) + (\varepsilon_t - \rho\varepsilon_{t-1})$$

(a) Let $Y_t^* = (Y_t - \rho Y_{t-1})$ and $X_t^* = (X_t - \rho X_{t-1})$. The first-differences estimates (when $\rho = 1$), using $n - 1 = 19$ observations, are:

$$\hat{Y}_t^* = 0.16871\, X_t^*; \qquad R^2 = 0.984$$
$$(0.0049)$$

Thus $\hat{\beta} = 0.16871$. The estimated intercept, using all $n = 20$ observations, is:

$$\hat{\alpha} = 24.569 - (0.16871)\, 147.625 = -0.337$$

(b) Using $d = 2(1 - \hat{\rho})$, we get $\hat{\rho} = 1 - (d/2) = 0.633$ approximately. For Y_1 and X_1, the special adjustment factor is

$$\sqrt{1 - \hat{\rho}^2} = 0.775$$

Thus $Y_1^* = 0.775Y_1$ and $X_1^* = 0.775X_1$. All remaining variables ($t = 2, 20$) are given by

$$Y_t^* = Y_t - 0.633Y_{t-1}$$
$$X_t^* = X_t - 0.633X_{t-1}$$

Regression of the model yields:

$$\hat{Y}_t^* = 0.119 + 0.1646X_t^*; \qquad R^2 = 0.998$$
$$(0.108) \quad (0.0018)$$

The estimated slope coefficient is about the same as the estimate in the chapter, using $n = 19$ observations, but the standard error is now smaller. To get a new estimate for α, you need to perform the final adjustment:

$$\hat{\alpha} = \frac{\hat{\alpha}^*}{(1 - \hat{\rho})} = \frac{0.119}{0.367} = 0.323$$

Thus the final estimated equation is:

$$\hat{Y}_t = 0.323 + 0.1646X_t$$
$$(0.0018)$$

Chapter 9 Check Solutions

9.1 The four components are trend, seasonal, cyclical, and random or irregular variation.

9.3 (a)

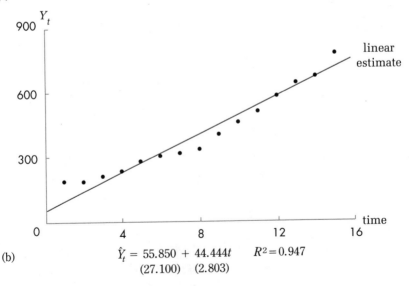

(b)
$$\hat{Y}_t = 55.850 + 44.444t \qquad R^2 = 0.947$$
$$(27.100) \quad (2.803)$$

where standard errors are in parentheses.

(c)
$$\hat{Y}_t = 181.001 + 2.724t + 2.454t^2 \qquad R^2 = 0.996$$
$$(12.954) \quad (3.507) \quad (0.201)$$

where standard errors are in parentheses. Notice that the estimated coefficient for t is not statistically significant.

(d) $\widehat{\ln Y_t} = 5.045 + 0.107t$ $R^2 = 0.995$
                       (0.020) (0.002)

where standard errors are in parentheses. If you try the exponential with both t and t^2, the coefficient for t^2 is not statistically significant.

(e) The exponential is more parsimonious, but the quadratic also fits well.

9.5 (a) The significance of $\hat{\beta}_1$ indicates that the series has a trend, and the lack of significance of $\hat{\beta}_2$ indicates that first differences should be sufficient to detrend the series.

(b) A series with trend cannot be stationary, and so it is not legitimate to use an AR model on this series.

(c) Create a new series $y_t = Y_t - \hat{Y}_t$ where $\hat{Y}_t$ is taken from one of the estimated models in Problem 9.3. One of the nonlinear models would probably be better than the linear model.

(d) Let $y_t = Y_t - Y_{t-1}$, so that the model becomes

$$y_t = \beta_0 + \beta_1 y_{t-1} + \varepsilon_t$$

(e) Least-squares regression yields:

$$\hat{y}_t = 29.369 + 0.450 y_{t-1} \qquad R^2 = 0.198$$
$$(0.262)$$

where the standard error is in parentheses. Notice that the coefficient on y_{t-1} is not significantly different from zero.

9.7 Parsimony; the $MA(q)$ model can be estimated with fewer parameters.

9.9   Skis $= \beta_0 + \beta_1$ SkiPrice $+ \beta_2$ LiftPrice $+ \beta_3$ Income $+ \beta_4$ Winter $+ \varepsilon$

where Winter is a dummy variable that takes a value of unity during the winter months of the ski season and zero otherwise.

Chapter 10 Check Solutions

10.1 The main differences between isoquants and indifference curves are:

(a) Indifference curves represent an ordinal ranking but isoquants represent a cardinal form of measurement.

(b) Indifference curves are strictly convex, with a continuously diminishing rate of substitution (MRS), but isoquants may have linear segments with a sectionally declining rate of input substitution ($MRTS$).

10.3 $T = \min[b_1', b_2/2, b_3, b_4/4]$. In other words, T is determined by the minimum of the terms in the brackets.

10.5 (a) The TP curve starts at the origin and increases at a decreasing rate but never reaches a maximum for this Cobb-Douglas production function.

(b) $AP = 100/\sqrt{L}$ and it falls continuously but at a decreasing rate.

(c) The MP falls continuously but at a decreasing rate and is everywhere below the AP curve. Notice that MP is one-half AP at every level of output.

10.7 The TP curve should consist of connected linear segments starting at the origin; the slope of each successive segment gets smaller, ending with the last segment, which has zero slope. Each kink in the TP curve corresponds to a corner point on an isoquant.

10.9 See Figure 10.10 in the text.

10.11 Diminishing productivity is usually said to begin when average product starts to diminish. Alternatively, you might say that diminishing productivity sets in when marginal product begins to diminish. Either way, total product continues to rise as long as marginal product is positive. Thus the variable input may be used efficiently until marginal product becomes zero or negative.

10.13 (a) Diminishing returns (also called the law of variable proportions or the law of diminishing productivity) is a short-run description of production technology that says the TP curve eventually will increase at a decreasing rate when at least one input is fixed.

(b) Decreasing returns to scale occur when output increases at a decreasing rate as all inputs increase but remain in fixed proportion (the firm moves along a ray).

(c) A diminishing $MRTS$ means that any isoquant is convex. Output is held constant but the inputs are variable.

(d) A diminishing MRT means concavity of the production possibilities curve. Increasingly large reductions in one good are necessary to produce incremental increases in another good as the firm (or the economy) moves along the production possibilities curve.

10.15 The log-linear seems to fit the data fairly well. The R^2s are both fairly high, and all the estimated coefficients are statistically significant. Of course, the equation for cotton fits better than the one for sugar. The coefficients are direct estimates of the output elasticities of the variable inputs, and all indicate diminishing marginal productivity of the inputs. The sum of the coefficients in each equation indicates the returns to scale. For cotton, $\beta_1 + \beta_2 = 1.04 > 1$ indicates slight increasing returns to scale. For sugar, $\beta_1 + \beta_2 = 0.92 < 1$ indicates slight decreasing returns to scale.

10.17 The optimality conditions are:

$$MP_{L_1} = MP_{L_2}$$
$$MP_{K_1} = MP_{K_2}$$
$$L_1 + L_2 = L$$
$$K_1 + K_2 = K$$

Therefore, try the given values in these equations to see if they are satisfied. Alternatively, show that $MRTS_1 = MRTS_2$.

10.19 When both goods have equal factor intensities (the same fixed input ratios), the efficiency curve is a straight line through the origin. Along this straight line a doubling of X will halve the output of Y because of constant returns to scale. Thus the transformation curve will be a straight line and the MRT is constant.

10.21 For a technological advance in producing X, the maximum of X that can be produced will be greater than before. The production possibilities curve will expand in the direction of X.

10.23 (d) $X^* = 3$

(e) The first activity gets $L = 4$ and $K = 1$; the second activity gets $L = 4$ and $K = 4$; the third activity gets $L = 0$ and $K = 0$.

(f) $X_1^* = 1$; $X_2^* = 2$; $X_3^* = 0$.

Chapter 11 Check Solutions

11.1 Accounting cost is a bookkeeping entry that does not necessarily equal an input's opportunity cost, the payment that an input would receive in its best alternative use—its economic cost. Two reasons explaining why accounting cost may be different are conformity to conventional accounting practice and conformity to legal requirements. A third reason is that opportunity cost is sometimes hard to measure.

11.3 (a) $X = \sqrt{L}$ when $K = 1$; $AP = 1/\sqrt{L}$; $MP = 1/2\sqrt{L}$. Stage II is everywhere because AP is diminishing while MP is positive for all levels of output.

(b) $L = L(X) = X^2$

(c) $VC = wL(X) = X^2$; $FC = rK = 4$; $TC = X^2 + 4$

(d) $AVC = X$; $AC = X + (4/X)$; $MC = 2X$.

11.5 (a) No change appears in AVC or MC, but ATC shifts up, leaving the stages of production unaffected.

(b) Both MC and AVC and ATC shift up, and the stages remain the same.

11.7 If the $MRTS$ is constant, the isoquant will be linear. When $MP_L/MP_K > w/r$, choose only L because you will be at a corner point. When $MP_L/MP_K < w/r$, choose only K because you will be at the other corner point.

11.9 (a) Linear models have constant returns to scale. For this linear model we have

$$X = 10 \min[L/2, K] = \min[5L, 10K]$$

Along the expansion path, $K/L = 1/2$ or $2K = L$.

(b) We are given $w = 3$ and $r = 1$, and so

$$LTC(X = 10) = 7 \text{ and } LTC(X = 20) = 14$$

These two points are sufficient to establish the LTC curve as $LTC = 0.7X$ because it is linear under constant returns to scale. Moreover, $LAC = 0.7$ is constant.

(c) At $K = 10$, $X = \min[5L, 100]$ or

$$X = 5L \text{ for } L \le 20 \text{ and } X = 100 \text{ for } L > 0$$

This statement means that:

$$L = L(X) = X/5 \text{ for } X \le 100$$

$$VC = wL(X) = 3X/5 \text{ for } X \le 100$$

$$TC = (3X/5) + 10 \text{ for } X \le 100$$

$$AC = (3/5) + 10/X \text{ for } X \le 100$$

(d) $MC = 0.6$ for $X \le 100$, and so MC graphs as a constant for $X \le 100$.

11.11 The LAC curve will be horizontal because LAC is constant. This condition follows because, with constant returns to scale, a doubling of output requires a doubling of all inputs, and hence a doubling of long-run total cost.

11.13 $LTC = 2X$ and $LAC = 2$

11.15 Economies of scale describe how cost changes in the long run when the firm increases one output. Economies of scope describe the case in which the total cost of producing two or more goods at the same time is less than the sum of the costs of producing those goods using separate production processes.

11.17 Firm A has greater difficulty in substituting inputs, and so its costs will increase more when the price of any input increases.

11.19 Long-run planning is crucial in any competitive environment if the firm is to remain in the industry. The LAC curve is called the "planning" curve.

11.21 Restricting the rate base to include only invested capital produces a bias toward choosing inputs that qualify. (This bias is called the Averch-Johnson effect.) The restriction tends to act as a subsidy on a qualifying input, reducing its effective price. This effect leads to substitution of capital for labor and the K/L ratio increases. The firm is motivated to move away from the cost-minimizing input ratio, thereby increasing the costs of production at any level of output. The result is an upward shift in the LAC curve. In Chapter 16, we consider in more detail the issues that arise in regulating utilities.

11.23 Technical progress in production means that fewer resources are needed to produce a given level of output. Thus both short-run and long-run cost curves will be lower than before.

11.25 Average transportation costs are likely to rise as the distance from point of departure to destination increases. Once average transportation cost is added to average cost, the AC curve will rise sooner than before. The optimal scale of plant will shrink, and so the number of plants in the industry will increase to keep average cost as low as possible.

11.27 Strong economies or diseconomies of scale will invalidate use of the linear model because it requires constant returns to scale and isoquants that remain parallel between rays. But any technology which has constant returns to scale, like the Cobb-Douglas, and which can be represented by a finite number of activities, can be described exactly or approximately by the linear model.

Chapter 12 Check Solutions

12.1 The profit-maximizing, price-taking firm will set output at $X = X^*$, where $MR = MC$ if $p \geq AVC$. Notice that $p = AR = MR$ for the price-taking firm. If $p < AVC$, then the firm will shut down to minimize the short-run loss. When $p = MR$ and the firm sets output so that $MR = MC$, it also sets output so that $p = MC$. Thus the supply curve coincides with the MC curve above the AVC curve (in stage II). See Figure 12.5 of the text for an illustration. This supply curve must have positive slope because MC is increasing due to diminishing productivity in stage II.

12.3 $R(L) = 32\sqrt{L}$; $ARP = 32/\sqrt{L}$; $VMP = 16/\sqrt{L}$

12.5 An increase in productivity of the variable input increases its VMP and thereby increases the demand for that input. Both the input's price and employment will increase in equilibrium.

12.7 (a) At $K = 1$, $X = \sqrt{L}$, so that $L = X^2$ and $MC = 2X$. Set $p = MC = 2X$ to get supply as

$$X = p/2$$

(b) At $K = 1$, $MP_L = 3/2\sqrt{L}$ and $VMP = pMP_L$. Set $w = VMP$ to get demand for L as

$$L = \frac{9}{4w^2}$$

12.9 The incentive system should tie salary to long-run profits. Stock options would do the trick for a corporation.

12.11 $LAC = LMC$ and are constant, and so there is no best scale. Firms will exit or enter until $p = LMC$, but the remaining firms may be large or small.

12.13 In the long run without interference, each firm selects a scale where $LMC = p$, resulting in minimum LAC and zero profit. In the diagram, as demand decreases to D_2, industry price will fall, each firm will adjust its output to X_2, where $p_2 = MC_1$, and firms experience short-run losses:

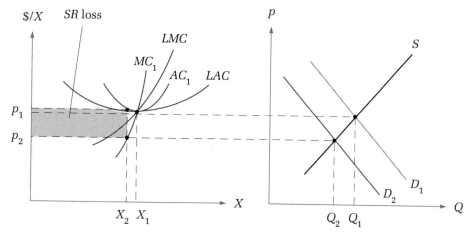

Ordinarily, the resulting losses would force some firms to leave the industry. Because that is prohibited, the firms' only response is to reduce their scale so that $p = LMC$ once more. As you can see in the next diagram, market supply shifts to the left as each firm decreases its scale. Market price will rise to p_3, and each firm produces less at X_3 units. But each firm still suffers a loss. Ultimately, some firms will be forced into bankruptcy.

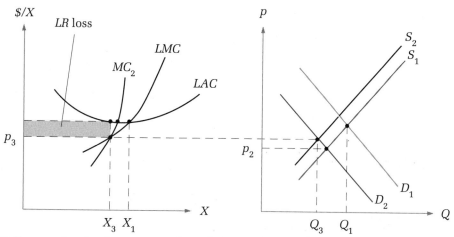

12.15 If economies of scale occur over the entire range of market demand, the industry will support only one large firm in the long run.

12.17 [See Figure 5.37.] The trading bundle T^* must lie on the contract curve (Pareto optimality) so that $MRS_a = MRS_b = p_X/p_Y$, and all markets must clear.

12.18 [See Figure 12.24 in the text.] Pareto optimality in production occurs when $MRTS_X = MRTS_Y = w/r$, and all input markets must clear. This outcome will put the economy on its production possibilities curve.

12.19 The contract curve in the Edgeworth-Bowley box diagram is a straight line through the two origins when the input ratios are the same in the production of both goods. Along this contract curve, a doubling of X will halve the output of Y when returns to scale are constant. Therefore, the production possibilities curve will be a negatively sloped straight line.

12.21 The initial distribution of wealth affects the initial endowments and hence influences their utility-maximizing choices regarding input supply and output demand. Thus, the general equilibrium set of prices depends on the initial distribution of wealth, which in turn affects the distribution of income among persons in the economy. Society may judge that distribution as inequitable even though it is Pareto optimal. The unbiased property of competitive equilibrium, however, says that any desired Pareto-optimal distribution can be achieved through competition by redistributing wealth.

Chapter 13 Check Solutions

13.1 (a)
$$TR = p(Q)Q = (a - bQ)Q = aQ - bQ^2$$

$$MR = \frac{\Delta TR}{\Delta Q} = a - 2bQ$$

(b)
$$MR = p\left[1 - \frac{1}{\eta}\right] = 0 \text{ when } \eta = 1$$

$$MR = a - 2bQ = 0 \text{ implies } Q = a/2b$$

(c) The elastic range is to the left of the midpoint of the AR curve because $MR > 0$. The inelastic range is to the right of the midpoint because $MR < 0$.

13.3 If $VC = 0$, then $MC = 0$, and the monopoly firm sets Q and p so that $MR = MC = 0$. Elasticity is unitary when $MR = 0$.

13.5 (a) Because $AR = 50 - 5Q$, $MR = 50 - 10Q$. Setting $MR = MC$ yields $Q^* = 4$ and $p^* = 30$.
   (b) $\eta = 1.5 > 1$ is elastic.
   (c) $D = 40$

13.7 The competitive equilibrium occurs where market demand cuts market supply, and market supply is the horizontal summation of the firms' marginal cost curves. At the firm level, each competitive firm will have a short-run AC curve such that $AC = MC = LAC = LMC$. When the cartel is formed, none of the firms' plants will be closed. The noncheating, market-sharing cartel views the inverse market demand curve as its AR curve, and the cartel will maximize profits where MR cuts the supply curve. The supply curve is the horizontal sum of all plants' MC curves, and so the supply curve is the same as before. Price is higher for the cartel and quantity lower because now MR is below AR. The deadweight loss will equal the area between the demand and supply curves over the range of the change in quantity. Converting the competitive firms into a pure monopoly would yield a different result because the monopolist would close some of its plants, causing the market supply curve to shift to the left. Price would be greater, output lower, and the deadweight loss is greater under monopoly than under the noncheating, market-sharing cartel.

13.9 The outcome will depend on where the LAC curve reaches a minimum. Let's start by assuming that the LAC reaches a minimum at a point halfway between that point and the market demand curve:

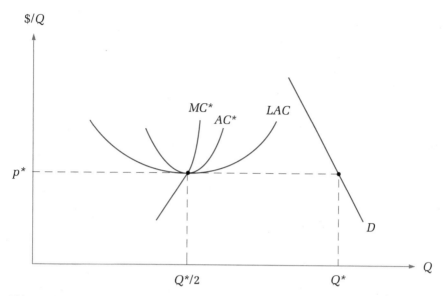

$/Q

p^*

$Q^*/2$ Q^* Q

MC^* LAC
AC^*

D

This market will support two identical firms at price p^*, and each firm produces $Q^*/2$ units. Notice that $\pi^* = 0$ because $p = LAC = AC = MC$. The results are the same as under perfect competition. If market demand cannot be divided equally between the firms, though, some firms will be forced to wait in the wings for a chance to contest the market. Then the incumbent firms will still not be able to charge a price greater than MC because the market is contestable. Thus profits are zero and price equals minimum LAC as before, but industry output is *lower* than under perfect competition.

13.11 Concentration ratio = 85 percent; $H = 0.3078$.

13.13 Set $MRP = MFC$ to find $L^* = 8$.

13.15 Choose the water monopoly because the consumer surplus is greater, so that the potential for monopoly profit is greater.

Chapter 14 Check Solutions

14.1 (a) The decrease in MC and AC caused by increased productivity or a decrease in input price leaves the MC curve within the gap in the MR curve, and so price remains unchanged.

(b) Both AR and MR shift to the right. If MC continues to cut within the gap in the MR curve, price remains the same and the kink in the AR curve occurs at that price. Output increases to the level where the new kink occurs.

14.3 Monopolistic competition is characterized by a large number of small firms producing differentiated products that are close but not perfect substitutes. Concentration ratios and the Herfindahl index should be small in such an industry, and cross-elasticities between the products should be positive and large. Profits and the Bain index should be small because of easy entry, and price should be close to long-run average cost, but LAC should not be at a minimum. Each firm's demand curve should be highly elastic. In contrast, oligopoly is characterized by a few relatively large firms in the relevant market. Concentration ratios should be large, but cross-elasticities may not be useful because the product can be homogeneous. Each firm's demand curve, however, is likely to have small elasticity. Both the Bain and the Learner indexes are likely to be fairly large. Any evidence of price leadership or followership is consistent with oligopoly; however, other explanations of such behavior are possible. Strategic behavior is the primary indicator of oligopoly as a market structure.

14.5 (a)
$$\pi_1 = 84X_1 - 0.1X_1^2 - 0.1X_1X_2 - 6,000$$

$$\pi_2 = 90X_2 - 0.1X_2^2 - 0.1X_1X_2 - 9,000$$

(b) Calculus is required to find:

$$\Delta\pi_1/\Delta X_1 = 84 - 0.2X_1 - 0.1X_2$$

$$\Delta\pi_2/\Delta X_2 = 90 - 0.2X_2 - 0.1X_1$$

Both firms are profit maximizers and have control of their own output only, and so each will set its marginal profit equal to zero, taking the other firm's output as given. The simultaneous solution is:

$$X_1 = 260, X_2 = 320$$

The equilibrium price will be $p = 42$, yielding total quantity of $Q = 580$.

14.7 A dominant strategy yields the best result no matter what an opponent does. When equilibrium of dominant strategies occurs, no player is motivated to make another strategic choice.

14.9 Negotiation costs will increase along with the complexity of the game as the number of players increases. With more than two players, enforcement is more difficult. Moreover, over long periods, market conditions change. Players' attitudes and motivations may change also. Cheating is more likely when the underlying conditions change, and so collusive agreements deteriorate.

14.11 In a game, a "first-mover" advantage may appear when players alternate moves and one player moves first. A first-mover advantage occurs in the game of chess as long as you don't make a "bad" move. Another example of first-mover advantage occurs in warfare, when one opponent starts play with a surprise attack. If successful, such a first strike can incapacitate an opponent so severely that the game is won on the first move. The first firm to establish a position in the market for a new product may also establish an almost insurmountable position.

14.13 For player I, the maximin $= 0$, the maximum of the row minimums. For player II, the minimax $= 0$, the minimum of the row maxima. Thus the saddle point occurs at the intersection of row 2 and column 1, and the value of the game is zero.

14.15 (a) Call the two firms players A and B. Assume that all sales go to the firm with the lowest price. When both players charge 50¢, the market demand is 1,000 and each firm sells 500 units. Profit to each firm is $50. If A charges 60¢ and B charges 50¢, then B sells 1,000 units and has a profit of $100 when A has zero profit. Likewise, if B charges 60¢ and A charges 50¢, then A sells 1,000 units and has a profit of $100 and B has zero profit. If both charge 60¢, market demand falls to 900 units and each firm sells 450 units, yielding a profit of $90 for each. The payoff table is:

		Player A	
		50¢	60¢
Player B	50¢	(50, 50)	(100, 0)
	60¢	(0, 100)	(90, 90)

(b) The solution to the noncooperative game is $p = 50$¢ and profits are $50 each.
(c) The solution to the cooperative game is $p = 60$¢ and profits are $90 each. This solution is likely to be unstable because either firm can gain by lowering price to 50¢ if the other firm continues to charge 60¢.

Chapter 15 Check Solutions

15.1 Cost-plus pricing is used frequently because it is easy to implement. If applied properly, cost-plus pricing does not invalidate the conclusions of the economic models of profit maximizing. If the firm is operating in the long run near minimal average cost, then fully allocated cost may be close to marginal cost. If the costing method closely approximates all inputs' opportunity costs, and if the markup closely approximates the opportunity cost of owners' equity plus a return on any monopoly power, then markup pricing will closely approximate marginal cost pricing.

Cost-plus pricing may also reflect demand conditions if discounts applied to list price are used to adjust price to changes in demand elasticity. The optimal markup is smaller as demand grows more elastic.

15.3
$$\pi = 90X - 7X^2 + 4X\sqrt{A} - A$$

The easy way to solve this problem is to set both derivatives equal to zero simultaneously:

$$\frac{\Delta\pi}{\Delta X} = 90 - 14X + 4\sqrt{A} = 0$$

$$\frac{\Delta\pi}{\Delta A} = \frac{2X}{\sqrt{A}} - 1 = 0$$

Substitution and algebra yield $X^* = 15$ and $A^* = 900$. Thus $p^* = 175$.

15.5 Price discrimination is *possible* when the seller has some monopoly power and if resale can be prevented. The *legality* of price discrimination is another matter, however.

15.7   The firm will maximize profit where $MR_1 = MR_2 = MC$, and so

$$p_1\left(1 - \frac{1}{\eta_1}\right) = p_2\left(1 - \frac{1}{\eta_2}\right)$$

Therefore,

$$\frac{p_1}{p_2} = \frac{\left(1 - \dfrac{1}{\eta_2}\right)}{\left(1 - \dfrac{1}{\eta_1}\right)}$$

Thus if $p_1 > p_2$, then $\eta_1 < \eta_2$. Demand is less elastic in the market with the higher price.

15.9   (a) $MR_1 = 500 - 16X_1$; $MR_2 = 400 - 10X_2$

(b) Set $MR = MC$ in each market when $MC = 20$:

$$MR_1 = 20 \text{ yields } X_1^* = 30 \text{ and } p_1^* = 260$$

$$MR_2 = 20 \text{ yields } X_2^* = 38 \text{ and } p_2^* = 210$$

(c) $Q = X_1 + X_2 = 142.5 - 0.325p$, and so $p = 438.46 - 3.077Q$. Thus

$$MR = 438.46 - 6.154Q$$

Setting $MR = MC$ yields $Q^* = 68$, $p^* = 229.23$, $X_1^* = 33.85$, $X_2^* = 34.15$.

(d) With price discrimination, profit is $\pi = \$4,420$. Without price discrimination, profit is $\pi = \$4,228$.

15.11 (a) AR_1 is the horizontal sum of AR_e and AR_2, and MR_1 is the curve marginal to the AR_1 curve. Therefore, first we need to express X_e and X_2 as functions of price:

$$X_e = 1,500 - 1.25p \text{ and } X_2 = 1,600 - 1.60p$$

$$X_1 = X_e + X_2 = 3,100 - 2.85p$$

Now we invert this last equation to get $AR_1 = 1,088 - 0.351X_1$. The curve marginal to the AR_1 equation is $MR_1 = 1,088 - 0.70X_1$.

(b) To find X_1^*, set $MR_1 = MC_1$, which yields $X_1^* = 826$ units

(c) To find X_e^*, set $MR_e = MC^*$, where $MC^* = MC_1(X_1^*) = 510$. This figuring results in $X_e^* = 431.25$ units. The price to be charged to the external market is $p_e^* = AR_e(X_e^*) = \$855$.

(d) The optimal transfer quantity X_2^* occurs where $MR_2 = MC^*$. This condition yields $X_2^* = 392$ units. The price to be charged for the transfer good is

$$p_2^* = AR_2(X_2^*) = \$755.$$

Chapter 16 Check Solutions

16.1 (a) The marginal social cost is $MSC = 3 + 6E$, and so when we set MSC equal to the MCA, we get $E^* = 0.40$ thousand tons or 400 tons.

(b) Evaluate either the MSC equation or the MCA equation at E^* to get the optimal fee of $f^* = \$5.4$ billion per thousand tons or $\$5.4$ million per ton.

16.3 In this diagram, the unregulated price is p^* where the firm maximizes long-run profit. If regulators were to set price at p_r, where $p = LAC$, a subsidy would be required equal to the area of the rectangle shown in the diagram.

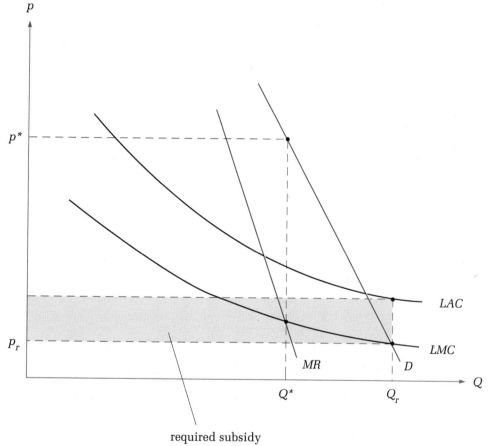

required subsidy

16.5 A fixed tax per unit of output, an excise tax, changes the variable costs of production, and so the MC curve shifts upward vertically by an amount equal to the tax, as shown in this diagram. Thus price is higher and output lower than before the tax was imposed.

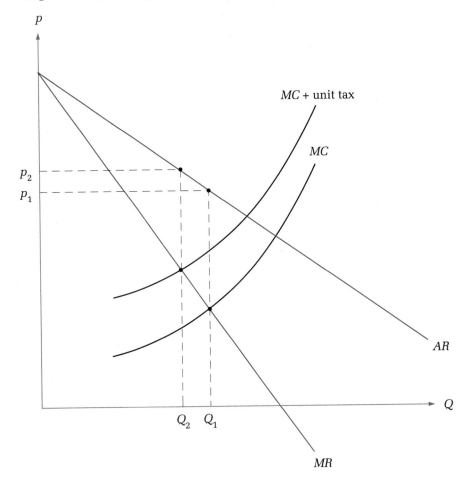

In contrast, a lump-sum tax is viewed as a fixed cost, and so the AC curve shifts upward but MC remains unchanged. Therefore, the lump-sum tax leaves price and output unchanged.

16.7 The natural monopolist sets output where $p = LAC$, where $\pi = 0$, or else entrants will capture any profit. The result is the same as if the firm were subject to regulated average cost pricing.

16.9   First, let's calculate the squared percentage shares:

Firm	S (% share)	S^2
1	20	400
2	18	324
3	15	225
4	10	100
5	8	64
6	8	64
7	6	36
8	5	25
9	5	25
10	5	25

(a) Before the merger, the HH index is $\Sigma S^2 = 1,228$. After the two largest firms merge, the 20 percent and 18 percent shares would be combined to yield 38 percent. Squaring this new share and replacing the first two squared terms, the HH index would become $\Sigma S^2 = 2,004$. The premerger index is above the 1,000 DOJ guideline. Moreover, the postmerger index is above the DOJ guideline of 1,800 and the increase in the index is above the 100 guideline, and so this merger is likely to be challenged.

(b) A merger of the third and fourth firms would result in the new firm's having a 25 percent market share, and so 25 percent would replace the 15 percent and 10 percent shares of those firms in the table. The postmerger index would be 1,588, which is below the guideline of 1,800, but the change in the index would be 360, which is above the guideline value. Because the premerger index was above 1,000 and the change in the index is greater than 100, this merger may well be challenged, but the DOJ will look at other possible consequences before making a final decision.

(c) A merger of two of the smallest firms would give the merged firms a 10 percent share rather than 5 percent each. This combination would result in a postmerger index of 1,278 because the change in the index would be 50. Thus, this merger is not likely to be challenged because the change is less than 100 and the postmerger index is less than the 1,800 guideline. The DOJ might, however, look at other consequences of the merger before it makes a final decision because the premerger index was above the 1,000 guideline.

(d) The DOJ might look at the potential for entry, the ability of firms to coordinate their pricing decisions, and any social gains or losses that might arise because of the merger.

16.11   Price discrimination is *possible* when the seller has some monopoly power if resale can be prevented, but price discrimination is *legal* when it does not lessen competition or tend to create a monopoly. Thus, price discrimination is allowable when no significant injury, actual or potential, is done to competition. Price differences caused by differences in cost or quantity are not considered to be price discrimination.

Glossary

absolute advantage the theory that specialization in trade is beneficial whenever each party has an absolute cost advantage (uses fewer resources) in the production of some product. Thus all parties can be made better off if each specializes in the production of goods where it is comparatively more efficient.

adverse selection a situation in which "less desirable" traders are more likely to participate in exchange, causing the outcome to be less efficient than otherwise.

agency relationship a relationship in which one hires an agent to perform a task that affects one's own welfare.

annuity a financial agreement consisting of a series of periodic payments over a fixed number of periods.

arbitrage the practice of selling one asset and buying another while earning a risk-free profit.

arc elasticity an elasticity computed at a midpoint of a secant line drawn between two points along a curve.

asymmetric information a situation in which some parties know more than others about relevant economic decision variables.

attainable set the set of all affordable combinations (bundles) of goods.

autarky the absence of trade.

autoregressive model $AR(p)$ a time series of a variable expressed as a linear function of p lagged values of that series.

autoregressive–moving average model $ARMA(p, q)$ a time series expressed as a linear function of p lagged values of that series plus q lagged values of a series of shocks to the series.

average cost (AC) total cost divided by output. AC is the sum of AFC and AVC.

average cost pricing the attempt by regulators to set price equal to LAC for a natural monopoly.

average fixed cost (AFC) the fixed cost per unit of output.

average product (AP) the total product divided by the amount of input required.

average revenue product (ARP) revenue per unit of the variable input. ARP of an input equals the AP of the input multiplied by the product price.

average variable cost (AVC) variable cost per unit of output.

Bain monopoly index accounting profit less an imputed return on owner's investment.

Bayesian rule the decision rule that, when objective probabilities are unknown, one should assign subjective probabilities to states of nature and then choose the action with the greatest expected value.

beta of an asset a measure of the risk of an asset relative to the market as a whole. It is computed by dividing the covariance of the asset's return with the market as a whole by the market variance.

bilateral monopoly the form of market structure in which there is a single seller and a single buyer.

bilateral pure exchange a model consisting of two agents, each endowed with a bundle of two goods.

bliss point the bundle in the model of individual consumer choice for which a consumer is satiated with respect to all goods simultaneously.

block pricing a situation in which the same customer pays a different price for different quantities of an identical good (also known as **second-degree price discrimination**).

borrowing the reduction of future consumption in order to increase present consumption.

budget line the equation that indicates all bundles of goods requiring a level of expenditure equal to money income.

capitalism the form of economic organization in which the means of production are owned primarily by individuals and decisions are decentralized.

cartel a formal collusive agreement.

certainty a situation without speculation and guesses.

certainty equivalent the amount of money whose utility is equal to the expected utility of a gamble.

CES production function a production function that has constant elasticity of input substitution everywhere.

change in demand a shift in the demand curve caused by changes in the determinants of demand other than the good's own price.

change in supply a shift in the supply curve caused by changes in the determinants of supply other than the good's own price.

coefficient of determination (R^2) the proportion of the total variation in the dependent variable explained by an estimated regression equation.

coefficient of variation a measure of risk equal to the standard deviation divided by the mean of a random variable.

coefficient of variation rule the decision rule that among risky alternatives, one should choose the alternative with the smallest coefficient of variation.

communism the form of economic organization in which the means of production are publicly owned and decisions are primarily centralized.

comparative advantage the theory that persons, firms, and nations should specialize in the production of goods for which their opportunity costs are lowest.

comparative statics sensitivity analysis based on changing only one thing at a time.

completeness in individual consumer choice, the assumption that a consumer can compare and rank any pair of bundles.

completeness and uniqueness in revealed preference, the assumption that there must be at least one set of prices and income at which each bundle is chosen and that except for proportional changes, there is only one set of prices and income at which each bundle is chosen.

concentration ratio a measure of monopoly power computed as the percentage of total industry sales, output, employment, value added, or assets associated with the largest firms ranked in order of market shares.

conglomerate merger a merger of firms from unrelated industries.

consistency in revealed preference, the assumption that if **A** is revealed as preferred to **B**, then **B** must never be revealed as preferred to **A**.

consistent estimator an estimator whose probability distribution collapses on its true value as the sample size gets larger.

constant cost industry an industry in which firms' cost curves are not affected by changes in industry output.

constant returns to scale a property of a production function for which output changes by the same scalar amount as the scalar change in all inputs.

consumer (buyer) surplus the total benefit, or value, that buyers receive beyond what they pay for a good.

contestable market the form of market structure in which even a lone incumbent will behave as if it were perfectly competitive because of the absence of sunk costs and entry barriers as well as a lag in the ability of incumbents to react to pricing initiatives of potential entrants.

contingent consumption plan a specification of what would be consumed under each state of nature that could occur.

contract curve the set of Pareto-efficient allocations within the trading set.

convexity of preference in consumer choice, the assumption that means are preferred to the lower ranked of two extremes and that means are preferred to equally ranked extremes. Convexity of preference is the same as a diminishing marginal rate of substitution between pairs of goods.

correlation a measure of the linear association between two random variables computed by dividing their covariance by the product of their standard deviations.

cost-benefit analysis the public-sector counterpart to private-sector investment decisions.

cost-plus pricing the pricing technique by which a firm estimates the average variable costs of producing and marketing a product, adds a charge for overhead, and then adds a markup for profits (also known as **markup pricing**).

covariance the expected value of the product of the deviations of the two random variables about their means.

cross-price elasticity the percentage change in the quantity demanded for one good divided by the percentage change in a second good's price.

deadweight loss the social loss, welfare loss, or efficiency loss caused by a departure from marginal cost pricing.

decreasing returns to scale a situation in which output changes by a smaller scalar amount than the scalar change in all inputs.

degree of scale economies (*DSE*) a measure of scale effects on the costs of production computed by dividing *LAC* by *LMC*.

demand curve the graph of quantity demanded as a function of price.

demand for a public good the vertical summation of all individuals' demand curves. The aggregate demand for a public good measures the total marginal benefit to society for each unit consumed.

demand price elasticity the percentage change in quantity demanded divided by the percentage change in price.

derivative the slope of a function at a point as measured by the slope of the tangent line at that point.

diminishing returns the principle of an eventual diminishing productivity of a variable input in the short run (also known as the **law of variable proportions**).

diseconomies of scale a situation in which average costs rise as the scale of production operation increases.

dominance in game theory, the assumption that no player will choose a strategy that yields worse results for all of the rivals' alternatives.

dominant strategy in game theory, a strategy that yields the best result no matter what an opponent does.

dummy variable a binary variable that equals unity when some characteristic is present and zero otherwise.

duopoly the form of market structure in which there are only two firms.

economic cost the payment that a resource would receive in its best alternative employment opportunity (also known as **opportunity cost**).

economic profit revenue less all opportunity costs.

economic region of consumption the region of positive marginal utilities for all goods.

economic region of production the region of positive marginal products for all inputs.

economic rent a payment to a resource in excess of its opportunity cost.

economies of scale a situation in which the average costs fall as the scale of production operation is increased.

economies of scope a situation in which the cost of producing two products jointly is less than the total cost of producing each product separately.

effective competition a situation in which buyers and sellers act independently even though the market is not pure or perfect. The competitive process needs to be open and free and the competitors must be comparable.

efficiency curve the set of all Pareto-efficient allocations of inputs in the two-input case.

efficient market hypothesis the theory that the stock market adjusts so quickly to news that no technique of selecting a portfolio of stocks can outperform a strategy of holding a diversified portfolio.

elasticity the percentage change in one variable divided by the percentage change in another variable.

elasticity of (input) substitution the percentage change in the input ratio divided by the percentage change in the marginal rate of technical substitution.

endogenous variable a variable that has its value determined by the solution of a model.

Engel curve quantity demanded as a function of money income.

entrepreneurs the risk takers, innovators, and organizers of the factors of production.

excess capacity the ability of a firm to reduce average cost by expanding output.

excess demand quantity demanded less quantity supplied.

exogenous variable a variable that has its value determined outside a system of equations.

expansion path (EP) the set of input bundles in which the isoquants are tangent to isocost lines.

expected utility in a chance at random payoffs, the sum of the utilities of the payoffs weighted by their probabilities.

expected value the weighted average of the possible values with the probabilities serving as weights (also known as **mean**).

expected value rule the decision rule that when a decision will be replicated many times, one should choose the action with the greatest expected value in order to maximize the expected payoff from the action.

external diseconomies a situation in which the cost curves for each firm shift upward as industry production increases (also known as an **increasing cost industry**).

external economies a situation in which the cost curves for each firm shift downward as industry production increases (also known as a **decreasing cost industry**).

externality a state in which the actions of one economic agent affect the welfare of others directly so that social costs or benefits diverge from private costs or benefits.

fascism the form of economic organization in which the means of production are primarily privately owned, but decisions are centralized.

firm's demand curve the curve that coincides with a firm's average revenue curve.

free-rider a person who enjoys a benefit without paying any share of its cost.

function a mathematical relationship in which the value of a dependent variable is determined from the values of one or more independent variables.

fundamental theorem of consumer choice the theory that any good (simple or composite) that is known always to increase in demand when money income alone rises must definitely shrink in demand when its price alone rises.

fundamental theorem of exchange the theory that voluntary trade is mutually beneficial.

futures contract a promise to deliver a fixed quantity of something at a future date at a fixed future price.

future value the computed value of an amount of money after compounding at an interest rate over a fixed period of time.

game theory a class of models that deal with strategic decision making by adversaries.

general equilibrium a state in which the entire economy is in equilibrium.

Giffen good a special inferior good that has a price-induced income effect larger in magnitude than its substitution effect. Thus the consumer's demand curve for the good has positive slope.

gross national product (GNP) the money value of all goods produced in the economy.

group price discrimination a situation in which different prices are charged to different groups of consumers with different price elasticities of demand (also known as **third-degree price discrimination**).

hedge a situation in which an individual simultaneously sells in the futures market and buys in the spot market in order to reduce the risk associated with an uncertain transaction.

Herfindahl monopoly index the sum of the squares of the market shares of all firms in an industry.

Herfindahl-Hirschman (HH) index a measure of monopoly power computed by summing the squared percentages of market shares of all sellers in the market.

heteroscedasticity a state in which there is a changing variance of the stochastic error term in a regression equation.

horizontal integration the merger of firms that produce the same product.

human capital the set of workers' skills that generates services that can be "rented out" to employers; investments in people's skills, knowledge, or health that directly affect their productivity.

income effect the change in quantity demanded when price increases because consumers' purchasing power falls. A pure income effect is the change in quantity demanded due to the change in money income. Income effects are associated with movements along an income expansion path.

income elasticity the percentage change in quantity divided by the percentage change in income.

income expansion path (*IEP*) the path of bundles chosen as income changes alone and relative prices remain constant.

increasing returns to scale a state in which output changes by a larger scalar amount than the scalar change in all inputs.

indifference curve a set of bundles among which the consumer is indifferent.

industry supply, long-run (*LS*) a graph of the long-run equilibrium price-quantity pairs after all demand-induced adjustments have occurred.

inferior good a good for which quantity demanded decreases when money income alone increases.

input requirement (*IR*) curve a graph of the minimum amount of a variable input required as a function of output when other inputs remain constant.

internal rate of return the discounting interest rate that makes an investment's net present value equal to zero (also known as the **marginal efficiency of investment**).

intertemporal decision decision that affects the future as well as the present.
inverse demand curve the demand curve inverted, yielding price as a function of quantity demanded.
inverse supply curve the supply curve inverted, yielding price as a function of quantity supplied.
investment demand schedule the relationship between the aggregate investment and the interest rate (also known as the **marginal efficiency of investment (MEI) curve**).
isocost a line showing the input combinations that yield equal total cost.
isoquant a curve showing the set of all input bundles that generate an equal quantity of output.
isoutility a curve showing the set of all bundles of goods that generate an equal level of utility.

Laplace rule the decision rule that in the absence of better information, one should assign equal probabilities to the states of nature and then choose the action with the highest expected value.
Laspeyres price index a weighted sum of prices using base period quantities as the weights.
law of large numbers the theory that when an event occurs k times in n identical trials (replications), then k/n approaches the probability of the event as n gets larger.
law of variable proportions the theory that diminishing productivity of variable inputs will occur eventually as successive increases in variable inputs are combined with fixed inputs.
least-squares regression the method of fitting a linear equation by minimizing the sum of squares of the residual errors for all observations.
Lerner monopoly index price less marginal cost, divided by price.
level of significance in inferential statistics, the probability of wrongly rejecting a true null hypothesis.
limit pricing a pricing practice intended to discourage entry into an industry or expansion by existing firms.
linear programming (LP) a practical technique for solving optimization problems that can be described in terms of a linear objective function and linear constraints.
long run the time period over which all inputs are variable.
long-run average cost (LAC) long-run total cost per unit of output (also called the **planning curve**).
long-run marginal cost (LMC) the change in long-run total cost divided by an incremental change in output as the firm moves along its expansion path.
long-run total cost (LTC) a graph of minimum cost as a function of output in the long run.
long-run total product (LTP) a graph of output as a function of all inputs given fixed input proportions.
lottery a gamble undertaken by buying a ticket.

marginal cost (MC) the change in cost for an incremental change in quantity.
marginal cost pricing a situation in which price is equal to marginal cost.
marginal factor cost (MFC) the change in cost divided by the incremental change in a variable input, holding other inputs constant.
marginal product (MP) the change in output divided by the incremental change in a variable input, holding other inputs constant.
marginal rate of substitution (MRS) the negative of the slope of an indifference curve. The MRS is a measure of the amount of one good that the consumer is willing to exchange for small amounts of another good in order to remain on the same indifference curve in the economic region of consumption.
marginal rate of technical substitution (MRTS) the negative of the slope of an isoquant. The MRTS is a measure of the amount of one input that can be substituted for another input while remaining on the same isoquant in the economic region of production.

marginal rate of transformation (*MRT*) the negative of the slope of the production possibilities curve. The MRT is a measure of the opportunity cost of an extra unit of one good in terms of a decrease in another good.

marginal revenue (*MR*) the change in total revenue for an incremental change in quantity.

marginal revenue product (*MRP*) the change in revenue divided by the incremental change in a variable input as that input changes alone. The MRP equals the marginal product of the input multiplied by the marginal revenue of the product.

marginal social cost the extra cost per unit to society for each extra unit produced, where social cost is measured as an opportunity cost of the next best foregone alternative.

marginal utility (*MU*) the change in utility divided by an incremental change in consumption of one good alone.

market complement a good whose demand is inversely related to the price of another good.

market demand the aggregation of all consumers' demands at every price.

market substitute a good whose demand is directly related to the price of another good.

market supply the aggregation of all firms' supplies at every price.

maximax rule the decision rule that one should choose the action that yields the best of the best payoffs.

maximin rule the decision rule that one should choose the action that yields the best of the worst payoffs.

mean elasticity an elasticity computed at the point of the means for an estimated function.

minimax criterion in game theory, the assumption that each player should make the best of the worst possible situation.

minimax regret rule the decision rule that one should choose the action that minimizes the opportunity cost of an incorrect action.

minimax theorem in game theory, the result that every mixed-strategy two-person zero-sum game is known to have a Nash equilibrium.

mixed-strategy in game theory, the assignment of probabilities to choosing pure strategies so that the choice of any strategy cannot be predicted with certainty.

monopolistic competition the form of market structure in which there are many relatively small firms producing differentiated but substitutable products.

monopoly, pure the form of market structure in which one firm produces a unique product that has no close substitutes.

monopoly power a situation in which a seller has some control over a good's price.

monopsony, pure the form of market structure in which there is only one buyer of an input or intermediate good.

monopsony index a measure of monopsony power computed by subtracting an input's price from its marginal factor cost and dividing by the input price (similar to the **Learner index**).

monopsony power a situation in which a buyer has some control over a good's price.

moral hazard a situation in which a probability distribution is affected by one agent's action and is not observed by another.

moving average model (*MA(q)*) a representation of a time series of a variable expressed as a linear function of a series of q shocks to the series.

multicollinearity a state in which a linear combination of explanatory variables is highly collinear with another explanatory variable.

Nash equilibrium a pair of strategies for which each player's choice is optimal given the opponent's strategies.

natural monopoly the form of market structure in which there are economies of scale over a substantial range of market demand so that a single firm can supply the entire market at a price lower than the minimum short-run average cost of smaller firms.

noncertainty a state in which the payoffs or outcomes of events are unknown.

nonexclusion a situation in which the consumption of the good cannot be confined to only those who pay for the good.

nonexhaustion a situation in which the use of the good by one person does not reduce its availability to others.

nonsatiation the assumption that the consumer must prefer more to less.

normal good a good whose quantity demanded increases when money income alone increases.

null hypothesis a statement about a value or a range of values that could occur if the researcher's theory is not correct.

oligopoly the form of market structure in which there are only a few relatively large firms producing substitutable products.

opportunity cost the cost of foregone alternatives.

Paasche price index a weighted sum of prices using reference period (rather than base period) quantities as the weights.

Pareto efficiency in exchange a situation that occurs for an allocation of goods between agents if any further exchange of goods will leave someone worse off.

Pareto efficiency in production a situation that occurs for an allocation of inputs between goods being produced if any further exchange of inputs will result in a decrease in the output of any good.

partial derivative the slope of a multivariate function with respect to one variable when all other variables are held constant.

payoff table a list of alternative actions and an array of their payoffs, which depend on different states of nature, along with their probabilities.

peak-load pricing the practice of charging higher prices during peak demand periods.

pecuniary economies or diseconomies states in which the cost curves shift because input prices change as production increases.

penetration pricing a situation in which price is set relatively low with the intent to establish a broad market base for a new product.

perfect competition pure competition plus perfect mobility of resources and perfect knowledge about the market.

perfectly competitive industry an industry in which there are no barriers to entry or exit and resources can move freely into or out of the industry.

perfect price discrimination a situation in which the price of each unit sold to each customer is set equal to each customer's marginal value of each unit (also known as **first-degree price discrimination**).

perpetuity an annuity that lasts forever.

persuasive advertising a form of product differentiation used to gain some degree of monopoly power.

point elasticity of demand the absolute value of the slope of the demand curve at a point multiplied by the ratio of price divided by quantity at that point.

point elasticity of supply the slope of the supply curve at a point multiplied by the ratio of price divided by quantity at that point.

predatory pricing a pricing practice intended to eliminate a competitor.

present value the current value of an amount of money that will be received some time in the future.

price discrimination the act of charging different prices for an identical good produced under unchanging cost conditions.

price expansion path (*PEP*) the path of bundles chosen as one price changes alone (also known as the **offer curve**).

price-induced income effect that part of the change in quantity demanded due to the change in real income as price changes.

price skimming the practice of setting a high initial price to "skim" the demand by limiting demand by those buyers willing to pay the higher price.

probability distribution a function that assigns a probability to each possible value of a random variable.

process innovation technical change that results in new and improved production processes.

producer (seller) surplus the total value that sellers receive beyond the amount required to supply the good.

product innovation technical change that results in a new and improved product.

production activity a technological relationship between output and input levels, where all inputs remain in fixed proportion to one another. The ray defined by the fixed proportion is called an **activity ray** or **production process**.

production function the boundary of the production possibilities set; the maximum levels of output that are attainable from all input bundles under the current technology.

production possibilities curve the technologically feasible combinations of products and services that can be produced under full and efficient employment of limited resources (also known as the **transformation curve**).

production possibilities set the possible combinations of production possibilities using limited resources under a given technology.

property rights legal conditions of ownership, that is, the right to own, use, and sell.

public good a good that is either nonexclusive or nonexhaustive in consumption.

pure competition the form of market structure in which there are many small buyers and sellers trading a homogeneous product.

pure public good a good for which the consumption by one consumer does not reduce the existing supply available to other consumers and when other consumers may not be excluded from the consumption of the good.

quasi-rent a short-run payment to any input in excess of its opportunity cost.

random variable a function whose value is determined by a probability.

regression analysis a statistical technique that attempts to "explain" movements in a dependent variable as a function of movements in explanatory variables.

rent seeking the behavior of individuals attempting to earn payments in excess of opportunity costs; the expenditure of scarce resources to capture an artificially created transfer.

resale price maintenance a situation in which a monopoly supplier forbids retailers to undercut a retail price floor (also known as **fair trade pricing**).

revealed preference in consumer choice, the assumption that when **A** is chosen over **B** when both are affordable, then **A** is revealed preferred to **B**.

risk a situation in which there is more than one possible outcome for an alternative, and the probabilities of the outcomes are known.

risk aversion the attitude that exists when the certainty equivalent of a gamble is less than the gamble's expected value. Diminishing marginal utility of money is implied, and the person is risk averse.

risk lover a person who has a certainty equivalent for a gamble that is greater than the gamble's expected value.

saving the decision to postpone consumption in the present period in order to increase future consumption.

savings the stock of money and asset values that can be converted into future consumption.

scale effects the impact of plant size on the costs of production. Scale effects show up in the shape of the LAC curve.

second derivative the derivative of the first derivative of a function.

Shepherd's lemma the theory that for the cost-minimizing firm, the derived demand for any input is equal to the change in total cost due to a small change in that input's price alone.

short run any period of time at which technology is constant and at least one input is fixed.

shut-down rule the theory that in the short run, a firm should shut down to minimize loss and incur fixed cost only if price is below average variable cost.

simplex method a technique for finding the optimal solution to an LP problem by systematically searching for the optimal solution from a finite set of feasible solutions.

slope the change in the dependent variable of a function caused by an incremental change in an independent variable.

social discount rate the public cost of capital; the discount rate used to calculate the net present value of a public project.

socialism the form of economic organization in which the means of production are publicly owned but decisions are primarily decentralized.

spot price the price of a good or asset in the current period.

standard deviation the positive square root of the variance of a random variable.

strategy a plan, method, or series of maneuvers for the purpose of obtaining a specific goal or result; the science or art of combining or employing resources in planning or directing large operations; a predetermined line of play that specifies completely how to respond to each possible circumstance at each stage of a game.

substitution effect the change in quantity demanded due to the change in relative price alone with real income held constant.

sunk cost an expenditure that has already been made and cannot be recovered.

supply curve the graph of quantity supplied as a function of price.

supply price elasticity the percentage change in quantity supplied divided by the percentage change in price.

tactical decisions decisions regarding how to use and deploy resources in production.

technical progress technological change that leaves inputs more productive because of the development of better production techniques.

tied sales sales in which a firm bundles products together and sets a single price for the bundle.

tit-for-tat in a repeated game, a strategy to induce cooperation by punishing an opponent for deviating from a jointly optimal series of moves but then returning to cooperation (forgiving and forgetting) until the opponent cheats once more.

total product (*TP*) curve a graph of maximum output as a function of a variable input when other inputs remain constant.

trade, terms of the quantity of one good that can be obtained per unit of another good as determined by the price ratio.

trading set a region of mutual advantage.

transfer pricing the practice of determining the price of an intermediate good transferred from one division of a firm to another division of the same firm.

transitivity in consumer choice, the assumption that if the consumer prefers **A** to **B** and prefers **B** to **C**, then **A** is preferred to **C** also; or if the consumer is indifferent between **A** and **B** and is indifferent between **B** and **C**, then the consumer is indifferent between **A** and **C** also.

trusts corporate holding companies.

two-part tariff a pricing scheme in which an initial "entry" fee or tariff must be paid as well as a price per unit in order to purchase the good.

unbiased parameter estimate an estimate for which the expected value of the estimator is equal to its true value.

unbiasedness property of competitive equilibrium the theory that any Pareto optimal state can be achieved through the competitive mechanism.

uncertainty a state in which outcomes cannot be described or probabilities cannot be assigned.

unitary elasticity a state in which elasticity equals unity.

utility function a numerical assignment made to every bundle once bundles have been ranked in accordance with a consumer's preferences.

utility of perfect information the difference between the expected utility of a perfect prediction based on information and the expected utility without the information.

value of marginal product (*VMP*) the marginal product of a variable input multiplied by the fixed price of the good being produced.

value of perfect information the maximum amount of money that will be paid for a perfect prediction.

variance the expected value of the squared deviations of a random variable about its mean; a measure of the dispersion of a random variable about its mean.

vertical integration a situation in which a firm that produces an intermediate good or supplies raw material is merged with another firm that uses that input.

weak axiom in revealed preference, the assumption that if **B** is affordable when **A** is chosen, then **A** must be too expensive when **B** is chosen, if consumer behavior is consistent.

zero-sum game a game in which the gains by some players equal the losses by other players so that the sum of all losses and gains is zero.

Index